CW01497507

BLACK AND ASIAN BRITISH WRITING

The Cambridge History of Black and Asian British Writing provides a comprehensive historical overview of the diverse literary traditions impacting on this field's evolution, from the eighteenth century to the present. Drawing on the expertise of over forty international experts, this book gathers innovative scholarship to look forward to new readings and perspectives, while also focusing on undervalued writers, texts, and research areas. Creating new pathways to engage with the naming of a field that has often been contested, readings of literary texts are interwoven throughout with key political, social, and material contexts. In making visible the diverse influences constituting past and contemporary British literary culture, this *Cambridge History* makes a unique contribution to British, Commonwealth, postcolonial, transnational, diasporic, and global literary studies, serving both as one of the first major reference works to cover four centuries of black and Asian British literary history as well as a compass for future scholarship.

SUSHEILA NASTA is Professor of Modern and Contemporary Literature at Queen Mary University of London. She is the founding Editor of *Wasafiri, the magazine of international contemporary writing*. A pioneer in the field of postcolonial writing, she received an MBE for her services to black and Asian literatures in 2011. She has published over thirteen books, directed major award-winning research projects, and judged numerous literary prizes.

MARK U. STEIN is Professor of English, Postcolonial, and Media Studies at Westfälische Wilhelms-University Münster where he founded the interdisciplinary MA in National and Transnational Studies. His research interests include diaspora, transnational, and postcolonial studies. He has published ten books, including *Black British Literature: Novels of Transformation* and *Locating African European Studies*.

THE CAMBRIDGE
HISTORY OF
BLACK AND ASIAN BRITISH
WRITING

*

Edited by

SUSHEILA NASTA

Queen Mary University of London

MARK U. STEIN

Westfälische Wilhelms-University of Münster

 **CAMBRIDGE**
UNIVERSITY PRESS

CAMBRIDGE
UNIVERSITY PRESS

University Printing House, Cambridge CB2 8BS, United Kingdom

One Liberty Plaza, 20th Floor, New York, NY 10006, USA

477 Williamstown Road, Port Melbourne, VIC 3207, Australia

314–321, 3rd Floor, Plot 3, Splendor Forum, Jasola District Centre,
New Delhi – 110025, India

79 Anson Road, #06–04/06, Singapore 079906

Cambridge University Press is part of the University of Cambridge.

It furthers the University's mission by disseminating knowledge in the pursuit of
education, learning, and research at the highest international levels of excellence.

www.cambridge.org
Information on this title: www.cambridge.org/9781107195448
DOI: 10.1017/9781108164146

© Cambridge University Press 2020

First published 2020

Printed in the United Kingdom by TJ International Ltd. Padstow Cornwall

A catalogue record for this publication is available from the British Library.

ISBN 978-1-107-19544-8 Hardback

To Maya, Alexander, and Lara
and the future mixings of cultural streams

Contents

PART II
UNEVEN HISTORIES: CHARTING TERRAINS
IN THE TWENTIETH CENTURY 95

Preface 96

(I)
GLOBAL LOCALS: MAKING TRACKS AT
THE HEART OF EMPIRE 97

(II)
DISAPPOINTED CITIZENS: THE PAINS
AND PLEASURES OF EXILE 193

Contents

Contents

Notes on Contributors

NICOLA L. ABRAM is Lecturer in Literatures in English at the University of Reading. Her research values literature in relation to global justice, and focuses on postcolonial and women's writing. Nicola's publications include the monograph *Black British Women's Theatre: Intersectionality, Archives, Aesthetics* (2019) and articles and chapters on plays by Helen Oyeyemi (in *'Telling it Slant': Critical Approaches to Helen Oyeyemi*, ed. Chloe Buckley and Sarah Ilott, 2017), Winsome Pinnock (in *Modern and Contemporary Black British Drama*, ed. Mary F. Brewer, Lynette Goddard, and Deirdre Osborne, 2014), and debbie tucker green (in *Journal of Contemporary Drama in English*, 2:1, 2014).

REHANA AHMED is Senior Lecturer in Postcolonial and Contemporary Literature at Queen Mary University of London. She is the author of *Writing British Muslims: Religion, Class and Multiculturalism* (2015), and the co-editor of *South Asian Resistances in Britain, 1858–1947* (2011), *Culture, Diaspora, and Modernity in Muslim Writing* (2012), and a special issue of the *Journal of Commonwealth Literature* on 'British Culture after 9/11' (2018).

ASHOK BERY is a Research Associate at the School of Oriental and African Studies (SOAS), University of London. He is the author of *Cultural Translation and Postcolonial Poetry* (2007) and the co-editor of *Comparing Postcolonial Literatures* (2000). His essays have appeared in a number of academic journals and critical works, and his poems in a variety of British magazines and anthologies, including *PN Review*, *Stand*, *The North*, and *Life Lines*. His research interests are mainly in modern poetry and Indian literature. He is currently working on a series of poems about the Indian Rebellion of 1857–1858.

ROGER BROMLEY is Emeritus Professor in Cultural Studies at the University of Nottingham, and was a Visiting Professor at Lancaster University until 2016. He worked for forty-four years in a range of UK Higher Education institutions, and is the author of *Lost Narratives: Popular Fictions and Politics* (1988), *Narratives for a New Belonging: Diasporic Cultural Fictions* (2000), *From Alice to Buena Vista: The Cinema of Wim Wenders* (2001), and four other books, as well as more than fifty scholarly articles. His current research interests include migration, diaspora, and literary/cinematic representations of refugees and asylum seekers.

SARAH BROUILLETTE is a Professor in the Department of English at Carleton University in Ottawa, Canada. She is the author of *Postcolonial Writers in the Global Literary Marketplace* (2007), *Literature and the Creative Economy* (2014), and a forthcoming book on the history of UNESCO's book-related programming.

J. DILLON BROWN is an Associate Professor in the Department of English at Washington University in St Louis, USA. He specialises in anglophone Caribbean, postcolonial, and world literatures. He is the author of *Migrant Modernism: Postwar London and the West Indian Novel* (2013) and the co-editor, with Leah Rosenberg, of *Beyond Windrush: Rethinking Postwar Anglophone Caribbean Literature* (2015).

ANTOINETTE BURTON is Professor of History and Swanlund Endowed Professor at the University of Illinois, Urbana-Champaign, USA, where she also directs the Illinois Program for Research in the Humanities. She is the author of *The Trouble with Empire* (2015) and *An ABC of Queen Victoria's Empire* (2017), and the editor, with Tony Ballantyne, of *World Histories from Below* (2016). Her most recent project is as editor of the six-volume series *A Cultural History of Western Empires* (2018). She is currently at work with Renisa Mawani on an anti-imperial bestiary.

CHRIS CAMPBELL is Lecturer in Global Literatures at the University of Exeter. He teaches and researches in the areas of world literature, environmental criticism, and postcolonial studies. He is co-editor of *The Caribbean: Aesthetics, World-Ecology, Politics* (2017) and has published articles on world literature and world-ecology, Caribbean writing, and broadcast culture and decolonisation.

VINCENT CARRETTA, Professor Emeritus of English at the University of Maryland, USA, specialises in transatlantic historical and literary studies during the long eighteenth century. Vincent has published two books on verbal and visual anglophone political satire between 1660 and 1820, as well as authoritative editions of the works of Olaudah Equiano, Quobna Ottobah Cugoano, and other eighteenth-century transatlantic authors of African descent. His most recent books are biographies of Equiano (2006) and Phillis Wheatley (2011), as well as authoritative editions of the writings of Philip Quaque (2010), Ignatius Sancho (2015) and Phillis Wheatley (2019).

COLIN CHAMBERS was Literary Manager of the Royal Shakespeare Company (1981–1997), and since 2014 has been Emeritus Professor of Drama at Kingston University, London. He co-edited *Granville Barker on Theatre* (with Richard Nelson, 2017) and edited the *Continuum Companion to Twentieth Century Theatre* (2002), which he is updating. He has written extensively on the theatre, including *The Story of Unity Theatre* (1989); *Peggy: The Life of Margaret Ramsay, Play Agent* (1997; winner of the inaugural Theatre Book Prize) and *Peggy to her Playwrights* (2018); *Inside the Royal Shakespeare Company* (2004); *Here We Stand: Politics, Performers and Performance – Paul Robeson, Isadora Duncan and Charlie Chaplin* (2006); and *Black and Asian Theatre in Britain: A History* (2011).

JOHN R. COLEMAN is a doctoral candidate in English at Carleton University in Ottawa, Canada. His thesis analyses the impact of neoliberal British education policies on contemporary British literature, particularly writing by authors from minoritised communities. He is interested in showing how neoliberal education policy has privileged a relatively homogeneous creative class, whose hegemony resonates across literary production. He is also concerned with discerning the lines of flight that have emerged to elude this class's control. *Wasafiri* published his article 'Making Readers: Book Trust's Multicultural Programming in the Creative-Economy Context' (2016).

DENISE DECAIRES NARAIN is Reader in Postcolonial Literatures at the University of Sussex. She is reviews editor for *Contemporary Women's Writing* and co-editor for Palgrave's Contemporary Women's Writing series. She teaches Caribbean and postcolonial writing with an emphasis on gender in the contexts of global feminisms. She has published widely on Caribbean and postcolonial women's writing, including two monographs, *Caribbean*

Women's Poetry: Making Style and *Olive Senior: Writers and their Work*. Her current research is on the representation of servants in postcolonial women's writing for a book project titled *Maids and Madams: Postcolonial Feminisms, Solidarity and Servitude*.

ALISON DONNELL is Professor of Modern Literatures in English and Head of School of Literature, Creative Writing and Drama at the University of East Anglia. She has published widely on anglophone Caribbean, diasporic, and black British writings, with a particular emphasis on challenging orthodox literary histories and recovering women's voices. Her current projects include General Editorship of *Caribbean Literature in Transition, 1800–2015* (three volumes) with Cambridge University Press and a monograph, *Caribbean Queer: Culturequeer Belonging, Creolised Sexualities and the Literary*. She is also leading a major research project, 'Caribbean Literary Heritage: Recovering the Lost Past and Safeguarding the Future' funded by the Leverhulme Trust (www.caribbeanliteraryheritage.com).

TOBIAS DÖRING is Chair of Literature in the English Department of Ludwig-Maximilians-Universität (LMU), Munich, Germany. His books include *Caribbean–English Passages: Intertextuality in a Postcolonial Tradition* (2002); *Eating Culture: The Poetics and Politics of Food* (co-edited with Markus Heide and Susanne Mühleisen, 2003); *A History of Postcolonial Literature in 12½ Books* (2007); *Postcolonial Literatures in English: An Introduction* (2008); *Edward Said's Translocations: Essays in Secular Criticism* (co-edited with Mark U. Stein, 2012); and *Meteorologies of Modernity: Weather and Climate Discourses in the Anthropocene* (co-edited with Sarah Fekadu and Hanna Straß-Senol, 2017).

MARKMAN ELLIS is Professor of Eighteenth-Century Studies at Queen Mary University of London. He is the author of *The Politics of Sensibility: Race, Gender and Commerce in the Sentimental Novel* (1996), *The History of Gothic Fiction* (2000), *The Coffee-House: A Cultural History* (2004), and co-author of *Empire of Tea* (2015). He co-edited *Discourses of Slavery and Abolition: Writing in Britain and its Colonies 1660–1832* (2004) and has published essays on Ignatius Sancho, slave narratives, and eighteenth-century Caribbean poetry.

FELIPE ESPINOZA GARRIDO is Associate Professor in English, Postcolonial and Media Studies at the University of Münster, Germany, where he received his PhD with a thesis on 'Post-Thatcherism in British Film'. Currently he is researching a book on empire imaginations in rediscovered women's sensation fiction. His research interests also include neo-Victorian studies and transmedia franchises, as well as adaptation studies. He has published on British popular fiction and co-edited *Locating African European Studies: Interventions – Intersections – Conversations* (with Caroline Koegler, Deborah Nyangulu, and Mark U. Stein, 2020).

KATE HOULDEN is Senior Lecturer in World Literature at Anglia Ruskin University, and has worked previously at Liverpool John Moores University, the University of Surrey, and Queen Mary University of London. Her book *Sexuality, Gender and Nationalism in Caribbean Literature* appeared in 2016 and a co-edited collection, *Popular Postcolonialisms,* in 2018. She is one of the founders of the international World Literature Network and her current research focuses on the intersections between queer studies, transnational feminism, and world literature. An essay on queer and world-literary approaches to the work of Anna Kavan appeared in *Women: A Cultural Review* in 2017, and she is currently working on her next monograph, *Queering World Literature.*

DELIA JARRETT-MACAULEY, the youngest daughter of Sierra Leonean parents, is a writer and arts consultant. She is the author of *The Life of Una Marson 1905–65* (1998) and *Moses, Citizen and Me* (2005). She has edited two academic collections: *Reconstructing Womanhood, Reconstructing Feminism: Writings on Black Women* (1996) and *Shakespeare, Race and Performance: The Diverse Bard* (2016). Since 2016, she has been the Chair of the Caine Prize for African Writing.

TABISH KHAIR, an Associate Professor at Aarhus University, Denmark, was born in Ranchi and educated in Gaya, Bihar, India. His scholarly books include *Babu Fictions* (2001), *The Gothic, Postcolonialism and Otherness* (2009), and the co-edited anthology *Other Routes: 1500 Years of African and Asian Travel Writing* (2005). He is also an award-winning poet and novelist. The chapter in this anthology was written with the support of the Leverhulme Trust when Khair was a Leverhulme guest professor at Leeds University.

MADHU KRISHNAN, Professor of African, World and Comparative Literatures, University of Bristol, is the author of *Contemporary African Literature in English: Global Locations, Postcolonial Identifications* (2014), *Writing Spatiality in West Africa: Colonial Legacies and the Anglophone/ Francophone Novel* (2018), and *Contingent Canons: African Literature and the Politics of Location* (2018). Her work centres on African and African diaspora writing, publishing, and culture, with a particular focus on 'making' of African literary institutions. She has published widely in the field of African literatures.

OLE BIRK LAURSEN is Lecturer in Postcolonial Indian Literature at New York University, London. His research concerns the literature and history of black and South Asian people in Britain and Europe, from the mid-nineteenth century to the present, with a particular focus on anti-imperialism and anarchism. He is co-editor of *Reworking Postcolonialism* (2015), *Networking the Globe* (2016), and of a special issue of *SubStance* on comics and anarchism (2017), and editor of M. P. T. Acharya, *We Are Anarchists: Essays on Anarchism, Pacifism, and the Indian Independence Movement* (2019). His monograph, *The Indian Revolutionary Movement in Europe, 1905–1918*, will be published in 2020.

SARAH LAWSON WELSH is Associate Professor and Reader in English and Postcolonial Literature at York St John University. Her most recent research focuses on writing and Caribbean food cultures with a new monograph, *Food, Text and Culture in the Caribbean*, published in 2019. She authored the first monograph study of the writing of Grace Nichols (*Grace Nichols*, 2007) and, more recently, a chapter on 'Black British Poetry' in *The Cambridge Companion to British Poetry 1945–2010* (ed. Edward Larrissy, 2015). She is one of the founding members of the international *Journal of Postcolonial Writing*.

BÉNÉDICTE LEDENT teaches at the University of Liège, Belgium, and is a member of the postcolonial research group CEREP (www.cerep.ulg.ac.be). She has published extensively on Caryl Phillips and other contemporary writers of Caribbean descent. She has also worked on several editorial projects, the latest of which are a volume entitled *Madness in Anglophone Caribbean Literature: On the Edge* (co-edited with Evelyn O'Callaghan and Daria Tunca, 2018) and a special issue of the *Journal of Postcolonial Writing* devoted to minor genres in postcolonial literature (edited in collaboration with Delphine Munos, 2018). She is co-editor of Brill's book series Cross/Cultures.

GAIL LOW's teaching and writing interests are in creative non-fiction, creative criticism, and book/publishing history; her research publications address the ways in which institutions and institutional practices help or hinder creativity. Author of *Publishing the Postcolonial* (2011), *White Skins/Black Masks: Representation and Colonialism* (1996), and co-editor, with Marion

Wynne-Davies, of *A Black British Canon?* (Macmillan, 2006), she is on the editorial board of the *Journal of Commonwealth Literatures* and is founder-editor of *DURA – Dundee University Review of the Arts*.

JOHN MCLEOD is Professor of Postcolonial and Diaspora Literatures at the University of Leeds. He is the author of *Life Lines: Writing Transcultural Adoption* (2015), *J. G. Farrell* (2007), *Postcolonial London: Rewriting the Metropolis* (2004), and *Beginning Postcolonialism* (2nd edn, 2010). He has published over fifty essays on black British, diasporic, and postcolonial literatures. His new book, *Global Trespassers: Permitted Migration, Prohibited Personhood*, is forthcoming.

JAVED MAJEED is Professor of English and Comparative Literature at King's College London. He is the author of several books on modern South Asia, including *Ungoverned Imaginings: James Mill's 'The History of British India' and Orientalism* (1992), *Autobiography, Travel and Postnational Identity: Gandhi, Nehru and Iqbal* (2007), *Muhammad Iqbal: Islam, Aesthetics, Postcolonialism* (2009), and *Nation and Region in Grierson's Linguistic Survey of India* and *Colonialism and Knowledge in Grierson's Linguistic Survey of India* (2 vols., 2018). He has co-edited *Hali's Musaddas: The Flow and Ebb of Islam* (with Christopher Shackle, 1997) and *India and South Africa: Comparisons, Confluences, Contrasts* (with Isabel Hofmeyr, 2016).

VIJAY MISHRA is Professor of English and Comparative Literature at Murdoch University, Perth, Australia. Among his book publications are *Dark Side of the Dream: Australian Literature and the Postcolonial Mind* (with Bob Hodge, 1991), *The Gothic Sublime* (1994), *Devotional Poetics and the Indian Sublime* (1998), *Bollywood Cinema: Temples of Desire* (2002), *The Literature of the Indian Diaspora: Theorizing the Diasporic Imaginary* (2007), *What Was Multiculturalism?* (2012), *Annotating Salman Rushdie: Reading the Postcolonial* (2018), and *Salman Rushdie and the Genesis of Secrecy* (2019). He is a Fellow of the Australian Humanities Academy.

PETER MOREY is Professor of 20th Century Literature at the University of Birmingham. He has written widely on colonial and postcolonial literature, with particular reference to South Asia and its diaspora. Most recently he has been working on literary and cultural representations of Muslims. He is the author of *Fictions of India: Narrative and Power* (2000), *Rohinton Mistry* (2004), *Framing Muslims* (with Amina Yaqin, 2011), and *Islamophobia and the Novel* (2018). He has co-edited four books on South Asian and Muslim writing, multiculturalism, and Islamophobia. He has also led two research-council funded projects into the media framing of Muslims and into the conditions for building intercultural trust through dialogue.

MPALIVE-HANGSON MSISKA is Reader in English and Humanities and Course Director for BA Arts and Humanities at Birkbeck, University of London. His main research interests are in African literature, especially Wole Soyinka and Chinua Achebe, Caribbean literature, and black British writing. Mpalive-Hangson has published the books *Post-Colonial Identity in Wole Soyinka* (2007), *Chinua Achebe's 'Things Fall Apart': A Study* (with David Whittaker, 2007), *Wole Soyinka* (1998), and *Writing and Africa* (co-edited with Paul Hyland, 1997), among others. He is a member of the editorial board of the *Journal of Southern African Studies* and the Council of the British Institute in Eastern Africa.

MONA NARAIN is Associate Professor in the Department of English at Texas Christian University, USA. She is the Scholarship Editor for *ABO: Interactive Journal for Women in the Arts, 1640–1830*. Her areas of expertise are eighteenth-century British literature, (post)colonial studies, gender, and critical race studies. Publications include her co-edited book *Gender and Space in British Literature, 1660–1820* (2014) and articles on eighteenth-century Indians writing about Britain in *Literature Compass* and *SEL*. She is currently working on a project on cross-cultural encounters, funded in part by a research grant from the National Endowment for the Humanities.

SUSHEILA NASTA MBE is Professor of Contemporary and Modern Literatures at Queen Mary University of London and Emerita at the Open University. Founding Editor of *Wasafiri*, the magazine of international contemporary writing she launched in 1984, she has published widely, especially on the Caribbean, the South Asian diaspora, and black Britain. From 2007 to 2013 she led a major research and public engagement project on South Asian Britain. Her books include: *Home Truths: Fictions of the South Asian Diaspora* (2002), *Writing Across Worlds* (2004), *India in Britain* (2013), and *Asian Britain: A Photographic History* (2013). She is currently writing a group biography, *The Bloomsbury Indians*, and was awarded the Benson Medal in 2019 by the Royal Society of Literature.

MEENAKSHI PONNUSWAMI is Associate Professor of English at Bucknell University, USA. Her research focuses on postwar black British, British Asian, and African American drama. Her recent publications include '*Dutchman* in the Drama Class' (in *Approaches to Teaching Baraka's 'Dutchman'*, ed. Matthew Calihman and Gerald Early, 2018) and 'British Muslim Feminism on Stage' (*Contemporary Theatre Review*, 2018). She is currently researching British Asian feminist performance and stand-up comedy; African American women's playwriting of the 1960s; and contemporary South Asian American theatre. Professor Ponnuswami teaches modern American drama, including courses on American masculinity in performance, the theatre of the Civil Rights Movement, and American ethnic comedy.

James Procter is Professor of Modern and Contemporary Literature at Newcastle University. He is the author of *Dwelling Places* (2003), *Stuart Hall* (2004), and *Reading Across Worlds* (with Bethan Benwell, 2014), and the editor of *Writing Black Britain* (2000) and *Out of Bounds* (with Jackie Kay and Gemma Robinson, 2012). He is currently completing a monograph as part of the Leverhulme-funded 'Scripting Empire' project on West Indian and West African radio writing at the BBC between the 1930s and 1960s.

Ruvani Ranasinha is Reader in Postcolonial Literature at King's College London. She specialises in postcolonial literature and theory, especially relating to South Asia and the South Asian diaspora. She is the author of *Hanif Kureishi* (2002), *South Asian Writers in Twentieth-Century Britain: Culture in Translation* (2007), and the lead editor of *South Asians Shaping the Nation, 1870–1950: A Sourcebook* (2012). Her most recent monograph is *Contemporary Diasporic South Asian Women's Fiction: Gender, Narration and Globalisation* (2016).

Pallavi Rastogi is Associate Professor of English at Louisiana State University, USA, where she teaches classes on postcolonial literature and culture. She has published numerous articles on South Asian and South Asian diaspora literature. In addition to editing a collection entitled *Before Windrush* (2008), she has also authored a monograph entitled *Afrindian Fictions: Diaspora, Race, and National Desire in South Africa* (2008). Her second book, *Postcolonial Disaster: Narrating Catastrophe in the Twenty-First Century*, will be published in spring 2020.

Susanne Reichl is Professor of Contemporary English Literature at the Department of English and American Studies at the University of Vienna, Austria. Her main research interests are black and Asian British literature, children's and young adult literature, teaching literature and culture in the foreign language classroom, cognitive approaches to literature, multimodal texts, and time travel stories. Publications include *Cultures in the Contact Zone: Ethnic Semiosis in Black British Literature* (2002), *Cheeky Fictions: Laughter and the Postcolonial* (edited with Mark U. Stein, 2005), and *Cognitive Principles, Critical Practice: Reading Literature at University* (2009). She co-ordinates the interdisciplinary research platform *#YouthMediaLife*, which investigates young people's media lifeworlds.

HENGHAMEH SAROUKHANI is Assistant Professor in Literatures and Cultures of the Black Atlantic at Saint Mary's University, Canada. She has published essays on dub poetry, contemporary black British literature, black British soldiers in British and Irish film, and the cultural politics of the car. Her work has appeared in the *Journal of Postcolonial Writing*, *Études Anglaises*, *Caribbean Quarterly*, and *British Literature in Transition, 1980–2000*. She is currently working on a monograph that examines the cosmopolitics of twenty-first-century black British texts.

ANNA SNAITH is Professor of Twentieth-Century Literature at King's College London. Her publications include *Modernist Voyages: Colonial Women Writers in London, 1890–1945* (2014), an edition of Virginia Woolf's *The Years* for the Cambridge University Press Edition of the Works of Virginia Woolf (2012), and of *A Room of One's Own* and *Three Guineas* for Oxford World's Classics (2015). She is currently working on a project on interwar modernism and noise, and is editing a volume on *Literature and Sound*.

FLORIAN STADTLER is Senior Lecturer in Postcolonial Literatures in the Department of English and Film at the University of Exeter. His research focuses on South Asia and its diasporas and he has published widely on Indian popular cinema, South Asian writing in English, and British Asian cinema, drama, history, and literature. His monograph *Fiction, Film and Indian Popular Cinema: Salman Rushdie's Novels and the Cinematic Imagination* was published in 2013. He is the Reviews Editor of *Wasafiri: The Magazine of International Contemporary Writing*.

MARK U. STEIN is Chair of English, Postcolonial and Media Studies at Westfälische Wilhelms-Universität (WWU) Münster, Germany. He specialises in diaspora, transnational, and postcolonial studies with a focus on phenomena such as porosity and translocation in anglophone cultural production. He is the author of *Black British Literature: Novels of Transformation* (2004) and has co-edited *Postcolonial Ideology* (with Katja Sarkowsky, 2020), *Edward Said's Translocations: Essays in Secular Criticism* (with Tobias Döring,

2012), *African Europeans* (with Lyn Innes, 2008), and *Laughter and the Postcolonial* (with Susanne Reichl, 2005). ptts.wwu.de / stein.

SARA UPSTONE is Professor of English Literature and Head of Humanities at Kingston University, London. She is the author of three monographs – *Spatial Politics in the Postcolonial Novel* (2009), *British Asian Fiction* (2010), and *Rethinking Race and Identity in Contemporary British Fiction* (2016) – and is also editor of three co-edited collections, most recently *Postmodern Literature and Race* (2015). Her most recent publication is *Literary Theory: A Complete Introduction* (2017).

JULIAN WACKER teaches English, Postcolonial and Media Studies at the University of Münster, Germany. His doctoral thesis focuses on space and identity politics in grime culture and examines its remediation in contemporary British inner-city fiction. His research areas include black and Asian British film in the twenty-first century, black neo-Victorian / neo-Edwardian imaginaries, and Afropolitan writing. He has previously published an interview with the Chinese Jamaican author Kerry Young titled 'Outside the Boxes' (2017) in *Wasafiri*. Articles on grime poetry and on obscurity in Teju Cole's work are forthcoming.

CHRIS WEEDON is Professor Emerita at Cardiff University where she directed the Centre for Critical and Cultural Theory. Her books include *Feminist Practice and Poststructuralist Theory* (1987), *Cultural Politics: Class, Gender, Race and the Postmodern World* (with Glenn Jordan, 1995), *Postwar Women's Writing in German: Feminist Critical Approaches* (1997), *Feminism, Theory and the Politics of Difference* (1999), *Identity and Culture: Narratives of Difference and Belonging* (2004), and *Gender, Feminism and Fiction in Germany 1840–1914* (2007). She is currently working on a collection of life stories from East Germany and a book on the cultural politics of memory.

Preface and Acknowledgements

We began work on this book in 2015 to consolidate the now significant body of academic scholarship which has sought for several decades to provide a wide-angled vision of Britain's mixed cultural heritage and to locate the history of black and Asian literary culture as a formative and integral element within it. As the development of the project coincided with a referendum called by the UK government in June 2016 for Britain to 'exit' the European Union (Brexit) and once more close its borders, the broader aims have become even more urgent. Ironically perhaps, given this context, this project has been built on the fruits of much cross-cultural exchange and communication: not only are the editors situated in different locations – one in Britain at Queen Mary University, London and the other in Germany at the University of Münster – but black and Asian British writing is featured prominently on the literature curriculum in both institutions.

A project of this scope could not have been brought to fruition without the generous assistance of many colleagues, friends, and family. We would especially like to thank our project administrator Julian Wacker, University of Münster, for his research assistance and his diligence in managing the many editorial files that have flown across continents; Marziyeh Sadat Ghoreishi for the scrupulous production of a booklet of draft chapters; Rachel Goodyear for her meticulous assistance with preparing the manuscript for publication; Maya Caspari and Emily Mercer for their readings and bibliographical research; Julia Debreceni and Sara Fedrich for their careful assistance, Felipe Espinoza Garrido and the MA National and Transnational Studies students Camille Vianey, Theresa Krampe, Cristina Calvopiña Heredia, and Janine Bonnekoh who supported our symposium with contributors to kick off ideas and discuss draft chapters. We were delighted that many of our contributors, so many of whom are pioneers in this field, were so generous in giving up time to travel, to share ideas, and to generate the exchange and collaborative spirit of friendly critical companionship that has been key to the evolution of this book.

An editorial project of this scale builds on the wealth of previous scholarship and the knowledge of many. Professor Lyn Innes has been formative, not only in her academic mentorship at early stages of both our careers but in her astute readings. We are also grateful to Rehana Ahmed, Antoinette Burton, Denise deCaires Narain, Alison Donnell, Tobias Döring, Kate Houlden, Ole Birk Laursen, Sarah Lawson Welsh, Gail Low, John McLeod, Peter Morey, and Florian Stadtler, as well as many others amongst our international community of forty-one scholars who not only committed to the vision of the project but have always been available to give advice.

Institutional support has been critical in terms of sabbaticals and funding. We thank colleagues at the Open University, Queen Mary University of London, the University of Münster, and the DFG German Research Foundation for generously supporting our work; especially the University of Münster for funding the Cambridge History of Black and Asian British Writing symposium. Finally, we must thank Cambridge University Press and their production and editorial teams, including Sharon McCann, Anna Oxbury; especially Ray Ryan for his commitment to the field and his energy in commissioning this book, a vision combined with steady editorial guidance which ensured the book got to the finish line.

Most importantly, we would like to thank our families who have lived with this project beyond the call of duty for the past four years: Conrad, Maya, and Alexander Caspari in Greenwich; Yomi Bennett and Lara Stein in Telgte.

Susheila Nasta and Mark U. Stein

Introduction

SUSHEILA NASTA AND MARK U. STEIN

Man Moses, you are still living in the Dark Ages!
You don't even know that we have created a Black Literature, that it have writers who write some powerful books what making the whole world realize our existence and our struggle.   Sam Selvon, *Moses Ascending* (1975)

Striving to be both European and black requires some specific forms of double consciousness.
Paul Gilroy, *The Black Atlantic: Modernity and Double Consciousness* (1993)

Despite all our desperate, eternal attempts to separate, contain and mend, categories always leak.
Trinh T. Minh-ha, *Woman, Native, Other: Writing Postcoloniality and Feminism* (1989)

The composition of this first substantial history of black and Asian British writing, which stretches from the eighteenth century to the present, is both a challenge and a provocation. It is a challenge in its aim to open new dialogues, highlight correspondences, and establish productive frames through which to read black and Asian British writing across a continuum of quite distinct historical, social, and political moments of cultural production. It is a provocation in its necessarily mediated reconfiguration of the often eclipsed, discontinuous voices of Britain's black and Asian past, present, and future. The assemblage of any history is inevitably partial, a reading of the past through the eyes of the present, which necessarily involves construction, selection, as well as the unavoidable omission of materials which might later come to light. Moreover, in relation to black and Asian British writing, a body of work still in the process of definition and deriving from an uneven and often occluded set of histories, the task is even more complex. For whilst any literary history must record and track key moments of literary and cultural expression, it should also be tasked with posing questions and

I

interrogating received frameworks of meaning, not only in order to chart new critical cartographies but also to embed such readings within specific cultural and material contexts. Aware of the pitfalls of producing an overly neat narrative of reclamation, this history nevertheless seeks to decompress the all-too-familiar narrative of post-World War II large-scale black and Asian migration and settlement, uniquely opening up an extended vista which will inevitably complicate understandings of the diverse and intrinsic contributions of black and Asian writing to Britain's literary culture.

One can tell a lot about a nation by the stories it invents, by what books it chooses to treasure, which paintings it displays at its galleries, and the nature of the histories it constructs. Yet, as Anthony Appiah reminds us in his recent study of contemporary identities, creeds, and colour, *The Lies that Bind* (2018), one can learn even more about a nation by what it chooses to forget.[1] Numerous cultural historians and literary scholars have drawn attention in past decades to what the acclaimed cultural theorist Stuart Hall once called the nation's wilful 'loss of historical memory', an amnesia that not only evacuated from plain sight the adjacent histories of Britain's pre-World War II black and Asian residents but also enabled the postwar myopic construction of Britain as a white 'island nation'.[2] As Bill Schwarz puts it in his introduction to *End of Empire* (2011), a study of the post-1945 novel, 'England' has always been a 'fabrication', its invention forcing out 'from the field of national vision awkward truths'. It has disconnected 'metropole from colony, white from non-white' and has reinforced the enduring myth of England as green and pleasant land.[3]

---

[1] Anthony Appiah, *The Lies that Bind: Rethinking Identity* (London: Profile Books, 2018), 102.

[2] Until the 1990s, this amnesia was reflected in the lack of any reference to Britain's black and Asian writers. Andrzej Gasiorek in *Post-War British Fiction: Realism and After* (London: Edward Arnold, 1995) draws attention to such absences more than evident in Margaret Drabble (ed.), *The Oxford Companion to English Literature* (Oxford: Oxford University Press, 1985) and Jenny Stringer, *The Oxford Companion to Twentieth-Century Literature in English* (Oxford: Oxford University Press, 1996); also, Bryan Appleyard, *The Pleasures of Peace: Art and Imagination in Post-War Britain* (London: Faber and Faber, 1989); Bernard Bergonzi, *The Situation of the Novel* (London: Macmillan, 1970); David Lodge, *The Novelist at the Crossroads* (London: Routledge, 1971); Malcolm Bradbury and David Palmer (eds.), *The Contemporary English Novel* (New York: Holmes and Meier, 1980); David Gervais, *Literary England: Versions of 'Englishness' in Modern Writing* (Cambridge: Cambridge University Press, 1993).

[3] Bill Schwarz, 'Introduction' in Rachael Gilmour and Bill Schwarz (eds.), *End of Empire and the English Novel since 1945* (Manchester: Manchester University Press, 2011), 1–37; 5; see also Timothy Brennan, 'Writing from Black Britain', *Literary Review*, 34:1 (Fall 1990): 5–11; 5, where Brennan discusses the relationship between 'Englishness', national identity, literature, and the formation of the canon.

In fact, Britain has had a black and Asian population for well over 400 years – at least as long, that is, as the history of its empire abroad. As W. E. B. Du Bois noted in 1911, not only was the 'Empire' a 'coloured' empire but the streets of London were increasingly revealing this fact.[4] The long history of black and Asian settlement has repeatedly been borne out by the writings of pioneering historians such as Peter Fryer, Rozina Visram, and, more recently, David Olusoga, who look back to the period of transatlantic slavery from the sixteenth to the nineteenth century, Britain's engagement with the East India Company in the 1600s, to empire, and as far back as the black population of Roman Britain. Nevertheless, it is frequently forgotten that the definition, composition, articulation, and identity of the present-day nation stem from this much longer series of complexly interwoven and distinctive histories.[5] Though not often evident in existing literary histories, it is clear that the long presence of Britain's empire 'within' was not only a crucial element of the nation's political and economic health but was also to become increasingly important in its cultural and literary life, responsible well before 1945 for a number of productive and transnational exchanges and connections which were to have major ramifications later in the century.[6] Even the rationale for the building of a national literary canon, a concept originally designed to transport the Victorian Arnoldian notion of the nation as 'home' of purity, order, cohesion, and stability to the colonies, was first conceived of in relation to the context of colonial India before becoming institutionalised as a field of study at British universities in the nineteenth century.[7] For not only was the formation of the nation built on the cultures of empire, but the subsequent construction, as Gauri Viswanathan presciently observes, of a narrow genealogy that attempts to 'confine the discipline' is 'belied' by

---

[4] See Susheila Nasta, '1940s–1970s' in Deirdre Osborne (ed.), *The Cambridge Companion to British Black and Asian Literature (1945–2010)* (Cambridge: Cambridge University Press, 2016), 23–39; 23.

[5] Peter Fryer, *Staying Power: The History of Black People in Britain* (London: Pluto Press, 1984); Rozina Visram, *Asians in Britain: 400 Years of History* (London: Pluto, 2002); James Procter (ed.), *Writing Black Britain 1948–1998* (Manchester: Manchester University Press, 2000); David Olusoga, *Black and British: A Forgotten History* (London: Macmillan, 2016).

[6] We are drawing here on Susheila Nasta's argument in '"Voyaging In": Colonialism and Migration' in *The Cambridge History of Twentieth-Century Literature* (Cambridge: Cambridge University Press, 2005), 563–84; 563–9.

[7] See Gauri Viswanathan, *Masks of Conquest: Literary Study and British Rule in India* (New Delhi: Oxford University Press, 1989).

such 'transcontinental movements' and influences whose 'multiple' origins are as 'diffuse as its current (and future) shape'.[8]

Drawing attention to how the confluence of such diverse and enmeshed
cultural tributaries have impacted on the literary imagination of the nation is
not always an easy process; not least, because of the 'bundles of silence'
which have most commonly enshrouded these sources.[9] The writing of any
history is not a given but a process and a construction. Moreover, silences, as
the historian Michel-Rolph Trouillot has observed, can enter 'historical
production at four junctures: fact creation (the making of *sources*); assembly
(the making of *archives*); fact retrieval (the making of *narratives*); and retrospective significance (the making of *history* in the final instance)'.[10] There are
several examples of this, some more graphic than others. At a critical
moment during World War II, to take one, Sir Winston Churchill delivered
a famous speech to the House of Commons, seeking to rouse the patriotic
spirit of the nation. Churchill was quoting liberally from a sonnet entitled 'If
We Must Die' by the Jamaican émigré poet and novelist Claude McKay, as
one of the authors of this introduction has argued elsewhere.[11] Whilst
Churchill clearly intended to boost the morale of British troops to rise up
and not surrender their 'precious blood' by dying 'like hogs penned in an
inglorious spot', McKay's 1919 poem was intended originally to resist the
traumatic violations inflicted on the black descendants of the Atlantic slave
trade in the United States.[12] A key figure in the Harlem Renaissance, McKay
had emigrated to the USA from Jamaica in 1912 and, unlike many other black
writers and intellectuals who settled in Britain prior to the end of World War
II in 1945, he only spent a brief and disillusioned spell in the country he had
once imagined to be his spiritual and intellectual homeland. However,
Churchill's alleged translation of these lines into one of the sustaining
narratives of the nation prior to the defeat of Germany and the winning of
the Battle of Britain in 1945 is not only interesting for its obvious ironies (the
source and original purpose of the poem have seldom been noted), but is also

---

[8] Gauri Viswanathan, 'Preface to the Twenty-Fifth Anniversary Edition' in *Masks of Conquest* (New York: Columbia University Press, 2014), xi–xiv; xi–xii.

[9] Michel-Rolph Trouillot, *Silencing the Past: Power and the Production of History* (Boston, MA: Beacon Press, 1995), 26.

[10] Trouillot, *Silencing the Past*, 26.

[11] See Nasta 'Voyaging In', 564–6; Claude McKay, *Selected Poems* (New York: Harcourt-Brace, 1953); see also Paula Burnett, *The Penguin Book of Caribbean Verse in English* (Harmondsworth: Penguin, 1986), 144, 402, who discusses Churchill's use of the poem in the House of Commons and its original publication in 1919. See also Fryer, *Staying Power*, 319.

[12] McKay, 'If We Must Die' in Burnett, *Caribbean Verse*, 144.

indicative of some of the challenges faced in attempting to unearth, untangle, and retrospectively construct a history of black and Asian British literary and cultural production.[13]

Such elisions continue even in more contemporary accounts. In September 2000, for instance, the *Times Literary Supplement* printed a review of the recently published modernist volume of the new *Cambridge History of Literary Criticism* (2000). Entitled 'How the Critic Came to be King', it appeared adjacent to a fascinating photograph, taken in 1942 on the occasion of a BBC broadcast by the Eastern Service monthly magazine programme *Voice*. In the original published version of this image, all the contributors to that programme were named, including several key black and Asian writers discussed in this history. They include: Una Marson (Caribbean poet and presenter), Venu Chitale (assistant producer and novelist), M. J. Tambimuttu (major poet and editor of *Poetry London*), Mulk Raj Anand (novelist and critic), Narayana Menon (writer and broadcaster) as well as T. S. Eliot, William Empson, Nancy Barratt, and George Orwell.[14] In the image reproduced by the *TLS*, no reference is made to any of the black and Asian contributors, who were not only significant literary figures in interwar London but were also to play an important part in presenting a wider-angled view on Euro-American modernity. The caption simply reads: 'among others – T. S. Eliot, George Orwell and William Empson'.[15]

New archival findings are increasingly coming to light, but few substantive material traces exist in print which make available the voices and inscriptions of Britain's early black and Asian writers. Yet, as several chapters here attest (Part I), some of the very first published works by Britain's black and Asian writers appeared towards the end of the eighteenth century, often as political tracts, autobiographical forms of testimony, letters, and diaries: notably, they include publications such as Ukawsaw Gronniosaw's *A Narrative of the Most Remarkable Particulars in the Life of James Albert Ukawsaw Gronniosaw, an African Prince, as Related by Himself* (1772), Olaudah Equiano's *The Interesting Narrative of the Life of Olaudah Equiano, or Gustavus Vassa, the African. Written by Himself* (1789), Ignatius Sancho's posthumously published *Letters of the Late*

---

[13] We note that there is at present no conclusive evidence of Churchill's use of McKay's lines.

[14] For a reprint of the photograph, see James Procter, 'Una Marson at the BBC', *Small Axe* 19:3 (2015): 1–28; 3 Available at https://muse.jhu.edu/article/602408.

[15] See Susheila Nasta, *Home Truths: Fictions of the South Asian Diaspora in Britain* (Basingstoke: Palgrave, 2002), 25 where this oversight is discussed in detail; also Stephen Collini, 'How the Critic Came to be King', *Times Literary Supplement*, 8 September 2000, 11.

Ignatius Sancho, an African (1782), and Sake Dean Mahomet's *The Travels of Dean Mahomet* (1794), arguably one of Britain's first published works by an Indian in English.[16] These books and compilations were in many cases self-consciously literary, engaging – as in Sancho's epistolary exchanges with the novelist Laurence Sterne or in the wide-ranging appeal of Equiano's strategically multigeneric and worldly text, which straddles autobiography, captivity narrative, and travelogue – directly with the literary culture of the day.[17] Whilst such texts cannot be seen to inaugurate 'a tradition', the many issues these early black British writers had to negotiate, whether having to seek the means, like Equiano, to self-publish and market their works or having to shift between deliberately self-constructed and multidimensional political, cultural, and personal identities, still pertain today.

While this history of black and Asian British writing strives to be comprehensive, it cannot be all-encompassing. Not only does this heterogeneous body of writing emerge from the confluence of a set of multifaceted lineages and cultural-geographic reference points, comprising the Caribbean, Africa, the USA, South Asia, and Europe including the UK, but the diverse and often fraught engagements of its histories have generated layered and intricate topographies. Owing to the shifting nomenclatures that have been attributed to the writing over time, the not unproblematic categories of 'black' and 'Asian' are used here as a convenient starting-point, gesturing broadly to a field of reference rather than implying narrowly imposed racial or ethnic affiliations across what are diverse forms of expression and complexly formed cultural identities.[18] In addition, whilst the overarching title *black and Asian British writing* is current in contemporary critical discourse, we are more than aware that the subject-matter and writers covered in this book (most of whom settled in, or spent significant periods of time in Britain) may well have

---

[16] *The Travels of Dean Mahomet: An Eighteenth-Century Journey Through India*, ed. Michael H. Fisher (Berkeley, CA: University of California Press, [1794] 1997). The spelling 'Mahomet' was used in the first published edition of this work in Cork in 1794. After moving to Brighton in 1812 'Mahomet' changed his name to 'Mahomed', setting himself up as Shampooing Surgeon to George IV.

[17] We are grateful here to John McLeod's insights in 'Postcolonial Writing in Britain' in Ato Quayson (ed.), *The Cambridge History of Postcolonial Literature* (Cambridge: Cambridge University Press, 2011), 571–603; 574–6; and C. L. Innes, *A History of Black and Asian Writing in Britain, 1700–2000* (Cambridge: Cambridge University Press, 2002), 17–18; Sukhdev Sandhu, *London Calling: How Black and Asian Writers Imagined a City* (London: HarperCollins, 2003), 41–5.

[18] See Innes, *History of Black and Asian Writing*, 2; Mark U. Stein, *Black British Literature: Novels of Transformation* (Columbus, OH: Ohio State University Press, 2004), 14–18; Gail Low and Marion Wynne-Davies (eds.), *A Black British Canon?* (Basingstoke: Palgrave Macmillan, 2006), 5–6.

6

been described or have wished to describe themselves otherwise: whether as British, Scottish, Irish, Indian, Caribbean, African, Sinhalese, Trinidadian, Ethiopian, 'Negro', Asiatic, African Briton, woman, queer, with mixed and multiple identifications such as BAME – or simply as writer. That a number of these writers have chosen over time to highlight their complexly formed subjectivities, strategically subverting the straitjackets of racial or political categories of definition, is not only evident in a range of distinctive historical contexts; it has been crucial in disrupting exclusionary constructions of British literary culture which have persistently located them in a parenthetical relationship to the 'nation' and its literary culture. As Caryl Phillips notes in *Extravagant Strangers: A Literature of Belonging* (1997), British writing has long been forged in the crucible of cultural admixture and fusion, yet: 'the once great colonial power that is Britain has always sought to define her people, and by extension the nation itself, by identifying those who don't belong'.[19] Examples of this double narrative of insider/outsider, focused on rights of citizenship and cultural 'belonging', abound in the rhetoric of politicians and their immigration policies. It is also more than evident in the articulations of writers past and present who have frequently been forced to negotiate the perhaps 'irreconcilable' gap between an enforced politics of cultural identity and 'literary aesthetics'.[20] The contradictions inherent in the implications of such positionings are clear: most obviously, perhaps, in the 2018 'Windrush scandal' in which the British government sought – in the same year as the seventieth anniversary celebrations and following the flagging of the 1948 arrival of *Empire Windrush* as an icon of Britannia's multicultural face at the 2012 London Olympics – to wrongfully deport significant numbers of its elderly black citizens.

The title of this volume is not meant to suggest one single history because, significantly, we are *not* dealing with a singular, unified historical object. Neither do we propose a dual history, one black, one Asian. Instead, this *History* represents and constructs a heterogeneous history in a comparative, panethnic, and panoramic fashion: a 'messy' history that cuts across a broad range of ethnic and cultural backgrounds, but without downplaying meaningful distinctions between them. Although proceeding from the beginnings in the eighteenth towards the contemporary in the twenty-first century, this book is characterised by historicist perspectives rather than a strictly linear order, eschewing reductive and neat linear evolutionary chronologies.

---

[19] Caryl Phillips, *Extravagant Strangers: A Literature of Belonging* (London: Faber and Faber, 1997), x.
[20] Osborne (ed.), *Cambridge Companion to Black and Asian Literature*, 7.

Individual chapters are of necessity not chronologically sequenced because of their engagement with phenomena that cut across time, be they of a formal, theoretical, political, or thematic nature.

This *History* traces the *plural* history of black and Asian British writing, an intertwined and polymorphous literary field characterised by both overlap and distinction. Moreover, as the use of 'black' and 'Asian' has only recently and retrospectively become part of common discourse to describe a key part of Britain's diverse cultural heritage, this history revises as it documents. As a history which has evolved from the inter-section of the multiple pathways which continue to criss-cross the various constituencies of the republic of letters – whether through conventional genres, the influence of orature, performance poetry, the influences of contemporary cultural theory, the wider networks of lit-erary culture which determine reputation, visibility, and taste – it is inevitably also a work in progress. As such, however, this *History* navi-gates the location (or locations) of these literatures within the various contexts of UK cultural production and beyond, reflecting on their contribution both to Britain's present-day postcolonial status and its contemporary international and transnational face.

Black and Asian British writing is not congruent with the contours of the UK; it extends beyond the borders of white British literary history. While constituting a key part of the UK's national literary history, it is at once larger, more amorphous, and translocal. This literary field inhabits and at the same time also exceeds the literary space of the nation. In that sense this literature challenges and expands narrow and insular definitions of the nation, remind-ing the UK of the lingering effects of empire, confronting it with its colonial past and postcolonial present, and representing the irrevocable entanglement with the peoples and cultures it once colonised and who have now, for many generations, made up the face of the nation. This *History* engages with texts whose belonging to Britain is frequently expressed with ambivalence; texts whose reception, as British texts, cannot be taken for granted. More impor-tantly, they are texts which can (and perhaps must) frequently be contextua-lised elsewhere too, in distinct literary and cultural traditions; texts which can point to and feed on a wide range of histories, geographies, languages, and cultures. Texts which *may* speak of and *may* be marked by diaspora and migration, displacement and exile, colonialism and postcolonialism, negotia-tions of exclusion and belonging. But even if none of these experiences are explicitly thematised, or formally encoded, in a given text, the sheer diversity, breadth, and pertinence of black and Asian writing from this country has meant that it, too, constitutes British literature, co-determining what Britain and Britishness are today.[21]

As has already been intimated, our usage in this volume of 'black' and 'Asian' references several highly diverse multilingual peoples and cultures with complex and fluctuating social, political, and cultural histories. In so far as *black* and *Asian British* are politically constructed categories, rather than specific references to a narrowly defined race or ethnicity, any critical language employed, any literary or cultural categorisations endorsed are necessarily interventions and acts in history. As has now been well documented, the use of the inclusive term 'black' (as comprising all British-based writers and artists of African, Caribbean, and South Asian ancestry, first popularised in the 1970s by CAM (the Caribbean Artists Movement), and later used as a political signifier against a constant barrage of racial injustices) soon shifted to the semantic distinction and political separation in the 1980s and 1990s of black and Asian British cultural production, a division that has more purchase today.

The solidity, then, of the terms 'black British' and 'Asian British' as literary categories is by no means complete, given the further complication that a wide variety of distinct nomenclatures are in circulation, with more than one label being applicable at times to the same text. CAM had deployed 'black British' in an overarching sense to refer to diasporic artists and writers in Britain with distinct backgrounds from Guyana, Trinidad, Jamaica, and so on. The concept was then extended, pointing beyond the Caribbean, in order to subsume 'the common experience of racism and marginalisation'.[22] Listing black and Asian Britons under one heading was a way of countering racism through a larger political alliance. This overarching concept had become increasingly problematic by the 1990s, as ethnicity could no longer be seen as grounds for cultural or political affinity.[23]

Cultural and linguistic distinctions notwithstanding, the historical and structural correspondences and connections between the distinct groupings referenced by the terms 'black Britons' and 'Asian Britons', and their cultural production, require the panoramic and comparative approach which can only be provided in a single – and yet plural – history. While the strategically

---

[21] Mark U. Stein, 'Cultures of Hybridity: Reading Black British Literature', *Kunapipi: Journal of Post-Colonial Writing*, 20:2 (1998): 76–89; 86–7.

[22] Stuart Hall, 'New Ethnicities' in Kobena Mercer (ed.), *Black Film, British Cinema*, ICA Documents 7 (London: Institute of Contemporary Arts, 1988), 27–31; 27.

[23] Leon Wainwright, 'Canon Questions: Art in "Black Britain"', in Low and Wynne-Davies (eds.), *Black British Canon*, 156.

inaccurate denomination 'black British' had its uses, the present moment requires a critical language which is not only 'sensitive to specific intersections between national and transnational modalities' but also 'adroit in its handling of the complexities of aesthetic modes'.[24] In this *History*, black and Asian British writing is used as a retrospective formulation when it comes to writing from preceding centuries. Instead of labelling, for example, Sake Dean Mahomet's books as 'Asiatic' ('Asian') or Equiano's as 'African', in accordance with eighteenth-century practice, our broad categories allow for diachronic development as well as synchronic overlap and distinction to emerge. These categories are marked not by closure but by *porosity* – they differentiate as much as they affiliate.[25]

Useful to navigate across this double bind of alliance and difference, which both connects and distinguishes the diverse histories of Britain's black and Asian communities, is Michael Rothberg's concept of 'multidirectional memory'.[26] This helpfully accounts for the *dynamics* of generating and transmitting memory, the productive exchanges and entanglements which characterise remembrance across community boundaries. Rothberg emphasises that cultural memory evolves not in narrow isolation but through acts of dialogue, negotiation, and borrowing, so that, for example, the memory of slavery can productively draw on the language and grammar of indentureship – and vice versa. Multidirectional memory, then, is another conduit between the distinct bodies of writing this *History* represents. Bringing the work by black and Asian British writers into dialogue, emphasising points of connection as well as distinction, does not conflate these texts; rather, the mesh of knotted histories and distinct traditions and cultures which constitute the writing need to be contextualised and historicised in particular ways, chapter by chapter, not only with respect to community or lineage but also with respect to specific intersections of class, gender and sexuality, generation, regional locations, and idiom.

This project works on the assumption that black and Asian British literatures' formal, generic, and cultural complexities can best be conceptualised as a refraction of the historical processes that have shaped the black and Asian presence in Britain. Historically, black and Asian literary culture has perhaps

---

[24] See Low and Wynne-Davies (eds.), *Black British Canon*, 5.

[25] On porosity in Mohsin Hamid's *The Reluctant Fundamentalist* and Teju Cole's *Open City*, see Mark U. Stein, 'Mobile Writers, Porous Texts' in Christiane Lütge and Mark Stein, *Crossovers: Postcolonial Studies and Transcultural Learning* (Zurich: LIT, 2017), 139–58; 149 and passim.

[26] See Michael Rothberg, *Multidirectional Memory: Remembering the Holocaust in the Age of Decolonization* (Stanford, CA: Stanford University Press, 2009).

necessarily presented itself as a challenge to what exactly one takes 'writing' to be. Given the history of the evolution of the writing as well as the wide remit of cultural production (ranging from the oral to the literary, from essays, life-writing, performance, TV, film, and visual culture to new media), we have chosen the broader term 'writing' as a vehicle to reflect the dynamism of a field that is still in evolution, revising as it reinvents. Whilst the use of 'literature' is perhaps more common in a history such as this – a descriptor enabling selection, valorisation, and even the canonisation of certain texts – 'writing' is more inclusive and offers engagement with the complex histories, communities, forms of expression, and genres this *History* of black and Asian British writing must navigate.

There is an emphasis here on the material underpinnings of the writing charted, so that one encounters key texts and writers always in relation to their vexed engagement with social and political contexts, whether direct or oblique, instead of being utterly or ultimately explained by them. We conceive of historical inquiry as an ongoing, open-ended, and indeed conflictual process, which explores contested terrains rather than providing mere context or background against which texts can be firmly 'set'. Our contributors take the opportunity to intervene in the field's ongoing development through acts of retrospective reformulation. From the terminology applied to the connections suggested and the distinctions drawn, this is a historicist project, which holds that 'every expressive act is embedded in a network of material practices' and that 'no discourse, imaginative or archival, gives access to unchanging truths'.[27] This *History* engages the material conditions which impinge upon black and Asian British writing and which it, in turn, seeks to affect. It also offers readers a wide-angled compass to read across what are distinctive histories and modes of cultural expression, encouraging active engagement with the debates generated between chapters, periods, and across theoretical and critical readings.

Although the evolution of black and Asian British writing itself has a long history, academic work in the field does not. Scholarly articles on black *and* Asian British writing first began to appear in periodicals and essay collections from the 1980s onwards. The body of black and Asian British literature began to grow exponentially from the late 1990s, which was in turn reflected by an increase in specialist academic publications and a growing number of undergraduate and postgraduate courses. Yet full-length monographs encompassing

[27] Harold Aram Veeser, 'Introduction' in Harold Aram Veeser (ed.), *The New Historicism* (New York: Routledge, Chapman and Hall, 1989), ix–xvi; xi.

both black *and* Asian British literatures have only been appearing regularly since the beginning of the twenty- first century, including C. L. Innes' foundational *A History of Black and Asian Writing in Britain, 1700–2000* (2002) and Gabriele Griffin's *Contemporary Black and Asian Women Playwrights in Britain* (2003).[28] They have been complemented by many thematic edited collections such as Gail Low and Marion Wynne-Davies (eds.), *A Black British Canon?* (2006) and Pallavi Rastogi and Jocelyn Fenton Stitt (eds.), *Before Windrush: Recovering an Asian and Black Literary Heritage within Britain* (2008), and most recently Deirdre Osborne (ed.), *The Cambridge Companion to British Black and Asian Literature (1945–2010)*.[29]

Specific elements and aspects of black and Asian British cultural production have also begun to appear in a range of different contexts: in companions, anthologies, edited collections, and even some thematic or generic histories. Here, chapters covering black and Asian British writing are often contextualised amongst discussions of the 'Literature of London', 'Postcolonial Literature', 'Modern British Women Playwrights', 'Twentieth-Century English Poetry', or 'the Modernist Novel', for example.[30] These are indeed

---

[28] Two of the earliest book-length studies are David Dabydeen and Nana Wilson-Tagoe's *A Reader's Guide to West Indian and Black British Literature* (London: Hansib, 1987) and Suzanne Scafe, *Teaching Black Literature* (London: Virago, 1989). Further monographs on black *and* Asian British writing are Susanne Reichl, *Cultures in the Contact Zone* (Trier: WVT, 2002); James Procter, *Dwelling Places* (Manchester: Manchester University Press, 2003); Sandhu, *London Calling*; John Clement Ball, *Imagining London: Postcolonial London and the Transitional Metropolis* (Toronto; London: Toronto University Press, 2004); Bruce King, *The Internationalization of English Literature* (Oxford: Oxford University Press, 2004); John McLeod *Postcolonial London: Rewriting the Metropolis* (London: Routledge, 2004); Stein, *Black British Literature*; Colin Chambers, *Black and Asian Theatre in Britain: A History* (London: Routledge, 2011).

[29] See also Lars Eckstein et al., *Multi-Ethnic Britain 2000+: New Perspectives in Literature, Film and the Arts* (Amsterdam: Rodopi, 2008).

[30] Lawrence Manley (ed.), *The Cambridge Companion to the Literature of London* (Cambridge: Cambridge University Press, 2011); Ato Quayson (ed.), *The Cambridge History of Postcolonial Literature* (Cambridge: Cambridge University Press, 2012); Elaine Aston and Janelle Reinelt (eds.), *The Cambridge Companion to Modern British Women Playwrights* (Cambridge: Cambridge University Press, 2006); Neil Corcoran (ed.), *The Cambridge Companion to Twentieth-Century English Poetry* (Cambridge: Cambridge University Press, 2008); Moragh Shiach (ed.), *The Cambridge Companion to the Modernist Novel* (Cambridge: Cambridge University Press, 2007). There have also been several studies by critics who contextualise some aspects of black and Asian British literature in different research contexts, such as Simon Gikandi, *Maps of Englishness: Writing Identity in the Culture of Colonialism* (New York; Chichester: Columbia University Press, 1996); Roger Bromley, *Narratives for a New Belonging: Diasporic Cultural Fictions* (Edinburgh: Edinburgh University Press, 2000); Ann Blake et al. (eds.), *England through Colonial Eyes in Twentieth-Century Fiction* (Houndmills: Palgrave, 2001); and Richard Lane, Rod Mengham, and Philip Tew, *Contemporary British Fiction* (Cambridge: Polity Press, 2003). British Asian literature has also been the focus of separate enquiries, from Susheila Nasta, *Home Truths* (2002), which

welcome and necessary inclusions which correspond to and underscore the *multiple* locations of black and Asian British cultural production. But they do not offer readers a comprehensive engagement with either black or Asian British writing, nor do they allow readers to gauge its crucial contribution to the constitutive makeup of postcolonial Britain today.[31]

Despite the ever-growing scholarly attention afforded to individual authors, specific texts, genres such as the *Bildungsroman*, aesthetic formations, and historical periods, the complex genealogy of black and Asian British writing requires a comprehensive and comparative historical account as offered by the scope of this *History*. The *longue durée* of black and Asian British writing, the sustained and multiple points of cohesion between individual authors and groupings, the deictic references to territories and histories elsewhere, the intertextual echoes of black and Asian British texts, of British writing, and of non-European literatures and oratures have not yet been systematically explored; the precedence frequently given to explorations of narrative has happened at the expense of sustained analyses of drama, poetry, and other cultural forms. The material conditions of book publishing and reviewing, of literary networks and prizes, of organisations and conferences, all critical to the evolution of this field, are therefore still in need of systematic archival exploration. This *History of Black and Asian British Writing* addresses and seeks to remedy some of these limitations.

This *History* not only fills an important gap in providing a four-centuries-long vista on a field most commonly compressed as a perennially 'new' post-1945 wave of black and Asian writing; it also intersperses the significant cultural and material contexts which have been key in sustaining it. Gaps in the archive aside, a line of advancement can be traced, taking readers from the eighteenth-century beginnings of black British cultural production to twentieth-century examples of black and Asian writing contending with the UK as imperial metropolis and, later, as decolonising nation, through to contemporary twenty-first-century articulations of such writing, shaping national futures beyond the reductive polarities of margins and centres, minority and host. Although historical thematics – including colonialism, slavery and indentureship, empire, migration,

---

problematises narrow categorisations, to work on *British Muslim Fictions* (ed. Chambers, 2011).

[31] The field also offers its own specialised research tools, including Alison Donnell's *Companion to Contemporary Black British Culture* (London; New York: Routledge, 2002), David Dabydeen and John Gilmore's *Oxford Companion to Black British History* (Oxford: Oxford University Press, 2007), Osborne's *Cambridge Companion to British Black and Asian Literature*, David Olusoga's *Black and British: A Forgotten History* (London: Macmillan, 2016), and Geoffrey Davis and Anne Fuchs' *Black and South Asian British Literatures* (Trier: WVT, 2018).

diaspora, transnationalism – have been formative, the strict order of such a neat chronology is problematic in this case.

Cognisant of the complexity of individual histories and their transversal moments of intersection, the porous structure of this book offers both a vertical and largely linear chronology, simultaneously enabling a more fluid horizontal and thematic narrative of predominant 'tropes' and 'preoccupations' to emerge.[32] This situates particular writers, groupings, and political and cultural movements in specific historical contexts, while simultaneously offering readers the chance to recognise common concerns which straddle different cultural/aesthetic dynamics and transnational contexts. At the same time, the structure enables the identification of interconnecting strands across the three parts of the *History* where links are often not linear or developmental but thematic, generic, theoretical, and/or political. This framework opens up false dichotomies and reconfigures boundaries between established periods and traditions. The organisation of this *History* not only lifts the curtain on Windrush, pluralising and extending orthodox accounts of the impact that Britain's black and Asian citizens have made on British literary culture, but also opens up and reconfigures the nature of the critical geographies by which it has most commonly been defined.[33]

A history of black and Asian British writing of this scale, range, and depth has not previously been attempted. The wide-ranging scope of this volume is unique in setting crucial historical, political, and material contexts alongside an in-depth examination of the emergence of aesthetic movements, forms, and genres, focusing on cross-cultural exchange, experimentations with voice and style, and specific spheres of influence. At the same time, it demonstrates how these distinctive historical moments, which form the backcloth to the evolution of this field, are interlinked by recurrent political themes and questions: such as Ignatius Sancho's prescient observation in his posthumously published 1782 volume of letters, that he remains a 'a lodger and [. . .] hardly that', echoed over 200 years later by Hanif Kureishi's mixed-race protagonist Karim Amir in *The Buddha of Suburbia* (1990) who opens his autobiographical *Bildungsroman* with the lines: 'I am an Englishman born and bred, almost.'[34] This question regarding rights of 'belonging' is echoed in

---

[32] Innes, *History of Black and Asian Writing*, 2.

[33] See Pallavi Rastogi and Jocelyn Fenton Stitt (eds.), *Before Windrush: Recovering an Asian and Black Literary Heritage within Britain* (Newcastle upon Tyne: Cambridge Scholars, 2008).

[34] Hanif Kureishi, *The Buddha of Suburbia* (London: Faber and Faber, 1990), 3.

different forms, by different writers, in different periods, and at different political moments across the book's variegated historical continuum. A range of other preoccupations concerning the straddling and inscription of multiple identities, the constant need to confront yet step outside an imposed burden of representation, and the difficulties of getting published and reviewed in contexts that do not only focus on racial and cultural identities also reverberates.

Whilst contributors have been tasked primarily with focusing on defined periods, cultural movements, groups of writers, and the social and political contexts of material histories, individual essays necessarily approach their subject-matter through a range of different disciplinary and/or theoretical lenses which both ground specialist discussions and enable reformulations which can reshape the plural provenance of this *History*'s subjects. Several chapters dialogue productively beyond the tripartite chronological structure: in some cases explicitly, through correspondences articulated broadly by genre, whether fiction, life-writing including political autobiography, drama, theatre, poetry (including dub and performance poems), cinematography, television, or music; in others through the parallel excavation of material histories which offer the reader a vital window into the often vexed and proximate social and political contexts from which black and Asian literary production was to emerge. Seeking to step outside the politics of a now perhaps overly comfortable retrospective narrative of reclamation, our aim is to enable the articulation of a history not constrained by existing and sometimes reductive cultural and theoretical paradigms.

The particular problematics of compiling this *History* are not only addressed through its historicist perspective and porous structure, but by making this wide-ranging project a collective and collaborative venture from the outset. More than conscious of the need to offer an inclusive history, we commissioned a group of international specialists (pioneers alongside up-and-coming scholars) who contribute their cutting-edge research and provide important insights on this fast-growing dimension of British writing as it is received within and beyond the UK. To encourage dialogue and collaboration, most contributors came together for a three-day symposium to participate in the book's composition. This enabled collective engagement and creative links to be generated across historical periods, chapters, texts, and writers, some of whom appear in more than one guise in different chapters.[35] Aware of continuing absences and silences

---

[35] Hanif Kureishi's work, for example, is discussed in all three parts of the book. First, in reading Dean Mahomet's work through the lens of *The Buddha of Suburbia*

within the existing archive as well as the dangers of imposing a 'genealogy' which cannot be so contained, our rationale for structuring this history draws on a debate raised by Alison Donnell on the parallel difficulties inherent in defining a black and Asian British canon. Arguing that the 'heterodox' (and often contested) conjunctures of black and Asian British writing may best be viewed as a 'collective autobiography' of the nation, she posits a model, adapting Aijaz Ahmad, of a multi-voiced collective, an ongoing 'theatre of exchange', not of 'authority and closure' but of interrogation and dialogue.[36]

Whilst the guiding principle of the three sections of this *History* is broadly chronological (with further thematic/period subdivisions), not all authors and texts, nor all contributions, can be forced into a singular *grand récit*. Instead a series of *petits récits* are assembled in three overlapping parts divided only, to quote the words of the contemporary poet Jay Bernard, by a 'translucent sheet' hanging 'between eras'.[37] Each part begins with a short explanatory preface providing further context and pointing readers to major preoccupations or moments.

Part I, 'New Formations: The Eighteenth to the Early Twentieth Century', comprises five chapters, each offering different points of departure and inter-sections. This part covers a historically copious span and contributors were tasked with the difficult brief of both embedding their subjects within the specifics of a historical period, whilst pointing to insights enabled by present-day readings. As such its extended timeframe deploys what we might term a 'promiscuous genealogy'. This term, which was coined by a contributor to the symposium as a way of avoiding the pitfalls of reading such discrepant histories through a single developmental narrative and of enabling connections realised by what we might call 'multidirectional' readings, is productive as a conceptual compass both in this first section and elsewhere.[38] Chapters 1 and 4 focus attention on the challenges facing eighteenth-century black writers as they navigate the discourse of abolitionism but nevertheless write in a state of interdiction. Significantly, their interventions also intersect with features that recur elsewhere: namely, the multidimensional roles these writers strategically

---

(Chapter 3); second, in discussions of Kureishi's writing from the 1990s; and third, in the context of reinventing the nation in the twenty-first century (Chapter 27).

[36] Alison Donnell, 'Afterword: In Praise of a Black British Canon and the Possibilities of Representing the Nation "Otherwise"' in Low and Wynne-Davies (eds.), *Black British Canon*, 191, 189–204; 201–2.

[37] Jay Bernard, *Your Sign is Cuckoo, Girl* (London: Tall-Lighthouse Productions, 2008), 10; cited in Denise deCaires Narain, Chapter 31 of this volume.

[38] Thanks to Denise deCaires Narain and the discussion at the symposium in Münster, 2016.

adopt as active participants in political and literary debates, and the variety of forms and voices – in this case, the epistolary, autobiography, political essay, diary – which Britain's black and Asian writers have used to articulate the diversity of their imaginative and political visions. Mona Narain's proximate discussion (Chapter 3), focusing on the travels of Sake Dean Mahomet as a self-created Indian (later Irish Indian), offers an illuminating counterpoint to readers more familiar with eighteenth-century scholarship on early black writing. It is clear that the rediscovery of Olaudah Equiano's eighteenth-century auto-biography by Paul Edwards in the 1960s (Chapter 1) inspired a revisionary historiographical trend in the fiction of late twentieth-century black British writing. Similarly, the presentation of Mahomed as skilled Asian 'ethnopre-neur', strategically playing the Orientalist 'exotic' against itself as he dons the role of Shampooing Surgeon to George IV (literally massaging his passage into the nation), connects with broader questions of colonial and postcolonial citizenship across the volume. Like others to follow, Mahomed shifts across identities, artfully deconstructing stereotypical notions of both India and Britain, critiquing negative views of Islam, and identifying himself in multiple roles: as 'black', as 'Asian', and as a 'Victorian British gentleman' (Chapter 3). Like the nineteenth-century Anglo-Indian photojournalist Olive Malvery and the Egyptian editor Duse Mohamed Ali (Chapter 5), who respectively exploited various media platforms to challenge colonial ethnographies and intervene in how Britain saw itself, Mahomed held complex and often contradictory cultural and political affiliations. Similarly looking backwards and forwards, Antoinette Burton's discussion (Chapter 2) of the specular writings of early nineteenth-century travellers and fugitives taking refuge in Britain reveals the nation to be a 'jumbled set of different religious, linguistic, and cultural communities', a small island with 'precarious borders' contrary to the common Victorian vision of Britain as the stable heart of empire. Navigating the diverse and contrasting literary voices of nurse Mary Seacole, British subject and Bombay journalist Behramji Malabari, and black American fugitives William and Ellen Craft, Burton points to the precarious 'inside–outside' locations of these writers, the strategies they adopt for survival (which include cross-dressing), and subversions of an already entrenched xenophobia, evident in the designation of Britain's Irish communities as 'non-white'. These 'namings' anticipate later conflations, such as the overt racism faced by Britain's black and Asian migrant citizens in the 1950s, literally and metaphorically excluded by the familiar accommodation signs ('No Irish, no Blacks, no dogs') designed to keep Britain 'white'.

Part II, 'Uneven Histories: Charting Terrains in the Twentieth Century', consists of twenty chapters, further broken into subdivisions to map distinct historical moments and shifting political contexts. The first, 'Global Locals: Making Tracks at the Heart of Empire' (1920s–1950s), provides a new lens onto the already evident diversification of British literary culture in the interwar period. As several essays note, the transnational aesthetics of these black and Asian moderns have been eclipsed until recently, along with their significant interventions into established institutions of British literary culture, which were to anticipate transnational developments both theoretically and in terms of poetics later in the century (Chapters 6, 7, and 9). Developing this *History*'s focus on drama and performance, the discussion in Chapter 11 concludes that whilst these years were vibrant in terms of dramatic activities, regrettably only a faint 'string of connections' remains which could possibly link to the more publicly visible era of black and Asian theatre to emerge in the 1980s (Chapter 22). Several new frames of interpretation are offered in terms of both genre and material context. Notably, Majeed's analysis of the political autobiographies of prominent British colonial subjects – Mohandas Karamchand Gandhi, Jawaharlal Nehru, Jomo Kenyatta, and Sarojini Naidu (all of whom lived or studied in Britain for significant periods) – is useful to reflect on the extent to which the postwar narrative of migration was only one side of the equation in terms of national and political self-invention, especially when combined with the complex challenge of disentanglement from conjoined and dual allegiances (Chapter 10).

'Disappointed Citizens: The Pains and Pleasures of Exile', the second subsection, spans the two decades after World War II (1950s–1970s). It opens with an analysis of the history of the 'Windrush' myth and interrogates its continuing influence (despite blind spots) as signifier of modern Britain as a multicultural nation (Chapter 12). This subsection moves on to depict a wide range of literary articulations of the disillusionment bred by a relentless sense of political and cultural exclusion. Often described as being 'in' but not 'of' the nation because of their bifurcated identities, this group of Caribbean migrant writers included Beryl Gilroy, Stuart Hall, George Lamming, Sam Selvon, Andrew Salkey, and James Berry, many of whom were formative in evolving a 'canon' of postwar black British writing. Their dynamic experimentations with form, genre, and language (Chapters 14, 16, and 18) resulted from the productive convergence of local and global influences and wide-angled, translocal modernities (Chapters 14 and 16).

The third subsection, 'Here to Stay: Forging Dynamic Alliances' (1970s–1990s), concerns the fraught years following the aftermath of the inflammatory racist rhetoric of Enoch Powell's 1968 'Rivers of Blood' speech in the writings of a new generation of black and Asian writers. They strategically united under the collective political identity of 'black', despite differences across ethnicity, gender, and class, in order to navigate an increasingly exclusionary xenophobic climate. The 1970s arrivals of South Asians expelled from East Africa were confronted with police violence as well as a series of increasingly rigid immigration acts. The heightened tension led to the uprisings in Brixton, Toxteth, and other major British cities in 1981. Inequalities on the streets led to the evolution of new cultural poetics, often making porous the traditional boundaries between writing, reading, and performance: from the sounds of 'dub', to performing resistance (Chapter 19), to creolisations of poetic voice and form (Chapter 20), there was a general move to confront the realities of a fraught politics of identity by making space for Britain's black and Asian citizens and moving the writing centre stage. Public funding and multicultural government initiatives also led to the writing and production of a number of new plays (Chapter 22); several anthologies appeared, made up of the diverse constituencies of different collectives and mixed racial/gender groupings. The plethora of such initiatives, however, also highlighted the increasing limitations of the political designation 'black' as writers began to vociferously express their need to disentangle themselves from a spectrum of sometimes misaligned alliances and identities (Chapter 24). As we have seen, by the late 1980s the shift from 'black' to 'black and Asian' (still contested as broad containers for such a vastly different series of British histories, subject-positions, and cultural influences) became increasingly marked. By the 1990s, a now substantive and increasingly visible field of black and Asian writing gained significant international recognition as a vital element of the late twentieth-century British literary landscape. However, despite the advent of postcolonial studies, its institutionalisation as an integral part of the English Studies curriculum remained (and remains) a protracted process (Chapter 25).

Our final part, 'Writing the Contemporary', uses the vantage point of the millennium as pendulum to capture some of the major preoccupations, poetics, and changing contexts of writing today. Conscious of the difficulties of recording history from the present moment, contributors offer a number of readings that look to the future as they interrogate the past. Whilst transnational concepts from the 1990s, like Diaspora and Black Atlantic Studies, still provide productive conduits to articulate the complexity of the writers' mixed and complexly layered affiliations, the conjuring of new imaginaries and experimentations within a proliferation of new and old forms (ranging from grime fiction and children's literature to new media, film and TV, life-writing, and the aesthetics of new realisms) develops alongside the disturbing re-emergence of the familiar soundtrack of an exclusionary xenophobia presented in new clothes (Chapters 31, 32, 33, and 36). Divisions bred by 9/11, 7/7, the ensuing rise of Islamophobia, and Britain's move to exit from the European Union, combined with a growing disenchantment with cultural pluralism, have inspired a wealth of writing seeking to break the recurrent halter of racial and religious framings in order to explore alternative cultural and literary affiliations as well as a post-secular ethics of representation (Chapter 38). Though such an unsettled political and cultural climate has sparked creative transformations, the millennial hype of a book industry keen to 'prize' diversity and 'Otherness' continues to disguise harsher political and cultural realities such as the triggers for the Black Lives Matter movement. Several chapters in this last part posit new critical frameworks to shift perspectives, proposing new ways of reading: these include the twenty-first-century interrogation of a contemporary generation of 'African Britons', the challenges of reading black and Asian Britain through 'post-ethnic' eyes, and the limitations of engaging 'difference' as common critical denominator across an increasingly wide spectrum of different verse forms and self-identifications (Chapters 37 and 39). In a provocative reading of the contemporary which offers productive new critical conduits to loosen and shift the boundaries of the past, we are given a glimpse into how a reading of black and Asian British writing through the lens of queer theory might further muddy the boundaries of the nation's literary culture, creating new intersections beyond the familiar binaries of race, gender, and class (Chapter 34).

As is perhaps inevitable in a project of this size, it has not been possible to cover all the individual writers or subjects we would have liked. Not only do significant gaps in the archives still remain but, even with the considerable range of material that is available, some omissions have been inevitable. We hope nevertheless that this first substantive history of black and Asian British writing will go some way towards setting a critical agenda, opening dialogues, and imagining a future, which will be unstable but productively and creatively so. Writing this introduction in 2018, the year which marks the seventieth anniversary of the arrival of the Windrush, the fiftieth anniversary of Enoch Powell's infamous speech, and the twenty-fifth anniversary of the murder of Stephen Lawrence, it is beyond doubt that the long continuum of black and Asian British cultural production is not only incontrovertibly integral to the hybrid cultures of British writing today but has long been part of its extensive and diverse cultural past, intertwined with the texture of the nation at its deepest level. As we are writing, the adaptation of Victor Headley's cult novel *Yardie* (dir. Idris Elba) has hit the screens, a film which effortlessly switches back and forth between Jamaica and London, in fact superimposing one on top of the other, creating a *translocal imaginary* that has been recognised as a distinctive feature of black and Asian British cultural production. The effortlessness with which the film draws on and forges these translocal connections, knowing its spectators will do the same, is highly significant because it represents the degree to which the many distinct but intersecting cultural tributaries inform the UK's cultural matrix. The texts we read, the images we see, the soundtracks we hear do not just generate fresh perspectives onto the past or indeed the present moment, as this *History* sets out to demonstrate. They have the potential to shape and transform the future of the nation, in which, one day, literary and cultural historiography will be marked by fully embracing its diverse and distinct components in one place – as opposed to adjacent volumes.

PART I

★

NEW FORMATIONS
The Eighteenth to the Early Twentieth Century

Preface

There has been a black and Asian presence in Britain for over four centuries. However, it was only in the mid-eighteenth century that a range of writings – whether letters, diaries, autobiographies, or political testimonies – by figures such as Ukawsaw Gronniosaw, Ignatius Sancho, Olaudah Equiano, Sake Dean Mahomed, and Mary Prince first began to gain notice. Whilst these writings highlighted specific cultural geographies and distinctive histories of arrival and settlement, interesting correspondences emerge which frequently point to and comment on the harshness of the political context of the times; in particular, issues of race, representation, and the conditions and the aftermath of slavery in an ever-growing global empire. The persistent identification of 'blackness' with 'slavery' and the economic profits of an exploitative and violent global trade generated a number of recurrent tropes and stereotypes, paradigms which shifted from hierarchical concepts of racial superiority and difference to commodified representations of the 'exotic' or the 'Other'. A similar series of figures began to emerge around early representations of 'Asians', who shift from being called 'coolies' or 'Asiatics' to exoticised 'Orientals'. As is evident from the surviving poetry, memoirs, letters, diaries, travel narratives, and journalism discussed in this part of the History, these writers were both insiders and outsiders, straddling multiple social and cultural identities, strategically manipulating their narrowly defined positions to subvert and resist easy framings in Britain. As literary and cultural historians of the eighteenth and nineteenth centuries have shown, these early black and Asian Britons were certainly operating in a social, cultural, and political context far removed from today; yet, there is no doubt that some of the forces driving their writing, combined with the urgent need to find public platforms to embed their voices at the heart of British culture, still reverberate. Several of the chapters in this section offer productive if 'promiscuous genealogies', enabling multidirectional readings of the works of these early Britons from the perspective of both the historical moment of their production and the present.

1

Narratives of Resistance in the Literary Archives of Slavery

MARKMAN ELLIS

The texts discussed in this chapter are 'narratives of resistance' to slavery, not only because of the stories they tell, but also because their mere existence is an act of resistance. In the context of eighteenth-century discourse on race, publications in English by writers of African descent were not meant to exist. They were written and printed under a state of interdiction: that is to say, a set of philosophical and political constructs that denied these authors the capacity to write. Yet a diverse group of writers, including Ukawsaw Gronniosaw (1710–1775), Ignatius Sancho (*c.* 1729–1780), Ottobah Cugoano (*b. c.* 1757), and Olaudah Equiano (*c.* 1745–1797), and later Mary Prince (*b. c.* 1788), presented to the public a complex and varied set of writings. This literary archive includes forms of life-writing – some of which can appear to later generations to be the earliest examples of 'slave narratives' – alongside a broad variety of genres including letters and correspondence, poetry, essays, and polemics (see Chapter 4). The 'Sons of Africa', as Cugoano was to call the earliest group of male writers, were born in various parts of the Black Atlantic diaspora, and all subsequently claimed the status of British subjects; and although the case of Mary Prince is different, her freedom was also achieved in and through her status in Britain. Faced with a culture of interdiction that denied them the right to speak, their writing and self-narrations were not only a victory of application and personal courage, but also voiced a considerable critique of slavery and its nascent racial system. This chapter begins by exploring the culture of interdiction with regard to the slave and the African in Enlightenment philosophy. It discusses resistance to those arguments by a series of writers in English of African descent, considering each text first as an argument in political history and then also as a work of literary creativity. Narratives of slave resistance in a variety of genres including letters, polemic, and life-writing engage with the political campaigns of abolition and emancipation, with Christian discourse on human equality, and with the culture of common feeling known as sensibility. The chapter ends by considering the legacy of this archive in black and Asian British fiction of the contemporary period.

Enlightenment Interdiction of Slave Humanity

Numerous European Enlightenment *philosophes* denied the intellectual and human equality between Africans and Europeans. David Hume, Thomas Jefferson, Immanuel Kant, Voltaire, James Monboddo, and Henry Home (Lord Kames) are some amongst the many *philosophes* who denied Africans and slaves – sometimes considered together – the same status as humans that they themselves enjoyed. These assertions were important in the emergence of the new conceptual formation or category known as 'race' or 'racism', even though as conclusions they were wrong and under-researched. The Scottish philosopher Hume is a representative example. In an essay, 'Of National Characters', published in 1753, he argued that

> I am apt to suspect the negroes, and in general all the other species of men (for there are four or five different kinds) to be naturally inferior to the whites. There never was a civilized nation of any other complexion than white, nor even any individual eminent either in action or speculation. No ingenious manufactures amongst them, no arts, no sciences.

In case his point was unclear, he continued: 'Not to mention our colonies, there are Negroe slaves dispersed all over Europe, of which none ever discovered any symptom of ingenuity; tho' low people, without education, will start up amongst us, and distinguish themselves in every profession.'[1] Following Hume, Immanuel Kant wrote in 1764 that

> [t]he Negroes of Africa have by nature no feeling that rises above the ridiculous. Mr. Hume challenges anyone to adduce a single example where a Negro has demonstrated talents, and asserts that among the hundreds of thousands of blacks who have been transported elsewhere from their countries, although very many of them have been set free, nevertheless not a single one has ever been found who has accomplished something greater in art or science or shown any other praiseworthy quality.[2]

---

[1] David Hume, *Essays: Moral, Political, and Literary*, ed. Eugene E. Miller (Indianapolis: Liberty Classics, 1987), 629–30.

[2] Immanuel Kant, 'On the Feeling of the Beautiful and Sublime', trans. Paul Guyer, in Günter Zöller and Robert B. Louden (eds.), *Anthropology, History, and Education* (Cambridge: Cambridge University Press, 2007), 23–62; 59.

Elsewhere in his moral philosophy, Kant argues that human freedom and equality are at the centre of Enlightenment values, and that these qualities are unalienable aspects of the status of being human. Yet in his comments on the accomplishments of people of African descent, he contradicts himself, and denies this. Kant's two positions are as historically entwined as they are inconsistent: which is to say, his comments give further evidence that the Enlightenment invented racism in the course of promoting its opposite. George Fredrickson, in *Racism: A Short History*, argues that 'What makes Western racism so autonomous and conspicuous in world history has been that it developed in a context that presumed human equality of some kind.'[3] Fredrickson argues that Enlightenment debate about human equality and autonomy encouraged the development of ideas that rationalised why some other humans were excluded from those conditions. Slavery alone does not produce racism: it needs Enlightenment debate about human equality to encourage race-based rationalisations.

In his claims about the alleged inferiority of people of African descent, Hume gave an example: 'In Jamaica, indeed, they talk of one negroe as a man of parts and learning; but 'tis likely he is admired for very slender accomplishments, like a parrot, who speaks a few words plainly.'[4] Hume, as many contemporary readers knew, referred to Francis Williams, who had been educated in England, perhaps at the University of Cambridge, and was admitted as a member of Lincoln's Inn in 1721 (the institution in London in which students were trained as lawyers, specifically barristers). He lived most of his life as a free black gentleman in Spanish Town, Jamaica, where he owned considerable property. Evidence of his writing, in the form of neo-Latin verse, was preserved in Edward Long's *History of Jamaica* (1774), despite Long's hostility to it and him.[5] Williams's erudite and refined poetry, written from the 1730s to the 1760s, clearly vindicated 'African capacity' and equality. As this debate established, evidence of intellectual activity and production among people of African descent, especially in the widely disseminated forms of print publication, was both highly compelling and ideologically fraught. In a state of interdiction, the pen and the printing press were significant weapons.

[3] George M. Fredrickson, *Racism: A Short History* (Princeton, NJ: Princeton University Press, 2002), 11.
[4] Hume, *Essays*, 629–30.
[5] Vincent Carretta, 'Who Was Francis Williams?', *Early American Literature*, 38:2 (2003): 213–37; John Gilmour, 'The British Empire and the Neo-Latin Tradition: The Case of Francis Williams' in Barbara Goff (ed.), *Classics and Colonialism* (London: Duckworth, 2005), 92–106.

A stream of diverse publications by black Africans in English in the mid-eighteenth century gave eloquent testimony against the *philosophes'* prejudiced view. In 1760, Briton Hammon (*fl.* 1747–1760) related his providential adventures in a pamphlet, *A Narrative of the Uncommon Sufferings and Surprizing Deliverance of Briton Hammon, A Negro Man*, published in Boston, Massachusetts. Hammon had been cast away in Florida, and then held prisoner in Cuba before he escaped to Jamaica and London. He later returned to the British colony of Boston, where his work was published.[6] In 1773, Phillis Wheatley (1753?–1784), a young woman enslaved in Boston, came to London to publish her collection of poems, *Poems on Various Subjects, Religious and Moral*, with a title-page that clarified that she was 'negro servant to Mr. John Wheatley, of Boston, in New England'.[7] In 1772, James Albert Ukawsaw Gronniosaw published a spiritual narrative relating the trials of his life: *A Narrative of the Most Remarkable Particulars in the Life of James Albert Ukawsaw Gronniosaw, an African Prince*. Born in Bornu in present-day Nigeria, Gronniosaw had been kidnapped on the Gold Coast and sold into slavery in Barbados and, later, New York. The thirty-nine page pamphlet described his spiritual and physical sufferings as a slave and a poor man on the road to Christian salvation and emancipation. The pamphlet had been 'committed to paper by the elegant pen of a young Lady of the town of Leominster', and was dedicated to the radical evangelical Christian Selina Hastings, the Countess of Huntingdon. Gronniosaw's pamphlet was a narrative of his life and of 'God's wonderful dealings' with him in allowing him to be saved, both in this world and spiritually.[8] Although their publications did not address the topic of slavery directly, Hammon, Wheatley, and Gronniosaw gave powerful witness to claims for the moral and intellectual equality of African people with Europeans.

Creativity in a Time of Slavery

The *Letters of the Late Ignatius Sancho, an African* (1782) was the first substantial volume published by a man of African descent. It is a deeply experimental

---

[6] Briton Hammon, *A Narrative of the Uncommon Sufferings, and Surprizing Deliverance of Briton Hammon, a Negro Man* (Boston, MA: Printed and sold by Green & Russell, in Queen-Street, 1760).

[7] Phillis Wheatley, *Poems on Various Subjects, Religious and Moral* (London: Printed for A. Bell, Bookseller, Aldgate; and sold by Messrs. Cox and Berry, King-Street, Boston, 1773).

[8] Ukawsaw Gronniosaw, *A Narrative of the Most Remarkable Particulars in the Life of James Albert Ukawsaw Gronniosaw, an African Prince, as Related by Himself* (Bath: Printed by W. Gye in Westgate-Street; and sold by T. Mills, bookseller, in King's-Mead-Square, [1772]), iv.

work. Cast in the form of a series of letters, it celebrated Sancho's anomalous status as free British gentleman, a grocer of some means, who voted in parliamentary elections for the Westminster electorate, and who took a full and robust part in metropolitan civil society. Sancho's letter-writing began as a private practice, but came to public knowledge through his correspondence between 1766 and 1768 with Laurence Sterne (1713–1768), author of the comic novel *Tristram Shandy* (1759–1767), which was published subsequently in Sterne's posthumous *Letters* in 1775.[9] Through Sancho's intermediation, Sterne wrote a sympathetic, though ambiguous, portrait of the sufferings of African slaves in the Caribbean colonies. Through Sterne's influence, Sancho adopted the sophisticated and ironic Shandean mode of epistolary writing. Sterne's style was embedded within the ambitiously egalitarian philosophical programme of sensibility, which reaffirmed that all human creatures, of whatever race, creed, or gender, had the same ability to feel. Emotional equality of experience was expressed in the Shandean mode through a flowing conversational writing style, with punctuation loosely supplied by dashes. This too equated Shandean sentimentalism with liberty and freedom: Sancho's letter-writing demonstrated, rather than claimed, his status as a free and franchised black British gentleman. However, although it can be argued that Sancho's chosen writing style, and his quotidian choice of epistolary topics, was an ambitious and creative response to his precarious social position, it has led some recent critics to accuse him of obsequious assimilation. As Sancho said of his own subject position, as both an African former slave and a British citizen and merchant, 'I am only a lodger – and hardly that.'[10]

Sancho's *Letters* imparts a strong sense of his self, and provides an intriguing portrait of his status in London as a black British citizen. Nonetheless, the *Letters* is not an autobiography in any conventional sense. He shows he is aware of, and uncomfortable about, his role in retailing sugar and tobacco through his shop in Westminster, products deeply implicated in the colonial system of chattel slave plantations. His hostility to slavery is consistent and clear, even though the *Letters* does not develop or present discussions of or arguments against slavery. In his book, his life was detailed in a biographical preface composed by Joseph Jekyll (1754–1837), a young lawyer and writer. Jekyll's biography claims that Sancho had been born in 1729 on a slave ship

<hr/>

[9] Lydia de Medalle (ed.), *Letters of the Late Rev. Mr. Laurence Sterne, To his Most Intimate Friends*, 3 vols. (London: T. Becket, 1775), 22–36.

[10] Ignatius Sancho, *Letters of the Late Ignatius Sancho, an African*, ed. Vincent Carretta (Peterborough, Ontario: Broadview Press, 2005), 231.

sailing from the Guinea coast of West Africa to Cartagena in the Viceroyalty of New Grenada, a Spanish colony in north-west South America (now Colombia), where he was baptised. His parents died while he was an infant, and in 1731, aged two years old, he was brought to England, and while a child served as a slave or servant to a family in Greenwich, London. He escaped their unkind treatment, and the threat of forcible return to slavery in the Caribbean, by becoming a servant to John, second Duke of Montagu (1690–1749). Montagu had already shown his interest in the cause of African learning by his patronage of Francis Williams. Montagu allowed Sancho to receive some education. On Montagu's death Sancho became butler to Mary, Duchess of Montagu, a position of authority and responsibility in an aristocratic household. In his time working for the Montagus, Sancho was free, or, by being paid, effectively so, although the precise moment of his manumission is obscure. Subsequently, after the death of the Duchess, Sancho was left with a legacy income. He reportedly did some acting, without much success, and became a proficient musician and composer.[11] In 1773, he took up trade as a grocer and merchant with his own family, at No. 20, Charles Street, Westminster. Sancho was well known in London's literary, musical, and artistic circles: he was a friend of Sterne, David Garrick, and the painter John Hamilton Mortimer, as well as Richard Payne Knight (the poet-aesthetician), John Ireland (a painter and Hogarth's biographer), and Joseph Nollekens (the sculptor). Gainsborough painted his portrait. The publication of his letters reflected this celebrity.

Life-Writing Against Slavery: Cugoano and Equiano

Ottobah Cugoano and Olaudah Equiano wrote and were published in the context of the campaign for the abolition of the slave trade. Both their writing projects were, in whole or part, autobiographical, resting on the argument that their lives were a testimony against slavery. Cugoano's *Thoughts and Sentiments on the Evil and Wicked Traffic of the Slavery and Commerce of the Human Species* (1787) is a trenchant polemic on the moral cost of slavery, not only to slaves but also to slave-owners. Cugoano argues that the slavery of the Africans in the Caribbean should be abolished, including but not limited to the trade in slaves from Africa. Cugoano makes this argument as

---

[11] Josephine R. B. Wright, *Ignatius Sancho (1729–1780) An Early African Composer in England: The Collected Editions of his Music in Facsimile* (London; New York: Garland, 1981).

a Christian, and a man of 'enlightened understanding', as must 'every man that has claim or affinity to the name of Christian'. For someone to ignore his argument, he concludes, would be to 'resign their own claim to any degree of sensibility and humanity, for that of barbarians and ruffians'.[12] His analysis of the politics of slavery is rigorous, and as he says, the consequences are harsh. His argument exploits the inconsistency between the British political identity that supported both slave-owning in British colonies and the civilising mission of Christian faith: for as he argues, if Christians were to truly apply the teachings of their faith to themselves, without hypocrisy or double standards, they would not tolerate slavery, in either its moral or practical dimension. At the end of his book, after many compelling lessons against slavery and slave-owners (whom he repeatedly denigrates as thieves, 'robbers of men', and kidnappers), Cugoano calls explicitly for the destruction of the slave trade and proposes the global emancipation of slaves, to be enforced by the redeployment of the British navy. Slave-owners, he goes on, should be punished by being made the slaves of those they have enslaved. This forceful view made Cugoano the most radical African British voice in the eighteenth century.

Cugoano's *Thoughts and Sentiments* is a trenchant and angry prose narrative addressed to a metropolitan audience. Henry Louis Gates, Jr argues, in *Figures in Black* (1987), that the typical condition of the written utterance of the ex-slave was that it 'was written or published for an essentially hostile auditor or interlocutor, the white abolitionist or the white slaveholder'.[13] This was certainly the case with Cugoano, who addresses his political opponents directly. In literary form, his book has been likened to a jeremiad, a form of religious protest writing, common in the Protestant Dissenting tradition, which presents a list of woes or complaints. Cugoano, also known as John Stuart or Stewart, situates himself within the burgeoning abolitionist discourse of the 1780s written against chattel slavery (especially as it was practised in the Americas) and the slave trade (the commerce in slaves between Africa and the Americas). This discourse was notably Christian: Cugoano's biblical rhetoric and phrasing, together with his frequent quotation of scripture, underline his location within abolitionist circles. The book begins with an introductory statement testifying to Cugoano's African status and his right to speak on the topic. 'To a man of my complexion', he says, 'it cannot but be very discouraging' to meet with men, like Hume and Long,

---

[12] Quobna Ottobah Cugoano, *Thoughts and Sentiments on the Evil of Slavery*, ed. Vincent Carretta (Harmondsworth: Penguin, 1999), 10.

[13] Henry Louis Gates, Jr, *Figures in Black: Words, Signs, and the 'Racial' Self* (Oxford: Oxford University Press, 1987), 105.

who argue that 'an African is not entitled to any competent degree of knowledge, or capable of imbibing any sentiments of probity'.[14] Cugoano finds his
voice by explicitly opposing the·Enlightenment interdiction of slave humanity.
His voice is reinforced by a short narrative account of his early life, explaining
how he was snatched away from his native country, kidnapped, and trafficked
to America. Life narrative, Cugoano discovered, was a rhetorically powerful
testimonial to his subsequent arguments about slavery (although modern
readers, habituated to the conventions of the nineteenth-century slave narrative, have sometimes been disappointed by the comparative brevity of this
autobiographical section). He relates that he was a Fanti, born in Agimaque in
present-day Ghana, in 1757. Aged thirteen he was sold into slavery and transported to the island of Grenada in the Caribbean, a British sugar colony
captured from the French in 1763, where he was forced to work on a sugar
plantation for more than a year. Although his truncated slavery narrative notes
some of the horrors of slavery he witnessed in Grenada, Cugoano does not
dwell on them, nor, for that matter, his passage to literacy, his conversion, or
his eventual emancipation. In 1772, he was purchased by Alexander Campbell,
an English merchant, and brought to England, where he taught himself to read
and write. There he apparently took advantage of the legal ruling against
slavery by Lord Mansfield in the Somerset case (1772), which established that
chattel slavery was not supported by English common law, though it was
tolerated in other English jurisdictions. So while the decision did not affect
slaves in the American colonies, it clarified that a person could not be removed
from England back to a slave-owning jurisdiction against his or her will. As
such, the judgment was widely interpreted as establishing that all slaves present
in England were free. Cugoano celebrated the case in the second edition of the
Thoughts and Sentiments.[15]

As a free man in Britain, Cugoano was employed, for wages, as a servant,
working from 1784 for the artists Richard and Maria Cosway. Through their
circles he met a wide range of artists and politicians active in London at the
time. He may have met Sancho before the latter's death in 1780, and certainly
came into contact with Equiano. In 1786 they joined forces with Granville
Sharp to defend the case of Henry Demane, an African who was threatened
with forcible return to the slave-owning territories of the Caribbean. Self-
styled the 'Sons of Africa', they continued their struggles against slavery
through letters to newspapers and public meetings. *Thoughts and Sentiments*

---

[14] Cugoano, *Thoughts and Sentiments*, ed. Carretta, 11.   [15] Ibid., 115–16.

was a contribution to this political campaign. In 1791 Cugoano published a shortened version of his account, with some additional material, in which he proposed opening a school to advance the education of black British children.

The full potential of life-writing as testimony against slavery and the slave trade was explored by Olaudah Equiano two years later. *The Interesting Narrative of the Life of Olaudah Equiano, or Gustavus Vassa, the African. Written by Himself* was first published in 1789 in London in two volumes, with an illustrated portrait frontispiece.[16] This was a remarkably successful publication, with nine British editions published during Equiano's lifetime, further editions in the United States, and translations into Dutch, German, and Russian by 1794. His book was 'printed and sold for the Author', meaning he took all the risk and made all the profit for the publication, while a bookseller, John Murray of Fleet Street in London, simply contracted for the printing of the volumes.[17] The book was accompanied by a list of 311 'subscribers' in the first edition, supporters of his work who had agreed to its purchase before publication. Equiano assiduously promoted the book, its sales, and his argument, through extensive lecture tours around the British Isles in the 1790s (see Chapter 4). All this was a major achievement.

In the text, Equiano's *Interesting Narrative* described itself variously as a life, a memoir, and a history. The title-page insisted on its status as autobiography with the phrase 'Written by Himself', though it gives the writer two names, Gustavus Vassa and Olaudah Equiano. In genre, the book is a creative response to a form of life-writing well established in the eighteenth century: the spiritual autobiography. This was a kind of prose biography, especially popular in Protestant writing from the mid-seventeenth century to the nineteenth century, which offered an account of a believer as he or she moves from a state of sinfulness to one of salvation and grace, typically through a repeating pattern in which recognition of sin leads to repentance, before renewed doubt ends in a fall into sin again. To the conventions of the spiritual autobiography, Equiano added a considerable repertoire of literary tools, successfully enhancing the narrative's value and power as rhetoric and entertainment. His book recalls, and has learned from, the narrative techniques of eighteenth-century travel writing and adventure stories, including prose fictions in the Defoe tradition that describe the trials of a self-made

---

[16] Olaudah Equiano, *The Interesting Narrative and Other Writings*, ed. Vincent Carretta, rev. edn (London: Penguin, 2003).

[17] Vincent Carretta, *Equiano, the African: Biography of a Self-Made Man* (London: University of Georgia Press, 2005), 272–5.

identity. It also borrows from other forms of self-writing, including the captivity narrative and apologia, and includes sections more familiar from moral philosophy and economic tracts. This polyvocal discourse helps to make Equiano's narrative the most readable and compelling account of slavery written in the period. That it was presented as if written by an eyewitness with personal experience of the state of slavery makes it doubly significant.

Equiano's narrative of himself explicitly served the political agenda of the nascent abolitionist movement, whose aim was the suppression of the Atlantic slave trade and eventually the abolition of slavery itself. Equiano's life served as testimony to that campaign: he wrote to expose the horrors and inequalities of slavery. The *Interesting Narrative* details that he was born an Igbo, in a village called Essaka in modern-day Nigeria. He paints a positive, even idyllic, image of his early life in Africa, before he and his sister were kidnapped into slavery to be sold to European slave-traders on the seacoast. He offers a historically significant account of the middle passage and the horrors he witnessed while a slave, first in Barbados and then in Virginia. Recent historical research has complicated this account: Vincent Carretta notes documentary evidence that suggests he was born in South Carolina in North America,[18] and parts of Equiano's account of Africa borrow scenes and ideas from previous travel writing, notably Anthony Benezet's *Some Historical Account of Guinea* (1788).[19] The fictionalised elements of his autobiography arguably show how important it was for Equiano that his writing would make a clear and significant contribution to the political cause of the anti-slavery movement. To this end, his narrative provides an account of life as a slave, and also relates how he learned to read and write, and tell accounts, key skills that transformed his slave life. It also details his conversion to Christianity, and his eventual manumission. This he achieved in 1767 by saving enough money to buy himself out of slavery, under conditions imposed on him by his then owner Robert King, a Quaker merchant from Philadelphia. As a free man, Equiano was employed as a sailor and served in a Royal Navy expedition to the Arctic in 1773, before settling in London in the early 1780s, where his political career in abolitionist circles began. He was actively engaged with the Society for Effecting the Abolition of the Slave Trade, founded in 1787 by Thomas Clarkson and Granville Sharp. His auto-biography was a document planned to be of use to this cause: 'I now offer this

[18] Carretta, *Equiano, the African*, 319–20, 350–3.
[19] Equiano, *Interesting Narrative*, ed. Carretta, 241–4; Carretta, *Equiano, the African*, 313–15.

edition of my Narrative to the candid reader, and to the friends of humanity, hoping it may still be the means, in its measure, of showing the enormous cruelties practiced on my sable brethren, and strengthening the generous emulation now prevailing in this country, to put a speedy end to a traffic both cruel and unjust.'[20]

Women and the Slave Narrative: Mary Prince

The early writings of black British writers provided eloquent testimony against the Enlightenment culture of racialised interdiction. The writings were, further, a significant contribution to the political campaign against the trade in slaves, broadly successful in Britain by 1807, and for the emancipation of slaves in British colonies in 1834. The campaigns and these texts provided significant impetus for the publication of *The History of Mary Prince* in 1831, the first narrative of a black woman and former slave published in Britain.[21] Prince was a woman of about forty years of age, who had endured very harsh treatment as a slave in Bermuda before being brought to London in 1828. There, as she tried to escape her status as a slave, she had appealed for assistance at the Anti-Slavery Society in Aldermanbury, in the heart of the City of London. The help she required was legal and monetary, and centred on her attempts to escape the state of slavery by avoiding the threat of forcible return to slavery in the Caribbean. Thomas Pringle, the secretary of the Anti-Slavery Society, gave her legal advice, arranged for the relief of her debts, and helped her find paid employment, as he detailed in his 'Supplement' to the text.[22]

The Anti-Slavery Society also agreed to support her case by assisting her to publish an account of her life, an idea 'first suggested by herself'. *The History of Mary Prince* is a self-told biography, for although she could read and write, Prince dictated her narrative to Susanna Strickland (1803–1885). Her amanuensis was an accomplished writer of books for children, who later, having moved to Canada, found some literary fame with her memoirs of pioneer life. To some extent, it is a spoken-word biography frozen in text, the oral dimension periodically reasserting itself. In the preface, Pringle explains how Prince's story was dictated to Strickland, who wrote out a full transcript, with 'all the narrator's repetitions and prolixities'. Pringle as editor reshaped the

---

[20] Equiano, 'To the Reader', *Interesting Narrative*, ed. Carretta, 5.

[21] Mary Prince, *The History of Mary Prince: A West Indian Slave*, ed. Sara Salih (London: Penguin, 2000).

[22] *History of Mary Prince*, ed. Salih, 39–63.

narrative for publication, cutting or 'pruning' extraneous material, but keeping 'Mary's exact expressions and peculiar phraseology'.[23] Mary's vocal idiosyncrasies occasionally disturb the smooth and confident flow of the late Regency prose. An example is her characteristic repetitions of key phrases: the triplet 'work – work – work' is repeated three times, and echoed in the Blakean 'weep, weep, weep'.[24] The account ends too with a call for emancipation, addressed to the King of England, calling for 'all the poor blacks be free, and slavery done up evermore'.[25] Although Pringle claimed 'no fact of importance has been omitted', he had cut away key aspects of her experience. Some of the omissions were revisited in the press after the text was published. The book had of course been intended to publicise the anti-slavery cause, and deep concern was raised by the awfulness of her experience, especially the extent to which Prince was repeatedly treated with cruelty and violence by unfeeling white slave-owners. But other readers were more hostile. James MacQueen, a former plantation overseer and anti-abolitionist campaigner, cast doubt on Prince's account in *Blackwood's Edinburgh Magazine*, accusing the abolitionists of exaggerating the suffering of the slaves, and making damaging *ad hominem* attacks on Mary Prince's character.[26] Thomas Pringle sued Thomas Cadell, the London publisher of *Blackwood's Edinburgh Magazine*, but was then countersued for libel himself. Prince gave evidence at Pringle's libel trial, providing further verification of her life story, but also revealing that her past was more complicated than her *History* had suggested. For legal reasons, and to respect religious scruples, key aspects of Prince's experience, especially around her experience of sexual abuse, were left unsaid in her narrative. In the cultural climate of the period, those events, and their omission from her story, lessened the value of her testimony. After three editions in its first year, *The History of Mary Prince* was all but forgotten until the feminist literary historian Moira Ferguson produced an edition for a trade paperback imprint in 1987.[27]

Prince's account of her suffering at the hands of the slave-owners works to personalise and sentimentalise the relation of slavery: she wants the reader to feel the trials of her experience along with her, exploiting the power of empathy. Like Sancho, Cugoano, and Equiano, her writing serves

---

[23] 'Preface', *History of Mary Prince*, ed. Salih, 3.
[24] *History of Mary Prince*, ed. Salih, 20, 21, 38, 16.   [25] Ibid., 38.
[26] James MacQueen, 'The Colonial Empire of Great Britain', *Blackwood's Edinburgh Magazine*, 30:187 (November 1931): 744–64.
[27] *The History of Mary Prince, a West Indian Slave; Related by Herself*, ed. Moira Ferguson (London: Pandora, 1987).

a polemic purpose. But the earlier male writers of the 1770s and 1780s were intent on establishing an intellectual equality, as co-religionists, cultural producers, and fellow citizens, with their implied British reader, as a way to counter the Enlightenment interdiction of African arts and letters. Mary Prince, by contrast, seeks, through a detailed account of her suffering, to demonstrate the emotional or sentimental equality she shared with her fellow Christians in England, using the commonality of feeling to beseech them for assistance in the wider struggle for emancipation.

The middle section of Prince's biography offers a series of scenes exposing the cruelties of slavery, developing a contrast between slave sensibility and the morally hardened depravity of the slave-owner. She shows how, on the one hand, the slave system harshly objectifies the slave body, which is simply a machine from which labour is extracted through the application of violence; on the other, the narrator reiterates that the slave body is a feeling body, subject to extended and extreme suffering, manifested through pain and tears. Her status as a woman underlines her capacity for feeling and suffering. The repeated scenes of weeping and tenderness, which some readers may now find mawkish, were a highly successful strategy in the literary culture of the period. Prince argues that the English slave-owners of Antigua have been corrupted by the slave system: 'Slavery hardens white people's hearts towards the blacks.' Prince explains that in this morally-depraved condition, slave-owners can see slaves only as objects and commodities. When she was sold at a slave auction, Prince explains, the 'vendue master' who conducted the auction offered her 'for sale like sheep, or cattle'.[28] Prince's narrative contrasts hard-hearted slavery and the shared humanity of feeling. In the cruel commercial logic of the slave-owner, the only motive is to extract the maximum amount of labour from the slaves, whatever the cost to their body and mind. Prince locates this commercial impulse behind the slave-owner's willingness to use, and perverse preference for, extreme violence meted out to the slave body. Against this, she describes the slave's capacity for feeling: the awful experience of the slave system leads the slave to feel more, to have more sensibility. This re-establishes a claim to humanity and the equality of experience between colonial slave and metropolitan subject. Prince expostulates:

> Oh the horrors of slavery! – How the thought of it pains my heart! But the truth ought to be told of it; and what my eyes have seen I think it is my duty to relate; for few people in England know what slavery is. I have been

[28] *History of Mary Prince*, ed. Salih, 11.

a slave – I have felt what a slave feels, and I know what a slave knows: and I would have all the good people in England to know it too, that they may break our chains, and set us free.

The first-person testimony about feeling slavery is offered as encouragement to activism. As Mary Prince says twice in the book, 'To be free is very sweet.'[29]

Conclusion: Historical Fiction in the Archive of Slavery

The archive of eighteenth-century black British writing about the experience of slavery in Africa and the Caribbean became the subject for renewed historical enquiry in the late twentieth century. In the 1980s and 1990s, a group of scholars, notably including Paul Edwards and Vincent Carretta, undertook research into eighteenth-century black British writers and their publications, producing critical editions of all the major works. David Dabydeen's *Hogarth's Blacks* (1985), which detailed the extensive presence of black figures in eighteenth-century British painting, performed similar work in the discipline of art history. These historical and editorial projects advertised and analysed the struggle undertaken by writers to overturn the culture of interdiction and encode their resistance to slavery. In their turn, this archive of narratives served as a significant resource for an extraordinary series of historical novels which appeared in the 1990s. Caryl Phillips's *Crossing the River* (1993) engages with Equiano's depiction of a bucolic African childhood, as the narrator reveals how he was forced to sell his children into slavery when his crops failed.[30] Fred D'Aguiar's *Feeding the Ghosts* (1997) novelises the history of the *Zong* slave-ship massacre, relating the story of a slave who survives being thrown overboard.[31] Slave experience of life on an eighteenth-century Caribbean sugar plantation informs further historical novels, such as Phillips's *Cambridge* (1991).[32] David Dabydeen's *A Harlot's Progress* (1999) takes the black servant figure from William Hogarth's eponymous visual satire and traces a complicated history for him between Africa and Britain, and slavery and freedom.[33] S. I. Martin's *Incomparable World* (1996) reimagines the experience of a community of former slaves, black Loyalist soldiers evacuated from North America after the rebellion of the slave-owners in 1776, living in London in the eighteenth

---

[29] Ibid, 21, 31, 38.   [30] London: Bloomsbury, 1993.   [31] London: Chatto & Windus, 1997.
[32] London: Bloomsbury, 1991.   [33] London: Jonathan Cape, 1999.

century, including not always flattering portraits of Sancho, Cugoano, and Equiano.[34] Drawing on the archives of black history, and the narratives of resistance encoded there, these works, both scholarly and fictional, provide a partial answer to Cugoano's lament, at the end of his *Thoughts and Sentiments*, that 'what I have said may appear as the rattling leaves of autumn, that may soon be blown away and whirled in a vortex where few can hear and know'.[35]

[34] London: Quartet, 1996.   [35] Cugoano, *Thoughts and Sentiments*, ed. Carretta, 110.

2

Writer-Travellers and Fugitives
Insider–Outsiders

ANTOINETTE BURTON

Travellers of African and Asian descent who came to and through Britain in the nineteenth century were a provocation. Their very presence collapsed the space between 'inside' and 'outside' and made visible the material consequences of global imperialism to native Britons, the vast majority of whom had not themselves travelled to British colonial possessions and would never do so in their lifetimes. For those travellers of colour who made it to the shores of England, Ireland, Scotland, or Wales, empire or its centripetal effects were likely the root cause of their mobility. Some came willingly, in search of work or education or fame or simply out of curiosity. Others arrived with differing degrees of agency, either in bonded service or as fugitives from slavery. Others passed through on their way to Europe or beyond, taking on the Grand Tour through colonial eyes and offering incisive ethnographies of metropolitan life. Regardless of their motives or their fates, they challenged the presumption that home and empire were segregated domains and invited all those who observed them or read their travel accounts to do the same.

Asian and African travellers were, then, doubly unsettling: they interrupted the fiction of the white Island Story *and* reminded residents of how comparatively local their own experiences of the world that Britain made were. As for their travel writing, it signalled the power of mobility to upend stereotypes and to create western audiences who wanted to see and hear the stories of people of colour on the move – if only mediated and from afar. Victorian readers followed those journeys and even made celebrities out of some travel writers, either because such figures fulfilled their fantasies about the mobile liberal self or because they believed in the causes of freedom, and freedom of movement, they appeared to embody. In many ways travel represented the ultimate expression of liberty in an age of emancipation, democracy, and progress – the triple bases of nineteenth-century English identity. In an era also defined by empire, those expressions could be limited, or were at the very least shaped, by colour prejudice and the systems of gender and class hierarchy that punctuated it at nearly every turn.

These drags on emancipation in the global field of Victorian imperialism notwithstanding, black and brown and mixed-race travellers helped to constitute a literary community of racialised life-writing that reflected the historical experience of one stratum of Britain's non-white 'subjects'. As such, they were also key players in an imperial reading commons that circulated well beyond the boundaries of empire per se. That reading commons created opportunities for a unique kind of deterritorialised sovereignty and authority for colonial travellers that was, arguably, unavailable in any other arena in the nineteenth-century anglophone world.[1]

The Work of Travel Writing in Configuring the Nation

By now it is a truism that Britain has been a crossroads of global travel and migration for centuries. Deep histories of maritime and commercial links have brought all manner of peoples – and goods and ideas – to the British Isles, throwing natives and newcomers together in perpetual encounter, embrace, collision, and conflict well before the modern period. Britain has not been a homogeneous or closed society since ancient times. It was, rather, an open and porous system, subject to pressures from both in- and out-migration in ways that could generate upward mobility for some and social alienation for others. As personal, kin, and occupational networks became embedded in urban and provincial cultures, belonging – and by extension Britishness itself – was mapped onto an insider–outsider axis cross-hatched by local–global co-ordinates.[2] Thus the social landscape that greeted nineteenth-century travellers to Britain was Victorian, but not necessarily in a self-evident way. Contrary to expectation, perhaps, what they found was a lively and dynamic blend of native Britons and short- and long-term residents from regions as close as the Netherlands to colonies as far away as Natal and New Zealand.

Any nineteenth-century traveller seeking a homogeneous British nation would have had her expectations quickly dashed by the demographic fact of

---

[1] See Antoinette Burton and Isabel Hofmeyr (eds.), *Ten Books that Shaped the British Empire: Creating an Imperial Commons* (Durham, NC: Duke University Press, 2014), 4.

[2] Laura Tabili, *Global Migrants, Local Culture: Natives and Newcomers in Provincial England, 1841–1939* (Basingstoke: Palgrave Macmillan, 2011), 62.

Irish out-migration alone. The Irish left Ireland for England and Scotland before the 1840s famine, of course, but the potato blight that killed a million people also sent hundreds of thousands of individuals and families in search of livelihoods and stable futures. That first generation developed multidirectional networks, which, in turn, continued to deliver Irish people to the cities and the countryside as skilled and unskilled labourers and domestics. Contemporary portraits were not flattering. The German traveller and socialist Friedrich Engels (1820–1895) quoted Thomas Carlyle's denunciation of the Irish as irredeemably benighted in his reformist travelogue, *The Condition of the Working Class in England* (1845), because for all intents and purposes, he agreed: 'The southern facile character of the Irishman, his crudity [. . .] places him but little above the savage.'[3]

The discourses that developed around the Irish established a hierarchy of inside-out that depended on images of savagery and helped to shape the grid of Victorian colonial difference that travellers of African or Asian descent encountered and to which they were often subject. Indeed, such was the power of Irish stereotypes – as alien, as savage, as drunken, as shiftless, and, most notoriously, as simian – that for Engels, as for other contemporaries, the Irish were often barely recognisable as white.[4] It is tempting, therefore, to privilege them as the quintessential 'Other'. But in fact, a host of colonial and ex-colonial people made their way to and through the British Isles during Queen Victoria's reign, to such a degree that the metropole itself may be thought of as every bit as multiracial as Britain's extraterritorial possessions. Coll Thrush, whose work tracks the visitations of natives from settler colonial locations to Britain from Pocahontas forward, goes so far as to make a claim for an 'indigenous London' as the right and proper way of understanding the metropole's demographic diversity.[5]

Meanwhile, Africans both slave and free had been in Britain at least since Elizabethan times.[6] People from India and China also came and went, either coerced by labour regimes or drawn to London and other cities by the promise of work or education or both. 'Travellers' in the strictest sense, they were not. But they too remind us of the long histories of heterogeneous,

---

[3] Friedrich Engels, *The Condition of the Working Class in England* (London: Penguin, 2005), 125.

[4] Noel Ignatiev, *How the Irish Became White* (New York; London: Routledge, 1995).

[5] Coll Thrush, *Indigenous London: Native Travelers at the Heart of Empire* (New Haven, CT; London: Yale University Press, 2016).

[6] And possibly before: there is evidence some Africans may have come to Britain via Roman armies; C. L. Innes, *A History of Black and Asian Writing in Britain, 1700–2000* (Cambridge: Cambridge University Press, 2002), 7.

racialised communities that travellers of colour encountered when they undertook their journeys to the metropole. These 'visible minorities' were embedded in the social and economic fabric. Their presence gave Britain a global cosmopolitan identity that belied its claims to be the exclusive heart of civilisation and whiteness, and underscores the precariousness of Britain's borders in the Victorian era. Precisely because Britain was home to scores of people who were not 'native', it was not a fully formed or accomplished 'national' space, let alone an ordered or stable one, in the time of Victoria's reign. It was, rather, an active contact zone: an often jumbled set of cultural, religious, and linguistic communities in which axes of difference cut a variety of ways – across divides of English–Irish, foreigner–native, Christian–heathen, wealthy–poor, to name just a few of the ways that spectres of inside-out were manifest.

The term 'street Arab' is one recurrent example of the kinds of civilisational and racial categories that were invoked to map the interior spaces of Britain over the course of the nineteenth century. Such terminology suggests that the nation was actually more of 'a category to be filled in' than a pre-existing order, and that the West itself was a geopolitical formation that had to be actively made through 'acts of configuration' like travel writing.[7] If we think of this uneven and dynamic terrain as the *mise en scène* of Asian and African travellers to the metropole, we appreciate the role their writing played in staking their claims to belonging *and* in shaping the very contours and parameters of that order – as much by their presence as by their writing, if not more so.

Destination Britain: Fugitives and Other Mobile Subjects

As the heart of the empire and the home to numerous port cities, Britain was the destination for runaway slaves across the long nineteenth century. Their eighteenth-century predecessors – most notably Olaudah Equiano (*c.* 1745–1797), Ottobah Cugoano (*b. c.* 1757), and Ignatius Sancho (*c.* 1729–1780) – combined autobiography with the slave narrative form to produce accounts of self-made men for whom visits to Britain were key to their social, cultural, and political formation. Abolitionism was critical to that formation; it structured the metropolitan experiences of these men and became the idiom in

[7] Saree Makdisi, *Making England Western: Occidentalism, Race and Imperial Culture* (Chicago, IL; London: University of Chicago Press, 2014), xvi.

which much subsequent slave and ex-slave writing was read by a domestic public eager for evidence to support their reformist convictions when it came to the future of slavery. Significantly, Equiano's narrative scarcely touches down in Britain. Though he receives important anti-slavery mentorship and spiritual guidance there, he represents London chiefly as a port of call for more far-flung adventures, a touchstone for points east and west, with only glimpses of its highways and byways. As a travelogue, *The Interesting Narrative* is more of an ocean story than a land-based one. Notwithstanding a few glimpses of London wharves and street locations (like Pall Mall, where he was employed as a hairdresser), it mainly captures Equiano's restless desire for the ship-deck, the open sea, and the utter freedom of movement associated with the restless pursuit of untrammelled personal liberty.

The History of Mary Prince, A West Indian Slave (1831) chronicles a quite different personal history into freedom, one as local and domestic and inward-looking as Equiano's was peripatetic and far-flung. Born in 1788 in Brackish Pond, Bermuda, Mary spent much of her early life exploited and abused as a domestic servant in Bermuda, Turks Island, and Antigua. After years of suffering and resisting the micro-aggressions of domestic confinement and enslavement, Mary came to Britain in 1828 with the Wood family, where she sought refuge in the Moravian Church in Hatton Garden, London. Because slavery was illegal in England itself she was technically free, but John Wood refused to manumit her or allow her to be hired by anyone else. As Markman Ellis details elsewhere in this volume, the Anti-Slavery Society took up her cause, publishing her story in a highly mediated way (see Chapter 1).

As travel writing, this is the story of a journey to and from what the poet Adrienne Rich calls the geography closest in: the body.

> I was a sickly body and the washing did not agree with me. But Mrs Wood would not release me from the tub, so I was forced to do as I could. I grew worse, and I could not stand to wash [...]. When I complained to my mistress of this, she only got into a passion as usual, and said washing in hot water could not hurt anyone; – that I was lazy and insolent, and wanted to be free of my work [...] I thought her very hard on me, and my heart rose up within me [...] But the English washerwomen who were at work there, when they saw that I was so ill, had pity on me and washed [...] for me.[8]

The witness of her fellow domestics, and their willingness to help her, is notable here. Household service was evidently a bond that weakened the inside–outside dichotomy; or, at least, it had the capacity to do so in the small,

---

[8] Mary Prince, *The History of Mary Prince*, ed. Sara Salih (London: Penguin, [1831] 2000), 32.

cramped spaces that threw servants and ex-slaves like Mary into proximity in the years immediately before abolition. By Mary's account, it was Mrs Wood's refusal to recognise Mary's pain and suffering 'that drove me out'. As she left, it was, again, the nurse and the servant girl from the household who witnessed her impassioned speech about the degradations of slavery. She concludes her narrative by arguing not only that slavery is wrong and freedom is 'very sweet' but that the model of English service is the ideal because servants 'have their liberty' to leave bad conditions and 'that's just what *we* want'.[9]

For Ellen (1826–1891) and William Craft (1824–1900), as for Mary Prince, Britain was a fugitive destination rather than the site of elaborate observation or experience. Their account of escape from southern US slavery is captured in the text *Running a Thousand Miles for Freedom* (1860), written from 12 Cambridge Road, Hammersmith, where they lived and raised a family for almost twenty years after their escape. The most remarkable feature of their narrative is the fact that Ellen dressed as a man so that she could accompany her husband on his flight without arousing suspicion. Her light-skinned complexion (she was the daughter of a mixed-race mother and a slave-holding father) meant that she might pass, or in this case be mistaken, for a white woman – which would have made their travel together impossible. Their account records that the disguise was Ellen's idea, but it seems that it was William who effected her transformation. He cut her hair, bought her a pair of glasses, and wrapped her in poultices, the latter to help guarantee that conversation with people they met along the way would be more difficult. 'I found', he wrote, 'that she made a most respectable looking gentleman'.[10]

What ensues is the breathless story of their passage, with Ellen pretending to be William's master, thereby leading them to freedom from Georgia to Boston and Canada until they finally board a ship to England. Through this wilful and performative act of gender inversion, Ellen turned herself inside out so that they could make the journey and live to tell the story. This inversion was not merely a gendered one. In order for the ruse to succeed, Ellen had to be believable as William's *white* master; she had to affect the mannerisms of an elite southern man to convince porters, hotel workers, and even a steamboat captain with whom she dined one night that she was a wealthy slave-holder striding confidently through the world. Unsurprisingly, the Crafts' story made

---

[9] Ibid., 38.
[10] William and Ellen Craft, *Running a Thousand Miles for Freedom: Or, the Escape of William and Ellen Craft from Slavery* (Mineola, NY: Dover Publications, 2014), 19.

them a transnational sensation, celebrated on both sides of the Atlantic for their daring and courage. But the challenges of turning gender identity inside out did not end with the travelogue. For decades, the book appeared only under the name of William Craft. Ellen did speak in public in the service of the anti-slavery cause, and she even wrote for an anti-slavery newspaper. But in the 1850s and 1860s, before the Victorian women's movement worked to challenge the custom, it was taboo for respectable women to talk from public podiums so she often remained silent, leaving her husband to be the bearer of their joint tale.

There were less well-known but equally impressive journeys by a variety of black travellers that did not garner as much attention in the nineteenth century but were consequential both locally and globally. One remarkable example is that of Amanda Berry Smith (1837–1915), an evangelist and itinerant preacher invited to Britain in the mid-1890s because of her involvement in temperance. Though not a fugitive, she was a former slave and washerwoman who travelled in England and Scotland at the invitation of Lady Henry Somerset (1851–1921) of the Woman's Christian Temperance Union. Her travel writing was neither extensive nor published between covers; she left her impressions serially, via letters to the evangelist periodical the *Christian Standard*, which archived her auto-ethnography of what it meant to be a black woman abroad. An earlier trip in the late 1870s had taken her from temperance work in Leeds to a mission trip to India and, from there, to Liberia and Monrovia, where she recorded not just her impressions of the continent but her frustration at the sight of 'backward' native customs and Africans' 'uncivilized' ways.[11] These travels were also reported serially via letters in the *Christian Standard*. Smith's dispersed and fragmented travel accounts represent the work of a variety of black Victorian evangelists in the global project of Christian conversion – itself a highly itinerant enterprise in which the boundary of inside-out was a starkly saved/not saved one, sometimes regardless of racial connection or common racial heritage.

Less common were fugitives of South Asian descent, at least in Britain itself. To be sure, in the wake of the Indian Mutiny of 1857, Muslim clerics and scholars were compelled to flee their homes, scattering as far as Cairo and Istanbul and Mecca: lurking, in other words, at the interstices of empire, between British and Ottoman imperial worlds. The historian Seema Alavi has called these men 'fugitive mullahs and outlawed fanatics' whose careers

---

[11] Adrienne M. Israel, *Amanda Berry Smith: From Washerwoman to Evangelist* (Lanham, MD: The Scarecrow Press, 1998), ch. 4. Thanks to Zach Sell for putting this book into my hands.

helped to build out networks of Muslim thinking and writing with implications for global Islamic community.[12] One such figure did actually make it to London: Jamal ad-Din al-Afghani (c. 1838–1897), an itinerant speaker and political agitator born in Iran who traversed the Middle East spreading sedition and anti-colonial ideas via fiery oratory, newspaper articles, and secret political societies. Wilfred Scawen Blunt, an anti-colonial sympathiser, befriended al-Afghani in Egypt just at the moment of British occupation. As a result of this acquaintance al-Afghani came to London in 1883, 1885, and 1892.[13] Like Amanda Berry Smith, al-Afghani's travel was powered by righteousness; like her, he could be impatient with what he saw as the failings of his fellow Muslims when it came to their capacity to advance themselves.[14] Al-Afghani's boundary-line was less the shores of Britain than the border between the British and the Ottoman empires. His fugitive life backlights not the binary of home and away but the inter-imperial landscapes that shaped the political lives and imaginative worlds of Muslim cosmopolitans in the age of empire.

Travelling Enterprise: The *Wonderful Adventures of Mrs Seacole in Many Lands*

Mary Seacole (1805–1881) was one of the most highly travelled women, regardless of colour or class, of the mid-Victorian period. She was a Crimean War heroine to Victorians and in the contemporary present. She has earned her place in the pantheon of British greats via a portrait in the National Portrait Gallery (not to mention a postcard in the gallery shop!) and, as of 2016, a statue in London. Her travelogue, published in 1857, chronicles her work as an itinerant medical warrior who not only offered accommodation, food, and drink in her 'hotel' but used her skill as a nurse and a provider of tinctures, bandages, and the occasional plum pudding to battle yellow fever, cholera, and a host of other afflictions that plagued mainly soldiers but also the down-and-out in the cities to which she travelled.[15]

---

[12] Seema Alavi, '"Fugitive Mullahs and Outlawed Fanatics": Indian Muslims in Nineteenth Century Trans-Asiatic Imperial Rivalries', *Modern Asian Studies*, 45:6 (2011): 1337–82.

[13] Pankaj Mishra, *From the Ruins of Empire: The Revolt Against the West and the Making of Asia* (New York: Picador, 2013), 96, 100.

[14] Mishra, *From the Ruins*, 70.

[15] Mary Seacole, *Wonderful Adventures of Mrs Seacole in Many Lands*, foreword by Harriet Washington (New York: Kaplan, 2009).

Seacole was such a peripatetic that calling her a traveller hardly does her justice: she was on the move constantly, sometimes picking up and putting down stakes at three-month intervals. She braved the hazards of the battle-field, whether it was to help carry out the wounded or to tend them once they had been seconded to her care. The testimonials that teem forth from the *Wonderful Adventures* speak to the gratitude that many men – young privates and established officers – felt for all she had done for them. Seacole's work brought her into intimate contact with people of many stations. She navigated the borders and boundaries of race and class and gender under the cover of professionalism: she was a medico and a good one, by all accounts. We might say that she managed the boundaries of colonial and racial difference, and of gender and status difference, as a professional before there was any such training for nurses, as the notorious struggle of Florence Nightingale (1820–1910) to have nursing even recognised as such in the wake of the Crimean War reminds us. Perhaps the most important boundary Seacole faced was the one between this life and the next; as she recounted time and again, she had become 'habituated' to 'death in its most harrowing forms'.[16] In the most existential sense, the deathbed, which was her daily workplace in war and peace, was and is the ultimate borderland, the final hyphen of inside-out.

Despite the word 'adventure' in the title of her travelogue, Seacole was not motivated by pleasure or curiosity. And though she professed herself a heroine, she was not moved only by duty or even exclusively by a sense of conviction about the rightness or wrongness of war. What the *Wonderful Adventures* registers is a notably unsentimental account of Seacole's travelling enterprise. For this heroine of the Crimea was driven, in fact, by economic necessity: by the need to earn a living and stay ahead of the spectre of poverty that dogged her writing and her life. It was the identity she assumed and actively cultivated as a shrewd and canny businesswoman-on-the-move that allowed her to manage the expectations she encountered of her as a mixed-race woman shorn of roots and family and the kinds of burdens that might otherwise be counted on to endorse her as respectable, let alone as a heroine.

Mary was hailed variously as 'Mother Seacole', 'Aunty Seacole', 'Mrs', and 'Madame' – familiar and familiarising terms used most often by patients and those who knew her. Such endearments blunted her rootlessness and fixed her in the Victorian firmament of respectability and even gentility. This was all-important as she was regularly the object of what she called 'colour

---

[16] Ibid., 60.

prejudice', which she attributed most commonly to Americans (northern and southern hemisphere). In an oft-cited scene from the book, where her attempts to get work as a nurse in a hospital were rejected, she asks readers point blank: 'Did these ladies shrink from accepting my aid because my blood flowed beneath a somewhat duskier skin than theirs?'[17]

Seacole reports being called a 'doctoress', which affirmed her medical skill and reputation as well as her identity as a woman. She was also referred to variously as 'the yellow doctoress', a 'yaller woman', and a 'nigger' woman, typically by strangers calling her out in the ports and on the streets of the cities she moved through as she peddled her services and her wares. Seacole makes no secret of these catcalls, nor of her status as an 'unprotected Creole woman'.[18] The book is a travelogue, to be sure, but it is also a series of stories designed to represent Seacole both as she was seen and as she wished to be seen: as an economically self-made, and self-making, woman who was one thing above all – the chief employer in and boss of a roving medical establishment.

As she travelled outward from Jamaica to South America and then to the battlefronts of the Crimea, Mary picked up all kinds of servants along the way. There was her manservant Mac and her maid; she hired a barber and a 'Greek Jew' whom she named 'Jew Johnny'. She had an off-site washer-woman near Balaclava as well. Seacole is at pains to tell her readers the personal servants are 'black' – presumably in contrast to her own light complexion, and presumably also to illustrate her appreciation for exactly how hierarchies of skin colour helped her to manage her own 'unprotected' status as an itinerant Creole woman. Seacole was clearly no shirker of work – 'I was doing the work of half a dozen men' – but the servants were necessary nonetheless.[19] They did the ancillary labour of running an establishment like her medical hotel at Spring Hill and of tending to her personal needs as she ran her one-woman clinic. Mary Seacole had aspirations. In the face of what ought to have been clear hierarchies and signposts of inside-out, she breezed past them towards disease and death, often at risk to her own health: she contracted yellow fever herself and we might even call her 'travel' feverish in more than a metaphorical way. She sought to be a 'woman-comrade' to the men whose wounds she tended. But she was also keen to display her own command over her patients, her customers, and her employees equally. Thieves and thievery were a constant concern; as is clear from her narrative, she relied partly on her servants to mind her stores and supplies and she was

---

[17] Ibid., 83.   [18] Ibid., 90.   [19] Ibid., 160.

quite sure she would have made more profit had she been able to hire more of them to look out for her inventory.

Seacole's travels were significant less for their affective than for their economic meaning. Or, her emphasis on the political economy of her heroism was a way of managing the inside–outside dichotomy that rendered women sentimental and vulnerable where she was, and/or wanted to be, hard-nosed and practical: a savvy and successful businesswoman, a heroine of her trade. Above all, the inside-out that Seacole saw, and lived, was the chasm between solvency and poverty. If they had been paying attention, Victorian readers could have seen how close she was to the edge, and how comparatively little the fame of being a travelling heroine actually bought her.

Pilgrim Reformers and the Traveller's Gaze

In 1872 Blanchard Jerrold (1826–1884) published *London: A Pilgrimage*, with extensive illustrations by Gustave Doré (1832–1883). The chronicle, which captured 'workaday London' from the docks to the West End to Whitechapel, was a decidedly secular pilgrimage. In an echo of that earlier book, the Parsi reformer Behramji Malabari (1853–1912) published *The Indian Eye on English Life: or, Rambles of a Pilgrim Reformer* in 1893. The 'rambles' of his subtitle was, of course, an echo of an earlier nineteenth-century tradition of walking accounts of the city (and countryside) in which typically unsophisticated folks approached the city with awe and wonder, tramping through its landscapes and leading readers across its neighbourhoods with an eye for the familiar and the strange. Malabari took up the same challenge, merging the pilgrimage and the ramble in a colonial ethnography at the heart of the fin-de-siècle empire.[20]

The Indian eye that Malabari cast was, by his own account, a reformist one. He was deeply involved in the Age of Consent Bill (1891), a piece of colonial legislation that grew out of concerns for the rights of Hindu women, especially girls and widows, whose freedom to marry (or not marry) was constrained by religious and cultural custom. Perhaps unsurprisingly, then, his travel account was filled with stories of his encounters with women on the street, in buses, and in other urban venues which threw men and women together in public in historically unprecedented ways. Having grown up in Bombay, Malabari was no stranger to the hustle and bustle of urban life.

---

[20] Blanchard Jerrold and Gustave Doré, *London: A Pilgrimage* (London: Grant and Co., 1872); Antoinette Burton, *At the Heart of the Empire: Indians and the Colonial Encounter in Late-Victorian Britain* (Berkeley, CA: University of California Press, 1998), ch. 4.

Yet the phenomenon of independent urban women was something he was not accustomed to. Nor was he prepared for the kinds of attention that the combination of his colour and his dress would attract in public thoroughfares. To add to this dynamic mix of gendered and racialised experience, Indian men were considered presumptively effeminate. As the work of historian Mrinalini Sinha has shown, they were viewed as not-quite-men by white Victorian middle-class standards.[21] As a result, Malabari took on a rather more defensive posture than native British 'ramblers', especially when it came to meeting the gaze of English women in the public sphere. His book archives some tense moments in the confines of the buses and even in the open street, where he records a variety of onlookers trying to make sense of just exactly who he is and whether his presence is menacing or innocent, curious or concerning.[22]

The Indian Eye was one of several urban ethnographies embedded in travel accounts by Indian men who made their way to the metropole in their capacity as reformers, students, and colonial nationalists in the making. Seen in this light, parts of Mohandas Karamchand Gandhi's My Experiments with Truth – those that chronicle his time as a barrister-in-training in London in the 1880s – might be added to the bibliography of colonial pilgrimages with, in his case, world-historical significance. But Indian men were not the only ones to turn the pilgrim's gaze onto British scenes. Probably the best-known Indian woman in the nineteenth century, Pandita Ramabai (1858–1922), was also the best-travelled one. A convert to Christianity, she spent time in Britain and the United States in the 1880s, during which time she recorded her observations of western life and demonstrated both her capacity as a canny observer and her ability to push back against Victorian expectations of what an Indian woman could and should be like. Ramabai travelled to Cheltenham Ladies' College, initially intending to be a doctor. Her letters to Sister Geraldine, of the Anglican community at Wantage, narrate her journey through the labyrinth of ecclesiastical hierarchy: a very particular byway of English life but one that brought her into contact with social reformers and opened out onto all kinds of Victorian political landscapes in the process.

Despite the pressure placed on her to return to India as a missionary for the Church of England, Ramabai persisted in her own quest to open a school for Hindu widows (of which she was one).[23] Her determination took her to the

---

[21] Mrinalini Sinha, Colonial Masculinity (Manchester: Manchester University Press, 1995).
[22] Burton, At the Heart, 169. [23] Burton, At the Heart, ch. 2.

USA in search of funds and other forms of support. There she travelled the length and breadth of the nation, archiving what she saw in a Marathi-language book whose title translates to *The Peoples of the United States*, which was published in 1889. As she had in her British travels, Ramabai pulled no punches. She offered Victorian readers a frank and often deeply critical assay of the government, social conditions, religious charities, and that most common of concerns in this period, the 'condition of women' question. Ramabai did not call herself a feminist, but as with Malabari, her pilgrim-tourism was rooted in convictions about the injustices visited on women and by a commitment to changing that state of affairs. Her boldness was noted by all those who heard her talk, as is evident in this headline from the *Philadelphia Evening Bulletin*: 'A Hindu Woman talks to American Women – A Unique and Striking Scene'. The fact that she spoke as a Christian in 'fluent idiomatic English' made her an insider in that crowd. That she spoke on behalf of 'millions of her Hindu sisters' lent 'a startling strangeness' to her wherever she went.[24] In that sense, her mobility and the responses it evoked were a provocation to any easy categories of inside/out – and to notions of what might count as travel writing in the context of the anglophone imperial worlds of nineteenth-century geopolitics.

Conclusion: Travelling Provocations

The archive left by the travellers I have gathered here is comparatively elite. Those that became books did so because of these networks and the support they offered in helping them write, frame, and sell their tales. Those that did not – like the letters of Amanda Berry Smith and the disparate writings of al-Afghani – have left a trace even though they were not 'upcycled' into texts between covers.[25] For each of the well-known figures examined here there are undoubtedly dozens, at least, whose movements to and from the metro-pole are not accessible to us, at least not in extended narrative form. The provocations they embodied, and the provocations they endured, are the untold stories of nineteenth-century anglophone travel, mobility, and migra-tion. Whether they were passing through or seeking to make a place for themselves in Britain 'proper', black and Asian travellers archived histories of

---

[24] Pandita Ramabai, *Pandita Ramabai's American Encounter: The Peoples of the United States*, trans. and ed. Meera Kosambi (Bloomington, IN: Indiana University Press, 2003), 4.

[25] For accounts of how that kind of 'upcycling' might shape a book's travels and historical impact, see Burton and Hofmeyr (eds.), *Ten Books*.

provocation that remind us how and why it has not been easy for people of colour to feel, or be, at home in Britain. The history of their writing foretells the challenges they pose to ready-made notions of inside-out in the age of Brexit.

3

Exoticisations of the Self
The First 'Buddha of Suburbia'

MONA NARAIN

Sake Dean Mahomet (1759–1851) arrived in Britain in September 1784 to start a new life far from his birthplace in northern India.[1] Ten years later, he published *The Travels of Dean Mahomet, A Native of Patna in Bengal, through Several Parts of India* (1794).[2] As he made a home and life in Britain, Dean Mahomet tried his hand at different occupations, first establishing a coffee-house in London and ultimately running a successful massage business in Brighton. Dean Mahomet's second and last known work, *Shampooing or Benefits Resulting from the Use of Indian Medicated Vapour Bath, as Introduced by S. D. Mahomed (A Native of India)* (1822), was about this business.[3] Michael Fisher, the modern editor of Dean Mahomet's *Travels*, argues that Mahomet was the first Indian to write and publish in English and as such his texts provide an important window into the life of an early Asian immigrant to Britain. These bookends of his British life, one written soon after his arrival and one written towards the end of his life, reveal Mahomet seeking to establish a positive identity and place for himself in a new country and later creatively asserting that identity through commerce, writing, and publication.

An examination of Mahomet's two texts contextualised within his eighteenth-century milieu reveals that, as an early 'Buddha of Suburbia', Dean Mahomet uses the trope of the 'exotic', specifically that which is Asian and/or black, as an entrepreneurship strategy to sell his immigrant status in England. Exoticism has been variously described by scholars as including the unfamiliar, the strange, the marginal, and the Other.[4] Importantly, it is both an aesthetic practice and a lived

---

[1] Variously spelled as Sake Deen Mahomed or Dean Mahomet.
[2] Dean Mahomet, *The Travels of Dean Mahomet: An Eighteenth-Century Journey through India*, ed. Michael H. Fisher (Berkeley, CA: University of California Press, 1997).
[3] Dean Mahomet, *Shampooing or Benefits Resulting from the Use of Indian Medicated Vapour Bath, as Introduced by S. D. Mahomed (A Native of India)* (Brighton: Printed by E. H. Creasy, Gazette-Office, North Street, 1822). Shampooing is a term for massage.
[4] See Victor Segalen, *Essay on Exoticism: An Aesthetics of Diversity*, trans. and ed. Yaël Rachael Schlick (Durham, NC: Duke University Press, 2002).

reality, often simultaneously, with slippage between aesthetics and lived experi-ence. Its historical trajectory is complicated and inflected by nationality, race, and gender, with distinctive differences before and after empire, as sketched out briefly below. An early border-crosser, Mahomet harnesses the exotic to bring together two different geographical locations, India and Britain, to begin to globalise British sensibility and create a space for the strange within it.[5] Paradoxically, the use of the exotically strange becomes the means for establish-ing his belonging in a new world. As an Indian in Britain who had to work hard to make new social, commercial, and literary spaces for himself, Mahomet deliberately uses his physical and cultural foreign markers to help establish what he perceives to be a developing, globally accented British culture. Mahomet, among other black and Asian eighteenth-century writers, represents the historic, diverse dimension of British identity. Like Dean Mahomet, early twentieth-century Indian writers Sarojini Naidu and Rabindranath Tagore interweave Asian themes with the English language and European genres. They utilise the power of the 'exotic' to educate the British reading public about India and to intervene in modernist discourses, but the reception of their work reveals the Orientalist framework within which British critics read their work. Late twen-tieth-century characters Haroon Amir and his son Karim Amir in Hanif Kureishi's *The Buddha of Suburbia* (1990) realise that their different skin colour is indelible in British culture and so they too, like their historical predecessors, come to exploit their Asianness.[6] Kureishi's modern day 'Buddhas' are ironic participants in their exoticisation by an intensely ocular society that has not quite scrubbed out the vestiges of colonialism.

This chapter takes a diachronic approach, with a brief synchronic foray, to illustrate aspects of the literary history of Asian immigrant writing in Britain. It highlights three distinct but related moments in this history, which corre-spond with the three parts of this volume. The primary focus of this chapter is the inaugural moment for Asian writing in Britain in the eighteenth century, when Dean Mahomet published *Travels* in 1794, with a short comparison with his predecessor Ignatius Sancho, to demonstrate similarities between the Asian and black experience in eighteenth-century Britain. The chapter exam-ines and follows Mahomet's hybridity and transnationalism, which continue to be visible in the early twentieth century, when Indian subjects of the British Empire, Sarojini Naidu and Rabindranath Tagore, 'write back' to

---

[5] Mona Narain, 'Familiarizing the Alien: Dean Mahomet's Travels, Border Crossings and the Narrative of Alterity', *Studies in English Literature 1500–1900*, 9:3 (2009): 693–716.

[6] Hanif Kureishi, *The Buddha of Suburbia* (New York: Penguin Books, 1990).

Britain, colouring British modernism with Asian themes.[7] The chapter concludes with examining the eighteenth-century resonances of Mahomet's life-writing, the first 'Buddha of Suburbia', in Hanif Kureishi's novel of the same name. Kureishi's interrogation of the Orientalist connotations of the modern-day 'exotic' leads to a delineation of the multiplicity of immigrant British identity and its satiric celebration of its own hybridity.[8] These writers and their texts reveal that the exotic functions not just as an Orientalist stereotype for Asian and black British identity but also as a productive concept strategically used and simultaneously subverted by writers, particularly in the eighteenth century, to articulate a hybrid immigrant subjectivity that necessarily straddles divisions of class, race, geography, and nationality. While there is no simple teleology to the embrace of the exotic by Asians in different time periods, the exotic recurs as a powerful trope in various forms in their writing, though its use and reception change after the establishment of empire with the ascendancy of Orientalism in the nineteenth century.

Christa Knellwolf and Ian McCalman have emphasised how the eighteenth century conceptualised 'the exotic' as an ideal 'relational concept, embracing the observer and the objects of observation', involving mutually respectful dialogue between different cultures.[9] Eugenia Zuroski Jenkins and Srinivas Aravamudan stress that exoticism can become an 'aesthetics of diversity' when untangled 'from the entwined discourses of imperialism and global capitalism', both of which were only nascent phenomena in the eighteenth century.[10] For Jenkins, exoticism is a desire to construct 'the ability to conceive otherwise', especially when coupled with cosmopolitan discourses, which demonstrates how 'eighteenth-century interest in foreign "worlds" exceeds imperial ideology'.[11] Aravamudan argues for locating a progressive dimension to exoticism, which is both pre- and post-Orientalist in its ability to create this desire for 'otherwise' before its 'functionalization [. . .] in the service of colonial rule by full blown Orientalism'.[12] Eighteenth-century

---

[7] Susheila Nasta, 'Introduction' in Susheila Nasta (ed.), *India in Britain: South Asian Networks and Connections, 1858–1950* (Basingstoke: Palgrave Macmillan, 2013), 1–11.

[8] Edward Said, *Orientalism* (New York: Pantheon Books, 1978).

[9] Christa Knellwolf and Ian McCalman, 'Introduction', *Eighteenth-Century Life*, 26:3 (2002): 1–9; 2.

[10] Eugenia Zuroski Jenkins, 'Introduction: Exoticism, Cosmopolitanism, and Fiction's Aesthetics of Diversity', *Eighteenth-Century Fiction*, 25: 1 (Fall 2012): 1–7; 1.

[11] Ibid., 1, 3.

[12] Srinivas Aravamudan, 'Response: Exoticism beyond Cosmopolitanism?', *Eighteenth-Century Fiction*, 25:1 (Fall 2012): 227–42; 228, 240. Graham Huggan's arguments in *The Postcolonial Exotic* (New York: Routledge, 2001) draw upon nineteenth-century colonial models. Using such contemporary postcolonial frameworks to 'read back' into the

fiction has a long history of engaging the exotic, seen in the work of writers from Aphra Behn to Jonathan Swift to Oliver Goldsmith, to assess and critique European world-views. When it breaks the material boundaries of the familiar, the radical potential of exoticism serves the purpose of narrating a new diverse and cosmopolitan subjectivity. Following a strong literary tradition, Dean Mahomet self-consciously uses the exotic for counter-hegemonic purposes, strategically experimenting with different versions of selfhood to engender 'multiple models of agency, affect, knowledge, and experience'.[13] The intimacy of the epistolary form, coupled with the credibility of the travelogue in Mahomet's first book and the testimonials in his second book, enables Mahomet to circumvent fiction's imaginative realm and assert authenticity through genre for new kinds of selfhood.

Though there are some important similarities, Mahomet's writing and experience in Britain are also quite different from the other eighteenth-century Indians who came as travellers to Europe and wrote about their encounters with the British upon their return to India. Mirza Sheikh I'tesamuddin, Joseph Emin, and Mirza Abu Taleb Khan wrote primarily for an Indian audience.[14] Mahomet's works address a British reading public. Mahomet's early affiliation with Britons and his later identification as a British subject resemble his predecessor Ignatius Sancho's life trajectory, demonstrating the early overlap between Asian and black experiences in Britain. C. L. Innes calls Sancho and Mahomet 'outsiders in the inside', describing how they performed different life roles to escape fixed definitions of identity.[15] Both were educated under British patrons and formed close associations with the literati and elite of British society. Each took to commerce and used writing to support their ventures and articulate their world-views.

Ignatius Sancho (c. 1729–1780), discussed in more detail by Markman Ellis (see Chapter 1), was brought as a slave to England at the age of two, educated by his patron, the second Duke of Montagu, and served as a butler and valet in his household. Later in life, he opened a grocery store in central London, while composing letters and music, and occasionally performing as an actor.

eighteenth century is problematic. Before the full establishment of empire, European views about Asians were much more fluid.

[13] Jenkins, 'Introduction', 4.

[14] Mona Narain, 'Eighteenth-Century Indians' Travel Narratives and Cross-Cultural Encounters with the West', *Literature Compass*, 9:2 (2012): 151–65.

[15] C. L. Innes, *A History of Black and Asian Writing in Britain, 1700–2000* (Cambridge: Cambridge University Press, 2002), 2; Susheila Nasta, *Home Truths: Fictions of the South Asian Diaspora in Britain* (New York: Palgrave, 2002), 1–13.

Sancho became well known as 'the extraordinary negro' owing to his accomplishments, and was the first person of African descent to vote in a British election. In the eighteenth century when vocational specialisations were fairly flexible, Sancho was able to craft multiple personae, which he used to great effect, modelling a strategy that Dean Mahomet followed a few decades later. Sancho employs the insider–outsider perspective in his letter to a friend, Jack Wingrave, in India, as he cautions against making stereotypical judgments about the 'treachery and chicanery' of Indians. Instead, he argues that European greed has been 'uniformly wicked in the East – West Indies – and even on the coast of Guinea', exploiting people and sustaining slavery; (see Chapter 4).[16] Sancho's adoption of both a black and a British sensibility represents an eighteenth-century 'citizen of the world' viewpoint.[17] Like his contemporary Olaudah Equiano, Sancho employs cosmopolitan perspectives to critique the British using western social and theological frameworks. Similarly, Dean Mahomet fashions a British identity and point of view informed by a transnational perspective.

Fashioning a Hybrid Identity

Mahomet was only eleven when he met his British patron, Godfrey Evan Baker, a new cadet serving in the East India Company Bengal Army. He joined Baker's household as a camp follower and served for fifteen years in the Bengal Army.[18] Later he followed Baker back to his home in Cork, Ireland, and upon Baker's death moved to England where he lived until his death in 1851. Mahomet published *The Travels of Dean Mahomet* through subscription, deliberately employing the novelty of the exotic to introduce India to the British public with a personal style and the familiar framework of an epistolary travel narrative. His involvement in the British imperial venture and his internalisation of British values makes him a unique interlocutor of both cultures. Residents of Cork at the time of publication included several connected to the East India Company or preparing to travel to India. Local readers as well as metropolitan Britons knew little of India beyond exotic

---

[16] 'Letter 1, To Mr. Jack Wingrave, 1778' in Vincent Carretta (ed.), *Letters of the Late Ignatius Sancho, an African* (Peterborough, Ontario: Broadview Press, 2015), 187–91.

[17] Vincent Carretta, 'Three West Indian Writers of the 1780s Revisited and Revised', *Research in African Literatures*, 29:4 (1998): 73–87; 80. He also notes that Sancho's living as a grocer depended on colonial slavery's products such as West Indian sugar and tobacco (83). Sancho, and Mahomet as a soldier of the East India Company's Bengal Army, were both implicated in British exploitation.

[18] Dean Mahomet, *Travels*, ed. Fisher, 22–3.

narratives, Company news, and imported items. They had no exposure to Indians beyond the few who served as lascars, ayahs, or mistresses of Company officials and their mixed-race families. Mahomet's task was to forge a new identity in this text. He intended *Travels* to become a guidebook connecting two geographical territories by narrating historical events that bound them together. Such connections would also allow later Asians to challenge the piety that 'home and empire were segregated domains' (see Chapter 2).

Border crossing two continents, Dean Mahomet writes his British identity as simultaneously local and cosmopolitan. In his ease with English, his embrace of Christianity despite a Muslim childhood, and his adoption of multiple cultural affiliations, including marriage to an Irishwoman, he represents an early cosmopolitan British subject who resists easy assimilation. From the beginning, Mahomet seeks to demonstrate his emotional affinity with and his loyalty to Baker, to the Company's Bengal Army, and to the British state more broadly by supporting Britain's expansion in India. Invited to live with Europeans and finding comfort in the 'humanity and affection' of his patron, Baker, Mahomet retrospectively identifies himself as both British and Indian, using the pronoun 'our' when he discusses British people and culture. Mahomet seeks the same benevolent and humane connection with the Irish in Cork, the primary audience for his book. While his criticism of putative Indian vices (fondness for opium, decadent luxury, and gambling) betrays Christian overtones, Mahomet pairs such critique with sympathetic understanding. Though a proponent of British control of India, an administration he perceives as fairer than that of local rulers, he implicitly pleads for tolerance from his readers for the strangeness of Indian customs and, by extension, for himself. Invoking biblical associations, Mahomet's Indians are people favoured 'by Providence'. His India sounds like Eden as imagined by one of England's greatest poets: 'the traveller beholds with admiration the face of this delightful country, on which he discovers tracts that resemble those so finely drawn by the animated pencil of Milton'.[19] Since he writes retrospectively about his time in India, Mahomet provides specific examples for readers to form associations. For instance, he compares 'our' Irish sedan chairs to Indian *palankeens*, the Ganges river 'ghats' to Sullivan's Quay, and an Indian bride to 'the sable Dulcinea'.[20] He employs intertextuality to integrate the non-commensurable and strange by framing them with British references.

---

[19] Ibid., 34.   [20] Ibid., 47, 80, 67.

Mahomet's descriptions of India are part of his process of integrating home and abroad and familiarising the strange. He describes Indian Muslims as temperate people given to healthy practices, something he would capitalise on later in his life as a shampooing surgeon in Brighton. He portrays Muslims meeting life's challenges and death with fortitude, a quality he himself displayed when he had to relocate in different professions.[21] Though his familiarity with Hinduism is limited, he offers an explanation of the caste system, countering claims that Hindu idolatry and polytheism are super-stitious. Mahomet explains that Hinduism professes that 'there is but one God infinitely perfect', even though God's divinity is represented in multiple anthropomorphisms.[22] His argument is part of a broader literary and philo-sophical movement in Britain at this time, joining fellow British writers such as Phoebe Gibbes and Elizabeth Hamilton (following Oriental philosophers like Sir William Jones) who sought to explain Hinduism's complex philoso-phy to the British public via popular writing and fiction.[23]

After moving to London from Ireland, Mahomet served as an apprentice to a bath-house business in 1808–1809 in London. Later he and his wife Jane set up an Indian coffee-house in a fashionable part of London to cater to East India Company officers and a British public intrigued with all things Oriental.[24] Though this business failed, Dean Mahomet recognised the untapped potential in the sale of exotic services to the London public, much as his *Travels* sought to sell India to the Irish and British reading public.

In Brighton, Mahomet capitalised on several Indian elements of his life experiences, claiming experience as a surgeon in the Company's Bengal Army. He also drew on his knowledge from working with wealthy patrons in Ireland and England as well as his business experiences in London. Brighton had become a popular location for seaside holidays, a favourite of the Prince of Wales, later King George IV. In 1787, the Prince commissioned the Brighton Royal Pavilion, an amalgamation of 'Eastern luxuries' combin-ing chinoiserie with Indian elements, a prime example of British royalty's fascination with the Orient. Mahomet established his Indian bath-house business in Brighton in 1814 and soon acquired royal patronage for his venture. In advertisements, he highlighted the use of special Indian

---

[21] Ibid., 68.   [22] Ibid., 82–3.

[23] Phoebe Gibbes, *Hartly House, Calcutta*, ed. Michael J. Franklin (New Delhi: Oxford University Press, [1789] 2007); Elizabeth Hamilton, *Translation of the Letters of a Hindoo Rajah*, ed. Pamela Perkins and Shannon Russell (Peterborough, Ontario: Broadview Press, [1796] 1999).

[24] Dean Mahomet, *Travels*, ed. Fisher, 150.

techniques and combinations of medicinal herbs and oils known only to him, distinguishing his establishment from other competitors. He fitted his bath-house with Indian paintings, linens, and Indian-style vapour baths, piping in hot and cold water for treatments. As Mahomet's fame as an Oriental shampooing surgeon grew, imitators started to spring up. The competition prompted him in 1822 to publish his second, lesser-known publication, *Shampooing or Benefits Resulting from the Use of Indian Medicated Vapour Bath*. Its purpose was both to advertise and to lay claim to his authentic training in and sole knowledge of Indian vapour shampooing.

In this second publication, Mahomet represents himself as both an English-trained surgeon and an informed Indian who possesses ancient knowledge that has proved transformative for many British patients. Mahomet establishes the roots of his art and vapour baths directly in India, writing, 'To the Hindoos, who are the cleanest and finest people of the East, we are principally indebted for the Bath [. . .] with them the medicated Bath has been brought to such perfection as to supersede the necessity of internal remedies for disease.'[25] The text provides case studies for various illnesses and each is followed by testimonials and newspaper articles that attest to the success and uniqueness of Mahomet's methods of treatment. Similar to the testimonials used to shore up the credibility of black slave narratives of the time, poems by grateful, locally well-known patients, such as Lady Louisa Cornwallis's encomium, are added to the text.[26] These testimonials applaud Mahomet as 'the dark sage' with ancient powers and support his subsequent dismissal of poor imitators and competitors. Mahomet emphasises that shampooing is the product of a combination of western and eastern knowledge that only he possesses. The text represents an early example of Asian immigrant self-fashioning based on an assertion of the exotic that refuses to be completely assimilated into the British commercial and cultural landscape.

Mahomet published three successful editions of *Shampooing*.[27] Through advertisements and extensive charitable giving, he fashioned a special, highly recognisable brand for his consumers. These public declarations of 'belong-ing' to his new home, Britain, were crucial to maintaining his royal patronage and his flourishing business. Psychologically, the gestures also helped Mahomet write his own new identity as an immigrant and become part of

---

[25] Mahomet, *Shampooing*, 11–12.   [26] Ibid., 83.
[27] Dean Mahomet, *Travels*, ed. Fisher, 167.

the Brighton community. This was all owing to his creation of an eccentric, different identity as an 'Asiatic' in Brighton that used the exotic as the basis for his brand of immigrant subjectivity.

Aligned with a British world-view, Mahomet's books demonstrate how he tames the unfamiliar and strange for his British readers, claiming authenticity for himself and empathy from his readers. As he carves a new translocal British Asian identity, Mahomet foregrounds his Asian past even as he gradually blends this identity with British allegiance.[28] His descendants continued to use his brand for practising medicine and retained his last name 'Mahomet' for several generations.

Globalising British Modernism

Mahomet is one of the earliest known Asian writers to bridge the gap between two worlds, but he is by no means the only one. Two of the best-known Indian writers of the early twentieth century, Sarojini Naidu (1879–1949) and Rabindranath Tagore (1861–1941), were writing at the height of the British Empire's control over India. In Naidu's and Tagore's work we witness the imaginative reduction of the geographical distance between home and colony, first visible in Mahomet's writing, through the bridges of language and literature. Though they are subjects of the Empire, they represent themselves first as Indians in their work. As children of highly educated Indian families, they learned English from a young age. Remarkably (because she was a woman) Naidu, and Tagore (less so because he was from an elite Bengali family), travelled to Britain to pursue higher education, coming into contact with British literati, though both returned to India without a degree. While Naidu and Tagore wrote in native Indian languages, they also wrote prolifically in English to express their blended, cosmopolitan notion of identity and literary tradition. Like Mahomet, they represent India from a native viewpoint and differently for example from their contemporaries E. M. Forster and Rudyard Kipling. They use exoticism productively to extend British modernism's diversity, and to challenge modernist notions of selfhood as universally western and male. As such, Naidu's and Tagore's works reveal the important role colonialism and the colonised played in the formation of modernity that Tani Barlow has described as

---

[28] Jahan Ramazani defines 'translocality' as the interlacing of the 'localities and nationalities with one another in a globally imagined space'; *A Transnational Poetics* (Chicago, IL: University of Chicago Press, 2009), 15.

'Colonial Modernism' and Susheila Nasta as 'Mulatto Modernities' (see Chapter 7).[29]

Naidu's collection of poetry, *The Golden Threshold* (1905), was introduced by the British writer Arthur Symons. Rabindranath Tagore's *Gitanjali* (1912) was published soon after with an introduction by fellow poet W. B. Yeats. Both Symons and Yeats praise the artistic achievement of the two Indian writers when they define the key themes of the poems they introduce. They also focus on the ultimate Oriental mysteriousness of Naidu's and Tagore's poetry, excusing the British reader from fully understanding the poems. Naidu's poetry, Symons writes, 'hint[s] [. . .] at a rare temperament, the temperament of a woman of the East, finding expression through a Western language and under partly Western influences. They do not express the whole [. . .] but [. . .] I think, its essence; and there is an Eastern magic in them'.[30] Writing for British readers, Symons configures woman and poem as embodiments of a gendered east or India under colonial rule, using this familiar trope to find a place for Naidu's exotic text within British literature.

In fact, Naidu *does* embrace the everyday experiences of Indian women and children as the subject of her poetry, while Tagore uses less gender-specific prisms. For this reason, Naidu's poetry occupies a special place for its delineation of female Asian identity in global modernist writing. 'The Village Song' poignantly expresses the adolescent Indian bride-to-be's desire to escape the 'sorrow' of patriarchal domesticity for the freedom of the 'champa-scented wild forest'.[31] 'Cradle Song' uses specifically Indian images to describe a mother's new infant and speaks of the broader experience of motherhood – 'From groves of spice, / O'er fields of rice, / Athwart the lotus-stream, / I bring for you, / Aglint with dew / A lovely little dream' – and familiarises and humanises Indian female subjectivity.[32] But Naidu also addresses more public themes of national pride in 'To India' and an ecumenical history of India, mixing Hindu, Muslim, Christian, and Zoroastrian references in 'Ode to H. H. The Nizam of Hyderabad'.[33] Both Naidu and Tagore use western poetic forms like the ode and Romantic imagery to write about pain and death. Tagore's *Gitanjali* vivifies the

[29] Tani Barlow, 'Introduction' in Tani Barlow (ed.), *Formations of Colonial Modernity in East Asia* (Durham, NC: Duke University Press, 1997), 1–20; Nasta, *Home Truths*, 1–13.

[30] Arthur Symons, 'Introduction' in Sarojini Naidu, *The Golden Threshold* (Hyderabad: Dodo Press, 1905), n.p.

[31] Naidu, *Golden Threshold*, 7.   [32] Ibid., 11.   [33] Ibid., 42, 19.

universal experience of death using western imagery coupled with Indian philosophy.

However, W. B. Yeats's introduction to *Gitanjali* describes Tagore's poems as the product of a 'supreme culture' and ascribes their exoticism to Tagore's metaphysical emphasis on the soul, in contrast with modern western poetry's more political and critical impetus. Echoing Arthur Symons's introduction to Naidu's volume, Yeats writes, 'we fight and make money and fill our head with politics – all dull things in the doing – while Mr. Tagore, like the Indian civilization itself, has been content to discover the soul and surrender himself to spontaneity'.[34] Yeats's reference to the everyday Indian subjects of Tagore's lyrics is reminiscent of the Prince of Wales's amalgamation of Chinese and Indian themes in the Royal Pavilion in Brighton, which visualised the British Empire's aggrandisement of a homogeneous, colonised east.[35] Contrary to Yeats's categorisation, both Naidu and Tagore were well-known political activists whose writing had a deep impact on the Indian independence movement, similar to Yeats's own critical role in Irish nationalism. Naidu's and Tagore's poetry was explicitly political in its efforts to resurrect a strong native Indian literary tradition. Their poetry was also political in its efforts to inflect British literature with Asian elements in ways similar to translocal black intellectuals' transnational, countercultural challenge to European modernity charted by Paul Gilroy.[36] Naidu and Tagore mix Indian themes and hybridise western literary forms to represent them, as first seen in Dean Mahomet's writing. Their production of such syncretic writing incorporates global elements into both Indian and British modern literature. On the other hand, Symons's and Yeats's reception of Naidu's and Tagore's poetry demonstrates their understanding of Asian cultures as relatively ahistorical and static, even as they sought to rectify the ethnocentrism of British modernism by the inclusion of Indian writers in it. Through the western reception of Naidu's and Tagore's poetry, we can observe late nineteenth- and early twentieth-century attempts by British and Irish critics to represent a cosmopolitan world-view that could not fully disentangle itself from colonial Orientalism.

---

[34] W. B. Yeats, 'Introduction' in Rabindranath Tagore, *Gitanjali* (Mineola, NY: Dover Publications, 2000), ix–xiv; xi, xiii.

[35] Ibid., xii.

[36] Paul Gilroy, *The Black Atlantic: Modernity and Double Consciousness* (Cambridge, MA: Harvard University Press, 1993).

Marketing Exotic Identities

Hanif Kureishi (1954–) depicts the extraordinary resilience of Orientalism's vestiges in late twentieth-century British culture in his novel *The Buddha of Suburbia,* more than forty years after the disintegration of empire in India. Written during the Thatcherite era and set against the backdrop of the 1982 Falklands War, the novel's critique of capitalism's excesses and British nationalism's strident turn is clear. Kureishi's own experience as a boy of mixed parentage, growing up in London's suburbs, serves as the autobiographical background for his novel. Tired of his suburban childhood experiences of being called 'Shitface and Curryface', and counting himself 'lucky to get home from school without serious injury', the protagonist Karim is propelled by his desire to finally 'make-it' as an actor in the highly competitive London theatre world and 'blend in' with white Britain.[37] Orientalism's vestiges are especially visible in the theatre director Shadwell's insistence that his only Asian cast member, Karim, lather on dark brown make-up and wear a loin cloth. Karim confesses the costume makes him look 'like a turd in a bikini bottom', when he plays Mowgli in a production of *The Jungle Book.*[38] Little wonder that Karim is deeply ambivalent about his typecasting as the 'Asiatic' in a play based upon Rudyard Kipling's novel of empire, even though this is his first big break. Previously, in order to move out of the conundrum of their dimly perceived Asian past and visible difference, teenagers Karim and his friend Jamila try out different ethnic affiliations to find solidarity against racism to no avail: 'The thing was, we were supposed to be English, but to the English we were always wogs and nigs and Pakis and the rest of it'.[39] It is Shadwell who finally, and explicitly, makes connections across Karim's fragmented, youthful sense of his own history by reminding Karim that he is the product of 'two hundred years of imperialism', an immigrant Everyman of the twentieth century who belongs nowhere.[40]

The problems of belonging nowhere and racial Otherness consistently confound and imprison the characters until they embrace these challenges in order to move forward. Mahomet's life as a border-crosser and Asian immigrant in Britain prefigures Haroon Amir's journey to Britain as a young boy. Haroon initially finds internal relief from his banal life by escaping into

---

[37] Kureishi, *Buddha of Suburbia,* 63.   [38] Ibid., 146.   [39] Ibid., 53.   [40] Ibid., 141.

eastern philosophy, Buddhism, and yoga. Through these 'native' practices, he rediscovers his self-confidence and uses them to create a new place for himself in English society, actively advocating eastern philosophy and yoga, first to his girlfriend Eva and then increasingly to other people.

In their efforts to compromise with the reality of being 'almost Englishm[e]n', the Amirs use exoticism to confront their own longing for belonging to Britain. Their selective enactment of Asian identity serves as a deliberate and playful subversion of the melancholy of racism.[41] As Karim struggles to find his place in Britain, he turns to his father and Haroon's friend Anwar, both of whom had immigrated to Britain together: 'Now as they aged [...] Anwar and Dad appeared returning internally to India, or at least to be resisting the English here. It was puzzling: neither of them expressed any desire to actually see their origins again.'[42] Observing the previous generation, Karim realises that the imaginative translocation of a British Asian identity, which shuttles from India to Britain, Bromley to central London, is inextricably bound with the collapse of distances between different places around the globe due to the legacies of colonialism and immigration, contracting both historical time and space. Similarly, though ambivalently, Haroon comes to embrace his Asianness more fully, later creating 'eastern practices', gleaned from multiple sources, to help lonely English people.

In the eighteenth century, Dean Mahomet had made it his business to heal English bodies. His late twentieth-century counterpart Haroon Amir makes it his business to heal English souls. However, his son Karim, the so called 'half-caste' as Shadwell labelled him, ends up both miserable and happy, caught between many worlds, trying to find his place in 'the centre of this old city that I loved, which itself sat at the bottom of a tiny island'.[43] The Buddha of Suburbia acknowledges the messiness of translocal, immigrant identity 'always in making' but is still hopeful because of Karim's desire for a future, deeper life. The novel artfully juxtaposes the experience of being an Asian immigrant in Britain (the father, Haroon) with being born Asian in Britain (the son, Karim) to paint the different challenges that different generations of Asians face in late twentieth-century Britain. Kureishi's playful 'Buddhas', Haroon and Karim, become translators and 'ethnopreneurs' of exotic Asianness in a way that echoes Dean Mahomet's entrepreneurship of

---

[41] Anne Anlin Cheng, The Melancholy of Race (Oxford: Oxford University Press, 2001).
[42] Kureishi, Buddha of Suburbia, 64.   [43] Ibid., 284.

the exotic in the eighteenth century. Dean Mahomet is an early representative of translocal Asians in Britain who inflect and colour modern British identity. In the late twentieth century, in addition to international migration, border crossings can simply be from the suburbs to the city. For Haroon and Karim, Asian Britons, and the many other lost 'buddhas of suburbia', it still takes a lifetime to figure out the journey.

4

Black People of Letters
Authors, Activists, Abolitionists

VINCENT CARRETTA

Introduction

During the roughly century-long period, ending in 1865, that saw movements in the anglophone world to abolish the transatlantic slave trade and the enslavement of people of African descent, apologists for slavery frequently asserted that the alleged lack of literary talent of the enslaved demonstrated their mental incapacity to handle freedom responsibly. Hence, the fact *that* people of African descent wrote was almost as significant as *what* they wrote. Phillis Wheatley (*c.* 1753–1784), Ignatius Sancho (*c.* 1729–1780), Olaudah Equiano (*c.* 1745–1797), and Robert Wedderburn (*c.* 1762–*c.* 1835) are best known for their respective magna opera: *Poems on Various Subjects, Religious and Moral* (London, 1773); *Letters of the Late Ignatius Sancho, an African* (London, 1782); *The Interesting Narrative of the Life of Olaudah Equiano, or Gustavus Vassa, the African. Written by Himself* (London, 1789); and *The Horrors of Slavery; Exemplified in the Life and History of the Rev. Robert Wedderburn* (London, 1824).[1] Publication by these and other writers of African descent was an important dialogic form of activism in the abolitionist era.

Once Wheatley, Sancho, Equiano, and Wedderburn were free, these formerly enslaved writers of sub-Saharan African descent chose to use letters to participate in contemporaneous dialogues about the plight of their fellow enslaved African Britons. They rhetorically transformed their positions at the margin of society into a vantage point from which to speak as supposedly

---

[1] On Equiano, see Chapter 1.

disinterested observers and critics of the societies that they were *in* but not fully *of*.[2] They did so by drawing on Judaeo-Christianity to authorise themselves to judge hypocritical self-styled Christians of European descent. They all represented themselves to varying degrees as prophetic descendants of 'Moses and the Prophets' designated to convey to their readers the Pauline doctrine that in the Christian community there 'are no more strangers and foreigners, but fellow-citizens with the saints, and of the household of God'.[3] Like Moses in the Old Testament, the archetypal Judaeo-Christian 'stranger in a strange land', Wheatley, Sancho, Equiano, and Wedderburn sought to lead an exodus of their people from slavery.[4]

Condemning Slavery: Phillis Wheatley

Enslaved in western Africa and brought to Boston in 1761 when she was about eight years old, Phillis Wheatley was given an extraordinary education by her owners. She was composing verse in English within four years. In 1770 she sent an apparently unsolicited elegy on the death of the evangelist George Whitefield to his English patron, the Countess of Huntingdon. The subsequent publication of the elegy in Boston and London brought Wheatley transatlantic fame, and earned her the Countess's patronage for her *Poems* in 1773. Prior to her manumission in the summer of 1773, Wheatley's criticism of slavery is so subtle that it went largely unappreciated for nearly two centuries.[5]

There is nothing subtle, however, about the letter with which Wheatley entered the public debate over slavery, and which established a precedent followed by succeeding authors of sub-Saharan African descent.[6] Wheatley, who describes herself in a private letter to a black correspondent as having

---

[2] The ways in which Wheatley, Sancho, Equiano, and Wedderburn position themselves rhetorically anticipate those of the later nineteenth-century authors that Antoinette Burton discusses in Chapter 2.

[3] *Letters of the Late Ignatius Sancho, an African*, ed. Vincent Carretta (Peterborough, Ontario: Broadview Press, 2015), 259: Ignatius Sancho to Jack Wingrave, 5 January 1780. Ephesians 2:19 (King James Version).

[4] Exodus 2:22.

[5] For a survey of the criticism, see John C. Shields, *Phillis Wheatley's Poetics of Liberation: Backgrounds and Contexts* (Knoxville, TN: University of Tennessee Press, 2008), 43–69.

[6] Phillis Wheatley, *The Writings of Phillis Wheatley*, ed. Vincent Carretta (Oxford: Oxford University Press, 2019), 119–20. Wheatley's letter is addressed to Samson Occom (1723–1792), a Presbyterian minister and member of the Mohegan people in Connecticut. Published first in the *Connecticut Gazette; and the Universal Intelligencer* on 11 March 1774, the letter was reprinted in nearly a dozen New England newspapers, as well as in the 3 May 1774 issue of the *Nova Scotia Gazette and the Weekly Chronicle* in Canada.

been 'a poor little outcast & a stranger' when she was brought to America, invokes the book of Exodus in her public letter.[7] Her 'Vindication of [the] natural Rights' of 'the Negroes', her first overt condemnation of slavery, appeared in numerous American newspapers in early 1774. Wheatley couples her appeal to reason with an invocation of biblical precedent and authority: 'the glorious Dispensation of civil and religious Liberty, which are so inseparably united, that there is little or no Enjoyment of one without the other: Otherwise, perhaps, the Israelites had been less solicitous for their Freedom from Egyptian Slavery'. Those who deny Negroes their natural rights render themselves 'our Modern Egyptians. [. . .] whose Avarice impels them to countenance and help forward the Calamities of their Fellow Creatures'. Wheatley turns to logic to note 'the strange Absurdity of their Conduct whose Words and Actions are so diametrically opposite'. Wheatley's own liberation authorises her to use an ironic tone bordering on sarcasm to close her indictment of slave-owners: 'How well the Cry for Liberty, and the reverse Disposition for the Exercise of oppressive Power over others agree, – I humbly think it does not require the Penetration of a Philosopher to determine.'

A Stranger in a Strange Land? Ignatius Sancho

Ignatius Sancho was the first person of African descent known to have commented on Wheatley's poetry. Brought to England as an enslaved toddler, Sancho eventually gained the patronage, as others in this volume have noted, of a nobleman whose legacy enabled Sancho to become the proprietor of a grocery shop. Like Wheatley before, and Equiano as well as Wedderburn after him, Sancho positions himself rhetorically as a stranger in a strange land to comment on English society from the perspective of an outsider, despite the fact that as a property owner in Westminster he was in the very small minority of Englishmen qualified to vote for Members of Parliament. Sancho disingenuously tells one correspondent, 'I am only a lodger – and hardly that' in England, even as he gives him a very circumstantial account of recent military affairs and their likely political consequences.[8]

---

[7] Phillis Wheatley to Obour Tanner, 21 March 1774; *Writings*, ed. Carretta, 120–1.
[8] Ignatius Sancho to Roger Rush, 7 September 1779; *Letters of the Late Ignatius Sancho*, ed. Carretta, 231. For ways in which Sancho's rhetorical use of various personae anticipated Sake Dean Mahomed's self-representations, see Chapter 3.

Sancho first gained widespread fame when the correspondence he began on 21 July 1766 with the novelist Laurence Sterne (1713–1768) appeared in Sterne's posthumously published *Letters* in 1775. Sancho's successful encouragement of Sterne to 'Consider Slavery' in his future writings was soon reprinted in London and provincial newspapers, as well as in the major contemporaneous magazines.[9] In his letter to Sterne and elsewhere in his posthumously published letters, Sancho embraces his dual identity as a black man in Britain to judge the corruption of England from a seemingly more innocent point of view. For example, when he criticises British imperialism and slavery in India, Africa, and the West Indies in a 1778 letter to Jack Wingrave, a white soldier stationed in India, Sancho rhetorically positions himself as simply 'a resident', or outsider, judging the sins of 'your country'. Sancho's objective stance also enables him to criticise the complicity of some Africans in the slave trade, though he effectively replaces his objective voice with his emotional response to the subject at the end of the passage:

> I am sorry to observe that the practice of your country (which as a resident I love [. . .]); I say it is with reluctance, that I must observe your country's conduct has been uniformly wicked in the East – West-Indies – and even on the coast of Guinea. – [. . .] – In Africa, the poor wretched natives – blessed with the most fertile and luxuriant soil – are rendered so much the more miserable for what Providence meant as a blessing:– the Christians' abominable traffic for slaves – and the horrid cruelty and treachery of the petty Kings – encouraged by their Christian customers – [. . .]. – But enough – it is a subject that sours my blood –[10]

Sancho represents Phillis Wheatley, too, as an outsider in her American society when he celebrates her poetry and censures the white readers who offer her praise but nothing else. He likens her to the stranger in Jesus's parable of the Good Samaritan in Luke 10:25–37: 'These good great folks – all know – and perhaps admired – nay, praised Genius in bondage – and then, like the Priests and the Levites in sacred writ, passed by – not one good Samaritan amongst them.'[11]

Strategically Embracing an African Identity: Olaudah Equiano

Sancho's posthumous fame was so great that Equiano identifies one of the subscribers to his *Interesting Narrative* in 1789 as 'William, the Son of Ignatius

---

[9] *Letters of the Late Ignatius Sancho*, ed. Carretta, 311.   [10] Ibid., 188.
[11] Ignatius Sancho to Jabez Fisher, 27 January 1778; ibid., 166.

Sancho', even though William was then only thirteen years old. By doing so, Equiano makes his claim to be working within the tradition of African British activism that Wheatley initiated. Equiano's connection to Wheatley is less overt than that to Sancho. They shared a patron in the Countess of Huntingdon, whose name appears on Equiano's subscription list. Through his subscriber Thomas Clarkson, Equiano was familiar with at least the Wheatley poems that Clarkson included in his *An Essay on the Slavery and Commerce of the Human Species, Particularly the African* (London, 1786).

Earlier in the 1780s, Equiano sent letters to newspapers to place himself at the forefront of the rapidly growing abolitionist movement.[12] He had followed with great interest the development of the abolitionist cause in the press and Parliament, intervening whenever he could. As he did so, his public identity evolved to match the temper of the times. Although he retained his legal name, Gustavus Vassa, even after the publication of his autobiography, he increasingly embraced an African identity in the two years between his dismissal in March 1787 from the project to resettle London's black poor in Sierra Leone, and his public claim in April 1789 of an African birth. As his public identity evolved he also increasingly came to be recognised as the spokesman for people of African descent in Britain.

In 1788 Equiano published epistolary book reviews in the *Public Advertiser* and in the *Morning Chronicle, and London Advertiser*, addressed to the authors under review. The reviews display a masterful rhetorician honing his skills. A book review is intertextual. It exists only because a prior text – the book reviewed – exists. The review must be read in light of the book reviewed, and the ways the book is subsequently read will be affected by the review. Through his reviews, Equiano joined the print exchange between his abolitionist friend James Ramsay and the apologists for slavery James Tobin and Gordon Turnbull that epitomises the intertexuality of the larger dialogue over abolition during the last decades of the eighteenth century.

Equiano entered the debate by taking on both Tobin and Turnbull within one week in the pages of the *Public Advertiser*. His letter addressed 'To J. T. Esq; Author of the BOOKS called CURSORY REMARKS & REJOINDER' appeared on 28 January 1788.[13] By calling him 'Esquire', Equiano acknowledges Tobin's superior social status as a gentleman. But his strictly *pro forma* recognition of Tobin's rank soon turns ironic. Equiano

---

[12] For Equiano's life, see Vincent Carretta, *Equiano, the African: Biography of a Self-Made Man* (New York: Penguin, 2006).

[13] Olaudah Equiano, *The Interesting Narrative and Other Writings*, ed. Vincent Carretta (New York: Penguin, 2019), 330–2.

immediately assumes the position of moral superiority to Tobin by invoking the Bible against him:

> Sir,
>
> That to love mercy and judge rightly of things is an honour to man, nobody I think will deny; but [quoting Psalm 49:20] 'if he understandeth not, nor sheweth compassion to the sufferings of his fellow-creatures, he is like the beasts that perish.' [. . .] Excuse me, Sir, if I think you in no better predicament than that exhibited in the latter part of the above clause; for can any man less ferocious than a tiger or a wolf attempt to justify the cruelties inflicted on the negroes in the West Indies? You certainly cannot be susceptible of human pity to be so callous to their complicated woes! Who could but the Author of the Cursory Remarks so debase his nature, as not to feel his keenest pangs of heart on reading their deplorable story?[14]

Equiano turns Tobin's own rhetoric against him. Tobin, a committed racist, had contended that blacks are less than fully human because they are incapable of the same degree of feeling as whites. To Equiano, Tobin, not black slaves, demonstrates 'unrelenting barbarity'. Consequently, Equiano tells him,

> for as you are so fond of flogging others, it is no bad proof of your deserving a flagellation yourself. Is it not written in the 15th chapter of Numbers, the 15th and 16th verses, that there is the same law for the stranger as for you?
>
> Then, Sir, why do you rob him of the common privilege given to all by the Universal and Almighty Legislator? Why exclude him from the enjoyment of benefits which he has equal right to with yourself? Why treat him as if he was not of like feeling? Does civilization warrant these incursions upon natural justice? No. – Does religion? No. – Benevolence to all is its essence, and do unto others as we would others should do unto us, its grand precept – to Blacks as well as Whites, all being the children of the same parent. Those, therefore, who transgress those sacred obligations, and here, Mr. Remarker, I think you are caught, are not superior to brutes which understandeth not, nor to beasts which perish.[15]

In Equiano's review, Tobin's actions and statements have transmogrified Tobin the gentleman into Tobin the beast.

But Equiano is far from done with Tobin. He calls him a liar who delights in misrepresentation: 'From your having been in the West Indies, you must know that the facts stated by the Rev. Mr [James] Ramsay are true; and yet regardless of the truth, you controvert them. This surely is supporting a bad

---

[14] Ibid., 330.   [15] Ibid.

cause at all events, and brandishing falsehood to strengthen the hand of the oppressor'.[16] Equiano appropriates the voice of God to curse Tobin and his fellow defenders of slavery, and in so cursing them Equiano overturns the current power relationship between whites and blacks.

> Recollect, Sir, that you are told in the 17th verse of the 19th chapter of Leviticus, 'You shall not suffer sin upon your neighbour'; and you will not I am sure, escape the upbraidings of your conscience, unless you are fortunate enough to have none; and remember also, that the oppressor and the oppressed are in the hands of the just and awful God, who says, Vengeance is mine and I will repay – repay the oppressor and the justifier of the oppression. How dreadful then will your fate be?[17]

From invoking divine authority to damn Tobin's immorality, Equiano shifts to using his own personal experience to undermine Tobin's credibility on the issue of whether West Indian slaves are treated well:

> The contrary of this I know is the fact at every one of the islands I have been, and I have been at no less than fifteen. But who will dispute with such an invective fibber? Why nobody to be sure; for you'll tell, I wish I could say truths, but you oblige me to use ill manners, you lie faster than Old Nick can hear them.

Cleverly, Equiano claims his readers as allies in the case against Tobin: 'the public can bear testimony with me that you are a malicious slanderer of an honest, industrious, injured people!'[18]

Even more shrewdly, Equiano closes his review with a response to Tobin's passionate condemnation of interracial sexuality, implying not only that Tobin may have hypocritically engaged in the practice himself, but may even be the product of such intercourse:

> Now, Sir, would it not be more honour to us to have a few darker visages than perhaps yours among us, than inundation of such evils? and to provide effectual remedies, by a liberal policy against evils which may be traced to some of our most wealthy Planters as their fountain, and which may have smeared the purity of even your own chastity?[19]

Equiano's readers would have recalled that Ramsay had earlier referred to 'some very near black and yellow relations' of Tobin's.[20] Equiano's response

---

[16] Ibid. [17] Ibid., 330–1. [18] Ibid., 331. [19] Ibid., 332.
[20] James Ramsay, *A Letter to James Tobin, Esq. Late Member of His Majesty's Council in the Island of Nevis* (London: printed and sold by James Phillips, George-Yard, Lombard-Street, 1787), 23.

to Tobin's dismay about racial pollution in England seems calculated to give Tobin apoplexy:

> As the ground-work, why not establish intermarriages at home, and in our Colonies? [. . .] That ancient, most wise, and inspired politician, Moses [. . .] established marriage with strangers by his own example – The Lord confirmed them – and punished Aaron and Miriam for vexing their brother for marrying the Ethiopian – Away then with your narrow impolitic notion of preventing by law what will be a national honour, national strength, and productive of national virtue – Intermarriages![21]

Equiano assumes the voice of the evangelist John to conclude his book review by threatening Tobin from the position of the highest human authority: 'If I come, I will remember the deeds which he doeth, prating against us with malicious words' (3 John: 10). Equiano ironically signs his review of Tobin's books as 'Your fervent Servant, GUSTAVUS VASSA, the Ethiopian and the King's late Commissary for the African Settlement'.[22] He calls himself an 'Ethiopian' no doubt because of the positive biblical associations with that identity. As an 'Ethiopian' he is a 'stranger' to his readers. But his reference to himself as 'the King's late Commissary' reminds them that at the same time he is also a fellow subject of the realm. He is 'Fervent', indeed, but not in the way that Tobin expected his slaves to demonstrate fervour. Equiano rarely expresses his opposition to slavery as fervently in his later *Interesting Narrative*. Like any great writer, Equiano was a great *reader* of his own audiences, knowing when he could afford to take a radical stance, and when a more moderate position would gain him an even wider readership.

He was in no mood to be moderate in 1788, however. Still writing as 'Vassa, the Ethiopian and the King's late Commissary', a week after he attacked Tobin, he turned his attention to Tobin's 'friend' Gordon Turnbull. In his 'To MR. GORDON TURNBULL, Author of an "Apology for NEGRO SLAVERY"', Equiano appropriates and polishes a passage from another African British opponent of slavery to compare Turnbull and Tobin to the pagan Demetrius in the New Testament:

> You and your friend, J. Tobin, the cursory remarker, resemble Demetrius, the silversmith, seeing your craft in danger, a craft, however, not so innocent or justifiable as the making of shrines for Diana, for that though wicked

---

[21] Equiano, *Interesting Narrative*, ed. Carretta, 332.   [22] Ibid., 332.

enough, left the persons of men at liberty, but yours enslaves both body and soul – and sacrifices your fellow-creatures on the altar of avarice.[23]

In Equiano's letter to Turnbull, also published in the *Public Advertiser*, he again uses the rhetoric of inversion. He had called Tobin inhuman. Turnbull's apology for slavery becomes in Equiano's second book review an 'Apology for oppression'.[24] Turnbull and Tobin are benighted, antichristian, and un-British:

> In this enlightened age, it is scarcely credible that a man should be born and educated, in the British dominions especially, possessed of minds so warped as the author of the Cursory Remarks and yourself. Strange that in a land which boasts of the purest light of the Gospel, and the most perfect freedom, there should be found advocates of oppression – for the most abject and iniquitous kind of slavery.[25]

Equiano sarcastically notes 'the ability and the modesty' that Tobin and Turnbull display in their treatment of 'that friend to the rights of mankind, the Rev. James Ramsay', and the 'noble' *Essay on the Treatment and Conversion of African Slaves in the British Sugar Colonies* that Ramsay had published in London four years earlier. In 1788 the terms *enlightened, liberty,* and *rights of mankind* did not yet have the radical implications they would acquire after the French Revolution the following year. But Equiano is sufficiently immoderate and radical in his review of Turnbull's book to call explicitly for 'the abolition of Slavery' itself, and not just the transatlantic slave trade.[26]

Equiano offers himself as a 'witness' against the abuses of slavery and in defence of Ramsay:

> Many of the facts he relates I know to be true, and many others still more shocking, if possible, have fallen within my own observation, within my own feeling; for were I to enumerate even my own sufferings in the West Indies, which perhaps I may one day offer to the public, the disgusting catalogue would be almost too great for belief.

To refute Turnbull's 'hypothesis, that the Negro race is an inferior species of mankind', he simply advises the 'fool' Turnbull to read Acts 17:26: 'God hath made of one blood all nations of men, for to dwell on all the face of the earth, &c.'[27]

[23] Ibid., 333. Quobna Ottobah Cugoano had earlier likened 'the Cursory Remarker' to Demetrius, the silversmith who made shrines for Diana; *Thoughts and Sentiments on the Evil of Slavery*, ed.Vincent Carretta (New York: Penguin, 1999), 18. On Demetrius, see Acts 19:23–41.

[24] Equiano, *Interesting Narrative*, ed. Carretta, 332.   [25] Ibid., 332–3.   [26] Ibid., 333.

[27] Ibid., 333–4.

Equiano invokes the 'law of Moses', presumably referring to the codifica-
tion of slavery in Exodus 21:1–11, as if the Bible indisputably supports the
abolitionist position.[28] Unfortunately, such is not the case, as the Reverend
Raymund Harris demonstrates in his 214-page *Scriptural Researches on the
Licitness of the Slave-Trade*, published in Liverpool early in 1788. When
Equiano published 'To the Rev. Mr. RAYMUND HARRIS, the Author of
the Book called – "Scripture Researches on the Licitness of the Slave Trade"'
in the 28 April 1788 issue of the *Public Advertiser*, he apparently did not know
what would soon become public knowledge. Harris, whose real name was
Don Raymondo Hormaza, was a Jesuit priest who had been expelled from
Spain in 1767. After wandering around Europe for several years he moved to
Liverpool, where he opened a school. There he soon found himself disagree-
ing with the Roman Catholic bishop, who relieved him of his priestly duties.
If Equiano did not know, he certainly correctly guessed that Harris was
a hired pen. The city of Liverpool awarded him £100 for his efforts on behalf
of the slave trade and slavery interests.

Harris effectively forced his many opponents, including Ramsay, to either
concede, at least implicitly, that a literal reading of Scripture did not support
abolition, or to resort to *ad hominem* attacks on him to divert attention from
the logic of his argument.[29] Equiano's review illustrates the difficulties
Harris's respondents faced. The closest Equiano comes to an *ad hominem*
comment is calling Harris an 'advocate' for 'the Worshipful Committee of
the Company of Merchants trading to Africa'.[30] As Equiano recognised, the
stakes in the abolition debate were higher in late April than they had been
when he reviewed Tobin and Turnbull before either the Privy Council or
Commons investigations into Britain's role in the transatlantic slave trade
had begun:

> The Subject of Slavery is now grown to be a serious one, when we
> consider the buying and selling of Negroes not as a clandestine or
> piratical business, but as an open public trade, encouraged and pro-
> moted by Acts of Parliament. Being contrary to religion, it must be
> deemed a national sin, and as such may have a consequence that ought
> always to be dreaded. – May God give us grace to repent of this
> abominable crime before it be too late![31]

---

[28] Ibid., 337.

[29] For a fuller discussion of the context and significance of Harris's argument, and
responses to it other than Equiano's, see David Brion Davis, *The Problem of Slavery in
the Age of Revolution, 1770–1823* (Ithaca, NY: Cornell University Press), 541–51.

[30] Equiano, *Interesting Narrative*, ed. Carretta, 337.   [31] Ibid., 337.

In trying to reclaim St Paul from Harris for the abolitionist cause, Equiano was compelled to defend the kind of loose interpretation of the Bible that Protestants normally accused Roman Catholics, and especially Jesuits, of practising. Rather than attending to what St Paul literally says about slavery, Equiano contends that we should be concerned with 'the whole tenor' of his writings, including what he 'plainly insinuates' and 'implied'.[32] Equiano has little choice but to argue that St Paul allowed political considerations to compromise his moral clarity:

> St. Paul in his epistles enjoins servants to submission, and not to grieve on the account of their temporal estate. For if, instead of this, he had absolutely declared the iniquity of slavery, tho' established and authorised by the laws of a temporal government, he would have occasioned more tumult than reformation [. . .] yet [. . .] he thought it derogatory to the honour of Christianity, that men [. . .] shall be esteemed slaves, and the private property of their fellow-men.[33]

Equiano believes that under different circumstances St Paul would have denounced slavery unequivocally: 'had Christianity been established by temporal authority in those countries where Paul preached [. . .] he would have urged, nay, compelled the masters, [. . .] by the most pressing arguments, to treat their quondam slaves, not now as servants, but above servants – a brother beloved'.[34] Equiano's St Paul sounds like an earlier version of Equiano himself and others who opposed slavery, but who for practical reasons chose to emphasise only their opposition to the slave trade.

Equiano's book reviews prompted an epistolary war among pseudonymous correspondents in the *Morning Chronicle, and London Advertiser* during 1788, which linked Equiano and Sancho. Responding on 19 August to his antagonist 'Christian', the pro-slavery 'Civis' writes,

> I will neither envy nor interrupt this gentleman in the enjoyment of all the amusement and instruction he can derive from the performances of Mr. Ramsay and Gustavus Vasa [*sic*]. [. . .] If I were even to allow some share of merit to Gustavus Vasa, Ignatius Sancho, &c. it would not prove equality more, than a pig having been taught to fetch a card, letters, &c. would show it not to be a pig, but some other animal. As to the Christian's wish to be pitted against the former of these blacks, I can only assure him, I am neither apprehensive nor ambitious of meeting him or his friend; and should I decline the contest, it would be from emotions of a very opposite nature from fear.

[32] Ibid., 338.   [33] Ibid.   [34] Ibid.

Robert Wedderburn

Like Wheatley and Equiano, Robert Wedderburn used the periodical press to enter the debate over slavery. But he goes much further than his predecessors in establishing himself in the prophetic tradition. He does not so much appropriate the tradition as expropriate it to serve his radical vision of the relationship between Judaeo-Christianity and slavery. He is less interested in accommodating his religious and political beliefs to those of his readers, than he is in estranging them.

Wedderburn never achieved the celebrity or success of Wheatley, Sancho, or Equiano. Wedderburn wrote almost all of his surviving works between Britain's abolition of its transatlantic slave trade in 1807 and its abolition of the institution of slavery in its American colonies in 1833. He was born in Kingston, Jamaica, around 1762, to Rosanna, a slave on the plantation of his father, James Wedderburn, a surgeon and slave-trader. Manumitted at the age of three, Robert Wedderburn was a seaman in the Royal Navy when he reached London in April 1779. There he married Elizabeth Ryan on 5 November 1781. When he responded in October 1795 to the charge that he was 'a Rogue and Vagabond', he testified that he was 'by Trade a Taylor and at present works as a Journeyman', and was 'legally settled in the Parish of Saint Leonard Shoreditch'. He was then too illiterate to sign his name.[35]

Within a few years he had become literate enough to establish himself as a radical anticlerical religious freethinker with the publication of *Truth Self-Supported; or A Refutation of Certain Doctrinal Errors Generally Adopted in the Christian Church* (London, [*c.* 1802]), which he addresses to 'Candid Reader'.[36] Wedderburn soon expressed equally radical social and political views after becoming a friend and supporter of Thomas Spence, who advocated the communal ownership of property. Following Spence's death in 1814, Wedderburn became increasingly prominent in the ultra-radical working-class political community. By participating in public debates, like Equiano before him, Wedderburn was an activist in person as well as in print. He was ordained a Unitarian minister in an ultimately unsuccessful attempt to avoid prosecution for the debates he officiated at his 'chapel' in Hopkins Street, Soho. He received a two-year prison sentence in 1820 on a charge of seditious blasphemy. He continued his radical career after his release, but less

[35] London Metropolitan Archive, MJ/SP/1795/10/034, 'Middlesex October Session 1795 The Examination of Robert Wedderburn a Rogue and Vagabond And the Witnesses against him'.

[36] *The Horrors of Slavery and Other Writings by Robert Wedderburn*, ed. Ian McCalman (Edinburgh: Edinburgh University Press, [1824] 1991), 66.

prominently than earlier, following the publication of his autobiographical *The Horrors of Slavery* in 1824. Wedderburn was sentenced in 1830 to twelve months in jail on the charge of 'keeping a disorderly house'. He was buried on 5 January 1835.[37]

Wedderburn's initial contribution to the anti-slavery movement was his short-lived epistolary periodical *The Axe Laid to the Root or A Fatal Blow to Oppressors, Being an Address to the Planters and Negroes of the Island of Jamaica*, which appeared in six issues in 1817. As Wedderburn's modern editor observes, '*Axe Laid to the Root* is a remarkable publication', best considered 'as a series of oral sermons designed to be read out to semi-literate audiences in alehouses and workshops', very different from the highly educated readers that Wheatley, Sancho, and Equiano address in their letters on slavery.[38] Wedderburn's inclusion of popular eighteenth-century sentimental anti-slavery songs in *The Axe Laid to the Root* is then very appropriate for a text with oral roots and a plebeian audience. Approaching Wedderburn's writings as if they are transcriptions of somewhat meandering oral presentations may also help to explain why his rhetorical position regarding slavery is often so much more difficult to identify than those of his African British predecessors. Moreover, as a recent critic has noted, to avoid prosecution Wedderburn designed his 'texts [to] always contain the potential for an intentional obfuscation of the real underlying intent behind them'.[39] Wedderburn's penchant for obfuscation may lie behind his apparently sincere ameliorationist and gradual emancipationist argument in his recently found 'last word on slavery', *An Address to the Right Honourable Lord Brougham and Vaux, Chancellor of Great Britain, by the Descendant of a Negro; Suggesting an Equitable Plan for the Emancipation of the Slaves* (London, 1831).[40]

As Wedderburn does in many of his writings, in *The Axe Laid to the Root* he combines fact and fiction, autobiography and intertextuality, as well as irony

---

[37] Ryan Hanley, 'A Radical Change of Heart: Robert Wedderburn's Last Word on Slavery', *Slavery & Abolition*, 37:2 (2016): 423–45; 425.

[38] *Horrors of Slavery*, ed. McCalman, 18.

[39] Eric Pencek, 'Intolerable Anonymity: Robert Wedderburn and the Discourse of Ultra-Radicalism', *Nineteenth-Century Contexts*, 37:1 (2015): 61–77; 65.

[40] Hanley, 'Radical Change of Heart', 433, argues that in *An Address to Lord Brougham and Vaux* Wedderburn rejects the abolitionist position that he takes in his earlier writings. Hanley, 441, quotes Wedderburn: 'I am so proud with the child of my imagination, that my enthusiasm would lead me to imitate the martyrs of old: the plan is just; it is founded on the very principle of inherent right. Without meaning to give offence, I am bold to challenge the collective wisdom of the universe, to produce any other that will prove effectual.' But rather than speaking *in propria persona*, Wedderburn may be unsuccessfully employing a fictional persona reminiscent of Jonathan Swift's ironic self-satisfied speaker in *A Modest Proposal* (1729).

and argument, to elide his ostensible addressees – the fictional editor, the 'slaves of Jamaica', and his possibly fictional slave-owning half-sister 'Miss Campbell' – with the British public, particularly the poor. *The Axe Laid to the Root* is multigeneric and multivocal: an epistle; a testimonial; a medley; an exhortation; a polemic against clericalism and slavery; a Spencean economic and political manifesto; a warning; a threat; a prophecy; and an exchange of correspondence. Wedderburn's inclusion of his correspondence with 'Miss Campbell', a woman of mixed parentage, within his letters to the ostensible editor gives the dialogic epistolary structure of *The Axe Laid to the Root* a nested effect. Wedderburn consequently introduces a first-person plural perspective through an act of apparent ventriloquism by having 'Miss Campbell' report on the successful implementation of his reform programme on her plantation in Jamaica.

Wedderburn establishes his ethos conventionally in *The Axe Laid to the Root*: he opens his first issue with a brief autobiography addressed to its 'editor'. But he also uses rhetorical ju-jitsu to ironically embrace his opponents' characterisations of his political and religious views to establish his ethos. He identifies himself as 'Wedderburn the deluded Spencean', who, 'being a Spencean Philanthropist, is proud to wear the name of a madman; if the landholders please, they may call me a traitor, or one who is possessed with the spirit of Beelzebub'.[41] He uses the voice of 'Miss Campbell' to evoke the account of Moses' righteous killing of a cruel slave-owner.[42] Wedderburn repeatedly invokes Moses to justify his beliefs and actions.[43] But unlike Wheatley, Sancho, and Equiano, Wedderburn does not simply place himself in the Mosaic prophetic tradition. He transforms that tradition to make it his own by, for example, calling Moses a liar, and promoting 'PURE CHRISTIAN DIABOLISM'.[44] At other times Wedderburn even more audaciously likens himself to David and Christ to combine his anticlericalism with his opposition to slavery.

Conclusion

Wheatley, Sancho, Equiano, and Wedderburn all use correspondence to engage in contemporaneous debates about slavery through the rhetorical

---

[41] *Horrors of Slavery*, ed. McCalman, 82, 83.

[42] Exodus 2:11–15. Equiano alludes to the same passage in his *Interesting Narrative*, ed. Carretta, 110–11.

[43] *Horrors of Slavery*, ed. McCalman, 85, 97, 108, 114. Exodus 2: 11–15. Equiano, *Interesting Narrative*, ed. Carretta, 110–11.

[44] *Horrors of Slavery*, ed. McCalman, 124, 153.

guise of what might be called paradoxically public epistolary intimacy. Allusions to Judaeo-Christianity, and especially to the Mosaic tradition of the book of Exodus, gave them the authority to enter the public forum. Publication of their letters gave their readers the illusion of eavesdropping on expressions of private, and therefore implicitly more sincere, thoughts. All four contributed to the movement that ultimately abolished slavery in the English-speaking world by engaging in the dialogue between the defenders and opponents of the enslavement of people of African descent. Wheatley, Sancho, Equiano, and Wedderburn offered their readers the first-person accounts of the horrors of slavery that the abolitionist movements needed. And the writings of Wheatley, Sancho, and Equiano have been cited since the eighteenth century as evidence that the intellectual capacity of people of African descent rendered their enslavement indefensible. Wheatley, Sancho, Equiano, and Wedderburn represent themselves as preachers in the Judaeo-Christian tradition to excoriate the hypocrisy of contemporaneous defenders of slavery. But like their prophetic predecessor Moses, none lived to enter the Promised Land in which all their enslaved brothers and sisters would be emancipated.

5

Engaging the Public
Photo- and Print-Journalism

PALLAVI RASTOGI

In the early twentieth century, a young Indian woman sailed to England with dreams of taking the London stage by storm with her extraordinary voice. Olive Christian Malvery (1876/7–1914) did not quite achieve the musical stardom to which she had aspired; yet she acquired fame of a different sort: as a photo-journalist who went undercover in the 'heart of the empire' to report on the seamy underbelly of London slum life. In the opening pages of her book of documentary reportage, *The Soul Market* (1907), Malvery writes:

> I began student life in India, hoping to qualify for a university degree, and towards this end I studied towards the matriculation – or, as it is called in India, the Entrance Examination to an Indian university. The studies were conducted under circumstances that almost seemed play, when compared *to the heart and blood studies of life* that I have since made [. . .] Later it was discovered that I had a voice, and it was urgently advised by those who understood these matters, that I should be sent to England to train as a singer [. . .] I came [to England] with a humble heart and absolute faith in everything that was English.[1]

Malvery dexterously constructs a somewhat multifaceted persona for herself that lingers over the entire book and in our consciousness as readers. In this short passage, she appears vain about her singing talent, displays humility towards the greatness of England in the face of her own insignificance, and also reveals the anglophilia that characterises her attitude towards her colonisers. She informs us that she is well-educated, especially for an Indian woman of her time. That gruelling education, however, was nothing compared to the grim reality – 'the heart and blood studies of life' – in England where she was exposed to horrors she had never seen in her relatively sheltered time in India. Malvery also foreshadows for her readers that her

[1] Olive Christian Malvery, *The Soul Market, with Which is Included 'the Heart of Things'* (London: Hutchinson, 1907), 9.

ideals – her 'absolute faith in everything English' – will be shaken by what she encounters in the English slums. In all her journalism, including photographic and print genres, Malvery would recycle western stereotypes of the non-western world, using imperial imagery as a mirror in which western civilisation could look at its own 'savagery' *within its own topography*. That reversal of imperial imagery would become her literary and photographic signature.[2]

Nearly two decades earlier – sometime in the 1880s – a young man arrived in England from Egypt. He too had aspirations of a life on stage, where he performed for nearly a quarter of a century. Yet for both these remarkable colonial subjects a life of theatrical glamour was not enough. Duse Mohamed Ali (1866–1945) took to editorialising, reportage, and journalism after he left the stage.[3] As founding editor of the British-published *African Times and Orient Review* and as editor of the *Islamic Review*, he sought to mould public discourse on empire, race, and religion through the medium of print-journalism.

This chapter examines how Duse Mohamed Ali and Olive Christian Malvery used the media technologies of their times, particularly those of print- and photo-journalism, in order to shape public discourses on a wide range of subjects, including those of race and empire. In the early twentieth century, Britain was at the highest point of its colonial domination. Imperial contact, the dialectical flow of culture, commodities, and people from metropolis to colony and from colony to metropolis, also perhaps reached its zenith then. Britain was host to a number of writers, students, intellectuals, journalists, artists, and performers who used the vast repertoire of expressive outlets at their disposal to mount diverse and subversive agendas, often against the empire that housed them. Many of them, such as Raja Ram Mohun Roy, Cornelia Sorabji, and Behramji Malabari, came to England as reformers and students and then returned 'home', sometimes only briefly. Others, arrived as visiting or exiled royalty or as holders of high political office, like Maharajah Duleep Singh and Sir Apolo Kagwa, Uganda's African Regent. Malvery and Duse Mohamed, however, voluntarily committed to

---

[2] I have already made this argument in my essay on Malvery in the anthology *Before Windrush*. See Pallavi Rastogi, 'An Easterner in the East End: Olive Christian Malvery's "Inverted Imperial Travelogue"' in Pallavi Rastogi and Jocelyn Fenton Stitt (eds.), *Before Windrush: Recovering a Black and Asian Literary Heritage within Britain* (Newcastle upon Tyne: Cambridge Scholars, 2008), 117–40.

[3] There have been different spellings over time, from Dusé Mohamed Ali to Duse Mohamed Ali. I will refer to Duse Mohamed Ali as Duse Mohamed, as he is more commonly known.

a permanent life in England, a choice that deepened their investment in writing about how England treated its Others within its national boundaries.

It was in this moment of high empire that these two extraordinary journalists of African and Asian heritage made their mark on the world of English letters in the Heart of the Empire. Duse Mohamed Ali was born in Egypt to a Sudanese mother and an Egyptian father. Duse Mohamed was much more of a political firebrand than the 'Anglo-Indian' Malvery who cultivated, indeed absolutely delighted in, her anglophile persona. Yet both these writers interjected themselves into metropolitan discourses of race and empire, shaping these conversations with surprising autonomy and agency. Duse Mohamed and Malvery appeared on the metropolitan stage – both of them literally so – at a time when 'print culture' and 'photo-journalism' began to enjoy mass appeal. Britain, claiming its reputation as 'the heart of the empire', to use Antoinette Burton's iconic phrase, hosted many immigrants, sojourners, students, and visiting royalty.[4] Duse Mohamed and Malvery both took strategic advantage of the rise in print culture, as well as the presence of colonial subjects in metropolitan England, to publish widely for their voices to be heard in the proliferating genres of print- and photo-journalism.

Duse Mohamed edited and wrote for publications such as the *Islamic Review*, the *Indian Sociologist and African Sentinel*, and *African Times and Orient Review* in which he sharply interrogated the hegemonic imperatives of the British Empire. He used the mode of print-journalism, primarily through his foundational work in the periodical *African Times and Orient Review*, to reformulate imperial perceptions of race, religion, and culture, especially to challenge stereotypes of the Islamic world. Malvery, however, deployed her flamboyant anglophile persona, carefully curating her Indian identity in order to show her British audience that an Indian woman could be as British as the British themselves. To gather primary research for her essays of photo-journalism, such as *The Soul Market with Which is Included the 'Heart of Things'*, Malvery went undercover in London's East End to write an exposé of the exploitation of women and children in the city's factories and sweatshops.

Duse Mohamed's and Malvery's works reveal complicated and complex ideological allegiances: the former was often *less* revolutionary than his obvious radicalism suggested whereas the latter imagined a *more* radical public role for anglicised Indians in Britain than her overt anglophilia may

---

[4] Antoinette Burton, *At the Heart of the Empire: Indians and the Colonial Encounter in Late-Victorian Britain* (Berkeley, CA: University of California Press, 1998).

have initially intimated. In a partial echo of discursive conventions of Edwardian urban reform, Malvery's journalism, paralleling that of Duse Mohamed, demonstrated the range of her political voice, undercutting her own obvious anglophilia. Both Duse Mohamed and Malvery attempted to engage their reading public in judicious ways in order to achieve their political agenda rather than merely launching into an outright diatribe against the evils of British imperialism or uncritically embracing British values and customs.

Duse Mohamed Ali and Subversive Print-Journalism

In an early edition of the *African Times and Orient Review* (June 1912), Duse Mohamed Ali, who often employed the nom de plume of Duse Mohamed, provided readers with wide-ranging information about Egyptians, Islam, race, and pan-African solidarities. Duse Mohamed, however, did not satisfy himself with simply disseminating information. The newspaper was structured in such a way that every article, photograph, or headline was undergirded by an interventionist agenda: to enter, alter, and challenge contemporary racial and imperial debates of the time. Duse Mohamed was no mere nationalist though. His purview exceeded that of Egyptian nationalism and pan-Africanism. He was a 'transnationalist' in the most open, inclusive, and diverse sense of the term. Even the title of his paper, the *African Times and Orient Review*, suggested a broad inclusivity across narrow racial or religious categories. The editorial in the 1912 issue of the journal opines, 'for, whereas there is an extensive Anglo-Saxon Press, devoted to the interests of the Anglo-Saxon, it is obvious that this vehicle of thought and information may only be used in a limited and restricted sense in its ventilation of African and Oriental aims'.[5] Yet Duse Mohamed Ali did not simply 'ventilate' African and Oriental aims; he conjoined east and south in his publications and pushed for a dialogue between the oppressed and their oppressors. Like Malvery, he too used his English audience to mould public opinion on his terms. This global and inclusive mission was embedded even in the masthead of the *African Times and Orient Review* (July 1913), which broadcast an inclusive and declarative subtitle: 'A Monthly Journal Devoted to the Interests of the Coloured Races of the World'.

---

[5] Foreword, iii. Retrieved from https://babel.hathitrust.org/cgi/pt?id=uc1.b3352514;view=1up;seq=13.

Duse Mohamed, somewhat immodestly, provided an entire page of coverage to his book *A Short History of Egypt: From the Fall of Ismail to the Assassination of Boutros Pasha* in this edition of the newspaper. A list of book reviews from prominent European papers followed. While this could be seen as shameless self-promotion, the reality is obviously a little more complicated. The words of those in power matter. In seeking metropolitan validation, Duse Mohamed also embarked on a clever marketing ploy, which had profound consequences for the more racially diverse world that he was seeking to bring into being. Who better, in some ways, to affirm the assertion of non-white equality with the Europeans than the Europeans themselves?

We will observe this later in the work of Malvery too, where what might seem like ethnic pandering and obvious anglophilia actually concealed a strategy oriented towards bringing about a deep and abiding racial diversity. In the same issue, Duse Mohamed asserted the agenda of the journal: 'THE AFRICAN TIMES AND ORIENT REVIEW, in stepping into the arena of Anglo-Saxon literature and politics, arrogates to itself no pretentions of superiority, neither does it gird itself with the weapons of offense.'[6] This editorial was careful and deliberate in its stance. The journal did not deploy verbal aggression to reveal its interventionist agenda. Neither did it attest to the 'superiority' of its agenda. Yet, this dissemblance is significant for it is precisely through its mild tone that the journal sought to build parity between the races. The paragraphs that follow, however, become increasingly strident in their call for equality by evoking the need for a journal 'which would lay the aims, desires, and intentions of the Black, Brown, and Yellow races – within and without the Empire – at the throne of Caesar'.[7] The reference to the British Empire as the throne of Caesar is a perfect encapsulation of Duse Mohamed's method of nestling slings and arrows in pieces of velvet prose. Remember that Caesar was an imperialist, who was acquiring dictatorial tendencies, before he was overthrown by the very people who had supported him. Duse thus deftly compliments as well as critiques, warning the British of the consequences of untrammelled imperial authoritarianism. But the subtle mode of his exegetical practice did not risk alienating his European readers.

The cover art of the *African Times and Orient Review* also validated its global agenda. For example, one cover includes artwork depicting a white woman atop a globe with the words 'Concordia' emblazoned across it. A bare-

[6] Retrieved from https://babel.hathitrust.org/cgi/pt?id=uc1.b3352514;view=1up;seq=13.
[7] Ibid.

breasted, ethnically ambiguous figure kneels at the bottom of the globe, holding hands with an Indian woman dressed in a sari. A straightforward analysis would suggest that the image is a plea for pro-imperial harmony across the British Empire. The vertical distance between Britannia and her imperial servants insinuates that concord is possible only if Britain maintains its spatially superior position. What if we choose to read this image differently though? What if the cover art deconstructs these imperial hierarchies by revealing the reality of the situation: that Britain has a stiff and strict hierarchical relationship with its colonies? What if real Concordia is not possible unless England abandons its position at the top of the imperial scheme? These questions may not have been suggested explicitly from within the image, but our well-trained eyes catch them quite easily today. Knowing Duse's politics, it is also quite possible that he was speaking the unspeakable in his usual coded vocabulary of compliment and critique.

The contents of the journal also validate the cover art's global scheme. Stories include articles on 'Native Lands and Crown Colonies, Japan's policy in China, The future of Persia, Appeal Law in British Guiana, The Great Buddhist and his College'. The table of contents includes essays on most of the British Empire but the journal's coverage also extends to Japanese imperialism, Persia, South America, and Buddhism. Duse Mohamed's vision as journalist and as editor was global and eclectic. He was able to showcase a cosmopolitan sensibility that was very different from Malvery, whose photo-journalism focused on a tiny subsection of London's East End population. Duse Mohamed cultivated an erudite persona that could aspire towards global citizenship, especially an *egalitarian* global citizenship, through its suave and urbane sophistication. Colonial subjects in the heart of empire often had to use metropolitan techniques in order to make themselves visible. Duse Mohamed similarly used print and visual culture to assert his place in the metropolitan scheme of things.

Yet, with the passage of time, the journal took on a heavier and more aggressive tone. The editorial in volume 2 discussed the situation in the Balkans and in West Africa in language that was more strident than usual:

> In South Africa they have not only annexed the lands of the Black Man, but they have refused to grant him a voice in his own country. The death rate has increased in the mines, and he stands an excellent chance of being blotted

from the face of Africa, in order that the Hebrew millionaire of questionable antecedents may batten in Park Lane and marry into an impoverished nobility [. . .] in West Africa the same system is being engineered.[8]

Duse Mohamed's otherwise flawless voice falters in this editorial with its obvious anti-Semitism and racial ideology, in which Malvery was also complicit. To be sure, he may have seen Jews as equal participants in imperial rule because they were white and also because of the tensions between Jews and Muslims over Palestine. Duse Mohamed's racial elitism shows up at a later point in the article when he says:

It is obvious that the so-called Native having progressed intellectually, cannot be expected to remain in the same condition of serfdom as his forefathers: and it is certainly ridiculous to treat all Natives, educated and uneducated, as on the same mental level. It is necessary either that the European should absolutely suppress all education among dependent races, or grant to the educated members those rights which their intellectuality demands. Until there is one measure for all sons of the Empire, whether Black, Brown, White or Yellow, there will be unrest and the time will come when the guiltless European will inevitably suffer for the sins of the guilty.[9]

Duse Mohamed was no fiery Frantz Fanon who argued for absolute equality for all black people. His statement certainly echoes the sentiments behind W. E. B. Du Bois's notion of the 'talented tenth' though.[10] Equality can only be expected by people who have attained a certain level of 'intellectuality'. Notice too how that equality is to be granted to the 'sons' of empire and not to its daughters, as well as the threat of violence at the end of the sentence. The journal's tone acquired more stridency as it became more and more established as a powerful voice for the colonised. Yet volume 4, published after a hiatus of two years and during the high point of World War I, took on a somewhat different tone. Duse Mohamed urged the colonised to support the empire in the time of war, with the caveat that payback would be expected when the time of judgement arrives. Evidently, he believed, like many others, that colonial support during the war would mean some measure of freedom or civil rights for the colonised afterwards.

---

[8] Retrieved from https://babel.hathitrust.org/cgi/pt?id=uc1.b3352515;view=1up;seq=14.

[9] Ibid.

[10] In his essay *The Talented Tenth* (1903), W. E. B. Du Bois argues that only 10 per cent of the most exceptional black men could lead their community. See W. E. B. Du Bois, 'The Talented Tenth' in Booker T. Washington (ed.), *The Negro Problem: A Series of Articles by Representative American Negroes of To-Day* (New York: James Pott, 1903), 35–77.

C. L. Innes also points to this shift in Duse's later writing. Even as his earlier journalistic pieces looked outwards to global solidarity, his later articles spoke more to a metropolitan British audience:

> now his writing is addressed just as much as to an audience outside as well as inside the United Kingdom, and he appeals directly to Britain's coloured population for support and contributions [. . .] just as the African business-men and politicians who supported *The African Times and Orient Review* saw the usefulness in setting up a journal in the heart of the empire, and manipulating the English cultural scene and its tools to express their own aspirations, so too a number of other Caribbean, African, and south Asian intellectuals and activists engaged in similar strategies.[11]

Duse's influence was thus profoundly global, emerging and extending itself outwardly even when nestled in the heart of the empire. In this way, he was far ahead of his time as his work went beyond pan-Africanism to embrace much of the colonised world.

Duse Mohamed Ali also moulded public opinion through the stage. He acted in many Shakespearean plays, and wrote and produced other dramatic works including *The Jew's Revenge* (1903), *A Cleopatra Night* (1907), and *Lily of Bermuda* (1909). Again, even the mere titles of the plays reveal not just his eclectic geographic range but also his interest in other regions and religions, although his anti-Semitism again raises its head in his portrayal of Josephus the Jew. According to Innes, 'reviewers commented both on his national dress and his appearance and the excellence of his English. As Ian Duffield concurs, this episode displays the divided identity imposed upon him: "the more 'British' he became, the more to the British he seemed a bizarre stranger"'.[12] Yet it is precisely in these spaces of divided identity, which Homi Bhabha would call 'almost the same but not quite', that the possibilities of subversion lie.[13] Moreover, they also reveal the conservatism behind this radical figure through the very titles of his plays: the Jew encompasses the stereotype of revenge, whereas Bermuda is associated with the white Lily and Cleopatra with the exotic and alluring night. Needless to say, the last two plays failed spectacularly on the London stage.

I would like to conclude the section on Duse Mohamed by quoting Innes's fine summary of his work: 'both as a journalist and as a commentator, Duse

---

[11] C. L. Innes, *A History of Black and Asian Writing in Britain, 1700–2000* (Cambridge: Cambridge University Press, 2002), 196.

[12] Ibid., 184.

[13] See Homi Bhabha's essay 'Of Mimicry and Man' in *The Location of Culture* (London: Routledge, [1994] 2004), 121–31.

Mohamed thus belongs more in the activist tradition of Cugoano and Wedderburn than the more conciliatory mode of Mary Seacole or Cornelia Sorabji'.[14] Duse's writings could be rousing, stirring, scathing, ironic, and biting. Unlike Malvery, he subverted from without rather than from within. He took on British colonialism and exposed it for what it was. The two writers form a striking contrast with each other in the way they sought to mould public opinion and intervene in imperial debates of their time. Obviously, their own positionality had a great deal to do with how they wrote about their subjects: Duse Mohamed was a black man from North Africa while Malvery was an 'Anglo-Indian', half-white and half-Indian. As with many writers who followed, both had to negotiate a different set of stereotypes that determined how they projected themselves to the world.[15]

Olive Christian Malvery and Subversive Photo-Journalism

Malvery revealed a different public persona from Duse Mohammed although, on closely examining the fine details of her photo-journalism, the difference between the two does not appear as radical as it may have seemed. While Malvery was ready to go undercover like many photo-journalists of her time, as I have pointed out elsewhere, the dramatic difference lay in her ethnicity.[16] Here was an Indian woman at the heart of the empire pointing an accusatory finger at the English, who had historically pointed accusatory fingers at *her* people. Malvery was undoubtedly an anglophile, as others, including Judith Walkowitz, have discussed at length.[17] Yet, anglophilia itself is never uncomplicated. Instead, following Bhabha's definition of colonial mimicry, quoted earlier, as 'almost the same but not quite', anglophilia is always wracked with internal inconsistencies, fissures, and doubts in which its subversive potential lies.[18] In the rest of this chapter, I will examine a few photos of Malvery, along with their accompanying text, in order to uncover the anti-imperialist tendencies that overtly imperialist texts may display. A cursory internet search of Malvery-related images reveals a stunning

---

[14] Innes, *History of Black and Asian Writing*, 187.

[15] Like Malvery, Duse married a white spouse and was also a proponent of mixed-race marriages; Innes, *History of Black and Asian Writing*, 174.

[16] Rastogi, 'An Easterner in the East End', 117.

[17] Perhaps the most pioneering work done on Malvery has been by the historian Judith R. Walkowitz. See 'The Indian woman, the flower girl, and the Jew: Photojournalism in Edwardian London', *Victorian Studies*, 42 (Autumn 1998/1999): 3–46.

[18] Bhabha, 'Of Mimicry and Man'.

diversity in how she presented herself. The captions often said more than the text itself. One stated: 'Miss Malvery serving in a cheap coffee house'.[19] This statement instantly elevates Malvery above the people she served through the prefix 'Miss' as well as emphasising that she is 'slumming' by describing her location as 'cheap'. The spatial arrangement of the photograph, with Malvery standing and the men she is serving sitting, also creates a visual hierarchy in which she has power over these men. But, obviously, while there is a tremendous inversion of authority with an Indian woman turning the tables on white men, power is merely inverted rather than subverted, transferred, or transformed. The men after all are relatively powerless themselves: poor working class in London's East End, an area in the imperial metropolis that was sometimes caustically called the greatest empire in the world.

In another picture, appearing in *Pearson's* magazine, Malvery is draped artistically across an ottoman in a sari with her head covered and bedecked in elaborate jewellery.[20] The class politics of such a framing cannot be over-emphasised. Malvery is veiled, her head is covered, but her face is bare. Her hand is also resting on her head-covering, asserting that she is in control of her headgear, which was always a contested symbol in the discourse and the powerplay of empire. In much of the photo-journalism in which she person-ally figured, Malvery made sure she had the agency to frame herself as a certain kind of subject: as Indian royalty and as a server at a cheap coffee shop who nonetheless extracts power from that position of patronage. In another picture in which she is dressed as an organ-grinder, Malvery wears the clothes of any working-class woman in Edwardian London.[21] But her arms are akimbo, in an almost combative posture, again giving herself power and authority through the optics of how she presents herself. These are subtle ways in which Malvery inserted herself visually into the archive of her times, unlike Duse Mohamed who spoke more through the printed word than through self-portraiture.

In a recent book entitled *Secret Commissions: An Anthology of Victorian Investigative Journalism*, the editors point out that 'Malvery's talent for thea-tricality and self-promotion sets her accounts apart from those of other social explorers, as did the unusual perspectives on English life conferred by her

---

[19] 'Olive Christian Malvery: Journalist, Lecturer, Reciter, and Social Worker', East End Women's Museum. Available at https://eastendwomensmuseum.org/blog/olive-christian-malvery-journalist.

[20] Available at http://www.hannahbruce.org/small-choices-gallery.html.   [21] Ibid.

Anglo-Indian ancestry.'[22] Perhaps Malvery's reasons for going undercover are best expressed by Rick Allen:

> Motivated for sure by Christian compassion and an indignant sense of justice, but probably also by adventurist and histrionic impulses, this remarkable young Indian woman pursued the role of social explorer much further, not merely visiting the poorest of the poor but temporarily joining their ranks [. . .] Malvery assumed false identities for essentially serious purposes, not least that of realizing for herself and her readers the classic maxim, *Nihil humanum a me alienum pute* (I regard nothing human as alien to me).[23]

This echoes, as well as inverts, the imperial mission of empire, which claimed a false equality, even though it was predicated on an unyielding binary between Self and Other.

In addition to her photo-journalism, Malvery also wrote depressingly titled books such as *Baby Toilers* (1907), *The Soul Market* (1907), and *The White Slave Market* (1914). The idea of the market, as well as of toilers in that market, appears as a repeated image in Malvery's work. Her purpose was clear-eyed and unflinching: she wanted to expose metropolitan corruption through the eyes of an outsider who could pass as a slum-dweller, thereby giving her depictions more credibility. She was equally relentless in showing the British the evils that existed before their eyes, in their own world, and how desperately the civilised world needed to clear its own 'jungle'.[24]

In *Britain and Transnational Progressivism*, David Gutzke mentions an incident in which Malvery personally took two smug 'missionaries' to the bowels of the London slums in order for them to understand that what was going on in England was not radically different from the colonies. Gutzke comments that 'Malvery was particularly horrified by "impure food." Her description of the London bakery evoked Dante's inferno.'[25] The literary reference was deliberate, of course. Like many black and Asian British writers after her, Malvery could mould the canon to suit her own purpose and her own political agenda. A closer and more nuanced look at Malvery's journalism reveals a persona at war both with itself and with the England which she so revelled in and reviled. I have shown the ways, here and elsewhere, in

---

[22] Stephen Donovan and Matthew Rubery (eds.), *Secret Commissions: An Anthology of Victorian Investigative Journalism* (Peterborough, Ontario: Broadview Press, 2012), 291.

[23] Rick Allen, *The Moving Pageant: A Literary Sourcebook on London Street Life, 1700–1914* (New York; London: Routledge, 1998), 19–20.

[24] I have made a similar point in 'An Easterner in the East End'.

[25] David Gutzke (ed.), *Britain and Transnational Progressivism* (New York: Palgrave Macmillan, 2008), 165.

which 'different disaffected groups [. . .] interact with each other in the heart of whiteness [. . . and] how her writing also highlights the rifts and fissures in a seemingly Anglophilic persona, showing [. . .] that colonized identities in the metropolis were multiple in their affiliation, always fraught with contradiction'.[26]

How then do we contrast Duse Mohamed Ali and Olive Christian Malvery, an African man and an Anglo-Indian woman? How do we compare them? Are they different not just in method but also in effect and agenda, both aiming for something different from the other? The answer, I would argue, lies somewhere in the middle. Duse Mohamed used the printed word along with artfully arranged visual text. Like Malvery, he was not unduly modest and gave himself credit whenever he needed to and sometimes even when he did not need to. But it could also be asserted that those deprived of credit have to be the most careful about promoting the value of their own work. Malvery was also no stranger to giving herself publicity. Unlike Duse Mohamed, though, she used her own body as a stage upon which a wealth of conflicting information could be projected. Gender and race complicate these conclusions further. As an Anglo-Indian, Malvery may have been more socially acceptable to the British, although, counterbalancing that argument, Duse Mohamed was perhaps given internal access to British society, based on gender, that Malvery was not. Ultimately, both writers and journalists sought the news media of their time to stage an intervention in the way Britain saw itself and its colonies. That they had to rely on different strategies of representation speaks more to their gender, their personalities, and the forums in which they were speaking than to a difference in objective. Both were subtle when subtlety was needed; both were ham-fisted upon occasion, making the point that needed to be made with a lack of nuance. Yet both interceded in metropolitan discourse to create a space for subaltern voices that was, consciously or unconsciously, thus made available to later writers. This political space allowed colonial and postcolonial writers to speak for themselves, often in the language of metropolitan codes and conventions, which nonetheless elaborately punctured the frames of those same codes and conventions. Dean Mohamed and Malvery certainly wrote back to the empire, holding its deficiencies as a promise to do better not only by the people it colonised but also by the people it colonised *within its inner sanctum*.

---

[26] Rastogi, 'An Easterner in the East End', 117.

PART II

★

UNEVEN HISTORIES
Charting Terrains in the Twentieth Century

Preface

Studies of the emergence of black and Asian literary culture in the twentieth century have focused almost exclusively on the decades following the end of World War II and the arrival of SS Empire Windrush at Tilbury Docks in 1948 as iconic signifier of Britain as a multicultural nation. There are a number of viable reasons for this, not least the widespread cultural amnesia that screened out the uncomfortable realities of the longue durée *of Britain's imperial past which was accompanied by a failure to recognise the existence of an already significant black and Asian British population. After 1947, with the Independence of India and the Partition of the subcontinent, Britain strategically averted its eyes from the uncomfortable realities of the global consequences of its imperial past as it sought to define a new identity as a postcolonial and island nation. Political turmoil abroad, labour shortages after the war, and the seeming 'open door' policy of the 1948 Nationality Act had prompted large-scale economic migrations from the Caribbean, Africa, and South Asia before successive Immigration Acts (1962, 1968, 1970, 1981) imposed increasing restrictions on Britain's non-white former colonial subjects and Commonwealth citizens. Whilst the post-1945 period was certainly prolific in terms of the number of black and Asian writers publishing in Britain, as writers migrated to the metropolis and another generation of British-born black and Asian artists were born, the uneven emergence of this now substantive body of work has to be read alongside some of the most turbulent political and social decades of the twentieth century. Issues of racial and social inequality, national and cultural identity, black power, gender and human rights – already contested by black and Asian Britons since the Aliens Act in 1919 – came increasingly to the fore in the 1970s and 1980s, as artists began to interrogate and challenge notions of 'Englishness', inclusion, and the orthodoxies of the canon. And whereas 'black' was first adopted in the 1970s as a strategic political signifier – a collective identity to unite the voices of Britain's marginalised black and Asian communities – by the mid-1980s, the necessary shift towards cultural diversity and pluralism enabled a recognition of more complexly defined identifications and affiliations, whether of class, race, gender, or sexuality. The twentieth century closes with a questioning of the liberal secular consensus presupposed by cultural pluralism, accompanied by the ascendancy of political Islam. However, it also saw the growth of a publishing industry keen to prize diasporic identities and 'Otherness', a move only temporarily bolstered by the wide commercial success of award-winning books by Zadie Smith and Monica Ali and the popular appeal of black and Asian British film, television, and drama.*

(1)

★

GLOBAL LOCALS
Making Tracks at the Heart of Empire

6

Between the Wars
Caribbean, Pan-African, and Asian Networks

DELIA JARRETT-MACAULEY AND SUSHEILA NASTA

During the twentieth-century interwar years, there was a marked rise in the number of black (Caribbean, pan-African) and Asian political and cultural groupings in Britain. These included left-wing activist groups challenging fascist warmongers, student bodies who questioned the impact of colonialism, and writers setting up their own publishing houses and discussion groups in order to challenge colonial and imperialist thinking and practice to reach new readers. From the mid-1920s onwards, a small but significant number of these networks involved black and Asian writers, some of whom resided, settled, and published in Britain for long periods, actively contributing to anti-colonial protests, before returning to, or in some cases settling in, their countries of origin in South Asia, the Caribbean, or Africa.[1]

The writers of this productive generation wrote novels, collections of poetry, plays, short stories, and non-fictional essays. Many works were first published in Britain, are still in print, and form the subject-matter of subsequent chapters in this *History*.[2] The focus here, however, is on the underlying sociopolitical networks that gave meaning and substance to these writers' lives and work. This chapter will demonstrate how these mixed constituencies of Asian, pan-African, and Caribbean writers who came together at the heart of empire between the wars were to generate a number of parallel creative and political projects that were of increasing significance in the formation of anti-colonial resistance and political independence movements. As Lyn Innes notes in her pioneering study which charts the background to

---

[1] See: C. L. Innes, *A History of Black and Asian Writing in Britain, 1700–2000* (Cambridge: Cambridge University Press, 2002); Kristin Bluemel, *George Orwell and the Radical Eccentrics: Intermodernism in Literary London* (Basingstoke: Palgrave Macmillan, 2004); and Susheila Nasta, '1940s–1970s' in Deirdre Osborne (ed.), *The Cambridge Companion to British Black and Asian Literature (1945–2010)* (Cambridge: Cambridge University Press, 2016), 23–39.
[2] See Chapters 7 and 8.

the emergence of black and Asian British writing from 1700 to 2000, global unrest following World War I, uprisings and strong anti-British sentiment in Ireland, the fallout from Amritsar in India, and race riots in the United States, all served to stoke the fears of the British government and feed a sense of militancy amongst all colonial peoples.[3] This growing resistance to and disenchantment with empire became increasingly evident amongst Britain-based colonial writers and intellectuals who turned towards socialism and Marxism as the most effective anti-imperialist stance. Notably, alliances developed with prominent figures of the left-wing British intelligentsia, including Sylvia Pankhurst, Nancy Cunard, Victor Gollancz, Fenner Brockway, Sidney and Beatrice Webb, George Bernard Shaw, George Lansbury, Keir Hardie, and the young Michael Foot.[4]

Such cross-cultural affiliations were productive, but it is important not to forget that a form of apartheid, commonly referred to as the 'colour bar', was still very much in operation during these years.[5] It prevented black people from entering certain public places, hotels, clubs, and pubs. Regularly flagged as a topic in popular newspapers, issues around the colour bar also reached the debating rooms at Oxford and Cambridge. As F. D. Karaka (1911–1974), first Indian president of the Oxford Union, was to observe ironically in 'A Barbarian is Born' (1935), one of the central paradoxes of western modernity is that whilst it opens new spaces for some, it simultaneously closes doors for others.[6] A talented journalist, non-fiction writer, and war correspondent, Karaka published widely on the colour bar as well as the lives of Indians in imperial Britain, most notably, *The Pulse of Oxford* (1933), *Oh! You English* (1935), and his collected essays, *All My Yesterdays* (1944). His words were prescient. Visible black and Asian minorities continued to be excluded from many areas of work until well into the 1950s and there was discrimination in public services, in nursing, education, the law, and the armed forces.[7] Given the losses suffered as a result of the colonial war effort, the prevalence of such overt discrimination was reason enough to prompt writers to congregate and voice their fellowship and solidarity. Initiatives, like the Coloured Men's Institute (CMI) in Canning Town, sprang up at grassroots level to counter discrimination against mixed-race marriages, common amongst lascar

---

[3] Innes, *History of Black and Asian Writing*, 175.   [4] Ibid., 175–6.
[5] See Learie Constantine, *The Colour Bar* (London: Stanley Paul, 1954).
[6] Cited in Susheila Nasta, *Home Truths: Fictions of the South Asian Diaspora in Britain* (Basingstoke: Palgrave, 2002), 25, 29.
[7] This discrimination was evident across all walks of life continuing well into the 1950s and 1960s as detailed in Beryl Gilroy's memoir, *Black Teacher* (London: Cassell, 1976).

seamen. Founded in 1926 by Kamal Athon Chunchie, a Ceylonese pastor of Malay origin, the CMI provided a safe sanctuary for working-class men and women. Formerly a Chinese lodging-house, the building offered rooms for social meetings and respite from the racism encountered on London's streets.

Many of Britain's black and Asian residents found themselves living in major seaport cities, Liverpool, London, Cardiff, and Hull, where the majority of the population were in low-paid or insecure jobs as lascar seamen, cooks, or hostel-owners.[8] It made sense therefore for the young, educated, and artistically inclined colonial students and intellectuals to band together and voice the injustices prevalent across the race and gender divides. This was more than evident in the life and work of Shapurji Saklatvala. One of Britain's first Asian MPs, he was elected as Labour Party member for Battersea in 1922. A nephew of the industrialist J. N. Tata, Saklatvala married Sarah Marsh, who came from a working-class English background in Derbyshire, and campaigned fiercely for workers' rights, launching the Workers' Welfare League (WWL) in 1917. Initially focusing on London's lascar seamen, the WWL soon widened its objectives, linking to the causes espoused by other activists such as George Padmore and Krishna Menon (discussed below). In addition to their common experience as disappointed colonial 'guests', individuals and groups rapidly built alliances, also comparing their frustrations with conditions 'back home'.

Perhaps not surprisingly, a number of organisations sprang up which began to promote the rights of the black and Asian population in Britain, also connecting to imperial inequalities and wider global issues. Bodies such as the West African Students Union (WASU, 1925), the League of Coloured Peoples (LCP, 1931), the Negro Association in Manchester, the India League (1916, formerly Annie Besant's Home Rule for India League, later Commonwealth of India League), the Coloured People's Associations in Edinburgh and Cardiff, and the African Service Bureau began to flourish.[9] Alongside, a number of small journals and newsletters began to circulate information, intervening in debates to reach a diverse readership and link different communities. These included, amongst others, the *African Times and Orient Review* (1912–1920), *The Keys*, arm of the LCP, the West African

---

[8] See: Georgie Wemyss, 'Littoral Struggles, Liminal Lives: Indian Merchant Seafarers' Resistances' and Rehana Ahmed, 'Networks for Resistance: Krishna Menon and Working-Class South Asians in Inter-War Britain' in Rehana Ahmed and Sumita Mukherjee (eds.), *South Asian Resistances in Britain 1858–1947* (London: Continuum, 2012), 35–54, 70–91.

[9] Innes, *History of Black and Asian Writing*, 167–77.

Students Union journal *Wasu* (first issue, 1926), and the various publications of the Indian Students Association (1877–1933).[10] Today, these and other enterprises, like *Indian Writing* (1940–1942), a literary magazine co-edited by four Asian writer-activists, Iqbal Singh, Ahmed Ali, Kirshnarao Shelvanakar, and Alagu Subramaniam, provide vibrancy and texture to the more broad-brush general histories that have to date documented the consistent patterns of racism and discrimination faced by black and minority people in Britain during the colonial period.

In attempting to map this complex area, the tools of the book and cultural historian – who might scrutinise letters, diaries, or limited editions of orga-nisational newsletters – are valuably combined with more formal published sources. Although this chapter will point to key networks, it should be noted that many writers and activists belonged to several organisations concur-rently and at different times. To provide a comprehensive breakdown of all the different groups to which these writers belonged would need to be the subject of a much longer study.[11] Many quite distinct cultural histories and individual life-stories are necessarily fused in this short appraisal. Some have already been the subject of extensive scholarly endeavour and are also addressed elsewhere in this volume (see Chapters 7, 8, 9, and 11). Together however these sources provide an insight into the complex interplay between these writers and offer a window on how particular writers or groups developed connections with cultural organisations and thinkers in the English literary and art worlds, including writers such as Leonard Woolf of the Hogarth Press, E. M. Forster of the Bloomsbury circle, academics such as the LSE professor Harold Laski, and George Orwell, the political novelist, journalist, and BBC broadcaster.[12]

Leading Writers and their Groups

The Urdu writer Sajjad Zaheer (1904–1973), son of a prominent Indian judge, was sent to Oxford in 1927 to study law. Like many others who

---

[10] Known as *The Journal of National Indian Association, The Indian Magazine and Review*. See www.open.ac.uk/researchprojects/makingbritain/content/journal-national-indian-association.

[11] See Rozina Visram, *Asians in Britain: 400 Years of History* (London: Pluto, 2002); some valuable archival work has also been made available by the George Padmore Institute (www.georgepadmoreinstitute.org) and the South Asians Making Britain project (www.open.ac.uk/researchprojects/makingbritain).

[12] Bluemel, *George Orwell* and Susheila Nasta, 'Sealing a Friendship: George Orwell and Mulk Raj Anand at the BBC (1941–43)', *Wasafiri*, 26:4 (2011): 14–21.

crossed the 'black waters' after World War I, Zaheer was to encounter many passionate South Asian intellectuals in the colonial heartland whose experiences in India and Britain urged him to consider a different career path. His Urdu novella *Ki Ek Raat* ('A Night in London', 1938; first published in translation in 2011) is set in Bloomsbury and depicts angst-ridden young men, like himself, frustrated by the injustices and hypocrisies of British rule and longing for a vision of a fairer society, both at home and abroad. Forging close links with the Communist Party of Great Britain, Zaheer met some key figures such as the poet and activist Ralph Fox, becoming one of the party's first South Asian members. At Oxford, he served as chief editor of *Bharat*, a journal of socialist politics run by South Asian students concerned with the struggle for independence. In 1932 he edited a collection of ten experimental Urdu short stories, titled *Anghare* ('Burning Coals'), which included writers such as Ahmed Ali, whose first novel, *Twilight in Delhi* (1940), was later published by the Hogarth Press. The progressive and iconoclastic content of the collection's stories caused considerable controversy and it was subsequently banned in India by the government of the United Provinces, further radicalising its editor and prompting him to build more formal links with fellow activists in both India and Britain and create a radical writers' group.[13] He devoted himself to this and, in 1954, several years after his return to his new nation of Pakistan, published his reminiscences of this time in *Roshnai*.[14]

One of Zaheer's most significant alliances was with the young Indian novelist Mulk Raj Anand (1905–2004) who, like him, was keenly aware of the pitfalls of colonial rule. Working for a short period for T. S. Eliot at *The Criterion* and for Leonard Woolf at the Hogarth Press, Anand was strategic in building contacts within Bloomsbury networks (as detailed in his belated memoir, *Conversations in Bloomsbury*, 1981) and also with the left-wing British establishment as well as Herbert Read and George Orwell at the BBC.[15] An accomplished polymath and public intellectual, he published extensively in Britain and India from the 1930s, carefully placing himself on and negotiating a number of cultural, literary, and artistic platforms. He was the author of ten novels well as poetry, essays, autobiographies, art criticism, and short

---

[13] See: Priyamvada Gopal, *Literary Radicalism in India: Gender, Nation and the Transition to Independence* (Abingdon: Routledge, 2006).

[14] Sajjad Zaheer and Amina Afzar, *The Light: A History of the Movement for Progressive Literature in the Indo-Pakistan Subcontinent* (Oxford: Oxford University Press, 2006).

[15] See Bluemel, *George Orwell* and Nasta, 'Sealing a Friendship'.

stories.[16] He also became heavily involved with broadcasting for the BBC Eastern Service, commissioning the content in Britain alongside George Orwell during the war years.[17] His commitment to leftist politics was both practical and theoretical: even though he earned a doctorate in Philosophy from London's University College, he chose to forgo academic work to become involved with the socialist Workers' Education Association. A committed member of the International Brigade during the Spanish Civil War, he worked as a war correspondent from Barcelona, completing whilst he was there an early draft of his powerful World War I novel which dramatises the often forgotten contribution of Indian sepoys to the trenches, *Across the Black Waters* (1940). It is not the object here to provide a literary analysis of Anand's fiction but it is worth remembering that whilst early novels, like *Untouchable* (1935) and *Coolie* (1936), adhere to forms of social realism in their depiction of the dehumanising contradictions within colonial Indian society, setting a generation of British and Indian readers thinking about the social evils perpetuated in the name of religion and tradition, they also self-consciously articulate Anand's evolving and 'prescient global alternative to a predominantly Euro-American vision of modernity, carving out a space to locate himself and his Indian subjects in history'.[18] Resident in Britain for over twenty years, Anand returned to India in 1945 on a troop ship, founding the fine arts magazine *Marg* (1946–) soon after.

Together, Anand and Zaheer established the All-India Progressive Writers' Association (PWA), which by all accounts they founded in 1935 in a basement at the Nanking Chinese restaurant in Fitzrovia. At this meeting, which included participants from across the Indian student circuit as well as figures like the poet Ralph Fox, Anand was elected President of the Association and asked to draft its manifesto. Early drafts were edited by Zaheer and Dr Jyotirmaya Ghosh (both co-founders) with the final version circulated to several thousand readers of the *Left Review* in 1936:

> Radical changes are taking place in Indian society [. . .] We believe that the new literature must deal with the basic problems of our existence today – the problems of hunger and poverty, social backwardness, and political subjection. All that drags us down to passivity, inaction and un-reason we reject as

[16] For a full discussion of Anand's networks see: Susheila Nasta, '"Negotiating a New World Order": Mulk Raj Anand as Public Intellectual at the Heart of Empire 1925–1945' in Ahmed and Mukherjee (eds.), *South Asian Resistances in Britain*, 140–60.

[17] Some of Anand's letters to Orwell are published in W. J. West (ed.), *Orwell: The War Broadcasts* (London: Duckworth, 1984); see also Nasta, 'Sealing a Friendship', 14–19.

[18] This case is made in detail in Nasta, *Home Truths*, 15–55.

re-actionary. All that arouses in us the critical spirit, which examines institutions and customs in the light of reason, which helps us to act, to organise ourselves, to transform, we accept as progressive.'[19]

Around the same time as these radical South Asians were forming the PWA, the League of Coloured Peoples, initiated some years previously in 1931, was going through seismic shifts, sparked by the activities of two young writers of Caribbean origin who were passionately writing tracts and publishing pamphlets about anti-colonialism and the challenges of racial discrimination in Britain.

In his powerful memoir, *Beyond a Boundary* (1963), the Trinidadian-born intellectual C. L. R. James (1901–1989) wrote: 'In March 1932 I boarded the boat for Plymouth. I was about to enter the arena where I was to play the role for which I had to prepared myself. *The British intellectual was going to Britain.*'[20] C. L. R. James was to become one of the foremost writers of his generation both in the colonial environment and in Britain. The role for which he had prepared himself meant making a leap out of the world of the nineteenth-century colonial intellectual to become a fringe member of the Bloomsbury group and eventually an ever more radical thinker and a close associate of fellow West Indian activist and writer George Padmore.

In the Caribbean, where he published some early short fiction, C. L. R. James had befriended the famous cricketer Learie Constantine. After arriving in Britain he resided with Constantine in Nelson, Lancashire before moving to London. Cricket was the central motif of his first book, *The Life of Captain Cipriani* (1932), which featured an outstanding West Indian political personality who asserted the readiness of West Indian society to assume self-rule. The text was eagerly snapped up by the Hogarth Press, run by Leonard and Virginia Woolf. As a result, the author agreed to abridge the work, which was published a year later under the more muscular title *The Case for West Indian Self-Government* (1933). The Hogarth Press was not the only English publishing house on the lookout for radical anti-colonial works. Martin Secker & Warburg Limited, for example, established in 1936, keenly promoted C. L. R. James's episodic novel *Minty Alley* (one of the first books on their new list). Set in the midst of Trinidadian barrack-yard culture, it depicts the contradictions of the author's West Indian childhood where 'the

---

[19] Mulk Raj Anand, 'Manifesto of the Indian Progressive Writers' Association, London', *Left Review*, 2:5 (1936): 240; see also Anand, 'On the Progressive Writers Movement' in Sudhi Pradhan (ed.), *Marxist Cultural Movement in India*, vol. 1 (Calcutta: National Book Agency, 1979), 1–22.

[20] C. L. R. James, *Beyond a Boundary* (London: Stanley/Hutchinson, 1963).

social ambience of a fused colonial community was analysed in terms of [. . .] class privilege and class oppression'.[21] Also offering British readers a critique of empire, Lawrence & Wishart, a left-wing publisher with Communist Party roots, published two of Mulk Raj Anand's early works. His first novel, *Untouchable*, which concerns a day in the life of a sweeper boy, was finally published in 1935 after nineteen rejections and was prefaced by E. M. Forster. It is now a Penguin Classic. Wishart also published the poetry of Anand's friend and associate, the English writer Ralph Fox, whose support was critical in the founding of the PWA. In other words, pan-African and Asian writers began to be actively supported by a number of the smaller English presses, which, in turn, had an impact on the thinking of the reading public.[22]

But in the mid-1930s it was C. L. R. James's boyhood friend George Padmore (1903–1959) who most closely shared his ideals. C. L. R. James won a scholarship to Trinidad's main government school. Padmore, another Trinidadian, was the son of a schoolteacher. A journalist and activist from an early stage, Padmore arrived in London, via New York and Moscow, in 1935. In England, he wrote for the Independent Labour Party's (ILP) weekly, the *New Leader,* and for other independent left-wing publications such as *Controversy, Left, Socialist Leader,* and *Tribune.* And in 1936, following Mussolini's invasion of independent Abyssinia, he published *How Britain Rules Africa,* which Fryer has heralded as a 'detailed and outspoken indictment';[23] *Africa and World Peace* followed in 1937. By the mid-1930s, Padmore and C. L. R. James were without doubt the leading anti-colonial figures writing and speaking about the attack on Abyssinia (now Ethiopia), the only free state in Africa.[24] Though Padmore did not ever formally join the Independent Labour Party, he collaborated closely with several of its members.[25]

Another writer from the Caribbean who came to Britain in 1932 was the Jamaican poet and playwright Una Marson (1905–1965). One of the few colonial women who travelled independently, Marson first resided in the

[21] Robert A. Hill, 'In England 1932–38' in Paul Buhle (ed.), *C. L. R. James: His Life and Work* (London: Allison & Busby, 1986), 61–80; 66.
[22] For a fuller discussion of the book history of this period see Ruvani Ranasinha, 'Talking to India: The Literary Production and Consumption of Selected South Asian Anglophone Writers in Britain and the USA' and Susheila Nasta, 'Between Bloomsbury and Gandhi? The Background to the Publication and Reception of Mulk Raj Anand's *Untouchable*', both in Robert Fraser and Mary Hammond (eds.), *Books Without Borders,* vol. 2: *Perspectives from South Asia* (Basingstoke: Palgrave Macmillan, 2008), 170–81, 151–70.
[23] Peter Fryer, *Staying Power: The History of Black People in Britain* (London: Pluto, 1984), 335.
[24] Ibid. [25] Ibid., 334, 336–7.

home of Harold Moody, the founder of the recently formed black-led organisation the League of Coloured Peoples. She soon became its assistant secretary, vociferously participating in meetings as well as contributing to its newsletter, *The Keys*. Her poem 'Nigger', a harsh critique of the street racism she encountered in Britain, appeared in the first issue, in July 1933. The LCP was not a radical organisation, but its entertainments – concerts, day trips, and sports events – and the publication of its regular newsletter provided a much-needed source of communication for many African and West Indian young people who were struggling against the colour bar. Like C. L. R. James, Marson wanted to find a metropolitan publisher. She placed great value on being at the centre of empire and longed to reach a British audience. Using the platform of the LCP, she was able to meet the Poet Laureate John Masefield as well as other English writers. She also promoted her first play *At What a Price*, mounting a production in London's West End in 1934. As a prominent activist in the League's affairs, Marson reached out to the wider community, finding new friends among feminists such as Winifred Holtby and making international contacts by her lectures to women's groups in Europe. She often joined public debates on the colour bar and spoke out as a black woman about the discrimination faced by black nurses and on women's issues at home in Jamaica.[26] It was rare to hear a woman of African and Caribbean heritage address such issues in England at this time; most of Marson's peers from the colonies were men – students, lawyers, and doctors in the making – amongst whom her intersectional concerns with race and gender stood out.

Although her activism was mainly cultural rather than political, Marson was deeply affected by the 1935 invasion of Abyssinia by the Italian dictator Benito Mussolini. Like other anti-colonial activists across the globe, she wanted to assist the apparently helpless African nation facing this seemingly unprovoked attack, and she volunteered to work for the Ethiopian Legation in London. Amy Ashwood Garvey (former wife of Marcus Garvey), Jomo Kenyatta, C. L. R. James, and others organised themselves into the International African Friends of Abyssinia (IAFA) with the main purpose of arousing the British public's support for the victim of fascist aggression, and when the defeated Haile Selassie arrived in London, the IAFA organised a reception for him at Waterloo Station.

---

[26] Delia Jarrett-Macauley, *The Life of Una Marson 1905–65* (Manchester: Manchester University Press, 1998). See ch. 7, 'Identity Politics', 68–79.

The Italian–Abyssinian war prompted the politicisation of the membership of the League of Coloured Peoples. While actively anti-racist and critical of the 'colour bar', their founder and leader Dr Harold Moody had initially drawn back from completely denouncing the British state. However, after Mussolini's attack, the League was deemed out of touch with the younger, more radical activists, led by C. L. R. James, who had no qualms about vehemently spelling out his opinion in *The Keys* in 1936:

> Africans and people of African descent, especially those who have been poisoned by British Imperialist education, needed a lesson. They have got it. Every succeeding day shows exactly the real motives, which move imperialism in its contact with Africa, shows the incredible savagery and duplicity of European Imperialism in its quest for markets and raw materials. Let the lesson sink in deep.[27]

In response to such shifts, Moody's stance changed. Una Marson's activities and those of other LCP members now dovetailed with those of the more radical West Indians, including C. L. R. James and Padmore, who had become the leading lights of the IAFA. In 1937, the IAFA was replaced by the broader-based International African Service Bureau (IASB), embracing the rights of all of those of African descent and representing them to the British public. This was evidenced in its leadership: Sierra Leonean I. T. A. Wallace-Johnson as General Secretary, Padmore as Chair, with many of the former members of the IAFA joining the ranks. At this time C. L. R. James was also editor of a monthly journal, *International African Opinion*, sold at IASB meetings. Padmore, equally prolific, continued to publish numerous books, pamphlets, and articles arguing the case against imperialism and in support of the global ideology of pan-Africanism.

Wider Visions: Changing the World

Marson returned to Jamaica in 1936. There, in addition to speaking and writing about her experience with the Ethiopian legation, she reported on the West Indian Labour rebellions and wrote anti-colonial articles for the *Jamaica Standard*. Marson also encouraged writers to discover platforms for their work in literary magazines abroad and at home. She created the Kingston Readers and Writers Club, a group that met to discuss books and manuscripts and to hear lectures, to encourage creativity and critical

---

[27] C. L. R. James, 'Abyssinia and the Imperialists', *The Keys*, 3:3 (January–March 1936): 32–40.

thinking.[28] Being back home afforded her the opportunity to join fellow Jamaican writers such as Roger Mais (1905–1955) in challenging the imperial Victorian ideals that had shaped their youth.

When Marson came back to London in 1938, her involvement with the BBC and her steering of the influential radio programme *Caribbean Voices* (1944) was pivotal in shaping what was to become a vision of Caribbean literary and cultural production after the war.[29] Originally invited to work as an assistant on *Calling the West Indies*, its predecessor and a programme designed to speak to West Indian servicemen, Marson was instrumental in shifting its content to a cultural agenda, drawing on West Indian writers and artists in Britain.[30] Over the next twenty-five years some of the most exciting Caribbean literary talents were to appear on that show, which launched the careers of writers like V. S. Naipaul, Andrew Salkey, Sam Selvon, and George Lamming (see Chapters 9 and 14).

Marson's key role at the BBC was captured in a famous 1942 photograph (specifically requested by George Orwell) of a poetry magazine programme he was producing during the war years entitled *Voice*. The photograph is remarkable for its unique capture of the programme's notable mixed participants. These included: George Orwell and T. S. Eliot, William Empson, Mulk Raj Anand, Venu Chitale, Narayana Menon, and M. J. Tambimuttu, the Ceylonese editor of *Poetry London* (1938–1951), a magazine that regularly featured the works of major British artists and sculptors, such as Henry Moore and Barbara Hepworth, and published soon-to-be major poetic voices like Kathleen Raine and Dylan Thomas. Marson is centrally located in the image as the presenter, the figure linking the writers and offering a vision of crucial pan-African, Caribbean, Asian, and British networks both at home and abroad.

When Marson returned to Jamaica again after World War II, she was a very different person from the young woman who had arrived in Britain as assistant secretary for the LCP in the early 1930s. Back home, Jamaican publishing became the focus. She established the Pioneer Press, which brought out a mixture of fiction and poetry for young readers. The first books were a volume of short stories, *Anancy Stories and Dialect Verse* (1950), largely the work of the young Louise Bennett (1919–2006), and *Maxie*

---

[28] Jarrett-Macauley, *Life of Una Marson*, 181–97.
[29] Different years have been given for the beginning of the BBC *Caribbean Voices* programme; however, archival research by James Procter, in 'Una Marson at the BBC' (*Small Axe* 19:3 (2015): 1–28; 3), suggests that the programme started in 1944.
[30] Ibid., 157.

Mongoose and Other Animal Stories (1950) by Laurice Bird. And, drawing on her understanding of the contexts for broadcasting and publishing in Britain, she helped young writers like Andrew Salkey and Vic Reid to launch their literary careers. (Vic Reid published his debut novel *New Day* with US publisher Alfred Knopf in 1949.) She also persuaded her London associate, the novelist and biographer Vera Brittain, to give a talk about writing at the Extra Mural Department of the University of the West Indies, promoting further collaborations by asking other London-based writers to provide challenging reading material to her young circle.[31]

Like Marson, Cedric Dover (1904–1961) was a writer who straddled several key political and cultural groups. Born in Calcutta in 1904, to an English father and an Indian mother, Dover first became a zoologist. Having dedicated his life to the study of race, he employed his scientific knowledge to write a series of sociological and anthropological books which importantly challenged common eugenicist myths, delivering several lectures on the subject across Europe. Shortly after his arrival in England in 1934, Dover was given a copy of Julian Huxley's *We Europeans: A Survey of Racial Problems* (1936), which inspired him, as some have argued, to write his first major work *Half Caste,* a novel published in 1937. Anticipating how the world was already changing with the intermingling of 'races', Dover drew on his knowledge of science, history, and literature as a way of illuminating and comparing the contemporary struggles of people of mixed ethnicity.

In his work Dover celebrated the richness of hybrid potentiality and he expressed solidarity with all ethnic minorities, publishing a manual in 1947, *Feathers in the Arrow: An Approach for Coloured Writers and Readers*, which reflected the depth of his thoughts. One of his most resonant poems, 'Brown Phoenix', the title poem of his 1950 collection, reflected his stance on mixed ethnicity, a vision prescient in its anticipation of the future:

> Listen brown man, black man
> Yellow man, mongrel man
> And you white friend and comrade:
> I am the brown phoenix – I am you.[32]

---

[31] *The Well of Loneliness*, Radclyffe Hall's novel about lesbian relationships, was discussed by the Readers and Writers Club in November, 1937. See Gemma Romain's *Race, Sexuality and Identity in Britain and Jamaica: The Biography of Patrick Nelson, 1916–1963* (London: Bloomsbury Academic, 2017), 52.

[32] Cedric Dover, 'Brown Phoenix' in *Brown Phoenix* (London: College Press, 1950).

In addition to writing poetry and contributing to numerous journals and newspapers, Dover, like many others, was commissioned during the early years of the war by the Indian Section of the BBC's Eastern Service. There, he encountered fellow Asian intellectuals such as Anand and Tambimuttu. It was here too that Dover also became acquainted with George Orwell, who invited him to present several talks at the BBC. Like G. V. Desani, author of *All About H. Hatterr* (1948), Dover worked for the home effort during the war, supporting Civil Defence and offering service as a lecturer with the Ministry of Information. During this period, he also edited the journal *Three*, a publication of the No. Three Army Formation College.[33]

One of Dover's most fervent political ambitions was for Afro-Asian solidarity, a mission he had pursued from the 1930s and which had been taken up by the Indian Prime Minister Jawaharlal Nehru after Independence in 1947. Chief among his beliefs was that India should achieve full independence and self-government. He moved across a number of black and Asian circles, being both member of the LCP and a supporter of Krishna Menon (1896–1974) who, following in the footsteps of Annie Besant and her Home Rule for India League (established 1916), grew what came to be known as the India League (1928–1947) from a small office in the Strand.[34]

Like many other interwar activists, Krishna Menon was multitalented. In 1934, he was called to the Bar, but he had also studied at the London School of Economics under Harold Laski, obtaining an MSc in politics. Through his leadership of the India League and his dedication to its mission to obtain freedom from imperial rule, Krishna Menon worked, like Padmore, alongside the left-wing British intelligentsia, regularly drawing on British contacts like Fenner Brockway, Harold Laski, and Michael Foot. He was also able to count on the support of major South Asian writers such as Anand, the Irish Indian novelist and dramatist Aubrey Menen, and Venu Chitale (then secretary to George Orwell at the Eastern Service) in the membership of the League. Although led by left-wing intellectuals and activists, the India League was primarily a British-based organisation and, while its mission was closely allied with events in India, it used its branches across Britain to educate the general public about the pitfalls of colonialism and garner support for freedom.

This broadening of the campaign beyond national boundaries to encompass both colonised subjects and the British population gave the India League its strength and vibrancy. Krishna Menon talked about India with a thrilling

[33] 'Cedric Dover', *Making Britain Database*. Available at www.open.ac.uk/research projects/makingbritain/content/cedric-dover.

[34] See Visram, *Asians in Britain*, 321–40.

combination of knowledge and passion. Not only a political figure, Menon was utterly committed to the local, acting as Labour Councillor for St Pancras from 1934 to 1947 and co-founding Pelican, the non-fiction educational imprint at Penguin books with Allen Lane in 1935. He was an enigmatic but always compelling speaker – as a member of his audience once remarked, 'You could almost hear the pounding of his heart.'[35]

Following the outbreak of World War II in 1939, Indian protests continued to gather pace in Britain. On 8 August 1942, at the All India Congress Committee session in Bombay, Mohandas Karamchand Gandhi launched the Quit India Movement. Earlier that summer, the leaders of the All India Congress had rejected the British offer of Dominion status presented by Sir Stafford Cripps. The decision to protest peacefully for the sake of full independence nevertheless led to thousands of arrests. Yet, by the end of the war, Britain's position on the world stage had changed so dramatically that India's Independence became almost inevitable. It was granted, finally, in 1947 and Krishna Menon, longtime friend of Nehru and literary editor of his memoir *Toward Freedom* (1936), became India's first High Commissioner to London.

It was a different kind of energy that had spurred the African-American philosopher W. E. B. Du Bois (1868–1963) to prophetically declare: 'the problem of the twentieth century is the problem of the colour line'.[36] Du Bois made this statement in 1903, the year before Cedric Dover's birth, and at a time when he was clearly highly conscious of the various ways in which humanity was graded according to skin colour in different societies, from the caste system in India to the prevalence of colourism in the USA, where some people chose to 'pass for white' even though they had black parentage because the advantages of belonging to the 'white' sector of society were emphatic. Du Bois was not only highly conscious of the widespread discrimination faced by black people in many parts of the world, he was also very aware of the challenges faced by people of dual heritage, like Dover, who were situated between the colonisers and the colonised, and wished to explore the significance of 'race' as a wider global phenomenon.[37] In 1947, the year of India's Independence and Partition, Dover moved to the United

---

[35] Quoted in Fryer, *Staying Power*, 354.

[36] W. E. B. Du Bois, 'The Forethought' in *The Souls of Black Folk* (New York: New American Library, 1969), xi.

[37] For a detailed discussion of Dover and race see: Nico Slate, 'Cedric Dover's Coloured Cosmopolitanism' in *The Prism of Race: W. E. B. Du Bois, Langston Hughes, Paul Robeson and the Coloured World of Cedric Dover* (Basingstoke: Palgrave Macmillan, 2014), 9–29.

States. A change of continent brought a change in focus: Dover began to turn his attention away from Britain to African American minorities and, although he held visiting posts in anthropology at Howard and Fisk universities until his departure from the USA in the late 1950s, his lifelong interest in African American art led to his influential 1960 study, *American Negro Art*.[38]

There was perhaps no better symbol of pan-African ambitions during the early twentieth century than the five Pan-African Congresses led by the African American Du Bois, pioneer of black African liberation. The first ran alongside the post-World War I Paris Peace Conference in 1919. This was followed by three further meetings, which took place between Lisbon, Paris, Brussels, London, and New York between 1921 and 1927, and whose delegates came to accept there could be little progress for the black populations of North America, the Caribbean, or Europe without liberation from colonialism and progress on the African continent itself. By far the most significant, however, in terms of scale, timing, and membership, was the fifth Pan-African Congress, which took place in Manchester on 15 October 1945.[39] Organised only months after the end of World War II, political allies were marshalled by Padmore, who attracted representatives from fifty different organisations for what was to become a landmark event. Among the eighty-seven delegates at the Chorlton-upon-Medlock Town Hall five-day Congress were many who would later take on leading roles in the fight for independence in Africa. Jomo Kenyatta was present (see Chapter 10). Kwame Nkrumah, who would go on to lead the movement in Ghana, was also prominent (see Chapter 9). The South African writer Peter Abrahams and Dr Hastings Banda, the first student to graduate from Nyasaland (now Malawi), attended. Caribbean activists, including the Jamaican lawyer Dudley Thompson and Amy Jacques Garvey, widow of Marcus Garvey, were also present; the West African Students Union sent a number of representatives. And Du Bois, organiser of the first 1919 conference, now in his late seventies, agreed to act as Chair.

The purpose was lofty.[40] Convened to demand that the European powers liberate the hundreds of millions of Africans still living under colonial rule,

---

[38] Cedric Dover, *American Negro Art* (London: Studio, 1960).

[39] A number of congresses were held, sometimes with multiple meetings in different cities: the inaugural conference (1900) was in London, followed by several other meetings, but mainly: 1919 in Paris (1st Pan-African Congress), 1921 in London (2nd Pan-African Congress), 1923 in London (3rd Pan-African Congress), 1927 New York City (4th Pan-African Congress), 1945 Manchester (5th Pan-African Congress).

[40] See for instance, Hakim Adi and Marike Sherwood (eds.), *The 1945 Pan African Congress Revisited* (London: New Beacon Books, 1995); M. Sherwood, 'Pan-African Conferences,

the body passed radical resolutions condemning imperialism, racial discrimination, and capitalism. Significantly given the timing, it was not only African freedoms that were being sought. The Ceylonese student T. Subasinghe, for example, an active member of the India League, helped with the organisation of the Congress and a large Indian delegation headed by Surat Alley of the Hindustani Social Club in London's East End also attended.[41]

Key topics on the agenda were 'The Colour Problem in Britain', 'Oppression in South Africa', and 'Problems in the Caribbean'. Perhaps not surprisingly, a number of radical British organisations like the Communist Party and black groups such as the Pan-African Federation and the Negro Association also sent delegates. In spite of its scale and significance, the Fifth Pan-African Congress received little coverage in the mainstream press, though *Picture Post* commissioned the celebrated Soho photographer John Deakin and the acclaimed war journalist Hilde Marchant to document the event. Their work was duly published under the heading 'Africa Speaks in Manchester', in November 1945.[42]

Two years later, and coinciding with the year of Indian Independence and the division of the subcontinent into the two new nations of India and Pakistan, Padmore summed up his view thus:

> The delegates of the Fifth Pan-African Congress believe in peace. How could it be otherwise when for centuries the African peoples have been victims of violence and slavery? Yet, if the Western world is still determined to rule mankind by force, then Africans, as a last resort, may have to appeal to force in the effort to achieve Freedom, even if force destroys them and the world.[43]

Though never a formal member of the Labour Party, Padmore was its colonial expert, collaborating like Menon with left-wing intellectuals Fenner Brockway and Reginald Reynolds, leaders of the pacifist No More War Movement. He became Kwame Nkrumah's personal representative in London during the struggle for Ghanaian independence and later Nkrumah's

1900–1953, What Did Pan-Africanism Mean?', *Journal of Pan African Studies*, 4:10 (January 2012): 106–26.

[41] See www.open.ac.uk/researchprojects/makingbritain/content/5th-pan-african-congress.

[42] 'Africa Speaks in Manchester', *Picture Post*, 10 November 1945. The London-based photography organisation *Autograph* held a groundbreaking exhibition, 'The Fifth Pan-African Congress', in summer 2015, curated by June Giovanni. Several photographs by Deakin were displayed which form part of the collection held by the Getty Archives.

[43] George Padmore, 'The Challenge to the Colonial Powers' in George Padmore (ed.), 'History of the Pan African Congress', 1947. The George Padmore Archive. Available at www.marxists.org/archive/padmore/1947/pan-african-congress/index.htm.

adviser on African affairs in Ghana. He earnt the title of the 'Father of African Emancipation' because he was the originator of the movement to achieve the political independence of African countries and people of African descent. Whilst Africa was the main focus, he remained appreciative throughout of parallel South Asian networks in Britain and the collaboration of other major groups in anti-racist and anti-colonial circles. In his 1957 book, *Pan-Africanism or Communism*, he specifically acknowledges the comradeship of Leonard Woolf and Saklatvala, 'the one Indian who had no time for opportunistic trimmers and sycophants'.[44]

As we have seen, black (African and Caribbean) and South Asian writers were instrumental in building several formative cultural and political groups and networks during the interwar years. Although affiliations shifted over time and some members moved between the colonies and Britain, these different constituencies gradually developed stronger and stronger anti-colonial stances, becoming staunchly vocal on issues of political and cultural independence. As activists and wordsmiths, many writers amongst them recognised the power of the word as a weapon to bring change across the world. Connections that emerged across these mixed cultural groupings, despite individual differences, continue to reverberate. This was especially evident, almost forty years later, with the launch of the International Book Fair of Radical and Black Books (1982–1995), an initiative which came to birth at a particularly difficult moment in British race relations following the Brixton uprisings in 1981 and the tragedy of the New Cross fire. Set up by a collective of black publishers led by John La Rose of New Beacon Books and influenced by Padmore's example, the fair highlighted the continuing need to fight for equality worldwide. Whilst Britain's black and Asian writers were strategically positioned as being integral to literary culture, the activities of the fairs also drew attention to the historically global dimension of the black struggle as British writers and publishers shared platforms with their international counterparts in the Caribbean, Africa, South Asia, and the United States.[45]

---

[44] Quoted in Susan D. Pennybacker, *From Scottsboro to Munich: Race and Political Culture in 1930s Britain* (Princeton, NJ: Princeton University Press, 2009), 101.

[45] See: Sarah White, Roxy Harris, and Sharmilla Beezmohun (eds.), *A Meeting of the Continents: The International Book Fair of Radical Black and Third World Books – Revisited* (London: New Beacon Books, 2005).

7

Mobile Modernisms
Black and Asian Articulations

ANNA SNAITH

Modernist literary production in Britain in the first decades of the twentieth century was distinctly multicultural and multiracial. Black and Asian writers were engaged in publishing, editing, reviewing, and broadcasting in a wide range of cultural and political organisations and venues. C. L. R. James wrote his 'Letters from London', published in the *Port of Spain Gazette*, from the lecture halls and student venues of Bloomsbury soon after his arrival from Trinidad in 1932. Jamaican Claude McKay wrote for Sylvia Pankhurst's periodical the *Workers' Dreadnought* and Una Marson's play *At What a Price* – performed at the New Scala Theatre in January 1934 – was the first black production in London's West End. In the pages of periodicals founded and edited by black and Asian writers, such as Egyptian Sudanese Duse Mohamed Ali's *African Times and Orient Review* or the League of Coloured Peoples' *The Keys*, colonial writers debated and responded to topical issues regarding race relations.[1]

But modernist London has not always been understood in these terms. In fact, the involvement of black and Asian writers was largely absent from the accounts of literary modernism that emerged in the mid- to late twentieth century. The recent 'transnational' or 'global' turn in modernist studies has begun to make visible and audible not only individuals and networks such as those described above, but the complex ways in which the impulses that generate modernist writing derive themselves from shifting relations within the empire, whether at local or geopolitical levels. Simon Gikandi has demonstrated in rich detail the ways in which modernist art forms 'derive their energy from their diagnosis of the failure of the imperial enterprise'.[2] In

---

[1] There have been different spellings over time, from Dusé Mohamed Ali to Duse Mohamed Ali. Preferred usage in this chapter is Duse Mohamed Ali.
[2] Simon Gikandi, *Maps of Englishness: Writing Identity in the Culture of Colonialism* (New York: Columbia University Press, 1996), 161.

the last few decades a wealth of scholarship has revolutionised our understanding of the movement of black and Asian texts and individuals between
colonial locations and Britain in this period.[3]

This serves to undercut the Eurocentrism of accounts of modernism, as
well as revealing the ways in which black and Asian modernists were
themselves articulating such paradigm shifts in the early twentieth century.
C. L. R. James, for example, in *The Black Jacobins* (1938), argues for the
inseparability of modernity and colonisation: 'When three centuries ago
the slaves came to the West Indies, they entered directly into the large-
scale agriculture of the sugar plantation, which was a modern system [. . .]
The Negroes, therefore, from the very start lived a life that was in its essence
a modern life.'[4] The relationship between plantation slavery and capitalist
modernity resonates through the work of Caribbean writers such as Claude
McKay, Una Marson, and Jean Rhys. If one way of approaching or defining
modernism is as an artistic response to political, social, and cultural modernity, then literary modernism emerges just as forcefully in Kingston as in
Bloomsbury. The recent overturning of the critical narrative that modernism
first developed in a number of European urban centres and moved outwards
or was mimicked in colonial locations was refused by colonial modernists
themselves in the early years of the twentieth century. The experiments of
black and Asian literary modernism in this period emerge between colony
and metropole, a result of the tensions and synergies between cultures and
literary traditions. One way in which these 'crossroad' texts bear witness to
their diverse points of origin is in their complex formal experiments with
voice, genre, language, and register.

This chapter will discuss single texts from the 1930s and 1940s by a cluster of
black and Asian writers living in London: Mulk Raj Anand (*Untouchable*, 1935),
Una Marson (*The Moth and the Star*, 1937), C. L. R. James (*The Black Jacobins*,
1938), and Aubrey Menen (*The Prevalence of Witches*, 1947). These focal points
are not so much representative as snapshots of a much wider literary terrain,
including writers yet to emerge from the archives or still to come into critical

---

[3] See, for example, Jessica Berman, *Modernist Commitments: Ethics, Politics, and Transnational Modernism* (New York: Columbia University Press, 2011); Laura Doyle and Laura Winkiel (eds.), *Geomodernisms: Race, Modernism, Modernity* (Bloomington, IN: Indiana University Press, 2005); Len Platt (ed.), *Modernism and Race* (Cambridge: Cambridge University Press, 2011); Urmila Seshagiri, *Race and the Modernist Imagination* (Ithaca, NY: Cornell University Press, 2010); Mark Wollaeger with Matt Eatough (eds.), *The Oxford Handbook of Global Modernisms* (Oxford: Oxford University Press, 2012); and the AHRC-funded project 'Making Britain: South Asian Visions of Home and Abroad 1870–1950'.
[4] C. L. R. James, *The Black Jacobins* (London: Penguin, [1938] 1980), 305–6.

prominence. London provided a generative topography for this diverse constellation of writers. Focusing on the metropolis may seem perverse: a reinforcement of the pre-eminence of the 'heart of empire' that concretises geographical hierarchies which render colonial spaces 'primitive' or deriva- tive. But this focus is in part to recognise that colonial intellectuals and artists did focus their sights on London in this period. This was to do with percep- tions deriving from their colonial education, as well as access to employment and publishing opportunities. Paradoxically, though, this focus serves to de- centre the hierarchies of empire, given London's role in this period as 'a unique incubator for radical black internationalist discourse'.[5] It was precisely the encounters with racism on London's streets, as well as proxi- mity to institutions of imperial power, that deepened the cultural nationalism or socialist politics with which writers like Marson and James arrived in the capital. Una Marson's poem 'Nigger', published in the first issue of *The Keys* soon after her arrival in London, was triggered by her experience of racist abuse (and her struggle to find accommodation and employment). Crucially, Marson places this experience within a history of racist constructions of blackness in Britain: 'from Curse to Clown'. The city was both catalyst and facilitator.

That said, it is important to acknowledge the ways London connected, for colonial modernists, with other sites of opportunity and influence. The period C. L. R. James spent in Nelson, Lancashire, for example, or Mulk Raj Anand's journey from London to report on the Spanish Civil War, were equally formative and create networks of journeys whose nodal points intersect at moments of serendipity and intention. Our cartographic under- standing of colonial modernism, often limited to the movement between two points, must be flexible, or versatile, enough to encompass other kinds of networks and journeys such as those between London and northern Britain for James or between London and Dublin or Spain for Anand. Cross-racial interactions, too, such as those between Mulk Raj Anand or Una Marson and George Orwell at the BBC, or Anand and Leonard Woolf via the Hogarth Press, were made possible because of London's cosmopolitanism. While it is important to differentiate between particular histories of black and Asian immigration and colonial relations, the cultural amnesia that saw black and Asian British writing as beginning with Windrush or the 'South Asian diaspora' cuts across cultures (see Chapter 12).

---

[5] Minkah Makalani, *In the Cause of Freedom: Radical Black Internationalism from Harlem to London 1917–1939* (Chapel Hill, NC: University of North Carolina Press, 2011), 194.

Formal experimentation has long been associated with literary modernism, but a startling feature that connects this group of writers is the multiplicity of genres and modes in which they wrote. A fluidity of form and genre operates across œuvres and careers as well as in relation to single texts. James's *The Black Jacobins* was a (recently discovered) play script (1934) and production (1936) before it was a non-fiction text. Anand wrote literary journalism, art criticism, food writing, short stories, radio broadcasts, novels, and autobiographies. Marson was a journalist, poet, dramatist, and broadcaster. These writers are proponents of what we might call a 'versatile modernity', one that shifted and adapted itself to a plurality of circumstances. Not only does this speak to the diversity of the political and cultural networks in which they moved, and to their polymath sensibilities, but also to the ways in which they wrote at the crossroads of multiple literary traditions. Their formal experimentation involved complicating or inserting themselves within British literary traditions, as in Marson's deliberate rewriting of Rudyard Kipling's 'If –' in her first collection, *Tropic Reveries* (1930), as well as bringing forms of cultural nationalism to the metropolis. Claude McKay's reshaping of the novel form around the sonic cultures of jazz and blues in *Home to Harlem* (1928) and *Banjo* (1929), for example, deserves attention in this context. So, too, Kenyan-born Indian G. V. Desani's career-long refusal of generic categorisation did much to influence and foreshadow the writing of postcolonial authors such as Salman Rushdie later in the century. Desani's *All About H. Hatterr* (1948) is a mock-epic, fictional autobiography that blurs the lines between novel, prose poem, play, and morality tale. Its Malay European protagonist, Hatterr, goes on a series of seven transcultural voyages to visit a number of gurus, the traversing of national boundaries mirroring the blending of languages and literary traditions evident in this playful and parodic text. Furthermore, those features so marked within Anglo-American literary modernism – fragmentation, temporal discontinuity, the interior turn – may generate additional meanings when employed to represent subaltern experience as, for example, in Anand's *Untouchable*.

Mulk Raj Anand, *Untouchable* (1935)

Mulk Raj Anand (1905–2004) arrived in Bloomsbury from northern India in 1925 following a brief period of imprisonment under the Civil Disobedience Act. He began studying for a PhD in philosophy at University College London and, by the late 1920s, was mixing with a range of London literary figures including T. S. Eliot (reviewing for his periodical, *The Criterion*) and

Virginia and Leonard Woolf (working as a proof corrector at the Hogarth Press). At a range of sites, such as Harold Munro's Poetry Bookshop and the British Museum Reading Room, he befriended writers and critics such as Aldous Huxley, Clive Bell, Nancy Cunard, and Herbert Read. By 1928, he was working on his first novel, *Untouchable*, an early example of Dalit literature given its focus on Bakha, an outcaste sweeper and latrine cleaner in a northern Indian town. *Untouchable* is a one-day novel (in the style of James Joyce's *Ulysses* or Virginia Woolf's *Mrs Dalloway*) and Anand wrote later about the direct influence of Joyce's *A Portrait of the Artist as a Young Man* in his depiction of the 'conflict-torn rhythms of [Bakha's] existence'.[6] While drafting the novel, however, he came across Mohandas Karamchand Gandhi's account of a young sweeper, Uka, in *Young India*, which prompted him to reconsider his own fictionalised representation and also to travel to meet Gandhi in 1929. As Anand recounts the meeting, Gandhi advised making Bakha less of a 'Bloomsbury intellectual' and suggested that Anand 'take off the mask of the "brown Sahib"' he had become in London.[7]

The published novel opens with a description of the 'outcastes' colony':

> a brook ran near the lane [. . .] now soiled by the dirt and filth of the public latrines situated about it, the odour of the hides and skins of dead carcases left to dry on its banks, the dung of donkeys, sheep, horses, cows and buffaloes heaped up to be made into fuel cakes, and the biting, choking, pungent fumes that oozed from its sides.[8]

Anand tackles the topical and controversial subject of untouchability head-on via an immersive, sensory rendering of this abject environment. Although Anand already had a diverse presence on London's publishing scene as a writer of short fiction, art criticism, and Indian cookery, the excremental content led to rejections from nineteen publishers.[9] Eventually, a letter of endorsement from E. M. Forster persuaded the publisher Wishart to accept the novel provided that Forster also pen an introduction to the book, which

---

[6] Mulk Raj Anand, *Roots and Flowers* (Dharwar: Karnatak University, 1972), 21.

[7] Mulk Raj Anand, 'Why I Write' in K. K. Sharma (ed.), *Perspectives on Mulk Raj Anand* (Ghaziabad: Vimal Prakashan, 1978), 1–8; 5.

[8] Mulk Raj Anand, *Untouchable* (London: Penguin, [1935] 1940), 9.

[9] For more detail on the publishing history of *Untouchable* see Ruvani Ranasinha, *South Asian Writers in Twentieth-Century Britain: Culture in Translation* (Oxford: Clarendon Press, 2007), 17–23; and Susheila Nasta, 'Between Bloomsbury and Gandhi? The Background to the Publication of Mulk Raj Anand's *Untouchable*' in Robert Fraser and Mary Hammond (eds.), *Books Without Borders*, vol. 2: *Perspectives from South Asia* (Basingstoke: Palgrave Macmillan, 2008), 151–69.

would, in editor Edgell Rickword's words, 'be the book's passport through the ordinary reviewer's latent hostility'.[10]

Written in free indirect speech, *Untouchable* traces Bakha's sensory responses to cold, hunger, and demeaning labour in intense detail. Anand counters an objectified or collectivised representation of the subaltern through this highly individualised and hyper-alert consciousness. The crisis point in the novel occurs when, distracted after a rare purchase of some sweets, Bakha forgets to warn of his presence and bumps into a caste Hindu. This moment of shock jars 'his nerves of sight, hearing, smell, touch and taste, all into a quickening' and prompts a moment of epiphany: 'I am an Untouchable!'[11] From here, Anand presents a series of 'solutions' to untouchability: Christianity in the shape of Colonel Hutchinson of the Salvation Army, disregard for the 'observance of untouchability' as proclaimed in a public speech by Gandhi, and technological modernity in the shape of the flush toilet as espoused by a young poet, Iqbal Nath Sarshar.[12] None is given especial priority and the novel ends with Bakha journeying homeward with all the voices echoing in his head.

It is too simplistic to suggest that *Untouchable* fuses Indian politics and subject-matter with the formal features of European modernism. Anand wrote later that 'the English writing intelligentsia of India was thus a kind of bridge trying to span, symbolically, the two worlds of the Ganga and the Thames through the novel', but those two worlds cannot be so easily distinguished.[13] His topic suggests also the social realist or proletarian novels of the 1930s as espoused in the Marxist reading groups that he frequented in London in this period. Anand himself has linked the flow of urban sensory experience to the serialised Urdu novel *Fasana-i-Azad*, by Ratan Nath Dhar Sarshar, which itself draws on Dickensian tropes as well as the Persian and Urdu epics.[14] *Untouchable* is a novel as highly conscious of its eclectic formal properties and influences as it is of its political contexts. Jessica Berman has drawn attention to the 'variety of styles and modes, from romance to patriotic monologue to psychological analysis, that periodically erupt through its ostensibly realist surface'.[15] This is tied to what Berman perceptively calls his 'rooted cosmopolitanism'.[16] Located firmly in the environs of an Indian village, the novel also connects the question of Dalit rights with the colonial subject more broadly. As Anand put it, the 'local personality

---

[10] Edgell Rickword to Mulk Raj Anand, 30 November 1934. Quoted in Ranasinha, *South Asian Writers*, 18.
[11] Ibid., 52. [12] Ibid., 149. [13] Anand, *Roots and Flowers*, 15. [14] Ibid., 20.
[15] Berman, *Modernist Commitments*, 112. [16] Ibid., 111.

becomes a universal type'.[17] The varied use of Punjabi words (translated, untranslated, Punjabi syntax rendered in English) makes visible, too, the vexed questions of access to subaltern experience in terms of language and literacy.

Through the 1930s and until his return to India in 1946, Anand continued to work in a range of genres and modes. He was a regular broadcaster on the BBC, he worked as a reviewer and essayist in periodicals such as the *Left Review*, he became involved with the International Congress for the Defence of Culture, and continued his engagement with Marxism, publishing his own *Letters on India*, with an introduction by Leonard Woolf, in 1942. As Susheila Nasta has explored, Anand's eclectic and often competing commitments in modernist London demonstrate not only his versatility but his 'multi-voiced position as insider and outsider [. . .] both authoritative informant and inter-locutor, who could not only infiltrate and mediate but also *change* and subvert' imperialist orthodoxies.[18]

Una Marson, *The Moth and the Star* (1937)

Una Marson (1905–1965), like Anand, was engaged in a wide range of net-works in 1930s London, having arrived in 1932 from St Elizabeth, Jamaica. From a black, middle-class family, she was educated as a scholarship student at the predominantly white Hampton High School. She had founded a periodical, *Cosmopolitan*, and published two volumes of poetry – *Tropic Reveries* (1930) and *Heights and Depths* (1931) – and had her play *At What a Price* staged in Kingston before embarking on the sea voyage to London. There she found lodgings in Peckham with Harold Moody, who had founded the League of Coloured Peoples (LCP) in 1931. She began to write for and then edit the LCP's magazine, *The Keys*, work which brought her into contact with figures such as C. L. R. James, George Padmore, and Paul Robeson.

Marson stayed in London until 1936: this was to be the first of two extended periods in the metropolis. Her collection *The Moth and the Star* was published on her return to Jamaica in 1937, the same year she staged her play *London Calling* about Caribbean students in the metropolis. Marson, too, was a versatile modern, continually moving between modes: journalist, political

---

[17] Anand, *Roots and Flowers*, 35.
[18] Susheila Nasta, 'Negotiating a "New World Order": Mulk Raj Anand as Public Intellectual at the Heart of Empire (1925–1945)' in Rehana Ahmed and Sumita Mukherjee (eds.), *South Asian Resistances in Britain 1858–1947* (London: Continuum, 2012), 140–60; 140.

activist, poet, dramatist, editor. *The Moth and the Star* parallels and emerges out of this versatility in its shifts between love poetry, political poems, odes, and dialect poems. The collection is divided into four sections – 'Poems Written in England' and Poems of 'Love', 'Nature', and 'Life' – but in many ways the poems defy and complicate this categorisation. The collection is self-consciously the project of Marson's transnational perspective, looking as it does to Ethiopia, the West Indies, and London from a mobile subject position.

A crucial negotiation in Marson's positioning emerges from her identity as a black woman, moving across and between organisations and institutions that invariably eclipsed one or both of these aspects of her identity. She was unusual as a woman within pan-African circles of the 1930s and her racial identity set her apart within feminist organisations like the British Commonwealth League, dominated as it was by white, middle-class women. A cluster of poems in the collection, including 'Kinky Hair Blues', 'Cinema Eyes', and 'Black is Fancy', speak directly to this intersection and underscore Marson's remarkable work as an inaugural figure in the history of black British women's writing. They also demonstrate her engagement in a Caribbean and African American tradition of vernacular poetry by poets such as Claude McKay and Langston Hughes. In 'Kinky Hair Blues', Marson explores the emulation of 'white' standards of beauty in the context of the marriage market: 'I like me black face / And me kinky hair. / But nobody love dem, I jes don't tink it's fair / I's gwine press me hair / And bleach me skin / What won't a gal do / Some kind a man to win.'[19] In 'Cinema Eyes', the worship of white stars is described as a 'cinema mind' in a prescient articulation of the internalising effects of the lack of representation of black people on screen. Women's voices articulate the inner tensions – across generations and across media – that constitute the struggle for black pride and self-assertion. Alison Donnell notes of Marson's poetic œuvre more broadly that the 'mixed bag of devotional sonnets, love lyrics, feminist parodies, Afro-blues and folk monologues that comprise her four volumes of poetry struggle to be identified with the clean, sharp edges of male nationalist writings that dominate the political project of Caribbean writing in the 1930s'.[20] This intersectional position is one of the reasons for her sustained omission from histories of black

---

[19] Una Marson, *The Moth and the Star* (Kingston: Gleaner, 1937), 91.
[20] Una Marson, *Selected Poems*, ed. Alison Donnell (Leeds: Peepal Tree Press, 2011), 11–39; 12.

British writing, of pan-Africanism in the 1930s, and of the BBC West Indian Service: an omission which is being vigorously rectified in renewed critical interest.[21]

Several of the poems in *The Moth and the Star* emerge directly out of Marson's political work in the 1930s. 'To Joe and Ben' is an elegy to the two sons of Hakim Warqenah (Charles Martin), an Ethiopian nationalist and statesman who was Ambassador to London in 1935–1936 during the outbreak of the Italo–Abyssinian War. Joseph and Benjamin Martin were assassinated in Ethiopia in 1937 by Italian forces after travelling from London to 'fight for a country, / Yours, and yet not yours'.[22] Marson's tribute repeats the phrase 'gallant sons of Ethiopia', inscribing the ties to the African continent that were evoked in pan-African discourse of the period. Marson's work for Warqenah led to her position as Haile Selassie's secretary during his exile in 1936.[23] Other political poems pay tribute to Marson's feminist collaborators and networks. 'To the I.A.W.S.E.C.' records her trip to Istanbul in 1935 as the first woman of African descent to attend the International Alliance of Women for Suffrage and Equal Citizenship conference. The more personal tribute, 'Winifred Holtby' – 'O valiant woman, author, speaker, friend' – speaks to their mutual interest in feminism and racial equality.[24]

Holtby urged Marson to write an autobiography but instead this became the poem 'Little Brown Girl'. The poem consists of a lengthy series of questions addressed by a metropolitan speaker to a young Caribbean woman: 'Why do you wander alone / About the streets / Of the great city / of London?', 'How is it that you speak / English as though it belonged / to you?'[25] The narrator's ignorance and stereotypical views about colonial peoples ('I guess Africa, or India, / Ah no, from some island / In the West Indies, / But isn't that India / All the same?')[26] write over the voice of the 'brown girl', which is characterised by silence. This contrasts with 'Quashie Comes to London', a creole poem that uses the 'letter home' genre to represent the male immigrant's perspective on the heart of empire.[27] The

---

[21] See work by Alison Donnell, Lawrence Breiner, Glyne A. Griffith, and James Procter.

[22] Marson, *Moth*, 81.

[23] See Delia Jarrett-Macauley, *The Life of Una Marson 1905–65* (Manchester: Manchester University Press, 1998), 102.

[24] Marson, *Moth*, 79. Marson met Holtby through the LCP in 1933 and Holtby spoke at LCP events, including the conference 'The Negro in the World Today' along with Paul Robeson and Jomo Kenyatta; *The Keys*, 2:3 (1935): 52.

[25] Marson, *Moth*, 11, 13.   [26] Ibid., 13.

[27] See Lee M. Jenkins, *The Language of Caribbean Poetry: Boundaries of Expression* (Gainesville, FL: University Press of Florida, 2004), 131–41, for a fuller discussion of the poetic contexts of this poem (and others in the collection). See also Denise deCaires

poem, like Sam Selvon's *The Lonely Londoners* after it, oscillates between celebration and deflation. Quashie starts by affirming the myth of the heart of empire: 'I tell you fuss 'bout London town, / Hi man, it big fe true'.[28] But when Quashie requests 'ripe breadfruit / Some fresh ackee and saltfish too' at a Lyons Corner House, nostalgia takes over: 'It not gwine be anoder year / Before you see me face'.[29] The poem ends with Quashie 'sick fe see white face'.[30]

It is easy to privilege Marson's political and creole poems within this collection, given their topical and pressing engagement with questions of black rights. But the conjunction of these with Marson's nature and love poems characterises the collection. The volume's epigraph and title come from Percy Shelley's 'One Word is Too Often Profaned', suggesting the influence of Romanticism routed through a Caribbean political and cultural consciousness. Deliberate rewritings ('Nostalgia' rewrites W. B. Yeats's 'Lake Isle of Innisfree') sit alongside broader gestures of influence. As Mary Lou Emery has argued, 'this complex relay of cultural influence, "Eastern" and "Western", "high" and "low", from colony to metropole to colony, and also across colonies' complicates traditional postcolonial binary models of connection.[31]

C. L. R. James, *The Black Jacobins* (1938)

In 1932, another black intellectual sailed from the Caribbean to London: the Trinidadian C. L. R. James (1901–1989). His colonial education at Queen's Royal College was to become formative in his later position as one of the twentieth century's most significant theorists of anti-colonialism. He sailed with two manuscripts: a novel, *Minty Alley*, to be published in 1936 and set in working-class Port of Spain, and a political biography of the Trinidadian Labour leader and Mayor of Port of Spain, Captain André Cipriani. He immediately began writing about his experience of the heart of empire in the form of 'Letters from London' sent back for publication in the *Port of Spain Gazette*. Here we see him negotiating his own relationship to Britishness and articulating his sense of disappointment at the betrayal of those values, such as freedom and equality, which he had associated with Britain's modernity. In his last 'letter', 'The Nucleus of a Great Civilisation'

Narain, *Contemporary Caribbean Women's Poetry: Making Style* (London: Routledge, 2002), 8–29.
[28] Marson, *Moth*, 17. [29] Ibid., 20–1. [30] Ibid., 21.
[31] Mary Lou Emery, *Modernism, the Visual and Caribbean Literature* (Cambridge: Cambridge University Press, 2007), 119.

(August 1932), James crucially shifts the focus from London, 'the peak, the centre, the nucleus of a great branch of western civilisation', to the northern, working-class community of Nelson, Lancashire where he had been writing the memoir of the West Indian cricketer Learie Constantine. He cites the townspeople's support of striking cinema operators as evidence of those values on which he had understood British civilisation to be premised.[32] It was in Nelson, with a small press, that he published *The Life of Captain Cipriani: An Account of British Government in the West Indies* in 1932. The following year an abridged version of this was published as *The Case for West Indian Self-Government* by Virginia and Leonard Woolf's Hogarth Press as No. 16 in their political pamphlet series, *Day to Day*. This slim volume set the tone for James's lifelong interest in the intersections between revolutionary politics and anti-colonialism. Not only that, as he was to argue of Caribbean peoples: 'cut off from all contact with Africa [. . .] they present today the extraordinary spectacle of a people who [. . .] are essentially Western and, indeed, far more advanced in Western culture than many a European community'.[33]

Versatility characterises James's entire œuvre but is a particularly apt descriptor for his 1930s writing: he was publishing fiction, sports journalism for the *Manchester Guardian*, biography, and essays in a range of genres and venues. In London, where he lived until 1938, James was on the executive council of the LCP and wrote for *The Keys* and was involved with the Independent Labour Party and was Chair of its Finchley branch (1935–1936).[34] But this versatility is particularly in evidence in the work that culminated in his major study *The Black Jacobins: Toussaint L'Ouverture and the San Domingo Revolution* (1938). The combination of James's commitment to the global struggle for black rights and his Marxist historiography drew him to the story of the slave uprising and revolution (1791–1804) that led to the first black republic outside Africa. James was keen to depict the 'transformation of slaves [. . .] into a people able to organise themselves and defeat the most powerful European nations of their day'.[35] In this way, he would counter narratives that linked abolition to European philanthropy. He conducted extensive research, including in Paris and Marseilles, so as to outline in

---

[32] C. L. R. James, *Letters from London*, ed. Nicholas Laughlin (Oxford: Signal Books, 2003), III.

[33] C. L. R. James, 'The Case for West Indian Self-Government' in Anna Grimshaw (ed.), *The C. L. R. James Reader* (Oxford: Blackwell, 1992), 49–62; 49.

[34] James wrote for the journal in 1933, 1934, and 1936. See issues 1:1 (1933), 1:4 (1934): 72, and 3:3 (1936): 4. The last is entitled 'Abyssinia and the Imperialists'.

[35] James, *Black Jacobins*, xviii.

meticulous detail the origins, setbacks, and achievements of the revolution as it unfolded in the Caribbean and was responded to in France.

His historical study has its origins in drama: the play *Toussaint Louverture* that James wrote and produced in 1936 at the Westminster Theatre with Paul Robeson in the title role (see Chapter 11).[36] The text's origins on the stage determined, in large part, its complexity of form and genre. Most often seen as a work of history, it shifts frequently into fiction, biography, autobiography, and drama. Paul Buhle, for example, has noted its 'extraordinary synthesis of novelistic narrative and meticulous factual reconstruction'.[37] James's decision to focus his narrative around the revolutionary leader and ex-slave Toussaint L'Ouverture allows investigation of the relationship between individual and collective. James sets up L'Ouverture's downfall, and ultimate surrender to Napoleon, as emerging from his 'hamartia' or 'tragic flaw' – a continued commitment to revolutionary France – which fuses biography (or collective biography) with Aristotelian tragedy.[38] Passages of direct speech and dialogue, as well as sections of figurative or descriptive language, complicate the simple categorisation of this text as one of historical record.[39]

Another feature of the text which complicates its categorisation is James's awareness (augmented in the preface to the first edition and the subsequent appendix and foreword) of his moment of writing: 'the booming of Franco's artillery, the rattle of Stalin's firing squads and the fierce shrill turmoil of the revolutionary movement striving for clarity' make themselves heard in *The Black Jacobins*.[40] Thus, the work becomes as much manifesto or manual as historical narrative. James is as conscious of the remarkable story of resistance that he has to tell, as of 'the violent conflicts of our age' in which 'the writing of history becomes ever more difficult'.[41]

Aubrey Menen, *The Prevalence of Witches* (1947)

While Indo-Irish Aubrey Menen (1912–1989) did not make the 'voyage in' – having been born and raised in London – his eclectic œuvre makes him very much a 'versatile modern'. The son of a Keralan father and an Irish mother,

---

[36] See C. L. R. James, *Toussaint Louverture*, ed. Christian Høgsbjerg (Durham, NC: Duke University Press, 2013).

[37] Paul Buhle, *C. L. R. James: The Artist as Revolutionary* (London: Verso, 1988), 59.

[38] James, *Black Jacobins*, 237.

[39] See, for example, James, *Toussaint Louverture*, 70–2 and 211.

[40] James, *Black Jacobins*, xx. In a Foreword to the 1980 Penguin edition James tells of the work's influence on young, black activists in South Africa in the 1950s (xvii).

[41] James, *Black Jacobins*, xix.

he traced his sociopolitical outlook to his multicultural origins: 'My parents were pioneers: I was the offspring of bold spirits who had opened the path to a new world where all the races of mankind could live in harmony together. It sustained me when English school companions called me the Rajah of Jampot and tripped me up so that I fell in the mud.'[42] After studying philosophy, like Anand, at University College London, Menen worked initially in the theatre: dramatising H. G. Wells's *The Shape of Things to Come*, serving as drama critic for *The Bookman* (1933–1934), and founding the Experimental Theatre in 1934 with André van Gyseghem (see Chapter 11). His own play, *Genesis II*, was censored when performed in 1934 and Menen was sued for blasphemy and obscenity.[43]

Much like Anand's memoir, *Conversations in Bloomsbury* (1981), Menen's later writing describes his time living on Charlotte Street in the 1930s and mixing with the Bloomsbury set: John Maynard Keynes, Virginia Woolf, Lytton Strachey, and Duncan Grant. He writes openly in *The Space Within the Heart* about his own homosexuality and the broader defiance of convention that characterised this milieu: 'any form of sexual self-expression was legitimate'.[44] Increasingly resistant to the privilege of the Bloomsburies, however, he gravitated towards the Strand and Krishna Menon's India League, and then moved to India in 1939. He went on to work in radio broadcasting as Head of the English Drama Department at All-India Radio, and to publish in a range of genres: travel writing, autobiography, books on religion, and a number of satirical novels.

The Prevalence of Witches (1947) was the first of these novels and Menen returned to London from India to supervise its publication by Chatto & Windus. It draws on his experience as education officer in Bulsar, Gujarat, working amongst the Dangi peoples: 'There was a post going for someone to do them good by setting up village schools and such. I took it [. . .] I set up a school among them but it was the Dangis who taught me a lesson.'[45] The novel tells the story of an unnamed education officer sent to a fictional British colony named Limbo in northern India. There, together with the British Governor Catullus, an American missionary Cuff Small, and Bayard Leavis, he becomes embroiled in a local dispute. The village headman has been imprisoned for murdering his wife's demon lover, sent by a local witch, Gangabai, who had been cursing the village. To ensure the headman's

[42] Aubrey Menen, *The Space Within the Heart* (London: Hamish Hamilton, 1970), 30–1.
[43] Menen, *Space*, 40. See also Mohammed Elias, *Kerala Writers in English: Aubrey Menen* (Madras: Macmillan India, 1985), 12.
[44] Menen, *Space*, 86.   [45] Ibid., 100–1.

release, the men have to persuade the 'rationalist' judge that witches exist. To do this, they plan a staged 'miracle' involving a Swami and a local village boy bribed to feign illness. The plans, and with it a rationalist perspective, are complicated when the 'fake' Swami learns that the boy was not acting after all.

As with Anand's Untouchable, Prevalence is a product of Menen's transnational position and the mediation of or movement between cultures and belief systems. But unlike Untouchable, the novel's focalising perspective is not a particular subaltern or indigenous position, but rather one which defamiliarises all. While early reviews stressed Menen's role as a cultural translator, and his novel as offering 'insight into the primitive mind', in fact the novel satirises all systems and privileges none.[46] Its mocking eye is all pervasive. This mobility characterises the novel's formal strategy of continuous swerves and displacements through digression and stories within stories. The real or 'authentic' is never so. When the headman begins the account of the murder, we learn that he will 'tell the truth, but in the way of a story' and his account of his wife's seduction by a shape-shifting demon is remarkably similar to the story of Adam and Eve.[47] The Governor, Catullus, trains the village children to produce 'primitive art': 'suppose we take the most promising boys and set them down to manufacture primitive art in considerable quantities. The world market is insatiable.'[48] The novel ends with Bay Leavis (whose name recalls F. R.) imagining the history he is going to write for Limbo including 'the first and rather eccentric King of the Limbodians that I have invented'.[49]

The Prevalence of Witches recalls Leonard Woolf's The Village in the Jungle (1913) for its focus on indigenous people's encounters with the colonial justice system. As reviewers noted at the time, Menen also drew on a Swiftian tradition of satire involving the traveller to an unfamiliar land as well as more contemporary satirists such as Aldous Huxley (who had published a short-story collection entitled Limbo in 1926) and Evelyn Waugh.[50] But none of these influences is straightforward and the novel is highly self-conscious of its inheritance. The Swami comes, not from India, but from London where he has been developing a business offering spiritual consultations over the

---

[46] Maurice Richardson, 'Review of The Prevalence of Witches', Times Literary Supplement, 6 December 1947: 625.

[47] Aubrey Menen, The Prevalence of Witches (Harmondsworth: Penguin, [1947] 1957), 47.

[48] Ibid., 85.   [49] Ibid., 216.

[50] For details of the novel's reception see Ruvani Ranasinha, 'Cultural Contestations in the Literary Marketplace: Reading Raja Rao's Kanthapura and Aubrey Menen's The Prevalence of Witches' in Shafquat Towheed (ed.), New Readings in the Literature of British India, c. 1780–1947 (Stuttgart: Ibidem, 2007), 279–99; 290–7.

telephone. He declares he owes it 'all to Aldous Huxley'.[51] As Ruvani Ranasinha has explored, reviewers tended to focus on the novel's satire of Limbodians, occluding the critique of empire that is so central to the novel.[52] Furthermore, the novel sends up various modes of masculinity and, through its focus on witches, can be read as a critique of violence against women. The novel goes into extraordinary detail about the duckings and beatings to which Gangabai is subject at the hands of the villagers. As Menen wrote in his memoir: 'their scientists were certain women, of all ages, who had a profound knowledge of magic. They were not crones or eccentrics. They were perfectly responsible working women, ready, like doctors, to serve the Community at all times.'[53]

Menen's novel, published just months after Indian Independence in 1947, acts as a hinge or pivot point between the modernist period and postcolonial writing of the latter part of the century. It belongs with a cluster of late modernist Asian novels that are Janus-faced in terms of influence and anticipation. G. V. Desani's *All About H. Hatterr*, for example, written during the 'warring years' and in part a mock-philosophical search for truth, is a refusal of stability or homogeneity of any kind: national, linguistic, formal. Framed with introductions, epigraphs, and postscripts that self-consciously undermine any attempt to situate the text, *All About H. Hatterr* is both a product of its multilingual, multicultural author as well as a response to its composition in interwar Britain when questions of national allegiance were paramount.[54] These texts and the diverse œuvres from which they emerge put pressure on narratives of literary production in twentieth-century Britain, as modernist and postcolonial overlap, extend, and intertwine.

Works of black and Asian modernism tend to be read in terms of content and political or biographical contexts. This can lead to an occlusion of the myriad experiments of form and genre that characterise this body of work, experiments which are of course the product of such contexts but also a transgression of their influence. The versatility shown in the careers of these writers is, in part, a response to the rapidly changing contours of capitalist, imperialist modernity as well as their authors' precarious position within the metropolis. But it is also about these writers' intersectional position at the nodal point of a mixture of cultures, ethnicities, and class positions. The formal multiplicity of their writing both marks these diverse

---

[51] Menen, *Prevalence*, 126.   [52] Ranasinha, 'Cultural Contestations', 292.

[53] Menen, *Space*, 102.

[54] G. V. Desani, *All About H. Hatterr* (New York: New York Review of Books, [1948] 1986), 13.

influences and braids them together in often surprising ways. Black and Asian modernists were already experimenting with a global outlook and frames of reference that came to be associated with post-World War II, postcolonial literature. Here, too, we have an alternative perspective on the 'newness' that has been so central to definitions of literary modernism.

8

Establishing Material Platforms in Literary Culture in the 1930s and 1940s

RUVANI RANASINHA

This chapter illustrates the extent and means by which disproportionately influential black and South Asian minority writers, intellectuals, and editors in Britain established material platforms and shaped British cultural, political, and intellectual life during the 1930s and 1940s. During this time, London was a hotbed of radical nationalist activity, and a cosmopolitan, dynamic site for contact between a wide variety of students, writers, intellectuals, and anti-colonial activists from a range of colonial and white British backgrounds. Broader networks forged connections between the injustices of British rule in Africa, the Caribbean, and India, with London providing an intellectual 'organising' space for nationalism for people throughout the colonies.[1] The Indian Labour MP Shapurji Saklatvala addressed the second Pan-African Conference held in London in 1921. As others note, the Jamaican Dr Harold Moody founded the League of Coloured Peoples in 1931: Britain's first significant black-led organisation set up to engage with the racism and prejudice facing arriving migrants. As discussed in previous chapters, Una Marson (1905–1965) worked for the League as its unpaid assistant secretary. Swiftly networked into black British circles, by 1937 she became not only the contributing editor of the League's journal *The Keys*, but its key spokesperson. *The Keys* 'had a circulation of over two thousand world-wide in 1934. It was well-designed, well-illustrated and comprehensive in its coverage of race issues both at home and abroad, from the case of the Scottsboro boys in the USA to the problems of colonial seamen in Cardiff.[2] Its wide coverage of pan-African issues included the education of black children in South Africa.

Similarly, South Asian writers and commentators in Britain deployed existing platforms *and* created new ones to counter and complement the

[1] See also the Anti-Colonial People's Conference held in Manchester in the 1940s.
[2] Delia Jarrett-Macauley, *The Life of Una Marson 1905–65* (Manchester: Manchester University Press, 1998), 54.

mainstream British press, which 'gives so little news of India and so little account of different Indian political views'[3] – notably, the short-lived, radical, sparsely produced *Indian Writing* magazine (1940–1945), edited by Iqbal Singh (1912–2001), Ahmed Ali (1910–1994), Alagu Subramaniam (1915–1971), and Krishnarao Shelvankar (1906–1996), to which the Indian writers and activists Mulk Raj Anand (1905–2004) and V. K. Krishna Menon (1896–1974) contributed. Although very different in terms of duration, circulation, and appearance, *The Keys*' and *Indian Writing*'s shared rationale was to engage with British indifference and ignorance of the colonies. *Indian Writing* aimed to inform readers of what was happening in the colonies in the context of 'rigorous censorship that prevents any real news of India from percolating into the outside world'.[4] A 1936 article in *The Keys* similarly documented that the 'British public seldom hears of the West Indian colonies, and hardly realizes their existence'.[5] This chapter traces black and Asian writers' political and literary aspirations in the newspapers and magazines with which they were so centrally involved.

The 1930s saw increasing political tensions between anti-colonial activists and the British. This period saw a shift away from a reformist agenda towards bids for independence, notably in the Round Table Conferences held in London (1930–1932) between British politicians and key Indians to discuss India's new constitution, dominion status, and the creation of separate provinces. At the Second Round Table Conference in 1931, Mohandas Karamchand Gandhi (1869–1948) represented the Indian National Congress, with the Indian poet and reformer Sarojini Naidu (1879–1949) voicing the concerns of Indian women. South Asian writers in Britain contributed to and facilitated the heightened political writing of this period; notably the politicised autobiographies by Gandhi and Jawaharlal Nehru (1889–1964) (see Chapter 10), produced when – as Naidu describes in 1931 – the 'Gandhi craze' was at its height in London.[6] Increasingly forceful critiques of British imperialism emerged in the late 1930s and 1940s: the *Indian Bulletin* monthly (1932–1939), published in Britain by the Friends of India Association, sought to

---

[3] Venu Chitale, 'An Interview with Kingsley Martin: The Man in the Street', broadcast 15 May 1942, Contributors Talks File 1, BBC Written Archives Centre, transcript: 1.

[4] Ahmed Ali, Iqbal Singh, Krishnao Shelvankar, and Alagu Subramaniam, 'Commentary', *Indian Writing*, 1:3 (March 1941): 125–9; 126.

[5] R. O. Thomas, 'Revolt in the West Indies', cited in Anna Snaith, *Modernist Voyages: Colonial Women Writers in London, 1890–1945* (Cambridge: Cambridge University Press, 2014), 159.

[6] Makarand Paranjape (ed.), *Sarojini Naidu: Selected Letters 1890s–1940s* (New Delhi: Kali for Women, 1996), 248.

persuade British readers of the inevitability of Indian self-governance, by charting the civil disobedience movement launched by Gandhi in the 1930s, and by drawing attention to the colonial government's repressive measures, which were erased from most mainstream British newspapers. In 1935, Mussolini's invasion of Abyssinia, the last truly independent African nation and the oldest African state, galvanised pan-Africanism and black people worldwide, but especially in London. Other minority figures engaged exclusively with white British and European literary culture. Influencing a more rarefied cultural sphere than his anti-colonial activist peers with their political pamphlets, the Sri Lankan poet and editor of the influential *Poetry London* literary magazine (1939–1951), M. J. Tambimuttu (1915–1983), published the leading English writers of the time and had a dynamic influence on the content and format of British publishing. Other minority writers produced critiques of canonical white literary figures such as Shakespeare and Yeats.

Building on the growing body of scholarship in this area, this chapter explores how certain minority figures created and deployed material platforms, not only to mediate representations of the colonies and the colonised to Euro-American readers, but also to reverse 'the colonial gaze' in a number of ways.[7] First, their positions on cultural borders enabled fresh views of Britain; these countered dominant British self-representations, particularly of colonialism. Secondly, they critiqued white literary portrayals of both the colonies and the colonised, and even the contemporary British literary scene. Furthermore, they promoted minority causes and writers, and countered dismissive, negative reviews of their work within the journals they created, as well as more broadly in British newspapers and mainstream periodicals such as the *Left Review*, *Life and Letters*, and the *New Statesman*.

This period saw a rise in the coverage of minority writers, particularly because of the ascendancy of left politics in response to the rise of fascism. So just as Mulk Raj Anand used broadly imperialist organisations such as the BBC for his own anti-colonial purposes, I will show how he, alongside other

---

[7] Including Jarrett-Macauley, *Life of Una Marson*; Bill Schwarz (ed.), *West Indian Intellectuals in Britain* (Manchester: Manchester University Press, 2003); Ruvani Ranasinha *South Asian Writers in Twentieth-Century Britain: Culture in Translation* (Oxford: Oxford University Press, 2007); Alison Donnell, *Una Marson: Selected Poems* (Leeds: Peepal Tree Press, 2011); Rehana Ahmed and Sumita Mukherjee (eds.), *South Asian Resistances in Britain, 1858–1947* (London: Continuum, 2012); Ruvani Ranasinha with Rehana Ahmed, Sumita Mukherjee, and Florian Stadtler (eds.), *South Asians and the Shaping of Britain, 1870–1950: A Sourcebook* (Manchester: Manchester University Press, 2012); Susheila Nasta (ed.), *India in Britain: South Asian Networks and Connections, 1858–1950* (Basingstoke: Palgrave Macmillan, 2013); Snaith, *Modernist Voyages*; Elleke Boehmer, *Indian Arrivals, 1870–1915* (Oxford: Oxford University Press, 2015).

minority writers, deployed British left journals to reach broader readerships.[8] Furthermore, this chapter emphasises how many of these key, prolific black and Asian writers and activists made several interrelated formative interventions: they established material platforms that enabled them to engage with broader sociopolitical inequities rather than solely with those that preoccupied the colonised. Thus this chapter places these black and Asian figures not as part of isolated 'minority traditions', but within the developing context of the historically local movements and cross-cultural milieus in which they found themselves. As we will see, these include the synergy and intersection between global feminism and anti-colonialism, black, Indian, and Irish cultural nationalism, as well as left politics and literature.

Literary Platforms

I want to begin by examining the different ways in which certain minority writers deployed their material platforms to reverse the colonial gaze. First, their 'insider–outsider' perspectives produced de-familiarising critiques of Britain. This kind of book flourished at the turn of the century: notably *An Indian Eye of English Life* (1893) by the Parsi poet, journalist, and reformer Behramji M. Malabari (1853–1912) and *England to an Indian Eye* (1897) by Rev. T. B. Pandian (*b.* 1863, *d.* unknown).[9] These are early examples of the countering of the dominant metropolitan gaze with the Indian writers' ambivalent commentary on English social mores. Their critiques of British slums and social inequality provided a reversal of British perceptions of India's poverty and lack of 'civilisation'. But in the 1930s and 1940s, minority writers began to critique British racist *behaviour* both in the colonies and in Britain. So even politically conservative anglophiles, such as the literary critic Ranjee G. Shahani (1904–1968), presented British readers with a critique of how the British behaved in India. In his memoir *Indian Pilgrimage* (1939) Shahani recounts his journey back to India in the 1930s as an expatriate. He observes that in Britain friendship between Indians and English is 'not only possible but really exists'. However, he argues that 'in India [. . .] the story is quite different: the Englishman in India becomes acutely

---

[8] Like the literary and publishing activities examined in this chapter, the BBC operated similarly as a contact zone: it facilitated and sustained the interaction between British and minority writers resident in Britain (especially Marson and Anand). See Chapter 9.

[9] Behramji M. Malabari made several visits to London from Bombay to win support for a reform of Hindu marriage customs from British reformers.

aware of his pigmentary aristocracy'. He behaves like a 'savage' to Indians, treating them with contempt and disdain.[10] This kind of contrast alerts British readerships to the broader discrepancy between notions of 'Englishness', of justice and fair play, and how these are distorted in praxis in the rule of the colonies: a contradiction that fuelled a dominant strand of the anti-colonial movement. A few years later, Shahani critiques growing racial prejudice and the challenges to mixed-race relationships in the west in his story *A White Man in Search of God* (1943).[11]

Such portrayals of Europeans marked a transgression of the role designated to the native informant: they were expected to confine themselves to depictions of colonised Others; parallel scrutiny of Europeans was implicitly discouraged. See, for example, the review praising Anand for 'wisely avoiding that stumbling block [depictions of] "the European"' in his novel *The Village*.[12] Similarly, during the 1930s, the prolific Indian Parsi journalist D. F. Karaka (1911–1974) studied law at Oxford (1930–1933) when he began to voice criticisms of racism in British society in the British press. He published an article on the colour bar in 1934 in the *Daily Herald*, one of the most widely read newspapers in the 1930s. He further dealt with the position of Indians in the British Empire and in Britain in several books and memoirs: *The Pulse of Oxford* (1933), *Oh! You English* (1935), and *I Go West* (1938). However, at a time of heightened Indo-British tensions, Karaka's criticisms of racism in British society were dismissed as jaundiced and unreliable: 'There is too much bitterness, too little thought in this book.'[13] Analogously, after complet-ing his doctorate from the University of London, Bhabani Bhattacharya (1906–1988) wrote *So Many Hungers!* (1947) to inform the British public about the Bengal famine (1943–1944) in which almost four million people died. He challenges dominant readings of colonialism by examining the sufferings of Indian villagers during the Bengal famine as the direct result of British rule: scarce food supplies were diverted to British troops and urban industrial areas, rather than to the rural poor. Just as the politically conservative *Times Literary Supplement* rejected Karaka's observations, it reviewed Bhattacharya's book as a 'sincere, bitter and prejudiced [. . .]

---

[10] Ranjee G. Shahani, *Indian Pilgrimage* (London: Michael Joseph, 1939), 39.

[11] See also Anna Snaith's discussion of Una Marson's critique of racism in her plays in London in *Modernist Voyages*, 167.

[12] Hilton Brown, 'Review of Anand's *The Village*', *Times Literary Supplement*, 15 April 1939: 215.

[13] Anonymous, 'Review of Karaka's *Oh! You English*', *Times Literary Supplement*, 18 July 1935: 468.

naïve expression of Indian nationalism'.[14] This reveals the dismissal of texts that challenge hegemonic notions of Englishness and offer transformative reflections. Thus any exploration of the building of material platforms must also recognise sections of the literary establishment's continued opposition to them.

Reversing the Gaze

Secondly, I wish to consider minority critiques of *white* literary portrayals of the colonies and the colonised as powerful reversals of the dominant white literary gaze. In his wide-ranging *Survey of Anglo-Indian Fiction* (1934) Bhupal Singh confidently questions the authenticity of British fictions on India: 'Anglo-Indian writers have a right to make fun of us, if it pleases them to do so. And no harm is done, provided it is understood that Anglo-Indian art is not always a faithful copy of life.'[15] He gives examples of their 'failure to lift the veil that hides real India from the eye of the foreigner'.[16] Cornelia Sorabji (1866–1954), Britain's first qualified Indian barrister, as well as a writer, activist, and social reformer, reviews key exponents of the genre of Anglo-Indian fiction, Rudyard Kipling and Flora Annie Steele, to a similar end.[17] As Madhumita Lahiri has shown, by identifying the limitations of their work, Sorabji promotes her own fiction and the insights into 'the real India' that, according to her, only an Indian author can provide: Kipling and Steele 'can describe what they have seen: Indian servants, the life of the bazaar, field or road [. . .] but life behind closed doors [. . .] the complexities of the innermost soul of reserved East [. . .] this neither of them really touches'.[18]

Anand goes further. He offers astute critical commentaries not only of Kipling but of more contemporary writers – Leonard Woolf, T. S. Eliot, Edward Thompson, E. M. Forster, Lionel Felden, Stephen Spender, and George Orwell – in a variety of British journals. In a particularly radical

---

[14] Anonymous, 'Review of Bhattacharya's *So Many Hungers!*', *Times Literary Supplement*, 7 February 1948: 46.
[15] Bhupal Singh, *Survey of Anglo-Indian Fiction* (Oxford: Oxford University, 1934), 305.
[16] Ibid., 80.
[17] Sorabji studied in Oxford and London (1889–1894) and settled permanently in Britain from 1938. She was the author of *Love and Life Behind the Purdah* (London: Freemantle, 1901), *Sun Babies: Studies in the Child Life of India* (1904), *Between the Twilights* (1908), *The Purdahnashin* (Calcutta: Thacker, Spink and Co. 1917), as well as a memoir, *India Calling: The Memories of Cornelia Sorabji* (London: Nisbet, 1934), and its part-sequel, *India Recalled* (1936).
[18] Sorabji cited in Madhumita Lahiri, '"Best Sellers": India, Indians and the British Reading Public' in Nasta (ed.), *India in Britain*, 134–8; 137.

move, Singh, Ali, Shelvankar, and Subramaniam provide a damning critique of the contemporary white British literary scene and leading writers of the day in their 'anonymous' review of John Lehmann's left-wing *New Writing* in their magazine *Indian Writing*. They acknowledge that Lehmann's editorship 'goes beyond the idiosyncrasies of a coterie [and] communicates a sense of larger urgencies shaping the destiny of the world'. However, their review also goes on to suggest that the new technique of reportage as literary technique 'has already reached a degree of monotony'. Furthermore, 'this is particularly noticeable in the English contributions [which] in spite of their undeniable competence and power often seem to develop on stereotyped lines and lack any compelling interest'. In a significant reversal of the usual comparisons, the review claims the most memorable stories in *New Writing* come from India, China, and the Continent: they possess 'greater individuality of observation and expression' than their British counterparts. Moreover, the leading British poets of the day are dismissed in no uncertain terms: 'look in vain for illumination [. . .] in the dreary neo-metaphysics of Day Lewis, the sentimental effusion of Spender, pseudo-elegiac tortuosity of George Barker [and] the facile and facetious topicality of Auden'.[19]

Narratives of Nationalism

Like Anand, all four *Indian Writing* editors were at the centre of anti-colonial activities with strong links to the India League, the Congress party, and the Indian Progressive Writers' Association. Although the magazine was called 'Indian' Writing, the co-editor Subramaniam, as well as several regular contributors including Pieter Keuneman (1917–1997) and J. Vijayatunga (*b*. 1902, *d*. unknown) were in fact Sri Lankan (or Ceylonese to use the terminology of the time). *Indian Writing* was based at Sasadhar Sinha's bookshop, 'The Bibliophile', in London's Little Russell Street, which opened in 1935 as a meeting place for politically minded South Asians. The editors perceived the need to literally create their own space within Britain in the form of a literary magazine, to articulate their own views on politics and culture, which would have been seen as radical and extremist at the time. *Indian Writing*'s opening editorial set out the aspirations of its founding editors:

> We are witnessing today a significant shift of the bases of culture, that initiative in cultural matters is passing to those vast masses of humanity

[19] Anonymous, 'Commentary', *Indian Writing*, 1:1 (1940): 61–3; 61.

who have so far served only as pawns for the profit of Western Imperialism. In this respect the awakening of India is one of the most important facts of contemporary history. No single magazine could possibly claim to represent this great movement in all its complex aspects. We only hope to interpret its specifically cultural implications.[20]

The magazine provided a radical critique of Indo-British relations from the perspective of these activists in London. *Indian Writing* charted the Stanley Cripps mission to India, and criticised Allied war propaganda and the BBC's staging of 'a mock debate on India, in which the BBC presented as representatives of Indian opinion, a number of abjectly illiterate non-entities, incapable of even representing themselves'.[21]

Poetry London

Indian Writing's forthright critique of Indo-British relations, politicised conceptions of 'culture', and nationalist, anti-colonial agendas contrast sharply with its contemporary *Poetry London* magazine, and with Tambimuttu's privileging of aesthetic and formal considerations. Nevertheless, Tambimuttu's and other writers' exclusive engagement with white literary culture marked a significant inroad into British publishing, and an important move politically: exceeding the role traditionally demarcated for minority writers to examine authors from their own cultural background as native informants. Not only did Tambimuttu publish the leading English and international writers of the time (Walter de la Mare, Stephen Spender, Louis MacNeice, and Dylan Thomas), he ushered in a group of emergent writers he later called 'The New Moderns': Kathleen Raine, George Barker, and David Gascoyne. In addition, he published some of the first books or volumes of poetry of Elizabeth Smart, Michael Hamburger, and the war poets Alun Lewis (stationed in India) and Keith Douglas (in North Africa).

Tambimuttu's imprint, Editions Poetry London, also published the first London editions of novels by Anaïs Nin and Vladimir Nabokov. Tambimuttu aligned himself with the New Romanticism of 1940s Britain as a robust rejoinder to the poetry magazines *New Verse* and *Twentieth Century Verse*, and to the poetry of political commitment of the thirties, such as John Lehmann's *New Writing*. He promoted a number of up-and-coming visual artists, such as Henry Moore and Barbara Hepworth, and commissioned Graham Sutherland, Lucian Freud, and Mervyn Peake to design covers for

---

[20] Ahmed Ali and Iqbal Singh, 'Editorial', *Indian Writing*, 1:1 (1940): 3–4; 3.
[21] Iqbal Singh, 'Indian Art at the Imperial Institute', *Indian Writing*, 1:3 (1941): 151–5; 155.

his publishing imprint and for his illustrated texts. These lithographs and illustrations were particular achievements given the constraints on paper publishing during the war. In spite of wartime conditions, financial difficulties, and irregular publication, Tambimuttu built up *Poetry London*'s circulation. It was the main poetry magazine of the war and for a long time afterwards retained its position as a leading vehicle for modern poetry, and a proving ground for promising younger poets. *Poetry London* (1939–1951) survived Geoffrey Grigson's *New Verse* (1933–1939), with its reputation for vitriolic criticism, John Lehmann's *New Writing*, distinguished by its socialist, anti-fascist stance (1936–1946), Julian Symons's short-lived *Twentieth Century Verse* (1937–1939), Alan Rook and Henry Treece's modernist *Kingdom Come* (1939–1942), and Cyril Connolly and Stephen Spender's *Horizon* (1940–1949), intended for readers formerly served by *New Verse*. Tambimuttu's crucial role in sustaining *Poetry London* is underlined by the fact that the magazine folded a couple of years after he departed for Sri Lanka in 1949.[22]

Academic Platforms

Other minority critics and writers forged inroads into British publishing through academia. With a DLitt from Paris, Shahani (mentioned above) published his thesis *Shakespeare Through Eastern Eyes* (London: Herbert Joseph, 1932) with an introduction by J. Middleton Murry and appreciation by Emile Legouis. Shahani was made a Fellow of the Royal Society of Literature in 1933. He subsequently published an influential reading of Shakespeare's allegorical poem about the death of ideal love 'The Phoenix and the Turtle' (1601) in *Notes and Queries* (1946). Shahani was one of the few Asian writers to interview T. S. Eliot in 'T. S. Eliot answers questions'.[23] As an anglophile and elegist of the English spirit at a time of postwar uncertainty, Shahani resumed a prewar call to the English to take up leadership of Europe in his book *The Amazing English* (London: Adam and Charles Black, 1948), which was reviewed in the *Times Literary Supplement* and in *Britain Today*.

The academic and scholar of Indian dance and classical music Narayana Menon (1911–1997) was Carnegie Scholar in English Literature from 1939 to 1941 at Edinburgh University where he graduated with a PhD in English for his thesis on William Butler Yeats. He published this fearless critique of Yeats

---

[22] For a fuller discussion of Tambimuttu's activities in Britain see Ranasinha, *South Asian Writers*, 103–44.

[23] Ranjee Shahani, 'Interview with T. S. Eliot', *John O' London's Weekly*, 18:1369 (19 August 1949): 497–8.

in his book, *The Development of William Butler Yeats* (Edinburgh: Oliver and Boyd, 1942). E. M. Forster reviewed it favourably on BBC radio.[24] Similarly, Balachandran Rajan (1920–2009), a scholar of poetry and poetics, wrote not on South Asian poets, but on Milton, as the author of *Paradise Lost and the Seventeenth Century Reader* (London: Chatto & Windus, 1947), and on *Modern American Poetry* (London: Dennis Dobson, 1950). Rajan was a Fellow of Trinity College, University of Cambridge from 1944 to 1948. During this period, he edited a series of volumes on literary criticism titled *Focus*, which had four issues between 1945 and 1948 published by Dennis Dobson. *Focus* engaged critically with work by some of the key literary names of the day, including Aldous Huxley, Jean-Paul Sartre, Christopher Isherwood, and Franz Kafka. Contributors of essays include Kathleen Raine, D. S. Savage, and Julian Symons, with poems by e. e. cummings, George Barker, John Heath-Stubbs, and Vernon Watkins, as well as Rajan himself. The fourth volume was collected into an influential book edited by Rajan entitled *The Novelist as Thinker* (London: Dennis Dobson, 1947) with key contributions from Savage on Huxley and the dissociation of personality and from H. Bantock on the novels of Isherwood. The series had its beginnings at Cambridge, where Rajan co-edited (with Wolf Mankowitz) a collection of criticism titled *Sheaf*, which was published by the university, and authored his own collection of poems, *Monsoon and Other Poems*. He went on to write four further books on Milton after he left England in 1948 for academic posts in Delhi University and later the University of Western Ontario where he lived until his death. Similarly, the less well known but no less important writer Sirdar Ikbal Ali Shah (1894–1969) provided a scathing critique of 'refined, soulless [. . .] English novels through Eastern eyes' in *The Bookman*.[25] Sarvepalli Radhakrishnan (1888–1975) was appointed as Spalding Professor of Eastern Religions and Ethics at All Souls College, Oxford from 1936 to 1952. Acting as a reader for the publisher Allen & Unwin, he facilitated the publication of key anglophone Indian narratives of nationalism, notably Raja Rao's *Kanthapura* (1938) but also Rao and Singh's edited collection *Changing India* (1939).[26]

For Anand and Singh, among others, their own literary output and critiques of white British writers formed only part of their ambition to produce and facilitate a re-evaluation of anglophone literary culture and of

---

[24] E. M. Forster, 'An Indian on W. B. Yeats', *The Listener*, 28:728 (24 December 1942): 824.

[25] Sirdar Ikbal Ali Shah, 'Review', *The Bookman* (December 1931): n.p.

[26] For a fuller discussion of Radhakrishnan's role in facilitating South Asian anglophone publications, see Ranasinha, *South Asian Writers*, 26–9.

South Asian anglophone literature's place within it. In 1946, Anand, Singh, and D. P. Chaudhuri (also deputy editor of *Asian Horizon*, 1948–1950) set up the New India Publishing Company in London with the aim of reconfiguring relations between India and the west on 'the basis of free and creative co-operation between India and the Western world'. To this end they would 'produce literature of permanent value written by Indians on various aspects of Indian culture, civilisation and particularly on modern trends of thought in relation to the Indian renaissance' in order to supplement the 'ephemeral [. . .] pamphlets, leaflets and news bulletins' produced by Indian organisations in Great Britain.[27] One of the few known volumes produced by this venture is a collection of *Indian Short Stories* (1946) edited by Anand and Singh. It features authors who considerably influenced South Asian writing in both English and indigenous languages: one of the great innovative figures of modern literature, the Bengali poet, playwright, and novelist Rabindranath Tagore (1861–1941); the novelist, critic, and poet Ahmed Ali; the pioneering feminist Urdu writer Ismat Chughtai (1911–1991); Alagu Subramaniam, short-story writer and editor of *Indian Writing*; and Attia Habibullah Hosain (1913–1998). Hosain settled in Britain in 1947 and worked for many years at the BBC. She published *Phoenix Fled* (1953), a collection of short stories on dispossessed Indian peasantry. Her novel *Sunlight on Broken Column* (1961) voices the conflicts of a daughter of the ruling classes caught between tradition and modernity in the context of the events leading to the Independence of India and the creation of Pakistan.

What is particularly striking about Anand and Singh's introduction to their collection is their positioning of Indian anglophone short stories as 'hybrid' products of the collision of Indian and European literary traditions, alongside their rationale for a new critical framework within which to evaluate these texts. Anticipating western readers' criticisms of these stories, the editors take on the role of mediators, preparing Eurocentric readerships to engage with culturally different texts and aesthetics. In contrast to 'the subtle interplay of situation and character of the Western short story [. . .] the background of life which [Indian writers] have to deal with does not lend itself to the same kind of formal treatment'.[28] But equally important was their aim to evaluate '*all progressive movements outside India*' (original emphasis) rather than only inter-preting Indian problems for the west. The founding editors of this first publishing venture run by Indians insisted that 'free and creative co-

[27] Mulk Raj Anand and Iqbal Singh (eds.), *Indian Short Stories* (London: New India Publishing Company, 1946), 8.
[28] Ibid.

operation between India and the Western world cannot be securely established' without 'such two-way traffic of disseminating ideas'.[29]

Role of British Left Journals

To this end, several black and Asian activists and writers looked to influence the direction of mainstream literary magazines and publishing houses. Some figures promoted minority causes and writers, and countered dismissive, negative reviews of minority writers' work not only within the journals they created,[30] but also more broadly in British newspapers and mainstream periodicals such as the *Left Review* (1934–1938), *Life and Letters*, and the *New Statesman*. Similarly, in the writer and activist Nancy Cunard's review in the *Left Review* of Prince Nyabongo's book *Africa Answers Back* (1936), which contrasts the discipline and logic of tribal life with the bigoted, sterile discipline of the missionary teacher in an East African mission school during the 1890s, she writes: 'After the prejudiced, the romantic, the paternal handling of the African theme by so many white writers, it is very good to have a book on Africa *by* an African.' Rather like South Asian writers acting as mediators, here Cunard anticipates the prejudices of white readerships and is careful to establish the credentials of the non-white author: the Prince 'who has studied at Yale and Oxford speaks and writes perfect English'.[31]

As noted above, the late 1930s and 1940s saw a flowering of Asian and black writing, particularly because of the growth of left politics as a form of political protest against the rise of fascism. These minority writers used British left journals to articulate a new politics to more mainstream readerships. For instance, Anand published several short stories and an essay on 'New Indian Literature' in the *Left Review*. One story, 'Bombay Mill', is particularly significant. It informs broader British readerships (those who may not have read Anand's powerful anglophone fictional explorations of Indian nationalism) of the realities of British exploitation of vulnerable oppressed Indian 'coolies': factory workers including women and children who work in harsh, Victorian conditions. The mill was:

> full of women with babies tied to their backs, in their laps or wallowing in the
> dust on the floor, crying, screaming, sobbing, precariously perched near the

---

[29] Ibid.

[30] See Anand's response to negative British reviews of Ahmed Ali's *Twilight in Delhi* (1940) in his own review of Ali's novel; Mulk Raj Anand, 'Review', *Indian Writing*, 1:3 (1941): 175–7.

[31] Nancy Cunard, 'Review', *Left Review*, 2:12 (1936): 469.

claws of the machine which softened cotton on the far side of steel planes and pistons and steam. Munoo wondered that all the children had not grazed their arms, knocked their heads or been cut into pieces by the parts of the machine which jutted out, without any wiring to keep them safe out of harm's way.[32]

The manifesto (drafted by Anand and Sajjad Zaheer) of the All-India Progressive Writers' Association (IPWA), established in London in 1935 by Indian writers with the encouragement of some British literary figures, was similarly published in the *Left Review* in February 1936. Its motivating aim was 'that the new literature of India must deal with the basic problems of our existence to-day – the problems of hunger and poverty, social backwardness, and political subjection'.[33] The *Left Review* was instrumental in supporting Indian writing in English, particularly under the editorship of Edgell Rickword from January 1936: he was an editor at Lawrence & Wishart and ushered in the publication of Anand's path-breaking novel *Untouchable* (1935). Other Indian writers soon followed Anand's lead in publishing in the *Left Review*. The magazine included articles on Nehru's campaign for Indian liberties and short stories by Subramaniam ('This Time the Fan'), Sarat Chandra Chatterjee ('The Drought', in a translation by Sasadhar Sinha), and Ahmed Ali ('Mr Shamsul Hasan'), as well as poetry by Fredoon Kabraji ('The Patriots'). The *Left Review* also reviewed the writings of Indian writers Iqbal Singh and Jawaharlal Nehru.

The work of several South Asian writers based in Britain also occasionally featured in *Life and Letters Today*: a monthly literary review magazine which published short fiction, essays on cultural issues, and book reviews. Several well-known British literary figures, including D. H. Lawrence, Dylan Thomas, and Julian Symons, contributed to the magazine. Mulk Raj Anand was a regular contributor of both fiction and reviews. There were three issues dedicated to Indian writing and featuring a range of short fiction and essays by writers such as Narayana Menon, S. Menon Marath, Iqbal Singh, and J. Vijayatunga, as well as reviews of their work, which tended to be more favourable than reviews in the more conservative *Times Literary Supplement*. A. Calder-Marshall offers a sympathetic view of Anand's novel *Across the Black Waters* and 'his extraordinary technique' in *Life and Letters Today*.[34] In

---

[32] Mulk Raj Anand, 'Bombay Mill', *Left Review*, 2:12 (1935): 374–7; 377.

[33] For more information on the IPWA see Priyamvada Gopal, *Indian English Novel: Nation, History, and Narration* (Oxford: Oxford University Press, 2009), 50.

[34] Arthur Calder-Marshall, 'Review', *Life and Letters Today*, 28:4 (1941): 83–8.

contrast, R. D. Charques reviews Anand's novel as 'tedious and pointless' in the *Times Literary Supplement*.[35]

The three Indian editions of *Life and Letters Today* highlight a degree of success on the part of South Asians in infiltrating an established mainstream British cultural product that showed an awareness of and sympathy with marginalised Indian writers in Britain. Contributions to the magazine by South Asians comprise mostly short fiction located almost uniquely in India and Ceylon rather than in Britain. Their short prose on South Asian history and culture often positioned these authors primarily as cultural informers. However, while Anand reviewed key South Asian texts such as Shelvankar's *The Problem of India*, Narayana Menon's *The Development of William Butler Yeats*, and Nehru's *Autobiography*, it is significant that he also reviewed key white British and European texts including Virginia Woolf's *The Death of a Moth*, T. E. Lawrence's *Oriental Assembly*, William Saroyan's *Razzle-Dazzle*, and Ignazio Silone's *The Seed Beneath the Snow*. S. Menon Marath reviewed Gustave Flaubert's *Letters*.

This kind of publication was a product of the synergy between the left, anti-colonial politics, and literature that characterises many of the literary endeavours of black and Asian writers at this time. For instance, the Left Book Club (1936–1948) constituted a nexus between left-wing anti-imperialist white British (Harold Laski, Sidney and Beatrice Webb, Leonard Woolf, George Orwell) and South Asian and black intellectuals (Rajane Palme Dutt, Ayana Angadi, Santha Rama Rao, Bhabani Bhattacharya, C. L. R. James, Paul Robeson, and Una Marson). It brought influential British metropolitan writers into contact with minority writers, whom they supported by writing reviews or prefaces to their work. During the period when Marson became involved with the Left Book Club she encountered the writings of Rabindranath Tagore. The Trotskyite C. L. R. James published *The Case for West-Indian Self-Government* with the Woolfs' Hogarth Press in 1933. As a member of the Left Book Club between 1927 and 1939, Robeson wrote articles championing African culture in the *New Statesman and Nation* as well as for the *Left Review*.

A distinct strand of left political writing on colonialism distinguished by rational analysis, logical argument, and accessible prose developed. This includes E. J. Thompson's *The Reconstruction of India* (1930), Krishna Menon's *Condition of India* (India League, 1932, with a foreword by Bertrand Russell), R. Palme Dutt's *India Today* (1940), and Nehru's (among others')

---

[35] R. D. Charques, 'Review', *Times Literary Supplement* (7 December 1940): 619.

numerous India League pamphlets. The journalist, translator, and editor Clemens Palme Dutt (who like his elder brother Ranjani Palme Dutt was an active member of the Communist Party of Great Britain) disseminated politics to left-wing readerships in his book *Labour and the Empire* (London: Communist Party of Great Britain, 1929), and as the editor of over nine volumes of Marx, Engels, and Lenin published by Martin Lawrence.

As noted, key black and Asian writers found ways to combat wider socio-political injustices, not exclusively those that preoccupied the colonised. Notably, the Jamaican feminist activist Marson addressed wider issues of women's rights in addition to her work on racial division, black liberation, and pan-Africanism. Marson spoke as the Jamaican delegate at the International Alliance of Women for Suffrage and Equal Citizenship conference in Istanbul in 1935 about both women's deprivation in Jamaica and the colour bar facing black people in London, including British citizens. She gave evidence to the Moyne Commission specifically on the conditions for women in Jamaica. As Snaith describes, during the interwar years Marson was 'the most significant black British feminist': she was involved with several feminist organisations whilst campaigning for the case for self-representation in the West Indies.[36]

Analogously, while addressing the pressing issue of colonial occupation, activist figures such as V. K. Krishna Menon engaged with broader socialist issues and penetrated wider British readerships. After studying law at the London School of Economics in 1928 Menon joined, and swiftly radicalised, the India League, campaigning for Indian Independence alongside key British and South Asian figures for the next two decades. As an editor at Bodley Head (1932–1935) Menon launched the Twentieth Century Library Series and commissioned the publication of Nehru's autobiography and the republication of Anand's *Untouchable* as a Penguin Modern Classic in 1940. But it is in his role as an editor at Penguin that Menon made economics, history, and political theories accessible to new British reading constituencies through his co-founding of the innovative and affordable non-fiction educational paperback imprint Pelican Books. Krishna Menon's key role has been written out of official accounts of the history of Pelican Books. In addition, serving as a Labour councillor for St Pancras from 1934 to 1947, Menon inaugurated an arts festival and extended the library service in this predominantly working-class area.[37]

[36] Snaith, *Modernist Voyages*, 155.
[37] For more details on Krishna Menon see T. J. S. George, *Krishna* (London: Jonathan Cape, 1964); Ranasinha, *South Asian Writers*, 23–8.

To conclude, while certain black and Asian writers (Krishna Menon, the *Indian Writing* editors, Marson) developed material platforms primarily in order to inscribe new imagined politicised communities, others (Tambimuttu and Sorabji) tended to deploy the inroads they created to emphasise their exceptionalism: the constructions and projection of the self in their life-writings focus on the individual rather than the collective.

9

Transnational Cultural Exchange
The BBC as Contact Zone

JAMES PROCTER

Among the many artists to converge at the BBC during and just after World War II was an extraordinary range of late colonial writers, editors, and intellectuals.[1] In the Eastern Service, these included the Kenyan-born Indian G. V. Desani (1909–2000), author of the late modernist classic *All About H. Hatterr* (1948); M. J. Tambimuttu (1915–1983), the Sri Lankan poet, editor, and founder of the literary magazine *Poetry London*; and Mulk Raj Anand (1905–2004), whose novels included *Untouchable* (1935) and *Coolie* (1936). The African Service hosted the leading West African writers of a generation, including Chinua Achebe (1930–2013), Wole Soyinka (1934–), Amos Tutuola (1920–1997), and Cyprian Ekwensi (1921–2007). Meanwhile the Caribbean Service employed or commissioned over 300 different literary contributors between the 1940s and 1960s, including the Jamaicans Una Marson (1905–1965) and Louise Bennett (1919–2006), the Trinidadians V. S. Naipaul (1932–2018) and Sam Selvon (1923–1994), the Barbadians George Lamming (1927–) and Kamau Brathwaite (1930–), the Guyanese Edgar Mittelholzer (1909–1965) and Jan Carew (1920–2012), and the St Lucian Derek Walcott (1930–2017). Alongside white British contemporaries such as George Orwell (1903–1950), E. M. Forster (1879–1970), and Henry Swanzy (1915–2004), this gathering of creative talents generated possibilities for exchange and collaboration on a scale unprecedented at the mid-twentieth century.

Scholarship has begun to reveal in this context the important role played by otherwise discrete areas of the corporation, notably the Indian Section of the wartime Eastern Service (1941–1945) and the West Indian literary

---

[1] For a fuller account of World War II and West Indian writing at the BBC, see James Procter, 'Wireless Writing, World War II and the West Indian Literary Imagination' in Gill Plain (ed.), *Postwar: British Literature in Transition 1940–60* (Cambridge: Cambridge University Press, 2018), 117–35.

magazine programme *Caribbean Voices* (1944–1958).[2] For instance, critics such as Susheila Nasta and Ruvani Ranasinha have elaborated on the friendships and literary connections between South Asian and late colonial writers including George Orwell and Mulk Raj Anand, or explored how the wartime Indian Section 'fostered intellectual networks in which diasporic Indian nationalism could be debated and critiqued'.[3] Similarly, Glyne Griffith and Peter Kalliney have shown how *Caribbean Voices* was characterised by 'friendships' and 'collaborative efforts' (Griffith), and described how the BBC 'incubated cross-racial and intercontinental collaboration' (Kalliney) within a wider climate of hostility and discouragement.[4] However, there has been little discussion to date of the exchanges *between* West African, West Indian, and South Asian artists across different programmes. Even less has been said

[2] For accounts of the Eastern Service, see for example Douglas Kerr, 'Orwell's Broadcasts: Colonial Discourse and the Rhetoric of Propaganda', *Textual Practice*, 16:3 (2002):473–90; Susheila Nasta, *Home Truths: Fictions of the South Asian Diaspora in Britain* (Basingstoke: Palgrave, 2002); Daniel Morse, 'Only Connecting?: E. M. Forster, Empire Broadcasting, and the Ethics of Distance', *Journal of Modern Literature*, 34:3 (Spring 2011): 87–105; 'An "Impatient Modernist": Mulk Raj Anand at the BBC', *Modernist Cultures*, 10:1 (Spring 2015): 83–98; Susheila Nasta (ed.) *India in Britain: South Asian Networks and Connections, 1858–1950* (Basingstoke: Palgrave Macmillan, 2013); Ruvani Ranasinha, 'South Asian Broadcasters and the BBC: Talking to India (1941–1943)', *Journal of South Asian Diaspora*, 2:1 (2010): 57–71; *South Asian Writers in Twentieth-Century Britain: Culture in Translation* (Oxford: Oxford University Press, 2007); Glyne A. Griffith, *The BBC and the Development of Anglophone Caribbean Literature, 1943–1958* (Cham: Palgrave Macmillan, 2016). For scholarship on *Caribbean Voices*, see for example Rhonda Cobham, 'The Caribbean Voices Programme and the Development of West Indian Short Fiction: 1945–1958' in Peter O. Stummer (ed.), *The Story Must be Told: Short Narrative Prose in the New English Literatures* (Bayreuth: Königshausen, 1986), 146–58; John Figueroa, 'Flaming Faith of these First Years: *Caribbean Voices*' in Maggie Butcher (ed.), *Tibisiri: Caribbean Writers and Critics* (Aarhus; Sydney; Coventry: Dangaroo, 1989), 59–80; Phillip Nanton, 'What Does Mr. Swanzy Want? Shaping or Reflecting? An Assessment of Henry Swanzy's Contribution to the Development of Caribbean Literature', *Kunapipi*, 20:1 (1998): 11–20; Glyne Griffith, 'Deconstructing Nationalisms: Henry Swanzy, *Caribbean Voices* and the Development of West Indian Literature', *Small Axe*, 5:2 (2001): 1–20; Laurence A. Breiner, 'Caribbean Voices on the Air: Radio, Poetry and Nationalism in the Anglophone Caribbean' in Susan Squier (ed.), *Communities of the Air* (Durham, NC: Duke University Press, 2003), 93–108; Gail Low, *Publishing the Postcolonial: Anglophone West African and Caribbean Writing in the UK, 1948–1968* (London: Routledge, 2011); Darrell Newton, *Paving the Empire Road: BBC Television and Black Britons* (Manchester: Manchester University Press, 2011); Peter J. Kalliney, *Commonwealth of Letters: British Literary Culture and the Emergence of Postcolonial Aesthetics* (Oxford: Oxford University Press, 2013); James Procter, 'Una Marson at the BBC', *Small Axe*, 19:3 (2015): 1–28.

[3] Susheila Nasta, 'Sealing a Friendship: George Orwell and Mulk Raj Anand at the BBC (1941–43)', *Wasafiri*, 26:4 (2011): 14–21; Ranasinha, 'South Asian broadcasters and the BBC', 57. See also Emma Bainbridge and Florian Stadtler, 'Calling from London, Talking to India: South Asian Networks at the BBC and the Case of G. V. Desani' in Nasta (ed.), *India in Britain*, 164–78.

[4] Griffith, *The BBC*, 13; Kalliney, *Commonwealth of Letters*, 30.

about the African Service, in terms of either its own distinct literary contribution, or its relationship to Indian and Caribbean broadcasting.[5] Despite
a growing critical consensus that the BBC was a transnational metropolitan
meeting place during the postwar decades, cross-cultural approaches to radio
remain in their infancy.

More broadly, our understanding of the pragmatic factors and power relations that underpinned collaborative cultures at the corporation remain little
understood. One reason for the lack of a joined-up narrative of cross-cultural
production at the BBC is the corporation's own compartmentalised development, the legacy of which lives on in its piecemeal, boxed off, and largely
uncatalogued archives. It is important to recognise in this context that the
BBC's organisational structures divided as much as they joined the
Commonwealth. The Home Service, the General Overseas Service, the various
sections of the Colonial Service: these were not automatically or inevitably
confluent and harmonious channels of cosmopolitan cultural communication.
They also separated both 'domestic' from 'overseas' transmissions, and colonial
territories from each other. Describing the 'topography' of the BBC after almost
a decade's work within the corporation, George Lamming's classic account of
migration, *The Pleasures of Exile* (1960), records that 'these services are run as
though they were foreign countries, each requiring a separate and certified
visa'.[6] The Colonial Service, he continued, was 'the arse-hole of the corporation'.
Certainly, the BBC was not averse to reinforcing a sense of cultural distinction
through what Lamming calls the 'mysterious [. . .] frontiers' of its myriad
services, sections, and departments. For example, a BBC memo assessing
R. K. Narayan's radio plays in 1956 concluded that 'The writing is stilted and
foreign like. They might do for one of our Far Eastern Services, but would not
come up to Home Broadcasting standards at all.'[7] When, in May 1952, the
Jamaican novelist and poet Andrew Salkey proposed a talk on the African
Service about the South African film-maker and actor Lionel Ngakane, he was
given short shrift by the producer Sheila Straddling: 'I am very sorry, but I am
afraid this simply is not suitable for inclusion in one of the *Calling West Africa*
programmes. As I explained on the phone to you, a talk by a West Indian about
a South African, will not be of interest to West African listeners.'[8]

[5] For a rare account of *West African Voices*, albeit one focused on Soyinka alone, see
   James Gibbs, 'Caribbean and African Writing in the BBC's Written Archives', *Yearbook of
   English Studies*, 20 (1990): 152–61.
[6] George Lamming, *The Pleasures of Exile* (London: Pluto Classics, [1960] 2005), 44.
[7] Hughes to Greenmalgh, 9 November 1956. BBC WAC, Narayan Rcont4.
[8] Letter from Sheila Straddling to Salkey, 28 May 1952. Andrew Salkey Papers, British
   Library.

Radio, Reciprocity, Friendship

Yet despite these imperious-sounding anecdotes of border control at the BBC, overseas broadcasters were by no means confined to the ethnic enclaves and partitions of the BBC's various departments. Andrew Salkey's stories were produced for listeners in both Africa and the Caribbean. Along with many of the more established late colonial writers, he could also be heard increasingly across all three programmes of the 'Domestic' Service: the Home Service (including the Regional Home Services), the Third Programme (associated with 'serious' cultural transmission), and the Light Programme (associated with more 'popular' entertainment programming). The Caribbean Service originally operated under the aegis of the African Service and not only did their respective programme schedules, *Calling the West Indies* and *Calling West Africa*, share occasional scripts, they shared many of the same literary producers and critical commentators, including the Irishman Henry Swanzy and the English novelists and critics L. A. G. Strong and Arthur Calder-Marshall. The aspiring West Indian writers Gordon Woolford, George Lamming, and V. S. Naipaul were regularly commissioned as readers on *Calling West Africa*: their Caribbean voices could be heard in both Lagos and Barbados. When the pan-Africanist revolutionary and Ghana's first president Kwame Nkrumah delivered his independence speech in March 1957, it was re-broadcast by the BBC two days later on *Calling the Caribbean*. Similarly, programmes on *Calling West Africa* explored what one series called the 'Caribbean Connection', including the history of the British slave trade and the rebellions it prompted. Short fiction and poetry from the Caribbean was spliced into West African literary broadcasts, while African authors would review Caribbean novels on *Calling West Africa* programmes, and vice versa.

These reciprocal arrangements were effectively triangulated by the presence of the wartime Eastern Service, which produced perhaps the most iconic image of collaborative transnational networks at the BBC: a studio photograph 'taken during the broadcasting of' the literary magazine programme *Voice* (1942) and first published in *London Calling* magazine in 1943.[9] The photograph shows the Jamaican poet and producer Una Marson sitting before the microphone, flanked by the likes of George Orwell, William Empson, T. S. Eliot, Mulk Raj Anand, Narayana Menon, Venu Chitale, and M. J. Tambimuttu. As Anna Snaith notes, '[t]his programme, and the

---

[9] *London Calling*, 175 (1943): 22. The photograph appears below programme details for the week 14–20 February 1943.

photograph which exists of it, encapsulates a symbolic moment: the meeting and sharing of colonial and metropolitan writers and texts'.[10] *Voice* aimed to bring wider attention to younger, relatively neglected artists and, in the fourth episode on American literature, Marson was asked to elaborate on African American poetry. She referred in the broadcast to the pioneers of the Harlem Renaissance, James Weldon Johnson, Countee Cullen, and Paul Lawrence Dunbar, before performing a poem of her own: 'The Banjo Boy'.[11] Though it was only short-lived, Orwell's literary series for Indian listeners is often credited with providing a blueprint for Marson's own literary magazine programme for West Indian listeners, *Caribbean Voices*, which began towards the end of the war.

Both *Voice* and *Caribbean Voices* exploited the eclecticism of the 'magazine' format in bringing to the airwaves a transnational constellation of writers. Calling for contributors to *Caribbean Voices*, Marson did not just reach out to listeners across the anglophone Caribbean, but invited submissions from West Africans via the *Calling West Africa* programme. While it tends to be assumed that literary contributions to *Caribbean Voices* were singularly Caribbean in content, programming throughout the 1940s and 1950s accommodated both British and (to a lesser extent) American authors in the construction of a cosmopolitan community on air. In one of the earliest surviving literary broadcasts by Marson, delivered in November 1942, the Jamaican poet worked to summon up the literary and cultural identity of the Caribbean by eschewing any definitive West Indian essence. Rather, she arranged literary content around the poetry and music of 'four races' that 'predominate in the West Indies': Chinese, Indian, European, and African. The programme's assemblage and orchestration of poetry and melody evoked the West Indies as a diasporic site; a transnational crossroads, rather than a series of self-contained islands. It drew not just on different musical and poetic traditions, but on different voices. For example, the Indian selection included Sarojini Naidu's poem 'A Challenge to Fate', which was read by Venu Chitale of the Eastern Service.[12] Tao Chien represented China ('Moving

---

[10] Anna Snaith, *Modernist Voyages: Colonial Women Writers in London, 1890–1945* (Cambridge: Cambridge University Press, 2014), 168.

[11] There were limits to how far such cosmopolitan experiments actually went. For example, Orwell seemed to seize some of the radical potential of radio for polyphonic literary co-production when he conceived of a hybrid short story format for radio that invited different authors to write consecutive instalments of the same narrative. But he missed the possibilities of this format for transnational or cross-cultural collaboration, inviting only white British authors to participate.

[12] Una Marson, 'At the Barbeque', *Calling the West Indies*, 26 November 1942. BBC WAC.

House'; 'Reading the Book of Hills and Seas'), Constance Hollar represented Europe ('The Poinciana Tree'), and J. E. C. Macfarlane, Africa ('Villanelle of Immortal Love'). The choice of Chien and Naidu (poets of China and India, rather than representatives of the Caribbean's Indian and Chinese communities) points to a lack of available local literary resources. However, it also suggests Marson's inclusive and international conception of 'West Indian' within the context of the wartime literary imagination.

In her opening programme remarks, Marson hints anxiously at the considerable debate over coverage and representation the arrangement caused, adding '[p]erhaps one day we'll have a listener come-back committee, and you'll help us plan our programmes, so share in the rejoicing, or in the distress if it doesn't quite come off'.[13] It is a comment that captures both the hard work of conveying friendly 'harmony' across a region and empire whose scattered population groups still tended to think of themselves as relatively autonomous island entities, and Marson's difficult delegatory role as a metropolitan editor charged with ensuring collective representation in spite of that fact.

Elsewhere, in the Indian Section, the Anglo-Indian author Cedric Dover (1904–1961) had emerged as an eloquent early advocate of interracial unity. He used his BBC broadcasts on the Eastern Service to promote many of the arguments to be found in his numerous studies of cultural and biological hybridity. Among the subjects of Dover's radio talks in 1942 was his friend the African American actor Paul Robeson. In broadcasts such as 'The Importance of Minorities' and 'Race Mixture and World Peace', Dover argued that 'History is, in fact, a long process of mongrelisation. How, then, can we talk of racial purity when all men are mongrels in a greater or lesser degree? How can we talk of half-castes when there are no full castes?'[14] In the same year, Mulk Raj Anand broadcast a series called *Meet My Friend*, which involved interviews with writers, painters, and film-makers who were presented precisely as friends and casual acquaintances. In the first episode, Anand outlined the rationale behind the series:

> I have stood between Europe and Asia now for some years as a kind of interpreter. I have tried to tell the English people something about life in India, specially about the life of the people [. . .] Now I want to present to India some of my English friends, so that Englishmen do not remain the

[13] Ibid.
[14] Cedric Dover, 'The Importance of Minorities', 25 February 1942, and 'Race Mixture and World Peace', 24 January 1942, on the series *Through West Indian Eyes*. BBC WAC.

collective 'they' of the 'Great British Nation' of Anglo-Indian controversy, but appear as human beings. You know, 'they' are quite human! Believe me they are.

Anand's appeal to the ideal of friendship served to humanise the English for India, as more than an undifferentiated imperial enemy and as subjects of empathy and identification with whom South Asians might also share a common cause during the war.[15] Personal and professional friendships more generally oiled the collaborative and cosmopolitan relations of these programmes from within London and across the corridors of the BBC.[16] While it is well documented that Marson appeared twice on Orwell's *Voice* programme, it tends to be overlooked that Orwell also appeared on Marson's *Calling the West Indies* programmes, as did Zulfiqar Ali Bukhari (Director of the Indian Section of the Eastern Service) and, as we have seen, Venu Chitale (Talks Producer, Indian Service).[17] Marson's successor on *Caribbean Voices*, Swanzy, first met Orwell during their two-week BBC training course, where he become a mutual friend of both Orwell and Marson. In his diaries, Swanzy records his shared affinities with Orwell: 'we seemed to agree on many points, romantic declasses, haters of Imperial Organisation, he from Burma, I from years in Whitehall'. It was Swanzy who put Orwell in contact with the English literary critic William Empson, a subsequent contributor to *Voice* and other Indian broadcasts. Swanzy himself contributed a forty-line meditation, 'Poem on Gandhi', which was read by John Arlott on the Eastern Service on 30 January 1948 following the assassination of the leader of India's independence movement. Though Swanzy seems destined to be remembered for the singular achievement that was *Caribbean Voices*, and even had to occasionally remind his colleagues that he was based in the African Service, he was also the first producer of *Caribbean Voices*' sister programme *West African Voices*, broadcast on *Calling West Africa*. In other words, there was a significant degree of literary exchange and echo *across* the various and putatively self-contained Colonial Services of the BBC.

---

[15] Anand, 'Mulk Raj Anand Interviews George Bishop', *Meet My Friend*, No. 1, 27 May 1942, on the series *Through West Indian Eyes*. BBC WAC, 38,521.

[16] In another series, *A Day in My Life*, Anand focused on everyday roles of Britons: nurses, soldiers, canteen workers, farmers, soldiers.

[17] Broadcast from London to the Caribbean on *Calling the West Indies*. The script from this interview is absent from the otherwise encyclopaedic *Complete Works of George Orwell*. Zulfaqar Ali Bukhari, Orwell's immediate boss, begins by extending a warm personal greeting to his Caribbean listeners: 'How do you do, West Indies?'; Bokhari and Marson 'Close Up', *Calling the West Indies*, 20 September 1942. BBC WAC.

London's Literary Headquarters

In his cultural history of black London, Marc Matera writes of the mid-century metropolis that it 'functioned as both a facilitator and provocateur', resourced colonial networks, and stimulated 'conversations, alliances and boundary crossings' while all the time generating 'tensions and conflicts'. Paraphrasing the autobiography of the black South African novelist Peter Abrahams, Matera notes that:

'London was the critical point of contact where Pan-African, socialist and anti-colonial ideas were shared and enlarged.' Intellectuals and activists from the colonies 'shared classes, meals, parties,' and in the process, they 'got to know each other [. . .] intimately and personally.' Quotidian encounters and activities yielded capacious political imaginaries and rerouted lives.[18]

This sense of London as both a potentially abrasive administrative centre of empire and a convivial site of gathering and social exchange speaks eloquently to the environs of the BBC. If the broadcaster lacked the street credibility of Notting Hill, Ladbroke Grove, Brick Lane, or Railton Road, the physical venues of the corporation constituted a significant crucible during those decades as a literary 'headquarters' that formed an undeniable part of the cultural and symbolic geography of black and South Asian London. Bush House, 200 Oxford Street, the Langham Hotel, Broadcasting House were, along with the 'BBC' pubs, canteens, cafés, and eating houses between them, routine sites of cross-cultural encounter. When, in December 1953, *London Calling* magazine described the experience of a journey around Oxford Street, it was presented as an adventure on the scale of a Jules Verne novel: 'Round the world in the BBC studios.'[19]

Peter Abrahams was among those writers to pass through the corporation's corridors during the 1950s, contributing variously as he did so to the Home Service, the African Service, and the Caribbean Service. In a diary entry dated 2 September 1955, the white Jamaican novelist John Hearne recalls his first meeting with Abrahams: 'Andrew [Salkey] invited me down to the BBC on Wednesday to meet Peter Abrahams. Abrahams slight, brown and tranquil looking. Very quick in speech; slightly affected in the way he searches for paradoxical statements [. . .] extraordinarily generous.' Abrahams had been helping to publicise Hearne's first novel, *Voices Under*

---

[18] Marc Matera, *Black London: The Imperial Metropolis and Decolonization in the Twentieth Century* (Oakland, CA: University of California Press, 2015), 2.

[19] Wynford Vaughan Thomas, 'Round the World in the BBC Studios', *London Calling* (10 December 1953): 26–7.

the Window (1955). The 'host' to this encounter, the fellow Jamaican Andrew Salkey, was another stalwart at the BBC, among the broadcaster's most prolific Caribbean contributors during the 1960s and 1970s. He had emerged during the 1950s as the unofficial broker, agent, and publicist of the major West Indian writers to arrive at the corporation, including Lamming, Mittelholzer, Selvon, and Carew. Even Naipaul, not known for his collaborative spirit, would subsequently acknowledge Salkey's help at the BBC with his first manuscript, *Miguel Street* (1959). The Jamaican intellectual Stuart Hall (another familiar BBC voice from this period) remembered Salkey's central contribution as follows:

> For a critical period, he was the key figure, the main presenter and writer-in-residence in the Caribbean section of the BBC World Service at Bush House, and his programmes became a glittering showcase for a generation of writers, including Sam Selvon and George Lamming, who had made London their second home. Established and aspiring authors were chivvied, cajoled, gently chastised, inspired and schooled to produce new work for radio on the Caribbean Voices programme over which Andrew Salkey often presided.[20]

Salkey himself would recall the 'at home' readings at Swanzy's Swiss Cottage flat as key catalysts in establishing this new literary community, lubricated by 'near endless bottles of rough cider, Worthington and Guinness to loosen our none too reluctant tongues [. . .] There we met Edgar Mittelholzer [the Guyanese novelist], Léon Damas [the French Caribbean poet, politician and co-founder of the Negritude movement], Cyprian Ekwensi [the West African novelist and short-story writer], David Diop [the French West African poet and contributor to Negritude movement]'. Recalling the same evenings, the Jamaican poet John Figueroa also mentions the presence of Peter Abrahams and the Guyanese painter Dennis Williams, while reflecting more generally on the significance of these encounters in the shaping of a transnational artistic community in London: 'The production of this programme offered to West Indians in London an opportunity to meet English and African writers and to discuss West Indian literature in particular and writing and art in general.'[21]

Something like a thick description of friendship begins to emerge across these distinct but overlapping anecdotes of social encounter and interaction.

---

[20] Stuart Hall, 'Obituary: Andrew Salkey', *The Independent*, 15 May 1995. Available at www.independent.co.uk/news/people/obituary-andrew-salkey-1619715.html.

[21] John Figueroa (ed.), *Caribbean Voices: An Anthology of West Indian Poetry*, vol. 2: *The Blue Horizons* (London: Evans Brothers, 1970), 3.

If, as Matera suggests, 'quotidian encounters' exposed 'capacious' imaginaries in twentieth-century London, then there is still a great deal to be learnt from these everyday exchanges among writers and artists at the BBC, during a critical moment in the flowering of cultural nationalism, pan-Africanism, and black internationalism. Not only did the circuits of the BBC draw together anglophone writers from across the dispersed islands of the Caribbean, who now began to think of themselves collectively as 'West Indian' for the first time, it put them in touch with South Asian nationalists, West African writers, and francophone African-Caribbean movements.[22]

However, we also need to be cautious in reconstructing the BBC as an idealised imagined community of singularly benevolent collaboration and encounter. If friendship implies volition, something freely chosen and beyond the professional or formal codes governing institutional protocols, it was more than just a spontaneous set of relations operating at the level of individuals and personalities. For one thing, as the beer-fuelled get-togethers described by Salkey and Figueroa suggest, friendships at the BBC were typically overdetermined by the common-sense codes of mid-century masculinity that placed women outside, or at the peripheries of, social and literary circles. Certainly, women played a significant, and indeed underestimated role in radio programming during and after World War II – as writers and broadcasters (Sylvia Wynter, Louise Bennett, Venu Chitale), as producers and editors (Una Marson, Mary Treadgold, Sheila Straddling), and as readers (June Grimble, Pauline Henriques). Well-known couples at the BBC during this period included Pearl and Edric Connor, and Sylvia Wynter and Jan Carew. Yet surviving correspondence suggests professional friendships between men and women more generally were limited. As Alison Donnell speculates, one of the reasons so few of the women writers on *Caribbean Voices* managed to convert their literary aspirations into published novels and more permanent literary careers was because 'respect, friendship, contacts and advice were traded among male writers and editors in the cause of the West Indian novel'.[23]

Secondly, associations and encounters between writers were marked by both conviviality and competition. As Pierre Bourdieu reminds us, in the field

---

[22] As Lamming put it in *The Pleasures of Exile*: 'no islander from the West Indies sees himself as a West Indian until he encounters another islander in foreign territory [. . .] In this sense, most West Indians of my generation were born in England' (214).

[23] Alison Donnell, 'Rescripting Anglophone Caribbean Women's Literary History: Gender, Genre, and Lost Caribbean Voices', in J. Dillon Brown and Leah Reade Rosenberg (eds.), *Beyond Windrush: Rethinking Postwar Anglophone Caribbean Literature* (Jackson, MS: University Press of Mississippi), 79–96; 82.

of cultural production writers compete for, among other things, 'cultural legitimacy', acknowledgement, pay, and prestige.[24] If the literary field represents a relational and conflictual site of ongoing struggle then this was intensified at the BBC, where the sheer number of writers and the finite opportunities for commission and transmission added to the friction. When they came together on air it was sometimes characterised by combative exchanges. Swanzy would speak of the first West Indian critic's circle in this context as a 'licensed massacre'. Meanwhile, a review of West Indian writing in the UK's *Guardian* newspaper said of a Third Programme discussion between Stuart Hall, Jan Carew, Errol John, George Lamming, Edgar Mittelholzer, and Sylvia Wynter that 'the air-waves still vibrate from the explosion'.[25] Radio was a crowded space, and both West Indian artists and white critics found themselves vying for airtime. When Arthur Calder-Marshall broadcast a tart review of Robert Herring's special Caribbean issues of *London Life and Letters* on *Caribbean Voices*, it suggested defensive gatekeeping of his *own* editorial role on the programme as much as anything else. Breaking with the unwritten rules of advocacy and side-taking associated with existing networks could have terminal consequences for relations among writers, as Sam Selvon's recollection of his brief friendship with Colin MacInnes reminds us:

> One day at the BBC I met the Australian novelist Colin MacInnes, who was bringing out a book called *City of Spades* [. . .] we became good friends [. . .] Then the book came out. I read it, and didn't like it [. . .] He hasn't spoke to me since that day. We met in Birmingham on a television programme to discuss the same book, together with an African writer [. . .] I lost his friendship because of my adverse review of his book.[26]

Before this falling-out, MacInnes had written to tell Selvon how he had advocated for him at *Encounter* magazine. Selvon would have known that the cost of giving his honest opinion would mean losing such support in the future. Friendships at the BBC were rarely unconditional when literary reputation was at stake.

Finally, due recognition of the artistic exchanges that were forged through the BBC also needs to go hand in hand with a consideration of the BBC's own construction of friendship and collaboration during and just after

[24] Pierre Bourdieu, *The Field of Cultural Production: Essays on Art and Literature*, ed. Randal Johnson (Cambridge: Polity Press, 1993).

[25] Peter Worsley, 'Colonial Culture', *The Guardian*, 29 July 1960: 4.

[26] Sam Selvon, undated, untitled typescript. Samuel Selvon Collection, St Augustine Library, Trinidad.

World War II. The war had prompted a more intimate mode of address from the BBC, and was a key factor in the joint emergence of the Colonial Services in the early 1940s. These services may have relied on different frequencies and disconnected networks, but they were ultimately informed less by a 'divide and rule' logic than by a desire to unify empire as the fracturing effects of World War II, creeping Americanisation, and the stirrings of anti-colonial nationalism began to take hold. Whatever its limits, bespoke, specialised programming across discrete services allowed the BBC to address the colonies regionally and intimately as friends rather than as anonymous, undifferentiated others. The unidirectional projection of information from metropole to margins that had characterised empire broadcasting in the 1930s gave way in the 1940s to a new strategy of what wartime Director of the Empire Service, R. A. Rendall, described as 'letting the people speak for themselves and their own country'. It was in bringing Commonwealth speakers to the microphone that the BBC also transformed itself into 'a microcosm of the empire itself'.[27]

The corporation's emphasis on convivial, reciprocal exchange reveals the extent to which appeals to friendliness were themselves performing significant ideological work at the BBC. Specifically, and by foregrounding the affinities of friendship over the obligations of loyalty, the BBC effectively modernised its mediation of empire from the early 1940s along the lines of egalitarianism, unity, and commonality, or what Wendy Webster has called the 'people's empire'. The Empire Service was associated in this context with what Sir Stephen Tallents called 'the comradeship in the ether'. 'Just being friendly' was, according to Grenfell Williams, the Director of the African Service in 1942, the 'life-blood' of overseas broadcasting.[28] The chimes of Big Ben greeting BBC listeners across the globe were described as 'our mutual friend': 'when, through our radio sets, we hear him we come perhaps a little closer together, in thought and feeling, linked by this familiar – above all by this most friendly – voice of London'.[29] As T. O. Beachcroft notes in *Calling All Nations*, a wartime study of the Empire Service published by the BBC, it was casual, rather than grand or formal social occasions that were able to stir feelings of 'unity and of sharing a common life [. . .] A joke, a melody, or a sporting event is a bond just as much as more conscious unity.'[30]

---

[27] Antonia White, *BBC at War* (London: BBC, n.d.), 39.
[28] Grenfell Williams, *BBC Yearbook, 1945* (London: BBC, 1945), 92–3.
[29] Howard Marshall, 'The Voice of Big Ben', *London Calling* (10 December 1953): 21.
[30] T. O. Beachcroft, *Calling All Nations* (London: BBC, 1942), 6.

If such accounts point to the interpellative work being performed by friendship in this period, it would be a mistake to assume the BBC was simply pulling the wool over the eyes of its colonial subjects. As the historian Anne Spry Rush has noted, the appeal of 'bonds of empire' among West Indian listeners was no straightforward capitulation to colonial authority.[31] On the contrary, West Indians seized upon the new discourses of cross-cultural friendship in renegotiating the very terms of their relationship with the metropole, as equals rather than subordinates. In other words, friendship was not simply a unidirectional master narrative, used by the metropolitan power to trick its conscripts into states of acquiescence. Narratives of friendship and reciprocal exchange were simultaneously used by West Indians to reframe power relations within a rapidly fading imperial setting.

The Case of Una Marson

The case of the Jamaican poet, playwright, and producer Una Marson is suggestive in this context because her wartime years at the BBC reveal much about both the possibilities and the limits of cross-cultural exchange at the corporation. Increasingly acknowledged as a pioneering producer at the BBC, the first figurehead of the *Calling the West Indies* series and founder of the now famous literary magazine *Caribbean Voices*, Marson worked in relative isolation within the West Indian Section during World War II. Perhaps partly because of this, she also forged extensive connections with black artists and white intellectuals working in the other services and sections of the BBC. Her programmes commanded the respect of, and were emulated in, the African Service by Grenfell Williams and Cecil Madden (Head of Empire Entertainments), both of whom saw the potential of the camaraderie they forged. Marson herself had turned to the BBC after trying to convince the Secretary for the Colonies that burgeoning numbers of West Indian servicemen and women needed more social venues to overcome isolation and loneliness. As the relaxed informality of her programme series suggest – 'West Indian Party', 'Caribbean Carnival', 'At the Barbeque', 'Rendezvous' – Marson saw her broadcasts as points of contact, social gathering, and exchange. In an unpublished manuscript, 'Friendliness in Wartime', Marson extolled the virtues of friendship as the 'moral sinews of war', capable of bringing an otherwise divided world together.[32] Radio's disembodied

---

[31] Anne Spry Rush, *Bonds of Empire: West Indians and Britishness from Victoria to Decolonization* (Oxford: Oxford University Press, 2011).

[32] Una Marson, 'Friendliness in War Time', MS 1944b, National Library of Jamaica.

technologies were equal in this context to the physical contact of the social club. As she put it to listeners one evening:

> The question is no longer, I wish I could see a West Indian, but how on earth can I find peas to cook with rice for all those hungry West Indians! And perhaps the Club that is doing the best service to you in the West Indies is the B.B.C. Message Party. Now I shall get slung out if I praise an organization for which I work – it's bad taste anyway. But I do want to tell you that some of your lads who keep missing someone they know at one club or another often startle Message Party with exclamations of joy.[33]

This sense of casual hospitality, emanating like a warm glow from the heart of London, did not always come off. Maurice Chargill candidly reported news of a somewhat less successful rice and peas story when Marson organised a lunch at the BBC for fourteen recently arrived Jamaicans:

> To begin with, it's difficult to convince an English cook that rice is a vegetable. It's most commonly served here in the form of rice pudding. Secondly, the chef at the BBC apparently didn't understand that rice and peas should be served in large quantities. Anyway, when the plates came to the table, about a tablespoonful nestled coyly upon each plate, hidden by a lettuce leaf.

Even anecdotes such as these converted cultural misunderstandings into illustrations of 'the hospitality and kindness of people here'.[34]

But, as I have argued in greater detail elsewhere, behind the scenes Marson's appointment had stirred 'what the director of Empire Services described as "jealousies," "dissentions," and "rivalry"'.[35] Some of her colleagues found it hard to accept that they now had to answer to a black woman. While travelling across the UK to host party programmes, she was subject to the whims of the colour bar in being denied accommodation at hotels. Meanwhile, West Indians in both the Caribbean and Britain felt that as a Jamaican she was overlooking their islands in favour of her own. Things came to a head when a bitter campaign of complaints, secretly organised by Aggrey House[36] and representing the interests of white colonial planters, eventually drove Marson from her role. These critics argued that Marson's broadcasts were biased towards black speakers and thus fell short of the

[33] Una Marson, *Calling the West Indies*, 3 September 1942. BBC WAC.
[34] Maurice Chagill, *Calling the West Indies*, 4 July 1944. BBC WAC.
[35] James Procter, 'Una Marson at the BBC', *Small Axe*, 19:3 (2015): 1–28; 4.
[36] Opened in 1935, Aggrey House was a club and boarding house for overseas students from the Commonwealth, funded with financial support of colonial governments in Africa and the West Indies.

egalitarian aural community they purported to represent. These were among the harsh realities silently underpinning cosmopolitan constructions of reciprocal and harmonious exchange on air.

To think critically about collaborative networks at the mid-century BBC is not necessarily to call for a more cynical understanding of friendship at the corporation. Marson herself would stay in personal touch with George Orwell, Henry Swanzy, and T. S. Eliot long after their time together at the BBC. Nevertheless, it is important that we take seriously the conflicted character of many of these otherwise amiable collaborations and literary exchanges. On the one hand, this chapter has presented examples of exchange that resemble Mary Louise Pratt's classic sense of the 'contact zone' as a hierarchical social site 'where disparate cultures meet, clash, and grapple with each other, often in highly asymmetrical relations of domination and subordination'.[37] In other regards, though, we have seen how the corporation helped ameliorate such asymmetries, fostering what Leela Gandhi has called 'affective communities': forms of cross-cultural interaction and affinity between what, in different circumstances, might have been antagonistic or binary relations between colonising and colonised forces.[38] Future research needs to take account of the fact that broadcasting both shaped and was shaped by these ideas and instances of literary collaboration, rather than trying to resolve the contradictions they leave behind through recourse to the imaginary coherence of 'the' BBC.

---

[37] Mary Louise Pratt, *Imperial Eyes: Travel Writing and Transculturation* (London: Routledge, 1992), 4.

[38] Leela Gandhi, *Affective Communities: Anticolonial Thought, Fin-de-Siècle Radicalism, and the Politics of Friendship* (Durham, NC: Duke University Press, 2006).

10

Political Autobiography and Life-Writing
Gandhi, Nehru, Kenyatta, and Naidu

JAVED MAJEED

For Asian and African thinkers and writers in the nineteenth and twentieth centuries, the impact of European colonialism raised fundamental questions about selfhood, the relationship between individuals and collective identities, the purpose of governance, and the overall movement of global history. As a literary genre signifying a retrospective narrative of the author's own life and reconstructing his/her personal development within historical, socio-political, and cultural contexts, autobiography enabled anti-colonial nationalists such as Mohandas Karamchand Gandhi (1869–1948), Jawaharlal Nehru (1889–1964), and Jomo Kenyatta (c. 1891–1978) to explore these questions in depth. While on one level autobiographies are 'non-fictional', they are also imaginative in nature. As such, their life-writing straddled empirically based narratives of the historicity of empire, and the processes of imagining the future nation as a community grounded in particular visions of the self. At the same time, this engendered tensions between the singularity of their selves and the communality of nationality. Sarojini Naidu (1879–1949) addressed similar issues in her letters, themselves a form of life-writing in which various senses of her selfhood were dramatised. For these four writers, their connections with and experiences of Britain were pivotal in their struggles to establish a sense of themselves. In their life-writing the transition from being British subjects of empire to the citizens of emerging states was key to their process of self-definition. Each writer to be discussed here had to negotiate this duality as anglicised subjects of the British Empire and their newly nationalised selves.

The Question of 'Self' and 'Rule'

Gandhi's *Hind Swaraj or Indian Home Rule* (1909) considers how the term 'Indian' should be disentangled from British colonial citizenship and outlines what form of rule is required to do so. One section of *An Autobiography, or, The Story of My Experiments with Truth* (1927–1929) depicts how he dissociates being Indian from 'Playing the English Gentleman'.[1] Each concept referred to in the title of *Hind Swaraj* (that is, 'Indian', 'Self', and 'Rule') is debated in the dialogue that makes up the book, which explores what constitutes a self, its relation to a collective identity, and its historical character. These questions also animate Gandhi's *Autobiography*, the subtitle of which signals the exploratory nature of the text, as it grapples with self-rule through questions of sexuality and embodiment, and the nature of violence and agency in colonial contexts.

Nehru's *An Autobiography* (1936) and *The Discovery of India* (1946) are also interrogative in tone. Nehru began his autobiographical venture 'in a mood of self-questioning'. What he described as 'doubt and difficulty about fundamental matters' marks his life-writing.[2] Disentangling being Indian from British colonial citizenship had deep personal ramifications for Nehru. As an upper-caste anglicised Indian who studied at Harrow and Cambridge from 1905 to 1910, Nehru confessed: 'Personally I owe too much to England in my mental make-up ever to feel wholly alien to her [. . .] All my predilections (apart from the political plane) are in favour of England and the English people, and if I have become what is called an uncompromising opponent of British rule in India, it is almost in spite of myself.'[3] His autobiographies demonstrate how the textual self-fashioning of his emergent Indian self did not completely reject anglicised aspects of his identity. On the contrary, an avowal of self-division rooted in the recognition of this duality characterises Nehru's anti-colonial life-writing and paradoxically grounds his nationalism.[4] This also led him to question his ability to represent and 'discover' India.[5] Nehru also formulates questions about identity from a universal point of view, rather than from an Indian perspective alone.[6] These are posed alongside the major question of his texts, namely, given India's heterogeneity what (or who, since India is frequently personified in his texts) is India? The question was especially critical because of the Montagu–Chelmsford reforms

---

[1] M. K. Gandhi, *An Autobiography, or, The Story of My Experiments with Truth* (London: Penguin, [1927–1929] 1982), Part 1, ch. 15.

[2] Jawaharlal Nehru, *An Autobiography* (New Delhi: Jawaharlal Nehru Memorial Fund, [1936] 1982), xv, 25.

[3] Ibid., 419.

[4] Javed Majeed, *Autobiography, Travel and Postnational Identity: Gandhi, Nehru and Iqbal* (Basingstoke: Palgrave Macmillan, 2007), ch. 4.

[5] Jawaharlal Nehru, *The Discovery of India* (Delhi: Oxford University Press, [1946] 1985), Epilogue.

[6] Nehru, *Discovery*, 31, 81, 558–9. For details see Majeed, *Autobiography*, 32–6.

of 1919 and the extension of separate electorates to Muslims, which was further endorsed by the Government of India Act 1935. Definitions of India and Indianness were obviously at stake in the territorial future of the subcontinent, especially by 1946 with the threat of Partition when *Discovery* was published. Hence Nehru's life-writing reflects the urgency of these questions.

For Naidu, too, her anglicised identity was an issue for her representativeness as an Indian politician and writer. As an anglophone Indian poet, her writings were composed in a period when there was a powerful Hindi language movement, which aimed to make Hindi the national language of India.[7] She was therefore writing in a context in which English was increasingly seen as an alien imposition, hence her anxiety to draw on the poetic inheritance of her birthright, such as the Sanskrit epics.[8] Moreover, her deep connections to strands of metropolitan literary culture, and her formative experiences as a student in England in the 1890s, mean that her anglophone identity can slip into anglophilia.[9] Her earlier letters express a need to be validated by the male metropolitan literary culture which launched her career. Her use of terms like 'godfather' for her publisher Heinemann and her patron Edmund Gosse, who is also addressed as the 'godfather' of her daughter, suggests a deep-felt need to be recognised by the British literary establishment in order to boost her legitimacy as an international figure in the republic of letters.[10] They may also reflect fragile self-worth and anxieties about self-assertion in the sphere of letters, as both a colonial British citizen and an Asian woman. Later, however, her relationship with England was more confidently self-assertive (see below), although the question of her representativeness as an anglophone poet and Indian politician persisted throughout her career, given the increasing politicisation of Indian linguistic identities against English in this period.[11]

For Kenyatta the form and the content of 'self' and 'rule' are also open to question as he tries to untie Kenyan nationality and polity from British colonial citizenship. The themes of self and national formation define

---

[7] For this movement, see Francesca Orsini, *The Hindi Public Sphere 1920–1940: Language and Literature in the Age of Nationalism* (New Delhi: Oxford University Press, 2002).

[8] Sarojini Naidu to Romesh Dutt, 17 February 1906, in Sarojini Naidu, *Selected Letters: 1890s to 1940s*, ed. Makarand Paranjape (New Delhi: Kali for Women, 1996), 49–51.

[9] Naidu to Leilamani Naidu, 4 March 1929, in *Selected Letters*, ed. Paranjape, 224–5.

[10] Naidu to Edmund Gosse, 6 October 1896, August 1899, 5 May 1904, 4 September 1905, and to Heinemann, 22 August 1911, in ibid., 27–30, 38–40, 42–3, 46–8, 62–3.

[11] For this, see J. D. Gupta, *Language Conflict and National Development: Group Politics and National Language Policy in India* (Berkeley, CA: University of California Press, 1970).

Suffering Without Bitterness (1968), and are paralleled by a concern with the 'Africanisation' of politics, the economy, and forms of self-rule. Hence his life-writing refers to concepts such as *Uhuru, Harambee, Ujamaa,* and 'African socialism'.[12] The partial homophony between the names Kenyatta and Kenya (Kenyatta's original name was Kamau wa Ngengi) underlines his self-creation as a national icon in *Suffering* and the consolidation of his status as a founding father, which was later crucial to his executive presidency in Kenya.[13] As a self-iconising text, *Suffering* slips between being a book that is 'a political portrait of one man' which 'does not pretend to be a political history of Kenya', and asserting that 'such themes are indivisible'.[14] But at the same time, the frequent (even obsessive) citations from the British press in *Suffering Without Bitterness* indicate his need to validate his own persona via Britain. In practical terms, he sought recognition by the colonial authorities as a leader with whom they could negotiate, especially after his release from prison.[15] However, there is also a deeper ambivalence here towards Britain as an intimate enemy, to use Ashis Nandy's phrase; he both defined himself against Britain and sought endorsement from it.[16]

The Regional, National, and Global

In their autobiographical disentanglement from British colonial citizenship, Nehru, Gandhi, Kenyatta, and Naidu negotiate regional, national, and global strands in their identities. Naidu's letters are marked by a flexible coalescence of all three strands. Her regional rootedness in Hyderabad is doubly framed. On the one hand, it is bound up with her self-Orientalising performances for her English correspondents, in which Hyderabad is presented in a set of Orientalist clichés that refers to the *Arabian Nights*.[17] (This also marks her juvenile piece 'Sunalini: A Passage from her Life'.[18]) In these letters Naidu plays with the 'exotic' preconceptions that her English literary sponsors and correspondents had of her as the 'Nightingale of India' and as an

---

[12] Jomo Kenyatta, *Suffering Without Bitterness: The Founding of the Kenya Nation* (Nairobi: East Africa Publishing House, 1968), x–xi, xv, lx.

[13] Charles Hornsby, *Kenya: A History since Independence* (London: I. B. Tauris, 2012), 165–6.

[14] Kenyatta, *Suffering*, 170.   [15] Hornsby, *Kenya*, 72.

[16] Ashis Nandy, *The Intimate Enemy: Loss and Recovery of Self under Colonialism* (Delhi: Oxford University Press, 1983).

[17] Naidu to Heinemann, 22 August and 7 September 1911, in *Selected Letters*, ed. Paranjape, 62–5.

[18] Sarojini Naidu, 'Sunalini: A Passage from her Life', British Library, Oriental and India Office Collection, EUR MSS A95.

'ethnopreneur'.[19] However, Hyderabad is also a centre of 'Hindu–Muslim unity and brotherhood',[20] and her letters are peppered with Perso-Arabic and Sanskritic phrases reflecting her unifying politics.[21] Her house in Hyderabad is a space for an informal Hindu–Muslim sociability.[22] This is combined with the formal politics of the conferences, committees, and delegations that she attended as a prominent member of the Indian National Congress and its first woman president, who also played a key role in the Indian women's movement. Naidu's regional rootedness, then, plays a dual role in her self-conception; it solidifies her relationships with her metropolitan literary sponsors, but it is also a crucible for a cross-communal nationalism.

Naidu's contribution to the emerging women's movement in India and globally, especially in the wake of the Katherine Mayo *Mother India* controversy, and her standing as an international figure who was India's quasi-official ambassador in the United States, have been discussed in detail elsewhere.[23] Naidu's epistolary self is multidirectional, facing Britain, India, and Hyderabad simultaneously, and this is reflected in her performative cosmopolitanism with its cultural and religious reframing of poems such as Shelley's 'To the Skylark' and figures such as Krishna and Gandhi.[24] Her letters express her personal sense of a transnational and mutually porous British Indian literary culture, with references to canonical English literary writers and poets,[25] the Sanskrit epics,[26] and Persian and Urdu poets such as Iqbal, Ghalib, Rumi, 'Attar, and Hafez.[27] Her aesthetic sensibility, then, also combines the regional, national, and global.

In his autobiographies, letters, essays, and public addresses, Nehru explores how his personal identity, India, and an emerging modern world

---

[19] See Chapter 3.

[20] Naidu to Gandhi, 6 March 1915, in *Selected Letters*, ed. Paranjape, 106; for her relations with Muslim leaders and her admiration for Jinnah, see ibid., xix–xx, xxiii.

[21] Naidu to Syed Mahmud, 10 November 1916 and 18 February 1919, and to Gandhi, 17 July 1919, in ibid., 119–20, 142–3.

[22] Naidu to G. K. Gokhale, 16 November 1914, in ibid., 96–9.

[23] Mrinalini Sinha, *Katherine Mayo: Mother India* (Ann Arbor, MI: Michigan University Press, 2000); *Specters of Mother India: The Global Restructuring of an Empire* (Durham, NC: Duke University Press, 2006); Geraldine Forbes, *Women in Modern India* (Cambridge: Cambridge University Press, 1996).

[24] Naidu to Heinemann, 27 July and 17 August 1911, and to Gandhi, 26 November 1925, in *Selected Letters*, ed. Paranjape, 57–9, 181.

[25] Naidu to Pamaja and Leilamani Naidu, 15 May 1932, in ibid., 272–4.

[26] Naidu to Romesh Dutt, 25 March 1906, in ibid., 49–51.

[27] Naidu to Syed Mahmud, 30 May 1917; to Pamaja and Leilamani Naidu, 26 June 1932; to Leilamani Naidu, 16 April 1935; and to Nehru, 29 March 1938, in ibid., 128–9, 275–7, 298–301, 302–3.

order are interconnected. In one letter he mentions how he tries to 'weave together' the 'numerous strains' of his identity into one pattern 'for my country and for the world', and he relates this to the 'emergence of a world order'.[28] For Nehru, becoming an Indian national also meant becoming a world citizen. The quasi-national differences between the different regions of India make it a microcosm of the modern world. The 'worldwide' development of a global culture connecting a variety of cultures is manifested in the subcontinent, where a new world civilisation combining 'East' and 'West' is prefigured.[29] This is captured in Nehru's own sense of himself in his *Autobiography*.[30]

There are also pan-Asian strands in Nehru's life-writing. One section of *Discovery* is dedicated to the historical, religious, and cultural connections between India and China.[31] India's isolation is the consequence of British imperialism, since the British 'barred all the doors and stopped all the routes that connected us with our neighbours in Asia'. Instead India was brought 'nearer to Europe' and especially to Britain.[32] The idea of 'Greater India', signifying an Indic cultural zone encompassing the Indian subcontinent and South-east Asia, was another strand in Nehru's depictions of India and himself as Asian.[33] The geopolitical imaginings in his life-writing about different forms of federation, often with a pan-Asian inflection, prefigure the idea of the Non-Aligned Movement, launched in 1961.[34]

For Nehru, then, globally oriented cosmopolitanism and being Indian were mutually constitutive. The publication history of his life-writing reflects this. *An Autobiography* was published in London in 1936, in New York in 1941, and in London again in 1942, while *Discovery* was first published in 1946 in both Calcutta and London. Given his cosmopolitanism, Nehru's regional identity as a Kashmiri was problematic. Rather than anchoring him in a specific locale, Nehru tries to make his Kashmiri roots a point of departure. He associates Kashmir with a self-forgetfulness that undermines the task of creating a pan-Indian identity. He also associates Kashmir with 'Nature' that needs to be overcome through technological progress, in which India has to

---

[28] Jawaharlal Nehru, 'To Eleanor F. Rathbone', 22 June 1941, in *Selected Works of Jawaharlal Nehru*, ed. S. Gopal (New Delhi: Orient Longman, 1972–1978), 11. 621.

[29] Nehru, 'Presidential Address at the All-Bengal students' Conference', 22 September 1928; 'On the Selection of the New Working Committee', 15 April 1936; 'To Syed Mahmud,' 24 September 1936; 'The Eastern Federation,' 28 October 1940, in ibid., 3. 189, 7. 198, 7. 392, 11. 192.

[30] Nehru, *Autobiography*, 28, 596.   [31] Nehru, *Discovery*, 192–200.

[32] Ibid., 149; Nehru, *Autobiography*, 608.   [33] Ibid., 200–12.

[34] Benjamin Zachariah, *Nehru* (London: Routledge, 2004), 154–60, 217–21.

participate by calling on its own philosophical, scientific, and cultural reserves.[35] In practical terms, after 1947 the creation of India as a federated union required giving sufficient scope to regional identities politically and linguistically, while countering the danger of subnational movements.[36] Nehru's negotiation of the regional strand of his identity in his definition of India and himself therefore reflects a larger process of nation formation, but the status of Kashmir remains an unresolved problem and questions about Nehru's handling of this issue persist.[37]

Kenyatta also negotiates his regional antecedents in his life-writing. His first book, *Facing Mount Kenya* (1938) was originally called *Voice of the Gikuyu: Echoes from Mount Kenya*.[38] In *Suffering* the term 'Kikuyu' represents an identity to move beyond for the sake of the 'people of Kenya as a whole' but it also anchors the independence struggle as 'firmly embedded in Kikuyu land'.[39] Kenyatta's release from prison in August 1961 is significant for an emerging Kenyan nation but especially for the Kikuyu, for whom this was 'an emotional experience and almost a mystical urge'.[40] Given the issue of land ownership and settlement schemes in Kenya since independence,[41] it is interesting to note his specific mention of his tour in June 1962 to the land scheme at Mugunga in which 500 Kikuyu families were settled.[42] The British arrested and imprisoned Kenyatta in October 1952 because of his alleged involvement with the Mau Mau, hence Kenyatta tried to distance himself from the latter's legacy.[43] After independence, he downgraded the Mau Mau's importance in the anti-colonial struggle. Their legacy was used to justify the Kikuyu's claims to a greater share of national resources, but they were sacrificed for the sake of national unity and Kikuyu elites claimed and disclaimed Mau Mau allegiances according to their own needs.[44]

Suffering also combines the global and transnational with the regional and national. Kenyatta refers to various federations and transnational organisations, such as the Treaty of East African Co-operation with Tanzania and Uganda of 1967 and the first Afro-Asian Solidarity conference at Moshi in February 1963.[45] In the Foreword he argues that 'nation-building' and 'Pan-

---

[35] Majeed, *Autobiography*, 143–6, 96–100.

[36] Uma Kant Tiwary, *The Making of the Indian Constitution* (Allahabad: Central Book Depot, 1967); Granville Austin, *The Indian Constitution: Cornerstone of a Nation* (New Delhi: Oxford University Press, [1966] 2004).

[37] Zachariah, *Nehru*, 178–9, 211–12, 232, 255–6.

[38] Jeremy Murray-Brown, *Kenyatta* (London: George Allen, 1970), 194.

[39] Kenyatta, *Suffering*, 43, 91.   [40] Ibid., 143.   [41] Hornsby, *Kenya*, 7–8.

[42] Kenyatta, *Suffering*, 172.   [43] Ibid., ch. 1.   [44] Hornsby, *Kenya*, 114–16.

[45] Kenyatta, *Suffering*, xi, 192.

Africanism' should be mutually dependent, and his early political career in the Kenyan African Union, of which he was made President in 1947, involved expanding it to achieve 'universal African objectives'.[46] However, the event that dominates his Foreword is the Congo Crisis of 1964. The immediate motive for writing *Suffering* is this international geopolitical crisis and the need to counter its depiction by the US ambassador to Kenya, hence global geopolitics was crucial to the very inception of the book.[47]

Some of Gandhi's Indian opponents sought to discredit him in terms of his regional identity. M. R. Jayakar depicted Gandhi as foisting a Gujarati regional identity on others,[48] while Gandhi's 'Gujaratiness' was used by intellectuals like K. M. Munshi to define Gujarat in the 1930s.[49] Gandhi, then, had to negotiate his regional identity carefully in his life-writing. Both *Hind Swaraj* and *Autobiography* were originally published in Gujarati, but Gandhi collaborated with their translation into English. *Hind Swaraj* was published in *Indian Opinion* by Gandhi's appropriately named International Printing Press in South Africa, staffed by a multilingual, multireligious, and multiethnic work force.[50] The Gujarati and English versions of his *Autobiography* were first published in serial instalments in journals, this time in India. The location of these publications illustrates how Gandhi's textual enactments of self-rule, while rooted in Gujarati, were multilingual events crossing geographical boundaries, reflecting a print culture that was both transnational and Indian. *Hind Swaraj* was also a response to the debate amongst Indians outside India on the justifiability of violence against imperial rule and the appendix lists texts by Plato, Mazzini, Tolstoy, and Ruskin, drawing together authors in a globalised intertextuality which crosses linguistic, cultural, and regional boundaries. Given the importance of dialogue as a philosophical method in both Sanskrit and European philosophy, the text's reworking of this form as a dialogue between an editor and reader has cross-cultural resonances. Gandhi's Gujarati identity, then, was embedded in a counter-modern but internationalist outlook.

---

[46] Ibid., vi, 43.   [47] Ibid., vi, viii.

[48] M. R. Jayakar, *The Story of my Life* (Bombay: Asia Publishing House, 1958–1959), 1. 362, 378–9.

[49] Nalin Mehta and Mona G. Mehta, 'Gujarat beyond Gandhi: Notes on Identity, Conflict and Society' in Nalin Mehta and Mona G. Mehta (eds.), *Gujarat beyond Gandhi: Identity, Society and Conflict* (Abingdon: Routledge, 2011), 1–13; 5.

[50] Isabel Hofmeyr, *Gandhi's Printing Press: Experiments in Slow Reading* (Cambridge, MA: Harvard University Press, 2013).

Travelling Identities

Thus, the life-writing of the figures considered here dramatised different forms of self-rule, combining global, transregional, and regional axes of identity as they sought to disentangle themselves from British colonial citizenship. Their travels to England played an important part in their self-conceptions but these travels were counterbalanced by their journeys to other regions of the world as part of their political education. As Gandhi outlines in his *Autobiography*, key elements of his political philosophy began to crystallise around issues such as caste, diet, sartorial politics, legality, and religiosity during his stay in England.[51] However, his lengthier stay in South Africa from 1893 to 1914 was particularly important for the development of *satyagraha*.[52] Gandhi's reimagining of India and the politics of self-rule were closely tied to his identity and experience as a traveller outside India, and his style of travel underpinned his political philosophy, as an expression of the ethics of simplicity and as a critique of modern technology.[53] His long marches after he returned to India, such as his Salt March from Ahmedabad to Dandi in March 1930, exemplified his ideology of mobility as a mode of protest and as part of his political philosophy.

Nehru's and Gandhi's travelling identities subvert dominant European perspectives on 'natives' as unselfconsciously rooted in territories, in contrast to the mobile freedom of European travellers.[54] Naidu's travelling identity is doubly transgressive because it also challenges European travel accounts of the 'Eastern' woman as immobilised by domesticity.[55] Her later travels to Britain as a nationalist and feminist politician signal a shift in emphasis in her relationship to England, as does her return of the Kaisar-i-Hind medal in protest at Jallianwala and its aftermath.[56] Her travels in the United States in 1928 and 1929 as Gandhi's and India's unofficial ambassador in the wake of the *Mother India* controversy reflect a confident cosmopolitan travelling identity, in which the roles of Indian nationalist-feminist and poet are conducted with

---

[51] Gandhi, *Autobiography*, Part 1, chs. 11–25.

[52] M. K. Gandhi, 'Satyagraha in South Africa (1924–1925)' in *The Collected Works of Mahatma Gandhi* (New Delhi: Ministry of Information and Broadcasting, 1968), vol. 29, 1–269.

[53] Majeed, *Autobiography*, 80–96.   [54] Ibid., passim.

[55] Anupama Arora, 'The Nightingale's Wanderings: Sarojini Naidu in North America', *Journal of Commonwealth Literature*, 44:3 (2009): 87–105.

[56] Naidu to Leilamani Naidu, 4 January 1920; to Nehru, 16 June 1920; to Gandhi, 15 July and 2 September 1920; and to Pamaja and Leilamani Naidu, 23 September and 27 November 1931, in *Selected Letters*, ed. Paranjape, 144–5, 145–7, 147–8, 151–3, 248–50, 261–3.

more assuredness.[57] However, these strands of her identity can be in tension with each other, testifying to the difficulties of managing her travelling persona. In one of her letters, for example, she says she rises 'to greater heights in international gatherings abroad than in India'.[58] In her Presidential Address at the All India Women's Committee in 1930 she refers to tensions between feminism and nationalism, as well as between different forms of feminism within and outside India. Her career as an Indian woman activist illustrates the complex place of feminism and women activists in Indian nationalism and the eventual triumph of sectional political identities in India over a cross-communal feminist solidarity.[59] The shifts between feminism as a critique of mainstream nationalism and the subordination of feminist goals to nationalism emerge in her endorsement of nationalised gender categories. Some of her letters invoke Sita and Padmini of Chitore as symbols of Indian and Hindu womanhood, and she exhorts her daughter to be an 'embodied symbol of Indian womanhood' by taking on a 'high burden of suffering and self-abnegation'.[60] When in Sacramento, she refers to how Indian settlers there came to see 'not my face so much as in me the face of India the Mother!'[61] She exhorts her son to be 'manly' and to do sports as 'I hate to see a soft man', and links an emerging India with 'splendid manhood'.[62]

Naidu's travels also dramatise her complex relationship with Gandhi. Her engagement with the Indian diaspora in South Africa, Kenya, and the United States, where she went as Gandhi's emissary, plays an important role in her sense of being Indian. For her, the diaspora in Africa has as legitimate a claim on India as Indians do at home, a view shared by Gandhi.[63] She was imprisoned in May 1931 for leading the raid on the Dharasan Salt Works as part of Gandhi's campaign against the Salt Tax.[64] However, her luxurious mode of travel as a cosmopolitan member of a global middle class at ease with modernity and Euro-American culture is at odds with Gandhi's austere style of counter-modern travels.[65] Her many references to Gandhi as 'little'

---

[57] Naidu to Leilamani Naidu, 17 November 1928, 4 March 1929, and 7 April 1929; to Gandhi, 19 November 1928, in ibid., 210–12, 224–5, 226–7, 212–16.

[58] Naidu to Leilamani Naidu, 7 April 1929, in ibid., 226–7. [59] Sinha, *Specters*, 205.

[60] Naidu to Leilamani Naidu, April 1922, in *Selected Letters*, ed. Paranjape, 164.

[61] Naidu to Leilamani Naidu, 24 January 1929, in ibid., 222–3.

[62] Naidu to Jaisoorya Naidu, 9 September 1913; to Ranadhera Naidu, 31 May 1924; and to Rajiv Gandhi, 16 October 1944, in ibid., 85–6, 175–6, 313–14.

[63] Naidu to Gandhi, 13 and 29 February 1924; to Leilamani Naidu, 3 April 1924, in ibid., 170–1, 172–3, 174.

[64] Forbes, *Women*, 134.

[65] Naidu to Leilamani Naidu, 4 March 1921, in *Selected Letters*, ed. Paranjape, 156; Arora, 'The Nightingale's Wanderings'; Majeed, *Autobiography*, 83–4.

and as 'Mickey Mouse' are simultaneously affectionate, patronising, and satirical.[66] She also makes insightfully critical remarks about his political philosophy.[67] At the same time, 'little' resonates with Gandhi's politics of self-reduction in his *Autobiography*, in which he expresses his aim to 'reduce myself to zero',[68] and Naidu repeatedly uses the term 'little' to refer to her own volumes of poetry.[69] Her poetic self-designation indicates the self-deprecation of an Indian woman poet in the colonial male world of letters. It may also reflect a tense relationship with Indian male nationalists who tended to view her poetry as casting doubt on her political substance.[70] However, 'littleness' was a source of strength for Gandhi, and so here Gandhian self-assertion through self-effacement is echoed in Naidu's own self-designated poetic 'littleness'. Her relationship with Gandhi was therefore both politically close but also critically distant.

Kenyatta interpreted his imprisonment in terms of 'subtle ways of breaking a widely-travelled man'.[71] In his capacity as Secretary to the Kikuyu Central Association he travelled to Europe in 1929, where he spent sixteen years. These travels shaped him as a 'world statesman'.[72] He depicts them as the technocratic and political education of a student of anthropology and economics who focused on political and technical issues of development, touring Russia and western Europe with the practical purposes of nation-building in mind.[73] One of his aims while travelling was to counter colonialism 'through propaganda and discussion and negotiation'.[74] During this stay he wrote his first book, *Facing Mount Kenya* (1938), described by one commentator as a 'masterly propaganda document'.[75] In Britain he assisted in the formation of African nationalist groups, including the Somali Youth League in Liverpool and Cardiff and the Pan-African Federation in London in 1935 in the wake of the Italian–Abyssinian crisis (see Chapter 6). He helped to organise the 5th Pan-African Conference in Manchester in 1945, which

---

[66] Naidu to Pamaja Naidu, 7 and 14 May 1930, 15 January 1931, 9 April and 9 May 1933; to Leilamani and Pamaja Naidu, 6 September and 8 October 1931; to Pamaja Naidu, 9 April and 9 May 1933; to Nehru, 29 March 1938; and to Leilamani Naidu, 3 March 1943, in *Selected Letters*, ed. Paranjape, 236–7, 239–43, 284–5, 288–9, 245–7, 250–2, 302–3, 308–9.

[67] Naidu to S. Satyamurti, 17 December 1922; to Pamaja Naidu 15 February 1930; and to Pamaja and Leila Naidu, 5 May 1933, in ibid., 167–8, 235, 285–6.

[68] Gandhi, *Autobiography*, 454.

[69] Ibid., 454; Naidu to Heinemann, 20 July, 27 September and 12 October 1911, 21 March and 11 April 1912; to Tagore, 16 November 1912 and 20 August 1917, in *Selected Letters*, ed. Paranjape, 54–7, 67–9, 71–2, 73, 77–8, 82–3, 132.

[70] Parama Roy, *Indian Traffic: Identities in Question in Colonial and Postcolonial India* (Berkeley, CA: University of California Press, 1998), 139.

[71] Kenyatta, *Suffering*, 68.   [72] Ibid., 42.   [73] Ibid., 33–4.   [74] Ibid., 33.

[75] Murray-Brown, *Kenyatta*, 191.

influenced his thinking on two issues: the need for outright Kenyan independence and the question of violence.[76]

Thus, Kenyatta's travels to Britain and Europe were important for his intellectual and political development as an anti-colonial leader who grappled with Kikuyu cultural identity, Kenyan nationalism, and pan-Africanism. While Gandhi's travels were imbricated with his critique of technological modernity and were underpinned by a spiritual search for 'Truth' to counter secular modernity,[77] Kenyatta's were framed by technocratic imperatives grounded in a critique of colonial thinking. The title *Suffering Without Bitterness* hints at the redemptive possibilities of suffering and his 'forgive and forget' attitude reassured British colonial officials pondering whether to release him.[78] Kenyatta read the Bible and the Qur'an in prison, and concluded that all religions could be reduced to one common theme, but there are few references to religion in *Suffering*.[79] When he was President he showed no religious interests. He praised the churches' contribution to Kenyan unity and development, but did not attend church services, and was buried non-denominationally.[80]

In his account of his stay in England Kenyatta frequently refers to and cites his letters to the British press. At times *Suffering* reads like a scrapbook of British press clippings about himself. The chapters on his trial, imprisonment, and release cite the British press on its injustice.[81] These citations suggest that a section of British public opinion is at odds with British colonialism in Kenya and the colonial establishment in London. British colonialism, therefore, is not just alien in Kenya; it does not completely reflect British public opinion. Like Kenyatta, Nehru also refuses to simplify the term 'Britain' to refer to an imperial oppressor alone, hence his discussion of two 'Englands'.[82] He also reworks the term Britain in other ways.[83] Nehru visited the USSR and Europe in 1926 and 1927, which was the beginning of his close relationship with the international left.[84] The USSR, not yet completely Stalinised, seemed to Nehru to offer solutions to global problems and influenced his concept of national planning.[85] His travels beyond Britain and India therefore testify to the range of his political influences beyond his ties to Britain, and to the importance of transnational imaginaries of solidarity in this period.[86]

---

[76] Kenyatta, *Suffering*, 41–2.   [77] Majeed, *Autobiography*, 80–96.   [78] Hornsby, *Kenya*, 72.
[79] Kenyatta, *Suffering*, 68.   [80] Hornsby, *Kenya*, 202.   [81] Kenyatta, *Suffering*, 79–83, 86.
[82] Nehru, *Discovery*, 287–8.   [83] Majeed, *Autobiography*, 161–2.
[84] Nehru, *Autobiography*, 16–20, 147–54; *Discovery*, 287–8.   [85] Zachariah, *Nehru*, 60–1, 96.
[86] Jane Burbank and Frederick Cooper, *Empires in World History: Power and the Politics of Difference* (Princeton, NJ; Oxford: Princeton University Press, 2010), 402–3, 414, 453.

Nehru's concept of travel in his life-writing was plotted in three ways. First, recovering historical memories of Indian travel was key to mobilising an India isolated by colonialism. The figure of the travelling Indian scientist was also crucial for his project to define India as a worthy participant in the global narrative of modernity. Thirdly, imaginary and mental travel during his imprisonment illuminated the paradox of prison as a site for the articulation of freedom, and showed how travel can dramatise complex relations between mind and body in which the two might not travel together at all.[87]

Composition

Sturrock stresses that a writer's style is 'an autobiographical statement par excellence', his or her 'signature',[88] and Clifford Geertz has remarked that new states are like apprentice poets or painters who are seeking their own proper styles.[89] How Naidu, Nehru, Gandhi, and Kenyatta stylise their texts affords clues to their self-conceptions in relation to their redefined communities. The mixed formal elements in Nehru's autobiographies and his technique of collage articulate his sense of self and his notion of India as a flexible amalgamation of diverse elements.[90] For Gandhi, self-authorship is closely related to the politics of translation and underpins the tree-like nature of 'Truth', which grounds *satyagraha*.[91] For these writers and for Naidu, incarceration was a key part of their senses of self, because it illuminated the questions of agency and constraint with which they grappled.[92] In *Suffering* a prison narrative and the international pressure for Kenyatta's release, as well as the injustice of his trial, dominate his self-presentation. Kenyatta compares his incarceration with that of Nehru and of 'many others from Colonial lands who were my friends in England'.[93] Kenyatta later used his imprisonment to legitimise his authoritarian regime and discredit his opponents in postcolonial Kenya; his prison narrative, therefore, was also used to justify a repressive and not just a liberating politics.[94]

---

[87] Majeed, *Autobiography*, 68, 99–100, 36–9.

[88] John Sturrock, *The Language of Autobiography: Studies in the First Person Singular* (Cambridge: Cambridge University Press, 1993), 224.

[89] Clifford Geertz, *The Interpretation of Cultures: Selected Essays* (London: Hutchinson, 1975), 278.

[90] Majeed, *Autobiography*, 152–4, 156–7.   [91] Ibid., ch. 7.

[92] Because of constraints of space, I can only discuss Kenyatta in this context. For Nehru in this context, see Majeed, *Autobiography*, 36–9, 180–2.

[93] Kenyatta, *Suffering*, 76–7, citing Paul Robeson.   [94] Ibid., 340–8.

Alongside press cuttings, *Suffering* incorporates transcripts and reports of Kenyatta's trial as part of its aim to shape 'the revelation of truth' and a 'fuller interpretation' of his trial and imprisonment. It operates with a notion of truth as empirically verifiable, rooted in publicly available texts, in contrast to the production of 'skilfully-propagated untruth' through the theatricality and melodrama of his trial.[95] The clash with colonial untruth is therefore also a clash between different genres of texts. *Suffering*'s notion of truth contrasts with Gandhi's expansive notion of the tree-like structure of 'Truth',[96] and this is underlined by its aesthetic of abridgement. Many of the documents, reports, and transcripts Kenyatta cites are abridged and the word 'condensed', or its synonyms such as 'précis', recur when these texts are reproduced.[97] Colonial productions of 'truth', on the other hand, are marked by 'verbose qualifications', the stringing together of 'qualifying phrases', and 'competent-seeming paragraphs and chapters'.[98] In a reversal of clichés British colonialism is associated with verbosity and overstatement, and Kenyan nationalist truths with clipped and condensed sharpness.[99] For Kenyatta an anti-colonial use of English is characterised by brevity and clarity.

Suffering's mode of authorship reflects Kenyatta' self-iconisation. Only the Foreword is written in the first person. The rest of the text refers to Kenyatta in the third person, sometimes very distantly so.[100] *Suffering* was co-authored with two other writers, both members of the government, one European and the other Kenyan; it was an officially authorised book.[101] The inclusion of a European author indicates Kenyatta's care not to alienate the white settler population after independence so as to ensure Britain's continued support for him as a moderate nationalist leader, in contrast to the perceived extremism of the Mau Mau.[102] Kenyatta is referred to variously in the text as Mzee Jomo Kenyatta, Mzee Kenyatta, Jomo Kenyatta, or just as Kenyatta. In his political career, he took on different names (the name Jomo Kenyatta first appeared in print as a 'new signature' as the author of *Facing Mount Kenya*).[103] These changing names in *Suffering* amplify his presence in the text and therefore also his iconic status.

---

[95] Ibid., 66, 24, 63.   [96] For which, see Majeed, *Autobiography*, ch. 7.

[97] Kenyatta, *Suffering*, 50, 58, 95, 120–1, 135–7, 167–8.

[98] This is how F. D. Corfield's report on the Mau Mau and some other government statements are characterised; see ibid., 101–7, 110–11.

[99] Ibid., 58, 95.   [100] Ibid., 145, 152.   [101] Kenyatta, *Suffering*, xvi.

[102] Hornsby, *Kenya*, 72, 103–4.   [103] Murray-Brown, *Kenyatta*, 194.

Suffering is self-conscious about its mode of writing. It is at pains to point out that it is 'not a novel',[104] but it also sanctions a departure from its aesthetic of careful control: 'it would still seem inadequate, in a work of this kind, to treat Kenyatta's home-coming merely as a factual incident, without attempting to paint in something of the surrounding colour and reaction and significance'.[105] In the pages that follow, cacophony, singing, carnival, ululations, dancing, shouts, tongues, accents, screaming questions, and pent-up feelings are given careful mention.[106] This controlled licence and catharsis, though, is not always effective. Written in a careful and even repressed English, there are hints in the text of a more energetic linguistic reality threatening to break through. The text ends with an appendix described as 'not [. . .] a set piece from formal script', but 'a conversation piece', marked by informality. As it was originally in Swahili there can be 'no precise reproduction of the substance and style' of the words, and what follows is a 'representation – no more – in English' of the text.[107] The carefully circumscribed nature of truth, linguistically policed in *Suffering*, ends on an almost Gandhian note about the necessity of translation. The appendix also suggests that *Suffering* is aware of the problematic status of English and its limits in a postcolonial multilingual society.

Naidu also grapples with the question of multilingualism in her letters, in which she expresses an ambivalence towards and a fear of Indian languages in textile similes. In a prison letter of 1932, her ambivalence to Indian languages is expressed in this way:

> the mixture of tongues are amusing and a little wearisome in their confusion and volumes of sound [. . .] the main fabric of speech is Gujarati [. . .] floating about in an endless length, like thin insipid magenta-pink *mull-mull* [muslin], unevenly faded [. . .] and on that surface there is now a dull blue and russet stripe of Marathi, an occasional yellow flick of Canarese and, every now and then, a sudden if strident orange dot and dash of colour from a powerful Punjabi voice.[108]

In another prison letter of 1933, the tension between her use of English and India as a multilingual entity threatens to unnerve her anglophone persona:

> You would presume it [Yeravda prison] is an idyll of Sabbath calm and repose [. . .] but not many yards away there are other iron-barred cages which you might well be pardoned for mistaking for parrot houses in the Zoo [. . .] such

---

[104] Kenyatta, *Suffering*, 139.   [105] Ibid., 139–40.   [106] Ibid., 140–4.   [107] Ibid., 340.
[108] Naidu to Pamaja and Leilamani Naidu, 15 May 1932, in *Selected Letters*, ed. Paranjape, 272–4.

a conflict of polyglot chatter issues forth in such a discord and medley of Sindi, Gujarati, Marathi, Hindi, not to mention the shrill and nerve-shattering Esperanto of a dozen wailing babies who act as an intermittent chorus! It seems almost impossible to collect one's mind long enough to write a coherent sentence – one is so assailed and assaulted by the confusion of tongues in every variety of sharps and flats.[109]

In prison India is not just a 'modern version of the Tower of Babel' where the 'world ebbs and flows [. . .] breaking into waves of Bengali, Gujarati, English and Hindi'.[110] It is a site where language is on the point of collapsing into a babble of pure sound. The references to parrots and infant sounds, while disparaging, also suggest a fear of regression into a pre-linguistic realm. Indian languages threaten Naidu's linguistic self-marshalling and the prospects of coherence in the English language. The question of how to define the relationship between English and Indian languages, and between Indian languages and Hindi, became an urgent one for the Indian state after 1947 and it continues to be an issue today. The irruption of this issue in Naidu's epistolary self, therefore, was of broader significance for the emerging Indian nation. Both Naidu's and Kenyatta's texts remind us of the irresolvable linguistic dimensions to the processes of disentangling emerging nationalist selves from British colonial citizenship. Naidu's textile similes also echo the symbolic, economic, and political significance of *khadi* and sartorial politics in Gandhi's philosophy of self-rule, and their usage in the context of language politics dovetails with her ambivalence towards Gandhi's politics, and possibly also to its linguistic aspects.

Conclusion

As writer-politicians, Naidu, Kenyatta, Nehru, and Gandhi used life-writing to reflect upon selfhood and governance in a context in which these were thrown open. All of them anticipate future struggles over defining postcolonial national identities. The question of who is an Indian remains an open one and continues to generate conflict in the present day.[111] In Kenya the issues of who is Kenyan and how Kenya is to be governed continue to be debated.[112] Moreover, in their attempts to disentangle their emerging national selves

---

[109] Naidu to Leilamani Naidu, 5 March 1933, in ibid., 282–4.
[110] Naidu to Nehru, 13 November 1937, in ibid., 301.
[111] Sunil Khilnani, *The Idea of India* (New Delhi: Penguin Books, 2012), ch. 4.
[112] Joyce Nyairo, *Kenya@50: Trends, Identities and the Politics of Belonging* (Goethe-Institut Kenya: Contact Zones NRB, 2015).

from British colonial citizenship, Nehru, Gandhi, and Naidu also anticipated questions about British postcolonial national identity, for which the 1948 British Nationality Act was key in separating out 'Britishness' from Indian and Pakistani nationality. After 1947 Britain had to rethink its ideas about nationality and the rights of its subjects in view of the new relationships linking the ex-colonies, old dominions, and Britain within the Commonwealth, and especially in relation to the successor states of the British Raj in South Asia.[113]

Through their travelling selves, Naidu, Kenyatta, Nehru, and Gandhi thread together regional, national, and global identities and show how the national and regional were necessarily global and transnational too. Their self-conceptions are tied to arguments for aspirational nationhood, hence they try to make themselves representative of the larger collective identities they sought to shape. This, however, makes their representativeness and the larger question of their authenticity, even the concept of authenticity itself, contestable. Such tensions are particularly evident in Naidu's and Kenyatta's linguistic handling of their texts against the multilingual backgrounds of their societies. As writer-politicians all four were both enabled and constrained by the conventions of life-writing. Their uniqueness renders their life-writing justifiable in the first place, but their singularity had to tie in with an emerging collective in heterogeneous societies with significant centrifugal tendencies. They thus had to simultaneously celebrate and tame their singularity to disentangle their national selves from their British selves. This disentanglement was also part and parcel of the larger process of the redefinition of Britishness itself in the postcolonial period.

---

[113] Sarah Ansari, 'Subjects or Citizens? India, Pakistan and the 1948 British Nationality Act', *Journal of Imperial and Commonwealth History*, 41:2 (2013): 285–312.

11

Staging Early Black and Asian Drama in Britain

COLIN CHAMBERS

British drama has represented the black and South Asian Other since early modern theatre began in Tudor times, and there is evidence of the presence in British theatre of African and Asian diasporic performers from that period on, but the beginnings of what can be regarded as a diasporic drama in its own right are not found until the nineteenth century when Britain was the centre of empire and diasporic communities lived the consequences of that reality.[1] In theatrical terms, for the black communities – African, African American, and Caribbean – this meant the dominance of a minstrelised entertainment industry, and for South Asian communities an exoticised one of fantasy Orientalism. Although minstrel and exotic theatrical phenomena were primarily reductive, restrictive, and negative, they were also inconsistent, contradictory, and fissured, and some practitioners found ways of exploiting unintended gaps in order to project an alternative representation.

The bulk of the career of the remarkable African American actor Ira Aldridge (1807–1867), who came to Britain in 1825 and honed his craft there, coincided with the craze for minstrelsy, and he turned the tables on his audiences by using their preconceptions against them.[2] He would, for example, juxtapose the stereotypical comic role of the black servant Mungo with the tragic dignity of Othello, the main representation in 'western' drama of the Other, and showed both to be a mask; he exploited the space he was allowed on stage to embody and animate ideas about his people that were not necessarily promoted by, or were even at odds with, the plays themselves. He revived *Titus Andronicus* and rewrote it with a white playwright to make

---

[1] For a study of this background, see Colin Chambers, *Black and Asian Theatre in Britain: A History* (London; New York: Routledge, 2011).

[2] For further information on Aldridge, see the four volumes of Bernth Lindfors's biography, *Ira Aldridge* (Rochester, NY: University of Rochester Press, 2011–2015).

Aaron the Moor, traditionally seen as the villain, a heroic figure, and in *The Black Doctor*, derived from a French melodrama in which a Creole doctor falls in love with a white aristocratic woman, Aldridge and his probable collaborator(s) moved the script away from the grotesqueries of minstrel-style representation to treat interracial marriage as a serious prospect. Other English versions existed, but a text published after his death is attributed to Aldridge, making it possibly the first time in Britain that a play was credited to a black author.[3]

Aldridge's exploitation of the inescapable emphasis on the black body in his performances was unsurprisingly taken up by other black performers, who found ways to demonstrate agency through their theatrical displays. An escaped Virginia slave, Henry 'Box' Brown, replicated his method of deliverance in a stage show when he posted himself from Bradford to Leeds in (what was said to be) the very crate in which he had fled. He was the author of several shows in the 1850s, such as his kinetic panorama *The Mirror of Slavery*, which used the latest technology and often included slave narratives.

Civil and National Rights

Just as Britain was central to the anti-slavery movement, by the end of the nineteenth and beginning of the twentieth centuries it was becoming a focal point of the diasporic struggle for civil and national rights and independence from empire. Political and social networks were formed, in which cultural activity and appreciation were valued, often in tension with European definitions, both as an aspiration for self-improvement and as a benchmark of universal equality, regardless of race or skin colour. Allied to the pan-African movement in Britain were the Egyptian actor, writer, and theatrical promoter Dusé Mohamed Ali (1866–1945),[4] who founded and ran the anti-colonial journal *African Times and Orient Review,* and the African American playwright Henry Francis Downing (1851–1928), probably the first person of

---

[3] The African writer and composer Ignatius Sancho (*c.* 1729–1780) was possibly the author of two plays but neither has survived. Dicks' Standard Play series (1883?, no. 460) attributes *The Black Doctor* to Aldridge, but whether or to what extent he was the author remains unclear. Keith Byerman in 'Creating the Black Hero: Ira Aldridge's *The Black Doctor*' in *Ira Aldridge: The African Roscius*, ed. Bernth Lindfors (Rochester, NY: University of Rochester Press, 2007), 204–15, suggests Aldridge did contribute, even if he was not the sole author.

[4] There have been different spellings over time, from Dusé Mohamed Ali to Duse Mohamed Ali. Preferred usage in this chapter is Dusé Mohamed Ali.

African descent to have a play of his or her own written and published in Britain.[5]

Ali came to Britain in the mid-1870s, and stayed until the early 1920s. He was apparently told that were he not a 'negro' he would be in the first flight of West End actors. Understandably, he turned to writing plays to provide himself with better parts (a motivation that recurs through the later history of black and Asian drama), and some of these plays garnered a few performances. He also founded a Hull Shakespeare Society with the leading actor of the day, Sir Henry Irving, as Patron. Ali became a literary and theatrical agent with an office off Shaftesbury Avenue, ghosting, doctoring, and giving advice on plays. He co-wrote the libretto of the musical comedy *The Lily of Bermuda* with the creator of the piece, Bermuda-born black actor Ernest A. Trimmingham. Ali's company produced the show in 1909 with a cast of almost seventy, opening at the Theatre Royal, Manchester on a pre-London tour to Middlesbrough, Sheffield, Liverpool, Bradford, Oldham, and Sunderland. Even though some of the actors were praised, the review in *The Stage* presaged failure ('the piece [. . .] did not go too well', and the familiar story of a rich American with an eligible daughter was deemed 'slender').[6] The leading actress left before the transfer to Middlesbrough where Ali cancelled further bookings and pawned the scenery to pay off the cast. He subsequently devoted his time to journalism and politics.

The journal Ali founded serialised Henry Downing's fiction and reviewed his plays, recognising them as part of the pan-African struggle. Downing, a former editor of a Brooklyn paper and US consul to Angola, came with his wife Margarita to London in 1895 where they lived until German bombing drove them back to New York in 1917.

During his time in Britain, Downing addressed the first Pan-African Conference in 1900, was a member of the executive committee of the short-lived Pan-African Association formed at the Conference, and attended the 1911 First Universal Races Congress. He managed poet Paul Laurence Dunbar's first recital with composer Samuel Coleridge-Taylor (both African Americans), and wrote fiction and drama as well as the lyrics for

---

[5] For further information on Ali, see Ian Duffield, 'Dusé Mohamed Ali and the Development of Pan-Africanism 1866–1945', unpublished PhD dissertation (Edinburgh University, 1971), available at www.era.lib.ed.ac.uk/bitstream/1842/7323/1/482134_vol1.pdf, and other sources listed in Chambers, *Black and Asian Theatre*, 217 n. 39. For Downing, see Brian Russell Roberts, *Artistic Ambassadors: Literary and International Representation of the New Negro Era* (Charlottesville, VA: University of Virginia Press, 2013), and sources listed in Chambers, *Black and Asian Theatre*, 216 n. 27.

[6] *The Stage*, 11 November 1909.

'Where the Paw-Paw Grows' by Amanda Aldridge, daughter of Ira Aldridge. In 1913 and 1914, Downing published at least eight plays, which are characterised by an anti-colonial literary utopianism. Two of the plays were self-published, and one was written with Margarita. In *A New Coon in Town: A Farcical Comedy Made in England*, Downing openly confronts racism and lampoons colonial attitudes in a multilayered, comic deconstruction of gender, class, and national stereotypes.

His precise theatrical activities are unclear but in the early 1910s he seems to have presided over the Players' and Playwrights' Association, which aimed to help dramatists have their work produced. Such bodies held competitions and organised performances of plays by their members. It is possible, especially given Downing's position, that some of his plays were seen in this kind of outlet, a speculation given substance by the action of a short comedy, *Placing Paul's Play*, which he wrote with Margarita about such an event. Sadly, the outbreak of war prevented the proposed production of some of his plays at the Royal Court Theatre, London and then he returned to the USA.

Asian Diasporas

The context for the Asian diasporas, particularly the Indian communities, differed significantly from the context for those of African heritage. There was a different cultural history as well as a different relationship to the 'mother' country, and one of the features of this difference was a larger middle-class and student body, which both actively sought to distance themselves from stereotypical views of their people. There was also an interest among certain sections of the British literati in eastern culture and philosophy. The classic Sanskrit play *Śākuntalā* by Kālidāsa had been translated into Latin and then English in 1789 but this was for the study not the stage. A version did not appear in a British theatre until 1868, and then only in scenes, which were performed by the Parsee Victoria Dramatic Company from Bombay. What is believed to be the British premiere was a full-length production staged in English in the open air in 1899 by the pioneering director William Poel, who enlisted the help of Indians resident in London on the translation, the costumes, and the posture and gesture of the actors; Indian performers were involved, although not in leading roles, along with an Indian singer and Indian musicians. Poel, again with Indian help, staged a revival in 1912.

That year also saw the first stirrings of an autonomous Indian theatre in Britain. Two performances were held at the Royal Court of Kālidāsa's poem

Kumārasambhava, presented as *The Birth of the War-God* in eighteen *tableaux vivants* acted anonymously by some thirty Indian women and children. Proceeds went to the Indian Women's Education Association, to train women to be teachers in India. Thanks to Poel, there was also at the Royal Court a production of *Buddha*, an adaptation by S. C. Bose of Edwin Arnold's narrative poem *Light of Asia*, presented 'under Indian management' (which was, in fact, Kedar Nath Das Gupta). The production featured six episodes from the life of the spiritual leader, who was played by white actor Clarence Derwent alongside a company of Indian actors, mainly composed of students of law and medicine. The run was extended from three to seven performances. As a result of *Buddha*, a group of Indian students formed the Hindusthan Dramatic Society, and, later in 1912 at the Whitney Theatre, Aldwych, it presented *Ayesha*, a dramatisation by Nirajan Pal and Harendra Nath Maitra of the romantic nineteenth-century Indian novel *Durgeshnandini* by B. C. Chatterjee.

The momentum in South Asian theatre was driven by Kedar Nath Das Gupta (1878–1942), an activist against British rule and the partition of Bengal who arrived in England from India in 1907 to avoid the possibility of imprisonment.[7] He formed the Union of the East and West, supported by several notable British figures, including H. G. Wells, and organised a number of often prestigious events, such as talks and lectures on Indian culture and politics. The majority of the Union's activities, however, were theatrical and were presented under the umbrella of the Union by the Indian Art and Dramatic Society (IADS, also known as the Indian Art, Dramatic and Friendly Society).

Buddha appears to have been the catalyst for the formation of the IADS in May 1912. It was based at 21 Cromwell Road, west London, which was owned by India House, a nationalist body, and run as a hostel and cultural centre for students from abroad. The first IADS venture came in July 1912 at the Royal Albert Hall when it presented an evening dedicated to Rabindranath Tagore, a friend of Das Gupta's. The IADS continued to present South Asian plays throughout the rest of the decade, including during the war, and into the 1920s. The IADS staged a remarkable collection of Indian plays in a wide range of venues, from town halls and art galleries to the West End. Performances were held mostly in the afternoons or when theatres were

---

[7] For further information on Das Gupta, see Colin Chambers, '"A Flute of Praise": Indian Theatre in Britain in the Early Twentieth Century' in Susheila Nasta (ed.), *India in Britain: South Asian Networks and Connections, 1858–1950* (Basingstoke: Palgrave Macmillan, 2013), 149–63; 151–8.

not being used commercially, and the productions involved both Indian and white British performers (the majority), some of whom were among the most famous names then in British theatre. Adaptations by Das Gupta and his musical play *Bharata* featured among the two dozen or so IADS productions, which included Sanskrit classics such as *Śākuntalā*, *Savitri*, *Ratnavali*, and *The Little Clay Cart*. Central to Das Gupta's vision of making progress through acceptance by the dominant culture was Tagore's work (aided by his being awarded the Nobel Prize for Literature in 1913 – the first non-European to be so honoured – and his knighthood in 1915): eight pieces by or based on Tagore's writings were presented, and this focus provides a link between the period of the 1910s to 1920s and the subsequent flowering of British South Asian theatre practice in the late twentieth century.

The activities of the IADS faded from the mid-1920s on as Das Gupta increasingly concentrated his energy on promoting world peace and interfaith unity. It did seem, briefly, as if the Indian Players might carry on his ground-breaking theatrical work, bringing a South Asian presence to British audiences as well as asserting cultural pride for Indians living in Britain. It is not clear whether the group was founded by Himansunath Rai (1892–1940), who was studying law, or Niranjan Pal (1889–1959), who was studying medicine, both of whom had worked with Das Gupta, or by the two together, but the group was created in 1922 to present Pal's play *The Goddess* for two matinees at the Duke of York's Theatre, with Rai in the lead.[8] In contrast to the work of the IADS, this production, though directed by a white American, had an all-Indian cast and Indian stage management, and also used Indian music.

The Goddess tells the story of a Brahmin priest who propounds rationalism in order to challenge deceit and pronounces a beggar woman with whom he is in love to be the incarnation of the goddess Kali. Despite being unhappy with the deception, she agrees to appear as Kali in order to please him, but she then commits suicide to atone for her sacrilege. This act brings much-needed food and rain to the village, an ending one reviewer called a 'compromise between faith and religious "reform"'.[9] Shorn of its prologue and epilogue but with enhanced musical and dance contributions, *The Goddess* also played at the Ambassadors' Theatre (evenings and matinees) and then transferred under the direction of B. N. Dey to the Aldwych Theatre for a remarkable run of sixty-six performances.

[8] For further information on Pal, see Chambers, '"A Flute of Praise"', 158–61, and Kusum Pant Joshi and Lalit Mohan Joshi (eds.), *A Forgotten Legend & Such is Life: An Autobiography by Niranjan Pal* (Hounslow: South Asian Cinema Foundation, 2011).

[9] *The Stage*, 22 June 1922.

Pal, who had been sent to Britain by his father, a leading Bengal nationalist worried by his son's extremist leanings, had met Das Gupta at India House where he became involved in independence politics. He appeared in *Buddha* and helped found the Hindusthan Dramatic Society, which presented *Ayesha*, co-adapted by him. He also wrote a satirical farce with an English setting called *The Magic Crystal*, which was performed in 1924 on tour for two months, as well as other plays such as *Singh Sahib*, but no texts or evidence of productions survive. A play of his called *Shiraz* was due to appear in the West End but instead was turned into a film with members of the Indian Players in the cast, including Rai. He and Pal had intended to found an Indian Repertory Theatre in London, but they returned to India and became pioneers of cinema there.

It is likely that there is more autonomous South Asian theatrical activity to be uncovered from the first half of the twentieth century. Indian students, who played an important role in the beginnings of British South Asian theatre, were well organised and ran their own cultural events in their hostels, but this phenomenon, along with the amateur work of groups like the India Office Drama Society, has not been adequately researched yet. For example, little is known about the Indian Students' Union Play-Reading Circle. There may also be more to discover about Cornelia Sorabji (1866–1954), a Christianised Parsi from western India who came to England to study at Oxford in 1889 and was asked to provide the leading English actress Mrs Patrick Campbell with a play. Sorabji turned to an ancient Sanskrit drama, but Mrs Campbell, whose role turned out not to be the lead, wanted changes that Sorabji refused to make. Her text was sent to George Bernard Shaw, who made what Sorabji took to be a disparaging comment, and she abandoned the play.[10] It is possible that Sorabji was active in one of the many amateur dramatic societies that flourished at the time, or was involved with student cultural activity. Her play *Gold Mohur Time: 'To Remember'* was published in Britain in 1930, but there is no record of its having been performed.

Between the Wars

In the years between the two world wars, the importance of social and cultural networks grew. Dance, music, different forms of writing – fiction and non-fiction – and theatre were shared and circulated through restaurants

---

[10] Details taken from her autobiography, *India Calling: The Memories of Cornelia Sorabji* (London: Nisbet, 1934), 46–7.

and clubs (sometimes run by individuals, sometimes by student bodies or political organisations) and through informal or non-professional networks.[11] They explored the experiences of the diasporic communities and promoted ideas of non-compliance, resistance, self-worth, and liberation. This phenomenon was strongest in the black communities that drew together the African American, Caribbean, and African diasporas.

The League of Coloured Peoples (LCP), for example, founded in 1931 as an integrationist, gradualist pan-African body, took the brave and unusual step in 1933 of producing a play: *At What a Price*, a formally conventional comedy, written by Jamaican Una Marson (1905–1965) when she was twenty-six.[12] It deals with women's experience in a male culture; spirited but naive young Ruth, daughter to a weak mother and patriarchal father, leaves her middle-class, countryside home to work as a stenographer in Kingston, falls for the charms of her white boss, and returns to her parents and a former admirer, pregnant, deceived, rueful. Though Ruth's attempt at independence fails, the play applauds her feistiness and rejection of women's domestic marital subjugation.

Mounting *At What a Price* was a huge undertaking, which Marson guided. It is a four-act play and calls for some twenty actors to play Jamaicans. Marson took the main role and was directed by Clifford Norman, who had to draw on people with little or no acting experience from different cultural backgrounds. Their original home was listed next to their name in the programme: Bermuda, British Guiana, England, Gold Coast, India, Italy, Jamaica, St Lucia, and West Africa, an indication of the spread of the diasporas and of LCP membership. The two white roles were taken by black actors. The production had one performance on 23 November 1933 at the central London YWCA and was deemed sufficiently successful to transfer for a three-night run on 15 January 1934 to the 1,130-seat New Scala Theatre nearby.

Although the production failed in its original aim – to raise money for the LCP – it did succeed in another aspiration, as a political statement that

---

[11] Among the outlets were the Indian Students Hostel, the West African Students' Union, which had a magazine and branches in the colonies, the Canning Town Coloured Men's Institute, the Coloured Workers' Association, the Florence Mills Social Club, the International Afro Restaurant, and the West Indian Students' Union. A play about students, *Colour Bar*, jointly written by Roland Ederisu Sawyer, a leading member of the Negro Welfare Association, and Anne M. Bagshaw, who was white, was privately published in 1939, but there is no record of it ever being performed.

[12] See Chapters 6 and 7 for the LCP and Marson.

demonstrated cultural autonomy. As the LCP journal said, the 'all-coloured' production aimed to:

> bring home to the British public the fact that we can manage our own affairs effectively and therefore need not to be for ever under tutelage. It will also bring our own people together and help us have more confidence in ourselves, dissipate from among us any inferiority complex in ourselves, and assist us to find a basis for fuller co-operation among ourselves. Its effect must also spread overseas and be a source of inspiration to our race.[13]

Marson later wrote two more plays, *London Calling* and *Pocomania*, neither of which was seen in Britain, and her drama output was overshadowed by her achievements as a poet. She became an important figure in British black culture, especially as the first black female programme maker at the BBC, working on *Caribbean Voices*, which remained an important influence until it closed in the late 1950s.[14] She returned to the Caribbean at the end of the war and continued her involvement in the anti-colonial struggle.

In contrast to the LCP production, most plays with 'black' subject-matter were authored by white writers and produced by white-led companies, such as Left Theatre, founded in 1934 by progressive theatre professionals, and Unity Theatre, founded in 1936 as an amateur left-wing group associated with the Communist Party. In 1934, Left Theatre produced *They Shall Not Die*, a play by John Wexley, a white American, depicting a notorious case in which black teenagers were falsely convicted of rape. The large black cast included Marson and two other members of the cast of *At What a Price*.

With members of Left Theatre, the Indian Irish writer Aubrey Menon (1912–1989) – who adopted the pen-name of Menen – founded the Experimental Theatre, which performed at the West End's Fortune Theatre on a Sunday evening in 1934 his anti-fascist and anti-racist play *Genesis II*.[15] It is an ambitious and sprawling reworking of the first books of the Bible, and led to Menon being sued for blasphemy and obscenity. The play deals with the oppression of one race by another, and journeys from Eden and the British Museum Reading Room to a swastika-clad German police station and an Indian tea plantation. Masks and make-up were

---

[13] *The Keys*, 1:3 (January 1934): 43.   [14] See Chapter 9 for discussion of *Caribbean Voices*.

[15] For further information on Menon, see his own *The Space Within the Heart* (London: Hamish Hamilton, 1970); his unpublished biography, *Graham and the Elephants*, Aubrey Menen Collection, Howard Gotlieb Archival Research Center at Boston University; Florian Stadtler, 'National Representations, National Theatres: Aubrey Menen and the Experimental Theatre Company', *Studies in Theatre and Performance*, 38:1 (2018): 23–35, DOI: 10.1080/14682761.2017.1303282; and sources listed in Chambers, *Black and Asian Theatre*, 225 n. 65. His novel *SheLa* (London: Hamish Hamilton, 1963) was also a play.

designed by the Bloomsbury set artist Duncan Grant. The group subsequently found its own premises in north London where, influenced by expressionism and constructivism, they converted a house into a 120-seat venue with a 'floating' stage, which appeared not to be fixed to the ground (it comprised two platforms at different levels and a cantilever support underneath entirely covered in black so that the audience could not see it). The group, which incorporated dance and music in its programme, responded to current events in Living Newspaper form as well as presenting a repertoire of plays.

The initial, twenty-week season opened with an evening that comprised three dance-drama 'News Reel' items ('Bread Queue', 'Eviction', and 'Factory'), and Menon's play *Pacific*, set on a Polynesian island and featuring Polynesian songs and dances; it was described by one critic as dealing in a semi-realistic way with 'the coloured problem' in an 'odd' production that had 'moments of interest and even power'.[16] Other offerings in the season included: a classical Chinese play; *Apu Ollantay* (an Aztec drama of revolt against the Inca); classics from Tibet and Java; and Kālidāsa's *Hero and Nymph* from India (which the Indian Art and Dramatic Society had produced). The Experimental Theatre's small auditorium, however, was not financially viable, and the venture, which had promised much, soon collapsed. It is not clear how much of the programme was achieved, although one item, *The Mysterious Universe*, Menon's adaptation of the astronomer James Jeans's popular science book, appeared at the Arts Theatre in 1935. The following year, a few weeks after the Battle of Cable Street in London's East End, he staged (in a private house) his satire *Requiem for an Idiot*, announced as an improvised play based on a newspaper headline, which exposed hypocrisy over the fate of a Jew shot in a street riot.

Menon, born in 1912 in London to a Malayali father from Kerala and an Irish English mother, prefigured the mixed heritage, hybrid perspective that became a striking feature of later British diasporic theatre in the second half of the century with writers such as Hanif Kureishi. He studied philosophy at University College London, where he was active in student theatre and set up his own student company, which staged his adaptation of H. G. Wells's *The Shape of Things to Come*. After graduating, Menon became the drama critic for *The Bookman* (1933–1934) and used his column to analyse British theatre and argue for a theatre that would be truly 'national'; he proposed a nationwide network of local theatre associations that would host a repertoire of touring

---

[16] George W. Bishop, *Hampstead and St John's Wood Advertiser*, 15 November 1934.

shows performed not in conventional auditoria but in circus tents. He toured Britain with the India League and its secretary Krishna Menon, campaigning for Indian Independence, and changed his pen name to Menen, apparently to avoid confusion with Krishna, before going to live in India, where he wrote at least one play for radio. An author of several novels, travel books, and other works of non-fiction, he returned to Britain after Indian Independence before heading for Italy and returning to India where he died in 1989.

Toussaint Louverture

It is within the same 'white theatre' context in which the Experimental Theatre operated that the most significant play of the interwar period to be written by a black writer came to be produced. The staging of *Toussaint Louverture* by C. L. R. James (1901–1989) has been celebrated as a milestone in both Caribbean and British theatre, not only because it marked the first time black professional actors had performed a play by a black playwright on a British stage but also because of its historical significance in reimagining resistance in the past and connecting that to resistance in the present.[17]

Born in Trinidad in 1901, the activist, essayist, and historian James came to Britain in 1932 and was cricket columnist for the *Manchester Guardian* from 1933. He was part of a Caribbean diaspora that he said formed a distinct group among other colonial subjects in London who were described by the Africans they knew as the 'Black Englishmen' or as the 'black white men'. He was part of a broader network of activists that included two future leaders of their countries, from Kenya Jomo Kenyatta (who appeared on screen as an extra) and Eric Williams from Trinidad, as well as other notable anti-colonial figures such as George Padmore, Sam Manning, and Amy Ashwood Garvey. Garvey and Manning ran the Florence Mills Social Club in London, which was a centre of diasporic radical life. By the time James's play was staged, fascist Italy had invaded Abyssinia (now Ethiopia) and *Toussaint Louverture* took on a topical note. James was a founder member of a group established to protest at the invasion, which developed into a wider pan-African body.[18]

---

[17] Christian Høgsbjerg, 'Introduction' in C. L. R. James, *'Toussaint Louverture': The Story of the Only Successful Slave Revolt in History; A Play in Three Acts* (Durham, NC: Duke University Press, 2012), 1–40 gives a full picture of the play's history. In the 1960s, with help from fellow Trinidadian Dexter Lyndersay, James reworked the play under a new title, *The Black Jacobins*. It had its premiere under Lyndersay's direction at the University of Ibadan in 1967 and was published in 1976. Fifty years after the first production of *Toussaint Louverture*, this new version was chosen by Yvonne Brewster to launch the London-based black company Talawa. The original playtext appeared to be lost, until, in 2005, Høgsbjerg discovered it during his PhD research on James.

[18] See Chapters 6 and 7 for discussion of James's writings and networks.

In writing about the origin of *Toussaint Louverture*, James said he thought a 'play was required'.[19] To compose it he drew on material he was collecting for a book called *The Black Jacobins* and the more general *A History of Negro Revolt*, both of which appeared in 1938. James said he conceived the idea of the play in 1932, the year he left Trinidad for Britain, and finished the script by the autumn of 1934, a period during which he had become more radical in a process that deepened during the following few years. While theatre in Trinidad never had particularly strong or popular roots, the young James seems to have taken an interest in what little there was, and involved himself in amateur dramatics. He also studied Shakespeare and ancient Greek drama, and was a cultural activist in the 1920s. In writing *Toussaint Louverture*, he was spurred by a dual desire. One was to counter imperial versions of history, as could be found, for instance, in the programme of British events commemorating the centenary of the 1833 Emancipation Act. The other was to validate black achievement, an example followed later by other black and Asian playwrights in the reclamation of the past.

Toussaint Louverture is an ambitious and exhilarating epic work in three acts running from 1791 to 1804, in which Toussaint establishes a free society in the name of the French Republic. On behalf of the white planters, Napoleon sends a force to Haiti, and tricks Toussaint, who dies in prison. In the face of attempts to re-establish slavery, a permanent Republic is created under the leadership of another black leader, Dessalines. The play's direct engagement with the birth of the modern European world at the time of the French Revolution challenges the history of the Enlightenment by focusing on the centrality of slavery to it. Yet the play is also conceived within an Enlightenment frame: Toussaint is a tragic hero in the classical mould, though his 'fatal flaw' is not psychological but political. James is issuing a call to arms in the contemporary anti-colonial struggle as well as exploring the difficulties that this struggle throws up.

The play was produced in 1936, and earned international interest, thanks to the portrayal of Toussaint by the renowned African American performer Paul Robeson, who spent much of the 1930s in Britain and, like James, became increasingly radicalised there. *Toussaint Louverture* received two performances on 15 and 16 March 1936 at the Westminster Theatre, then boasting a modern profile through its association with the experimental Group Theatre. The play's director was Peter Godfrey (white), who, with his wife Molly Veness, had founded and run the pioneering Gate Theatre.

[19] Programme note, *The Black Jacobins*, Talawa Production, Riverside Studios (1986).

Casting a large number of black parts was becoming easier, even if the skill levels remained drastically inconsistent. James later wrote of Peter Godfrey's absences and having to rehearse the cast himself. He came under pressure to make cuts, not least from Robeson (three scenes, including those dealing with Toussaint's personal life, were dropped), but James remembers a good collaboration with him. James freely admitted that he lacked 'the instinct of the playwright' – 'I am not a dramatist by nature or inclination', he said – and dedicated the rest of his considerable writing life to other forms of expression.[20]

It is clear from these experiences that, in order to progress, diasporic playwrights needed a body of skilled diasporic theatre workers to present their work, and in order for that to happen, there was a need for training and the opportunity to practise the theatrical crafts. The struggle for such conditions continued through the war, chiefly at Unity Theatre, and, growing out of that, in Robert Adams's short-lived Negro Repertory Theatre in 1944, which staged Eugene O'Neill's *All God's Chillun Got Wings* at Colchester Repertory Theatre before folding. Although Adams's further plans for a Negro Theatre did not materialise, impetus was sustained after the war, albeit sporadically, in the context of significant new immigration. A string of valiant though often isolated initiatives grew in the 1960s and 1970s featuring the work of many playwrights, including Errol John, Barry Reckord, Mustapha Matura, and Michael Abbensetts, until in the 1980s it reached a point at which a black and Asian theatre had arrived in Britain to stay.[21] There was, however, little if any continuity between these later initiatives and the earlier phenomena described here. Nevertheless, despite this lack of connection or memory, they share much in common: a struggle for autonomous expression and recapture of history, and the energy of a new, hybrid aesthetic that not only produced a new body of work but also transformed long-held notions of what constitutes theatre itself.

---

[20] First quotation, Paul Buhle, *C. L. R. James: The Artist as Revolutionary* (London: Verso, 1988), 22; second, programme note, *The Black Jacobins*.

[21] These initiatives are described in Chambers, *Black and Asian Theatre*.

*

DISAPPOINTED CITIZENS
The Pains and Pleasures of Exile

Looking Back, Looking Forward
Revisiting the Windrush Myth

ALISON DONNELL

The arrival of *SS Empire Windrush* at Tilbury Docks in 1948 and the disembarkation of '492' West Indians from that ship has remained a significant and tenacious signifier within black British history. Indeed, just the single word 'Windrush' is now the accepted shorthand for calling into view post-World War II mass migration from the Caribbean to Britain and an attendant narrative of the cultural shift towards a multicultural nation. In terms of a literary history, Windrush is similarly invoked as a defining moment when the presence and influence of West Indian (and sometimes also South Asian) writers working and publishing within an English domestic literary landscape gained visibility and recognition. As a powerful focalising motif, Windrush helped to bring certain writers, literary works, and networks into view, but it has also often eclipsed the much thicker history of black British literary cultures that earlier chapters have detailed. This chapter is interested in how such a powerful association between a decommissioned troopship and the changing demographics of Britain's national, cultural, and literary landscapes came to be established, consolidated, and refreshed into the contemporary moment. To this end, it examines which factors influenced the writers and works that came to prominence and gained an enduring currency as Windrush narratives, and also attends to works that have been less celebrated. The particular focus is on how the construction of the Windrush experience within literary works has aligned with wider political narratives to emphasise the ongoing challenges around the recognition and accommodation of black subjects within British culture and society. Two important blind spots within the literary framing of the Windrush experience to be addressed here are writings that emphasise transnational attachments and cultural mobility, as well as writings by women.

The arrival of the *SS Windrush* as an entrance point for black subjects into British history has been widely contested. The elevation of the *Windrush* over other ships and landings is one obvious point of myth creation, critiqued by Sukhdev Sandhu:

> Six months earlier and completely unheralded, the Almanzora had docked at Southampton with 150 Jamaicans aboard. The state did not offer them hand-outs or cheap accommodation; they spent the weeks after disembarking trying to stave off the coldest winter this century by loitering for as long as possible in the Underground and in Lyons Corner Houses.[1]

Sandhu might equally have called on the *Ormonde* that carried West Indians to Liverpool, also docking in 1947. While these earlier non-metropolitan arrivals clearly tell a different and lesser-known story, significantly they were not subject to the same cultural and political responses that hailed the arrival of the *Windrush*.

When Pathé News handed their microphone to the suave and assured young Trinidadian calypsonian Lord Kitchener (Aldwin Roberts; 1922–2000), as he walked off the gangplank, his homecoming serenade 'London is the Place for Me' initiated with flair the creative expression of Caribbean migrants' sense of belonging to the colonial motherland. While Kitchener's later works relate the harsher realities of life in Britain, his initial claiming of Britain as a place of anticipated belonging remains iconic. For the journalist Peter Fryer, sent to report on the docking of *Windrush* as his first by-line for the *Daily Worker*, his interviews with passengers made a clear case to the British public for welcoming these West Indians.[2] Fryer's article, with the headline 'Five Hundred Pairs of Willing Hands', chronicled Windrush as a positive moment in national postwar history – a historical claim he would later complete in his landmark 1984 study *Staying Power: The History of Black People in Britain*.[3] Cementing the idea that West Indians on board had travelled and often returned to Britain to make a contribution, Fryer was keen to report that they possessed relevant skills and had a pre-history as servicemen. These early narratives of national alignment and enrichment from both the migrant and the host were not, however, uncontested. By 5 July, Prime Minister Attlee felt compelled to send a letter in reply to a group of eleven MPs, defending the policy of free

---

[1] Sukhdev Sandhu, 'Welcome Home', *London Review of Books*, 21:3 (4 February 1999): 25–7. Available at www.lrb.co.uk/v21/no3/sukhdev-sandhu/welcome-home.

[2] Peter Fryer, *The Politics of Windrush* (Richmond, Surrey: Index, 1999), 57.

[3] See Peter Fryer, *Staying Power: The History of Black People in Britain*, introduction by Paul Gilroy (London: Pluto, [1984] 2010).

admission to the UK for all British subjects.[4] He also sought to dismiss the alarm raised around immigration by arguing that 'it will be shown that too much importance – too much publicity too – has been attached to the present argosy of Jamaicans'.[5] From a contemporary vantage point, Attlee's prediction is evidently flawed – in terms of both the continued concentration on Windrush as the illustrative experience of Commonwealth immigration and the attention this particular ship continued to attract in the public and political imagination.

Loosening the imaginative hold of Windrush as the definitive beginning of a multicultural Britain has been key to many scholars and researchers seeking to make space for an expanded and pluralised account of black British subjects and the impact they have made. Acclaimed Jamaican British cultural theorist Stuart Hall, whose essays have been so central to theorising diasporic cultural identities and their changing political contexts, disputed Windrush as '"the" inauguration of black Britishness':[6]

> The Windrush, which is often given an originary status in the narrative of the formation of a black British diaspora, was not really the origin of anything [. . .] Instead, the Windrush's arrival served as an important hinge between the large numbers of black men and women already represented in many walks of British social life before the war [. . .] and the later arrival (in significantly enlarged numbers) of black people as an identifiable group.[7]

Hall's call for the acknowledgement of Windrush as the scripted beginning of a migration that reaches back across the several centuries of Britain's colonial

---

[4] See Clement R. Attlee, 'Letter from Prime Minister Attlee to an MP about Immigration to the UK', 5 July 1948 (HO 213/ 715), National Archives Education Resources. Available at www.nationalarchives.gov.uk/ education/ resources/ attlees-britain/ empire-windrush-2/. For more relating to this incident and the role played by the Trinidadian anti-imperialist George Padmore, see David Olusoga, *Black and British: A Forgotten History* (London: Macmillan, 2016), 49.

[5] Attlee, 'Letter from Prime Minister Attlee to an MP about Immigration to the UK'.

[6] In key essays, such as 'New Ethnicities' (1988), Hall identifies a shift in 'black cultural politics' as marked by the 'change from a struggle over the relations of representation to a politics of representation itself'; in Houston A. Baker Jr., Manthia Diawara, and Ruth H. Lindeborg (eds.), *Black Cultural Studies: A Reader* (Chicago; London: University of Chicago Press, 1996), 163–72; 165. See also 'The Local and the Global: Globalization and Ethnicity' (1989) in Anthony D. King (ed.), *Culture, Globalization, and the World-System: Contemporary Conditions for the Representation of Identity* (Minneapolis, MN: University of Minnesota Press, 1997), 19–40; and 'Cultural Identity and Diaspora' (1990) in Patrick Williams and Laura Chrisman (eds.), *Colonial Discourse and Post-Colonial Theory* (London: Harvester Wheatsheaf, 1993), 392–401.

[7] Stuart Hall, 'Preface' in Paul Gilroy, *Black Britain: A Photographic History* (London: Saqi: 2011), 5–10; 7.

involvements, identifies an important dimension of its now mythic status that needs to be revisited in terms of literary historical understandings too.

The record of black subjects writing themselves into the global history mapped by England and its empire through a domestic publication outlet reaches back to the mid-eighteenth century and Ignatius Sancho. Yet, as Pallavi Rastogi and Jocelyn Fenton Stitt argue in the introduction to their edited collection, tellingly entitled *Before Windrush: Recovering an Asian and Black Literary Heritage within Britain*, the contributions made by Mary Prince, Mary Seacole, Behramji Malabari, R. C. Dutt, Olive Christian Malvery, Mulk Raj Anand, Lao She, and C. L. R. James still too often constitute a 'forgotten aspect of British literary history'.[8]

Bringing due recognition to this pre-Windrush literary presence does not only involve acknowledging the contributions of a sizeable and diverse population of black people in Britain before the era of mass migration, although this is not to be dismissed.[9] It also involves confronting the powerful asymmetry of the historical record that the colonial world-view endorsed. Every schoolchild growing up in a British colony was imprinted with favourable representations of Britain: its peoples, places, history, and literature. Such representations were inevitably and often intentionally freighted by ideological claims for the legitimacy of colonial rule. There was no reciprocal 'colonial education' at the heart of the empire. Instead, colonial subjects were silenced or stereotyped. The clear deficit in terms of Britain's domestic understanding of how cultural encounters and exchanges with British subjects in its colonies and former colonies might unfold productively was notable as late as the 1930s and 1940s. The Guyanese writer Eric Walrond (1898–1966), employed as a journalist in London and writing for Marcus Garvey's *The Black Man* in the mid-1930s, made the cutting observation that 'It is indeed a paradox that London, capital of the largest Negro Empire in the world [. . .] should be extremely inexpert in the matter of interracial relations.'[10] Writing towards the end of the war, the Jamaican writer, broadcaster, and journalist Una Marson (1905–1965) made the more optimistic but equally revealing remark that 'The people of England are gradually waking

---

[8] Pallavi Rastogi and Jocelyn Fenton Stitt (eds.), *Before Windrush: Recovering an Asian and Black Literary Heritage within Britain* (Newcastle upon Tyne: Cambridge Scholars, 2008), 11.

[9] One example of research and database initiatives that significantly contribute to disseminating the cultural impact of South Asian writers and artists in Britain is the 'Making Britain' research project led by Professor Susheila Nasta (www.open.ac.uk /researchprojects/makingbritain/).

[10] Eric Walrond, 'The Negro in London', *Black Man*, 1:12 (March 1936): 9–10; 10.

up. They have been uneducated about the coloured people for a long time but they are now beginning to wake up and learn about us.'[11] The illiteracy described by Walrond and Marson returns as a question to contemporary British readers in *Small Island*, the 2004 Windrush novel by Andrea Levy (1956–2019), when the Jamaican serviceman Gilbert Joseph asks, 'How come England did not know me?'[12] Maintaining a narrow, exclusive notion of Englishness was doctrinally necessary to the imperial project, and also shaped cultural politics such that important contributions by black and Asian British writers passed seemingly unnoticed and unrecorded within accounts of British life before the mid-twentieth century.

Another important factor in thinking about the oversight around earlier acts of black British writing is their investment in political projects of lateral solidarity that undermined Britain's nationalism. The defining politics of nationalism for Caribbean and South Asian subjects was anti-colonialism and the character of pre-Windrush networks and movements was often decidedly supranational with a privileging of anti-colonial alliances, such as pan-Africanism and Garveyism, or counter-nationalisms, such as the Free India campaign. The inclusive horizon of cross-cultural configurations that gave character to black creative endeavour in Britain pre-Windrush can be glimpsed in the 1934 review of Una Marson's play *At What a Price*, staged at London's New Scala Theatre. This first all-black West End production was remarked on for its diversity of voice: 'Some spoke the heavy, rich language of the African coast, others in the staccato, sing-song tones of Jamaica, and a few, natives of London, with a genuine Cockney accent.'[13] Marson's production, under the auspices of the League of Coloured Peoples, clearly signalled the multiple histories and geographies that black subjects brought to the colonial metropolis, but by not staking a claim for national inclusion her work was not readily recognised as black and British. Indeed, despite significant and sustained critical attention directed at recovering earlier writers and thereby making visible the longer trajectory of black British literature, the imprint of 1948 as a founding moment of black British life and literary expression remains remarkably resilient.

Given that the tenacity of the post-World War II narrative around the emergence of black British writing cannot be explained by the evidence of literary cultures or publications involving West Indian and South Asian

[11] Una Marson, 'Friendliness in War Time'. Ms. 1944b. Una Marson Collection, National Library of Jamaica, Jamaica.
[12] Andrea Levy, *Small Island* (London: Review, 2004), 117.
[13] *The Forum Quarterly* (Barbados, 1934), 22.

writers – both of which are far more extensive and expansive than the Windrush rubric and canon represent – it remains to ask when and why this compressed focus emerged. A more satisfying explanation for the mythic status accorded to this moment and these writers surfaces when we consider the nexus of political and cultural narratives that have retrospectively shaped the historical meaning of Windrush as a transition point from 'black in Britain' to 'black British' in terms of both identity and writing. There were important factors that made 1948 a noteworthy year in terms of migration, multiculturalism, and minority rights in Britain, creating a powerful correspondence with the *SS Windrush*. The 1948 British Nationality Act gave British citizen status to all Commonwealth subjects and confirmed their right to settle and to take employment in the UK. These legal entitlements allowed for the imagined prospect of a nation being co-created by its colonial subjects who arrived in significant numbers during the 1950s, usually with a prior sense of cultural belonging to a fictional England imagined via Shakespeare, Wordsworth, and Dickens.

While this expansion of citizenship may reflect Britain changing its story of itself, for those writers who travelled during the late 1940s and 1950s in search of professional authorship and the publishers, readers, and reviewers needed to sustain a writing career, Britain was still often neither their subject nor their primary concern. Those often identified as the Windrush generation from the 1950s onwards – Wilson Harris (1921–2018), George Lamming (1927–), Roger Mais (1905–1955), Edgar Mittelholzer (1909–1965), V. S. Naipaul (1932–2018), Andrew Salkey (1928–1995), and Samuel Selvon (1923–1994) – produced writing that mainly focused on imaginatively resisting the coloniser's perception of Caribbean people and places. When their literary works did bring attention to British life it was often in a discomforting and deliberately difficult fashion. Lamming's 1971 *Water with Berries* and Salkey's 1960 *Escape to an Autumn Pavement* both rendered the West Indian encounter with Britain in abrasive, extreme terms that could not be recognised or purposed as narratives of national accommodation. Works like Harris's 1960 *Palace of the Peacock*, with its dazzling magical realism and Guyanese world-view, and Mittelholzer's 1950 *A Morning at the Office*, with its modernist poetics and irreverent, brash depiction of ethnic stereotyping in Trinidad, issued a serious challenge to the literary definition of the novel in English. These writers' assured sense of their distinctive contribution was far removed from a call for accommodation to the imperial centre. Their works collectively foregrounded literary ingenuity and cultural particularity, as well as the linguistic force of knowing and accomplished vernacular

Englishes – traits also found in the work of South Asian writers of this same period such as Nirad Chaudhuri (1897–1999), M. J. Tambimuttu (1915–1983), Mulk Raj Anand (1905–2004), Attia Hosain (1913–1998), Raja Rao (1908–2006), and Aubrey Menen (1912–1989). Although the pluralising of black British culture through the intersections and commonalities between writers of West Indian and South Asian descent came as a later gesture, provoked by the compelling need for political solidarities and a move away from essentialising and discriminatory discourses, works by these earlier generations provide critical insights into the transnational exchanges and aesthetics shaping black British subjectivities quite differently to the Windrush 'arrival' template.

How the Myth Was Made

So if at this turning point in Britain's historical entanglements with its colonies, which Louise Bennett famously coined as 'Colonization in Reverse',[14] literary efforts did not centre on the realities and challenges of becoming black British, how did the Windrush myth take such hold? It would seem that what is now characterised as 'Windrush writing' was in fact styled both by critics and publishers in the 1980s and 1990s as a way of defining and affirming the black British experience within a climate of exclusionary nationalism. As Chris Weedon explains, it was the experience of institutional racism and other forms of violence and discrimination (as well as the first political efforts at developing inclusive multicultural policies) that emphasised the relevance of articulating and bringing visibility to the interrelated terms 'black' and 'British'.[15] The changing political landscape, anti-immigration rhetoric, and the racism of Enoch Powell and the National Front in the 1970s, followed by Thatcherism with its politics of exclusion and institutional racism in the 1980s, brought into sharp focus the task of representing and claiming a place for black subjects in Britain – a task that remains incomplete, as starkly revealed by the 2018 scandal of state derecognition for Windrush descendants. The 1971 Immigration Act that insisted on a prior family link to the UK for residency and the 1981 British Nationality Act created three categories of citizenship that effectively ended primary

---

[14] Louise Bennett, *Jamaica Labrish* (Kingston, Jamaica: Sangsters, 1966), 179. For a rich discussion of Bennett's poem 'Colonization in Reverse' see Denise deCaires Narain's *Contemporary Caribbean Women's Poetry: Making Style* (London: Routledge, 2004).

[15] Chris Weedon, 'British Black and Asian Writing Since 1980' in Deirdre Osborne (ed.), *The Cambridge Companion to British Black and Asian Literature: (1945–2010)* (Cambridge: Cambridge University Press, 2016), 40–56; 40–4.

immigration for Commonwealth citizens. With the rise of exclusionary politics constructed through a notion of Britishness rooted in white ethnicity, works that represented the social realities of being black in Britain came to the fore.

Many of the scholarly texts published in the 1980s addressed themselves to the need to recover and to record those black lives now in danger not only of misrepresentation and erasure but also of their violent consequences.[16] Creative attention was also increasingly negotiating the difficulties of being black and British. Most memorably, Linton Kwesi Johnson (1952–) in *Dread Beat and Blood* (1975) and *Inglan is a Bitch* (1980) combined literary activism and a lyrical, urban counter-history to articulate – to a reggae beat – the frustration and struggle of black youth against a hostile British establishment. *The Heart of the Race: Black Women's Lives in Britain* (1985), edited by Beverly Bryan, Stella Dadzie, and Suzanne Scafe, combined testimony, poetry, and cultural history to bring forward the situation of black women in Britain within a clear historical context of centuries of exploitation and racism.

The favoured focus on metropolitan experiences of migration shaped the emergent canonicity of certain narratives from the Windrush generation. Not only is the most popular novel in Selvon's Moses trilogy, *The Lonely Londoners* (1956), now 'the' foundational text in the corpus of Windrush literature with its episodic depiction of the animated urban encounters of West Indian men, but readers may not even know of *Moses Ascending* (1975) and *Moses Migrating* (1983) where Moses attempts to reconnect with his Caribbean home. It is also the case that several significant writers and their works that did not engage the British experience directly, such as John Hearne, fell out of critical sight. Most notable among these are nine novels by Roy Heath who lived in Britain for over fifty years and whose work, *The Murderer*, won *The Guardian* fiction prize in 1978.

Attempts at consolidating the presence and value of black British subjects and voices peaked in the fiftieth anniversary year and in 1998 Windrush came ashore to play a lasting role in the place-making of black British history. The 1997 election of New Labour engendered another decisive shift in the context

---

[16] See Fryer, *Staying Power*; Paul Gilroy, *There Ain't No Black in the Union Jack* (London: Routledge, [1987] 2010); Bill Ashcroft, Gareth Griffiths, and Helen Tiffin, *The Empire Writes Back: Theory and Practice in Post-Colonial Literatures* (London: Routledge, [1987] 2010); Salman Rushdie's critical essays 'The New Empire within Britain' (1982) and 'A General Election' (1988) in *Imaginary Homelands: Essays and Criticism 1981–1991* (London: Vintage, [1991] 2010), 129–38 and 159–62; and R. Victoria Arana, 'Sea Change: Historicizing the Scholarly Study of Black British Writing' in R. Victoria Arana. and Lauri Ramey (eds.), *Black British Writing* (New York: Palgrave Macmillan, 2009), 19–46.

of national redefinition, and the imaginative possibilities of inclusive and diverse communities were revived. But in the wake of the Stephen Lawrence enquiry (see Chapter 25), such hopes unfolded cautiously in the full knowledge of the racialised violence and continued injustice of British institutions. Several publications capturing postwar Caribbean migration refreshed the link between personal narrative and national belonging that Kitchener had inaugurated. *Windrush: The Irresistible Rise of Multi-Racial Britain* (1998), edited by Mike Phillips (1941–) and Trevor Phillips (1953–), drew together personal accounts by known authors and unknown passengers alongside archival material from media, governmental, and institutional sources. Vivienne Francis's *With Hope in their Eyes* (1998) similarly collated the testimonies of those whose hopes and expectations were often unfulfilled. Tony Sewell's *Keep on Moving: The Windrush Legacy* (1998) afforded comprehensive coverage of the influential role that writers and artists played in recording black British history through their work. Onyekachi Wambu's 1998 anthology *Hurricane Hits England: An Anthology of Writing About Britain* gathered poetry, short fiction, excerpts from novels, and essays to represent an extended timeline of Windrush experience. This hallmarking of black British history through Windrush affirms Matthew Mead's argument for the way in which a partial and selective history of immigration comes to stand as 'the' inaugurating history that 'validates and values the arrival and continuing presence of a Caribbean community'.[17]

The connections between this scripted past and present were further marked in 1998 by a number of creative commissions weaving Windrush into the contemporary scene of black British writing. The BBC commissioned works by John Agard (1949–), Jackie Kay (1961–), and Benjamin Zephaniah (1958–). Agard's commission, a poem titled 'Remember the Ship', plays on the ability of *Windrush*, a literal ship, to transform understandings of citizenship and kinship in a revival of the Windrush spirit of inclusive belonging. Zephaniah's poem 'The Men from Jamaica are Settling Down' takes its title from Fryer's follow-up article on those who had arrived on the *Windrush*, and seeks to celebrate and activate the memory of Windrush as a foundational event for black Britons in the present. Both works gesture to the importance of bringing Windrush back into historical consciousness as a reminder of migrant dreams and the ongoing hopes for (and obstacles to) social inclusion. Kay's story 'Out of Hand' is a much more

---

[17] Matthew Mead, 'Empire Windrush: The Cultural Memory of an Imaginary Arrival', *Journal of Postcolonial Writing*, 45:2, (2009): 137–49; 144.

intimate Windrush account narrated by Rose McGuire Roberts as she thinks back over her fifty years in England and 'that huge fiction of a ship'.[18] Her memories of her initial excitement to be coming 'home' and the thrill of seeing herself captured on the Pathé newsreel disembarking from the *Windrush* when she makes her first visit to an English cinema are tempered by those of the following years when Rose had to resign herself to demeaning supporting roles in a racist British society. Despite being a skilled nurse, she was allocated night shifts and the unskilled work of emptying bedpans. Unlike Agard's and Zephaniah's works, Kay's story presents an internal monologue of what was consciously unrecorded by the Windrush generation: 'She would never tell her twin granddaughters about all that now. She doesn't want them to know. She didn't even tell her own children.'[19]

Expanding the Windrush Literary World

While Kay's work fictionally restored the unrecorded experience of the Windrush woman, the retrospective construction of a Windrush canon has been especially limited in terms of its masculine bias. George Lamming's 1960 classic *The Pleasures of Exile* portrays the West Indian literary scene in London as an almost exclusively male enterprise, failing to acknowledge and represent the intellectual engagement and contribution of women writers. Jo Stanley's recent research has established that of the 492 West Indian passengers on board the *Windrush*, there were '45 women settlers and 25 "maybes", coming from Trinidad, Jamaica and Bermuda to make a new life'.[20] Apart from the daring female stowaway on the SS *Windrush*, the historical traces of these women and of black women writers in Britain from the 1940s through the 1960s have almost slipped from view.

Black Teacher (1976) by Beryl Gilroy (1924–2001) and *Brown Face, Big Master* (1969) by Joyce Gladwell (1931–) are two memoirs that have only recently received wider critical attention, even though they engage centrally with the issues that have defined the Windrush experience. Donette Francis discusses how Gilroy, who came to Britain from Guyana in 1951, waited a decade to garner interest in her autobiography after many editors rejected it for being 'too psychological'.[21] This dismissal again corroborates the template of black

---

[18] Jackie Kay, 'Out of Hand', *Soundings*, 10 (Autumn 1998): 103.   [19] Ibid., 102.

[20] Stanley's research also draws attention to the difference in cost and company that female travellers experienced. Jo Stanley, 'Women of Windrush: Britain's Adventurous Arrivals that History Forgot', *New Statesman*, 22 June 2018. Available at www.newstatesman.com/politics/uk/2018/06/women-windrush-britain-s-adventurous-arrivals-history-forgot.

[21] Donette Francis, '"Neither Pathological nor Perfect": Joyce Gladwell's Late Autobiographical Challenge to the Windrush Generation' in J. Dillon Brown and

British narrative which fashioned the Windrush story from a much more eventful and assorted literary history. It also points to the negatively gendered assumptions around autobiography that second-wave feminism would take up with its rallying call: 'the personal is political'. In fact, no phrase is more accurate in its description of *Black Teacher*, as Gilroy explains: 'My autobiography resulted from a fit of pique. After hearing the older generation of blacks in Britain being pilloried as "Topsies and Toms", I decided to set the record straight. There had been Ted Braithwaite's *To Sir, With Love* and Don Hind's *Journey to an Illusion*, but a woman's experiences had never been published'.[22] It is also not insignificant that when women's writing is included in Windrush narratives it is on the same terms of migration and the metropole. Tellingly, Beryl Gilroy's 1989 novel *Boy Sandwich* and her 1996 *In Praise of Love and Children* have received most critical attention alongside novels by Joan Riley (1958–), *The Unbelonging* (1985) and *Romance* (1988), whereas those with a more Caribbean focus such as Gilroy's 1986 *Frangipani House* and Riley's 1987 *Waiting in the Twilight* remain marginal.

Given the exclusion of women from the dominant Windrush narrative and canon, it is interesting that younger, British-born women writers have returned to the experience of migration that underpins their parental heritage by consciously looking for ways to resist the orthodox story of Windrush. In *Connecting Medium* Dorothea Smartt (1963–) invokes the seamstress figure to represent the second generation's literary task of crafting something distinctive and new from the material of that iconic ship and its settlers: 'dreaming to change the pattern, / undo the seams, re-style / the suits you wore / as you step off the boat, / Windrush style'.[23] Bernardine Evaristo (1959–) reimagines the fabric of Windrush narratives in order to tell a queer history in *Mr Loverman* (2013). This novel delivers a fresh perspective on the striking homosociality of Selvon's *The Lonely Londoners* and reminds us again of the notable critical silence which met Andrew Salkey's 1960 novel *Escape to an Autumn Pavement* – a fascinating narrative that queered the story of metropolitan migration. A differently gendered recovery informs *Kitch* (2018) by Anthony Joseph (1966–), a wonderfully textured narrative that draws on both fact and fiction to restore the story of Lord Kitchener's diasporic life and career, set mainly between Trinidad and the UK.[24] Drawing on the

Leah Reade Rosenberg (eds.), *Beyond Windrush: Rethinking Postwar Anglophone Caribbean Literature* (Jackson, MS: University Press of Mississippi, 2015), 97–112; 99.

[22] Beryl Gilroy, *Black Teacher* (London: Cassell, 1976), 199.

[23] Dorothea Smartt, *Connecting Medium* (Leeds: Peepal Tree Press, 2001), 12.

[24] Anthony Joseph, *Kitch* (Leeds: Peepal Tree Press, 2018).

testimonies of friends and rivals, as well as archival material like newspaper clippings, *Kitch* shows how such a life comes to be known and told from multiple perspectives in different places and times. With respect to a rebalancing of historical accounts, an important dimension of the inclusive ethics of this work is its focus on Kitchener's wife Marjorie, a white Irish woman, and the barriers to inclusion she faces in Trinidad.

The expansion of black British literary studies within university curricula also reinscribed Windrush as a mythic unified literary tradition. As Hannah Lowe points out, 'Post-1998 literary criticism often retells the arrival of the *Windrush* as a straightforward contextualising strategy and some critics employ the metonymic construction of "Windrush writers" or "Windrush writing" to collectively describe those writers who migrated to Britain from the Caribbean in the post-war period and pursued literary careers.'[25] This established chronicle of black British literary belonging, in which Windrush holds a defining place, has established a canonical story of migration to Britain, but there is a risk that, as Matthew Mead has observed, 'a history of mobility is in danger of becoming immutable'.[26]

Indeed, the power of the Windrush myth helps to explain the phenomenal success of Andrea Levy's 2004 novel, *Small Island*, chosen as one of the most significant books of that decade by *The Guardian*. This novel garnered huge popular appeal and a BBC television adaptation with its historical focus on World War II and Windrush Britain. For Levy, this fictional turn to her parents' generation was about finding a point of shared national interest through which 'to explore my British Caribbean ancestry, and to place that heritage where I think it belongs – squarely in the mainstream of British history'.[27] Yet the novel also revealed the long history of entwined Jamaican and British histories and identities.

Windrush as Transnational Story

While the *Windrush* is often represented as a ship in the dock, James Procter's research in BBC radio archives has issued a recent reminder that the *Windrush* was itself in motion and had made a 'prior journey to return West Indian war veterans from motherland to homeland'. As Procter goes on to discuss, this fuller context complicates the political inflection of the iconic narrative:

[25] 'Writing the Empire Windrush and Chan' (unpublished PhD thesis, School of English Literature, Languages and Linguistics, Newcastle University, 2016), 33.
[26] Mead 'Empire Windrush', 112.
[27] Andrea Levy, 'Interview', *Mosaic Magazine*, 6 November 2011, n.p.

What has subsequently been understood as a story of postwar influx and accommodation, was also once a story of exodus that points to the wartime presence, and active participation of West Indians (and the wider Commonwealth) in the war effort. With their war wounds and medals, Officers Smythe and Blair are potent embodiments of an alternative Windrush narrative which registers Britain's indebtedness and dependency to its colonies, rather than the other way around.[28]

In fact, archival records at the National Maritime Museum in Greenwich record the itinerary for *Windrush* as sailing from Southampton on 7 May 1948 and calling at Trinidad; Kingston, Jamaica; Tampico, Mexico; Havana, Cuba; and Bermuda before setting sail for Britain. What the *Windrush's* homeward journeying *around* the Caribbean shows is the wider Atlantic context, intra-Caribbean migrations, and the two-way flow of metropolitan–Caribbean journeys through which Caribbean British identities have always been forged whether during the Windrush period or after.

Restoring this more mobile dimension to Windrush reinstates the distinctiveness of Caribbean British narratives in which creative negotiations around the production of identity are not solely focused on Britain. In an interview with Kwame Dawes, the Jamaican/black British poet James Berry (1924–2017) addressed the inherently multiply-located nature of his Windrush identity:

> the Caribbean landscape holds me. But at the same time, I realize that I have been very much enmeshed with England. The experiences of these two landscapes hold me to their histories, both with agonies and a love I must not allow to get swamped by pain. I feel I must somehow try and link these two places together, as my home on earth.[29]

Unlike the commissioned engagements with this history, Berry's 2007 poetry collection *Windrush Songs* is a personal tribute to his own 1950s generation and tells a self-consciously Caribbean story. As Berry explains: 'It was a way of going back and retrieving my Caribbean experience [. . .] a way of hearing and preserving Caribbean village voices, of juxtaposing them. I found these characters in myself.'[30]

---

[28] James Procter, 'Wireless Writing, World War II and the West Indian Literary Imagination' in Gill Plain (ed.), *Postwar: British Literature in Transition, 1940–1960* (Cambridge: Cambridge University Press, 2018), 117–35; 135.

[29] Kwame Dawes (ed.), *Talk Yuh Talk: Interviews with Anglophone Caribbean Poets* (Charlottesville, VA: University of Virginia Press, 2001), 5–6.

[30] James Berry, *Windrush Songs* (Tarset: Bloodaxe Books, 2007), 11.

Interestingly, in this work Britain figures more as an imagined destination, with just four of the fifty-two poems relating to 'New Days Arriving'. As a whole, the collection traces the poverty and resilience of Jamaican life, the tidal emotions of disillusionment with Jamaica, and the expectations of England that swell the pushes and pulls of migration dreams, the loss of a homeland's natural hold when at sea, and the aspirations for status, money, and historical reconnection in the motherland. Berry's sense of Caribbean British migration is holistic, expressing how it is experienced in both locations and at sea. It is perhaps telling that, despite the very intimate character of the poetic sketches that give the collection an auto/biographical feel, Berry calls his work *Windrush Songs* when he, in fact, travelled on the *SS Orbita*.

This transatlantic focus on memory, history, and identity connecting both sides of the Atlantic is also poetically evoked by Grace Nichols (1950–) in *Startling the Flying Fish* (2005), an overlooked work which tackles postwar migration as part of the wider, longer Caribbean story of immigration and emigration from all over the globe. Nichols opens with a dedication to 'the memory of my mother who stayed. And to those overseas who still carry the *Cariwoma* spirit',[31] highlighting the ways in which Caribbean and South American folklore, culture, sounds, and memories travel through migration to new places of settlement, and stay with the migrant in ever-present, yet shifting ways. This characterisation of Windrush as a part of a larger history of journeying and cultural mobility is also evident in the critically under-explored 1998 work by Ferdinand Dennis (1956–), *Duppy Conqueror*, and *The Final Passage* (1985), the acclaimed debut novel of Caryl Phillips (1958–).

Whilst the transnational focus emerges strongly in recent Windrush writings, I want to end with a reading of the unheeded pulp fiction *Because They Know Not* (1959). Written by Alvin Gladstone Bennett (1918–2004), a Jamaican journalist who became a social worker in England, this work offers an inventively supple, satirical, and distinctively sociopolitical negotiation of the connections and journeys between Jamaica and Britain during the Windrush years. Described on the front cover as 'a powerful story on the colour problem', and on the back as 'a novel that will long be remembered', this work has not as yet been included in any discussions of Windrush narratives. As it opens, the book witnesses Jamaican Tom Hendon leaning over the rails on the deck of a steamship carrying him away from his beloved homeland, wife, and children to London with its promise of employment and prosperity. The novel's account of Tom's struggle to find work and housing

---

[31] Grace Nichols, *Startling the Flying Fish* (London: Virago, 2005), n.p. Emphasis mine.

in Britain commensurate with his status in Jamaica is familiar enough. However, the narrative's insistent interest in how life in Jamaica is impacted by migration generates a more completely realised Windrush story. While Tom's adjustment to an England that destroys the myth of a welcoming motherland unfolds throughout, a significant portion is also devoted to his wife Emma's life back home. For Emma, a teaching vocation in Jamaica binds her to the myth of the mother country and its colonial bearings. Just as Tom discovers the reality of England, Emma teaches her children the mythic version:

> England was so kind as to send people to take the best jobs in Jamaica. Jamaicans could not rule themselves, and England had to send wise people to administer all the affairs of the country. [...] England had been taking Jamaican workers in her factories, giving them work and treating them nicely altogether. The children learned too, that England was Jamaica's best customer, taking bananas, citrus fruits, spices, rum, cocoa, coffee and all the surplus manpower Jamaica could produce [...]
>
> She felt quite satisfied that she was making them good Jamaican citizens of the future by telling them every good thing about England and nothing about their own country.[32]

As the narrative traces the parallel attempts of Tom and Emma at social progress, both eventually stray into sexual infidelities: Tom with a fellow Jamaican immigrant, Marie, and Emma with the mixed-parentage anglophile school inspector Max Crost. The clashing narratives of Britain's promise of belonging and advancement, narrated from the perspectives of Brixton and Montego Bay, finally collide in melodramatic fashion when Crost is murdered by Marie's husband and Marie dies shortly after delivering Tom's son Rupert. The novel concludes in Jamaica where Emma and Tom return to Kingston's salubrious Upper St Andrew neighbourhood with their 'adopted son' and the social capital ironically accrued through their discouraging time spent in London. After Tom's failed and arrogant foray into Jamaican politics and the revelation that Hilda, the young woman they had hired as Rupert's carer, is actually his sister, the novel turns its focus back onto class hierarchies in colonial Jamaica. Tom and Emma reflect on the way Jamaican society is also divided, prejudiced, and soaked in secrets: 'We speak of the hypocrisy of the English and we are no better.'[33] The novel is also brilliantly subversive in its depiction of women's sexual autonomy, which remains largely undetected

---

[32] Alvin Gladstone Bennett, *Because They Know Not* (London: Phoenix Press, 1959), 42.
[33] Ibid., 159.

by the men in the novel. Its critique of Tom's inflated sense of masculinity, caustically undermined by his mistaken guilt at 'deceiving two simple and sweet angels',[34] is a refreshing corrective to the masculine-centred narratives of the Windrush canon. Although uninterested in being a literary master-piece, Bennett's forgotten novel presents a curiously rewarding combination of melodrama and satire to foreground the serious ramifications of Britain's false promise of belonging.

The tenacious hold between the history of black peoples' lives in Britain and 'Windrush' has been forged by the privileged status this ship and its passengers accrued across cultural and political narratives. Even within literary historical accounts, those publications that challenge the primacy of the Windrush generation, looking both *Before* and *Beyond*, repeat and thereby ratify Windrush as the primary historical marker.[35] There is no doubt that this focus has created a powerful myth of origin, sustained by retrospective investments in its landmark status in articulating the journey towards black British belonging, and that this myth has held other stories and voices in abeyance. All the same, the force this signifier has gathered within historical memory has enabled a vital space for the discussion of black British migra-tion, life, and cultural contributions to be carved out. The inclusion of Windrush in the historical timelines promoted by the British Library, the BBC, and the Imperial War Museum suggest its confirmed place within institutional/official versions of national history. All the same, revelations in April 2018 regarding the British government's hostile treatment of the children of the Windrush generation, who have been denied their right to employment, healthcare, and settlement, indicate an enduring institutiona-lised racism seventy years after *Windrush* docked.[36]

What is perhaps more valuable than contesting the dominant focus on Windrush is paying due attention to the continued task of releasing and recognising the long-standing and multidimensional history of black British writings that have engaged the realities and the myths around migration and citizenship. The literary value of these works in terms of innovation, whether in form or language, should also not be downplayed in favour of their social relevance. For it is often in their aesthetic experimentations that black British

---

[34] Ibid., 105.

[35] See Rastogi and Stitt (eds.), *Before Windrush* and Brown and Rosenberg (eds.), *Beyond Windrush*.

[36] See www.theguardian.com/uk-news/2018/apr/20/the-week-that-took-windrush-from-low-profile-investigation-to-national-scandal and www.theguardian.com/commentis free/2018/apr/20/theresa-may-windrush-equality.

literary works are able to shift the terms and scope of political and historical literacies most powerfully – from Caryl Phillips's *Cambridge* (1991), to Zadie Smith's *White Teeth* (2000), and Anthony Joseph's *The African Origins of UFOs* (2006).

A more inclusive account of the diversity of creative voices that founded and continued the project to articulate the identities and histories of West Indians and South Asians, women and men, queer and non-binary subjects would clearly enrich and thicken the assemblage of black Britishness for which Windrush is usually tasked to speak. The continued urgency of representing black lives in Britain as equal, consequential, and irreplaceable – some seventy years after Windrush – speaks volumes about the compromised and hesitant nature of official discourses around immigration and multiethnic life in Britain today. The momentary and heady promise of national co-belonging that Windrush captured is conspicuously nostalgic from the vantage point of 2019. The rise in racist and anti-immigrant rhetoric in the wake of the Brexit vote to leave the European Union threatens to establish a thicker wedge of insecurity and tension between being black and being British. For recent immigrants to Britain whose belonging is contested, the camp has replaced the ship and the spectre of indefinite detention and state tracking mount obstacles to accommodation unimagined by Windrush migrants. In this context, the ongoing project of researching, voicing, and acclaiming the long-standing and inclusive tradition of black British writings and writers remains vital. The creative power of the Windrush myth to reprise the successful, if hard won, reality of Britain as a multiethnic nation is understandably compelling but shifting our gaze backwards and forwards from the fulcrum of the Windrush moment enables a much richer appreciation of black lives lived and denied, stories told and untold, solidarities built and broken. This knowledge not only provides the fabric of future narratives, but it confirms that stories matter and that building cultural literacy by rendering black British lives on their own terms can work to challenge exclusionary world-views and enable new grammars of national belonging to take shape.

13

Double Displacements, Diasporic Attachments

Location and Accommodation

J. DILLON BROWN

The years immediately following World War II mark a crucial period of emergence for black and Asian British writing. Indeed, the era's remarkable profusion of publications by migrant anglophone authors has led critics to apotheosise this moment as the dawn of multiethnic Britain and its literature. The essays in this history cumulatively attest to the incompleteness of such a view: black and Asian people have a long history of both residing and producing literature in Britain.[1] Nevertheless, these postwar years retain a decisive importance to the formation of the more racially, ethnically, and even nationally ecumenical sense of what constitutes 'English literature' today. The themes and preoccupations of these mid-century writers making the voyage into their purported mother country anticipate many of the scholarly debates that currently animate the study of immigrant, postcolonial, and world literatures, while also resonating with contemporary works of British literature, obliged as they are to continue wrestling with issues of identity, belonging, and cultural proprietorship.

The roots of this importance are not hard to locate: due to the British Nationality Act of 1948, which guaranteed British citizenship (and hence undisputed right of entry) to all Commonwealth citizens, as well as official efforts to recruit workers from the colonies and ex-colonies of the Commonwealth in the face of labour shortages caused by World War II, approximately half a million black and Asian people came to Britain to live and work until the restrictive Immigration Act of 1962

---

[1] The classic accounts of the black and Asian presence in Britain are: Peter Fryer, *Staying Power: The History of Black People in Britain* (London: Pluto, 1984) and Rozina Visram, *Asians in Britain: 400 Years of History* (London: Pluto, 2002). For these populations' literary production, see C. L. Innes, *A History of Black and Asian Writing in Britain, 1700–2000* (Cambridge: Cambridge University Press, 2002).

decisively slowed this population transfer.[2] Although proportionally not much different from the non-white population in the eighteenth century,[3] this newly arrived postwar population represented the largest numerical influx of people of colour into Britain in its history, a fact made more perceptible by news stories announcing their arrival in sensationalist terms. The most heralded example is the docking of the former troop transport ship *SS Empire Windrush* at Tilbury on 22 June 1948, carrying 492 passengers from the Caribbean, an event now memorialised as the inaugural moment of a multicultural Britain (see Chapter 12). At the time, there was intense media interest in the story. Indeed, the *Evening Standard* ostentatiously sent a plane out to greet the returning 'sons of Empire' the day before the boat arrived, while the day after, *The Times* provided its report on the ship's landing under the nervous headline 'Jamaicans Arrive to Seek Work'.[4] These two examples emblematise the approach Britain took to this unprecedented mid-century migration, including the symptomatic oscillation between viewing the newcomers as fellow citizens or as exotic outsiders; the anxiety over where these 'dark strangers' (as even the sympathetic sociologist Sheila Patterson dubbed them) would find housing and employment;[5] and, finally, the emphasis placed on the West Indians as the population of primary concern.

By statistical measure, black Caribbean people – who were often mistakenly typecast as 'Jamaican' by the host population – did arrive at this time in much higher numbers, so the enhanced attention accorded them was not entirely unwarranted.[6] In terms of literary production, too, the West Indian migrants have a reasonable claim to prominence: between 1950 and 1962, Caribbean writers published over seventy novels in the United Kingdom,

[2] For a useful policy-oriented overview of immigration in this period, see Randall Hansen, *Citizenship and Immigration in Post-War Britain: The Institutional Origins of a Multicultural Nation* (Oxford; New York: Oxford University Press, 2000). For a more critical account, see Kathleen Paul, *Whitewashing Britain: Race and Citizenship in the Postwar Era* (Ithaca, NY: Cornell University Press, 1997).

[3] Ron Ramdin, *Reimagining Britain: 500 Years of Black and Asian History* (London: Pluto, 1999), 165.

[4] Cited in Sam Walker and Alvin Elcock (eds.), *The Windrush Legacy: Memories of Britain's Post-War Caribbean Immigrants* (London: The Black Cultural Archives, 1998), 5.

[5] Sheila Patterson, *Dark Strangers: A Study of West Indians in London* (Harmondsworth: Penguin, 1963).

[6] Hansen's statistics on Commonwealth immigration indicate substantially more Caribbean migrants than Indian and Pakistani ones – between double and quadruple the total each year, across the 1950s up until right before the 1962 legislation. Hansen, *Citizenship*, 265.

generating outsized interest among postwar British literary commentators and creating something of a 'boom' in West Indian writing.[7] While their Asian and African counterparts in Britain were not inactive during this time, the emergence of a comparatively consolidated set of West Indian authors is unmistakably of a different order. As scholars such as Glyne Griffith and Philip Nanton demonstrate, the decisive factor in the establishment of Caribbean literature in Britain at this time was the British Broadcasting Corporation's radio programme *Caribbean Voices*, an on-air literary magazine broadcast on the Overseas Service.[8] Launched by Una Marson and dynamically edited in succession by Henry Swanzy and V. S. Naipaul, the programme became, as we have seen, an important institutional base for virtually every author of the incipient anglophone Caribbean canon, attracting many of these writers to London and offering a vibrant network of British critics, agents, and publishers with whom to interact.[9] For various reasons, then – not least superior numbers and the devotion of formidable resources from the BBC – Caribbean writers emerged as leading literary figures in this heady postwar period of large-scale migration and anti-colonial organisation.[10]

The Formative Works

From the perspective of the formation of a black and Asian British canon, the foundational texts of this period are undoubtedly *The Emigrants* (1954), by the Barbadian George Lamming (1927–), and *The Lonely Londoners* (1956), by the Trinidadian Sam Selvon (1923–1994). These two novels directly take up the tensions experienced between Commonwealth migrants, expecting to find a warm welcome from what they had been educated to consider their mother country, and their suspicious English hosts, who were wholly unprepared to acknowledge or accept these migrants as equals. Lamming's novel,

---

[7] See the appendix listing West Indian publications in Kenneth Ramchand, *The West Indian Novel and its Background*, 2nd edn (London: Heinemann, 1983).

[8] Glyne Griffith, 'Deconstructing Nationalisms: Henry Swanzy, *Caribbean Voices*, and the Development of West Indian Literature', *Small Axe*, 5:2 (2001): 1–20; Philip Nanton, 'What Does Mr. Swanzy Want – Shaping or Reflecting? An Assessment of Henry Swanzy's Contribution to the Development of Caribbean Literature', *Caribbean Quarterly*, 46:1 (2000): 61–72.

[9] For a sense of the importance of this artistic and economic milieu, see Gail Low, *Publishing the Postcolonial: Anglophone West African and Caribbean Writing in the UK, 1948–1968* (New York: Routledge, 2011).

[10] While the migrant novelists from the Caribbean being published at the time were almost exclusively male, the Windrush generation included women who published later and became important voices, including Beryl Gilroy and Joyce Gladwell.

his second, is a dark, brooding, and fragmented work that follows the experiences of a group of migrants from the Caribbean travelling to England together by boat.[11] The novel delineates the multitudinous differences between the passengers, but shows them united in their shared desire for a more comfortable existence: 'They were all in search of the same thing which in a way they couldn't define. A better break. Broadly speaking it was little more than a desire to survive with a greater assurance of safety.'[12] Close to half the narrative is taken up by the slow journey to Britain, focusing on the fitful, uncertain way in which the passengers come to terms with each other and their shared identity as West Indian colonials suffering the same precarious colonial life.

Their hard-won unity, however, is shattered upon arrival, a point made clear by the novel's depiction of the boat-train to London as an elliptical jumble of snatches of conversation, confused apprehensions, and ominous announcements over the train's PA system. The section ends, aptly enough, in terse, perplexed opacity:

> What, man, what?
> When we get outta this smoke.
> When we get outta this smoke, w'at happen next?
> More smoke.[13]

As the novel continues, these inauspicious beginnings are realised: the titular characters scatter across London, struggling to survive in a claustrophobic and alien landscape.[14] Lamming puts pointed focus on the migrants' interactions with the host community, ranging from the well-meaning but ultimately futile attempts at sociability between a black West Indian character and a white English factory owner, to the horrifying sexual objectification of another black character by his white English landlady. The book ends on a dark note, with one of the emigrant characters driving away a newly arrived group of fellow emigrants led by a former shipmate hoping to find them shelter for a night. Although it contains numerous tenuous moments of

---

[11] It is requisite to note here that, famously, the Afro-Barbadian Lamming and the Indo-Trinidadian Selvon travelled together on the same boat to Britain in 1950. Traces of their friendship can be found in his novel's depiction of the sea journey.

[12] George Lamming, *The Emigrants* (Ann Arbor, MI: University of Michigan Press, [1954] 1994), 86.

[13] Lamming, *Emigrants*, 125.

[14] James Procter details how these novels take place in the cramped, dark physical surroundings in which postwar immigrants were typically compelled to live. See James Procter, *Dwelling Places: Postwar Black British Writing* (Manchester: Manchester University Press, 2003).

almost grasped possibility, *The Emigrants* ultimately emphasises, quite literally, the lack of accommodation made for its new arrivals, suggesting that the stresses of migrant life in London fracture even the most intuitive in-group solidarities.

Selvon's representation of these mid-century migrants is markedly different from Lamming's in style and tone, but the issues raised in his novel are consonant.[15] *The Lonely Londoners*, too, tracks the tenuous communal ties of migrants as they struggle to find jobs, housing, and acceptance in the urban swirl of postwar London. The novel's characters have rightly been celebrated for the trickster's verve and wit with which they address the unfriendly white world they encounter, and Selvon's mode – as it is in a later, slighter novel on a similar topic, *The Housing Lark* (1965) – is largely comic. Nevertheless, the book closes, as Lamming's does, with a profound sense of alienation and centrifugal isolation. Sitting by the Thames, the central figure, Moses, observes:

> he could see a great aimlessness, a great restless, swaying movement that leaving you standing in the same spot. As if a forlorn shadow of doom fall on all the spades in the country. As if he could see the black faces, bobbing up and down in the millions of white, strained faces, everybody hustling along the Strand, the spades jostling in the crowd, bewildered, hopeless.[16]

While some redemption may be found in the fact that Moses has finally taken a step back to consider the dire situation of himself and his fellow migrants (who, as the title suggests, do lay some claim to belonging in the city), the sharp notes of despair are hard to dispel.[17] Even the book's famous 'summer-is-hearts' episode, a gushing, unpunctuated, ten-page paean to the sensory and amatory delights of London as summer arrives, is laced through with alarming accounts of racist objectification and exploitative sex, ending when 'Moses sigh a long sigh like a man who live life and see nothing at all in it and who frighten as the years go by wondering what it is all about.'[18] Deceptively light-hearted, *The Lonely Londoners* at its base portrays its roster of characters as barely subsisting in a cold, alien city, too distracted with basic survival to build anything more prosperous or permanent.

---

[15] Interestingly, Selvon's novel scrupulously refuses to identify the race or ethnicity of its protagonists, prefiguring the 1970s British understanding of blackness as a coalition of people of African and Asian descent. Most of his Caribbean-set writings, however, engage explicitly with Indianness and the complexities of South Asian diasporic identity.

[16] Samuel Selvon, *The Lonely Londoners* (Harlow: Longman, [1956] 1985), 141–2.

[17] Kenneth Ramchand, 'An Introduction to this Novel' in Selvon, *Londoners*, 3–21.

[18] Selvon, *Londoners*, 110.

Together with Lamming's influential collection of bitingly honest, experimental essays, *The Pleasures of Exile* (1960), *The Emigrants* and *The Lonely Londoners* mark an important milestone in black and Asian British writing, mixing the period's rising anti-colonial energies with a clear look at the state of Britain from putative visitors who nevertheless had both the official political status and the cultural training to qualify as insiders. Caryl Phillips, the St Kitts-born, Leeds-raised author, has named Selvon and Lamming as crucial 'literary antecedents', enthusing that 'Those of my generation who were going to write found in the work of these two authors recognisable subject-matter and a restlessness associated with formal invention, which meant that there was no longer any necessity for us to keep looking to New Jersey or Chicago or Detroit for our literary fixes.'[19] By juxtaposing Lamming and Selvon with African American writers, Phillips's endorsement already presumes the two authors should be thought of as black British. He goes on to celebrate them as 'writers who knew not only the names of the flora and fauna, but [. . .] also knew the pages of London's *A-Z*. They knew also the front and back door of the BBC.'[20] Moreover, Phillips singles out the experimental leanings of Lamming and Selvon, a crucial feature of their canonical importance. The two authors approach this differently, but in both cases the visible experimentalism of the writing works to register the constructedness of any – and thus, pointedly, of British – identity.[21] This aspect of Lamming's novel manifests primarily in its halting, elliptical, multiperspectival mode of presentation, which lays bare the workings of ideology on individual consciousness and action in even the most quotidian events. Selvon's novel, on the other hand, advances its point via the carefully fabricated vernacular Caribbean language of its narration: while the language asserts a marked syntactical difference from standard English, it also never fully violates the normative rules that allow its enunciations to be comprehensible to anglophone readers.[22] A key moment in this regard emerges in the novel when Galahad, one of Selvon's central characters, responds to a British woman's complaint that she is having trouble understanding him with the riposte: 'What wrong with it? [. . .] Is English we

---

[19] Caryl Phillips, *A New World Order* (New York: Vintage, [2001] 2002), 237.

[20] Ibid. Although Selvon would best be described as an Indo-Trinidadian, Phillips seems here to understand the two West Indian authors within the 1970s British conception of blackness (i.e. including both Asian and African descent).

[21] For examinations of the important experimental investments of the Windrush authors, see J. Dillon Brown, *Migrant Modernism: Postwar London and the West Indian Novel* (Charlottesburg, VA: University of Virginia Press, 2013) and Simon Gikandi, *Writing in Limbo: Modernism and Caribbean Literature* (Ithaca, NY: Cornell University Press, 1992).

[22] See also Sarah Lawson Welsh's discussion of vernacular in Chapter 20.

speaking.'[23] Here, with Galahad's syntax standing partially athwart the English of his interlocutor, Selvon slyly suggests a foundational mutability at the heart of the English language, with English and Caribbean people seen as collaborators in its continued evolution.

In this way, Selvon's novel resembles that of his fellow diasporic South Asian, G. V. Desani (1909–2000), whose 1948 novel *All About H. Hatterr* was perhaps the most celebrated Indian-authored book in mid-century Britain.[24] Reminiscent of Laurence Sterne (and providing inspiration, most famously, to Salman Rushdie), Desani's text is an exuberant, linguistically playful account of its titular character's serio-comic pursuit of truth via conversations with seven Indian sages. The novel's ludic linguistic incursion on English is made plain in the narrator H. Hatterr's account of his decision to go to England: 'All my life I wanted to come: come to the Western shores, to my old man's Continent, to the Poet-Bard's adored Eldorado, to England, to God's own country, the seat of Mars, that damme paradise, to Rev. the Head's mother and fatherland, to the Englishman's home, his Castle, his garden, fact's, the feller's true alma mammy and apple-orchard.'[25] Gleefully mixing together garbled clichés and literary allusions – and implicitly calling the English both warmongers and mamma's boys – Desani expresses a pointed politics of language, representing, in Rushdie's view, Anglo-Indian literature's 'first genuine effort to go beyond the Englishness of the English language'.[26] Like Selvon's, Desani's novel works to relativise and deflate the pomposity of received English, arguing instead for a more freewheeling, ecumenical sense of how the language might work, and for whom. At stake, as in so much black and Asian British writing, is what kind of language – and hence what view of the world – gets consecrated as appropriately literary.[27]

Other Currents

A different sort of engagement with cultural accommodation is played out in the writing of E. R. Braithwaite (1912–2016), an understudied, but extremely

---

[23] Selvon, *Londoners*, 93.

[24] Desani was actually born in Kenya but spent two periods of time resident in Britain, as a young man in the late 1920s into the 1930s, and then again in the 1940s until his return to India in 1952. For further discussion of Desani, see Chapter 7.

[25] G. V. Desani, *All About H. Hatterr* (New York: Farrar, Straus, and Giroux, [1948] 1970), 36.

[26] Salman Rushdie, 'Introduction' in Salman Rushdie and Elizabeth West (eds.), *Mirrorwork: 50 Years of Indian Writing 1947–1997* (New York: Henry Holt, 1997), vii–xx; xvi.

[27] For an insightful, contextualised overview of Desani and other early Asian British writers' work, see the first chapter in Susheila Nasta, *Home Truths: Fictions of the South Asian Diaspora in Britain* (Basingstoke: Palgrave, 2002).

popular writer at the time. Instead of highlighting the contingency or mutability of English mores, Braithwaite's works suggest that it is the English *themselves* who fail to embody them, in sharp contrast to the nation's colonial subjects, whose education had immersed them enduringly in such values. Braithwaite's first and most famous book, *To Sir, With Love* (later made into a highly successful film starring Sidney Poitier), appeared in 1959, and it manifests the unusual combination of conservatism and forthright honesty regarding race relations that typifies his writing. A non-fiction work based on his own experience as a highly educated, former Royal Air Force pilot in London after the war, the book traces Braithwaite's time as a teacher at a poor, East End secondary school, a post he is obliged to take after being consistently denied higher paid work (for which he is particularly trained) owing to racism. The book's opening scene captures Braithwaite's amused superciliousness towards London's white working class, as well as the racial tensions his presence provokes. On a bus to the school, the narrator describes the 'overload of noisy, earthy charwomen it had collected on its run through the city – thick armed, bovine women, huge breasted, with heavy bodies irrevocably distorted by frequent childbearing', wondering, with some obvious condescension, at 'the essential naturalness of these folk who were an integral part of one of the world's greatest cities and at the same time as common as hayseeds'.[28] Braithwaite here positions himself as the haughty (and typically patriarchal) observer and thus reverses the traveller-native motif typical of imperial travel narratives, exoticising and universalising what the book figures as metropolitan peasants.[29] Immediately after, however, his narrator is confronted with the racial power of whiteness, when a newly embarked passenger pointedly refuses to sit in the empty seat adjacent to him. To this affront – as with others he records – the narrator responds with restrained dignity, and the narrative arc of the book takes shape as one in which students and even fellow teachers are eventually cowed by the narrator's well-bred propriety into modifying their own comportment towards him, finally accepting him, as the title implies, as somebody worthy of respect and admiration. Here, albeit from a particular class

---

[28] E. R. Braithwaite, *To Sir, With Love* (Englewood Cliffs, NJ: Prentice-Hall, 1959), 1, 3.

[29] Joshua [Jed] Esty, *A Shrinking Island: Modernism and National Culture in England* (Princeton, NJ: Princeton University Press, 2003) observes this kind of oppositional anthropological lens employed in the London-based works of Lamming and Selvon as well. For further discussions of exoticism and modes of representation, see Chapters 2 and 5 in this volume.

perspective, Braithwaite asserts that it is the English who actually need to be taught what it means to be English.

From a literary perspective, Braithwaite's most intriguing contribution in this vein remains his 1965 novel, *Choice of Straws*. While it takes up the same theme of embattled cross-racial understanding, it departs from his non-fictional, autobiographical works by adopting the voice of a young white working-class man, Jack, as the book's narrator. A predominantly stream-of-consciousness narration, the novel traces Jack's progression from a thoughtless tough who beats up (and, as the story opens, accidentally kills) solitary 'spades' to a self-conscious, inept wooer of a posh, British-born black woman. Braithwaite takes pains to illustrate the many complexities of race relations of the time and underscores the subtle (and not-so-subtle) hurdles to interracial comity at mid-century. While somewhat condescending towards the naivety and intellectual obtuseness of its poorly educated narrator, the novel nevertheless shows Jack slowly emerging into awareness of the basic humanity – and complex British identities – of the nation's black and Asian subjects. At one point, Jack realises how much he has overlooked due to racism, thinking to himself:

> I'd see Spades, lots of them, but all that happened was that, well, it sort of registered that there was a black face, but I didn't want to look at it, to see if it was young or old or handsome or ugly or happy or sad. Even when we'd knocked some fellow about I merely saw his blackness, not any feature.[30]

Earlier, on a tube train and eavesdropping on a set of schoolgirls (one black, the rest white), Jack realises with a shock the essential Englishness of those he has considered Other: 'A tight, closed group, the Spade as much a part of it as any other. And funny to hear the ordinary English voice coming out of her. Just to make sure I closed my eyes, and they all sounded alike.'[31] Braithwaite thus offers up an early instance in literature of the inexorable logic of national identity slowly forming across racial and ethnic lines as the second generation of Commonwealth-descended people comes to maturity. Of equal interest, Braithwaite's bold authorial decision to ventriloquise a white narrative voice marks a confident claim to his own sense of belonging, whatever the external resistance to recognising it.[32]

---

[30] E. R. Braithwaite, *Choice of Straws* (Indianapolis, IN: Bobbs-Merrill Company, [1965] 1966), 84.

[31] Braithwaite, *Choice of Straws*, 78.

[32] Braithwaite's efforts in this novel contrast interestingly with those of the white English author Colin MacInnes, who wrote several novels about the influx of black migrants to Britain but always from a native English narrative perspective. See especially

Displacement and Disaffection

The resistance, of course, was not inconsiderable, as many literary works of the era reveal, and Britain's new residents from Africa, Asia, and the West Indies experienced substantial amounts of prejudice, ignorance, and rejection in a place they had been educated to believe was the centre of enlightened, humane civilisation.[33] Mike and Trevor Phillips describe migrants' feeling of being 'more or less crushed by the country's indifference, coupled as it was with casual discrimination'.[34] More devastatingly, as Lamming has Collis express it in *The Emigrants*, for these newcomers 'there was a feeling [. . .] that England was not only a place but a heritage. Some of us might have expressed a certain hostility to that heritage, but it remained, nevertheless a hostility to something that was already a part of us.'[35] It is to this intimate betrayal that Braithwaite's works register such a poignant protest, and their palpable sense of indignation underscores the double sense of displacement felt by black and Asian migrants to Britain: not only were they removed from their original homes, but they were also made to feel alien in their new one, despite all the political, educational, and cultural preparation for belonging the colonial system had inculcated in them. Edward Kamau Brathwaite (1930–) makes a similar point in describing his initial arrival in England: 'When I saw my first snowfall I felt that I had come into my own; I had arrived; I was possessing the landscape. But I turned to find that my "fellow Englishmen" were not particularly prepossessed with me.'[36] As Brathwaite archly suggests here, the triumphant sense of returning to the birthright of the colonial subject's putative mother country was quickly dispelled by the indifference – and often the active hostility – of the natives.

Brought up to be 'a potential Afro-Saxon',[37] Brathwaite met with such resistance and apathy in Britain that he turned instead to Africa for succour.

Colin MacInnes, *City of Spades* (London: MacGibbon & Kee, 1957) and *Absolute Beginners* (London: MacGibbon & Kee, 1959).

[33] Histories and sociological works also delineate the struggles endured by postwar migrants of colour in Britain. For first-hand accounts, see Henri Tajfel and John L. Dawson (eds.), *Disappointed Guests: Essays by African, Asian, and West Indian Students* (London: Oxford University Press, 1965) and Donald Hinds, *Journey to an Illusion: The West Indian in Britain* (London: Heinemann, 1966).

[34] Mike Phillips and Trevor Phillips, *Windrush: The Irresistible Rise of Multi-Racial Britain* (London: HarperCollins, 1998), 96. This book, too, provides a wealth of first-hand accounts of the migrant experience.

[35] Lamming, *Emigrants*, 237.

[36] Edward Brathwaite, 'Timehri' in Orde Coombs (ed.), *Is Massa Day Dead?: Black Moods in the Caribbean* (Garden City, NY: Anchor Books, 1974), 29–46; 32.

[37] Ibid., 32.

While he famously found there the very root of his aesthetic persona, his near-namesake (E. R.) Braithwaite had a far different experience, as the ambivalent title of his travel memoir about Africa, *A Kind of Homecoming*, aptly expresses.[38] Several of their fellow Caribbean authors traced a similar path, exploring an aspirational identification with Africa with varying degrees of earnestness, irony, or despair.[39] Their Indo-Trinidadian contemporary, V. S. Naipaul (1932–2018), strikes a comparable note along a different diasporic route – to India. His earliest novel, *The Mystic Masseur* (1957), makes light of the faux-Indianness of the Indo-Trinidadian community, ridiculing the literal-mindedness of the protagonist Ganesh's belief that he can walk to Benares from Trinidad after his coming-of-age ceremony and satirising his later efforts to cultivate a Gandhian image of holiness, among many other targets.[40] Naipaul's metropolitan masterpiece *The Mimic Men*, published in 1967, is likewise haunted by a sense of isolation and deracination that, while encompassing both London and the fictional Caribbean island of Isabella, finds its deepest roots in the protagonist's absent relation to India. As a young boy, Ralph dreams of being an ancient Aryan ruler:

> I lived a secret life in a world of endless plains, tall bare mountains, white with snow at their peaks, among nomads on horseback [. . .] And I would dream that all over the Central Asian plains the horsemen looked for their leader. Then a wise man came to them and said, 'You are looking in the wrong place. The true leader lies far away, shipwrecked on an island the like of which you cannot visualize.'[41]

Sheltering in London after the implosion of his Isabellan political career, an older Ralph relates similar fantasies: 'I have visions of Central Asian horsemen, among whom I am one, riding below a sky threatening snow to the very end of an empty world.'[42] Expressing a subtly different form of longing, chastened by the experience of time, Ralph nevertheless articulates the fundamental rift that structures almost all of Naipaul's work: a desolation born of British imperialism's sundering of ancient roots across its empire.[43] While something of an extreme (and notoriously nihilistic) example,

---

[38] E. R. Braithwaite, *A Kind of Homecoming* (Englewood Cliffs, NJ: Prentice Hall, 1962).
[39] A list of similarly inclined novelists would include O. R. Dathorne, V. S. Reid, and Denis Williams.
[40] V. S. Naipaul, *The Mystic Masseur* (London: André Deutsch, 1957).
[41] V. S. Naipaul, *The Mimic Men* (New York: Vintage, [1967] 2001), 118.   [42] Ibid., 98.
[43] One of the more recuperative, if wistful iterations of this tendency can be found in Naipaul's quasi-autobiographical account of settling – both physically and psychologically – into the Wiltshire countryside, where he lived, for the most part, since 1970: *The Enigma of Arrival* (New York: Knopf, 1987).

Naipaul's work nonetheless illustrates the pronounced sense of multiple displacements – from notional ancestral home, from actual birthplace, and from Britain – felt by mid-century writers from the Caribbean.

Naipaul's affective links with primal Indo-Aryan culture distinguish him from Selvon, his fellow Indo-Trinidadian, who generally expressed more fealty to a creolised, cosmopolitan sense of identity. Nevertheless, there seems to have been an extra layer of diasporic alienation experienced by the era's migrating Caribbean-born authors that may help explain the particular resilience of these authors in articulating an (at least partial, if agonistic) affiliation with Britishness: they, unlike other late colonial migrants, had no real sense of an autochthonous, sovereign culture in which they could find alternative accommodation. Even Brathwaite, one of the generation's fiercest advocates of Caribbean cultural nationalism, admits that in the early 1950s he 'was not then consciously aware of any other West Indian alternative' to his inherited English cultural values.[44] While postwar Caribbean writers did portray the Caribbean islands of their lived experience, they also seem to have felt obliged to engage in a more overt questioning of Englishness on its home ground, given the poignantly embattled relation they experienced to it there.

Approaching Home

Indeed, their most prominent authorial counterparts from Africa and Asia living in Britain focused almost exclusively on portraying their home societies. The Nobel prize-winning Nigerian author Wole Soyinka (1934–), who lived in Britain between 1954 and 1960, produced plays and novels that focus on life on the African continent, both during and after his time abroad. Similarly, the novelist Ngũgĩ wa Thiong'o (1938–), who arrived as a student in the early 1960s, concentrates on conflict in his home country of Kenya in his foundational works of the time, including *Weep Not, Child* (1964), *The River Between* (1965), and *A Grain of Wheat* (1967). It is not until Buchi Emecheta (1944–2017) publishes *In the Ditch* (1972) and *Second Class Citizen* (1974) that the African novel in English takes up the encounter between ex-coloniser and ex-colonised in the metropolitan centre.[45] The most prolific British-based Asian writer of the time, Kamala Markandaya (1924–2004), likewise

---

[44] Brathwaite, 'Timehri', 32.
[45] The Nigerian Dillibe Onyeama's scathing memoir, *Nigger at Eton*, also appeared in 1972 and takes up similar issues of racism.

stuck close to home, thematically speaking, in her earliest work. Markandaya's first (and most widely known) novel, *Nectar in a Sieve*, appeared in 1954, tenderly tracing the story of a woman living in an Indian village and beset by poverty, natural disasters, and familial tragedy.[46] Markandaya steadily published novels over the next few decades, returning consistently to the topic of life in India, a life her novels depict in fine-grained detail with an eye toward the everyday complexities generated for her characters by competing (and imperially inflected) systems of thought, law, religion, and morality.

Not until 1972's *The Nowhere Man* does Markandaya directly confront such issues in her long-time home of Britain.[47] In this novel, the depiction of immigrant experience is harrowing, as Markandaya traces the slowly building alienation of her Indian protagonist, Srinivas. Fleeing his family's brutal dispossession by colonial officials in India, Srinivas settles in London and gradually grows, over a residence of nearly thirty years, to feel a part of his adopted home. So much so, in fact, that he responds to an implication of his foreignness late in life with a bold statement of national allegiance: "'This is my country now,' he said with some pride [...] 'My country,' he repeated. 'I feel at home in it, more so than I would in my own.'"[48] His telling adherence to notions of his 'own' (originary) country, however, is ultimately validated, as, in the crucible of the rising racial antipathy of the late 1960s, Srinivas's hard-won sense of belonging becomes unsettled by the xenophobic aggression of his neighbour's son, Fred, who embarks on a campaign of harassment. Contemplating his own status in the face of such intolerance, Markandaya's protagonist has a bleak, blunt epiphany: 'For what, at the end of these assimilating years, can the terminal product be said to be? Srinivas asked himself [...] An alien, he replied [...] An alien, whose manners, accents, voice, syntax, bones, build, way of life – all of him – shrieked *alien*!'[49] As this brutal, almost biological truth emerges over the course of the novel, Markandaya is careful to link her protagonist's

---

[46] A notable contemporary of Markandaya is Attia Hosain, whose one published novel captures the tensions of pre-Independence Lucknow in intricate, feminist-inflected detail: *Sunlight on a Broken Column* (London: Chatto & Windus, 1961).

[47] One exception might be her 1963 novel *Possession*, which is set primarily in England. However, it is not deeply concerned with immigration or immigrant life in London, using the temporary expatriation of an Indian artist as something closer to an allegory exploring the incommensurability of East and West.

[48] Kamala Markandaya, *The Nowhere Man* (New York: John Day, 1972), 60–1.

[49] Ibid., 241.

experience of violence in London back to his original suffering at the hands of colonial power in India, suggesting that there is, literally, nowhere Srinivas could go to escape from such cruelty. With its stark, fatal ending, the novel makes plain the fiercely visceral, immutable sense of unbelonging characteristic of the Asian immigrant's experience of Britain.[50]

Carrying it Forward

It is unsettling to observe that the experience depicted by Markandaya so closely resembles that found in the works of Braithwaite, Lamming, and Selvon twenty years earlier; it is disheartening to recognise eerily similar strains of dislocation in much later novels on the black and Asian experience in Britain such as Abdulrazak Gurnah's *Dottie* (1990) and *By the Sea* (2001), Hanif Kureishi's *The Buddha of Suburbia* (1990), Andrea Levy's *Small Island* (2004), and numerous works by Caryl Phillips, including *Foreigners: Three English Lives* (2007), *In the Falling Snow* (2009), and *The Lost Child* (2015). Critical treatments often emphasise the transformative possibilities unleashed by the rise of black and Asian British literature as it emerged into undoubted prominence after World War II.[51] The continuity of the pronounced themes of alienation and disaffection that extend in the literature from mid-century to the present day, however, suggests that there is some wisdom in Caryl Phillips's refusal to 'underestimate the impervious nature of British society, both then and now'.[52] Regardless, it remains the case that the immediate postwar years were a pivotal era in the evolution of black and Asian British writing, representing a time of sustained and unprecedentedly voluminous authorial production in the midst of a pronounced shift in Britain's geopolitical standing and influence. While in some cases looking outward, towards home, and thus establishing a basis for the study of what has come to be called postcolonial literature, many of the era's Britain-based black and

[50] Both Lamming and Selvon return, in a similarly despairing key, to the immigrant experience around this time as well. See Lamming, *Water with Berries* (London: Longman, 1971) and Selvon, *Moses Ascending* (London: Davis-Poynter, 1975).

[51] The most prominent, insightful surveys include: John Ball, *Imagining London: Postcolonial Fiction and the Transnational Metropolis* (Toronto: University of Toronto Press, 2004); John McLeod, *Postcolonial London: Rewriting the Metropolis* (London: Routledge, 2004); Sukhdev Sandhu, *London Calling: How Black and Asian Writers Imagined a City* (London: HarperCollins, 2004); and Mark U. Stein, *Black British Literature: Novels of Transformation* (Columbus, OH: Ohio State University Press, 2004).

[52] Phillips, *New World Order*, 236.

Asian writers also memorably turned their attention to their immediate surroundings. These writers, in laying bare the fluctuating consequences of British racial prejudices and directly confronting the contradictions inhering in their own Commonwealth citizenship, pointed up the arbitrariness and permeability of supposedly innate categories of identity and thus helped establish a set of concerns about belonging and alienation that have continued to haunt black and Asian British writing into the twenty-first century.

14

Wide-Angled Modernities and Alternative Metropolitan Imaginaries

MPALIVE-HANGSON MSISKA

Introduction

The 1950s witnessed an efflorescence of fiction by writers from the Caribbean.[1] At the forefront of this phenomena were: Edgar Mittelholzer (Guyana), George Lamming (Barbados), Vidiadhar Surajprasad (V. S.) Naipaul (Trinidad), Sam Selvon (Trinidad), and Wilson Harris (Guyana). Most of them arrived during the early postwar period, lived in London, and later came to be known as the 'Windrush generation'. Though this prominent grouping was predominantly male, several Caribbean women were also publishing, including Jean Rhys (1890–1979) and Beryl Gilroy (1924–2001), who came to prominence in the 1960s.[2] This chapter will argue that the works of these writers constituted themselves in different ways as a radical cultural formation that both challenged the traditional orthodoxies of modernism and worked within it, as a founding platform for their global vision and move towards a wider-angled modernity.[3]

This grouping has rightly been studied under a variety of rubrics: as part of the wider Commonwealth literary tradition, as 'migrant modernism', or as the representatives of an inaugural moment in modern Caribbean writing.[4] Noticeably, even though such readings include the writers' engagement

---

[1] George Lamming, *The Pleasures of Exile* (London: Michael Joseph, 1960), 29.

[2] Please note that the scope of the chapter does not allow for an in-depth account of the causes of male dominance among Caribbean writers, a topic that would require engaging with debates on the links between gender, education, culture, and the development of writing as a practice in the 1940s and 1950s Caribbean. Readers might find the following book on the topic useful: Joan Anim-Addo (ed.), *Framing the Word: Gender and Genre in Caribbean Women's Writing* (London: Whiting & Birch, 1996).

[3] Simon Gikandi, *Writing in Limbo: Modernism and Caribbean Literature* (Ithaca, NY: Cornell University Press, 1992), 8–11.

[4] Frank Birbalsingh, 'An Interview with Samuel Selvon' in *Passion and Exile: Essays in Caribbean Literature* (London: Hansib, 1986), 142–6; J. Dillon Brown, *Migrant Modernism*

within a British formation, they are primarily viewed as exiles. From the 1970s onwards, some of these works have begun to be seen as constitutive of an emergent black British canon.[5] Such approaches emphasise not only these writers' physical location in Britain, but also their respective efforts to create a liveable place and aesthetic space within the wider culture and community there. Since the 1990s, with the interventions of scholars such as Simon Gikandi and, more recently, J. Dillon Brown, the writings of this group have begun to be read as integral to a wider global modernity or what is sometimes termed new modernisms.[6] This marks a significant shift for, rather than placing such artists as Caribbean outsiders on the fringe of key metropolitan aesthetic debates, they are instead regarded as keenly attentive to such issues. This chapter will develop that perspective further, focusing specifically on how the expression of this wider-angled vision of Caribbean modernity not only impacted on but is demonstrably integral to Britain and its cultural geography.

As Raymond Williams once famously put it, 'immigrants' can be seen as catalysts of the avant-garde, and this gives the metropolis a greater capacity than non-metropolitan areas to challenge established ideas about the arts and engender new ones.[7] Even so, Williams does not especially register the contribution of immigrants from the British colonies in the rise of new currents of literary practice in Britain. That might be an excusable blind spot in an essay otherwise addressing the rise of modernism in the metropolis, but nonetheless his perspective betrays the kind of ethnocentric cultural monolithism that this early generation of writers from the Caribbean were challenging. Williams was right in urging that 'the metropolitan interpretation of its own processes as universals' needs questioning.[8] Thus, the writers were 'de-universalising' not only the monolithic idiom of British modernism, but also demonstrating their intrinsic multiple modernities, an approach posited by new modernist critics such as Marshall Berman, who contends that since the rise of capitalism, the world has been brought into new international social relations of production and consumption that emphasise

---

(London: University of Virginia Press, 2013); and Alastair Niven (ed.), *The Commonwealth Writer Overseas* (Brussels: Didier, 1976).

[5] John McLeod, *Postcolonial London* (London: Routledge, 2004) and James Procter, *Dwelling Places* (Manchester: Manchester University Press, 2003).

[6] Two contributors to this volume, Snaith and Dillon Brown (see Chapters 7 and 13), further explore this notion.

[7] Raymond Williams, 'Metropolitan Perceptions and the Emergence of Modernism' in *Politics of Modernism* (London: Verso, 1989), 37–48.

[8] Ibid., 47.

the notion of progress as *modernisation*.[9] However, as is now clearly evident, the experience of such *modernisation* and its overall cultural and material condition *modernity* is experienced differently in diverse geographical and cultural sites. In this context, these 1950s writers can be viewed as having created a *global and historical modernism* as counter to the reigning orthodoxies of British *national modernism*.

The emergence of these writers was helped by both their colonial formation and openings within British cultural hegemony. Nearly all had benefited from a colonial education prior to their arrival in Britain.[10] This familiarity with English literature would permeate their styles and force them, to some degree, to identify with metropolitan norms, whilst also proposing new regimes of representation. As other contributors to this history detail, the BBC programme *Caribbean Voices* was pivotal to their formation. Launched by the Jamaican poet and dramatist Una Marson in the 1940s, it was produced from 1948 to 1954 by Henry Swanzy, an Englishman of Irish descent, whose resourceful editorship transformed it into a full-scale literary forum on air (see Chapters 9 and 15). His colonial origins and left-wing leanings made him empathetic to the writers' creative ambitions as well as their social disadvantage after arrival in Britain. As he recalls: 'what one was interested in was not the kind of thing that somebody like a Philip Larkin [...] would write'.[11] Swanzy's mention of Larkin is not coincidental – it touches on key fault-lines in 1950s British writing. Larkin and others, described as 'Movement' poets, defined themselves by an ardent opposition to modernism, which they saw as pretentious and elitist. They wanted a literature that was authentic, written in contemporary language and without experimentation.[12] For Seamus Heaney, Larkin was the epitome of 'urban modern man, the insular Englishman' who 'responding to the tones of his own clan [was] ill at ease when out of his environment'.[13]

This pioneering group of Caribbean writers contested the postwar tendency in English letters towards insularity, especially as manifested in an anti-immigrant nationalism.[14] Their works proffered a transcultural and

---

[9] Marshall Berman, *All that is Solid Melts into Air* (London: Verso, 2010), 24.
[10] Bruce King, 'Introduction' in *West Indian Literature* (Basingstoke: Macmillan, 1995), 2–8; 2.
[11] Glyne Griffith, 'Deconstructing Nationalisms', *Small Axe*, 5:2 (2001), 1–20.
[12] Philip Larkin, 'The Art of Poetry', *The Paris Review Interviews, II* (New York: Picador, 2007), 233–5.
[13] Seamus Heaney, 'Englands of the Mind' in *Finders Keepers: Selected Prose 1971–2001* (London: Faber and Faber, 2002), 77–95; 94.
[14] Robert Miles and Annie Phizacklea, *White Man's Country* (London: Pluto, 1984), 148–9.

transnational literary consciousness and aesthetics, which insisted on the values of a cosmopolitanism rooted in a shared history and culture and broke down notions of a nationalist monolithic modernity. In doing so, they foregrounded the extent to which Britain's deployment of a nationalist discourse was oblivious to the constitution of modernity in the Caribbean as well as the region's long material contribution to imperial and global progress.

Mittelholzer: Telescopic Objectivity and Networks of Empire

Edgar Mittelholzer (1909–1965) was perhaps the most prolific of this group, having published over twenty-two novels.[15] His work is distinctive for its insistence on the representation of the Caribbean as part of a European modernity that had fashioned itself as a racial and ethnic cosmopolitanism. Mittelholzer's exploration of the legacy of the transatlantic slave trade in the formation of Caribbean subjectivity and social structure is evident for instance in his *Kaywana* trilogy, where historical romance is used to trace the history of modern Guyana, including the 1763 slave uprising against Dutch plantation owners.[16] Through several generations of the Van Groenwegels – originally from Holland, but of mixed African, American Indian, and English heritage – Mittelholzer reveals how European economic modernity in the Caribbean was a form of social Darwinism, with the supposedly physically and culturally fittest gaining ascendancy. Mittelholzer's white-supremacist leanings have often been criticised, even by his Caribbean peers.[17] The truth is that Mittelholzer is a contradictory figure – critical of racism in the Caribbean whilst also exhibiting the internalisation of the idea of whiteness as superior that, according to Frantz Fanon, is at the heart of colonialist hierarchies in slave plantation societies.[18] This is illustrated in Mittelholzer's biography, where he admits that his father found his African features repulsive, preferring his European-looking siblings.[19]

[15] Michael Gilkes, 'Edgar Mittelholzer' in Bruce King (ed.), *West Indian Literature* (Basingstoke: Macmillan, 1995), 127–38; 127–38; 127.

[16] Edgar Mittelholzer, *Kaywana Heritage* (London: Corgi, 1976).

[17] George Wagner, 'Edgar Mittelholzer: Symptoms and Shadows', *Bim*, 9:33 (July–Dec 1961): 29–34, and John Figueroa, 'Introduction' in Edgar Mittelholzer, *A Morning at the Office* (London: Longman, [1950] 1974), xv–xvi.

[18] Frantz Fanon, *Black Skin, White Masks* (London: Pluto, 1986), 44.

[19] Edgar Mittelholzer, *A Swarthy Boy* (London: Putnam, 1963), 11.

However, it is his theory of 'telescopic objectivity', which focuses on the ways in which objects connect subjects, that fundamentally informs Mittelholzer's assertion of a distinctive Caribbean modernity.[20] As the maverick writer-figure in *A Morning at the Office* (1950) says: 'we shouldn't devote attention only to human characters but we ought to tell the stories behind dumb objects like chairs and beds and doors'.[21] Exploring how characters and spaces are linked by objects, the novel is set in the Port of Spain, Trinidad office of 'Essential Products Limited', a British import and export company. The office is presented in terms of *telescopic objectivity*, a space for the global circulation of material signifiers of modernity in a national and international circuit of production and distribution connecting Port of Spain to its peripheral sites of production in far-flung rural areas as well as the company headquarters in London. It distributes sugar, oil, and other products from Trinidad to London and brings back various manufactured goods. It is such products that connect the various individuals and communities in Trinidad with those in Britain. The novel exemplifies Stuart Hall's now well-known observation that 1950s Caribbean immigrants were following the terminus of their own and ancestral labour: 'The notion that identity [...] could be told as two histories, one over here, [...] is simply not tenable any longer in an increasingly globalised world. [...] I am the sugar at the bottom of the English cup of tea.'[22] Thus, modernity could not be regarded as the exclusive property of one nation, as suggested by 1950s English writers like Larkin, but rather, as asserted by their Caribbean and later black British contemporaries, a contingent historical as well as a globally diverse phenomenon that required a rethinking of modernity in the double and multiple time of the British national formation alongside empire and its legacy.

Further, the novel draws attention to the notion of the office as a marker of both Caribbean and British modernity, a cosmopolitan site where men and women from diverse backgrounds are brought together in a practice particular to modern forms of labour and industry. It is a physical, psychological, and cultural elaboration of the global modern, one determined not only by the contemporary politics of colonialism, but also the old plantation economy and slavery which mark the identities and relations of the workers in the office and the world. The top jobs are preserved for the British regardless of qualifications, with the key recruitment model being racial kinship or the collusions of the old boys' network: for instance, the British accountant,

---

[20] Mittelholzer, *Morning at the Office*.   [21] Ibid., 82.
[22] Stuart Hall, 'Old and New Identities, Old and New Ethnicities' in Anthony D. King (ed.), *Culture, Globalization, and the World-System* (Basingstoke: Macmillan, 1991), 41–68; 48.

unqualified for the job, is appointed because of family connections. The fact that his incompetence is covered up by his junior, a qualified East Indian, additionally reveals how Caribbean modernity expressed the Manichean divides of colonial racism as the means of bureaucratic management. Significantly, although the office is an exploitative space with feudal and capitalist relations, it also demonstrates Trinidad's mastery of modern forms of bureaucratic rationality.[23] It is therefore a veritable site of modernity, altogether challenging the monolithic view of modernity that equates it with Britishness.

It needs to be noted that Mittelholzer also contests racism, for example, when we are presented with a British plantation manager based outside Port of Spain who turns up at the office to loudly condemn the racist ideology of the company and Trinidad colonial society. He is treated as an oddity, and Othered, to contain his oppositional potency. Moreover, there is resistance from below, though the workers themselves subscribe to the ideology. For instance, Mrs Hinckson, the light-skinned secretary to the General Manager, considers herself almost on par with white people and even above them on occasion because she is of an old mixed-race family locally perceived as aristocratic. Furthermore, there is opposition through transgressive desire, when Horace, the black messenger, declares his love for Mrs Hinckson – the ultimate outrage to the established hierarchical racial norm. As Mittelholzer's novel first appeared in 1950, its message must have had an immediate relevance to prevailing racial attitudes in the metropolis, particularly with regard to interracial sexual relationships, as expressed in the 1949 *Royal Commission on Population*.[24]

Mittelholzer's contestation of the orthodoxies of a monolithic modernity is also evident in the way he approaches subjectivity and representation. His characters are portrayed as modern subjects amenable to current models of selfhood. Whether through psychoanalysis or forms of representation such as stream-of-consciousness, once seen as avant-garde, they assert their claim to the universal categories of modern subjectivity. In identifying with modernism, Mittelholzer made clear his acquisition of metropolitan cultural capital, but challenged any lingering doubt that such techniques should only be applied to European characters. Like fellow Caribbean writers, he was keen to place such European radical ideas of subjectivity and narrative in dialogue with those from Caribbean culture, hybridising them into a specific

---

[23] Max Weber, *The Protestant Ethic and the Spirit of Capitalism* (London: Penguin, 2002).

[24] Colin Homes, *John Bull's Island: Immigration and British Society 1871–1971* (London: Macmillan, 1988), 116.

Caribbean modernity reflective of that now borne by the black British subject. Mittelholzer's attempts in his fiction to articulate a globalising modernity beyond the immediate bounds of his British location were equally central to Lamming's vision.

Lamming: Modernity as a Way of Seeing

George Lamming (1927–) has been variously described as a writer of the 'peasant consciousness' and an 'anti-colonial' writer.[25] Rarely is he seen in terms of his passionate commitment to modernity as defining the shared experience of both the Caribbean and Britain as colonial metropole. Modernity for Lamming is not simply a matter of participating in its global formation, of capitalist production and its ideology; rather, it offers a *new way of seeing*.[26] Shakespeare's *The Tempest* provides him with a foundational conception of subjectivity, consciousness, and location of modernity that is both historical and contemporary: contending that 'what is at stake is the historical result of our thinking; what is under tragic scrutiny is our traditional way of seeing'.[27] He argues there are two main ways of seeing – the traditional and the modern. This distinction corresponds to two fundamental subjectivities, Prospero's and Caliban's, with the former representing the colonial and slave-owning mentality that evolves into racism in 1950s Britain, and the latter a consciousness transcendent of the past and contemporary racialised consciousness. The traditional is inculcated into enslaved and colonised subjects, whereby Caliban is culturally and materially dispossessed by Prospero and *interpellated* or socialised into the latter's subject of ideology and relations of production.[28]

Lamming's vision in *The Pleasures of Exile* (1960) anticipates much writing that was to follow and he explores the complex production of such subjectivity in several novels, especially in his acclaimed *Bildungsroman, In the Castle of my Skin* (1953).[29] The relationship between the house on the hill, owned by several generations of the Creighton family since the days of slavery, and those on the plain below, predominantly of black and mixed parentage, encapsulates the feudal power structure in Creighton village. The villagers'

---

[25] Michael Gilkes, *Racial Identity and Individual Consciousness in the Caribbean Novel* (Georgetown, Guyana: National History and Arts Council, 1975), 123 and Sandra Pouchet Paquet, *The Novels of George Lamming* (London: Heinemann, 1982), 1.

[26] Lamming, *Pleasures of Exile*, 63.   [27] Ibid., 63.

[28] Louis Althusser, 'Ideology and Ideological State Apparatuses' in *Lenin and Philosophy and Other Essays*, trans. Ben Brewster (London: New Left Review, 1970), 121–76.

[29] George Lamming, *In the Castle of my Skin* (London: Michael Joseph, 1953).

acquiescence is due to their lack of understanding of the real conditions of their existence and awareness of their historical connection to the land – through slavery. The protagonist, Boy G, and his fellow pupils have no idea that Barbados had slaves. They are alienated from the past, the knowledge of which might enable them to develop a *different way of seeing* themselves and reveal their location in modernity as a site of cumulative historical dispossession and repression. Instead, they are immersed in English history, which excludes the experience of their ancestors. In Lamming's categories, they manifest a *Prospero mode* of modernity. So Boy G feels cognitively and affectively alienated from his society because he knows there is more to what is normalised as the *way of seeing*.

Boy G's alternative perception emerges from listening to the unconventional history told by the oldest couple in the village, who embody what might be described as a *critical peasant consciousness* that grasps more than it publicly declares and is authorised by the hegemony. This oral history re-incorporates the community into global and historical modernity and it is through them that Boy G acquires the notion of modernity as a critical consciousness. This 'peasant' view, as Lamming terms it, 'of seeing' is Caliban's new attitude to the world and it is this that can radically modify the Caribbean writer's view of modernity and the world.[30] Yet, Boy G's Caliban consciousness is contrasted with Trumper's more essentialist perspective, garnered in the USA: where, he has found his 'people [...] – the negro people'.[31] For Boy G (and for Lamming), that is a Prospero 'way of seeing', rather than that of a truly radicalised Caliban who can transcend the Manicheanism of racialised and essentialist ideologies.

Boys G's universalist and inclusive vision has to do with his own formation – his immersion in a colonial English education amidst the multiracialism and multiculturalism of Barbados. That experience imbues him from the outset with a cosmopolitan consciousness and the sense of being a citizen of the world. It is widely recognised that *In the Castle of my Skin* is autobiographical and that Boy G parallels the author himself. Importantly, too, Lamming was more than aware that an urbane, inclusive, and inherently cosmopolitan modernity was not widely shared in the 1950s Britain he encountered.[32]

His next novel, *The Emigrants* (1954), reflected on the factors that prompted the wave of Caribbean migration to Britain after the war.[33] Economic

---

[30] Lamming, *Pleasures of Exile*, 44.   [31] Lamming, *In the Castle*, 287.
[32] Lamming, *Pleasures of Exile*, 12.
[33] George Lamming, *The Emigrants* (London: Allison & Busby, [1954] 1980).

hardship in the islands was combined with the demand by the British government for cheap labour to assist with postwar reconstruction. However, the fundamental reason lay in the longevity of the connections between the Caribbean islands and Britain as 'mother-country', a relationship that stretches beyond empire to the early modern period. Though Lamming and Sam Selvon (fellow passengers by chance on the boat) sought employment like many other migrants, they were also already acculturated and cosmopolitan Caribbean subjects, writers-to-be on a literary pilgrimage to a country they had hitherto only imagined through books. *The Emigrants* highlights the range of differences amongst the voyaging immigrants, whether of race, class, or expectation.

Collis, autodidact and aspiring writer of an indeterminate class, is propelled, for example, by a deep sense of alienation. Educated for the world, he feels forced to live within restricted cultural horizons. His intellectual upbringing had inculcated the importance of cultural life, leaving him out of place within a growing Caribbean middle class which had been trained, says Lamming, 'to regard education as something to have and not to use' and refused 'to respond to any activity [...] not honoured by money'.[34] His dream of a cosmopolitan existence is frustrated: Collis is precluded from getting jobs befitting his education and takes up manual work. Dickson cannot find employment in Britain as a schoolmaster and is horrified when he is the object of cruel sexual voyeurism by an English doctor he thinks is romantically interested in him. His intrinsic sense of equality between educated black and white people is profoundly shaken, leading to a mental breakdown.

From Lamming's perspective, migrants from the Caribbean and other colonies arrive with a fundamental cosmopolitan identity which most Britons lack. This leads to huge disappointments and misunderstandings. As Tornado, an ex-soldier, explains: 'if they'd just show one sign of friendship, just a little sign of appreciation for people like me an' you who from the time we born, in school an' after school, we wus hearin' about them, if they could understan' that an' be different, then all the hate [...] would disappear'.[35] Despite this, the migrants and some British friends begin to create a new human geography of the city in terms of their own imaginaries, anticipating the evolution of new spaces for a multicultural identity.[36]

---

[34] Lamming, *Pleasures of Exile*, 42.   [35] Lamming, *The Emigrants*, 186.
[36] Michel de Certeau, *The Practice of Everyday Life*, trans. Steven Rendall (London: Verso, 2010).

Naipaul: Modernity as Adaptation and Excess

Still a somewhat controversial figure in the field of Caribbean and black British letters, despite his now Nobel Laureate status, V. S. Naipaul (1932–2018), an East Indian, left Trinidad for Oxford in 1950 to read English on a government scholarship, graduating in 1954. Following on from Henry Swanzy as editor of the influential BBC *Caribbean Voices* programme (1954–1958), his contribution has sometimes been criticised for shifting the programme away from literary experimentation to more traditional writing.[37] Additionally, Naipaul's satirical perspective, even in early satires such as *Miguel Street* (1959), pointed to what some readers and peers already saw as an incipient racism towards his fellow colonised. As Edward Said, a major postcolonial scholar, was to harshly put it almost thirty years later: Naipaul remained 'a third worlder denouncing his own people, not because they are victims of imperialism, but because they seem to have an innate flaw, which is that they are not whites'.[38] However complex Naipaul's racial politics, his importance in the emergence of black and Asian writing in Britain cannot be gainsaid nor indeed can his engagement with the question of modernity.

In his most famous novel *A House for Mr Biswas* (1961), sometimes viewed as a critique of the nineteenth-century canonical novel of the house, he was to contest the notion of a singular modernity then dominant in Britain.[39] It focuses on a traditional East Indian family in Trinidad, examining their place in and contribution to the workings of imperial modernity. For all his foibles, Naipaul thus also proffered the heterogenisation of the narrative of modernity. Highlighting the plantation as the inaugural point of entry for East Indian indentured labourers in Trinidad registers and recovers their history and place within the colonial economy and global modernity. These indentured labourers, such as Mr Biswas's father, are the hidden abode of global capitalist production, as their labour is unrecorded in the official production annals, yet they produce the material signifiers of modernity, such as sugar.[40] Moreover, in writing about the lives and histories of such workers, Naipaul recuperates their repressed agency in narratives of imperial modernity,

---

[37] Dillon Brown, *Migrant Modernism*, 172–3.
[38] V. S. Naipaul, *Miguel Street* (London: André Deutsch, 1959) and Edward Said, 'Intellectuals in the Post-Colonial World', *Salmagundi*, 70/71 (Spring–Summer 1986): 44–64.
[39] V. S. Naipaul, *A House for Mr Biswas* (London: André Deutsch, 1961).
[40] Stuart Hall, 'The Problem of Ideology: Marxism without Guarantees' in David Morley and Kuan-Hsing Chen (eds.), *Stuart Hall: Critical Dialogues in Cultural Studies* (London: Routledge, 1996), 24–45.

especially as racial antipathy replaces any historical understanding of the Caribbean presence in postwar Britain.

The novel focuses on the evolution of the community from a tightly knit one of indentured labourers, clutching onto lost ancestral traditions of home, to a cosmopolitan one with a distinct place in the colonial formation in Trinidad and Britain. In this process certain aspects of traditional Hindu culture are discarded or modified; for example, Mr Biswas's birth at the rural plantation is attended by elaborate Hindu rituals, but that is not the case with his children. The tension between tradition and modernity is further manifested as the community moves into the urban sphere – for instance, Mr Biswas's marriage is underwritten largely by his family's desire for social mobility.

Naipaul's text can be seen to echo Georg Simmel's view that obsession with money and the calculability of things is the hallmark of modernity.[41] Even religious values are subject to the calculation of surplus value in the novel. The Tulsi family does not only seek economic benefit from arranged marriages, but also the preservation of caste. All the poor men to whom they marry their daughters are Brahmins, the highest Hindu caste. Caste and money override other considerations, including affiliation to other religions such as Christianity, illustrated by the approval of the elder son's marriage to a Presbyterian Hindu.[42] Through his detailed portrait of this family, Naipaul thus demonstrates how the Trinidadian East Indian community forges its own diasporic and hybrid modernity, which entails accepting a certain degree of cultural mixing. It is one that conforms to the traditional Hindu religious class-structure which is itself translated into the general capitalist structure of modernity. It is worth noting that this novel does not extend its vision of cultural hybridity to race, as mixing with creolised Trinidadians of African or Chinese backgrounds, for example, is disapproved.

Whilst maintaining its cultural distinctiveness as Indian, the upper class has adopted English as its main language of expression, with Hindi downgraded to a minor language used mostly by the lower classes. In this regard, the novel presents Trinidad as a hierarchically structured world which is committed to ideas of relentless material progress – a notion central to modernity – as was the case in Britain. Naipaul thus

---

[41] Georg Simmel, 'The Metropolis and Mental Life' in Richard Sennett (ed.), *Classic Essays on the Culture of Cities* (New York: Prentice Hall, 1969), 47–60.

[42] Savi Naipaul Akal, *The Naipauls of Naipaul Street* (Leeds: Peepal Tree Press, 2018).

universalises modernity to contest the perception that he and fellow Caribbeans may have come from backward countries; instead he portrays Trinidad as a participant in the global capitalist economy with its citizens aspiring to modernity and the good life it promises. Though Mr Biswas protests against such changes, he is equally a cosmopolitan citizen who adores British writers and American thinkers. However, his bourgeois individualism is oppositional and cultural rather than economic as with the rest of middle- and upper-class Indians in Trinidad.[43] He attempts to disengage from the herd mentality that both traditional communalism and modern capitalism exert on the individual.

In the end, though, Naipaul seems to empathise with Mr Biswas's refusal to be taken in by a mimetic modernity that seems to be a version of Britishness. His decision to buy any old house is a symbol of his ardent rebellion against the oppressive and bullying in-laws and their narrow vision of progress. He hankers after a modernity that is deeply cultural and intellectual, like Lamming's character Collis or Selvon's Tiger in *A Brighter Sun* (discussed below). However, whilst Naipaul presents the possibility of a bicultural and more cosmopolitan vision of modernity in Trinidad, the world of the Tulsis in *A House for Mr Biswas* remains haunted by materialism and ethnic absolutism.

Sam Selvon: The Black Metropolis

For Sam Selvon (1923–1994), modernity is not simply a matter of highlighting the existence of a plurality of cultures in each national formation, but of an active incorporation of difference as a positive value in national consciousness. Like Naipaul, he was a Trinidadian from an East Indian background but, unlike him, his concerns go beyond those of the East Indian community to fully embrace a vision of creolisation and the heterogeneity of Caribbean cultural and ethnic identities. Speaking of *A House for Mr Biswas*, he once remarked, 'I could not write a book like that. That has not been my experience, the Indian family thing.'[44] Instead, he describes himself as having been '"creolised" from a very early age'.[45] He grew up in a rural environment and went to the city at fifteen after leaving school, later becoming a journalist for the

---

[43] Dilip Parameshwar Gaonkar, 'On Alternative Modernities', *Public Culture*, 11:1 (1999): 1–18.
[44] Birbalsingh, 'An Interview with Samuel Selvon'.   [45] Ibid., 146.

Trinidadian Guardian. He migrated to Britain in 1950 and, like his co-traveller and friend George Lamming, wished above all to improve his existing prospects as a writer: he was prolific and by 1960 had published six novels as well as a collection of short stories, *Ways of Sunlight* (1957). *The Lonely Londoners* (1956), an episodic, picaresque novel, is well known for its remapping of the city of London, consolidating his status as an innovator now key to any study of black British writing.[46] To fully understand his exploration of Caribbean modernity and its eventual relation to black British settlement, it is best to examine his first novel.

In *A Brighter Sun* (1952), Selvon traces the modernisation of Trinidad from the nineteenth century to the postwar period and the changes in modes of production and consciousness.[47] Although engaged with the local development of modernity, he is keen to locate it in the global context of empire and the postwar world. The contemporaneity of the global and the local is manifest in the novel's narrative style, exemplified from the outset where several key concerns are simultaneously foregrounded: Port of Spain's multiracial cosmopolitanism and its modernity – with its rich and poor – as well as the city's everyday link to history and the global.[48] It is remarkable how Selvon depicts the multiracial character of Trinidad as a natural aspect of a modern city, a vision that would have contrasted greatly with his experience in 1950s London.

There is serious resistance to multiracial cosmopolitanism in Trinidad as well; illustrated by Tiger's Afro-Trinidadian neighbour who reprimands his wife for befriending Tiger's wife and by Tiger's parents who disapprove of his friendship with the couple. Tiger, the main character, is himself discriminated against by an Afro-Caribbean shop assistant and her white customer in Port of Spain. Nevertheless, Tiger's experience and optimism indicate the possibility of transracial multicultural co-operation. His humane treatment by a supposedly socially superior person, the white doctor who rushes to his wife's aid after a black and an Indian doctor have declined his request, and the enormous help his black neighbour gives his wife when she is in labour, make him believe that Trinidad can transform its multiracialism into a modern inclusive society. That attitude is shared by other characters such as Boysie, an East Indian, who publicly carries out a romantic relationship with an Afro-Trinidadian woman and tells Tiger: 'that is the way to live,

---

[46] Susheila Nasta, 'Introduction' in Susheila Nasta (ed.), *Critical Perspectives on Sam Selvon* (Washington, DC: Three Continents, 1988), 1–13.
[47] Sam Selvon, *A Brighter Sun* (London: Allan Wingate, [1952] 1971).   [48] Ibid., 3.

especially in Trinidad'.[49] Tiger thinks of him as 'mixed up good and proper with the cosmopolitan atmosphere of the city'.[50]

The inherently inclusive vision of modernity in *A Brighter Sun* is not only limited to the internal character of Trinidad, but reverberates outwards: it is about being simultaneously in the world and in history, a global vision that was, perhaps, lacking in Britain when Selvon completed the novel. References to World War II and the arrival of Jewish refugees from Europe also record the global historical context that frames the quotidian of national life in Trinidad, whilst the country's continuing material and moral contribution to the 'mother country' is seen in its oil supply to Britain.

The difference in response to the mystery of the international economic order marks two forms of subjectivity globally: between the *interpellated subject*, who accepts things as they are and valorises modernity as signified by the hegemony, seeing it in nationalist or consumerist terms, and others who want to know more about the enabling conditions of modernity. Tiger wonders if Trinidad's economic contribution is generally known about or appreciated in Britain.[51] The response of Tiger's friend, Boysie, is intriguing as it indicates the impersonal nature of international capitalism – Boysie asks: 'You tink about who make de shoes you wearing?'[52] He alludes here to the fact that the world economic system privileges commodities rather than the human beings who make them, underwriting the extent to which such subjects, whether in Trinidad or Britain, are alienated from the social meaning of their labour and consumption. For Boysie, who focuses merely on consuming modernity, one should not ask difficult questions about one's place in the world, saying: 'I for one don't want to know which part it come from, as long as Ah cud get it.'[53] It is a similar amnesia and unwillingness to know the real conditions of modernity afflicting them that confronts Selvon's black immigrants in 1950s Britain.

Tiger offers an alternative in the novel, embarking on self-education, learning to read and write and, above all, learning to interpret ideas and situations critically in a manner reminiscent of what Paulo Freire once called 'self-conscientisation'.[54] Tiger's education is directed towards understanding the world and his possible role in it rather than simply being the repository for the material symbols of modernity. As the novel progresses, Tiger's desire to leave diminishes, as he contemplates returning to the cane plantations to share his knowledge with the labourers and propagate a future that is

---

[49] Ibid., 78.   [50] Ibid.   [51] Ibid., 88.   [52] Ibid.   [53] Ibid.
[54] Paulo Freire, *The Pedagogy of the Oppressed* (Harmondsworth: Penguin, 1996).

inclusive and transformative. Boysie leaves for America, but as one character warns, the idea of an inclusive modernity garnered from watching Hollywood films in Port of Spain is likely to be contradicted by the reality of racism in America.

The Lonely Londoners (1956) illustrates the magnitude of that contradiction for Caribbean migrants who imagine America and Britain are paradigms of cosmopolitanism.[55] All the characters in the book pursue the immigrant's dream of material well-being, conveyed through British education and popular culture. Galahad, for example, epitomises an egalitarian modernity, where the pursuit of money and materiality is a unifying factor. He and the other 'boys' – all with two-dimensional and mythical nicknames – suffer from racial discrimination, affecting their jobs and their accommodation. In a moving and illuminating episode, Galahad condemns his skin, saying: 'is you that causing all this, you know. Why the hell you can't be blue, or red or green, if you can't be white?'[56] Galahad counters his objectification by de-objectifying himself, drawing attention to the difference between the subject of skin-signification and that of his cosmopolitan outlook and agency. Part of settling thus involves the psychic transcendence of this split, which is coupled with a desire to create an uncompromising, multicultural imaginary of an accommodating city.

The novel portrays how Selvon's immigrants unwittingly invent London as a space of cultural hybridity, an in-between space, to use the concept of the theorist Homi Bhabha, which offers an alternative to the hegemonic space.[57] That entails mixing traditional Caribbean cultural forms with British ones to fashion a distinctly alternative cosmopolitan modernity. Newcomers change customer relations and ways of exchange in their sphere of influence. Tanty's introduction, for instance, of a Caribbean informal credit system at an English grocer's, ensuring that this community does not need to starve if they do not have cash, offers a more humane model of economic exchange than the existing one, thus making London a more intimate and liveable place.[58]

Selvon's immigrants, just as those in Lamming's The Emigrants, importantly appropriate parts of London, fashioning an alternative map of the city with their own matrix of significant places and routes, reminiscent of de Certeau's idea of the contestation of urban spaces between officialdom and the people.[59] They lay symbolic claim to certain streets and names, so that Bayswater becomes 'the Water', for example. Inclusive modernity is further

---

[55] Samuel Selvon, The Lonely Londoners (London: Allan Wingate, 1956).   [56] Ibid., 88.
[57] Homi K. Bhabha, The Location of Culture (London: Routledge: 1994), 1.
[58] Selvon, Lonely Londoners, 79.   [59] De Certeau, Practice of Everyday Life.

suggested by their alliance with other minorities, whether Jewish tailors in the East End or the Polish.[60] This connection with previous migrant communities indicates how old communities of immigrants provide a threshold for the arrival of new ones. And it is perhaps not remarkable that Selvon's black Londoners locate themselves in working-class areas for, as the narrator explains: 'It have a kind of communal feeling with the Working Class and the spades.'[61]

Selvon's ideology of form in *The Lonely Londoners* is predominantly modernist as it simultaneously creates a space for a distinctly Caribbean aesthetic, subordinating it to languages, such as creole or the vernacular, which were considered the antithesis of literary language within colonial cultural ideology.[62] Like many of his peers, Selvon sought both affiliation with and differentiation from modernism, intervening as both modernist and counter-modernist. They can thus be described as broadly experimental, a term abhorred by emergent 1950s literary peers such as Kingsley Amis, whose condemnation of Caribbean writers for their experimentalism inaccurately placed them too firmly in the modernist camp, without attending to their complex affiliation to earlier traditions of English writing, such as realism, as well as to indigenous Caribbean cultural forms.[63] However, in Wilson Harris's case the charge of experimentalism is fully deserved.

Wilson Harris: Modernity as the 'Literate Imagination'

Wilson Harris, who came to Britain in 1959 and died here in 2018, is distinctive in his aesthetics and approach. Born in Guyana (then British Guiana) in 1921, he won a scholarship to Queens College in Georgetown. He worked from 1942 to 1959 as a government forestry and hydrological surveyor, which had a lasting influence on his global vision and creative practice. Harris's principal contention was that modernity was not only about material development, but also the necessary transformation of consciousness into what has come to be called a 'literate imagination', that recasts humans' understanding of themselves, space, and time.[64] He distinguishes between 'garden illiteracy',

---

[60] Selvon, *Lonely Londoners*, 77.   [61] Ibid., 75.

[62] Edward Kamau Brathwaite, *History of the Voice: The Development of Nation Language in Anglophone Caribbean Poetry* (London: New Beacon Books, 1984), 5–6.

[63] Kingsley Amis, 'Fresh Winds from the West', *Spectator* (2 May 1958): 565–6.

[64] A. J. M. Bundy (ed.), *Selected Essays of Wilson Harris* (London: Routledge, 1999), 75–85; Michael Gilkes's edited collection *The Literate Imagination: Essays on the Novels of Wilson*

the failure to read and write, and 'cultural illiteracy', the inability to interpret the world beyond received categories. For Harris, the post-Columbian conquest of the Americas and the subsequent enslavement of the Amerindians, Africans, and East Indians – the latter by indentured labour – was based on a view of power and civilisation characterised by 'cultural illiteracy'.[65] He regards the traditional realist novel as reworking the values of conquest associated with the historical global deployment of power and therefore an unsuitable model for enabling any radical reconceptualisation of modernity. Thus, Harris's 'literate imagination' explores the multiple and non-linear metamorphoses of existence and form.[66]

That view lies at the heart of his first and best-known novel *Palace of the Peacock* (1960), in which the conquistador Donne (a direct allusion to the English metaphysical poet) and his crew are on a journey to his exotic mistress, Mariella, an object of both sexual desire and fear, the symbol of El Dorado – the mineral-rich city of legend that inspired the voyages of exploration by, among others, Walter Raleigh (another metaphysical poet).[67] Donne and his crew die in the opening sentences but he lives on to undertake the voyage by being dreamt back into life by his twin brother. He thus becomes a character in his brother's imaginative narrative, raising the question of the comparative modes of being of his two selves. For Harris, the permeability of the two levels at which Donne exists is legitimised by a belief in the notion of subjectivity as a point of transition between different moments of being.[68] This implies that the idea of modernity as culturally monolithic is a refusal to countenance trans-spatial modernity and the capacity of subjects to traverse different cultural and physical geographies.

As a mark of its transgressive nature, the novel also appropriates and transforms the colonial narrative of the 'venture into the interior' at the centre of Joseph Conrad's *Heart of Darkness* (1899), subverting its Manicheanism and representation of racial difference as an innate and absolute opposition.[69] Harris challenges both the formal and ideological aspects of Conrad's novel, its adoption of the realist mode of representation and

---

Harris (London; Basingstoke: Macmillan, 1989) significantly contributed to contouring 'the literate imagination' as a critical framework.

[65] Charles H. Rowell, 'An Interview with Wilson Harris', *Callaloo*, 18:1 (Winter 1995): 191–200; 194.

[66] For more information on Wilson Harris's theoretical work, see Chapter 23.

[67] Wilson Harris, *Palace of the Peacock* (London: Faber and Faber, 1960).

[68] Rowell, 'An Interview with Wilson Harris', 194.

[69] Joseph Conrad, *Heart of Darkness* (London: Blackwood, [1899] 1902) and Frantz Fanon, *The Wretched of the Earth* (London: Penguin, [1961] 2002), 30–3.

narrative linearity as well as its ideology of progress and the civilising mission. Instead, the real and the unreal intermingle in a metafictional narrative as Donne learns that he is a split subject, both self and other. This element of self-reflection is absent from Conrad's Kurtz, since he is unable to move beyond the innate duality and ethics of the subject caught between 'civilised' Europe and 'Dark' Africa. His moment of epiphany is the perception of utter negativity – 'The horror! The horror!'[70]

On the other hand, much as Harris reworks the notion of Conradian negativity, especially in relation to power, in his view it can be transcended if, unlike Conrad's Kurtz, the protagonist cultivates a 'literate imagination', which would make him or her recognise the desire for power as the impossibility of absolute self-mastery and the domination of the Other.[71] That is aptly exemplified in the epiphany Donne has, in his second death, when the indigenous people he has been pursuing for slave labour appear more like gods than the 'savages' of his *conquistador* project when he looks up at them from the bottom of the waterfall where he is dangling precariously to certain death. Thus, Harris asserts himself as the inheritor of modernist poetics, as well as one who supersedes and transforms it into an inclusive discourse of different and multiple experiences of modernity.

Conclusion

With Harris, then, Caribbean writing of the 1950s firmly advances a wide-angled modernity, not as a progressive accumulation of new knowledges and material products, but rather as the struggle for a 'literate imagination' that always seeks to transcend the received notions of modernity as a Eurocentric model of the conquest of nature and the Other. Thus, from Mittelholzer to Harris, one is presented with an impressive variety of perspectives on what it means to be located in modernity by the black Caribbean subject in 1950s Britain. In his notion of 'telescopic objectivity' Mittelholzer conceptualises modernity as a global network in which subjects are linked by the objects circulating among them through production, reproduction, and consumption. In Lamming's view of modernity as 'a way of seeing', 1950s monolithic modernity is quintessentially anti-modern, since it reconstitutes the racialised and authoritarian mentalities rooted in slavery and colonialism, and proposes

---

[70] Conrad, *Heart of Darkness*. Available at http://www.gutenberg.org/cache/epub/526/pg526.epub?session_id=76ca7f54bb0884eec65f814b45370ba7581e52af.
[71] Hena Maes-Jelinek, 'Wilson Harris' in Bruce King (ed.), *West Indian Literature* (Basingstoke: Macmillan, 1995), 139–51; 146.

the racial and cultural plurality of the Caribbean as a constructive basis for a postwar British modernity. As for Naipaul, he offers the example of the achievement of an ethnicised modernity in the Caribbean, through the experience of people of East Indian origin, as exemplary cosmopolitan embrace of the Otherness of place and culture, but he finds its imitative materialism destructive of the cultivation of a cultural modernity. Selvon's modernity is, like Mittelholzer's, predicated on the need to recognise the extent to which the Caribbean and Britain are historically, economically, and culturally linked through slavery and colonialism, a process that has made Caribbeans fundamentally subjects of global modernity, attesting to transnational modernities. However, that experience of modernity necessarily produces a desire to know and experience the world beyond one's own. The presence of the Caribbean subject in 1950s Britain is a function of that desire and helps Britain become a truly cosmopolitan and multicultural place, perhaps a little like the Caribbean.

15

Forging Collective Identities
The Caribbean Artists Movement and the Emergence of Black Britain

CHRIS CAMPBELL

CAM at the Crossroads

The lifespan of the Caribbean Artists Movement (1966–1972) belied both the scope and the intensity of the intellectual and political formations it fostered. Over these six years it acted as a vital forum for Caribbean cultural production, staging debates around the work of artists and writers resident in Britain and stimulating interest amongst a wide section of the British public. It marked a significant moment in the development of new directions in and perspectives on Caribbean culture at a period when new critical and conceptual frameworks were being defined in order to bridge 'the transformation of Britain's West Indian community from one of exiles and immigrants to black British'.[1] As Anne Walmsley observes in her comprehensive chronicle, the term 'black British' was employed within CAM circles in a collective, connective sense. It encompassed migrants from the anglophone Caribbean including Trinidad, Jamaica, Guyana, and Barbados, each with its own distinctive historical and cultural background. Partly as a legacy of CAM and a symptom of the self-reflective debates it rehearsed, the concept expanded during the 1970s to reference not only Britain's postcolonial citizens from Africa and South Asia, but also the legacy of pan-African identity. In providing a forum for those writers and artists who recognised a broader sense of their shared Caribbean identity in Britain, but who felt marginalised there, CAM contributed significantly to the growth of collective identities. It fostered alliances cutting across regional and ethnic divides and set the

---

[1] Anne Walmsley, *The Caribbean Artists Movement 1966–1972: A Literary and Cultural History* (London; Port of Spain: New Beacon Books, 1992), xviii.

foundations for the burgeoning of black British art that would flourish in the following decades.

Founded by Kamau (then Edward) Brathwaite (1930–), Doris Brathwaite (1926–1986), John La Rose (1927–2006), and Andrew Salkey (1928–1995) and constellated initially around meetings in the Brathwaites' London flat – 47(B) Mecklenburgh Square – the group drew together writers, artists, theatre practitioners, students, and scholars. Following the *West Indian Gazette* and the BBC's *Caribbean Voices*, both of which had ceased activity, in 1958 and 1965 respectively, CAM offered the opportunity for a discursive space for cultural engagement both reaffirmed and, crucially, recalibrated.[2] The roll call of those drawn into the orbit of CAM's activities is an exhaustive one. Writers of successive generations and diverse literary modes, including Michael Anthony, James Berry, Wilson Harris, Linton Kwesi Johnson, Evan Jones, and Orlando Patterson, circulated with artists working in diverse mediums, including Karl Craig, Paul Dash, Althea McNish, Ronald Moody, and Aubrey Williams. Theatre was represented by Marina Maxwell, Ram John Holder, Lloyd Reckord, and Pearl Connor. From the outset academics were involved too: Elsa Goveia, C. L. R. James, Louis James, Kenneth Ramchand, and Gordon Rohlehr; as CAM developed, the voices of activists from the West Indian Students Centre (WISC), including Richard Small and Locksley Comrie, became increasingly significant.[3] During its course, the crucible created by CAM's activities represented a contradictory dynamic of critical reflection, fusion, friction, and crisis out of which emerged an enriched and potent new form of cultural practice, a formative legacy for new generations of artists, writers, and scholars.

Walmsley identifies the movement as operating at a crossroads, drawing on Brathwaite's own vision of the organisation in just such a crucial position.[4] CAM's work might best be understood as both being at the crossroads of a specific historical conjuncture and as navigating the crossroads of struggle over the symbolic field. The intellectual ferment of CAM was pivotal for defining and articulating Caribbean and black British aesthetic practices – practices that operated within, and at times strained against, the circuits of

---

[2] The *Caribbean Voices* broadcasts ran from 1944 until 1958 (see Chapter 9). The *West Indian Gazette*, established by the Trinidadian Marxist journalist/activist Claudia Jones, was an instrumental cultural force, circulating news between the Caribbean and its British-based diaspora. The *Gazette* was also a coherent voice for black Britons blending political coverage of decolonisation and Cold War politics with a cultural purview that featured the work of many future CAM members. See Chapter 24.

[3] For a fuller range of CAM contributors, see Walmsley, *Caribbean Artists Movement*, 341–6.

[4] Walmsley, *Caribbean Artists Movement*, xvii.

power and the institutions that structured the politics of cultural life in Britain. Reflecting on what was to be CAM's first major conference, Brathwaite observed:

> It didn't get as far as the summit effect with the Establishment [. . .] But it didn't matter, because what happened was that West Indians themselves discovered that they had so much to say [. . .] at this time of crossroads, we realised that it might not really have been a good idea to have attempted both things at the same time.[5]

Before the 1967 conference (15–17 September at the University of Kent), Brathwaite had written to publishers, newspaper editors, and figures representing the British arts establishment to invite attendance. This move echoed earlier entreaties to Bryan King and Edward Lucie-Smith: influential, well-connected white West Indians embedded within the artistic world of London at the time. Brathwaite was motivated by a keen sense both that Caribbean writing was now receiving markedly less attention from established British critics than it had during the 1950s and that, around Caribbean art specifically, there was virtual critical silence. The aim was clear. CAM's founders hoped to harness the structural mechanisms and platforms for expression accessed through such institutions as the West Indian Commission, the BBC, and the mainstream print media. CAM might thus serve as a summit between West Indian and British writers, artists, and critics. Discernible in these invitations too, is an attempt not just to gain access to increased visibility via established institutional circuits, but moreover to shape or reshape the constitution of the artistic and critical field itself.

It will be helpful here to turn to Pierre Bourdieu's contention that any successful sociology of culture must consider a wider array of social agents which shape 'the conditions of production of the field':

> It therefore has to consider as contributing to production not only the direct producers of the work in its materiality (artist, writer, etc.) but also the producers of the meaning and value of the work – critics, publishers, gallery directors and the whole set of agents whose combined efforts produce consumers capable of knowing and recognizing the work of art as such.[6]

Brathwaite's 'summit' should be understood then as an engagement with the longer history of the gatekeeping practices of dominant colonial cultural

---

[5] Kamau Brathwaite, quoted in Walmsley, *Caribbean Artists Movement*, 96.
[6] Pierre Bourdieu, *The Field of Cultural Production: Essays on Art and Literature* (New York: Columbia University Press, 1993), 37.

forces, and as an intervention into 'the most disputed frontier of all [. . .] the one which separated the field of cultural production and the field of power' in British life.[7] This process of negotiating symbolic and political fields did not just manifest itself externally in the terms of the Caribbean presence situated in relation to British institutional cultural power. It manifested itself internally too, in the substance and tensions of the debates staged amongst CAM members themselves from the very outset.

Seen in this dual way, the debates of CAM, the alliances it fostered, and the connections it forged were inextricably enmeshed in wider, often competing visions of the history of black Britain at the time. For instance, we can trace the emergence of the notions of Commonwealth culture (with its attendant retrenchment of certain imperial values) as well as the formative pressures of radical black political thought, which was itself a co-constitutive part of the world-revolutionary moment that cohered across the globe in 1968. How best to navigate such a defining tension can be read through many CAM discussions: on the possibilities and potential of a decolonised Caribbean aesthetic; on the role of white patronage and universities within the movement; and about literary purpose and political engagement.[8]

If, as Louis James has noted, CAM in its affiliations, membership, media, and political trajectories was always 'too diverse to be easily defined', it is nonetheless possible to trace the common concern that underwrote the activities of its participants and interlocutors.[9] This concern might be best encapsulated as the pressing need to bring about a Caribbean aesthetic that was decolonised on every level. To think of decolonisation in an expansive manner necessitated an opening up of new domains of cultural life and thought. These domains needed to be better attuned to the lived experience of the Caribbean as well as migrant subjectivity, and to the prestige value ascribed to different cultural forms. This recalibration was only ever partially achieved by CAM 'where the question of creating appropriate popular forms was incessantly addressed' and caused 'incessant disputation'.[10]

---

[7] Bourdieu, *Field of Cultural Production*, 43.
[8] The differing positions on the function and form of literature were most stridently witnessed at the CAM colloquy, 5 May 1967. The heated debate on Orlando Patterson's novels, scathingly attacked for being sterile sociology by John Hearne, and Patterson's defence of his art provided an exemplar for Brathwaite of how it was the job of artists not to 'slap each other on the shoulders, but to confront each other with what they hold to be the truth of their art and discipline'; see Walmsley, *Caribbean Artists Movement*, 79.
[9] Louis James, 'The Caribbean Artists Movement' in Bill Schwarz (ed.), *West Indian Intellectuals in Britain* (Manchester: Manchester University Press, 2003), 209–27; 213.
[10] Bill Schwarz, 'The Predicament of History' in *West Indian Intellectuals*, 248–57; 252.

In order to address the range, scope, and influence of CAM's formation, and eschewing any attempt at comprehensive coverage already provided in depth and precision by others, this chapter will primarily focus on two areas. First, it will examine what is seen here as a 'long dialogue' or relationship between Brathwaite and Henry Swanzy (1915–2004) who, in his capacity as producer of *Caribbean Voices* (between 1948 and 1954), was one of CAM's metropolitan interlocutors and represents that fraction of the cultural establishment with stated interests in Caribbean culture. Second, it will consider the ways in which we might understand the 'worlding' of CAM, focalised through the interventions of the dramatist Marina Maxwell (1934–) and the dialogues fostered by CAM members with revolutionary Cuba. Significantly this moved attention beyond the confines of British imperial legacy and beyond the anglophone world. These two elements are highlighted here as they illustrate moments and case histories that depict the processes and progress made by the organisation in defining the shape of a realisable decolonised Caribbean culture at the end of the 1960s. They also help define the specific ways in which CAM can be understood to have been 'at the crossroads'. First and foremost they offer a view on how instrumental to the definitions of an emerging sense of black British culture the movement was. Either explicitly or through its relationship to growing literary and artistic networks (notably New Beacon Books and *Savacou*[11]), CAM influenced a wide range of black British writers, artists, and theorists including Linton Kwesi Johnson, Lorna Goodison, Stuart Hall, and Paul Gilroy.

From Swanzy to Stokely: Egalitarian Imperialism and Black Power Radicalism

The BBC's radio programme *Caribbean Voices* was established, as others in this volume have noted, under the guidance of the Jamaican journalist, poet, and writer Una Marson. Following Marson's return to Jamaica due to ill health in 1946, the programme passed on to the stewardship of Irish producer Henry Swanzy. Whilst a crucial part of the cultural machinery of metropolitan influence that placed London as the centre for Caribbean literary production in the 1950s, *Caribbean Voices* nonetheless played an instrumental role in the development of Caribbean literature, creating 'a significant and influential cultural arena in which personal friendships and alliances between

---

[11] *Savacou* was the journal of CAM. It took its name from the bird-god in Carib mythology who controlled thunder and strong winds. Issue 1 was published in June 1970, edited by Kamau Brathwaite, Kenneth Ramchand, and Andrew Salkey.

writers could be built'.[12] Gail Low describes how the programme connected the literary world of the anglophone Caribbean to London and 'became especially important for the development of regional creative writing, culti-vating strong links with regional literary journals such as *Bim*'.[13]

Philip Nanton has observed that scholarship has tended to assess the operations of the programme in 'two mutually exclusive ways': either as a 'concealed form of colonial imposition', refining and re-presenting an image of the region to itself, or as a facilitating agent offering 'opportunities for developing literary authorship for a wide range of writers'.[14] The double-edged capacity of the programme was embodied by Swanzy's role. While his personal investment in materially and intellectually supporting and launching migrant West Indian writers is well known, he had always been aware of the paradox of his own position.[15] Whether in the introductory segments to individual broadcasts of the programmes, his correspondence, or his own compendious diaries, Swanzy frequently acknowledged the obstructions his role as gatekeeper of Caribbean cultural life had produced. For example, the BBC programme script for 11 January 1947 dramatises this dilemma. Swanzy prefaces his 'Talk' on the direction of the programme with self-deprecating acknowledgement of his 'un Caribbean' voice (altered on the script from 'didactic, Oxford voice'), and 'slightly supercilious nose' which has poked into Caribbean culture.[16] In a letter to Frank Collymore, following his only trip to Jamaica, he writes: 'I fully realise that an outsider like myself is one of the real obstacles that presumably stand in the way of the island attaining some integrity.'[17] Similarly, diary entries often mention fears of being seen as little more than a 'CMG' (colonially made gent), all testament to an unease at

[12] Alison Donnell, 'Heard but not Seen: Women's Short Stories and the BBC's *Caribbean Voices* Programme' in Lucy Evans, Mark McWatt, and Emma Smith (eds.), *The Caribbean Short Story: Critical Perspectives* (Leeds: Peepal Tree Press, 2011), 29–43; 30.

[13] Gail Low, *Publishing the Postcolonial: Anglophone West African and Caribbean Writing in the UK, 1948–1968* (London: Routledge, 2011), 97–8. See Chapter 17 in this volume.

[14] Philip Nanton, 'Political Tensions and *Caribbean Voices*: The Swanzy Years, 1946–1954' in Michael Bucknor and Alison Donnell (eds.), *The Routledge Companion to Anglophone Caribbean Literature* (London: Routledge, 2011), 585–90; 589.

[15] For example, see George Lamming, *The Pleasures of Exile* (London: Pluto, [1960] 2005) and V. S. Naipaul, *Letters Between a Father and Son*, ed. Nicholas Laughlin and Gillon Aitken (London: Picador, [1999] 2009). For a cogent analysis of Swanzy's insider/outsider status see Glyne Griffth, 'Deconstructing Nationalisms: Henry Swanzy, *Caribbean Voices* and the Development of West Indian Literature' in *Small Axe*, 5:2 (2001): 1–20.

[16] *Caribbean Voices*. Script 160. BBC Caribbean Service, 11 January 1948. Transcript of Radio Broadcast. BBC Written Archives Centre, Caversham, UK.

[17] Letter from Henry Swanzy to Frank Collymore, 20 May 1952. Papers of Henry Swanzy, Yesu Persaud Centre for Caribbean Studies, University of Warwick.

making professional profit out of processes that might be considered, if not actually named, cultural imperialism.[18] It is in light of this that Swanzy saw his position as a place-holding one, moving towards a time when the steward-ship of Caribbean literary culture might pass beyond him. This moment seemed to arrive with the advent of CAM in 1966.

In a letter of 20 March 1975 (some twenty-one years after Swanzy left *Caribbean Voices* and seven after the second CAM conference), Swanzy replies to Brathwaite, looking back at their long correspondence: 'It was nice, as always to hear from you, the latest stage of a long relationship in Cambridge, London, Ghana, the University of Kent in Canterbury. And now, six weeks from my retirement under the age limit.'[19] This conversation attests to the depth of personal engagement between the men, but equally to the need to acknowledge the realignment of the field and the political energies of the times. It is clear Brathwaite still explicitly values Swanzy's helpful editorial eye. Here, for instance, debates over issues of poetic form in what will become the first two parts of his long poem *The Arrivants* are rehearsed:

> How very kind of you to send me a copy of *Rights of Passage*. I think it reads admirably, no holes of any kind in all the well-built structure; and although I myself do not altogether like the very short, rhetorical line I thought you manipulated it with great mastery.
>
> (Swanzy to Brathwaite, 20 January 1967)

> I'm glad you liked the 'final' version of *Rights*, reservations and all [. . .] *Masks*, I'm afraid does not contain any of my Mediterranean poetry. It's all brand new, but I think you'll like it, because a) it's about one aspect of my experience of W. Africa esp. Ghana and b) in it, I restore the Parnassian line.   (Brathwaite to Swanzy, 12 February 1967)[20]

If Brathwaite is preoccupied with the creation of a poetry that can better bear the weight of Caribbean historical experience and musical rhythms, Swanzy seems caught between admiration for Brathwaite's innovative style and a critical attach-ment to canonical poetic standards. In this we can see a microcosm of the larger pressures and tensions over literary value that defined the discussions of CAM.

As far as CAM was concerned, Brathwaite's continued relationship with Swanzy served a practical purpose beyond his editorial eye. Part of Brathwaite's mission was to secure and illuminate the archive of Caribbean

---

[18] Henry Swanzy Diaries (Ichabod), 1 January 1952. Papers of Henry Swanzy, YPCCS, University of Warwick.

[19] Letter from Henry Swanzy to Kamau Brathwaite, 20 March 1975. Papers of Henry Swanzy, YPCCS, University of Warwick.

[20] Letters. Papers of Henry Swanzy, YPCCS, University of Warwick.

culture in the present, a task essential to the preservation of historical memory and the forging of contemporary collective cultural identity. By inviting Swanzy to become an honorary member of CAM and in seeking to try to secure a run of the *Caribbean Voices* scripts for the University of the West Indies at Cave Hill (Barbados) to complement the Mona (Jamaican) archive, he formalised important connections between CAM's present and the work of earlier decades.[21]

Swanzy's institutional position and his professional judgements can be read as part of the larger circuits of institutional power and the metropolitan institutions which mediated the politics of Caribbean cultural life in Britain. Indeed, it is possible to read Swanzy's participation as an embodiment of what Anne Spry Rush defines as 'egalitarian imperialism'. Attempts by the BBC to project out to the world an idea of the Commonwealth, with relationships based on notions of shared identification, common purpose, and equality, see the shackles of empire newly transformed into more ambiguous 'bonds'.[22] His self-conscious but nonetheless conflicted position represents a microcosmic example of the role of the BBC itself in relation to its colonial cultural producers and audiences in the years after World War II. As Michael Niblett suggests, Swanzy's work can be seen as a cultural refraction of a political–economic impetus towards fostering a distinct West Indian culture *within* the framework of the British imperial system. This is a relationship constitutive of a wider world-historical move: 'Britain's attempts to recalibrate its imperial position [in the postwar era] by stressing an ideal of "commonwealth" that nominally ceded greater equality to its dominions without overturning the system as a whole'.[23]

Brathwaite's CAM conversations with Swanzy and the BBC over the course of the 1950s, 1960s, and 1970s demonstrate the pressures brought to bear on this 'Commonwealth' institutional matrix. The historian Rob Waters identifies how the politics of radical blackness worked to rethink and reorder the production and consumption of culture in the Black Atlantic world of the late 1960s. He argues that 'this was a transnational process which played out beyond just the former colonies and declining metropole' and situates CAM as central to this transformation in Britain. If CAM was a prime mover in

[21] Letter from Kamau Brathwaite to Henry Swanzy, 28 February 1975. Papers of Henry Swanzy, YPCCS, University of Warwick.
[22] Anne Spry Rush, *Bonds of Empire: West Indians and Britishness from Victoria to Decolonization* (Oxford: Oxford University Press, 2011).
[23] Michael Niblett, 'Style as Habitus: World Literature, Decolonization and *Caribbean Voices*' in Raphael Dalleo (ed.), *Bourdieu and Postcolonial Studies* (Liverpool: Liverpool University Press, 2016), 119–36; 128.

wider attempts to shift the dominant sites for decolonising cultural production, its internal operations and debates also became a key site of struggle
over this transition.[24]

It was at the second CAM conference in 1968 that this struggle announced
itself as a moment of crisis. Members were confronted and urged to acknowledge the evolution of the Black Arts Movement in the United States, to
connect political activism with cultural expression, and to resituate their
activities in more working-class, communal black locales. These assertions,
coming to CAM from members who represented the position of the West
Indian Students Centre and who were responding to the rapidly changing
shape of black politics in Britain, were a radical challenge to the traditional
institutional locus of cultural power in Britain. Against the backdrop of
successive anti-immigration legislation (the Commonwealth Immigrants
Acts, 1962, 1968) and the Powellite infection of political rhetoric that had
fuelled racism on the streets of Britain, the urgency for a politics of black
solidarity was announcing itself in new ways. From the visit of Malcolm X in
1965 and the foundation, in the same year, of the Campaign against Racial
Discrimination, through to the confrontations following the police raid on
the Mangrove restaurant in 1970, the latter half of the 1960s saw a shift in
the centre of gravity for responses to issues of metropolitan racism. The
watershed moment for this emergent militancy, however, came with the
arrival in July 1967 of the Trinidadian-born civil rights leader Stokely
Carmichael (1941–1998) who, in a whirlwind ten-day tour, spoke at WISC,
Africa House, Hyde Park's Speakers' Corner, and in Camden, Brixton, and
Dalston. The effects of the tour catalysed support for Black Power groups and
proved effective in pulling together splinter groups, which, as Brathwaite
recalled, possessed 'splintered feelings that had [. . .] long [. . .] been seeking
a node'.[25]

Seen through the optic of Black Power, the politics of culture in Britain and
the Caribbean was connected to the wider global radicalism of the time. The
wider political landscape encompassed Garveyite and Rastafarian politics in
Jamaica; the Black Power uprising in Trinidad; student revolts in Paris and
Mexico City; and, more broadly still, the anti-imperialist ideological struggles
across the world-system – the Vietnam War and guerrilla resistance across

[24] Rob Waters, 'Henry Swanzy, Sartre's Zombie? Black Power and the Transformation of
the Caribbean Artists Movement' in Ruth Craggs and Claire Wintle (eds.), *Cultures of
Decolonisation: Transnational Productions and Practices, 1945–70* (Manchester: Manchester
University Press, 2016), 67–85; 68.
[25] E. [Kamau] Brathwaite, 'Timehri', *Savacou*, 2 (1970): 35–45; 40.

Latin America. The radical energy in Britain was felt by many in CAM to be a constitutive element of a crucial moment of world-revolutionary possibilities. The endeavours of Caribbean artists were energised through this connection, speaking to the real possibility of a 'black International'.[26] In Canterbury, over that weekend at the end of August 1968, seizing the opportunity for CAM to precipitate the decolonising of the British arts establishment seemed as impossible to forgo as it was hotly contested. It was here that the confrontation between divergent visions for the future of CAM played out. The divide centred on those insisting on the essential autonomy of the individual artist, and others who backed Richard Small's calls for 'a new conception of art and culture' which carried with it all the political immediacy of the world-revolutionary moment. Small, a leading activist of WISC and a former law student, envisaged a course that would see CAM work much more closely with the Student Centre, democratising its focus. It should, he argued, take performances and exhibitions to the emerging centres of black British life, and more directly engage with the experiences of institutional discrimination and brutalisation by the police.

Commentators have identified this moment as a schism which brought CAM to a moment of crisis and it was certainly the case that some individual members felt that they could not continue to associate with the movement. Brathwaite, however, has stressed that a lack of consensus surrounding artistic practice had always been integral to CAM: it debated and discussed but never enforced or formalised a particular central line.[27] This discussion over the scope and depth of political commitment could be understood as a fractious part of a longer, dialectical process of development for Caribbean arts within Britain. This process entailed a rejection of the patrician structures of an 'egalitarian imperial' centre, which had a hand in enabling Caribbean artists and writers to produce work in Britain. Nonetheless, such a separation was the prerequisite of a movement towards the definition and legitimisation of black British artistic production. The draft resolution penned at the end of the conference represented as much of a resolution to the split as was possible. Small had proposed that the movement contact the Jamaican government in protest at the banning of Black Power literature. An amended version was then suggested by Bryan King, which included reference to the free expression of ideas as a way of framing the condemnation of the ban on Malcolm X and Stokely Carmichael. This deftly registered the terms of the split within the organisation itself and balanced insurgent politics with the

[26] Ibid.   [27] Walmsley, *Caribbean Artists Movement*, 188–9.

long-standing commitment to artistic autonomy. Passed by an overwhelming majority of members, it symbolises a significant moment in the reorientation of the powers of consecration for Caribbean culture.

The 'Worlding' of Caribbean Arts

If it seemed impossible after this point for CAM to continue along previous lines, other configurations were emerging out of the political ferment. With the Brathwaites leaving for the university campus in Jamaica, the putative leadership of the committee now included James Berry (1924–2017) and Donald Hinds (1934–) who, working in Britain with John La Rose and Andrew Salkey, offered a formalised acknowledgement of the need to reorientate cultural institutions to respond to a wider constituency. As the centre of activity shifted from the University of Kent to the Student Centre (site of the third CAM conference), Salkey observed that 'our own Caribbean communities must become the new centres of which we must first seek approval of the fruits of our imagination'.[28] Waters sees Salkey's intervention at this point as an explicit refusal of the 'earlier links to the British arts establishment' and a demand for revolution '*defined* by blackness'.[29] The work and (in certain respects) the guiding mission of CAM did not completely collapse under the weight of the debates at Kent, but rather continued more surely along a particular course.

Heading the calls for a more global vision of the decolonising power of Caribbean art was the Trinidadian writer and theatre practitioner Marina Maxwell. Maxwell became secretary of CAM – taking over from Brathwaite at the start of 1968 – and later, from Jamaica, founded the Yard Theatre. This project sought to concretise the decolonising and democratising potential of culture. It took theatre to the people of Kingston by performing outside, working within communal spaces, and bringing together professional and untrained writers and performers. Many CAM members embraced such moves (Brathwaite collaborated with Maxwell on his arrival in Jamaica) and CAM's newsletter, now edited by Donald Hinds, devoted the majority of its tenth edition (April–June 1969) to Maxwell's challenge that, pre-empting Salkey's conference talk by five months, urged members 'Towards a Revolution in the Arts'. This text, a draft of the talk Maxwell gave at Mona, was later reprinted in Brathwaite's *Savacou* and marked another

---

[28] Andrew Salkey, 'The Negritude Movement and Black Awareness', 1969. George Padmore Institute GB 2904 CAM/4/3/4.

[29] Waters, 'Henry Swanzy, Sartre's Zombie?', 79.

crucial intervention in debates surrounding the direction for Caribbean artistic practice. Brathwaite's attempts to reformulate CAM in Jamaica were frustrated, as Mervyn Morris (1937–), Poet Laureate of Jamaica from 2014 to 2016, explains, because it 'could not easily establish a distinctive image' in light of the wider cultural arenas for discussions of Caribbean art which were already operating around the university campus at the time.[30] However it was in the Brathwaites' endeavours and Maxwell's eagerness to continue conversations begun in London that important new directions emerged. The joint venture undertaken by CAM and the New World Group offered perhaps the best platform through which debates surrounding the decolonising capacities of Caribbean art might now be staged and realised. The New World Group comprised an increasingly influential aggregation of intellectuals drawn from across the anglophone Caribbean. Thinking across the disciplines of development, politics, and economics, the group steered the intellectual processes of decolonisation in the region. Lloyd Best, Kari Polanyi Levitt, Clive Thomas, Trevor Munroe, and Norman Girvan amongst others created new conceptualisations of the postcolonial era, attending to the legacies of plantation economics, structural violence, and continued economic dependence. The New World Group response to the historical conjuncture, grounded in political economy, both complemented and counterpointed CAM's culturalist focus.

Importantly, Marina Maxwell's talk kicked off a weekly Sunday seminar series (running from early March 1969 through to the end of April) with a clarion call for new expressions of Caribbean cultural nationalism that reframed and redirected much of the activity of CAM members in radical directions outwards. The aims of Maxwell's Yard Theatre and the ongoing debates in CAM were distilled in her inaugural talk. Her vision sought to thoroughly 'world' the Caribbean not only by rejecting aspects of the European theatrical tradition, but by offering a viable, historicised, and theorised alternative. After the malaise of the post-federation 'drought' years, she declared this new moment as 'a time of serious provocation' in which Caribbean cultural practices were 'vital' to 'the Third World', and must be connected to 'the upheavals, revolutions, new attitudes and thought' of global black radicalism.[31] Emphasising the multiplicity of cultural forms able to speak the Caribbean to the world, Maxwell's tour-de-force piece wove together calypso, literary fiction, carnival, poetry, the sound system yards,

---

[30] Mervyn Morris, *Making West Indian Literature* (Kingston, Jamaica: Ian Randle, 2005), 18.
[31] Marina Maxwell, 'Towards a Revolution in the Arts', *CAM Newsletter*, 10 (April–June 1969): 1–12; 1.

and theatre. These, she argued, were the connecting cultural threads of the Americas, stretching from New Orleans to Argentina, with the capacity to stitch together the insurrectionary histories of Latin America with those of a rapidly decolonising Africa.

By casting artists as 'cultural guerrillas' and calling for the consolidation of a 'poetry of steel' and, moreover, its transformation into a 'poetry *in* steel', Maxwell's talk was world-revolutionary in its range.[32] It is telling, nevertheless, that such a vision was grounded in the work of CAM authors: in particular, Harris, Walcott, and Brathwaite. In drawing on such figures, she argued for a powerful re-emphasis of specific currents in CAM, not for a thorough washing-away of its previous focus. In all this, Maxwell provided a pronounced, but by no means singular, expression of the Black Power politics current within CAM at the time.[33] Equally telling was the prominence that Maxwell gave to those women thinkers and cultural practitioners who had intersected with and helped to define CAM's work from the very start. The aptly titled 'Towards a Revolution in the Arts' draws to a conclusion by paying tribute to the work of Beryl McBurnie (1913–2000), whose Little Carib supplied a model for Maxwell's own Yard Theatre work and who more broadly symbolised 'the ferment beginning in West Indian culture', a creativity that needed to be sustained into the future.[34] Maxwell also traced the formative intervention of Elsa Goveia (1925–1980), keynote speaker at the first CAM conference at Kent in 1967. Goveia had set out a compelling vision for the role of Caribbean creative artists as the region emerged from colonial rule. Notably, too, Goveia had called for the overturning of racial classification and for cultural forms that could both cross over class boundaries and cross out class-bound attitudes. The talk was later published in the fourth edition of the CAM newsletter.[35] Maxwell's bookending of McBurnie and

---

[32] Maxwell, 'Towards a Revolution in the Arts', 8–9.

[33] Foregrounding Maxwell's intervention offers a useful corrective to analyses that perhaps underplay the radicalism of the movement. Kalliney in his illuminating study describes how 'CAM borrowed from the language of radical anti-imperialist and minority politics, but fitted this political discourse within its program for the arts.' Participants of CAM were more deeply invested in the *creation* of a cultural politics of Black Power and decolonisation than the tone of this assertion might suggest. Peter J. Kalliney, *Commonwealth of Letters: British Literary Culture and the Emergence of Postcolonial Aesthetics* (Oxford: Oxford University Press, 2013), 251.

[34] Maxwell, 'Towards a Revolution in the Arts', 9. McBurnie, Trinidad's foremost choreographer, dance teacher, and folklorist, founded Little Carib Theatre in 1948 very near her home in Port of Spain. It became a key site for the staging of local productions, provided a vision of national performance practices, and served as a model for later theatrical projects in the region.

[35] Elsa Goveia, 'The Caribbean: Socio-Cultural Framework,' in *CAM Newsletter*, 4 (August–September 1967): 2–8.

Goveia underscored the essential, continuous, though not always fore-grounded contributions that women had made to CAM's direction and formations of decolonising thought.

Walmsley's detailed postscript to her CAM history acknowledges the 'apparently small but significant' part played by women, and cites the contributions not just of Goveia and Maxwell but also of Yvonne Brewster, Doris Brathwaite, Pearl Connor, Althea McNish, and Jean Franco – also referenced by Maxwell in her influential talk, 'Towards a Revolution'.[36] It is clear that, although women contributed to, shaped, and facilitated many of the debates in CAM sessions and were prime actors in the facilitation of its activities, they occupied subordinated space in orthodox narratives about CAM, which was, despite some coverage, perceived to be 'an exclusively male club'.[37] In this light it is possible to view both the gendered division of labour within CAM and the tendency of scholarly approaches to it as exemplifying the masculinist mode of challenges to colonialism that dominated Caribbean cultural nation-alisms at the time. As has been argued, 'the complex gender politics of anticolonial literary nationalism' created an 'exclusionary paradigm' which has cast a shadow over subsequent narratives.[38] Recentring the contribution of women to CAM can form part of a longer revisionary critical project of which 'gender will necessarily be a central element', and can usefully throw new light on practices of Caribbean cultural consecration and processes of canonisation.[39]

The 'worlding' of CAM might best be understood as the situating of historical Caribbean experience within international networks of relation and the re-routing of an exclusive focus on the metropolitan 'mother coun-try'. Such a process, which had found new revolutionary expression and emphasis in an alignment with the radicalism of 1968, had of course been a constituent part of CAM's initial vision. As well as bringing together distinct

---

[36] Anne Walmsley also celebrates the 'most valuable work' undertaken by founding members' wives and partners Nerys Patterson, Pat Salkey, and Sara White (*Caribbean Artists Movement*, 307). It is important to recognise at this point the work done by Walmsley herself, both in her capacity as an editor at Longman in the late 1960s and as the seminal chronicler of the movement.

[37] Sandra Courtman, 'Caribbean Artists Movement' in Richard M. Juang and Noelle Morrissette (eds.), *Africa and the Americas: Culture, Politics and History*, vol. 1 (Santa Barbara, CA: ABC-Clio, 2008), 234–5; 235.

[38] Leah Rosenberg, 'The Canon/Canonicity: Anglophone Caribbean Literature' in Michael Bucknor and Alison Donnell (eds.), *The Routledge Companion to Anglophone Caribbean Literature* (London: Routledge, 2011), 347–55; 350.

[39] Rosenberg, 'Canon/Canonicity', 354. The work of Rosenberg can be situated alongside recent work by Alison Donnell, whose focus on the women participants of *Caribbean Voices* marks a significant moment in this revisionary critique of a Caribbean canon.

fields of cultural production and critical scholarship, CAM had always insisted on formulations that drew in more than anglophone territories. The commitment to and promotion of work from the francophone and Hispanic territories typified the endeavours of many founder members, La Rose in particular.[40] While CAM activities engaged prominent scholars of Latin America, the Caribbean island Cuba and its revolution loomed largest in such debates.

January 1968 saw the landmark Cultural Congress of Havana; notably, several of CAM's key figures took up invitations to attend. The focus constellated with CAM's concerns, centring on continuing imperialism, cultures of independence, and the role of artists and intellectuals in understanding and reshaping 'the underdeveloped world'.[41] Andrew Salkey's *Havana Journal* documents with clarity the interventions and reflections of C. L. R. James, John La Rose, and Robert Hill as they attended as spokespersons for the anglophone Caribbean. Indeed, a poignant subplot of the journal was the conversation between CAM delegates about the position of the English-speaking West Indies in the broader politics of anti-colonial revolution. The contested position of the anglophone Caribbean in conventional conceptions and definitions of Latin America fed the feeling that the English-speaking West Indians occupied a certain peripherality or 'not thereness'. As Salkey summarised to his fellow travellers: *"Limbo like we ... "* I parodied, perhaps in bad taste'.[42] Despite such misgivings, the informal session set up by La Rose with Aimé Césaire, with Nancy Morejón in attendance, went some way to consolidate and extend cross-linguistic collaborations. For Salkey, the whole experience of the Havana Congress allowed for a deeper rumination on the role of the artist in society. In concluding the journal, he presents the Cuban painters René Portocarrero and Wilfredo Lam as emblems for the revisionary capacity of the Caribbean artist:

> Portocarrero I had chosen as my human symbol of the West Indian artist who was rooted at home, in Cuba, in the West Indies, and with an international appeal and fame, and Lam the symbol of the distinguished artist who was living abroad and contributing both to Cuban and European art, in unequal measure.[43]

---

[40] See James, 'Caribbean Artists Movement', 217.
[41] Andrew Salkey, *Havana Journal* (Harmondsworth: Penguin, 1971), 98.   [42] Ibid., 107.
[43] Ibid., 295.

It may be possible in retrospect to view this symbolic reading by Salkey of the work of these two Cuban painters as a synthesised model for CAM's contributors and its overall collective of work.

Accounting for Conflict and Collectivity

The discursive frictions between CAM's members and the loosely articulated structure of the movement itself were central to providing a forum in which resistance to imperialism could be imagined and enacted. As Susheila Nasta argues, CAM had 'both an international and local agenda'; it sought 'to enable a more unified sense of Caribbean culture' while also engaging with new formulations of black British culture. It was transnational, but also solidly grounded in the local politics of both Britain and the Caribbean.[44] CAM's double-faceted nature thus placed it at the interstices of the imperatives of a rapidly decolonising world and the increasingly urgent task of forming a postcolonial Britain worthy of the name.

The Caribbean Artists Movement has taken up a position of pre-eminence in canonical narratives about twentieth-century Caribbean culture. Along with political and literary magazines in the Caribbean, the BBC's *Caribbean Voices* programme, and the development of the University of the West Indies, CAM forms one of the key institutional sites around which critical readings of Caribbean art have constellated. In light of this focus, Leah Rosenberg suggests that the task for scholars of the twentieth century now is to deepen understandings of 'the length and complexity of Caribbean literary [cultural] history and its relation to material and political history'.[45] If the tendency of retrospectives of CAM has been to account for and underscore the crises and the failures, this might now be usefully balanced by an understanding that the search for a unified sense of Caribbean culture, which might cohere and continue across generations, is matched in value by the energetic movement of intellectual and cultural practices exploding out across the world stage. From a critical perspective that considers the internationalist aspect of CAM's history, the fractious brevity of the movement's beginnings in Britain can be more fully understood, not only in terms of the fractures and fissures of an emerging arts collective but as a constitutive part of a more fully realised radical globalism. Despite its brief formal lifespan, then, it is unarguable that

---

[44] Susheila Nasta, '1940s–1970s' in Deirdre Osborne (ed.), *The Cambridge Companion to British Black and Asian Literature (1945–2010)* (Cambridge: Cambridge University Press, 2016), 23–39; 33.

[45] Rosenberg, 'Canon/Canonicity', 354.

CAM burned brightly and contributed to the struggle for cultural decolonisation in Britain and the Caribbean. It anticipated and contributed to the forging of black British self-representation and collective cultural identity, exemplifying processes that were anchored in frameworks of Black Atlantic radicalism, and in many cases, more widely, in a politics of world-revolutionary solidarity.

16

Breaking New Ground
Many Tongues, Many Forms

ASHOK BERY

Translocal Tongues

The writers and performers discussed in this chapter – Louise Bennett, Kamau Brathwaite, the calypsonian Lord Kitchener, Dom Moraes, John Figueroa, E. A. Markham, Wole Soyinka – do not fit neatly into a book on *British* writing. They all spent periods living in Britain during the two decades or so after World War II, but only Markham really settled and even he spent considerable periods abroad. Nonetheless, their respective experiences in Britain helped shape their work, and, in turn, their explorations amongst a variety of literary, vernacular, and oral influences and forms affected later generations of British writers.[1]

These poets form a rather disparate group. Although five are of Caribbean origin, they differ considerably in the linguistic and stylistic choices they make out of the range of Englishes available to them, the so-called 'Creole continuum'. Moraes (India) and Soyinka (Nigeria), on the other hand, generally write in standard English but come from countries where it coexists with a variety of vernaculars, the languages of everyday use for most people. James Clifford's concept of the 'trans-local' offers a useful comparative framework within which to explore such different contexts and writers. For Clifford, the term refers to 'theoretical paradigms [which] explicitly articulate local and global processes in relational, non-teleological ways'. In a discussion of black British poetry, Jahan Ramazani has applied the notion to work 'that reconceives and remaps widely disparate geocultural spaces and histories

---

[1] A helpful survey of the literary and cultural contexts of this period is Susheila Nasta's essay '1940s–1970s' in Deirdre Osborne (ed.), *The Cambridge Companion to Black British and Asian Literature (1945–2010)* (Cambridge: Cambridge University Press, 2016), 23–39.

in relation to one another'.[2] These helpful formulations are extended here through a more specific focus on language.[3]

Seamus Heaney describes the writer as being 'poised between his own idiolect and the vast sound-wave and sewage-wash of the language's total availability'. To explore this state, he draws on an essay by Ted Hughes, for whom each literary work is fixed at a point 'on a continuum between some sub-group's (the author's) system of shared understandings [...] and the most inclusive, ideally global wave-length of a multicultural lingua franca'.[4] In the present context, the lingua franca is standard English, while the sub-groups consist of the many varieties of English used in different parts of the world, such as the 'nation language' that Kamau Brathwaite has studied in detail.[5] (In Soyinka's case one must add the influence of Yoruba.) Although standard English is itself the language of a particular (and powerful) sub-group, exerting a hegemony that many writers have tried to contest, it can be more easily understood across a wider range of English-speaking cultures than, say, the language of the Jamaican performance poet Louise Bennett.

Any language is both enabling and restrictive. It embodies nuances unavailable to other languages, yet it can also constitute a prison: as George Steiner puts it, other languages allow us to conceive of 'alternities of being', other possibilities.[6] These possibilities may, Heaney points out elsewhere, open up the idea of 'an escape route [...] into some unpartitioned linguistic country, a region where one's language would not be simply a badge of ethnicity [...] but an entry into further language'.[7] This 'unpartitioned linguistic country' is utopian, of course, but it symbolises an attempt to circumvent the dualities of language and culture that are legacies of colonialism.

---

[2] James Clifford, *Routes: Travel and Translation in the Late Twentieth Century* (Cambridge, MA: Harvard University Press, 1997), 7; Jahan Ramazani, 'Black British Poetry and the Translocal' in Neil Corcoran (ed.), *The Cambridge Companion to Twentieth-Century English Poetry* (Cambridge: Cambridge University Press, 2007), 200–14; 200.

[3] The next two paragraphs draw on ch. 1 and p. 129 of my book *Cultural Translation and Postcolonial Poetry* (Basingstoke: Palgrave Macmillan, 2007).

[4] Seamus Heaney, 'The Drag of the Golden Chain,' *Times Literary Supplement*, 12 November 1999: 16; Ted Hughes, 'Metres, Myths, Rhythms' in *Winter Pollen: Occasional Prose*, ed. William Scammell (London: Faber and Faber, 1994), 310–72; 312.

[5] 'Nation language' is the term Brathwaite prefers to 'dialect' because of the 'pejorative overtones' of the latter: *History of the Voice: The Development of Nation Language in Anglophone Caribbean Poetry* (London: New Beacon Books, 1984), 13.

[6] George Steiner, *After Babel: Aspects of Language and Translation*, 3rd edn (Oxford: Oxford University Press, 1998), 497.

[7] Seamus Heaney, *Beowulf: A New Translation* (London: Faber and Faber, 1999), xxv.

These remarks highlight two themes that will recur in what follows: the tension between the lingua franca and the languages (and cultures) of the sub-groups, and the resistance to compartmentalisation within a particular language and culture. This chapter will explore how the writers discussed negotiate such pressures.

'If You Look for Me, I am not Here': Wole Soyinka and Dom Moraes

As indicated earlier, the poets can be divided into two broad groups: Moraes and Soyinka, on the one hand, and those of Caribbean origin on the other. There are, however, significant differences between Moraes (1938–2004) and Soyinka (1934–). Because English is not usually the primary language of daily life in India or Nigeria, its development in those countries is uneven and restricted; consequently, standard English can exert a pressure that is more difficult to contest than it is for the Caribbean writer, who is able to draw on living and changing varieties of English, including nation language. Multilingual Indian and Nigerian writers in English can turn to their other language(s), an option available to Soyinka but not to Moraes, who came from the relatively small Roman Catholic minority of India, and was not comfortable in any indigenous Indian language or culture. His cultural and linguistic resources were largely English; in consequence, he has sometimes been depicted as a 'brown sahib'. This view, Ranjit Hoskote has argued, is a caricature: Moraes should rather be seen as someone who 'struggled with the consequences of postcoloniality without fully recognizing this to be his predicament'.[8] One manifestation of this struggle is the sense of homelessness pervading his work.

Moraes often represents this homelessness through wandering, in-between mythological personae (including literary and historical figures who take on a quasi-mythical force), such as the Argonaut Jason, Frankenstein, Dracula, and the Emperors Babur and Alexander. In the poems that bear their names, Alexander, for instance, feels 'exiled from two countries I hated and loved'; Babur describes himself as 'lonely in all lands'. But, for Babur, the homelessness is mitigated by a different sense of belonging; towards the end of the poem, he says: 'If you look for me, I am not here. / My writings will tell you where I am.'[9] While it expresses a sense of

---

[8] Dom Moraes, *Selected Poems*, ed. Ranjit Hoskote (New Delhi: Penguin Books, 2012), xvii, xvi.
[9] Ibid., 169, 133.

dislocation, the first of these lines simultaneously makes allusive connections across time and space. In the Gospel of Matthew, when the door of Christ's sepulchre is opened, the angel tells the two waiting Marys: 'He is not here: for he is risen, as he said.' And Walt Whitman ends *Song of Myself* with the lines:

> I bequeath myself to the dirt to grow from the grass I love,
> If you want me again look for me under your boot-soles.
> [...]
> Missing me one place search another,
> I stop somewhere waiting for you.[10]

The two emperors seem to be oblique self-portraits. Moraes may have felt homeless everywhere but, the allusions in 'Babur' suggest, it is possible that he found a provisional home in an 'unpartitioned linguistic country'. The poem reverberates with what Heaney calls the 'sound-wave [...] of the language's total availability'.

Wole Soyinka spent several years in Britain during the late 1950s, and a number of poems from this period deal, in a realistic, satirical vein, with experiences of racism and discrimination. The most successful is the widely anthologised 'Telephone Conversation', in which the speaker satirises a potential landlady's prejudice through a witty literal-mindedness. Asked 'HOW DARK' he is, the speaker proceeds to list the colours of different parts of his body, concluding with:

> ' [...] Friction, caused –
> Foolishly, madam – by sitting down, has turned
> My bottom raven black – One moment, madam!' – sensing
> Her receiver rearing on the thunderclap
> About my ears – 'Madam,' I pleaded, 'wouldn't you rather
> See for yourself?'[11]

The politeness of the repeated 'madam' is undercut by the double-edged 'wouldn't you rather / See for yourself?', which refers both to the speaker as a whole and, in an insolent gesture, to the last-mentioned part of him, his 'bottom'.

At around the same time, however, Soyinka was also writing very different kinds of poems, which drew on the Yoruba myths and rituals that became prominent in his mature work. An interesting example is 'Abiku', a Yoruba term which mythologises the phenomenon of child mortality. Soyinka

[10] Walt Whitman, *The Complete Poems*, ed. Francis Murphy (London: Penguin, 1975), 124.
[11] *Times Literary Supplement*, 10 August 1962: 569; the poem originally appeared in the journal *Ibadan* in 1960.

defines the term in one of his essays: 'When a child dies to a mother twice or thrice, it becomes the same child returnee, whose "earthing" can only be guaranteed by sacrifices and rituals in propitiation of the obstinate child or in confrontation with his or her siblings on "the other side".'[12] Douglas McCabe describes the *àbíkú* as a '"club" (*egbé*) of "heaven-people" [...] whose founding purpose is to siphon off riches from [...] the "houses" (*ilé*) of the "world-people"'. An *àbíkú* is born into an *ilé* where, after accumulating wealth, it dies 'by a certain method prearranged secretly with its *egbé*', taking the 'spiritual portion of its loot back to heaven'; it then re-enters the world to repeat the process in 'the same or another *ilé*'. The contrast between *egbé* and *ilé* is one between 'voluntary membership, mutual benefit, pursuit of a shared non-reproductive purpose, and group secrecy' and 'marriage, lineage, procreation, geography, and hierarchical structures of seniority and inheritance'; in short, between loyalty to a group and loyalty to a lineage, between individual choice and collectivity. The way to stop an *àbíkú* continually returning to rob an *ilé* is to 'fetter' it spiritually (the process Soyinka describes as 'earthing').[13]

Soyinka's poem is a monologue spoken by an *àbíkú* who insists forcefully on his individuality (the word 'I' resounds throughout the poem), rejecting the family and its attempt to 'earth' the *àbíkú* in this world:

> In vain your bangles cast
> Charmed circles at my feet;
> I am Abiku, calling for the first
> And the repeated time.[14]

The casting of bangles refers to one of the rituals that the family into which the *àbíkú* has been born use to 'fetter' it and keep it alive. The *àbíkú* rejects this as it rejects all other rituals and domesticity:

> Must I weep for goats and cowries
> For palm oil and the sprinkled ash?
> Yams do not sprout in amulets
> To earth Abiku's limbs.[15]

As McCabe shows, the poem's concern with 'the relationship between Soyinka's Western present and his Yoruba past, between Western-style political individualism and Yoruba-style familial rule', with staging a drama

---

[12] Wole Soyinka, *Art, Dialogue and Outrage: Essays on Literature and Culture* (Ibadan: New Horn Press, 1988), 257. I have corrected misprints in spelling and punctuation.

[13] Douglas McCabe, 'Histories of Errancy: Oral Yoruba *Àbíkú* Texts and Soyinka's "Abiku"', *Research in African Literatures*, 33:1 (Spring 2002): 45–74; 46, 48.

[14] Wole Soyinka, *Idanre and Other Poems* (London: Methuen, 1967), 28.   [15] Ibid., 29.

of 'individualistic dissent from the norm of Yoruba family rule', operates on the level of form as well as content. It puts the point of view of the *àbíkú* through a mixture of genres, the western lyric (the poem is in quatrains) and the verbal textures of Yoruba oral traditions (particularly *oríki*, or praise poetry).[16] While being rooted in Yoruba forms, it bears the traces of the western culture in which it was composed during the late 1950s.

In his essay 'Neo-Tarzanism', Soyinka criticises the nativist 'bolekaja' critics who had attacked him and others for their obscurity, 'Euromodernism', and deracination; these critics, he argues, oversimplify the opposition between African tradition and the European modern, and 'subvert the principle of imaginative challenge which is one of the functions of poetry'.[17] Poems such as 'Abiku' pose this imaginative challenge by bringing different contexts and forms together, avoiding compartmentalisation within one frame of reference.

Creolised Modernities

Kamau Brathwaite (1930–) is an appropriate point of departure for a discussion of the Caribbean writers. He embodies, and has played an important role in articulating, the forces that have shaped the cultures of the islands and of Caribbean writing in Britain. Born in Barbados, he studied in the UK and spent a formative period working in Ghana, thus completing the 'triangular trade of [his] historical origins'. Ghana, he says, gave him 'a sense of place, of belonging; and that place and belonging, I knew, was the West Indies'.[18] As we saw in the previous chapter in this volume, Brathwaite was also a key figure in the Caribbean Artists Movement, which had a significant impact on the development of Caribbean arts in Britain during the late 1960s and early 1970s.[19] The term 'translocal' aptly describes Brathwaite's work, so closely does it fit a major concern of his throughout his career, the process of creolisation (the intermingling of different cultural influences) in the

---

[16] McCabe, 'Histories', 59, 60, 64.

[17] Soyinka, *Art*, 327. The best-known nativist critique is Chinweizu, Onwuchekwa Jemie and Ihechukwu Madubuike, *Toward the Decolonization of African Literature*, vol. 1: *African Fiction and Poetry and their Critics* (London: KPI, 1985).

[18] Rosalie Murphy and James Vinson (eds.), *Contemporary Poets of the English Language* (London: St James Press, 1970), 129.

[19] See Edward Brathwaite, 'The Caribbean Artists Movement', *Caribbean Quarterly* 14:1–2 (March–June 1968): 57–9. Brathwaite later changed his name to 'Edward Kamau Brathwaite' and then to 'Kamau Brathwaite'. When citing his works, I use the name under which they were first published.

Caribbean, a process which, in his view, involved a 'friction' which was 'cruel, but [...] also creative'.[20]

Such themes permeate his 'New World Trilogy' (1967–1969; published in a single volume as *The Arrivants* in 1973), which is also underpinned by a triangular movement.[21] As Brathwaite has explained, the first book, '*Rights of Passage* [...] is about the black diaspora'; the second, *Masks*, 'is the [...] return of scattered psyches to the ancestral homeland'; while the third, *Islands*, explores 'the certainties/uncertainties of the Caribbean, taking up the theme of "the gains and the losses", implicit in *Masks*'.[22] Brathwaite is often described as a modernist; Caribbean modernism, however, is a creolised phenomenon, 'fertilized by figures of the "other" imagination which colonialism has sought to repress'.[23] Like other cultural forms in the region, it produces what Antonio Benitez-Rojo describes as 'an ethnologically promiscuous text that might allow a reading of the varied and dense polyphony of Caribbean society's characteristic codes' (which include the European components).[24]

The modernist writer whom Brathwaite has repeatedly acknowledged is T. S. Eliot.[25] There are many links with Eliot in *The Arrivants*, both on a local level (such as verbal echoes) and on a structural level (the quest theme). Some of these threads will be drawn together here by focusing on one aspect of Brathwaite's modernism – fragmentation, a feature central to the history and cultural experience of the Caribbean. Unlike Eliot's fragments, however, which are defensively 'shored against [his] ruins', Brathwaite's are connected with the creative friction of creolisation; Benitez-Rojo's phrase 'varied and dense polyphony' emphasises the creativity, avoiding the potentially negative connotations of the term 'fragmentation'.[26] The polyphony of *The Arrivants* is visible on a number of levels. The narrative is dispersed amongst a variety of

---

[20] Edward Brathwaite, *The Development of Creole Society in Jamaica 1770–1820* (Oxford: Clarendon Press, 1978), 307.

[21] Edward Brathwaite, *The Arrivants* (Oxford: Oxford University Press, 1973).

[22] Quoted by Mervyn Morris, 'Overlapping Journeys; *The Arrivants*' in Stewart Brown (ed.), *The Art of Kamau Brathwaite* (Bridgend: Seren, 1995), 117–31; 119–20.

[23] Simon Gikandi, *Writing in Limbo: Modernism and Caribbean Literature* (Ithaca, NY: Cornell University Press, 1992), 4. On Brathwaite's modernism, see, for instance, Keith Tuma, 'Edward Kamau Brathwaite's *X/Self* and Black British Poetry' in *Fishing by Obstinate Isles: Modern and Postmodern British Poetry and American Readers* (Evanston, IL: Northwestern University Press, 1998), 244–64.

[24] Antonio Benitez-Rojo, *The Repeating Island: The Caribbean and the Postmodern Perspective* (Durham, NC: Duke University Press, 1996), 189.

[25] For instance, Brathwaite, *History of the Voice*, 30 and Murphy and Vinson (eds.), *Contemporary Poets of the English Language*, 129.

[26] Brathwaite discusses the aesthetic of fragmentation in 'An Interview with Kamau Brathwaite' in Brown (ed.), *The Art of Kamau Brathwaite*, 18–19.

settings, personae, characters, and voices. This dispersal, however, is also a kind of unification: the multiplicity represents the 'ingathering of the multitudes' of the African diaspora.[27] Polyphony is also evident in the variety of musical and literary forms used or alluded to (including jazz, calypso, folk songs, hymns, prayers, sermons) and in the variety of languages on which Brathwaite draws.

Some of these aspects of the trilogy are evident in two well-known poems, 'Negus' and 'The Dust', which start from different points on the linguistic continuum.[28] 'Negus' opens as follows:

> It
> it
> it
> it is not
> [...]
> it is not
> it is not
> it is not enough
> it is not enough to be free [...]

Although the poem is written almost entirely in standard English, creolisation is evoked in a number of ways. The repetition of 'it' – a feature brought out in Brathwaite's own readings of the poem – sounds like a beating drum, an instrument that *The Arrivants* regularly associates with Africa and with New World cultures.[29] 'Negus' also draws on stylistic features of the oral tradition, such as additive repetition: the 'it' of the first line gradually expands into 'it is not enough to be free'. The interweaving of languages can be seen in the concluding lines, an invocation in French creole to Attibon Legba, the 'Dahomean/Haitian god of the gateway', as Brathwaite defines him:[30]

> *Attibon Legba*
> *Attibon Legba*
> *Ouvri bayi pou' moi*
> *Ouvri bayi pou' moi*

---

[27] Morris, 'Overlapping Journeys', 119–20. Brathwaite uses the phrase to describe the second book in the trilogy, *Masks*, but it is relevant to the entire work.

[28] Brathwaite, *Arrivants*, 222–4; 62–9.

[29] As in 'The Making of the Drum', a multipart poem towards the beginning of *Masks* (94–7). In his notes to a recording of *Islands*, Brathwaite speaks of the 'raindrop drumbeats' of 'Negus'; quoted by Gordon Rohlehr, *Pathfinder: Black Awakening in 'The Arrivants' of Edward Kamau Brathwaite* (Tunapuna, Trinidad: Gordon Rohlehr, 1981), 263.

[30] Brathwaite, *Arrivants*, 273.

Poems such as 'The Dust' and 'The Stone Sermon' begin by using speech patterns and other elements derived from the nation language end of the spectrum, but go on to incorporate different aspects of the creolised culture.[31] Both titles allude to *The Waste Land* ('I will show you fear in a handful of dust' and 'The Fire Sermon' respectively); and, in its conception (a group of women talking in a grocer's store), 'The Dust' echoes the pub scene in 'A Game of Chess'. Eliot's 'Goonight Bill. Goonight Lou. Goonight May. Goonight' reverberates at the beginning of Brathwaite's poem:

> Evenin' Miss
> Evvy, Miss
> Maisie, Miss
> Maud.[32]

The 'varied and dense polyphony' of such poems is testimony to the creative friction of Caribbean culture; as Brathwaite puts it in the concluding lines of the trilogy, the Caribbean peoples are engaged in:

> making
> with their
>
> rhythms some-
> thing torn
> and new.[33]

City Calypsos: Lord Kitchener and Louise Bennett

In *History of the Voice*, Brathwaite discusses many predecessors in the use of nation language, including the calypsonians and Louise Bennett, to whom I turn in this section. The calypso, a creolised form associated with Carnival, became, according to Lloyd Bradley, 'the official sound-track of black Britain' during the 1950s and 1960s.[34] Lord Kitchener (1922–2000), like Bennett, was living in Britain during the 1940s and 1950s (indeed, he arrived in Britain on the *Windrush*, the vessel emblematic – as other contributors to this history have noted – of that period of Caribbean migration). The ironic and satiric features of the calypso tradition do not feature much in Kitchener's British songs, which record a trajectory common amongst West Indian migrants at the time: an initial surge of optimism followed by disillusion. The calypso

---

[31] Ibid., 254–7.   [32] Ibid., 62.   [33] Ibid., 270.
[34] Quoted by Stuart Hall in 'Calypso Kings', *The Guardian*, 28 June 2002 Available at www.theguardian.com/culture/2002/jun/28/nottinghillcarnival2002.nottinghillcarnival.

'London is the Place for Me' was begun in a rush of anticipation before he had set foot in Britain. As he put it in an interview years later, the song emerged from 'the feeling I had to know that I'm going to touch the soil of the mother country [...] a wonderful feeling':[35]

> To live in London you are really comfortable
> Because the English people are very much sociable.
> They take you here and they take you there
> And they make you feel like a millionaire.[36]

This optimism was soon eroded by realities in London, such as those described in 'My Landlady':

> No chair, no table,
> The convenience is terrible,
> And on the other part
> No hot water to take a bath,
> And believe you sleep like a rabbit
> Under the sheet with half of a blanket.[37]

However, 'London is the Place for Me' also depicts a slow creolisation taking place – the migrants adapt to London, and the city begins to adapt to them:

> You can take a walk down Shaftesbury Avenue
> There you will laugh and talk and enjoy the breeze,
> And admire the beautiful scenery
> Of London – that's the place for me.

These lines display a feeling of anticipatory belonging, even of taking imaginative possession of London, as he sees himself, to use the Trinidadian expression, 'liming' in Shaftesbury Avenue.[38]

Unlike Kitchener, Bennett (1919–2006) came from a middle-class background and had to contend with snobbery over the use of nation language, the 'social stigma attached to the kind of person who used dialect habitually'.[39] Her poem 'Bans O' Killing' mocks such attitudes; here, the speaker confronts a man, Mass Charlie, who has expressed a wish to 'kill

---

[35] 'Lord Kitchener: The Singer and the Song' [interview with Lord Kitchener] in Mike Phillips and Trevor Phillips, *Windrush: The Irresistible Rise of Multi-Racial Britain* (London: HarperCollins, 1998), 65–6; 66.

[36] *London is the Place for Me*, vol. 1 (London: Honest Jon's Records, 2012). The punctuation is mine.

[37] Ibid.

[38] Ramazani discusses Kitchener's creolisation of London in 'Black British Poetry', 205.

[39] 'Bennett on Bennett: Interviewed by Dennis Scott', *Caribbean Quarterly*, 14:1–2 (March–June 1968): 97–101; 101.

dialect', which he sees as inferior to standard English.[40] Her response exposes the absurdity of this stance by pushing it to extremes. 'Yuh gwine kill all English dialect', she asks Charlie, 'Or jus Jamaica one?' Standard English is itself a dialect, she points out: 'Dah language weh yuh proud o', / [...] Yuh noh know sey / Dat it spring from dialect!' English as a whole is *composed* of dialects, so that if he wants to kill dialect, he will also have to 'tear / Out Chaucer, Burns, Lady Grizelle / An plenty o' Shakespeare' from *The Oxford Book of English Verse*.

Another famous poem, 'Back to Africa', adopts the same literalising strategy to satirise nativist movements.[41] Here, addressing a regular interlocutor in Bennett's poems, Miss Matty, the speaker points out that, if extended universally, the desire for return would lead to an absurd situation:

> Wat a debil of a bump-an-bore,
> Rig-jig an palam-pam!
> Ef de whole worl' start fe go back
> Weh dem great granpa come from!

Pointing out that Matty's ancestors include Africans, Englishmen, Jews, and Frenchmen, the poem emphasises the creolisation that has shaped the Caribbean. Matty's place is Jamaica:

> But de balance o' yuh family
> Yuh whole generation
> Oonoo all bawn dung a Bun grung
> Oonoo all is Jamaican!

As these poems show, one tendency of her writing is to destabilise the linguistic and racial hierarchies entrenched in colonial cultures.

A Mug's Game: John Figueroa, E. A. Markham, and the Refusal to Be 'Ethnicked'

Although both John Figueroa (1920–1999) and E. A. Markham (1939–2008) make strategic use of nation language, they tend to gravitate towards the standard English end of the spectrum. Figueroa's satirical poem 'Problems of a Writer Who Does not Quite ... ', however, counterpoints both varieties in

[40] Louise Bennett, *Jamaica Labrish: With Notes and Introduction by Rex Nettleford* (Kingston, Jamaica: Sangster's Book Stores, 1966), 218–19.
[41] Ibid., 214–15.

its response to what Figueroa sees as a condescending review of Derek Walcott's *The Fortunate Traveller*:[42]

> Bwoy, yu no hear wa de lady say?
> Watch di pentameter ting, man.
> Dat is white people play!

Walcott is enjoined to conform to a particular stereotype of the Caribbean poet and to break up his lines:

> Bruck it
>
> up
>
> man   an' wid de drums
>   de drums

Here, in resisting what he takes to be the review's metropolitan *hauteur*, Figueroa also seems to be invoking Brathwaite, who often divides his lines in this way (as in 'Negus'), and for whom the drum is a recurrent symbol. Towards the end of the poem, Figueroa switches to standard English:

> No more of the loud sounding sea
> Or the disjecta membra
> Homer, Horace are not, are not for you and me

The phrase 'disjecta membra', an allusion to Horace, is used also by Walcott in 'Ruins of a Great House'.[43] Figueroa sees the review as representative of exclusionary attitudes to Caribbean poetry and identity; he claims the right to use any and all literary and cultural resources, even, as in this poem, those strongly associated with upper-class British imperial culture, such as the Classics.

A consistent feature of E. A. Markham's literary career was his resistance to dualities of identity:

> The dramatic revelation that poets [...] in and from the Caribbean had two voices – nation-language and Standard English – released many energies; but we had to be sure that this wasn't to be interpreted that we had *only* two voices, *only* two modes of expression: for this might gel into two modes of

---

[42] John Figueroa, *The Chase: A Collection of Poems 1941–1989* (Leeds: Peepal Tree Press, 1992), 137–8; the review (by Helen Vendler) seems to be 'Poet of Two Worlds', *New York Review of Books*, 4 March 1982: 26.

[43] Derek Walcott, *Collected Poems 1948–1984* (New York: Farrar, Straus and Giroux, 1986), 19.

perception, the one antagonistic to the other; [...] the possibilities of a different mode unexplored.[44]

In order to test 'the whole range of voices that were possibly real for me', he adds, he 'experimented with personae'.[45] This experimentation is evident in the poems that he published under the *nom de plume* Paul St Vincent (many about a West Indian called 'Lambchops'). Paula Burnett points out that these ventriloquised poems are 'carnivalesque' and 'festive' (as indeed is much of Markham's work).[46] These qualities are seen in one of the best known of the 'Lambchops' poems, 'A Mugger's Game', which confronts the stereotype of the young West Indian as criminal. The perspective here is that of what appears to be a composite policeman-judge, 'the Pig in the wig', who enjoins someone to 'Chase him [the supposed mugger] down the alley / put him behind bars'. What underlies this punitive attitude, the poem suggests, is fear:

> Black them here stop them there

> before they get too cheeky

> too second-generation aware.[47]

While it deals with a serious situation, the poem itself is playful. Markham associates the 'mugger's game' with the trickster figure Anancy: 'Lambchops looks as if he is running away; what he is actually trying to do is to draw the policeman out so you can see what is going on in his head. That's an Anancy pose'.[48] Behind the title lurks the expression 'a mug's game', and this in turn evokes a famous statement by T. S. Eliot that 'poetry is not a career, but a mug's game'.[49] This allusion adds a different dimension to the poem: the mugger is not only Lambchops but also the poet. We might therefore translate the title as 'A Poet's Game', so that the poet can be seen as mugging (playing a game with) the policeman (perhaps a stand-in for the reader), who is being tricked into revealing

---

[44] E. A. Markham, 'Many Voices, Many Lives' in *Hinterland: Caribbean Poetry from the West Indies and Britain* (Newcastle upon Tyne: Bloodaxe Books, 1989), 193–6; 194.

[45] Ibid.

[46] Paula Burnett, 'Introduction' to E. A. Markham, *Lambchops with Sally Goodman: The Selected Poems of Paul St Vincent and Sally Goodman* (Cambridge: Salt, 2004), xv–xviii; xviii.

[47] E. A. Markham, *Human Rites: Selected Poems 1970–1982* (London: Anvil Press, 1984), 105.

[48] Quoted at https://literature.britishcouncil.org/writer/e-a-markham.

[49] T. S. Eliot, *The Use of Poetry and the Use of Criticism: Studies in the Relation of Criticism to Poetry in England* (London: Faber and Faber, 1933), 154.

his prejudices. Both Lambchops and the poet are simultaneously mugs (victims, objects of prejudice) and Anancy-like muggers.

In this poem, Markham focuses on stereotypical views of West Indians found in Britain. 'Roots, Roots', one of a group of 'West Indian Myths', resists the opposite stereotype, the pressure to define oneself only as West Indian or black:[50]

> My grandmother's donkey had a name
> I can't recall. It's not important
> for the donkey, a beast of burden
> like my grandmother, is dead.
> And I am in a different place.

The doubling of the word in the title gives it an edge of mocking weariness. This first stanza of the poem evokes a past that appears to resemble Markham's own Montserrat childhood, largely spent with his grandmother.[51] Even as the poem begins to strike roots in its first line (the act of naming), it extirpates them with the line division: 'a name / I can't recall'. The way the syntax unfolds across the ensuing lines also constantly forces the reader to revise meaning. Does 'It's not important' refer to the name, or the speaker's inability to recall it? And then, in the lineation of the second and third lines it seems that these things (the name, the failure to recall) are not important *for the donkey*. As we read on, however, we see that 'for' here means 'because': the reason it doesn't matter is *because* the donkey and grandmother are dead. The play of meaning continually undermines the act of remembering/naming/striking roots with which the poem began. The second stanza brings this out more explicitly:

> Perhaps the donkey was a horse, a status symbol
> or a man, married to my grandmother;
> and he lives on with my name.
> But then, suppose there was no donkey
> no grandmother, no other place?

The possible rootedness symbolised in grandmother and donkey proves to be fragile, with the donkey becoming a horse, then a man, and finally – perhaps – disappearing altogether. As Omaar Hena puts it, the poem is founded on a tension: 'even as the speaker creates the illusion of excavating

---

[50] Markham, *Human Rites*, 20.
[51] See E. A. Markham, *Against the Grain: A 1950s Memoir* (Leeds: Peepal Tree Press, 2008), chs. 2 and 4.

familial-cultural origins, such excavations are bound to fail'.[52] In both poems, Markham demands 'the right [...] not to be "ethnicked"'.[53]

The writers discussed in this chapter have left diverse legacies for those who came later. In their use of nation language and the oral tradition, Brathwaite and Bennett paved the way for successors such as Linton Kwesi Johnson. Others – including John Agard, Grace Nichols, and Fred D'Aguiar – have followed Brathwaite, Markham, and Figueroa in moving between different points on the Creole continuum. While it is less easy to trace specific British literary successors of Soyinka and Moraes, they too embody strategies available to later writers. Soyinka's 'Abiku' is one example of a hybridising method open to bicultural and bilingual writers – the fusion of English and vernacular forms and cultures. Moraes's impact is more diffuse; nonetheless, he shows another way forward by contesting fixities of cultural and linguistic definition while still working within the grain of standard English. All the poets discussed here display an impatience with compartmentalisation, criss-crossing linguistic and cultural boundaries to create the textures of their poems. They refuse to be 'ethnicked'.

---

[52] Omaar Hena, 'Multi-ethnic British Poetries' in Peter Robinson (ed.), *The Oxford Handbook of Contemporary British and Irish Poetry* (Oxford: Oxford University Press, 2013), 517–37; 525.

[53] E. A. Markham, 'Roots and Roots', *PN Review*, 29:3 (January–February 2003): 22–8; 28.

17

The Lure of Postwar London
Networks of People, Print, and Organisations

GAIL LOW

In Pursuit of the English, Doris Lessing's memoir of her years as a penniless writer newly arrived in postwar London, recounts an anecdote when a friend from Cape Town accosts her with, 'Hey, Doris, man . . . how are you doing and how are you getting on with England?' Lessing's riposte was, 'I don't think I've met any. London is full of foreigners.' In this account, London, after World War II, is a place of transnational, cosmopolitan population flows living cheek by jowl with white working-class Londoners. This chapter moves across the three postwar decades to present a materialist history of London as it grappled with – however fitfully and unevenly – the legacy of empire. In addressing the diverse and discrepant material histories of broadcasting, cultural organisations, publishing, bookselling, and bookshops, it describes the multivarious experiences connecting local spaces with global cultural production, all within commercial, social, educational, and political imperatives. This chapter cannot but give a selective portrait of London during these decades, but such a narrative is vital for understanding the role that individuals and organisations have in creating a cosmopolitan city space.

Radio Days

Because of its ability to reach beyond its broadcast location, transforming print into the spoken word and hence widening its range, radio is perhaps the most logical place to begin. At once real and virtual, the airwaves constitute an imaginary space that makes material *and* substantive London's presence and its connection with other far-flung spaces. Debates over postwar programming at the BBC were marked by contradictory pulls towards and away from the Commonwealth: a 'continuing adjustment to imperial decline'; 'public apathy' towards the Commonwealth in favour of Europe; anxieties regarding the rise of American cultural and political influence.[1] The BBC's *Caribbean Voices* was no different in its embeddedness in a Reithian value system and a new more regional, decolonising transnationalism.

Many scholars have explored the impact on the literary landscape of the Caribbean of the BBC's *Caribbean Voices*.[2] As we have seen, *Caribbean Voices* was a twenty-, then thirty-minute programme launched by Una Marson in 1944 and later edited by Henry Swanzy (see Chapter 6). An influential radio series, it supported a developing literary ecology on the islands, mentoring writers and developing literary-institutional frameworks. As *Caribbean Voices* gathered creative work sent in from the BBC agent in Jamaica and also from regional little magazines, it both acted as publisher and forged a pan-island anglophone imagined community over the airwaves at a time when publishing did not easily transcend regional and national locations or offer writers payment. The programme sought to professionalise debates on Caribbean writing modelled in part on the BBC's 'home' arts broadcasts on the Third Programme, thereby growing a network of relationships between Caribbean writers and the London establishment that, unsurprisingly, challenged both stakeholders.

The programme's literary-critical developmental work, which included the creation of 'The Critics' Circle', was vital. Charges of neo-colonialism were inevitably levelled at the series. In reply to the Trinidadian writer Rodwell Debysingh, who criticised the English poet and critic Roy Fuller's contributions to one such programme (Fuller presented regularly on the Third Programme), Swanzy wrote reminding him that literature was a republic of letters. The formation of literary traditions, heritages, and public intellectual and literary-critical forums was necessary. Swanzy provocatively contrasted local island 'schoolmasters' with 'literary men', arguing that literature needed the full weight of educational, critical, and cultural apparatuses to support its development. Patronage may be neo-colonial, 'the imposition of alien standards on a regional culture which ought to develop of itself', but was necessary to 'help build up a better tradition' at a time when

---

[1] Simon J. Potter, *Broadcasting Empire* (Oxford: Oxford University Press, 2012), 201–2.

[2] Phillip Nanton, 'What Does Mr Swanzy Want? Shaping or Reflecting? An Assessment of Henry Swanzy's Contribution to the Development of Caribbean Literature', *Kunapipi*, 20:1 (1998): 11–20; Rhonda Cobham, 'The Caribbean Voices Programme and the Development of West Indian Short Story Fiction: 1945–1958' in P. O. Stummer (ed.), *The Story Must be Told* (Würzburg: Königshausen & Neumann, 1986), 146–58; Gail Low, *Publishing the Postcolonial* (London: Routledge, 2011); Glyne A. Griffith, *The BBC and the Development of Anglophone Caribbean Literature, 1943–1958* (Cham: Palgrave Macmillan, 2016).

local literary-critical culture was only coming into its own with the creation of the University of the West Indies.[3]

For some writers who gravitated towards London, *Caribbean Voices* provided employment as they became paid readers of broadcast material. As printed texts became the spoken word, the emphasis on sound and voice was pronounced. This led to complaints about regional accents but, as Glyne A. Griffith and Laurence Breiner both note, the differing patterns of speech and accents had the effect of sensitising writers and authorities to the spoken word.[4] Broadcast voices therefore opened up debates about authenticity, form, and voice, and encouraged writing poetry for performance after independence.

Swanzy's role as mentor to this circle of Caribbean writers in London, which included figures such as V. S. Naipaul, Wilson Harris, George Lamming, and Sam Selvon, has been well documented elsewhere.[5] Swanzy's introduction to the London literary elite enabled a productive network of connections between these individuals and English writers, publishers, reviewers, and editors in the London literary establishment. These informal networks were important to the metropolitan patronage of the Caribbean, which helped facilitate publication. Arthur Calder-Marshall and Walter Allen encouraged and championed Lamming, which led to the publication of *In the Castle of my Skin* (Michael Joseph); Roy Fuller, William Plomer, and Alan Ross's support of the young Derek Walcott (working then in Trinidad) smoothed the path towards his poetry debut, *In a Green Night* (Jonathan Cape). Francis Wyndham and Diana Athill, both with André Deutsch, supported V. S. Naipaul's early work; Charles Montieth, advised by Andrew Salkey, published Wilson Harris's first novel, *Palace of the Peacock* (Faber). These friendships and the contradictory, complex networks of patronage enabled Caribbean writers to be 'celebrated literary figures in metropolitan highbrow circles throughout the decade'.[6]

The importance of *Caribbean Voices* as a transnational metropolitan nexus of cultural activity is mirrored by that of the Transcription Centre (1962–1978) – albeit less influentially and more problematically, given the latter's reliance on external, private funding. The organisation was founded

---

[3] Henry Swanzy to Mr Debysingh, 18 October 1948, Swanzy Box 1 (1945–52), Henry Swanzy Papers MS 42.

[4] Griffith, *The BBC*, 41; Laurence Breiner, *Black Yeats: Eric Roach and the Politics of Caribbean Poetry* (Leeds: Peepal Tree Press, 2008), 55.

[5] Low, *Publishing the Postcolonial*; Griffith, *The BBC*.

[6] Peter J. Kalliney, *Commonwealth of Letters* (Oxford: Oxford University Press, 2013), 117.

by Dennis Duerden, whose interests and connections with West Africa were sparked by working as an education officer in the Nigerian colonial administration and as director of the Hausa BBC World Service. The Centre functioned primarily to create cultural radio recordings on African arts for distribution in Africa and beyond (including North America and the Caribbean), and as a result raised awareness about things African via London. It comprised a radio studio and a cultural centre containing a library, exhibition space, and reading room in, initially, central London, and then west London.

Its flagship programme, *Africa Abroad*, spread news of African cultural activities in Europe, the United States, the West Indies, South America, and beyond. Presented and edited from 1962 by Lewis Nkosi, the South African novelist, and then the Nigerian critic Aminu Abdullahi, from 1964, the weekly magazine offered a mixture of reviews, theatre, music, literature and art, and politics. The Transcription Centre also made other notable series, including *African and Afro-American Literature, African Music as an Art Form, African Vernacular Literature,* and *English-Speaking Caribbean Novelists,* as well as programmes on poetry in different African languages.[7] Duerden also recorded interviews with emerging West African writers and anglophone Caribbean writers for sale and radio broadcast in Africa and the USA. As Samantha Pinto observes, *Africa Abroad*'s 'eclectic mix' was a way to 'self-consciously' situate culture at the 'centre of diaspora identity and politics' in London, as well as contribute to the positive representation of the continent abroad.[8]

London: Cosmopolitan Nexus

Duerden wanted to 'break down the barriers' between what he considered the 'self-centred cultural worlds of Europe and Africa' and, much like Swanzy, to offer assistance to newly arrived African writers.[9] Duerden recognised that London's location at the centre of a nexus of relationships

---

[7] Transcription Centre Programmes (Appendix G); 21.2 CCF Financial Correspondence 1961–1966, Transcription Centre Archives, Harry Ransom Center, University of Texas at Austin.

[8] Samantha Pinto, 'Decolonizing the Radio: Africa Abroad in the Age of Independence', *Sounding Out!*, 17 December 2012. Available at https://soundstudiesblog.com/tag/the-transcription-centre/.

[9] Transcription Centre Programmes (Appendix N); 21.2 CCF Financial Correspondence 1961–1966, Transcription Centre Archives, Harry Ransom Center, University of Texas at Austin.

between diverse cultural bodies, and the constant and consequent traffic of visitors in the arts from abroad, made the city if not unique then certainly crucial to a literary cosmopolitanism. The Transcription Centre published a monthly informational newsletter, 'Cultural Events in Africa', with events listings, news items, reviews of new books, press releases, general reviews, and short pieces, including those by black writers of African descent. As Gerald Moore notes, the Centre 'became a first port-of-call for most African and West Indian writers, artists, or musicians'.[10] These networking opportunities were significant and the Centre's archive contains many appreciative letters of thanks. Similar to *Caribbean Voices*, the Centre connected with local West African arts organisations like *Mbari* and pioneering West African little magazines such as *Black Orpheus* and *Transition*.

The Centre's drama workshop, Transcription Theatre Workshop, filmed a production of Wole Soyinka's *The Swamp Dwellers* and staged readings of other African plays and poetry at the ICA (Institute of Contemporary Arts) and at the Little Hampstead Theatre Club, where Athol Fugard's *Sizwe Bansi is Dead* and Wole Soyinka's *The Trials of Brother Jero* were performed. The workshop in turn led to the formation of Ijinle Theatre Company, hosted by the Centre and formed to produce Soyinka's plays with African actors.

Scholarship on the reach and influence of the Transcription Centre is in its infancy. Yet what is clear is the troubled and difficult path it trod between pleasing its secret funders, firstly the CIA-backed Congress for Cultural Freedom and then later the Fairfield and Ford Foundations, and undertaking the genuine cultural work necessary to create awareness of Africa and African diasporic culture. While Congress funding was directed at resisting the spread of communism, especially among intellectuals in a decolonising world, the Centre did give voice, as Jordanna Bailkin observes, 'to various registers of transnational black solidarity'.[11] Duerden believed that London's distance from Africa, its cosmopolitan mix of visitors, organisations, and research libraries, countered narrowly nationalistic concerns in a decolonising Africa. Yet if London was imbricated in the future of a decolonising Africa, the reverse was also true as a cosmopolitan post-imperial future was imagined on British soil by such organisations as *Caribbean Voices* and the Transcription Centre. London's location and connections were paramount as the Centre entered into a collaboration with the ICA, located on the same west London

[10] Gerald Moore, 'The Transcription Centre in the Sixties: Navigating in Narrow Seas', *Research in African Literatures*, 33:3 (2002): 167–81; 170.
[11] Jordanna Bailkin, 'The Sounds of Independence? Lessons from Africa and Beyond at the Transcription Centre Archive', *History Workshop Journal*, 78 (2014): 229–45; 234.

street. Members of the Centre were granted ICA membership and ICA galleries were sometimes available for the exhibitions and lectures that the Centre organised. Some joint programming included 'The European Image of Africa', 'African Literature', 'Africa and Jazz', a reading of Lewis Nkosi's play *Rhythm of Violence* as well as a screening and discussion of a Centre-produced film, *African Writers of Today*.

A progressive postwar bastion of twentieth-century art, the ICA was an ideal partner with overlapping interests. Part museum, art gallery, and educational centre and part members' club, the ICA's interest in African art (music and dance) came from its avowed Euro-modernist preoccupations with primitivism and with anthropology. It cultivated a deliberately eclectic openness to internationalist writers and artists with exhibitions in the 1950s and 1960s including not only James Joyce and Pablo Picasso but also Roberto Matta and Wilfredo Lam, paintings from Haiti and India, film screenings of African plays, and readings by 'British Caribbean Writers' chaired by Stuart Hall. Lamming had already read his poetry at the ICA open series for emerging poets, 'Platform for Poets'; while he was critical of the literary patronage evident at these meetings, he was also aware that different kinds of partnership could emerge.[12]

In his welcome speech at the ICA launch in 1950, Herbert Read, a founder, emphasised the Institute's distinctive location at the heart of Britain and the Commonwealth. The ICA would be a meeting ground where 'foreign intellectual[s] and "visiting artists"' might gather, where different cultures and artistic fields might 'mutually inspire each other'. As Anne Massey and Gregor Muir write in their retrospective, the founders 'styled' the ICA as potent broker of 'challenging art, high culture and intellectual endeavour[s]' that sought to actively trouble the conventional and 'restrictive hegemony' of the postwar period.[13]

The ICA was not, of course, the only metropolitan institute positioning itself as breaking with imperial cultural legacies. The Commonwealth Institute, newly opened in 1962 in Kensington High Street, made a gradual, if fitful, transition from imperialism to post-imperialism, postcolonialism, and multiculturalism. Despite its past, the renamed Institute represented a 'co-operative effort' by all Commonwealth nations to 'create a physical expression in London' of a 'constructive' shared legacy, where culture and

---

[12] George Lamming, *The Pleasures of Exile* (London: Michael Joseph, 1960), 85.
[13] Anne Massey and Gregor Muir, *ICA London 1946–1968* (London: Institute of Contemporary Arts, 2014), 11.

educational activities were put above the narrow confines of politics or trade relations.[14]

The building's modern design was significant. It contained a central space – a raised marble platform under a distinctive tent-like canopied roofing – where visitors could glimpse three tiers of gallery displays devoted to diverse Commonwealth nations. Critics have argued that this positioning interpellated the everyday visitor as British, confirming Britain as the invisible centre, for the galleries contained no displays on Britain itself. Yet the Institute's archival papers attest to individual Commonwealth nations' resistance to centrist and neo-colonial paternalistic demands; many updated their displays, saw the networking opportunities as useful, and considered the organisation as offering a productive space for exhibiting their 'visualising and materialising' independent national identities in a changing global world.[15]

Sited not far from those very neighbourhoods which in the fifties and sixties were seen to be enclaves of postwar immigration, the Institute became a landmark with significant visitor numbers. Ruth Craggs cites visitor numbers upwards of 612,000 a year after its opening. The educational opportunities and activities co-ordinated by the Institute meant that several London schools visited the building regularly, allowing children from areas with significant 'new' Commonwealth populations – Notting Hill, Kensal Rise, and Bayswater – to locate themselves as integral to the shared and larger narrative of imperialism, colonialism, and decolonisation. The Institute thus enabled many local minority ethnic schoolchildren and visitors to affirm themselves as part of a larger Commonwealth history that provided a narrative and rationale for their continued presence in Britain.[16] This reimaging of a modern, cosmopolitan post-imperial Britain represented a coming to terms with the legacy of empire as a distinct problem of Britain's making and not one exclusively created by immigrant flows fetching up on its shores.

In the decades of the 1970s and 1980s, the Commonwealth Institute's sustained investment in multicultural arts and education meant a direct engagement with the changing face of London's diverse population, and with promoting literatures from other parts of the world. Not only did the

---

[14] Sir Kenneth Bradley, 'The New Commonwealth Institute', *Journal of the Royal Society of Arts*, 111 (1963): 403–11; 404.

[15] Claire Wintle, 'Decolonising the Museum: The Case of the Imperial and Commonwealth Institutes', *Museum and Society*, 11:2 (2013): 185–201; 193–4.

[16] Ruth Craggs, 'The Commonwealth Institute and the Commonwealth Arts Festival: Architecture, Performance and Multiculturalism in Late-Imperial London', *London Journal*, 36:1 (2011): 247–68.

Institute's resource centre and library offer important portals to the histories, geographies, arts, and cultures of the nations it represented, but the Institute became a unique repository for many foundational reports: the *Handbook of Library Holdings of Commonwealth Literature: UK and Europe* (1977), *Critical Writings on Commonwealth Literatures: A Selective Bibliography to 1970*, pamphlets, bibliographies, booklists, and resource booklets for the teaching of African, Caribbean, South Asian, and black literatures in Britain produced by the Association of the Teaching of Caribbean, African, Asian and Associated Literatures (ATCAL). In 1986, the Institute staged a Caribbean Focus Year with special events, film screenings, music, talks, and educational programmes linking the Caribbean islands with the black British community in London, and with major cities such as Liverpool, Bristol, and Leicester.

The Caribbean Transnational

London played a key role in the growth of Caribbean transnational movements. As discussed earlier in this volume, the Caribbean Artists Movement (CAM) became an important forum on Caribbean arts and letters, and an enduring influence long after its organisational demise (see Chapter 15). The Bajan poet Kamau Brathwaite, surprised at not finding local organisations with transnational links with Commonwealth nations or the wider non-anglophone Caribbean when he was a student in London, initiated a critical forum at the West Indian Students Centre (WISC) to remedy this lack. Initially, CAM's focus on carving out a 'space' within 'the existing metropolitan system of artistic production, consumption and criticism' was key, or as Brathwaite observed, why Caribbean literature was being 'marginalised into West Indian or black literature [sic]' instead of being treated simply as literature.[17] CAM's early concerns were centred on mutual contributions, literary cross-fertilisations between the Caribbean and Europe, but this changed as black identity politics strengthened in Britain. An enthusiastically received public reading of Brathwaite's poem *Rights of Passage* in 1967, staged in a theatre in Holborn, was followed shortly by the first public CAM meeting at the WISC in Collingham Gardens.

The location was important. Established over a decade earlier, WISC was funded by West Indian governments to provide a hub of leisure, social, and cultural activities for Caribbean students. WISC was the location of Wilson

---

[17] Brian Alleyne, *Radicals against Race: Black Activism and Cultural Politics* (Oxford; New York: Berg, 2002), 34.

Harris's seminal talk, 'Tradition and the West Indian Novel', a lecture subsequently published by the organisation; it was also where the Ugandan poet Okot p'Bitek's *Song of Lawino* was first performed. WISC was closely associated with CAM in the early years, and some of CAM's office-bearers were also appointed to the board of WISC. The benefits were felt by both organisations. CAM brought intellectual and cultural programming to WISC, and WISC provided CAM with a widening audience of students and activists drawn from local communities. Informal discussions became more structured with accompanying newsletters, bibliographies, cultural programming, and the election of office-bearers. The bimonthly newsletter, much like the Transcription Centre's 'Cultural Events in Africa', put local activities in London alongside those on the islands, including lecture transcriptions, notes, and news of creative activities taking place on two sides of the Atlantic. While details of CAM, including its journal *Savacou*, are addressed elsewhere in this volume, it is important to remember that CAM's presence on the London scene helped grow and catalyse the formation of a number of important activist, creative, and publishing enterprises that followed. These included: Creation for Liberation, South East London Parents Organisation, the Nigerian Society of African Artists, and perhaps most significantly New Beacon Books, which survives to this day.

Publishing and Bookselling in London

New Beacon, founded by CAM member John La Rose, had already brought out its first book by the time of the 1967 inaugural CAM meeting; the two organisations developed in tandem throughout the sixties. La Rose was a scholar, teacher, writer, and trade union activist and he believed that owning the means of literary production was vital to Caribbean literary development. He saw publishing as a 'vehicle' for cultural validation and a means to overcome the discontinuities and the overt suppression of information that characterised the colonial period.[18] In addition, publishing independently afforded small presses such as New Beacon flexibility and enabled them to eschew profitability as a main driving force; as Brathwaite put it, this was 'a publishing adventure' not in hock to 'commercial jagguarnauts [who] wd never

---

[18] First International Book Fair of Radical Black and Third World Books programme brochure (1–3 April 1982).

touch & therefore scissored, silenced out [sic]' what was real, diverse, experimental, and committed writing.[19]

La Rose published three books in two years: *Foundations*, a book of poetry written by himself, *Marcus Garvey 1887–1940*, and *Tradition, the Writer and Society: Critical Essays*, the latter a reprint of Wilson Harris's WISC pamphlet. In the decade that followed, Ivan Van Sertima's collection of essays *Caribbean Writers* was published; this comprised recorded radio broadcasts (including some produced by the Transcription Centre). Reprinting out of print work by Caribbean authors was part of a programme to assert the continuity of Caribbean intellectual and literary life. Brathwaite's doctoral work, *Folk Culture of the Slaves in Jamaica*, and Bernard Coard's pamphlet *How the West Indian Child is Made Educationally Sub-Normal in the British School System* were also published, the latter in association with the Caribbean Education and Community Workers' Association. La Rose did not hive off the political from the aesthetic (or vice versa) and the wide range of New Beacon's titles – literature, criticism, education, politics, history – was characteristic of the press's broad mission even as his selling and networking trips to the Caribbean and to Africa testify to transnational commitments.

New Beacon's bookselling arm, first based at the La Rose flat in Hornsey and later at Albert Road and Stroud Green in north London, was another factor in building an alternative publishing and bookselling dynamic focused on politically left and 'Third World' black and Asian concerns. The New Beacon Book Service, as it was then called, started as service provider for CAM.[20] Later, as a high street shop with a mail order service, it became a lively and welcoming community centre and meeting place for anti-colonial and anti-racist activities. Growing alongside the emergence of the black British community in London, the shop provided important organisational focus, combining local engagement with transnational Caribbean awareness as visitors were both local and international, the latter drawn by the La Roses' activist and intellectual connections. Jeremy Poynting, who founded Peepal Tree Press, a black British and Caribbean independent publishing house, in Leeds in 1985, was a frequent visitor from the 1970s on, commending its unique 'complex of commitments': bookselling, publishing, and a 'grassroots political activism' and awareness that 'made [simultaneous] sense of what

---

[19] Kamau Brathwaite, 'John the Conqueror' in John La Rose Tribute Committee (ed.), *Foundations of a Movement* (London: John La Rose Tribute Committee, 1991), 20–3; 21.

[20] Anne Walmsley, *The Caribbean Artists Movement 1966–1972* (London; Port of Spain: New Beacon Books, 1992), 90.

was happening in London, the Yorkshire coalfields, Port of Spain, Lagos, Soweto, New York'.[21]

Much like New Beacon, Bogle-L'Ouverture also began life in the living room of its founders, Eric and Jessica Huntley, later moving to rented premises in east London. Like New Beacon, the building in Chignell Road, west London became both publishing house, specialist bookshop, and grass-roots cultural, political, and intellectual activity hub. As a press, Bogle was formed in 1969 to publish the lectures of Walter Rodney, the Guyanese historian and University of the West Indies lecturer. Rodney was a close friend and associate of the Huntleys through their joint political activities. When Rodney was prevented from re-entering Jamaica on account of his political activism, the Huntleys launched a London campaign to publicise Rodney's work. Rodney's lectures, *The Groundings with My Brothers* and *How Europe Underdeveloped Africa*, addressed to ordinary black people, represented a Black Power-inflected indictment of poverty and underdevelopment as a consequence and legacy of imperialism in Africa, the Caribbean islands, and North America.

Bogle continued to bring black history, politics, and literature to public attention, publishing work by what are now canonical black British writers such as Linton Kwesi Johnson, Valerie Bloom, and Lemn Sissay. It also made available a range of political, educational, and children's writing. As with New Beacon, the bookshop became a community space where artists, writers, activists, students, teachers, and parents met to promote, sustain, and protect black cultural interests in London and beyond. Both Bogle and New Beacon can be located as part of a vein of alternative radical (and feminist) bookshops with community interests, though many of these are now no longer in operation. The list includes: the Black Panther Bookshop (Sabarr), Compendium, Collets, Silver Moon, Sisterwrite, Central Books, and Gay's the Word in London, Grassroots in Manchester, News from Nowhere in Liverpool, Frontline in Leicester, Greenleaf in Bristol, and Mushroom in Nottingham.

Given Bogle's and New Beacon's grounding in the local communities and activist politics, which included support for the Black Parents Movement (BPM), the Black Youth Movement (BYM), and supplementary schools and police injustices campaigns, it was perhaps natural that they would work together to mount the influential International Book Fair of Radical Black

---

[21] Jeremy Poynting, [untitled] in John La Rose Tribute Committee (ed.), *Foundations of a Movement* (London: John La Rose Tribute Committee, 1991), 149–50; 149.

and Third World Books in London between 1982 and 1995. New Beacon, Race Today Publications, and Bogle inaugurated the Book Fair committee in 1982 with Education for Liberation and Griot International Books joining them in 1987. These London-based, annual, self-financing book fairs were staged to grow 'radical ideas and concepts' given the 'failure of the post war settlements' to address minority ethnic communities' needs and aspirations,[22] though some satellite events spread to Manchester, Bradford, Leeds, and also to Glasgow after 1985.

The International Book Fair and Other Small Presses

The Book Fairs were not only bookselling and exhibition events but provided networking and consciousness-raising opportunities, platforms, and debates on film, theatre, art, poetry, criticism, and publishing. They included specific local political campaigns; they staged music and live poetry events. The initial roll call of publishers that attended the Book Fair may read like a who's who of presses with black and Asian, feminist, or political left interests, but by the nineties, while never losing their radical political impetus, the Book Fairs included exhibits from many more international and mainstream publishers. Stalls ranged from small and medium-sized London-based community publishers – such as Black Ink, Karnak House, Shakti, Allison and Busby, Nubia, the Leeds-based Peepal Tree Press, and *Wasafiri*; African presses such as Ikenga and Nok; Caribbean presses such as *Savacou*, Susan Craig, and Sangam Books; Indian presses such as Vikas; feminist presses such as the Women's Press, Virago, and Kitchen Table – to larger commercial presses such as André Deutsch and educational presses such as Longman, Heinemann Educational Books/Heinemann International, Oxford University Press, Routledge, and the University of the West Indies Press.

The Book Fairs can be located within a growing movement of small publishing collectives in the late 1970s and early 1980s, many of which were run by self-help, democratising, and consciousness-raising networks devoted to radical cultural, postcolonial, and sexual–political struggles. Well-known feminist presses also attended the fairs; Virago and the Women's Press were perhaps the biggest and best known of the women's publishers that started

---

[22] Inaugural flyer reproduced in Sarah White, Roxy Harris, and Sharmilla Beezmohun (eds.), *A Meeting of the Continents: The International Book Fair of Radical Black and Third World Books – Revisited* (London: New Beacon Books and George Padmore Institute, 2005), 74.

life in the 1970s, but smaller collectives such as Onlywoman Press and Teeth Imprints also thrived and were important in encouraging and growing an audience for women's writing. The Black Ink Collective, founded in 1978 to give a platform to young black British writers, also exhibited at the Book Fairs; with its Black Writers Workshop arm, the Collective provided a mentoring environment for a new generation of black British writers such as Benjamin Zephaniah, S. I. Martin, Desmond Johnson, and Michael McMillan.[23]

Initially, feminist presses in the late seventies published mostly white women's writing but criticisms of the absence of black and Asian women in their publishing output led to the formation of other presses that served to remedy this lack. Smaller independent presses such as Sheba, established in 1980 as a not-for-profit workers' co-operative, sought to prioritise 'writing by women of colour, or lesbians, or working-class women'. Other notable smaller London houses include Karnak House, the publishing arm of the Intef Institute, an African Caribbean arts and culture organisation formed in 1975, which published Grace Nichols's award-winning poetry collection *i is a long memoried woman* (1983); Karia Press, which published Claudia Jones; Ogwugwu Afo, started by Buchi Emecheta as a self-publishing venture for her own works *Double Yoke* (1982), *The Rape of Savi* (1983), and her autobiography, *Head Above Water* (1986); Tamarind, launched by Verna Wilkins in 1987 to address diversity in children's book publishing; the Asian Women Writers' Workshop (later Collective) inaugurated in 1984, which, with the Women's Press and Virago, produced *Right of Way* (1988) and *Flaming Spirit* (1994); Mango Publishing, formed in 1995 by Joan Anim-Addo and Diana Birch to promote literature from British, Caribbean, and Latin American traditions both in English and in translation. The international dimension of the women's movement meant that prominent black American authors such as the cultural theorist bell hooks and the writers Audre Lorde and Jewelle Gomez were published in Britain; such transnational dimensions were informed by continuities between Black Atlantic cultures and a preoccupation with identity politics within a growing local agenda of multiculturalism.[24]

---

[23] Desrie Thomson-George, 'The Legacy of Black Ink', *The Bookseller*, 7 November 2016. Available at http://thebookseller.com/blogs/legacy-black-ink-426351.

[24] Gail Low, 'Publishing and Prizes' in Emma Parker and Mary Eagleton (eds.), *The History of British Women's Writing 1970–Present* (Basingstoke: Palgrave Macmillan, 2015), 81–95; 89–90.

Not all London presses had political agendas writ large; Allison and Busby, founded in 1967 by Margaret Busby and Clive Allison, initially to produce affordable paperback poetry, published a diverse and eclectic list of international writers of fiction, non-fiction, poetry, and children's books (including books by Jill Murphy). Allison and Busby also published many transatlantic writers of African descent including C. L. R. James, Nuruddin Farah, Buchi Emecheta, Ishmael Reed, and Chester Himes before being acquired by W. H. Allen in 1987. After leaving the company, Busby, one of the first black women in publishing, went on to edit the influential *Daughters of Africa* (1992). This Jonathan Cape anthology offered a literary ancestry of black women's writing across continents and historical periods and has now been supplemented by *New Daughters of Africa* (2019), published by Myriad, a small independent publishing house in Sussex.

Mainstream and Educational Presses

Mainstream presses based in London, particularly during the 1950s and 1960s, published many writers from Africa and the Caribbean – Chinua Achebe, Wole Soyinka, Ngũgĩ wa Thiong'o, George Lamming, Derek Walcott, Wilson Harris, Edgar Mittelholzer, and Sam Selvon, among others – who are now established writers in their respective national and international world literature and postcolonial canons (see Chapters 13 and 14). The networks of friendship and patronage provided gateways into a metropolitan republic of letters, but many were also subsequently dropped by their publishers when publishing fashion moved on. Mittelholzer, for example, found it increasingly difficult to find a publisher for his work and some reviewers complained of the construction of 'a composite Caribbean author', for instance, a 'V. Selvon Mittelholzer' writing 'sunnily of quaint brown lives'.[25] While these networks flourished, writers were sought after for overseas trips, and the extended cultural and educational networks already linking Britain, the Caribbean, and West Africa assisted in the traffic of literary material. There were overlapping interests between writers of the nationalist period from abroad and London publishers and intellectuals. These synergies allowed the former to be incorporated into the latter in mutually beneficial ways.

Educational and textbook publishing contributed to the boom. Decolonisation had ironically paved the way for the flourishing of

---

[25] Ronald Bryden, 'Review', *Sunday Telegraph*, 26 May 1963: 13.

a metropolitan-produced textbook trade that catered for a changing curricular market abroad.[26] The formation of the West African Examinations Council (1952) and the Caribbean Examinations Council (1973) led to a demand for textbooks with local interest and appeal, which in turn contributed to the flourishing fortunes of Heinemann Educational Books' pioneering African Writers Series (AWS) and Caribbean Writers Series, and a rash of similar work published by Longman, Nelson, Collins, and Macmillan. Launched in 1962 with Chinua Achebe, Cyprian Ekwesi, and Kenneth Kaunda in a newly created cheap paperback format modelled on Penguins, AWS would, over the course of the next twenty-two years, publish a total of 270 titles, including now well-known names such as the Kenyan writer Ngũgĩ wa Thiong'o, the Ghanaian writer Ayi Kwei Armah, the Botswanian writer Bessie Head, and the Nigerian-born British writer Buchi Emecheta. The series predominantly published anglophone fiction but also included poetry, plays, and non-fiction, as well as some literature in translation. The success of the African Writers Series afforded Heinemann Educational Books, a new and relatively small player in the postwar West African market, the opportunity to compete with the bigger, well-established educational publishing companies such as Oxford University Press and Nelson, strengthening Heinemann's brand and enabling a generation of African writers to gain international recognition.[27]

Between 1966 and 1968, foundational anthologies by London-based publishers for an educational but also a general readership appeared. Many educational firms had appointed specialist Caribbean editors to develop their lists. In the early 1970s, both Longman and Heinemann began reissuing Caribbean classics from the fifties. Longman republished George Lamming's and Samuel Selvon's novels in paperback and Heinemann launched reprints of novels by Michael Anthony and Edgar Mittelholzer, V. S. Naipaul and Vic Reid. Later, Longman would commission original titles such as Lamming's *Water with Berries* (1971) and *Natives of My Person* (1972), and Roy Heath's *A Man Come Home* (1974). The first title in Longman's Drumbeat Series, a cross-market educational series of fiction, poetry, and drama for Africa and the Caribbean, appeared in 1979. The fortunes of educational and literary publishing linked up; publishers made general trade books widely available,

[26] Caroline Davies, *Creating Postcolonial Literature* (Basingstoke: Palgrave Macmillan, 2013).
[27] James Currey, *Africa Writes Back: The African Writers Series and the Launch of African Literature* (Oxford: James Currey, 2008); Olabode Ibironke, *Between African Writers and Heinemann Education Publishers: The Political Economy of a Culture Industry* (Ann Arbor, MI: UMI Dissertation Publishing, 2009); Low, *Publishing the Postcolonial*.

applying the standards of mass production and suitability for school audiences to works of literary value, and in turn affecting adversely, or favourably, the economic, symbolic, and cultural capital accruing to these texts.

Multicultural London

Literary and educational publishing histories are therefore imbricated in the rise of postcolonial and black British writing for both the general and higher education markets. Decolonisation turned into a commercial opportunity for mainstream metropolitan educational publishers both abroad and at home. A series that serviced parts of Africa, the Caribbean, or Asia could also be commercially viable in Britain. Such crossovers were fortuitous: as with the AWS, for example, the Nigerian economic collapse in the late 1970s and early 1980s, and the currency restrictions put in place to deal with the crisis, meant that dwindling overseas orders resulted in the change of the market focus from Nigeria to the USA and the UK as schools and higher educational curricula were beginning to feel the pressure towards cultural diversity.

Multiculturalism appeared to be gaining ground. Naseem Khan's groundbreaking study *The Arts Britain Ignores: The Arts of Ethnic Minorities in Britain* (1976), sponsored by the Commission for Racial Equality and the Arts Council of Great Britain, led to the formation of Minorities' Arts Advisory Service (MAAS) which in turn contributed to a flourishing of the black arts movement, with magazines such as *Echo* and *Artrage* providing valuable forums for intercultural and intermedia activities. A new Ethnic Minority Arts Unit was created within the Arts Council of England, and in 1986 a two-year Ethnic Minority Arts Action Plan was launched, leading to a further report, *Towards Cultural Diversity*. A major British 'Conference on Ethnic Arts' was staged in 1982, sponsored by the Greater London Council (GLC). Following the findings, GLC funding was made available for small minority presses like Kala Press, Black Ink, and *Wasafiri* and for workshops such as the Asian Women Writers' Collective.

The Association for the Teaching of Caribbean, African, Asian and Associated Literatures (ATCAL) was formed in 1978 to 'advance the education of the British public in the works of authors of African, Caribbean and Asian origin'.[28] ATCAL staged annual conferences, organised workshops,

---

[28] ATCAL, undated 'draft proposal for possible funding organisations'.

compiled booklists for schools (many lodged at the Commonwealth Institute), and submitted recommendations to examination boards effecting change to GCSE and Advanced-level syllabuses. A 1982 publicity pamphlet draws attention to its intention to 'promote and encourage new writing by [. . .] Black British artists'.[29] ATCAL's 1985 conference theme was 'Black British Experience in Literature'. Amongst other measures, ATCAL campaigned effectively in the 1980s to include African, Caribbean, Asian, and black British writers across the school and university curriculum (see Chapter 25). *Wasafiri*, a little magazine launched by Susheila Nasta at the 1984 ATCAL conference, offered serious critical and pedagogic space to promote these literatures, which were not gaining adequate notice in the mainstream press. It outlived ATCAL and is now a National Portfolio Organisation funded by Arts Council England. *Wasafiri* continues to sustain transnational cultural dialogue between an international community of diasporic writers and their audiences.

Conclusion

The spatial turn in cultural geography, following the work of Henri Lefebvre, David Harvey, and Donna Massey, has encouraged us to see place not simply as physical terrain but as a web of social constructions and processes that constantly makes and remakes the environment. In this sense, London is a constellation of competing forces – dynamic, contested, and diverse territorialisations and de/re-territorialisations – put into motion by different infrastructures, diverse social processes, and everyday activities, drawing on varying histories and practices. Heterogeneous but also hierarchical postwar London(s) were formed from institutions, organisations, communities, and diverse groups of individuals making material their entitlement to inhabit, to belong, to change, or to imagine a different future.

Once the heart of an empire, the centre of a vast global traffic of capital, services, goods, and people, postwar London was, and still is, a city of migration, diasporic settlements, and cultural heterogeneity. In his 1986 assessment of the arts in Britain, Kwesi Owusu argues that 'Black arts' in London have benefited from the flow and 'highest and most exciting concentrations of [resident and visiting] Third World artists' and that London's artistic efforts have in turn served as a 'strategic resource' for Britain as

[29] Committee Notes, *ATCAL Newsletter*, 6 (June 1982): 1.

a whole.[30] In this chapter's exploration of postwar London staged by institutions, organisations, and individuals all *performing* their contradictory and conflicting visions of a post-imperial city within a global cultural trajectory, we have a dream of cosmopolitan post-imperial Britain imagined and then, fitfully, worked into being.

[30] Kwesi Owusu, *The Struggle for Black Arts in Britain* (London: Comedia, 1986), 78.

18

Looking Beyond, Shifting the Gaze
Writers in Motion

BÉNÉDICTE LEDENT

Itinerant Writers and Authentication

At the beginning of *An Unfinished Journey* (1986), Trinidadian-born Shiva Naipaul (1945–1985), who in the 1980s decided to write on Australia, tells us about the 'curiosity teetering on suspicion' that usually meets 'itinerant writers' when they set out to address a country or a society that is not obviously part of their ethnic or national background.[1] In a humorous but sensible tone, the prematurely deceased author views the cross-examination triggered by what some regard to be an unexpected artistic choice as an invitation 'to categorise, to reduce to the abstractions of convenient, easily digested formulae an unprocessed and incomplete experience'.[2] Clearly, for him, the question 'But *do* tell me why you chose [. . .] Australia of all places?'[3] is just a variation on the awkward but standard 'Where're you from?',[4] also addressed to him by two Australians on board the plane taking him to Sydney.

Without any doubt the writers tackled in this chapter, from the Naipaul brothers to Caryl Phillips (1958–) and Bernardine Evaristo (1959–), have all had to field similar queries about their origins, again and again. This might explain why these black and Asian British authors have opted to explore in their writing places that are beyond the binary identity framework imposed by colonialism – a framework which comprises their ancestral homelands, on the one hand, whether Africa, the Asian subcontinent, or the Caribbean, and on the other, Britain. After examining the general implications of such a transnational scope and a few significant examples of the genre, I will compare a selection of texts, which, in order to avoid generalisations, will be

[1] Shiva Naipaul, 'Why Australia?', *An Unfinished Journey* (London: Abacus, 1986), 1–10; 1.
[2] Ibid.   [3] Ibid. Italics in the original.
[4] Ibid., 10. See also Caryl Phillips, *The Atlantic Sound* (London: Faber and Faber, 2000), 98.

read with a view to highlighting their authors' specific slant. The overarching argument will be that, in spite of – or perhaps thanks to – their ex-centric locations, the travel narratives discussed here have much to tell us about their authors, not only as writers in motion, but mainly as British writers attempting to come to terms with their own multifaceted postcolonial identities. One should keep in mind, however, that the works examined in this chapter are not emancipatory by default; they can also display ambiguous overtones, as Patrick Holland and Graham Huggan have shown in their now classic study of the travel writing genre. So whereas travel narratives belong 'to a wider structure of representation within which cultural affiliations [. . .] can be analyzed, questioned and reassessed', they can in some cases, as we will see, also harbour 'complacent, even nostalgically retrograde' values.[5]

British black and Asian writers are certainly not the only artists who have attempted to escape the postcolonial identitarian straitjacket whereby authors from former colonies are automatically aligned with the locales in which they have roots or where they have settled. As Sarah Brouillette reminds us, there has been a resistance to such reductive 'biographical positioning' among postcolonial writers.[6] She gives the example of Zulfikar Ghose, who has refused in some of his writing to identify directly with his native South Asia and has focused on South America instead. This, Brouillette argues, might account for his relative absence from critical radars. She further views Ghose's blurring of affiliative lines as a means on his part of critiquing a fashionable brand of cosmopolitanism that paradoxically goes hand in hand with an insistence on biographical 'authentication'.[7]

The Caribbean Legacy of Cosmopolitanism and Travel Writing

While some of these comments may apply to the black and Asian British literary scene, it is also necessary to look at it from a more specific perspective, one which involves cosmopolitanism too, but of a different, more benign kind than the one targeted by Ghose. In *The Pleasures of Exile* (1960), Barbadian George Lamming famously declares that Caribbean history,

---

[5] Patrick Holland and Graham Huggan, *Tourists with Typewriters: Critical Reflections on Contemporary Travel Writing* (Ann Arbor, MI: Michigan University Press, 1998), viii–ix, viii.

[6] Sarah Brouillette, *Postcolonial Writers in the Global Literary Market Place* (Basingstoke: Palgrave Macmillan, 2007), 9.

[7] Ibid., 144.

painful though it was, has made 'The West Indian [. . .] the most cosmopolitan man in the world'.[8] This Caribbean legacy of multiculturalism, and the
interest in foreign cultures it has engendered, might be a first way of
explaining why there is a majority of artists from the region among the
'writers in motion' at the heart of this chapter.[9] Jamaican-born Andrew
Salkey has addressed this inherited sense of placelessness and adaptability in
some of his work, especially his *Anancy, Traveller* (1992), a collection of stories
around the figure of the legendary spider of West Indian folklore. As
a trickster and a shape-shifter, Anancy is at ease everywhere and, following
his forced transportation to the New World, cunningly adapts to various
environments and displays in all situations a worldly-wise mind.[10] But there
might also be a less positive side to these travelling writers' sometimes
obsessive need to engage with other cultures, one which still relates to
their complex backgrounds but has more to do with their sense of not
belonging in Britain than with a sense of rootlessness inherited from history.
The consequence of such a feeling of exclusion can indeed result for the artist,
especially when foreign-born, in an imperative to sort out this identitarian
predicament or, as St Kitts-born Caryl Phillips puts it in his first travelogue,
The European Tribe (1987), to 'reconcile the contradiction of feeling British,
while being constantly told in many subtle and unsubtle ways that I did not
belong'.[11] What better way of doing this than looking elsewhere and comparing one's sense of domestic outsiderness with what is taking place in societies
outside one's immediate national or cultural remit? The reflections generated
by Phillips's wanderings around the old continent in the 1980s not only
allowed him to take the full measure of its colonial legacy of racism but
also to maintain that, for all their invisibility, black people were 'an inextric-
able part' of Europe, and as such had a moral right to be heard and participate
in its future.[12] Such an inherently protesting tone explains why this book has
been described by Holland and Huggan as a form of '*counter* travel writing'
because it questions, if only in its title, 'the privileges that accrue historically
to the genre'.[13] Recently, Phillips has revisited this early essay and concluded
that were he to make the same journey again today, he might very well

---

[8] George Lamming, *The Pleasures of Exile* (London: Allison & Busby, [1960] 1984), 37.
[9] Exceptions to the overwhelming Caribbean presence among 'roaming' writers include
Helen Oyeyemi's *The Opposite House* (London: Bloomsbury, 2007), a novel with links to
Cuba, and Salman Rushdie's *The Jaguar Smile* (London: Picador, 1987), a non-fiction
book about Nicaragua.
[10] Andrew Salkey, *Anancy, Traveller* (London: Bogle-L'Ouverture, 1992).
[11] Caryl Phillips, *The European Tribe* (London: Faber and Faber, 1987), 9.   [12] Ibid., 129.
[13] Holland and Huggan, *Tourists with Typewriters*, 50.

'arrive at basically the same conclusions', in spite of the dramatic changes that have taken place on the continent.[14] Testifying to Phillips's ongoing sense of realism, this pessimistic comment nevertheless also demonstrates how pioneering and perceptive his provocative travel essay was, and still is, in a Europe that, he writes, 'has chosen either not to see us, or to judge us as an insignificant minority, or as a temporary, but dismissible, mistake'.[15]

While Phillips is possibly one of the most conspicuous representatives of this cosmopolitan streak among contemporary postcolonial British writers, he is neither the first nor the only one to step outside his identity comfort zone in search for answers to what he has called the 'high anxiety of belonging'.[16] An early example of this approach, and possibly a model for Phillips's European travelogue, is that of Jamaican Claude McKay's *A Long Way from Home* (1937), a narrative that takes its author to Russia, France, and Morocco and is written in the tradition of African American autobiographies 'in which more intimate aspects of the autobiographer's personal experience are subordinated to social commentary'.[17] This combination of a personal quest with the examination of larger societal questions in the context of travelling can be found in several books published over the years by peripatetic black and Asian British writers, always providing challenging reflections on their own brand of Britishness. One example is that of Andrew Salkey's diaries, both *Havana Journal* (1971) and *Georgetown Journal* (1972), which take the author, as a visitor curious for Otherness, to other Caribbean societies than the one he grew up in. Interestingly, his encounters with Cubans and Guyanese people trigger thought-provoking considerations about class and race but also about Caribbeanness and literature, and shed light on the writer's own complex identity as a British intellectual of Jamaican descent born in Panama.

Focus on Three Travel Writers

The two Naipaul brothers, Shiva and V. S., are also well-known practitioners of the travel narrative genre. Both have written books that look beyond the Trinidad of their birth, the India of their ancestors, and the Britain where they

---

[14] Caryl Phillips, 'Revisiting *The European Tribe*', *Wasafiri*, 29:3 (2014): 4–7; 6.

[15] Phillips, *European Tribe*, 128–9.

[16] Caryl Phillips, *A New World Order* (London: Secker & Warburg, 2001), 303–9.

[17] St Clair Drake, 'Introduction' in Claude McKay, *A Long Way from Home* (London: Pluto, [1937] 1985), ix–xxi; x.

live, and which, as such, can provide us with insights into their own sense of being in the world.

Of 'Full-Blooded' Indian Ancestry: Shiva Naipaul

Shiva Naipaul's last, posthumous book is a collection of essays that is partly devoted, as mentioned above, to his visit to Australia. He also has an earlier travelogue to his name, *North of South: An African Journey* (1978), where he recounts his tour of eastern Africa. In his short introduction he explains how this volume, 'whose nature and purpose might so easily be misunderstood', arose from his 'own concerns – or, if you prefer, obsessions' with politics, colonialism, its impact on identity, and 'the relationship of black and white and brown', as he wrote to his English publisher in the early stages of the project.[18] In these preliminary intentions Shiva Naipaul seems animated by a desire to come to a personal understanding of other peoples, and eventually of himself, as a man who had 'inherited no culture; no particular outlook; no particular form. [. . . who] was nothing' when he left his native Trinidad at the age of eighteen.[19] The final product, however, does not live up to these worthy expectations, for, to quote Tom Odhiambo, Shiva Naipaul's African travel piece 'follows faithfully in the footsteps of those Western writers [. . .] preceding it who had constructed an essentialised Africa using images of absence of progress, degeneration and primitivity'.[20] Shiva Naipaul's dependence on colonial prejudices to represent the continent results in a binary vision, dismissing blacks and whites as enemies who 'deserved each other' for, he writes, 'Civilized man, it seems, can no more cope with prolonged exposure to the primitive than the primitive can cope with prolonged exposure to him'.[21] This embittered conclusion, which conveys Shiva Naipaul's distrust of cross-cultural relationships but also his realisation of the marginalisation of Indians, and therefore himself, in the black versus white confrontation, is compounded by the fact that Africans in his book are not really given a chance to speak for themselves. Such an imposition of voicelessness seems to be in contradiction to Shiva Naipaul's indignation in *An Unfinished Journey* where he deplores the 'Great Australian Silence' that was enforced by white settlers on the Aboriginal population.[22] At the same

---

[18] Shiva Naipaul, *North of South: An African Journey* (London: Penguin, [1978] 1980), 13, 14.

[19] Ibid., 104.

[20] Tom Odhiambo, 'Holding the Traveller's Gaze Accountable in Shiva Naipaul's *North of South: An African Journey*', *Social Dynamics*, 30:1 (2004): 51–68; 53.

[21] Naipaul, *North of South*, 347.

[22] Naipaul, 'Flight into Blackness' in *Unfinished Journey*, 11, 14.

time he advises the indigenous Australians 'to break free from the sublimated racism that would imprison people in their imagined essence', for, he concludes, 'Racial metaphysics is a cul-de-sac.'[23] Unsurprisingly, he applies this reflection to himself as well and offers a frank but ironical appraisal of his own identitarian quandaries:

> I am, after all, a man of 'full-blooded' Indian ancestry. Should I therefore put on a dhoti? Should I take myself up to a cave in the foothills of the Himalayas and surrender myself to the contemplation of the transmigration of souls? After a century of separation from the motherland, a century of confusion and disintegration, my racial essence has offered no clues to the dilemmas I have had to face.[24]

While the younger Naipaul brother's ambiguous travel narratives may be an index to his own development from a rather binary view of history in *North of South* to a subtler vision in *An Unfinished Journey*, they also point to the difficulty of achieving self-knowledge, especially as a diasporic individual, and they are suggestive of an unresolved tension. As a traveller in search of self-definition he is indeed divided between a genuine desire to 'clear up misconceptions' about the postcolonial world,[25] and a tendency to regard his subjects with some contempt, an attitude that often translates into a scathing tone reminiscent of that adopted by his elder brother in his own travelogues.

In an essay from *An Unfinished Journey*, entitled 'My Brother and I', Shiva Naipaul comments on his relationship with his more famous sibling and expresses his objection to being regarded as his double, in a form of 'doppelgänger absolutism', adding: 'Our being brothers is interesting. But it is not intrinsically so. In the end, it is the work that matters, not the relationship.'[26] This remark about establishing problematic genealogical connections in the literary field should alert us to the danger of placing writers together because of their common origins; it also highlights the need to look at the texts themselves instead of banking on biographical clues. So even if it can be said that the two brothers' tone is at first sight strangely similar in its bluntness and disregard for political correctness, it is nevertheless necessary to take a closer look at some of the texts where V. S. Naipaul discusses his interest in societies that are not part of his own heritage, as these can enlighten us about his sense of himself as a British writer of Indo-Trinidadian descent.

---

[23] Ibid., 21.   [24] Ibid.

[25] Douglas Stuart, 'Introduction' in Naipaul, *Unfinished Journey*, n.p.

[26] Shiva Naipaul, 'My Brother and I' in *Unfinished Journey*, 28, 29.

V. S. Naipaul's Exceptionalism

Like his younger brother, V. S. Naipaul (1932–2018) wrote non-fiction about travelling to Africa, but his posture comes across as more confident than Shiva's. An interesting example is his essay 'The Crocodiles of Yamoussoukro', which was published as one of the two narratives making up *Finding the Centre* (1984) and relates the Nobel Prize-winner's short stay in Ivory Coast, at the beginning of the 1980s.[27] According to the foreword, the account of this visit 'shows this writer [. . .] travelling, adding to his knowledge of the world, exposing himself to new people and new relationships' but, as is the case with his brother, these opening remarks are rather deceptive.[28] Indeed, the text does not reveal the traveller's thirst for newness as much as his obsession with the idea of Africa as a place imbued with magic, and as a society viscerally attached to the 'realm of the spirit', whereby, in the older Naipaul's book, it is refused access to reason and modernity.[29] Instead of trying to meet locals, V. S. Naipaul spends much of his time with expatriates, who more often than not come up with statements that confirm his own antiquated and biased vision of the place that, he claims, he is trying to get to know. For example, he is told about 'severed heads' allegedly used in the context of sacrifices, and he hardly questions the veracity of this urban legend with Conradian echoes.[30] But, as David J. Mickelsen rightly points out, the outcome of V. S. Naipaul's disquisition on Ivory Coast is 'autobiographical rather than anthropological'; that is, it reveals more about its author than the society he describes.[31] This confirms the close links that bind travel writing to life-writing, two genres which, in Bart Moore-Gilbert's words, 'traditionally involve personal quests, whether literal or metaphorical'.[32] With this in mind, it is interesting to focus briefly on the expatriates mentioned by V. S. Naipaul, who, he writes, 'are not unlike myself. They were trying to find order in their world, looking for the centre.'[33] Interestingly, what the author says about one of them, Janet, could very well apply to V. S. Naipaul himself. Of Guyanese origin, Janet is black, beautiful, and classy, and speaks unproblematically of herself as 'someone "from England"'.[34] Significantly, like V. S. Naipaul in a sense, 'she had no

[27] V. S. Naipaul, 'The Crocodiles of Yamoussoukro' in *Finding the Centre: Two Narratives* (Harmondsworth: Penguin, [1984] 1985), 73–160.

[28] V. S. Naipaul, 'Author's Foreword' in *Finding the Centre*, 9–12; 10.

[29] Naipaul, 'Crocodiles of Yamoussoukro', 130.   [30] Ibid., 156.

[31] David J. Mickelsen, 'V. S. Naipaul's "The Crocodiles of Yamoussoukro"', *World Literature Written in English*, 27:2 (1987): 269–74; 269.

[32] Bart Moore-Gilbert, *Postcolonial Life-Writing: Culture, Politics and Self-Representation* (London: Routledge, 2009), 83.

[33] Naipaul, 'Author's Foreword', 10.   [34] Naipaul, 'Crocodiles of Yamoussoukro', 123.

anxieties about "belonging"', the only certainty being that she does not belong to barbaric Africa or to the equally problematic Caribbean, but to the civilised world.[35] Clearly, in his travel writings, V. S. Naipaul claims for himself a form of exceptionalism that separates him from people of African descent, unless they are of a sophisticated kind, like Janet. This contempt is particularly visible in the way he represents some African American women visiting Ivory Coast: 'They had also come to Africa as to the motherland. They were ill-favoured, many of them unusually fat, their grossness like a form of self-abuse, some hideously bewigged, some dumpling-legged in short, wide, flowered skirts. They were like women brought together by a common physical despair.'[36] While this quotation betrays V. S. Naipaul's profound disdain for women, it also conveys his irritation at African American returnees who visit their ancestral continent in the hope of civilising it.

Caryl Phillips's Engagement with Returnees

Caryl Phillips has expressed a similar exasperation at the cultural arrogance of African Americans and Jamaicans going on a pilgrimage to West Africa in *The Atlantic Sound* (2000), a book-length essay where he explores the notion of 'home' by visiting Liverpool in England, Elmina in Ghana, and Charleston in South Carolina, three places historically associated with the slave trade but not always recognised as such today. After attending a Ghanaian cultural festival celebrating 'the arts, creativity and intellectual achievements of the Pan African world',[37] Phillips lashes out at

> People of the diaspora who expect the continent to solve whatever psycho-
> logical problems they possess. People of the diaspora who dress the part,
> have their hair done, buy beads, and fill their spiritual 'fuel tank' in prepara-
> tion for the return journey to 'Babylon'. They have deep wounds that need
> to be healed, but [. . .] Africa cannot cure. Africa cannot make anybody feel
> whole. Africa is not a psychiatrist.[38]

Although Phillips's observations, like Naipaul's, are critical of certain manifestations of pan-Africanism, they do not make fun of the physical features of
his targets. Indeed, his remarks focus on what the returnees do rather than
what they look like and, by implication, Phillips's less essentialist comments
do not suggest the same desire as Naipaul's to mark himself off from all

---

[35] Ibid., 123. Note how this phrase echoes Phillips's own 'high anxiety of belonging', which conveys a form of apprehension that V. S. Naipaul does not seem to share.
[36] Naipaul, 'Crocodiles of Yamoussoukro', 157.   [37] Phillips, *Atlantic Sound*, 133.
[38] Ibid., 172–3.

people of African descent whom he meets during his visit and who do not display evidence of what he regards as civilisation.

V. S. Naipaul and Caryl Phillips on South Carolina

It would be interesting to pursue the comparison between these two key figures of postcolonial travel writing in Britain by examining their respective approaches to the south of the United States, in particular to Charleston, a place that they have both visited and commented upon and which, on the surface at least, and unlike Africa for Phillips, does not directly relate to the authors' roots, in spite of the city's often concealed Black Atlantic identity. Putting side by side these two commentators' impressions of Charleston can provide us with a clearer sense of their use of the travelogue genre as a tool for personal quest and for the exploration of general issues relating to society and identity, while at the same time enlightening us on the differences that may exist between their world visions.

V. S. Naipaul writes about the capital of South Carolina in *A Turn in the South* (1989), a book that is devoted to the racial questions plaguing the south of the United States and is obsessed with the irrationality that, for Naipaul, characterises the actors of the historical drama that still shapes the former slave states. The second chapter of *A Turn in the South* focuses on Charleston. In typically Naipaulian fashion, the author's main informant is a white man, Jack Leland, a descendant of an old Charlestonian family that is now impoverished but looks with nostalgia to the splendours of the past, to a time when it owned plantation houses and the human 'cattle' that went with them. Significantly entitled 'The Religion of the Past', the chapter is essentially made up of Leland's explanations about life in the area, then and now, but with surprisingly few interventions from Naipaul himself, even when Leland's statements are clearly racist. We are told, for example, of Leland's ancestors' generosity to the newly arrived slaves, whom they 'kindly' helped to adapt to their new surroundings by asking an older, trusted slave to 'present the new life to [them] as one of ease and plenty', which in Leland's mother-in-law's terms 'showed the trouble planters went to, to make things easier for their slaves'.[39] Should Naipaul's lack of reaction to such pronouncements be viewed as reserve or silent approbation? If Naipaul does not openly question Southern prejudice, he nonetheless

---

[39] V. S. Naipaul, *A Turn in the South* (New York: Vintage, [1989] 1990), 82.

registers black people's 'spectral presences',[40] 'the lack of reference to Negroes' in white Charlestonian society,[41] but does not do anything to remedy this invisibility or silencing, for example by making sure that he also interviews someone from the black community (which he does in other parts of the book). One feels that here Naipaul is almost sorry for the embattled white people who, another white informant tells him, 'have this terrible burden of an alien population in their midst', a remark that has been uttered with variations by chauvinist politicians elsewhere, including Britain.[42] What is interesting in Naipaul's perception of the American South is that it mirrors his own vision of a racially and socially divided society, which is past-oriented and scared of mixing.[43] The historical links between Charleston and the Caribbean, especially Barbados and Trinidad, that Naipaul uncovers on his visit to the South recall for him the place he was born in, which, he concludes, 'came to nothing' because 'the slave-owners or their successors had finally to go'.[44] In other words, 'looking beyond' is also for Naipaul a paradoxical chance to reconsider his native land. As Arnold Rampersad points out, in *A Turn in the South* (with, he adds, the possible exception of *The Middle Passage*) 'Naipaul has never been closer to home in his travel writing.'[45]

In his review of Naipaul's *A Turn in the South*, Caryl Phillips regrets the limitations of his elder's approach to the South, which he finds uninspiring and 'wistful'.[46] Predictably, the younger writer's account of his visit to Charleston in his *Atlantic Sound* projects a more ambiguous, less static image of the capital of South Carolina, one in which the slave past still plays a significant role but which also gives us a glimpse of a less racially divided present and future, where young white and black people, 'dress[ed] alike', attend the same African and Caribbean art festival.[47] If the difference between the two perspectives, Naipaul's and Phillips's, might in part be due to the fact that the former's trip to the South took place some ten years before the latter's, it should mostly be linked to Phillips's narrative focus:

[40] Simon Lewis, 'Slavery, Memory, and the History of the "Atlantic Now": Charleston, South Carolina and Global Racial/Economic Hierarchy', *Journal of Postcolonial Writing*, 45:2 (2009): 125–35; 125.
[41] Naipaul, *Turn in the South*, 104. [42] Ibid., 105. [43] Ibid., 109. [44] Ibid., 89.
[45] Arnold Rampersad, 'V. S. Naipaul: Turning in the South', *Raritan*, 10:1 (Summer 1990): 24–47.
[46] Caryl Phillips, 'The Traveler Grows Wistful on His Last Turn: A Turn in the South by V. S. Naipaul', *Los Angeles Times*, 5 March 1989.
[47] Phillips, *Atlantic Sound*, 211.

a controversial figure from Charleston, Judge Waties Waring, who died in 1968 (and is only given a passing mention in Naipaul's account).[48] Coming from a privileged Charlestonian background, very much like Naipaul's interviewees, Waring, together with his wife Elizabeth, a liberal divorcee from the North, was socially ostracised by his community because of his rulings in favour of equality between blacks and whites. As a man able to go beyond 'the prejudices of his birth and status',[49] this judge provides Phillips with an interesting entering wedge into South Carolinian society, for it allows him to challenge its apparent stagnancy while also enabling him to express his own faith in human beings' ability to overcome the injustices inherited from history and to evolve towards a fairer world. Which is not to suggest that Phillips's view is unquestioningly optimistic, for it is important in this respect to register the many questions that remain in his text, most notably concerning the motivations underlying the close friendship between the judge's wife and a black woman, Ruby Cornwell, who also features among Phillips's informants. What is certain, however, is that unlike Naipaul's view of the American South, which, in line with his own conceptions of identity, is essentially inward-looking and imperialist in spirit, Phillips's is more open and testifies to what Justin D. Edwards and Rune Graulund have defined as travel writing's potential for 'transformative dialogue, one that is rooted in one place but that opens up to other places for the future'.[50]

Travelling Fiction

This chapter has so far concentrated on non-fiction, which is the predominant genre in which black and Asian British writers, overwhelmingly male ones too, have explored territories located outside the binary framework of postcolonial identity.[51] Yet black and Asian British fiction has also been the site of such spatial and cultural 'transgression', keeping in mind that overlaps between non-fictional and fictional writing are not uncommon when writers 'look beyond'. An early example of this would be Jan Carew's *Moscow is not my Mecca* (1964), a novel which tells the story of a Guyanese student sent to Russia on a scholarship provided by the Communist Party. Echoing its

---

[48] Naipaul, *Turn in the South*, 95.   [49] Phillips, *Atlantic Sound*, 192.

[50] Justin D. Edwards and Rune Graulund (eds.), *Postcolonial Travel Writing: Critical Explorations* (Basingstoke: Palgrave Macmillan, 2011), 10.

[51] Holland and Huggan have underlined the male predominance in travel writing, pointing out that travel writing can nevertheless 'transgress [. . .] the gender codes of heroic male adventure, clearing a space in the process for the subjectivities of women travellers'; *Tourists with Typewriters*, 110.

author's own experience as a West Indian scholar in Prague in the late 1940s, this text offers a reflection on the racism experienced by black men outside the colonial context and dismantles the myth of the Communist brotherhood that had encouraged them to go and live beyond the Iron Curtain.[52]

Unsurprisingly, some of the writers discussed above have also written novels expressing their interest in how societies outside their obvious lineage can provide a foil to their own identity dilemmas. One thinks of V. S. Naipaul's *A Bend in the River* (1979), a novel with Conradian ramifications taking place in post-independence Congo and reflecting some of the neo-colonialist ideas that the author had already put forward in his essays on Africa, as suggested earlier in this chapter.[53] Caryl Phillips too has written novels set in countries to which he is not historically linked, but which can play a meaningful part in his ongoing study of displacement and his creative exploration of the rejection of one human by another. This is the case of *The Nature of Blood* (1997), a structurally daring novel which juxtaposes stories taking place in Germany, Italy, and Israel and which allows Phillips to explore Europe's age-old fear of the Other that resulted in the Jewish Holocaust.[54]

Transcultural Flows in Evaristo's *Lara*

This chapter concludes by focusing on Bernardine Evaristo's *Lara* (1997, revised 2009), a novel in blank verse exploring its eponymous heroine's complex transnational heritage, which, very much like the author's, includes German, Irish, Nigerian, and Brazilian roots.[55] Lara has to face racism in her native London, where even one of her closest friends, a white girl called Susie, asks her 'Where're'you from, La?'[56] In response to this question (which, as suggested at the beginning of this chapter, haunts most of the texts discussed here) and propelled by a desire to put together the pieces of her personal puzzle, Lara travels to Africa then to South America in search of her father's family. However, if her trips to the lands of her ancestors are fruitful in the sense that they provide her with self-knowledge and an awareness of her Black Atlantic connections, it seems that it is a journey taken with her friend Trish across Europe and ending in Turkey, thus outside her own biographical strictures, that proves the most enlightening for her.

---

[52] Jan Carew, *Moscow is not my Mecca* (London: Secker & Warburg, 1964).
[53] V. S. Naipaul, *A Bend in the River* (New York: Alfred A. Knopf, 1979).
[54] Caryl Phillips, *The Nature of Blood* (London: Bloomsbury, 1997).
[55] Bernardine Evaristo, *Lara* (1997; rev. edn, Tarset: Bloodaxe Books, 2009).
[56] Ibid., 119.

Acquiring a better understanding of where she belongs, Lara concludes: 'We become more British, Trish and I, darker with the Turkish sun, yet less / aware of race for we are simply: Ingiltere.'[57]

Starting with its protagonist's full Yoruba name, Omolara, which means 'the family are like water', *Lara* is significantly replete with aquatic images: references to rivers, seas, and islands abound.[58] In keeping with this central metaphor, the novel promotes a vision of identity which is fluid and refuses to be contained within traditional national and ethnic parameters, a rationale also confirmed by the novel's generic uncertainties, its protagonist's multi-cultural experiences, and its non-linear narrative which gives voice to a myriad of characters outside Lara. This allows Mark U. Stein to conclude that 'Lara's travels are marked by [. . .] transformations [. . .] Like water, Lara is evolving, in flux. She is not *one* thing [. . .]; her cultural identity is relational; the tenets of constructivism are driven home by her experience.'[59] More generally, Evaristo's novel celebrates Britain's age-old transcultural nature and thereby exposes 'the fallacy of notions of original belonging and undoubted origin' which have regularly been used to circumscribe the British writers of immigrant heritage mentioned in this chapter.[60] Clearly, then, like Shiva Naipaul's, V. S. Naipaul's, and Caryl Phillips's writing, Evaristo's extols the virtues of reaching beyond one's limited identity frame-work, yet her world vision is more optimistic and more humorous than those of her male fellow writers, whose travel accounts and novels tend to look at the darker side of human nature and provide little redeeming compensation for it, especially in the case of the elder author from Trinidad. There is also something iconoclastic, almost trickster-like, in the way Evaristo's *Lara* handles the travel genre, which provides a twist on traditional travel accounts and demonstrates that form itself can be a way of looking beyond and being in motion.

If the texts discussed here, both fiction and non-fiction, are ideal means for their authors to come to terms with their own identity conundrums, they are also timely reminders for readers not only of the futility of authenticity, but also of the UK's rich cultural potential: not just because of its imperial past, it has access to incredible though all-too-often ignored cultural and human wealth. These texts, whether of the progressive or of the more conservative kind, all provide us with what John McLeod has called, in relation to

---

[57] Ibid., 150.   [58] Ibid., 98.

[59] Mark U. Stein, *Black British Literature: Novels of Transformation* (Columbus, OH: Ohio State University Press, 2004), 86.

[60] Ibid., 88.

Evaristo's *Lara*, a 'transcultural optic',[61] that is a lens through which we can better perceive the political stakes of Britain's problematic relationship with those of its inhabitants who are regarded as racially, ethnically, or historically Other. And at a time when Brexit could see Britain close its doors to the outside world, such concerns are more important than ever before.

---

[61] John McLeod, *Postcolonial London: Rewriting the Metropolis* (London; New York: Routledge, 2004), 183.

(III)

★

HERE TO STAY
Forging Dynamic Alliances

Sonic Solidarities

The Dissenting Voices of Dub

HENGHAMEH SAROUKHANI

> young blood
> yout rebels:
> new shapes
> shapin
> new patterns
> creatin new links
> linkin   (Linton Kwesi Johnson, 'Yout Rebels')

The history of black Britain in the 1970s and 1980s is often defined by targeted structural and physical violence against black and Asian communities. As black youths struggled to find decent and fair employment during the 1970s recession, headlines in the media stoked fears of the rise in black street crime or 'muggers'. These 'youth rebels' – vilified, generalised, and ostracised in contemporary political discourses – were subject to aggressive state-sanctioned policing tactics, where stop-and-search ('sus') laws and affray (public order) charges would lead to an ever-increasing black prison population. Appellations such as the Mangrove 9 (August 1970), the Metro 4 (May 1971), the Cricklewood 12 (October 1974), and the Bradford 12 (July 1981) indexed topographic flashpoints of police brutality aimed at disrupting black organisation and demonstration. Black community and leftist bookshops were firebombed or vandalised with racist signs, white power slogans, and National Front literature. White youths in areas such as east London harassed and abused the growing South Asian community. In 1976, Gurdip Singh Chaggar, an 18-year-old Punjabi, was murdered outside the Dominion Theatre in Southall. Two years later in Brick Lane, in another racially motivated attack, three teenagers stabbed to death Altab Ali, a Bangladeshi textile worker who was walking home from work. At stake in these confrontations was the presence of the racialised body in Britain's communal and civic spaces: in streets, shops, restaurants, parks, nightclubs, and places of work. The attack on black and Asian corporeality reflected the troubled transformation of Britain's increasingly visible multiethnic body politic, one that exposed protracted histories of racial violence and atrocity.

Wrought from these contentious times, a significant yet variegated front-line solidarity developed between a new generation of black and Asian dissidents who were galvanised, as Leila Hassan has suggested, by a consciousness not of being 'black-and-British' but of being 'black-in-Britain – of being black in a white society'.[1] While the term 'black' was beginning to challenge the notion of a unified Afro-Asian political subjectivity, this coming-to-consciousness nevertheless mobilised parallel movements that would enunciate the entangled rebellious energies of *both* black and Asian communities in Britain at the time. For second-generation Afro-Caribbean youths, rebellion was realised through wagelessness. As Darcus Howe and the Race Today Collective provocatively argued in 1975, there remains a 'distinct grouping of unemployed [West Indian] young men and women' who refuse to be the 'reserve army of labour' for 'London Transport, Fords, night cleaning agencies, hospitals and all other employers of black immigrant labour': theirs 'is an overwhelming refusal of shitwork'.[2] Unemployment, according to the Collective, became an active stance against racial prejudice, capitalist subordination, and the presumed accommodating condition of migrancy. The black working/workless classes emerged as a refigured, positive, even fetishised, subject position – nourished by the Civil Rights and Black Power movements in the United States – that articulated a 'new form of "negative consciousness"' through wilful unemployment.[3] This embodied resistance shaped the political activism of British Asian communities who also withheld their labour. The strikes at Imperial Typewriters (1974), Chix Bubblegum (1979), and particularly the Grunwick film processing plant (1976) became paradigmatic sites of political mobilisation between black, Asian, and white working classes. If 'black' as a signifier productively united these disparate causes, then it was because of the term's ability to mark tactical revolutionary cross-alliances that connected the frustration of South Asian youths in Southall, who received little to no state protection against the rising incidents of 'Paki-bashing', with the indignation of the black Notting Hill

---

[1] Leila Hassan, 'Reviews: Chris Mullard's *Black Britain*', *Race Today*, 5:6 (1973): 168.

[2] Race Today Collective, 'Editorial: The Police and the Black Wageless', *Race Today*, 7:2 (1975): 27.

[3] Stuart Hall et al., *Policing the Crisis: Mugging, the State, and Law and Order* (New York: Holmes & Meier, 1978), 356.

community, who could no longer take the consistent police harassment of the activist-oriented Mangrove restaurant in Ladbroke Grove.

It was during this kairotic moment that dub poetry as a distinctive *black British* literary genre began to flourish. Transplanted from the culture of its inception in post-independent Jamaica, the poetics of dub carried with it subversive and subcultural inflections that were forged through the Afro-Caribbean rhythms of reggae. The intermixture of creole with 'standard English' alongside the sonorous, politically conscious, often socialist verses enabled the genre to capture a uniquely multimodal revolutionary art form. Coining the first iteration of the term in 1976, Linton Kwesi Johnson argued that the 'dub-lyricist' was 'the dj turned poet', 'inton[ing] his lyrics rather than sing[ing] them' as a means to create 'a new form of (oral) music-poetry'.[4] The 'lyricism' of DJs such as Big Youth, I Roy, and Dillinger was conceived through the overdubbed articulation of their verses onto the rhythmic track of popular reggae and dancehall songs. The words and the rhythm formed the basis of a new euphonious poetic practice that would develop in ways that privileged the crafting of each line and the production of original music. Indeed, despite competing definitions of the term – particularly between two of the field's 'founding' practitioners, Linton Kwesi Johnson and Oku Onuora – dub poetry remains grounded within two distinguishing material realities: the page and the sound. It is a genre that relies upon the incommensurability between textuality and aurality. As a lyrical praxis, dub poetry exists largely in between differing sensorial modes of expression (sight, sound, feeling) in ways that emphasise centrally kinaesthetic utterances. The dub poem, moulded through the pulsations of the reggae beat, becomes sonic versification.

This chapter explores how dub poetry's epistemology of sound has constituted a crucially rebellious and coalitional genre that captures the sensibility of its times. The development of black British dub in the 1970s is both timely in its ability to articulate a demotic poetics accessible to the communities from which it speaks, and untimely in its politically impertinent capabilities. While Afro-Caribbean poets dominate the genre, the writing often remains committed to questioning the boundaries of race and nation. The form itself is constituted by a variety of mediums which shape an inherently hybrid poetic expression. Through an interrogation of the work of three influential black British dub poets – Linton Kwesi Johnson (1952–), Jean 'Binta' Breeze (1956–), and Benjamin Zephaniah (1958–) – this chapter

---

[4] Linton Kwesi Johnson, 'Jamaican Rebel Music', *Race and Class*, 17:4 (1976): 397–412; 398.

seeks to trace the means by which these poets cultivate manifold insurgent sonic solidarities. Their poetry remains firmly located within the frame of the written word and the materiality of the printed page in ways that are structured by the sonic and at times performative qualities of the poet. This attention to poetic voice enables a modality of understanding that, as Julian Henriques has insightfully contended in relation to reggae dancehall sessions, 'avoids being entirely bound up with language, notation and representation'.[5] In other words, the writing of Johnson, Breeze, and Zephaniah produces its lyrical alliances through the ineffable intermixture between the text and the sound.

The connection between dub poetry and Afro-Caribbean music, specifically, marks not only the textured context of the genre's inauguration but also the circumstances through which 1970s and 1980s black British identity was stylistically and politically transformed. As the authors of *Policing the Crisis* remind us, it was the anti-materialist, anti-colonial 'apocalyptic religio-politics of Ras Tafarianism' alongside the 'rocksteady, Blue-beat, ska and reggae' rhythms of Anglo-Caribbean cultures that 'provide[d] a new vocabulary and syntax of rebellion' for the disillusioned black youths of Britain: 'through the revivalist imagery of the "dreadlocks", the music of the dispossessed [...] and the insistent, driving beat of the reggae sound systems came the hope of deliverance from "Babylon"'.[6] This insurgent aesthetics combined North American influences of black resistance, through figures such as Angela Davis, Stokely Carmichael, and Malcolm X, with syncretic Afro-Caribbean musical cultures in ways that 're-routed' the diasporic construction of black British rebelliousness. Such a renewed 'syntax of rebellion', however, noticeably excluded Asian communities whose cultures had been suggested to be 'more cohesive and supportive for its youth'.[7] The specific trajectory of Asian resistance and industrial action in Britain, *Policing the Crisis* tells us, indicates a divergent development of urban dissent informed by differing histories of colonisation. While recognising the complexities of racialised social formations remains essential, I want to suggest that it is the cross-cultural solidarities amongst these groups that constitute not only the radical coalitional nature of the moment, but also the substance of black British dub poetry itself. Stewart Brown has argued that at the 'heart' of the musical/oral tradition of dub poetry

---

[5] Julian Henriques, *Sonic Bodies: Reggae Sound Systems, Performance Techniques, and Ways of Knowing* (New York: Continuum, 2011), xvii.
[6] Hall et al., *Policing the Crisis*, 357. [7] Ibid., 348.

lies 'the protest function, the duty of the poet to voice the concerns of the community'.[8] For black British dub practitioners, community has rarely been constricted to the boundaries of one distinctive ethnic group. As the pivotal 1980s uprisings demonstrate – where black *and* Asian youths took to the streets in Brixton, Handsworth, and elsewhere – the power of resistance movements comes from the intersection of differing struggles through which race, class, and the materialities of belonging converge. The black youths of this moment, as Linton Kwesi Johnson writes in his poem 'yout rebels', were crucially forming 'new shapes [. . .] creatin new links' *between* communities.[9]

Linton Kwesi Johnson

While the dissident nature of dub poetry contributes to its pronounced politico-poetics, the genre's civic inclinations have provoked critiques that depreciate its aesthetic and coalitional value. In *The Oxford Companion to Twentieth-Century Poetry in English*, dub poetry is seen as having 'Rage and belligerent overstatement' as 'its keynotes'.[10] '[A]t its worst', Gordon Rohlehr contends, dub poetry is 'a kind of tedious jabber to a monotonous rhythm.'[11] Based on his review of Christian Habekost's *Dub Poetry: 19 Poets from England and Jamaica* (1985), Victor Chang derides the collection for exposing the problems of dub as a poetic category: 'Its strengths lie in shrill denunciation and protest, polarized stances, confrontational postures [. . . which is why] we cannot often expect any subtlety of approach.'[12] The Jamaican-born British dub poet Linton Kwesi Johnson challenges these assertions through a body of work that establishes a recognisably critical poetics of timbre and feeling. His writing represents what Rohlehr deems the 'best' of dub poetry – not 'tedious jabber' but rather 'the intelligent appropriation of the manipulative techniques of the DJ for purposes of personal and communal signification'.[13] Born in Chapeltown, Jamaica in 1952, Johnson followed his mother at the age of eleven to Brixton, south London. Growing up as a black youth in 1960s

---

8 Stewart Brown, 'Dub Poetry: Selling Out', *Poetry Wales*, 22:2 (1987): 51–4; 52.

9 Linton Kwesi Johnson, *Dread Beat and Blood* (London: Bogle-L'Ouverture, 1975), 21.

10 Ian Hamilton (ed.), *The Oxford Companion to Twentieth-Century Poetry in English* (Oxford: Oxford University Press, 1994), 258.

11 Gordon Rohlehr, 'Introduction' in Stewart Brown, Mervyn Morris and Gordon Rohlehr (eds.), *Voice Print: An Anthology of Oral and Related Poetry from the Caribbean* (Harlow: Longman, 1989), 1–23; 18.

12 Victor Chang, 'Reviews', *Jamaica Journal*, 21:3 (1988): 49–52; 50.

13 Rohlehr, 'Introduction', 18.

Britain, he developed an acute understanding of classism and anti-black racism in the British metropolis. He would go on to join the youth wing of the British Black Panther movement as a way of immersing himself within a deeply rooted yet transatlantic history of black political consciousness. After graduating from Goldsmiths' College, University of London with a degree in Sociology, Johnson began establishing himself as a community artist and activist. As one of the younger members of the Caribbean Artists Movement (CAM) and later a journalist and music critic for the Race Today Collective, he soon became the leading creative voice of black Britain.

Johnson's writing and music remain consistently emblematic of the powerful multimodality of dub poetry in ways that have facilitated connective commentaries on the everyday condition of black and Asian communities: his is a *nuanced* and coalitional expression of 'rage' and 'shrill enunciation'. Like most dub poets, the interpretation and feel of his work can shift according to the physicality of the poetry; that is, the textual and sonic contexts from which the verses spring. It is through such contexts and modes of 'communal signification' that coalitions are engineered. Johnson's 'It Dread Inna Inglan' consummately captures this hybrid and multilayered expression of solidarity. The poem is dedicated to George Lindo, who on 5 August 1977 was wrongfully arrested for robbing a Bradford betting office. With evidence from a discredited detective, Lindo was sentenced at the Leeds Crown Court to two years in prison, a decision that spawned the lengthy 'Free George Lindo Campaign' led by the local black community and the George Lindo Action Committee. On 1 April 1978, over 300 protesters marched to the Tyrls Police Station in Bradford where Johnson read the poem aloud. The performance of 'It Dread Inna Inglan' produced what has become an iconic image of the poet: standing in between the crowd and two policemen, Johnson stoically amplifies his verses through the booming sound waves of a megaphone. Using call-and-response techniques that explicitly assert the circumstance of the poem's creation – 'dem frame-up George Lindo / up in Bradford Toun / but di Bradford Blacks / dem a rally roun' – the words move beyond the text as they constitute the organising sound of the protest.[14] The blaring vocalisation of the poem on the steps of the police station intensifies the solidarities claimed in the poetry. The text is replaced by the acoustic rhythms of a rallying cry.

'It Dread Inna Inglan' was first published in the 1978 May/June edition of *Race Today* and released on the LP *Dread Beat an' Blood* that same year; it

---

[14] Linton Kwesi Johnson, *Inglan is a Bitch* (London: Race Today, [1980] 1981), 14.

featured again in Johnson's third poetry collection, *Inglan is a Bitch* (1980). Each iteration of the poem represents a specific material site of articulation, whether at a demonstration, on an LP, in a political magazine, or in a book of poetry. Taken as an accumulation of utterances, the sonic and notational aspects of the poetry serve to deepen the black and Asian affiliations sought out in the verses. Following the rally cry, the poet goes on to claim that: 'African / Asian / West Indian / an' Black British / stan firm inna Inglan / inna disya time yah / far noh mattah wat dey say, / come wat may, / we are here to stay.'[15] In its textual version, the poem establishes an ethnic archive of alliances. The annotation of what comprises black Britishness is constitutive yet open: black British operates alongside the categories of African, Asian, and West Indian. These identities are lyrically brought together at a particular location of protest to set up the stakes of the battle. Borrowing the slogan of the Asian Youth Movements at the time, 'Come what may, we are here to stay', the poet versifies alliance by conjugating differing contexts and activities of dissent. We are invited to align the Southall Youth Movement, which came together after the 1976 murder of Gurdip Singh Chaggar, with the black communities demonstrating at the Tyrls Police Station. These political and somatic associations, which connect the insistent defence of black bodies, are not imaginatively deferred into idealised spaces of solidarity; rather, they exist 'inna disya time', coevally with each other. The battles are more than analogous. They are fighting the same system.

In musical form, 'It Dread Inna Inglan' sonically actualises affiliative communal organisation. The track begins with Johnson's distorted voice shouting through a megaphone, technologically mediating the words of the poet. When the crowd on the track chants 'George Lindo', Johnson replies with an adjoinder: 'him is a working man' or 'him nevah do no wrang'.[16] The call-and-response grows louder as it develops into a crescendo of anger and indignation. The last line spoken by Johnson, 'dem bettah free him noowww!', booms with the shrill cries of a poet on the frontline.[17] Breaking with his trademark stolid intonations, Johnson creates a raucous noise as he finishes the chant (which importantly also breaks the order of lines from the textual version). The immediacy and recorded spontaneity of this rendition contributes to what Peter Hitchcock has insightfully identified as the 'dread' in Johnson's poetry. Beyond its Rastafari connotations, dread becomes here a modulation of pressure and

---

[15] Ibid.
[16] Poet and the Roots, *Dread Beat an' Blood*, Front Line Label, FL 1017, 1978, compact disc.
[17] Ibid.

crisis where 'sound [is uttered] as syntax'.[18] The noisy voice critiques the 'harmful status quo by not being quiet'.[19] The disturbance of sound captured in the introduction to the track discordantly sits next to the melodic syncopation of the ensuing reggae beat. This shift from the disruption of a 'noisy protest' to poetic lines dubbed over harmonic reggae beats signifies two differing sonic modalities of solidarity. With each contrasting yet complementary enunciation of the verses, we find the subtleties of forged alliances enacted in the multimodal form of the poetry.

Such associative connections, sought by the writing and music, are further cemented through Johnson's phonetic use of vernacular language. In the anti-fascist poem 'Fite Dem Back', Johnson plays with speech and sound in order to mark the confrontational boundaries that urgently compel coalition. On both sonic and textual levels, the poem performs the communal possibilities enabled by dub poetry. First released on the LP *Forces of Victory* (1979) and subsequently in the collection *Inglan is a Bitch* (1980), the poem privileges aurality to stress the exigent aggression that informs these boundaries. Similar to 'It Dread Inna Inglan' the track begins with a chanting crowd, albeit differently figured. In unison with an uninflected rabble of voices, Johnson's recognisable tone sounds the first two lines: 'we gonna smash their brains in / cause they ain't got nofink in 'em'.[20] Mimicking a mob of fascists, these beginning verses capture Rohlehr's definition of the 'worst' of dub – the crowd intones a 'tedious jabber to a monotonous rhythm'. The soporific chant enacts an impoverished dub aesthetics in ways that align the crowd with a problematic and impoverished political position. The fascists, in their monotony, are not 'noisy'; they represent the actualisation of systemic violence rather than a disruptive resistance against the status quo. The aural and textual articulation of the Cockney accent set against Jamaican creole marks the significance of language on the frontlines by dramatising conflict. As the poet (now Johnson's lone voice) tells us: 'fashist an di attack / noh baddah worry 'bout dat / fashist an di attack / wi wi' fite dem back'.[21] The 'wi' here signifies those subjected to the fatal aggression of the 'paki bashah' and the 'black beatah'.[22] Black and Asian strife are again connected in the verses through language. The sounds and spelling of Jamaican creole are used to articulate the concerns of multifarious black and British Asian

---

[18] Peter Hitchcock, '"It Dread Inna Inglan": Linton Kwesi Johnson, Dread, and Dub Identity', *Postmodern Culture*, 4:1 (1993): n.p.
[19] Ibid.
[20] Linton Kwesi Johnson, *Forces of Victory*. Island Records, RRCD 32, 1979, compact disc.
[21] Ibid.   [22] Ibid.

communities. While the music politicises sound and rhythm, the text signifies orthographic sites of lyrical coalition.

Johnson's attention to the subtle cadences of the politics and linguistic aesthetics of his work obliged him, early in his career, to resist the genre of dub poetry. Since his craft was primarily concerned with the words, he instead embraced the title of reggae poet, or simply poet. Because of dub's innate association with rhythm, the assumed always already politicised poet appeared secondary to the technologies that sounded his verses. While the Jamaican dub poet Oku Onuora argues for the genre's limitless possibilities – 'you can dub een a South African riddim, you can dub een a kumina riddim, you can dub een a nyabinghi riddim, you can dub een a jazz riddim, you can dub een a funk riddim, you can dub een, you can dub!' – as a poetic category it necessarily produces limits.[23] The voice of the poet is always understood through the activity of dub or dubbing-over, a form of sonic doubling that makes composite various expressive mediums. The poet is also nearly always performing a demotic politics of rebellion. As Stewart Brown reminded us earlier, 'the duty of the [dub] poet [is] to voice the concerns of the community *rather than* to explore his own private neurosis'.[24] The dub poet, for Brown, is the extension of his immediate community; as 'the voice of popular discontent', he writes in a way that is 'exclusive to the experience of that community'.[25] The boundaries of the genre seem to be determined, then, by the necessity of (musical) rhythm and the urgency of a dissident politics connected to an immanent public sphere.

Jean 'Binta' Breeze

Jean 'Binta' Breeze, 'the first female dub poet in the male-dominated field', has challenged these limitations in ways that have centralised the discursive, personal, and universal concerns of her art.[26] As a poet, actress, choreographer, teacher, and theatre director, Breeze brings a distinctive multimodality to her work that dramatises the complex interpretive gestures required of dub. The 'audio/visual/kinetic integrity' inherent in her music, writing, and performances represents a poetic œuvre that is generically difficult to

---

[23] Oku Onuora, quoted in Christian Habekost, *Verbal Riddim: The Politics and Aesthetics of African-Caribbean Dub Poetry* (Amsterdam: Rodopi, 1993), 4.

[24] Brown, 'Dub Poetry', 52; my emphasis.   [25] Ibid., 52–3.

[26] Jean Binta Breeze, 'Can a Dub Poet be a Woman?' in Alison Donnell and Sarah Lawson Welsh (eds.), *The Routledge Reader in Caribbean Literature* (London: Routledge, 1996), 498–500; 498.

define.[27] While Breeze has been living mainly in the UK since 1985 (she was born in Jamaica in 1956 and studied at the Jamaican School of Drama), the majority of her poetry focuses on rural Jamaica and a category of writing she terms 'domestic dub'.[28] In Breeze's hands, the masculinity of dub poetry is broken down through the exploration of dub as an ontological poetic state, a *'personal* neurosis', that signifies sound and movement as 'a hermeneutical act'.[29] Her writing and performance invert Johnson's definition of the 'dub lyricist'. The poet is now the DJ as *she* manipulates her text and her body into an apparatus of sound. Her voice is the 'instrument' of a poetic practice that sounds the everyday lives of gendered, classed, and racialised bodies.[30] The subject of Breeze's poetry rarely prioritises black British life. ('The Arrival of Brighteye', 'The Wife of Bath Speaks in Brixton Market', and 'Anthem for Black Britain' are a few exceptions.) In this sense, it is hard to trace Breeze's explicit construction of Afro-Asian alliances. Since her formative years were spent in Jamaica (she came to London at the age of thirty), her work remains foundationally shaped by the Caribbean. Yet, Breeze's poetry demonstrates that dub has the potential to inspire sonic sites of dissent and solidarity without historical notation. The focus on sound and rhythm, even on the page, constitutes a poetics that frequently moves beyond its subject-matter. As Breeze herself explains, she strives to create 'work so simple in its truth and in its details that it becomes as big as the universe'.[31] The practice of dub becomes the subject of the poetry through which Breeze is able to encapsulate the rebellious mood of 1970s and 1980s black Britain.

Breeze's 'simple' free-verse poem 'dubbed out', featured in the 1988 collection *Riddym Ravings*, textualises the performance of sound and the desire of the poet to compose melody through the word.

> i
> search
> for words
>
> moving
> in their music
>
> not

---

[27] Carolyn Cooper, *Noises in the Blood: Orality, Gender, and the 'Vulgar' Body of Jamaican Popular Culture* (Durham, NC: Duke University Press, 1995), 68.

[28] Jenny Sharpe, 'Dub and Difference: A Conversation with Jean "Binta" Breeze', *Callaloo*, 26:3 (2003): 607–13; 611.

[29] Robert Beckford, *Jesus Dub: Theology, Music and Social Change* (Abingdon: Routledge, 2006), 2.

[30] Breeze, 'Can a Dub Poet', 498.   [31] Ibid.

broken

by

the

beat[32]

The visual representation of each line articulates the poet's seeming claim for the primacy of the word over the sound. Clear and harmonic stanzas mark the quest for the inherent musicality of language, while the disrupted and broken lines that follow reiterate the destructive nature of composition based on isolated rhythm. Optically, the print poet (who also happens to be a dub poet) rejects the foreign sounds of an overlaid beat. She is not 'dubbing een' but 'dubbing out' rhythm by exposing the ways external noise can destructively break the text into pieces. Her rejection of sound hinges on the word 'not', which becomes the poem's frontline, setting up the boundaries between the text and the sound, the words and the beat. This rebellion against genre ironically reconfirms the interpretative value of dub poetry since the poet uses the sense-based techniques of dub (sight, sound, and performance) in order to make her point. 'Dubbing out' is, in many ways, a synaesthetic poem that relies upon the built-in solidarities between the senses. As Carolyn Cooper eloquently suggests, in this space, 'Poetry becomes verbal dance, transmitted word-of-muscle.'[33] The poet in effect imprints the performance on the page and through this new 'stage' offers a complex resistance that deploys the tools of the system it rejects. The frontline transforms into a creative site of textual modulation that moves beyond what appear to be the binary concerns of the poet.

Dub poetry functions for Breeze as a machinery of sound. It is less a category of definable political and aesthetic guidelines and more of a device that concedes multitudinous forms of expression for the 'noisy' poet. Sound is not so much used in the service of public or political coalitions, but rather as a means to explore the limits of these connections on a personal or psychic level. In 'Riddym Ravings (the mad woman's poem)', Breeze demonstrates how such connections, which remain crucially gendered and classed, can move beyond the realm of the human. Through the trope of the radio (a literal sound machine), she exhibits how electronic sound has the potential to both extinguish and engender life and solidarity. Through her own voice, the poem delineates 'the mad woman's' troubled life as she is

---

[32] Jean Binta Breeze, 'Riddym Ravings' and Other Poems (London: Race Today Publications, 1988), 29.

[33] Cooper, Noises in the Blood, 68.

repeatedly placed in Jamaica's Bellevue Asylum. Thrown out 'fi no pay de rent', she hungrily seeks connection with those in town, in the markets, on the streets, on the bus.[34] As she bemoans: 'wen mi fus come a town / mi use to tell everybady "mawnin" / but as de likkle rosiness gawn outa mi face / nobady nah ansa mi / silence tun rags roun mi bady'.[35] It is the lack of sound that drives her 'stark raving mad', compelling her to 'tear up newspaper fi talk to'.[36] Silence becomes one of the most oppressive forces in the poem. This is why the 'de dactar an de landlord' operate on her head, removing the 'radio plug' that sounds the chorus of the poem, the singing DJ in her mind.[37] The metaphor of the organic radio establishes a form of sonic healing for the poet/'madwoman' (who always 'plugs' herself back in) while concomitantly registering a troublesome patriarchal history of medical practice. Before receiving her 'electric shack', 'the mad woman' reconnects: 'an wen dem gawn / mi tek de radio / an mi push i up eena mi belly / fi keep de baby company / fah even if mi nuh mek i / we waan my baby know dis yah riddym yah'.[38] As a conduit for rhythm, the pulse of the radio transforms into the pulse of embryonic life. The poet's/'madwoman's' dependence on sound (electronic or otherwise) enables a transmission of consciousness that turns the sonic waves of the verses into a mode of being. The technology that breeds this filiative connection is destructive in the hands of institutions. Through the anatomy of a woman's body, the machine, in contrast, births (re)productivity.

'Riddym Ravings' was released in 1987 on the album of the same name and published in the collection 'Riddym Ravings' and Other Poems a year later. It is in Breeze's performance, however, that we find the distillation of this embodied relationship to sound. Recounting the electrifying power of Breeze's reading of the poem in London in October 1986, Mervyn Morris describes his response to the 'derelict psychotic': 'I remember, for example, feeling shivers when, with a very sudden gesture, the woman pushes in the plug again.'[39] This somatic and notably voltaic reaction to Breeze's sound is impossible to replicate. Citing Walter Ong's lyrical contention that 'Sound [. . .] exists only when it is going out of existence', Morris suggests that the 'aural-visual' event of the performance always disappears.[40] Faced with the irretrievability of the performance, we nonetheless have access to Breeze's voice on her album, which allows an examination of the most crucial aspect of the poem: the 'raving'. Breeze's languid delivery of 'the mad woman's'

---

[34] Breeze, 'Riddym Ravings', 58.   [35] Ibid., 59.   [36] Ibid.   [37] Ibid., 58.   [38] Ibid., 60–1.
[39] Mervyn Morris, 'Printing the Performance', Jamaica Journal, 23:1 (1990): 21–5; 23.
[40] Ibid., 22.

verses allies with the slow ambient beats. As the track progresses, the poet's/ 'mad woman's' tempo speeds up as it becomes out-of-sync with the rhythm. Her raving is not loud and incoherent – indeed she is remarkably lucid – but rather revitalising. Her quickened pace, set against the music, intones a focused and animated ramble. The poet's/'mad woman's' raving signifies the boundaries between sanity and insanity, rationality and irrationality. Breeze challenges these categories by rejecting schematised notions of sound quality. She embraces the 'jabber' of her 'mad woman' by granting such noises intelligence, wit, and pleasure.

Benjamin Zephaniah

If 'raving' bespeaks the vital unintelligibility of personal and political rebel-liousness, then Benjamin Zephaniah's self-proclaimed dub 'ranting' takes this spirit of incongruent noise further. The Rastafarian dub poet, novelist, play-wright, actor, and activist emblematises a pivotal break in the genre. As one critic controversially put it, Zephaniah has 'in effect taken over from Linton Kwesi Johnson as the innovator and pathfinder of dub poetry'.[41] Born in 1958 in Handsworth, Birmingham to a Jamaica/Barbadian migrant family, Zephaniah's work is demotic in the fullest sense of the term: his art is profoundly informed by the everyday experiences of black British youths in the 1970s and 1980s. Unlike Johnson and Breeze, Zephaniah had no tertiary education. He came to dub poetry through an incensed political conscious-ness that was galvanised by police harassment and corruption. With the pervading influence of the sound system scene and dancehall music, Zephaniah developed a singular poetic, performative, and musical persona that would garner remarkable underground and mainstream success. However, his mass appeal and the forthright political nature of his verses have inspired much critical derision. While his writing has been lambasted as 'Pure greeting-card doggerel',[42] his commercial success has courted calls of 'selling out'.[43] Zephaniah's nomination for the Oxford Poetry Professorship in 1989, in addition to his endorsement by establishment venues such as the British Council, the BBC, and The Guardian, has led some to regard him to be 'hardly [. . .] a revolutionary'.[44] This preoccupation with Zephaniah's 'con-taminated' political credentials has unfortunately discouraged serious

---

[41] Habekost, Verbal Riddim, 31.   [42] Cooper, Noises in the Blood, 72.

[43] See Brown, 'Dub Poetry', 53.

[44] Bruce King, 'Review of Verbal Riddim: The Politics and Aesthetics of Afro-Caribbean Dub Poetry', Research in African Literatures, 26:2 (1995): 221–3; 222.

engagements with the aesthetics of his work. His style of dub 'ranting' flaunts the affective noises of an alienated generation in ways that are conceivably more inclusive than any other poet in the field. Because 'black' for Zephaniah signifies 'Romany, Iraqi, Indians, Kurds, Palestinians, all those that are treated Black by the united white states', his work necessarily attempts to forge these solidarities.[45] The limits of this poetics, especially on the page, might be read in terms of the textual constraints of capturing this specific artist's expansive proclamation of dissent.

Zephaniah's first poetry collection, *Pen Rhythms* (1980), inaugurates a developing dub voice that is marked not only by political inflection and rhythmic concern, but also an unapologetic consciousness of difference. The poet in these verses acts as a historical interloper, aware of his outsider position in the community. The pamphlet engages with the immediate sociopolitical issues of its moment by examining social injustices and resistance movements across a diversity of geographic locations. In the short collection, the poet interrogates global capitalism, poverty in England, crime, the National Front, and war. He references conflicts in Northern Ireland, Yugoslavia, India, Jamaica, Zimbabwe, Cambodia, and Australia. He connects the struggles of 'dem fighting in Angola' with 'dem fighting in Manchester'.[46] He creates near frenzied citational solidarities between vast communities around the world. On the back cover of the pamphlet, the last poem, 'According to My Mood', encapsulates the poet's recognition and enactment of this assertively unpolished and deeply dissident aesthetics:

> I have poetic licence, i WriTe thE way i waNt.
> i drop my full stops where i like . . . .
> MY CAPITAL LeteRs go where i liKe,
> i order from MY PeN, i verse the way i like (i do my spelling
>   write)
> Acording to My Mood.[47]

Spelling mistakes, grammatical inconsistencies, and stylistic idiosyncrasies constitute the unexpected beauty of the poem. This is an early evocation of Zephaniah's 'ranting' style where immediacy and a *seeming* lack of craft create a poetic mode that refuses cunning artistry. This is deliberate 'doggerel' through its awkward rhythms and irregular cadences. The declaration that 'poetic licence' is determined by disposition indicates a shifting and temperamental philosophy of writing that rejects convention. The poet's

---

[45] Benjamin Zephaniah, *Too Black, Too Strong* (Tarset: Bloodaxe Books, 2001), 13.
[46] Benjamin Zephaniah, *Pen Rhythms* (London: Page One, 1980), n.p.   [47] Ibid.

commitment to social justice and solidarity lies exposed in the form of the writing. He is attempting to do something different.

The sonic clarity that purposefully fails to reverberate off the page is instead articulated through Zephaniah's music. With the success of his first two albums, *Rasta* (1981) and *Us an Dem* (1990), Zephaniah transformed into a dub poet-cum-popular musician, a move that some critics felt diluted the politics of his work. Like his poetry, both albums serve the notational function of addressing foundational moments in black Britain and beyond. *Rasta*, for instance, covers the 1981 New Cross Massacre, the indignities of 'sus' laws, and protests against Apartheid. Unlike the work of Breeze or Johnson, Zephaniah's music rarely correlates with a written text. The words, then, become less important than the sound. It is not the texture of the poet's intonation that is of interest, but rather the rhythmic dubbing of his voice onto the track. The *music* carries the weight of cross-cultural connection.

The title track from the album *Us an Dem* offers one of the more provocative examples of Zephaniah's composition of Afro-Asian rhythm. The lyrics delineate a frontline society split into 'us' and 'dem'. There are no specifics: 'dem' denotes an elusive category of the powerful while 'us' signifies 'anyone who suffer'.[48] The abstraction of the pronoun 'us' creates radical inclusivity. There are seemingly no ethnic, class, or gender boundaries in the verses. The music intervenes to nuance the lyrics as Zephaniah's collaboration with the British tabla player Talvin Singh establishes a discernible investment in South Asian sound. Fusing classical Indian music with the sonorous baseline of drum and bass, 'Us an Dem' transmutes into a hybrid composition of Afro-Asian beats harmonised by the synthesised lilt of the Arabian mizmār. This British Asian influence (also featured in *Rasta* with the use of the sitar) is actualised in the music video for the track where the presence of black and South Asian bodies enacts the sonically inspired solidarity. The music reiterates what the video can only tell us belatedly: through sound Zephaniah finds a medium from which to euphoniously trace the cross-cultural alliances that have invariably shaped his verses.

Zephaniah's 'ranting', Breeze's 'raving', and Johnson's 'chanting' orchestrate sonic modes of dissent that compel sociopolitical and aesthetic change. Their 'noisiness' speaks to the ways in which the acoustics of dub poetry transforms the divide between various modalities of thought, expression, and

---

[48] Benjamin Zephaniah, *Us an Dem*. Universal Music Operations, CDMRED 406, 1990, compact disc.

being. Despite pronouncements of 'the genre's death' in the twenty-first century, the pioneering development of dub poetry in Britain exposed the revolutionary capacity of poetry, music, and performance as a *composite form*.[49] The sonic innovations of the genre continue to influence diverse artistic categories within and outside of Britain, from literature to music to theatre. Linton Kwesi Johnson's induction into the Penguin Modern Classics series (2002) further attests to the abiding significance of a form of sonic writing that has transcended its time, place, and expected audience.[50] While remaining a distinctive poetic category, the genre endures through both its aesthetic singularity and new improvisations that reaffirm the entanglement of art, community, and protest as multimodal rebellion.

---

[49] Kei Miller, *Writing Down the Vision: Essays and Prophecies* (Leeds: Peepal Tree Press, 2013), 87.

[50] See Henghameh Saroukhani, 'Penguinizing Dub: Paratextual Frames for Transnational Protest in Linton Kwesi Johnson's *Mi Revalueshanary Fren*', *Journal of Postcolonial Writing*, 51:3 (2015): 256–68.

20

Vernacular Voices
Fashioning Idiom and Poetic Form

SARAH LAWSON WELSH

Introduction

When, in his 1984 'electronic lecture' *History of the Voice*, Kamau Brathwaite famously declared, 'It is *nation language* in the Caribbean that, in fact, largely ignores the pentameter [...] English it may be in terms of some of its lexical features. But in its contours, its rhythm and timbre, its sound explosions, it is not English',[1] he outlined what will be the three main concerns of this chapter: the key role played by language experimentation and the use of 'vernacular voices' in Caribbean/black British and Asian British writing from the 1930s to the present day; the relationship of such writing to an English canonical model of poetry (a model dominated, formally, by the iambic pentameter and, ideologically, by monologic concepts of Englishness); and the centrality of orality and/or a performance aesthetic to many of these poets. The moment of Brathwaite's manifesto was a significant one, reflecting a recent upsurge in vernacular, 'nation language' writing within the Caribbean and Britain in the 1970s and early 1980s. However, as his lecture (originally given in 1979) makes clear, he was intent on excavating a much longer history in which nation language (also known as creoles) emerged from the historical contact between African slaves and European 'conquering peoples' in the contact zones of Caribbean plantations.[2] Africans were deliberately split up by slave-owners, disregarding tribal affiliation and language community in order to minimise the potential for slave insurrection. African languages were effectively pushed underground as forbidden, 'submerged' idioms.[3] In contact with European languages, they developed over time to

---

[1] Edward Kamau Brathwaite, *History of the Voice* (London: New Beacon Books, 1984), 13.
[2] Ibid., 7.   [3] Ibid.

become stable, fully functioning creole languages with their own native speakers, expanded linguistic forms and grammars, and unrestricted contexts of use.

'After-Dinner Jokes or Tropicism[s]': Early Accounts of Vernacular Forms

Historically, both popular and scholarly accounts of vernacular forms in the Caribbean have tended to be negative or derogatory. Many of the first accounts of vernacular voices come from early European travellers' accounts of visits to the Caribbean.[4] '[M]any of [these] early accounts of pidgins and creoles come from the pen of gentlemen travellers and administrators whose attention they had attracted because they appealed to them as caricatures of the civilized European tongues', as Peter Muhlhausler observes. Vernacular voices were viewed 'at the lowest levels' as entertaining curiosities, 'an after-dinner joke or [...] "tropicism"'.[5] In the mainly white-authored sources that have survived, we see the radical unfamiliarity of new world vernacular forms to many western ears and a fundamental lack of understanding of their linguistic origins. At this time, black vernacular forms were repeatedly relegated to a childlike, simplistic, comic status. Rather than being regarded as language systems in their own right, a status accorded to Caribbean creoles by modern linguists, they were viewed as debased or degenerate versions of standard English: 'Broken English'.[6]

---

[4] See for example, Edward Long, *A History of Jamaica*, 3 vols. (London: T. Lowndes, 1774); Mrs Carmichael, *Domestic Manners and Social Condition of the White, Coloured and Negro Population of the West Indies*, 2 vols. (London: Whittaker, Treacher & Co., 1833); Maria Nugent *A Journal of a Voyage to, and Residence in, the Island of Jamaica from 1801 to 1805, and of Subsequent Events in England from 1805 to 1811*, 2 vols. (London: private circulation, 1839); Anthony Trollope, *The West Indies and the Spanish Main* (London: Chapman & Hall, 1859); Charles Kingsley, *At Last a Christmas in the West Indies* (London; New York: Macmillan, 1872); Anthony Froude, *The English in the West Indies or the Bow of Ulysses* (London: Longmans, Green and Co., 1888).

[5] Peter Muhlhausler, *Pidgin and Creole Linguistics* (Oxford: Blackwell, 1986), 25.

[6] See for example, Dell Hymes (ed.), *Pidginization and Creolization of Languages* (Cambridge: Cambridge University Press, 1971); R. B. Le Page and Andrée Tabouret-Keller, *Acts of Identity: Creole-Based Approaches to Language and Ethnicity* (Cambridge: Cambridge University Press, 1985); John Rickford, *Dimensions of a Creole Continuum: History, Texts and Linguistic Analysis of Guyanese Creole* (Stanford, CA: University of California Press, 1987); Suzanne Romaine, *Pidgin and Creole Languages* (Harlow: Longman, 1994); Mark Sebba, *Contact Languages: Pidgins and Creoles* (Basingstoke: Macmillan, 1997); Peter Muhlhausler *Pidgin and Creole Linguistics*, expanded and revised edn (London: University of Westminster Press, 1997). Standard English itself, it should be remembered, is a historico-cultural construct. What is variously known as the 'Queen's English' or formerly as 'BBC English' originated in the English variety spoken

There are also many examples of white manipulations of black vernacular voices in published and written accounts in the nineteenth and early twentieth centuries (including translation, collection, and anthologisation of folk texts). From the very start, these texts had a transatlantic currency and circulation: rather than being discretely contained within national borders, ideas about new world vernaculars, as well as their speakers and texts, circulated in a transnational flow (as they did in relation to the abolitionist cause in Britain and the United States). Some were well-meaning but misguided attempts to bring such voices to a wider audience, apparently guided by the editorial exigencies of tempering some of the extremes of these language forms for white audiences. Others were quite deliberate appropriations of black vernaculars, exaggerated for parodic effect or wider political uses, whether sympathetic to the actual speakers or not. The net result was the same: to underscore the belief that black vernacular forms were *inherently* inferior to standard English and reflected the moral, cultural, intellectual, and technological inferiority of their speakers. In nineteenth-century India too, as Javed Majeed demonstrates, British Indologists' and administrators' choice of English as a 'unifying framework' and their promotion of Roman script (itself closely allied to a print rather than oral or manuscript culture) in the transliteration of 'vernacular' Indian languages ensured that Roman script became a 'culturally charged symbol' of modernity, justified in terms of economic efficiency and privileged within a wider colonial epistemology.[7] It is against such powerful and pervasive attitudes that the 'vernacular voices' of speakers and writers have had to fight. Indeed, the first Caribbean writers to make use of vernacular forms in their poetry all did so against a barrage of negative popular attitudes to the use – and especially the *literary* use – of the vernacular.[8]

in the London and south-eastern region of England, which by the fourteenth century was beginning to emerge as the hegemonic variety of English spoken at Court. The term is used in this chapter to denote a hegemonic variety against which 'non-standard' vernacular varieties are explicitly or implicitly compared and contrasted. The term 'vernacular' is often used of the Latinate or Romance languages which emerged from Latin (the official language of the Roman Empire and the Christian Church) in the eighth and ninth centuries and which more accurately represented the speech of ordinary people. The role of English as a colonial language imposed by the British in a range of global contexts added another dimension to this complex history. Importantly, vernacular languages are usually spoken as a mother tongue as opposed to imposed or learned (and often written) languages such as Latin or Sanskrit.

[7] Javed Majeed, 'Modernity's Script and a Tom Thumb Performance' in Michael S. Dodson and Brian A. Hatcher (eds.), *Trans-Colonial Modernities in South Asia* (London; New York: Routledge, 2013), 95–115; 100, 95.

[8] See for example, Claude McKay, *Constab Ballads* (London: Watt & Co., 1912) and *Songs of Jamaica* (Kingston, Jamaica: A.W. Gardner & Co., 1912); Una Marson, *The Moth and the*

A History of Denigration and Disavowal

The history of Caribbean vernacular voices is one of repeated denigration and disavowal: first by external observers, second by the colonial masters, and third through the agency of a powerful colonial educational apparatus. Everywhere the British went they implemented colonial systems of government, law, and education, all of which publicly upheld the primacy of a standardised form of English. Colonial subjects and speakers were themselves encouraged to regard vernacular forms as contemptible and inferior (rather than merely different) to standard English. As the Jamaican poet Louise Bennett recalls, they were considered 'not respectable', suitable for the yard or the street perhaps, but not for the classroom, the court, or the government building. In turn, there was 'a social stigma attached to the kind of person who used dialect habitually'.[9] Indeed, Bennett famously recalls an audience member shouting out at one of her early Jamaican performances: 'Is dat yuh modder sen yuh a school fa?'[10] As late as 1990, Merle Hodge commented: 'We speak creole, we need creole, we cannot function without creole, for our deepest thought processes are bound up in the structure of creole, but we hold creole in contempt.'[11] In 1999 Mervyn Morris summed it up thus: 'Linguistics tries to teach us equal respect for Creole and Standard English [... but] the historical legacy lingers. Facility in Standard English – the language of the masters, originally – confers a measure of social status.'[12] This history of high status for standard English and low status for vernacular voices has had tumultuous consequences for the emerging *literary* use of creoles. As Brathwaite's coinage of the affirmative term 'nation language' suggests, such vernacular forms, from their very earliest uses, gained the status of a subversive, frequently politically charged 'guerrilla' language, a vital source of anti-colonial cultural resistance, and also, for many, a source of Caribbean authenticity.

Star (Kingston, Jamaica: the author, 1937); Louise Bennett, *Jamaica Humour in Dialect* (Kingston, Jamaica: Jamaica Press Association, 1943).

[9] Louise Bennett, 'Bennett on Bennett: Louise Bennett Interviewed by Dennis Scott', *Caribbean Quarterly*, 14.1–2 (1968): 97–101. Reprinted in E. A Markham (ed.), *Hinterland: Caribbean Poetry from the West Indies and Britain* (Newcastle upon Tyne: Bloodaxe Books, 1989), 45–50.

[10] Louise Bennett, *Selected Poems*, ed. Mervyn Morris (Kingston, Jamaica: Sangster's Bookstores, 1982), xii–xiii.

[11] Merle Hodge, 'Challenges of the Struggle for Sovereignty: Changing the World versus Writing Stories' in Selwyn R. Cudjoe (ed.), *Caribbean Women Writers* (Wellesley, MA: Calaloux Publications, 1990), 202–8; 204.

[12] Mervyn Morris, *'Is English We Speaking' and Other Essays* (Kingston, Jamaica: Ian Randle, 1999), 7.

Experimenting with Vernacular Voices: Black
British Poetry

This history notwithstanding – indeed, perhaps partly because of it – the use of non-standard language forms by Caribbean, black British, and Asian British writers in the twentieth and twenty-first centuries has been one of the most important revolutions in contemporary British poetry. Black British poetry is the province of experimenting with voice and recording rhythms beyond the iambic pentameter. Not only in performance poetry and through the spoken word, but also on the page, black British poetry constitutes and preserves a sound archive of distinct linguistic varieties. In *Slave Song* (1984) and *Coolie Odyssey* (1988), David Dabydeen employs a form of Guyanese creole in order to render linguistically, and thus commemorate, the experience of slaves and indentured labourers respectively with the earlier collection providing annotated translations into standard English. James Berry, Louise Bennett, and Valerie Bloom adapt Jamaican creole to celebrate Jamaican folk culture and at times to represent and record experiences and linguistic interactions in the postcolonial metropolis. Grace Nichols and John Agard use modified forms of Guyanese creole, with Nichols frequently constructing gendered voices whilst Agard often celebrates linguistic playfulness. Indeed, the collective use of creole by many contemporary black British poets has shown it to be a rich and versatile medium. Their work has also helped break down a number of stereotypes surrounding the use of nation language: first, that it is employed primarily for comic effect; second, that it is used merely to effect 'authenticity' or verisimilitude;[13] and third, that it is limited to a 'syntax of rebellion'[14] and the medium of politicised 'protest' poetry alone – often, it is argued, of the most mediocre kind. On the contrary, as this chapter demonstrates, creole has proved a medium versatile enough to encompass a range of poetic effects. That vernacular voices have been central to the articulation of a 'demotic poetics accessible to the community from which [such poetry] speaks' is arguably something to celebrate, but this factor has also sometimes been harnessed in critiques which suggest that the use of the vernacular limits audience.[15]

---

[13] See also John Figueroa (ed.), *Caribbean Voices: An Anthology of West Indian Poetry*, vol. 2 (London: Evan Brothers, 1970), 14–16.

[14] Henghameh Saroukhani in Chapter 19 of this volume.   [15] Ibid.

Adapted Idioms and 'Synthetic Vernacular'

Part of the problem is that despite the emergence of well-respected dictionaries of Caribbean English from the 1960s onwards there is still not a uniform orthography for transcribing creoles into written form.[16] Mervyn Morris has reflected on the editorial misunderstandings that a lack of standard orthography can give rise to when transcribing primarily oral performance poems into print.[17] Other writers have found their own ways of 'modifying the dialect' and transferring their own vernacular voices into print.[18] Consequently, all literary use of creole is necessarily the use of an adapted idiom which can vary greatly from writer to writer. But this is not necessarily a disadvantage to the writer wanting to use creole in their work. Indeed, David Dabydeen has argued that:

> In the brokenness of language resides [...] the capacity to be experimental with a language; it is almost like Shakespearean English. You can make up words, play with words and you can rhyme in much more adventurous ways than you can in Standard English. The brokenness has a capacity to convey a greater sense of tragedy and pain, of energy, but you can also reconstruct it in your own way, you can play with the language with a greater degree of freedom.[19]

In *Nations of Nothing But Poetry* (2010), Matthew Hart proposes a potentially useful category of 'synthetic vernacular' based partly on the Scottish poet Hugh MacDiarmid's use in the 1920s of what he called 'synthetic Scots' – a kind of 'invented literary dialect' that combined actual Scots and 'regional expressions' as well as 'contemporary idioms' in a constructed amalgam.[20] Hart is fascinated by the modernist use of 'synthetic vernaculars' by poets including the early Brathwaite and shows how the 'double-voiced' trope of the synthetic vernacular 'troubles the border between [...] difference and universality [...] vernacular self-ownership and the wilful appropriation of language that will forever be foreign'.[21] For Hart, as for the present

---

[16] See R. B. Le Page, *Jamaican Creole* (London: Macmillan, 1960); F. G. Cassidy, *Jamaica Talk: Three Hundred Years of the English Language in Jamaica* (London: Macmillan, 1961); B. L. Bailey, *Jamaican Creole Syntax* (Cambridge: Cambridge University Press, 1966); F. G. Cassidy and R. B. Le Page, *Dictionary of Jamaican English* (Cambridge: Cambridge University Press, 1967).

[17] In Michael Smith, *It A Come*, ed. Mervyn Morris (London: Race Today, 1986), 10.

[18] See Morris, *'Is English We Speaking'*, 45–52.

[19] David Dabydeen, 'Interview with Wolfgang Binder', *Journal of West Indian Literature*, 3:2 (1989): 67–80; 76.

[20] Matthew Hart, *Nations of Nothing but Poetry* (Oxford: Oxford University Press, 2010), xi.

[21] Ibid., 7.

argument, 'conversations about vernacular language are inseparable from questions of political sovereignty and social inequality'.[22]

The Post-Creole Continuum and 'London Jamaican'

The 'post-creole continuum', a theoretical model derived from creole linguistics and used to explain variation in individual speakers' (or writers') uses of creole, is also relevant here. It posits a continuum of different forms within a single creole (such as Jamaican creole) from the broadest (*basilectal*) varieties at one end of the spectrum, through *mesolectal* varieties in the middle, to those which most closely resemble standard British English at the other end (*acrolectal* varieties). The type and extent of creole spoken by an individual speaker depends on a number of factors including the speaker's geographical location, educational background, and social status. Most speakers exhibit a linguistic competence, or ability to speak a range of creole along a section of this 'creole continuum'. Crucially, this model is not fixed but dynamic, allowing for linguistic change and development at both ends of the continuum. So, for example, standard English can be modified by creole forms and vice versa. Indeed, in a British diasporan context, the vernacular resource of nation language is continuing to change and develop, as speakers and writers continue to experiment with the resources of Caribbean creoles and standard English. The borders between linguistic varieties are porous rather than absolute or static, as the emergence and marked growth of what the sociolinguist Mark Sebba has termed 'London Jamaican' indicates.[23] Indeed, 'London Jamaican' is an important example of this fluidity and change at the edge of the post-creole continuum. The post-creole continuum can also be used as a model for a wider, equally mobile and fluid continuum of use as black British writers draw from those vernacular resources available to them in the linguistic, formal, and aesthetic choices in their poetry.[24]

Saroukhani argues in this volume that dub and black British protest poetry's 'powerful multimodality' has always allowed creative cross-

---

[22] Ibid., xiii.

[23] See Sebba, *Contact Languages*; Mark Sebba and Susan Dray, 'Making it Real: "Jamaican", "Jafaican" and Authenticity in the Language of British Youth', *Zeitschrift für Anglistik und Amerikanistik*, 60:3 (2013): 255–73.

[24] See Sajae Elder's recent online post 'Where Did Drake's "Jamaican" Accent Come From?' for further discussion of the politics of cultural appropriation and authenticity in another diasporan context: that of Toronto, Canada. Available at www.buzzfeed.com/sajaee/some-ting-borrowed?utm_term=.mrBA2q5W76#.xil4n5JbdL.

fertilisation of forms (such as bhangra, rap, and dancehall) and 'cross-cultural solidarities'.[25] Asian British writers, such as Daljit Nagra, creatively take liberties with English in different ways than the dub poets, but Nagra's poetry is 'promiscuously porous' enough to embrace dub rhythms in certain poems.[26] Nagra's heteroglot poems frequently emulate 'Punglish', the English of migrants whose first language is Punjabi. Whilst it is the language prestige of London Jamaican that has been significantly enhanced since the 1990s, a fact not only confirmed by linguistic research but also by its *transethnic* uses both in the streets and on the page,[27] Nagra's substantial success and the mainstream attention he receives also indicate the clout of vernacular voices in poetry more generally. Vernacular voices have the potential to connect with oral traditions and cultural memories, to record linguistic varieties, and to endow authors and texts with 'street cred'. Importantly, these multi-voiced poetic languages can also be read as signs of resistance against residual monologic ideologies of Englishness.

Sebba argues that 'From the early days of "London Jamaican" through to recent remarks by the historian David Starkey that rioters in English cities were communicating in "wholly false … Jamaican patois", authenticity and ownership have been problematic for both linguists and users of Creole in Britain.'[28] He continues:

> Second-generation speakers of Creole in London in the 1980s were conscious that they could not pass for natives when in the Caribbean, but could nevertheless claim to be authentic 'black British' by virtue of commanding both the local British vernacular and a local version of Jamaican Creole […] By the end of the century, claims of authenticity linked to ethnic identity had been undermined by the emergence of a non-ethnically specific youth variety incorporating Creole grammatical and phonological features, as parodied by the fictitious character Ali G […], sometimes called 'Jafaican' by the media.[29]

Sebba concludes that '"Creole" manifests itself less and less as a linguistic system and more and more as an additional linguistic resource in a complex semiotic system' – that is, '"authenticity" is achieved through practices rather than inherited ethnicity or native-like use of a specific variety'.[30]

---

[25] See Chapter 19.   [26] See Chapter 31.   [27] Sebba and Dray, 'Making it Real'.
[28] Abstract to Sebba and Dray, 'Making it Real'.   [29] Ibid.   [30] Ibid.

Orality and the Sounded Voice

From its very beginnings, nation language has been closely associated with orality and the spoken voice. In literature, its use has often been coupled with a holistic, communal, kinetic context of performance in which the speaker's location, voice, body, and interactions with his/her audience all are of central importance. As Walter Ong and Ruth Finnegan have shown, understanding oral expressive forms demands a critical awareness of an oral mindset or 'psychodynamics of orality'.[31] Orality is not merely the absence of literacy or an abstract aesthetic choice on the part of the writer (poetry for the 'stage' rather than the 'page'). In the case of black and Asian British poetry it is useful to think of an *oraliterary continuum of literary practices* in which both orality and writing, audio and print feature. Importantly this is not a simple binary: not all performance poems use vernacular voices or vice versa. Contemporary black British poets such as Agard and Nichols draw inspiration from African and Caribbean oral traditions in their work.[32] This privileging of orality and the sounded voice is also important in contemporary Britain, where spoken word performance is currently enjoying something of a renaissance. It thus makes sense to speak not only of a textual archive but of a *sound archive* as well.[33]

Louise Bennett: Pioneering Poet

The first black British poets to experiment with creole in Britain were undoubtedly inspired by the pioneering 'vernacular voice' of Louise Bennett (1919–2006). A prolific writer and performer, Bennett started performing her Jamaican nation language poems, short stories, and monologues in 1936, broadcasting on radio and publishing books and

---

[31] Walter Ong, *Orality and Literacy: The Technologizing of the Word* (London: Methuen, 1987) and Ruth Finnegan, *Oral Poetry* (Cambridge: Cambridge University Press, 1977); Ruth Finnegan, *Oral Literature in Africa* (Oxford: Clarendon Press, 1970; Nairobi: Oxford University Press, 1976; revised and enlarged edition, Cambridge: Open Book Publishing, 2012).

[32] See Grace Nichols in Kwame Dawes, *Talk Yuh Talk: Interviews with Anglophone Caribbean Poets* (Charlottesville, VA; London: University Press of Virginia, 2001), 140.

[33] See Julia Novak, *Live Poetry: An Integrated Approach to Poetry in Performance* (Amsterdam; New York: Rodopi, 2011). This sound dimension was explicitly recognised in *Voiceprint: An Anthology of Oral and Related Poetry from the Caribbean*, selected and edited by Stewart Brown, Mervyn Morris, and Gordon Rohlehr; with an introduction by Gordon Rohlehr (Harlow: Longman Caribbean, 1989), which included poems, songs, elegies, laments, calypsos, and other forms expressing the wide range and different styles of the oral tradition.

regular newspaper columns from the 1940s onwards.[34] Fellow Jamaican poet James Berry recalls: 'The "people's language" was first opened up by Louise Bennett. She dared to speak Creole – as the majority of people spoke – on the radio in the 1940s, and absolutely shook the whole island. She shook us into a new awareness of our Caribbean consciousness.'[35] Although Bennett uses the English quatrain form, the rhythms and cadence of her poems are rarely contained by iambic pentameter and, at best, she makes the form absolutely her own. For many years she faced opposition and critical censure for what was dismissively called 'doing dialect'.[36] She originally wrote in standard English but, after a revelatory moment, decided to switch to the vernacular voices heard all around her on a daily basis.

In 'Bans a Killing' her persona addresses 'Mas Charlie', a man who wants to 'kill' off all dialects in favour of standard English. Bennett draws parallels between Jamaican 'dialect', the origins of the English language as a vernacular of Latin, and the long existence of regional dialects in English:

> wha meck
> Yuh gwine go feel inferior when
> It come to dialec?
> [...]
> Dah language weh yuh proud a,
> Weh yuh honour an respect –
> Po Mas Charlie, yuh no know se
> Dat it spring from dialec!
>
> Dat dem start fi try tun language
> From de fourteenth century –
> Five hundred years gawn an dem got
> More dialect dan we![37]

[34] See Louise Bennett, *(Jamaica) Dialect Verses* (Kingston, Jamaica: Herald, 1942); *Jamaica Humour in Dialect; Anancy Stories and Poems in Dialect* (Kingston, Jamaica: Gleaner, 1944); *Mis' Lou Sez* (Kingston, Jamaica: Gleaner, 1949); *Anancy Stories and Dialect Verse* (Kingston, Jamaica: Pioneer Press, 1957); *Laugh with Louise* (Kingston, Jamaica: City Printer, 1961); *Jamaica Labrish* (Kingston, Jamaica: Sangster's Bookstores, 1966); *Anancy and Miss Lou* (Kingston, Jamaica: Sangster's Bookstores, 1979); *Selected Poems; Aunty Roachy Seh* (Kingston, Jamaica: Sangster's Bookstores, 1993).

[35] Asher Hoyles and Martin Hoyles, *Moving Voices: Black Performance Poetry* (London: Hansib, 2002), 204.

[36] See Mervyn Morris, 'On Reading Louise Bennett Seriously', *Jamaica Journal*, 1:1 (1967): 69–74.

[37] Bennett, *Selected Poems*, 4–5.

James Berry: Intimacy and Reflective Lyricism

The influence of Bennett is very clear in the poetry of James Berry (1924–2017), who came to Britain in 1948. Like Bennett (and McKay and Marson before her), Berry makes extensive use of the 'letter home' creole voice portrait, notably in *Lucy's Letters and Loving* (1982). Berry also edited two key anthologies of black British poetry – *Bluefoot Traveller* (1976) and *News for Babylon* (1984) – in which a new generation of vernacular voices is recorded. However it is his own poetry, with its crafted use of nation language and standard English, its experimentation with different poetic forms (the haiku, Jamaican proverb, love lyric, letter home, and creole monologue), that has done most to challenge stereotypical notions that black British poetry is overwhelmingly public rather than personal, a voice only of protest and rage rather than of reflective lyricism. As Berry's work shows, nation language is particularly suited to lyrical uses as part of an open and intimate style. Unlike standard English it is an informal and emotive language, strongly associated with intimacy and group solidarity amongst speakers. It facilitates a refreshing directness in place of the abstraction of standard English; sometimes, as David Dabydeen puts it, 'the English fails where the creole succeeds'.[38] In poems such as 'Ol Style Freedom'[39] and 'Words of a Jamaican Laas Moment Them'[40] Berry makes lyrical use of creole as the quiet, almost reverential medium of intimacy between speakers:

> Mek all the Island wash –
> wash away the mess of my shortcomings –
> all the brok-up things I did start.
> Mi doings did fall short too much.
> Mi ways did hurt mi wife too oftn.[41]

Valerie Bloom: Nation Language as Mother Tongue

Jamaican-born Valerie Bloom (1956–) was one of the young poets anthologised in Berry's *News for Babylon*. Her own first collection, *Touch Mi! Tell Mi!* (1983), was heralded by Linton Kwesi Johnson as an 'important and welcome' collection of 'oral poetry'.[42] In it, like Berry and Bennett before her, Bloom

---

[38] David Dabydeen, *Slave Song* (Mundelstrup: Dangaroo, 1984), 14.
[39] James Berry, *Hot Earth Cold Earth* (Newcastle upon Tyne: Bloodaxe Books, 1995), 49.
[40] Ibid., 72.   [41] Ibid.
[42] Valerie Bloom, *Touch Mi! Tell Mi!* (London: Bogle-L'Ouverture, 1983), 9.

uses an adapted Jamaican creole to celebrate Jamaican folk culture and at times to represent and record experiences and linguistic interactions in the postcolonial metropolis. In 'Language Barrier' Bloom addresses the issue of nation language directly, as her persona reveals her delight in the 'sweet' potentialities of 'Jamaica language':

> Jamaica language sweet yuh know bwoy [...]
> Is not dat wi don' like English'
> But wi lub wi modda tongue.[43]

Now, this open expression of nation language as 'wi modder tongue' is a new and important one, the logical corollary of Brathwaite's contemporaneous message in *History of the Voice*. Though Bloom uses the English quatrain form and writes about similar topics to Bennett, she belongs to a later generation of poets who were able to use vernacular voices more explicitly and more confidently than ever before.

David Dabydeen: Creolised Songs of Resistance

However, not all black British poets use vernacular voices in the same way. In his first collection, *Slave Song* (1984), David Dabydeen (1955–) takes as his starting point the historical perception of the 'vulgarity'[44] of creole languages as 'broken English', 'degenerate' linguistic forms that were thought to reflect the alleged depraved, uncivilised, or childlike status of their speakers. *Slave Song* consists of a series of Guyanese creole voice portraits, each accompanied by a standard English translation and the poet's own commentary. Dabydeen's observation that 'it is surprising [...] that very little Creole poetry exists' given 'the potentiality for literature is very great indeed' resonates with Brathwaite's manifesto.[45] Indeed, as he later reflected: 'People like Brathwaite have been arguing for years that Creole is a different language, sufficiently different from English to be considered its own language. So therefore the logic would be to provide a translation, which is what I did.'[46] Although it was not the first collection to use vernacular voice portraits, *Slave Song* was important in ushering in a new self-consciousness about the literary uses of creole, in opening up debates about its relation to standard English and an English canon, and in demonstrating how vernacular voices could be used for varied poetic effect.

---

[43] Ibid., 41–3.   [44] Dabydeen, *Slave Song*, 13.   [45] Ibid., 15.
[46] Dabydeen, 'Interview with Wolfgang Binder', 75.

Indeed, the poems in *Slave Song*, like those of Bennett or Berry, are more than Browningesque voice portraits transferred to a Caribbean context. They are, as the title suggests, first and foremost songs: songs of resistance. Dabydeen writes in his introduction of the 'brokenness' of creole as a 'naturally tragic language [...] no doubt reflecting the brokenness and suffering of its original users – African slaves and East Indian indentured labourers'.[47] However, this concept of a doubled brokenness is resisted in practice by the dominant and defiant voices of the poems themselves: fluent rather than faltering voices which refuse to be broken. Read collectively, the intensely imagined experiences of the individual speakers form a powerful examination of what Wilson Harris terms the 'pornography of Empire', an exploration of the brutalities enacted on the slave and the various means of resistance (linguistic, cultural, and sexual) open to him or her.[48] The collection mediates between these experiences and speaks with a thoroughly creolised as well as creole voice.

Dabydeen's adaptation of Guyanese creole is not a naturalistic or even necessarily a representative one. His literary reconstruction of particular 'vernacular voices' is deliberately artificial, as part of an artful and self-conscious process. Dabydeen writes of a 'criss-cross of illusions' between England and Guyana, mythically figured as 'El Dorado', and this notion of illusion as public mythology is neatly mirrored by the admission that the poems are, in part 'an imaginative rendition [...] a private fantasy'.[49] *Slave Song*'s 'vernacular voices' *do* seem to confer a certain 'authenticity', even as we acknowledge their artifice as the poet effectively returns to his creole-speakers an agency and voice which was denied to their historical counterparts.

In a collection so full of illusion and fantasy, perhaps the greatest irony is that such speakers and their vernacular voices are also illusory. Arguably, they are ultimately contained, challenged, and even silenced by the translations and notes in standard English. Indeed, we might read such standard English translations as the ironic legacy of a colonial history of vernacular voices being re-presented and mediated through the coloniser and, in the process, attenuated or obfuscated. Dabydeen has spoken of a painful 'unsheathing of the tongue' in preparation for a 'language uncomfortably raw', yet paradoxically the energy and radicalism of the poems themselves, so

---

[47] Dabydeen, *Slave Song*, 13.
[48] Wolfgang Binder, 'Interview with David Dabydeen' in Kevin Grant (ed.), *The Art of David Dabydeen* (Leeds: Peepal Tree Press, 1997), 159–76; 168.
[49] Dabydeen, *Slave Song*, 9, 10.

powerfully disruptive of linguistic hegemonies and canonical modes, are 'smothered' by the standard English translations and the Eurocentric critical apparatus that encases them.[50] It is as if 'the reader's need to consult the scholarly appendages to the poems was essentially in order to distance and detoxify the emotional effects of their message'.[51] The notes and translations are, in their own way, as insistent as the creole voices of *Slave Song* and, as competing voices, they act as a kind of meta-commentary on the asymmetries of power involved, as the images of conspicuous consumption of 'peasant' poetry by Oxbridge diners at the end of 'Coolie Odyssey' make even more explicit. '*Slave Song* [draws] attention to interesting problems of poetic form and voice, of the ways in which the projected audience of the poem modified the craft itself.'[52] Ultimately, Dabydeen deliberately assumes different roles and discursive modes – historian, polemicist, poet, and critic among them – in order to subvert conventional genre boundaries and to foreground the porous relationship between historical documentation and imaginative reconstruction, primary voices and scholarly apparatus, orality and literacy, vernacular voices and standard language translation.

The title poem to Dabydeen's second collection, *Coolie Odyssey* (1988), is even more explicit in its articulation of the politics of vernacular language. With a nod to the preoccupation with 'dialect' and 'the folk' in both a Caribbean and a British context, black British nation language poets, and more canonical contemporary voices who use regional dialects in their work (Seamus Heaney, Tony Harrison, Tom Leonard, Basil Bunting), the poem opens:

> Now that peasantry is in vogue,
> Poetry bubbles from peat bogs,
> People strain for the old folk's fatal gobs
> Coughed up in grates North or North east
> 'Tween bouts o'living dialect,
> It should be time to hymn your own wreck.
> Your house the source of ancient song[53]

The 'you/r' of this poem is 'Ma', Dabydeen's late grandmother. Indeed, the poem is in part an elegy to her as the poetic persona muses on the deep contrast between her life as an uneducated Indo-Caribbean peasant and his own life of privilege life in Britain:

[50] Ibid., 14.
[51] Mark McWatt, 'Review of *Coolie Odyssey*', *Journal of West Indian Literature* (September 1989): 86–90; 87.
[52] Ibid., 87.   [53] David Dabydeen, *Coolie Odyssey* (London: Hansib/Dangaroo, 1988), 9.

> We mark your memory in songs
> Fleshed in the emptiness of folk,
> Poems that scrape bowl and bone
> In English basements far from home,
> Or confess the lust of beasts
> In rare conceits
> To congregations of the educated
> Sipping wine, attentive between courses –[54]

These final, knowing – but also terribly poignant – lines reveal the personal and communal cost of consuming 'the folk' and their 'vernacular voices' in this way, as the poet reflects on the tension between his subject and his art, the Guyanese peasant life of his grandmother and the performance of his poems to an educated, mannered, sophisticated elite in Britain. Despite the speaker's skill in constructing the 'rare conceits' of his poetry, he is aware that not far beneath the surface reside some enduring colonial stereotypes: the 'bowl and bone' and 'lusts of beasts'. As Jamaica Kincaid might say, 'there is a world of something in this' and Dabydeen captures it perfectly.

Fred D'Aguiar: Retelling History, Rethinking 'Britishness'

A black British poet who has also drawn on Guyanese creole is Fred D'Aguiar (1960–) who is based at UCLA in California. His first collection, *Mama Dot*, was published to critical acclaim in 1985. Reminiscent of James Berry's similar experimentation, it consists of a series of vernacular voice portraits that centre around the inimitable figure of Mama Dot, a grandmother and household matriarch. The opening poem is especially effective in its renarration of the wider history from African enslavement to Caribbean emancipation within a pared-down poetic structure reminiscent of traditional oral forms such as the revivalist hymn or children's rhyme game. Representing the traumatic collective history through evocative details of a personal history, projected onto the forever recurring days of the week, its lightness of touch and disarmingly simple structure make the poem all the more powerful:

> Born on a sunday
> in the kingdom of Ashante

---

[54] Ibid., 13.

Sold on monday
into slavery

Ran away on tuesday
cause she born free

Lost a foot on wednesday
when they catch she

Worked all thursday
till her head grey

Dropped on friday
where they burned she

Freed on saturday
in a new century.[55]

D'Aguiar's later collections tend to use fewer vernacular resources, a notable exception being the long narrative poem *Bill of Rights* (1998), which combines more standardised language with modified Guyanese creole in order to retell the story of the 1978 Jonestown massacre in Georgetown, Guyana. Again, the versatility of vernacular voices comes to the fore as 'a gallimaufry of linguistic registers and moves through an exhilarating range of rhythms from the repetition of biblical language to the riffs of popular music'.[56] Perhaps the most pertinent of D'Aguiar's collections for an interrogation of black and British Asian identities is his punningly titled 1993 collection *British Subjects*, with the poem 'Home' a particular highlight.[57]

John Agard: Mugging the Queen's English

Not all poems using 'vernacular voices' absolutely necessitate a performative mode even if they do continue to privilege the speaking voice. A good example is John Agard (1949–), known for his lively, kinetic performances but whose poems also work well in print form. 'Palm Tree King' (1983) playfully utilises a vernacular idiom for serio-comic effect. By means of a bold dialogue with an imagined interlocutor (a technique also used by Bennett and

---

[55] Fred D'Aguiar, *Mama Dot* (London: Chatto & Windus, Hogarth Press, 1985), 9.

[56] Back cover to *Bill of Rights* (London: Chatto & Windus, 1998).

[57] See Sarah Lawson Welsh, '(Un)belonging Citizens – Unmapped Territory: Immigration and Black British Identity in the post 1945 period' in Stuart Murray (ed.), *Not On Any Map: Essays on Postcoloniality and Cultural Nationalism* (Exeter: Exeter University Press: 1997), 43–66 for a close reading of this poem.

Bloom), the poem's speaker mobilises and then disarms a series of stereotypes of the West Indian, including the notion of creole inarticulacy. 'Listen
Mr Oxford Don' (1983) addresses similar kinds of popularly received beliefs
but the subject is now vernacular language itself. The poem channels the
popular fear of nation language as an anarchic, alien language with a battery
of broken and bastardised forms potentially waiting to erupt on the quiet
tranquillity of standard English, as symbolised by that great repository, the
Oxford English Dictionary. The poem also plays upon a series of anxieties about
the figure of the immigrant in Britain, which are as timely today as they were
when the poem first appeared in 1983:

> Me not no Oxford don
> Me a simple immigrant
> From Clapham Common
> I didn't graduate
> I immigrate[58]

This is Agard's starting point: the imagined threat posed by a 'simple
immigrant' to the 'Oxford don', establishment figure and upholder of the
'Old Order' of standard English. The poem explicitly articulates the Oxford
don's (and other Britons') unspoken fear: that vernacular voices such as this
one threaten to subvert the quiet echelons of 'Oxbridge English', to ripple the
surface of the undying myth of English pastoral, to erupt in like the barbarians at the gate. This is not the threat of physical violence (another popular
fear), but by more insidious, invisible means. As the persona proclaims, in a
kind of dread 'prophesay':

> I ent have no gun
> I ent have no knife
> but mugging de Queens English is the story of my life.
> I don't need no axe to split
> up yu syntax I don't need no hammer to mash
> up yu grammar.[59]

Much of the poem's power derives from its playful exploitation of the
imagined threat to the English language. The speaker is incredulous that a
'concise, peaceful man like' him should be accused of 'assault / on de Oxford
dictionary'.[60] However, he, like many other black British poets, does exactly
this: harnessing the peaceful but also powerful medium of words in order to

---

[58] John Agard, *Mangoes and Bullets: Selected and New Poems, 1972–84* (London: Pluto, 1985), 44.
[59] Ibid.   [60] Ibid.

subvert the hegemony of standard English from within. Ironically, the 'immigrant' is also British and the English language has always been subject to change – while the *OED* is tasked with recording its ongoing development. The poem offers powerful insights into the ways in which language variation is perceived as a treacherous threat to hegemonic Englishness.

Grace Nichols: A Fusion of Languages

Fellow Guyanese writer Grace Nichols (1950–) also combines both standard English and nation language in her poems. *The Fat Black Woman's Poems* (1984) builds, in part, upon its resilient female personae and the nation language experimentation of Louise Bennett. Nichols's treatment of gendered experience in this and in *Lazy Thoughts of a Lazy Woman* (1989) is tinged with the same 'good-natured humour [...] shading into satire' that is found in many of Bennett's poems.[61] Certainly, the Fat Black Woman has much in common with some of Bennett's female personae but Nichols's poems are also freighted with deliciously playful and erotic overtones. As Nichols says of her use of the erotic: 'poetry, thankfully is a radical synthesising force. The erotic isn't separated from the political or spiritual.'[62] However, it is in her long poem cycles, *i is a long memoried woman* (1983), the title poem of *Sunris* (1996), and *Startling the Flying Fish* (2005), with their many-voiced, self-fashioning female personae, that Nichols's use of an adapted creole is most effective. In the epilogue to *i is a long memoried woman* Nichols famously reflects on the origins of nation language:

> I have crossed an ocean.
> I have lost my tongue,
> from the root of the old one
> A new one has sprung.[63]

Nichols claims that her choice of language is not a conscious decision: 'the language, like the form and rhythm, dictates itself'.[64] Her assertion that 'when I'm writing creole it's a kind of creole that I naturally speak'

---

[61] Carolyn Cooper, '"That Cunny Jamma Oman": The Female Sensibility in the Poetry of Louise Bennett' in Kwesi Owusu (ed.), *Storms of the Heart: An Anthology of Black Arts and Culture* (London: Camden Press, 1988), 135–51; 138.

[62] Grace Nichols in Lauretta Ngcobo (ed.), *Let it be Told: Black Women Writers in Britain* (London: Virago, [1987] 1988), 95–104; 103.

[63] Grace Nichols, *i is a long memoried woman* (London: Karnak, 1983), 87.

[64] Grace Nichols, 'Home Truths' in E. A. Markham (ed.), *Hinterland* (Newcastle upon Tyne: Bloodaxe Books, 1989), 296–8; 297.

importantly signals the proximity of creole to a wider oral matrix of 'songs
[...] proverbs, rhythms and so on', what Berry has called 'our voices with
their own wisdom'.[65] Creole is thus in part a language of intimacy, familiarity, and sincerity. Nichols has also acknowledged that the 'social stigma'
attached to nation language:

> is one of the main reasons why so many Caribbean poets, including myself,
> are now reclaiming our language heritage and exploring it. It's an act of
> spiritual survival on our part, the need (whether conscious or unconscious)
> to preserve something, that's important to us. It's a language that our
> foremothers and forefathers struggled to create and we're saying that it's a
> valid, vibrant language. We're no longer going to treat it with contempt or
> allow it to be misplaced.[66]

However, she stresses that this is not the only reason for her use of creole; she
also finds the language 'genuinely exciting' and enjoys writing in both
standard English and creole, seeking to 'fuse the two tongues because I
come from a background where the two worlds, creole and Standard
English, were constantly interacting'.[67]

Jackie Kay: Vernacular Scots and Family Histories

In Jackie Kay's first poetry collection, *The Adoption Papers* (1991), similar tensions
between multiple belongings are explored within the context of transnational
adoption. In this long sequence, Kay deploys a variety of voices, including a
modified Scottish vernacular. The text also uses different typefaces to signify
the intercutting, antiphonal, and sometimes overlapping voices of daughter,
adoptive mother, and birth mother as they come to terms with their individual
and collective histories in a poignant and powerful exploration of the politics
and experiences of transracial adoption: 'After mammy telt me she wisnae my
real mammy / I was scared to death she was gonnie melt / or something or
mibbe disappear in the dead / of night ... '.[68] In later collections, Kay's use of a
Scottish vernacular is less prominent and tends to be restricted to individual
poems but she has also experimented more widely with an African American
vernacular, not only in poems such as 'Black Ann',[69] but also in her fiction, for
example in writing the voice of transgender protagonist Joss Moody in her
novel *Trumpet* (1998) (see Chapter 28).

---

[65] Dawes, *Talk Yuh Talk*, 5.   [66] Nichols in Ngcobo, *Let it be Told*, 97–8.   [67] Ibid., 97–8.
[68] Jackie Kay, *Darling* (Newcastle upon Tyne: Bloodaxe Books, 2007), 27.   [69] Ibid., 213.

Daljit Nagra's Vernacular Cosmopolitanism

Linton Kwesi Johnson's wryly ironic 1996 poem 'If I Woz a Tap Natch Poet' is perhaps the best-known text exploring the relationship of black British vernacular voices to a western literary canon. However, other black and Asian British poets have also explored this relationship in different ways. *Look We Have Coming to Dover!* (2007) by Daljit Nagra (1966–) is an extraordinary first collection in which Punjabi family histories, migrant dreams, and the language and political ideologies surrounding UK immigration are mapped onto a poetic landscape which is both familiar and startlingly defamiliarised. From what he terms 'our babbling [...] lingoes',[70] Nagra creates a kind of adapted 'Punglish' – a combination of Punjabi and Ungregi (English) to which he provides a brief glossary at the end. He is also attuned to other vernacular resources (for example, Yorkshire English in 'Parade's End').

One of the striking features of this collection is its complex dialogue with canonical English writers such as Matthew Arnold ('Look We Have Coming ... '), Dr Johnson, and Shakespeare ('The Furtherance of Mr Bulram's Education'). In the title poem, Nagra returns to Arnold's most famous poem, 'Dover Beach', registering both the town's iconic place in British cultural nationalism and its centrality as a site of border-crossing for more recent migrant histories:

> Swarms of us, grafting [...]
> banking on the miracle of sun –
> [...] passport us to life. Only then
> can it be human to hoick ourselves, bare-faced for the clear.
> Imagine my love and I,
> our sundry others, Blair'd in the cash
> of our beeswax'd cars, our crash clothes, free,
> we raise our charged glasses over unparasol'd tables
> East, babbling our lingoes, flecked by the chalk of Britannia![71]

Nagra's 'Kabba Questions the Ontology of Representation, the Catch 22 for "Black" Writers' is a 'meta-poem' which examines the politics of representation and reception for black and Asian British poets; the role of colonial education; and the continuing power of the English canon with particular reference to the category 'Poets From Other Cultures' in the UK National Curriculum for English.[72] In an exasperated and crowded demotic, a Punjabi father asks on behalf of his son:

---

[70] Daljit Nagra, *Look We Have Coming to Dover!* (London: Faber and Faber, 2007), 32.
[71] Ibid., 32.   [72] Ibid., 42–3.

Vy giv my boy
dis freebie of a silky blue
GCSE anthology with its three poets
from three parts of Briten – yor HBC
of Eaney, Blake,
Clarke, showing us how
to tink and feel? For Part 2, us
as a bunch of Gunga Dins ju group, 'Poems
from Udder Cultures
and Traditions.' 'Udder' is all
vee are to yoo, to dis cuntry –
'Udder'? To my son's kabbadi posseee, all
Yor poets are 'Udder'!'[73]

In his essay 'The Vernacular Cosmopolitan' (2000), Homi K. Bhabha writes of 'the double life of British minorities' as 'mak[ing] them "vernacular cosmopolitans", translating between cultures, negotiating traditions from a position where "locality" insists on its own terms, while entering into larger national and societal conversations'.[74] This is a productive way of framing Nagra's poems in this and his later collection (2011). As Bhabha stresses, 'this is not a cosmopolitanism of the elite variety' trading in 'universalist patterns of humanistic thought that run gloriously across cultures', but rather that 'vernacular cosmopolitans are compelled to make a tryst with cultural translation as an act of survival. Their specific and local histories, often threatened and repressed, are inserted "between the lines" of dominant cultural practices'.[75]

Moniza Alvi: Seeing the Extraordinary in the Quotidian

Moniza Alvi's poetry deserves more space than this chapter permits. Born in Lahore, Pakistan in 1954, she was brought up in the UK and now lives in the north of England, writing poetry that has found a wide readership and does not easily inhabit categories such as 'British Asian' or 'postcolonial'. Thematically, her work often focuses on her dual cultural inheritance; in terms of form, it inhabits a mainstream English poetic tradition. Her earliest

---

[73] Ibid., 42.
[74] Homi Bhabha, 'The Vernacular Cosmopolitan' in Ferdinand Dennis and Naseem Khan (eds.), *Voices of the Crossing: The Impact of Britain on Writers from Asia, the Caribbean and Africa* (London: Serpent's Tail, 2000), 133–42; 139.
[75] Ibid.

collections, *The Country at my Shoulder* (1993) and *A Bowl of Warm Air* (1996), look back to family memories and wider migrant histories of Indian Partition in a series of intimate and vividly imagined poems. Alvi's gift in these first two collections is in seeing the extraordinary in the quotidian, and in capturing the delicate calibrations of a migrant sensibility, though her poems are not restricted to these themes. Indeed, in later collections such as *How the Stone Found its Voice* (2005), which reimagines a series of creation myths in the wake of 9/11, and *Europa* (2008), a dark reworking of the myth of Europa for contemporary times, her work is demonstrably more surreal and experimental. In 'England, I am Gazing at your Body' the speaker scrutinises the landmass from above, descending slowly, poring over colours, smells, and rhythms. Once England has shrunk down to the size of the speaker and the 'weakened' land is 'thrown back on [the speaker's] mercy', the two bodies become one:

> I press the weight of my body
> against the bulk of yours.
> The wind blows across our contours,
> the black-dog rocks, the winking lights,
> the peopled parks, an unforgiving street.[76]

This intimate act not only suggests an empowered outsider but also a fruitful embrace: the bodies are prised apart only when 'it's time / to call the children in'.[77] A speaker endowed with power and agency generates a grotesque perspective on England. As Reda Shehata has noted, Alvi writes 'geographical, feminist, or philosophical [...] accounts of the body [...] reflecting a diasporic consciousness'.[78]

Patience Agbabi's Cultural Translations

In *Telling Tales* (2014), Patience Agbabi (1965–) engages with the kind of 'cultural translation as [...] survival' that Bhabha describes and enters into a dialogue with a canonical tradition of English letters, central to which is Chaucer's *The Canterbury Tales*.[79] A gleeful cast of modern-day black British poets and would-be poets turns Chaucer's world upside-down in *Telling Tales*,

---

[76] Moniza Alvi, 'England, I am Gazing at your Body' in *How the Stone Found its Voice* (Newcastle upon Tyne: Bloodaxe Books, 2005), 28.

[77] Ibid.

[78] Reda A. Shehata, 'Moniza Alvi and Representations of the Body', *Contemporary Women's Writing*, 11:2 (2017): 168–83; 180–1.

[79] Bhabha, 'Vernacular Cosmopolitan', 139.

a collection comprising fully imagined speakers who satirically capture the zeitgeist of the contemporary British poetry scene. The inclusion of brief fictional biographies at the end of the book makes the characters seem even more convincing than Chaucer's originals; in this way, Agbabi encourages us to read both texts in dialogue in new and provocative ways. Thus Harry Bailey, the host of Chaucer's poem, becomes Harry 'Bells' Bailey who 'worked as a bouncer when studying at London Guildhall Uni. Ended up managing pub. Now owns five gastropubs, including the legendary Tabard Inn in Southwark. There hosts monthly storytelling night, *Plain Speaking*, which mixes live performance with Skype'.[80] Amongst the speakers is the vernacular voice of Mrs Alice Ebi Bafa, a modern-day Nigerian in Britain who brings her own unique story to an updated 'Wife of Bath's Tale'. Hers is a transnational voice, as Agbabi creatively mines the rich verbal resources, the cadences and timbre of a vernacular 'which is English and African at the same time'.[81] Moreover, Alice's Nigerian English also carries the tell-tale traces of a transethnic London black vernacular:

> My name is Mrs Alice Ebi Bafa,
> I come from Nigeria.
> I'm very fine, isn't it?
> My nex' birthday I'll be twenty-nine
> I'm a business woman.
> Would you like to buy some cloth?
> I've all the latest styles from Lagos,
> Italian shoe an' handbag to match,
> lace, linen an' Dutch wax.
> I only buy the bes'
> and I travel first class[82]

Conclusion

This chapter has examined the role and status of vernacular voices within a series of historical, cultural, linguistic, and literary contexts, tracing them, where possible, from their origins, through a history of frequent misunderstanding, denigration, and disavowal to a renewed sense of their linguistic validity and immense creative potential in the hands of contemporary Caribbean, black British, and British Asian poets. The focus has been on those figures who have made the most significant critical and creative

---

[80] Patience Agbabi, *Telling Tales* (Edinburgh: Canongate, 2014), 115.
[81] Brathwaite, *History of the Voice*, 13.   [82] Agbabi, *Telling Tales*, 31.

interventions in debates about the literary use of 'vernacular voices' and whose work has been crucial to the rehabilitation and creative refashioning of a wider range of language varieties in British poetry. One notable omission is any detailed discussion of Linton Kwesi Johnson, a key figure in these debates whose role and poetic practice is explored more fully elsewhere in this volume.[83] Together, these voices constitute a vibrant archive of sound and print, one which engages fully with the power of the sounded word and the potentialities of vernacular forms used as part of a fluid continuum of innovative aesthetic practices. In their creative plumbings of a whole spectrum of oral, musical, literary, linguistic, and other cultural influences, these poets engage with a western canon and monologic notions of Englishness in exciting and transformative ways – bringing new vernacular 'clout' to contemporary British poetry.

[83] See Chapter 19.

21

Narratives of Survival
Social Realism and Civil Rights

CHRIS WEEDON

This chapter looks at social realist writing published between 1959 and 1987 by Indian-born Kamala Markandaya (1924–2004), Guyanese-born E. R. Braithwaite (1912–2016) and Beryl Gilroy (1924–2001), and Nigerian-born Buchi Emecheta (1944–2017), pioneers of postwar writing who focus on the first-generation, adult, migrant experience. It also addresses work by Indian-born Farrukh Dhondy (1944–) and Jamaican-born Joan Riley (1958–), who write about growing up and living in Britain and include memories of life before migration. These authors use realism to address the effects of the widespread culture of interpersonal and institutional racism in postwar Britain. Like later British black and Asian writers, they draw on autobiographical, family, and community memories of migration and settlement. The chapter highlights how thematic, contextual, and stylistic correspondences emerge across a range of different writers whose primary concern is exposing the racism shaping six decades of black and Asian experience from 1920 to the beginning of the Thatcher era in 1979.[1] The chapter covers key themes – legacies of empire, race and class, realist imaginative fiction, and challenges for the second generation. It contests any easy narrative about the struggle for a tolerant, multiethnic Britain, the history of which remains highly relevant for understanding the present.

Britain has a long tradition of social realist writing by working- and middle-class authors, including other black and Asian writers in this volume, which depicts aspects of everyday life in ways that raise social and moral issues as problems that call for urgent social change. This writing relies for its effects on long-established liberal humanist assumptions about the power of knowledge and empathy to raise consciousness,

[1] Markandaya's *The Nowhere Man* also encompasses formative experiences in colonial India.

challenge and change attitudes and beliefs, and help bring about reform. At the same time, it shows how subjectivities are context-specific, materially discursively produced, and can and do change. It can be distinguished from forms of socialist realism in its rejection of specific political and ideological positions, such as Marxism, in favour of a broad humanism and a belief in the equal value and rights of people, whatever their colour, gender, or ethnicity. Some texts discussed in this chapter use a first-person, often autobiographical voice, others an omniscient narrator, but in most cases it is the power of testimony that is central to the ideological and affective power of the narratives.

World War II marked a period of relative tolerance of difference among white Britons, although oral history research suggests a much less rosy picture than the popular image, even for black and Asian people whose families had been in the UK for generations.[2] Testimonies from the Windrush generation of migrants describe how quickly the climate changed after 1945, when concerns arising from postwar austerity, a severe housing crisis, and the reassertion of a myopic white conception of the British nation became central. The immediate postwar decades were traumatic for both non-white Britons whose families had lived in the UK for generations and new black and Asian settlers. With an increase in numbers of immigrants, as the British government recruited workforces from the colonies and post-colonies, white British attitudes to migration and settlement became increasingly hostile, spawning new far right organisations and culminating in the type of racist discourse and politics most infamously represented by Enoch Powell and his 'Rivers of Blood' speech of 1968.[3] The immigrant experience was marked by racism, rejection, and the absence of basic rights to equality in work, housing, education, health, and welfare. Change would require an ongoing struggle for freedom from discrimination of all kinds, including racial abuse and racialised violence. For social realist writers the challenge was to make explicit and visible both institutionalised racist discourses and practices and the taken-for-granted everyday racism that appeared normal to the white population.

[2] See, for example, Glenn Jordan and Chris Weedon, 'The Construction and Negotiation of Racialised Borders in Cardiff Docklands' in Jane Aaron, Henrice Altink, and Chris Weedon (eds.), *Gendering Border Studies* (Cardiff: University of Wales Press, 2010), 222–42.

[3] Available at www.youtube.com/watch?v=mw4vMZDItQo.

Key Themes

The writing discussed here focuses on the London immigrant experience. It documents discrimination and offers insights into the effects of racism on black and Asian subjectivities and white British attitudes in the era before multiculturalism became government policy (beginning in 1965). It describes the early years of what Stuart Hall has termed the 'multicultural drift' that gradually reshaped ideas and realities in Britain in the second half of the twentieth century.[4] Taken together, the authors evoke horizontal and linear chronologies of racialised discourse and the incumbent fluctuations in white attitudes and practices at both individual and institutional levels.

For the colonial subjects who came to live and work in the 'mother-country' (Britain) in the twentieth century, the rejection that they encountered on arrival marked them profoundly. For example, in *To Sir, With Love* (1959), a first-person account of his early experience as a schoolteacher, Braithwaite describes the effects on his own immigrant subjectivity of the disjunction between expectations and lived reality in the changing climate in Britain after 1945:

> I had believed in an ideal for all the twenty-eight years of my life – the idea of the British Way of Life [. . .].
> Because of it, I had never sought to acquire American citizenship, and when [. . .] I came to England for postgraduate study in 1939, I felt that at long last I was personally identified with the hub of fairness, tolerance and all the freedoms [. . .] I volunteered for service with the Royal Air Force in 1940, willing and ready to lay down my life for the preservation of the ideal which had been my lodestar. But now that selfsame ideal was gall and wormwood in my mouth.[5]

This profound disenchantment, a response to racism and the absence of civil rights, figures centrally in social realist texts as they explore how the legacies of empire affected life in the UK, as Britain became increasingly diverse. Texts address racialisation, class, black–white relations, and the forms of non-belonging, alienation, and exclusion experienced by first-generation migrants. They use realism to detail the effects of class, racism, and ethnic difference on subjectivity and life chances, often with explicit attention to gender. They facilitate understanding of how racism works at the level of individuals,

---

[4] Zoe Williams, 'The Saturday Interview: Stuart Hall', *The Guardian*, 11 February 2012. Available at www.theguardian.com/theguardian/2012/feb/11/saturday-interview-stuart-hall.

[5] E. R. Braithwaite, *To Sir, With Love* (London: Vintage, [1959] 2005), 35.

institutions, and in the public sphere, soliciting empathy with the subjective effects of racialisation while raising important moral and political questions. They address the barriers to acceptance and equality and the many forms of oppression to which postwar immigrants from the Caribbean, Africa, and South Asia were subject.

The focus on human and civil rights relates to the writers' middle-class, colonial formations and their shock at the hostility and discrimination encountered by well-educated immigrants from British colonies and former colonies on arrival in Britain. The intersection of race, class, and gender is central: for Markandaya, Braithwaite, Gilroy, and Emecheta, it is confrontations between gendered forms of class difference and racism that produce vivid evocations of the effects of racism on black, South Asian, and white subjectivities. Their work exposes the raw racist attitudes and beliefs among the white British, which appeared normal to a white society rooted in both explicit and implicit assumptions about white racial superiority. In both Markandaya's and Braithwaite's texts, blatant racism and the denial of human and civil rights come to dominate everyday life. Challenges are largely individual and moral; only later would political responses to the embedded institutionalised racist discourses and practices that both Braithwaite and Gilroy docu-ment so clearly emerge.

Legacies of Empire

In *Black Teacher*, Gilroy describes how:

> At the end of each day [. . .] I realised afresh that I belonged in a cultural no-man's-land. However often I had sung 'I vow to thee my country' on Empire day in the pouring rain, I wasn't English. Brought up as we were under a faraway flutter of the Union Jack, I believe that at that time, we West Indians did think of ourselves as English. But Englishness, I now realise, contained elements of history, culture and perception to which I could lay no claim. I wasn't African either. I was of the generation of West Indians who regarded 'Africanness' as something morbid – a backward step that must be avoided at all cost. Until my 20th birthday I had never seen an African outside my school textbooks. When I dined with an African student from the Agricultural College in Trinidad, I'd found myself wondering if he really ate people as the schoolbooks said.[6]

---

[6] Beryl Gilroy, *Black Teacher* (London: Bogle-L'Ouverture, [1976] 1994), 34.

Like the other writers discussed here, Gilroy was educated in a colonial system that imparted high moral expectations of Britain and a sense of entitlement as a British citizen. These expectations were shattered by the racism, physical environment, and poverty that immigrants encountered in the 'mother country' in the immediate postwar years. Thus, passing bomb ruins and semi-derelict housing on his way to his East End school in *To Sir, With Love*, Braithwaite recalls how his image of London's East End had been shaped by both classical and contemporary literature. He describes, in a way not dissimilar to those nineteenth-century travellers discussed in Chapter 5 of this history, how his 'naïvely romantic ideas about London's East End, with its cosmopolitan population and fascinating history', contrast with the poverty and squalor that he sees around him.[7] This shock and disappointment felt by immigrants as they faced insanitary housing conditions, hostility, and discrimination remained largely invisible in the public sphere until the 1980s.[8] The social realism published before the 1990s filled an important lacuna and has immediacy, particularly in its evocation of white racist language and behaviour, which is rooted in personal experience and testifies to strategies of survival.

In the immediate postwar years, the legacies of empire shaped the subjectivities of both immigrants and the white host society. They were embedded in teaching materials used in schools and in the ways in which many children and adults imagined black and Asian people, and they were refracted through class. They underpinned everyday racist practices in housing and the workplace, and hindered the development of mutual tolerance and positive evaluations of cultural difference. Moreover, cultural and ethnic differences between and within immigrant groups further complicated this problem, as can be seen clearly in Emecheta's novels, most especially in *Second Class Citizen*, which is set in Lagos before migration and among first-generation Nigerians in London.[9] This novel directly addresses issues of gender, including the ways in which migrant women's expectations come into conflict with traditional masculinity, ethnic norms, and informal structures of power among diasporic communities.

---

[7] Braithwaite, *To Sir, With Love*, 5.

[8] A few attempts were made at the time to document the experience of migration, for example, 'Has Britain a Colour Bar?' (BBC, 1955). More recently history, photography, film, and writing have all addressed the postwar decades, e.g. Mike Phillips's four-part documentary, *Windrush*, on the history of black people in postwar Britain (BBC, 1998), available at www.youtube.com/watch?v=YGTm_Gsvyzw.

[9] Buchi Emecheta, *Second Class Citizen* (Oxford: Heinemann Educational Publishers, [1974] 1994).

Race and Class

The racial tensions that arose in the wake of postwar waves of inward migration to Britain were fuelled by a deep-rooted and unquestioned racism and ethnocentrism among white Britons, which pervaded much British culture and had its roots in ideas from racial science and empire. As Stuart Hall recalls, this was compounded by the feeling among many whites that the newcomers were taking things such as housing, jobs, and sexual partners that were by rights theirs.[10] At the same time, the government failed to explain to white Britain why migrants were arriving in large numbers in the context of postwar poverty and an acute housing crisis. As historical, literary, and visual accounts of the postwar decades demonstrate, overt racism was a common experience for non-white people, who found themselves defined as alien Others. Then, as now, the pervasiveness of discourses that ground Englishness and Britishness in whiteness rendered anyone who was not white, seemingly 'foreign', however many generations of their families had lived in Britain. Black resistance to racism and discrimination took the form of protests and riots, often directed at racist attacks, harassment, and oppressive, discriminatory policing (Nottingham 1958, Notting Hill 1958, and Brixton 1981 being the most well known). Yet the story told in these realist texts is for the most part one of neither violence nor organised resistance, although aspects of both can be found in other writing from the period such as Sam Selvon's *Moses Ascending* (1975).[11]

The importance of London as a locus for incomers from British colonies and postcolonies is well documented.[12] Its role as an often reluctant, multi-ethnic, cosmopolitan space and site of anti-colonial struggle (as seen in writing by Selvon, George Lamming, Andrew Salkey, and V. S. Naipaul) figures less in the work discussed in this chapter, which is set in working-class areas of London and often focuses on black–white relations.[13] The centrality of issues of class is an effect of racialisation: highly educated black and Asian incomers found themselves confronted with a racist employment and housing market that forced them to live and work in the poorest areas of the capital. The colonial experience, black–white encounters, racism, and white subjectivity emerge with a heightened clarity that comes from often

---

[10] See Hall's interview for Phillips, *Windrush*, Part 1.

[11] Samuel Selvon, *Moses Ascending* (London: Heinemann, [1975] 1991).

[12] See, in particular, John McLeod, *Postcolonial London* (London: Routledge, 2004) and James Procter, *Dwelling Places: Postwar Black British Writing* (Manchester: Manchester University Press, 2003).

[13] See Susheila Nasta, *Home Truths* (Basingstoke: Palgrave, 2002).

contrasting social classes and levels of education between the main protagonists and the white people that they encounter on a day-to-day basis.

Poor education among the white population is compounded by racist stereotypes in children's books and popular culture. For example, Gilroy recalls the fearful reaction of her first class of 7-year-olds when she arrived unannounced in the classroom:

> So when I opened the squeaking door and the class came face-to-face with me, there was a gasp of terror, then a sudden silence. A little girl broke it with a whimper. Some children visibly shook with fear, and, as I walked across the room, the whole lot – except for two boys – dived under the tables.[14]

These white, working-class children hold ideas about black people that are, like her own youthful assumptions about Africans, deeply racist. The narrative that follows describes how Gilroy is able to win the love and respect of her class. This battle for acceptance in the face of widespread racialised fear and a constant barrage of abuse from parents, children, and even some colleagues continues throughout her teaching career. The institutionalised nature of this racism affects the school curriculum and infuses the speech and artworks produced by the children. Motifs such as 'primitive' black people, living in trees, recur, while even schools that ostensibly reject racism often unthinkingly reproduce racist assumptions and practices. It is this all-pervasive climate that convinces Gilroy to send her own children to private schools where: 'They never had to defend their colour or their hair, or bother about identity. Nor were the traditional names of affection, like Sambo, Topsy or Fuzzy, ever used to them.'[15]

The intersection of class and race is central to Braithwaite's accounts of his time as a teacher and social worker in London between 1950 and 1960. Despite his Cambridge education and five years as a fighter pilot, Braithwaite was unable to find employment as an engineer and eventually worked as a schoolteacher in the East End. Introducing the 2005 edition of *To Sir, With Love*, Caryl Phillips calls attention to what he terms 'an unmistakable, almost anthropological sneer' in Braithwaite's depiction of the poor, white working class.[16] If this is true of some descriptions in the novel, Braithwaite also writes of his growing respect for the poor, white people around him and even love for the difficult teenagers he teaches. It is precisely the detailed accounts of the subjective processes of change that the narrator undergoes in response to racial and class prejudice that are important. As with race, it is the

---

[14] Gilroy, *Black Teacher*, 47.   [15] Ibid., 160.   [16] Braithwaite, *To Sir, With Love*, vii.

recognition of the fundamental humanity of others – in this instance of poor, working-class, white people – that reshapes his perceptions. This recognition of the humanity of the Other is a consistent message in Braithwaite's writing.

Class and race are also fundamental to depictions of the workings of the welfare state in texts from this period, most centrally Braithwaite's *Paid Servant* (1962) and Emecheta's *In the Ditch* (1972).[17] *Paid Servant* details Braithwaite's life as a welfare officer working for the London County Council where he is tasked with finding foster homes and adoptive parents for black children and those of mixed parentage. His work takes him to many parts of London and the south-east, visiting homes that range from the most deprived, crowded, working-class slums to middle-class suburbs. Encounters with clients, colleagues, superiors, and his middle-class intellectual friends and acquaintances show how ingrained negative assumptions shape discourses and practices, even among white people who believe themselves above prejudice. In dealing with the senior social workers in his department, he meets prejudices that have long been widespread in popular culture and can be traced directly back to classical racism and theories of heredity. Racist assumptions include the supposed 'nature' of mixed-parentage people, the imagined dangers of placing black boys in families with white girls, and the belief that the 'natural background' for a 'coloured' child is a 'coloured' family. The most unthinkingly and immovably racist of his colleagues appeal to their own experience: 'I've had to work among Asians and Africans and West Indians in London and before that in Cardiff, and I know how they feel about things like sex, quite different from the way we English people feel.'[18]

Paid Servant confronts issues of mixed-parentage children and cross-racial adoption that would be taken up again much later by British-born writers. While the authorities categorise mixed-parentage children as 'coloured', Braithwaite argues that consideration should be given to their white heritage. Braithwaite's humanistic belief that 'there must be many white Britons who would be willing to give [. . . non-white children] a home' bears little fruit and is compounded by the unwillingness of black families to adopt orphans of mixed parentage. Braithwaite's positive picture of aspects of life in children's homes in *Paid Servant* contrasts strongly with later texts, written from the perspective of the child. Riley's *The Unbelonging* (1985), for example, highlights the racism, alienation, and non-belonging experienced by a black child who

[17] E. R. Braithwaite, *Paid Servant* (New York: Open Road, [1962] 2014); Buchi Emecheta, *In the Ditch* (Oxford: Heinemann Educational Publishers, [1972] 1994).
[18] Braithwaite, *Paid Servant*, 8.

has come from the Caribbean at the age of eleven and is placed in a children's home following damaging parental abuse.[19]

Emecheta's *In the Ditch* (1972) documents the welfare state from the perspective of educated, middle-class Nigerian Adah Obi who is forced to depend on welfare after leaving her abusive husband and becoming the single parent of five young children. It details everyday life in a block of dilapidated council flats soon to be redeveloped in north-west London where the building is ridden with damp, overflowing rubbish chutes, dog faeces, and the smell of human urine on the dark staircases. This is where so-called 'problem families' are sent. Some have lived there for decades and, despite all the dilapidation and decay, a community has developed. Forced to resign from her well-paid job at the British Library by the lack of pre- and post-school childcare, Adah joins the ranks of women on welfare. Mostly white and working class, they form an underclass in which social differences and even race become unimportant, a community that offers companionship, mutual help, and 'joy in communal sorrow [. . .] Adah stopped being homesick. She was beginning to feel like a human being again.'[20]

In the Ditch is both appreciative and critical of the welfare system. The student volunteers, who help with childcare in the evenings, enable Adah to study and they gradually become a surrogate extended family. Her neighbours and the welfare officer offer 'a warm chat, a nice cup of tea and solidarity against any foe'.[21] The price paid for this is a culture of dependency, in which the women find themselves reliant on the favour of the welfare officer for the essentials of everyday life. As Adah prepares to move to new council accommodation in middle-class Regent's Park, she seeks to liberate herself from what she now perceives as a 'state of apathy, inadequacy and incompetence'.[22]

Both Braithwaite and Emecheta published later books that reflect on the experiences described in their early texts and are significant for understanding the immediate postwar decades. Braithwaite's *Reluctant Neighbours* (1972) uses a conversation on a train to New York to explore Braithwaite's past life.[23] The white passenger who has reluctantly taken the last vacant seat beside Braithwaite questions him closely. This encourages reflection on the different ways in which racism has shaped Braithwaite's life and subjectivity since leaving the then colony of British Guiana to study at Cambridge in 1939. The text retraces some of the material covered in *To Sir, With Love* and *Paid*

[19] Joan Riley, *The Unbelonging* (London: Women's Press, 1985).
[20] Emecheta, *In the Ditch*, 61.   [21] Ibid., 71.   [22] Ibid., 125.
[23] E. R. Braithwaite, *Reluctant Neighbours* (London: Bodley Head, 1972).

Servant. It touches on Braithwaite's early life in British Guiana (now Guyana), his higher education in New York and at Cambridge, his war service in the RAF, and the bitterness induced by his repeated rejection for the engineering posts for which he was more than qualified. It reflects on his years in London as a schoolteacher in the East End and as a welfare officer, his move to Paris and then to New York, where he is an ambassador at the United Nations. Whereas the earlier texts detailed day-to-day encounters in school and in the social services, *Reluctant Neighbours* uses specific incidents to examine aspects of black and white subjectivities.

Describing the visceral reluctance of his fellow passenger even to sit beside him, Braithwaite recounts the white man's reactions to hearing about his place in the white world of Connecticut, the RAF, his success as a writer, and his current status as a diplomat. The text is framed by Braithwaite's central concern: the ways ingrained racism shape subjectivities, making it difficult for white people to fully acknowledge the humanity of black people. The conversation ultimately fails to overcome white prejudice, since Braithwaite refuses to exempt anyone from the effects of structural racism and the white passenger refuses the idea that he, as a liberal, could be racist.

Emecheta's autobiography *Head Above Water*, like *Reluctant Neighbours*, revisits the years and experience that shaped the author's earlier works.[24] Recalling her uncertainty about the existence of an audience for *In the Ditch*, Emecheta describes how she uses a third-person narrator in her 'documentary realism' as a way of distancing herself from a narrative that is about 'fifty percent autobiographical', thus giving it a more 'objective' tone. Emecheta tells how other social realist texts of the period, particularly Nell Dunn's *Poor Cow* and Monica Dickens's *One Pair of Hands* and *One Pair of Feet*, convince her that there is readership for a book on 'the life of an unfortunate black woman who seemed to be making a mess of her life'.[25]

Realist Imaginative Fiction

While perhaps best known for her novels about India,[26] Markandaya published an important and insightful novel about London in 1972, *The Nowhere*

---

[24] See Buchi Emecheta, *Head Above Water* (Oxford: Heinemann Educational Publishers, [1986] 1994).
[25] Ibid., 58.
[26] *Nectar in a Sieve* (1954), *Some Inner Fury* (1955), *A Silence of Desire* (1960), *Possession* (1963), *A Handful of Rice* (1966), *Two Virgins* (1973), *The Golden Honeycomb* (1977), and *Pleasure City* (1982/1983). Most recent scholarship on Markandaya is by Indian critics.

Man, that traces the workings and effects of racism and colonialism on everyday life in Britain for an Indian migrant settler over six decades between the 1920s and the early 1970s.[27] Centrally concerned with the ways in which racism affects subjectivity and shapes behaviour, the novel traces one man's attempt to integrate and be fully accepted by the host society, a process that ultimately fails due to an all-pervasive racism, temporarily masked by more inclusive and accepting attitudes during World War II. The novel both explains aspects of Indian culture and history to western readers and traces shifts in English racism and continuities between white–Indian relations established in colonial India and reaffirmed in postwar Britain. At issue here, as in Braithwaite's work, is the recognition of the Other as fully human.

The Nowhere Man opens in 1968, when Powellism and racist assaults are rife. The central protagonist, Srinivas, survives a racist attack in which he is tied to a lamp-post and tarred and feathered by the son of one of his long-term neighbours. This incident is followed some months later by an arson attack on his home in the course of which he dies from shock. Moving between past and present, the novel covers life in India before and during World War I, Srinivas's move to Britain to escape the consequences of his anti-colonial activities, married life in Britain, World War II in which his younger son is killed, and the death of his Indian wife. Key motifs in the text are increasing alienation and loss as Britain refuses its immigrant citizens full acceptance, and the depression and loneliness these bring with them. Srinivas is partially rescued from his state of deep depression by a developing relationship with an ageing white woman. These two socially marginalised people offer each other a quiet form of love and companionship over two decades as the world around them changes. Shortly before his death, he develops leprosy, a visible manifestation of the way he has been treated by most white people all his life.

The narrative depicts changing social and individual perceptions and values, as Britain recovers from war and from postwar austerity. It shows how fluctuating discourses of race affect people, and how humanity is lost in the process. *The Nowhere Man* uses character, plot, and temporality to produce realism with a strong moral agenda. It relies on a narratorial voice that sees and understands much more than either individual characters or the reader. It tackles issues of class, the role of wealth or lack of it, and how this affects social status, especially if one is black or Asian. It addresses the strengths and limitations of second-generation strategies of belonging, the importance of day-to-day contact to breaking down racialised barriers, and

[27] Kamala Markandaya, *The Nowhere Man* (Harmondsworth: Penguin, [1972] 1973).

the ways in which the changing racialised climate, in this instance brought about by Enoch Powell and his supporters, polarises people who have tolerated one another until then.

In contrast, Braithwaite's *Choice of Straws* (1965) is an imaginative exploration of young, white, working-class male subjectivity.[28] The novel opens as twin brothers Dave and Jack wait among the bomb ruins of Stepney to attack a black man. Since a first revenge attack, after their father was seriously injured by a group of black men at the time of the Notting Hill riots, they have repeatedly attacked individual black men for the sheer feeling of exhilaration that engaging in violence gives them. Encountering resistance on this occasion, they use a knife, leaving their victim dead. Badly injured and in the process of escaping the crime scene, one twin dies in an unsolved motor accident together with the black doctor who has given him a lift.

The main focus of the narrative is the developing relationship between twin brother Jack and black, middle-class Michelle, the doctor's beautiful sister whom Jack meets while identifying bodies in the mortuary. The text analyses the intricate relationship between attraction, prejudice, and hatred in an overwhelmingly racist environment, offering insights into the psychological and physical effects of verbal, gestural, and violent racism on black subjectivity. Jack's initial resolve to hunt Michelle down as sexual prey becomes a form of love that is circumscribed by both class and racialised difference and his predatory attitude towards women. In the events that follow, Jack swings between attraction, love, and hatred. In the process, he is forced to see black people as human and to recognise that his own mother is profoundly racist. The conclusion of the novel, however, offers no grounds for supposing that Jack will put racism behind him.

Challenges for the Second Generation

The lives of second-generation children of postwar settlers, a sub-theme in *The Nowhere Man*, is a central focus in the 1980s work of Dhondy and Riley. Dhondy's anthologies of social realist short stories offer vivid insights into questions of cultural and generational difference, racism, and gender issues.[29] His evocative use of language captures the biculturality of South Asian and white, working-class, East End teenagers, their aspirations and the conflicts

---

[28] E. R. Braithwaite, *Choice of Straws* (London: Bodley Head, 1965).

[29] Farrukh Dhondy, *East End at Your Feet* (Basingstoke: Macmillan Education, 1976) and *Trip Trap* (London: Gollanz, 1982). For stories of the author's early life in India see *Poona Company* (London: Harper Perennial, [1980] 2008).

they have to negotiate in and outside of school. Some stories detail Asian relations with young white people with a particular focus on the problems of girls caught between Indian and British cultural and gender norms. Others are set in India, seen through the eyes of both Indian and British-born young people. As in the documentary and autobiographical literature discussed above, relations between South Asian and white young people are depicted as both positive and negative, if always circumscribed by broader race relations.

In contrast, there is little positive interaction between black and white in Riley's 1980s novels about Afro-Caribbean families in London, which offer a bleak picture of the struggle for survival.[30] While *The Unbelonging* depicts how everyday racism, paternal abuse, and an all-white children's home deprive a teenager of any positive sense of identity or belonging, *Waiting in the Twilight* powerfully details the combined effects of gender, class, and racism on one family. It shows how racism affects masculinity, formed in Jamaica and transplanted into racist Britain, and how Jamaican cultural, moral, and religious norms further hinder the main protagonist, Adela, from achieving even limited forms of happiness. Riley's novels show how memories of the home country can both serve as a resource for resisting the effects of white racism and inhibit changes that might enable her protagonists to achieve a better life. These are issues that are taken up by many subsequent writers.

Concluding Reflections

The realism discussed in this chapter shows how subjectivities are shaped and reshaped by the wider society and raises social and moral issues that call for social change. The texts discussed do not advocate specific political and ideological positions, but rather the recognition of the fundamental humanity of individuals, whatever class, racialised, or gendered positions they occupy. They advance a broad humanism and belief in the equal value and rights of people, whatever their colour, gender, or ethnicity. A key issue here is what Kobena Mercer has termed 'the burden of representation'.[31] Gilroy offers a clear illustration of what is meant by this term. She writes of how, when she was finally appointed to her first teaching post in London at a Catholic infants' school, the clerk at the divisional educational office wished

---

[30] Riley, *Unbelonging* and *Waiting in the Twilight* (London: Women's Press, 1987).
[31] Kobena Mercer, 'Black Art and the Burden of Representation', *Third Text*, 4 (1990): 61–78.

her luck, adding: 'I'm sure you're going to make a fine ambassador for your people.' She comments: 'I was to hear a lot of that one from then onwards. It was like carrying an unfair weight in a highly competitive steeple chase.'[32] The texts discussed in this chapter all suggest that white society insists on seeing individual black or Asian people as representative of larger stereotyped, racialised groups. In the twenty-first century this practice applies most clearly to Muslims and refugees.

The writers discussed use distinct and related forms of social realism to encourage readers to move beyond stereotyping and to feel and understand the effects of racialisation on subjectivity. They explicitly take on the burden of representation in order to highlight individual struggles against the material, psychological, and affective effects of being treated as a racialised 'second-class' citizen and the materiality of racist discourse and discriminatory practices. The texts are concerned with depicting strategies for survival. They document racism and its effects, and urge a humanism that does not stereotype but dispels the burden of race, allowing people to be seen as individuals shaped by the society in which they live. For all their differences, these texts share one central theme: the way in which ingrained racism dehumanises, shaping subjectivities in ways that make it difficult to acknowledge fully the humanity of others.

This issue is no less relevant today than it was in the immediate postwar decades and realism remains an important mode of representation in the expansion and diversification of black and Asian writing since 1990. Recent writing has moved away from a centralised focus on race to seeing racialisation as one factor among many shaping black and Asian lives in Britain. As later chapters here demonstrate, this includes realist, autobiographical novels that document the search for biological parents or family roots overseas. It is also a feature of the explosion of historical fiction, including major novels about migration, the slave trade, plantation slavery, and indentured labour in the Caribbean. These more recent forms of realism often open up competing viewpoints and sometimes invoke imaginative uses of dreams and myths. Another important form of realism to emerge in the 1990s and 2000s is what Modhumita Roy calls the 'brutalist realism', found in the London novels of Courttia Newland, Akinti, and Alex Wheatle. Like the texts discussed in this chapter: 'The novels identify and amplify the determining structures – lived as race, class and gender, and expressed through them – that are constitutive of "blackness". Indeed, each novel bears, in its own way, the marks of the

---

[32] Gilroy, *Black Teacher*, 46.

"ugly history" of raced discourse, which produces an exclusive definition of Britishness.'[33] Unlike the earlier writing, these texts are much less optimistic about the power of humanism to counteract racism and lessen the burden of representation. Yet the power of realism to transpose the reader into another world where she or he encounters other subjectivities remains important in the ongoing struggle to defeat racism, and the writing discussed in this chapter still has much to offer readers.

[33] Modhumita Roy, 'Brutalised Lives and Brutalist Realism: British Black Urban Fiction (1990s–2000s)' in Deirdre Osborne (ed.), *The Cambridge Companion to British Black and Asian Literature (1945–2010)* (Cambridge: Cambridge University Press, 2016), 95–109; 102.

22

Black and Asian British Theatre Taking the Stage

From the 1950s to the Millennium

MEENAKSHI PONNUSWAMI

This chapter traces the evolution of black and Asian British theatre as it moved from the fringes in the 1960s and 1970s towards specifically-funded and dedicated ethnic spaces in the 1980s, finally gaining a profile on some mainstream platforms by the 2000s. Postwar diasporic theatre operated in the shadow of the British Empire, where the performance of the black body had been part of 'ethnological show business' in its various forms.[1] Traditions of blackface dominated representations of black and Asian Britons in the nineteenth and twentieth centuries, persisting well after World War II; indeed, it was only in the 1970s that the BBC's *Black and White Minstrel Show* was finally taken off the air.[2] As Colin Chambers demonstrates in *Black and Asian Theatre in Britain*, 'images of difference produced by white theatre significantly shaped the environment of ignorance and prejudice in which diasporic theatre practitioners' worked throughout the postwar era. Even today, 'opportunities for black actors remain constrained by the legacy of stereotypes inherited from minstrelsy'.[3] Today's theatres thus confront both the racism of their own time and an inheritance of embodied misrepresentation which has accumulated over centuries. Referred to as a *'theatre of trespass'*, diasporic theatre can be seen as a story of struggle, survival, and radical self-fashioning which has the capacity 'to redefine ideas of the periphery and the centre'.[4]

---

[1] Bernth Lindfors's term from his edited collection *Africans on Stage: Studies in Ethnological Show Business* (Bloomington, IN: Indiana University Press, 2000).

[2] Michael McMillan and SuAndi, 'Rebaptizing the World in Our Own Terms: Black Theatre and Live Arts in Britain' in Geoffrey V. Davis and Anne Fuchs (eds.), *Staging New Britain: Aspects of Black and South Asian British Theatre Practice*, Dramaturgies No. 19 (Brussels: Peter Lang, 2006), 47–65; 47.

[3] Colin Chambers, *Black and Asian Theatre in Britain: A History* (London: Routledge, 2011), 4, 56.

[4] Ibid., 9.

Although black and Asian theatres often assumed a countercultural relationship to the mainstream, they adopted a great variety of aesthetic and political strategies: some were inward-looking and community-centred, providing refuge from racism; others insisted on inclusion within the mainstream but were accused of pandering to white tastes or prejudices; yet others remained devoted to the nurturing of new practitioners and the evolution of hybrid identities and styles. Despite this diversity, several common preoccupations emerged: issues of postcolonial, diasporic, and multicultural identities; the relationship between minority drama and the mainstream; questions of mentorship and training; the importance of social and professional networks; the value and hazards of state subsidy; differences between migrants and their British-born descendants; and, last but not least, explorations of form and aesthetics, including questions of tradition and individual talent.

Scholars did not substantially engage with the field until the mid-1990s. As Michael Pearce notes, archives remain 'incomplete, records are scattered, and perhaps crucially recordings of live performances are rare or difficult to access'.[5] Despite such gaps, studies published since the early 2000s have begun to provide substantive overviews, offering critical readings of performances, interviews with practitioners, and analyses of policy documents.[6] This has been strengthened by archival initiatives such as Future Histories, the Black and Asian Theatre archive, the oral history project British South Asian Theatre Memories, the online Black Plays Archive at the National Theatre, the Foundation for Indian Performing Arts, and the South Asian Diaspora Literature and Arts Archive (SALIDAA).[7] Individual theatres such

---

[5] Michael Pearce, *Black British Drama: A Transnational Story* (London; New York: Routledge, 2017), 4.

[6] These include Gabriele Griffin, *Contemporary Black and Asian Women Playwrights in Britain* (Cambridge: Cambridge University Press, 2003); Lynette Goddard, *Staging Black Feminisms* (London: Palgrave Macmillan, 2007) and *Contemporary Black British Playwrights: Margins to Mainstream* (London: Palgrave Macmillan, 2015); Dominic Hingorani, *British Asian Theatre* (London: Palgrave Macmillan, 2010); Chambers, *Black and Asian Theatre*; Rodreguez King-Dorset, *Black British Theatre Pioneers: Yvonne Brewster and the First Generation of Actors, Playwrights and Other Practitioners* (London: McFarland, 2014); and Pearce, *Black British Drama*; and essay collections edited by Davis and Fuchs (eds.), *Staging New Britain*; Dimple Godiwala (ed.), *Alternatives within the Mainstream: British Black and Asian Theatres* (Newcastle upon Tyne: Cambridge Scholars, 2006); Graham Ley and Sarah Dadswell (eds.), *British South Asian Theatres: A Documented History* (Exeter: University of Exeter Press, 2011); and Mary F. Brewer, Lynette Goddard, and Deirdre Osborne (eds.), *Modern and Contemporary Black British Drama* (London: Palgrave Macmillan, 2015).

[7] The Black and Asian Theatre archive was spearheaded by Susan Croft in the late 1990s; its online publication *Black and Asian Theatre: A User's Guide* includes valuable lists of

as Tara Arts and Talawa Theatre Company have also built their own archives.

This belated record has focused in the main on rapidly evolving social and historical circumstances, including generational, political, and demographic shifts within the 'specificities of the British socio-political and cultural landscape'.[8] As many scholars have observed, black and Asian British theatres evolved in three distinct chronological waves. The first is the so-called 'Windrush' period (1950s–1970s), which includes the activities of the Caribbean Arts Movement and is also the time when emerging African playwrights such as Wole Soyinka came to prominence. The second largely covers the Thatcher era of the 1980s, during which several new minority ethnic theatre companies were established (following the Scarman Report) and highlighted the transition from immigrant to second-generation perspectives. Finally, while the most recent period has witnessed the recruitment of a new generation of mainstream artists, it has also seen the breakup of some older networks, communities, and coalitions.[9]

The 'Windrushers' Take the Stage: 1956–1979

The mid-1950s witnessed a distinct upswing in the fortunes of the black British stage. This coincided with a moment when conventional theatre appeared to pivot sharply away from upper-class audiences and narratives. In 1956–1957, as John Osborne's Jimmy Porter famously stormed the English stage in *Look Back in Anger*, Errol John's *Moon on a Rainbow Shawl* won him *The Observer*'s prize for best new playwright; the BBC aired John Elliott's *A Man from the Sun*, a docu-drama about Caribbean immigrants; Pearl and Edric Connor opened the Edric Connor Agency, in recognition of a growing need for organised representation of black theatre workers; and Yvonne

---

black and Asian people involved in British productions from 1825 onwards. The South Asian Diaspora Literature and Arts Archive, an online resource, was established in 1999. The Foundation for Indian Performing Arts was established in 2006; its videotaped oral history project, 'British South Asian Theatre Memories', consists of extensive interviews conducted by Hi Ching and Avaes Mohammad with practitioners in the field. Kwame Kwei-Armah initiated the important resource Black Plays Archive at the National Theatre in 2009.

[8] Pearce, *Black British Drama*, 2. Pearce's study challenges this 'prioritisation of the nation' by proposing 'transnational frameworks to trace the ways the people, cultures and ideas from the US and from countries in Africa and the Caribbean have converged in the UK and how these find dramatic representation' (1–2).

[9] Goddard, *Contemporary Black British Playwrights*, 212. Recent scholarship by Chambers (see Chapter 11) highlights a wide range of black performance before World War II; see *Black and Asian Theatre*.

Brewster arrived from Jamaica to join the Royal Academy of Music and the Rose Bruford School of Speech and Drama.[10] Warned on her first day by Bruford that she would never find work, Brewster went on to found Talawa Theatre Company, direct scores of productions, earn an OBE, and serve on the London Arts Council and boards of many arts organisations, including the Rose Bruford's.[11]

Several major black British plays were produced in the 1950s and 1960s, including Edric Connor's cabaret *Caribbean* (1952), John's *Moon on a Rainbow Shawl* (1958), Derek Walcott's *Sea at Dauphin* (1960), and Soyinka's *The Lion and the Jewel* (1962). The Jamaican writer Barry Reckord was particularly active during this period, with *Flesh to a Tiger* in 1958, *You in Your Small Corner* in 1960, and *Skyvers*, with an all-white cast, in 1963. Inter-Action's lunchtime theatres featured black writers such as Mustapha Matura and the African American Black Arts Movement pioneers Ed Bullins and Amiri Baraka.[12] By the end of the 1960s, a first wave of black theatre had been established by writers including Brewster, Soyinka, Matura, Walcott, and Reckord. In 1970, the Institute for Contemporary Arts (ICA) conducted a season dedicated to Black Power. Plays of this decade, set in the xenophobic context leading up to the Kenyan Asian Act of 1968 and, in the same year, Enoch Powell's 'Rivers of Blood' speech, repeatedly express what Helen Thomas has called the 'disillusionment of black subjects within the imperial centre [. . .] as they found themselves the targets of [. . .] anti-black marches, racist attacks, open-air fascist meetings and "Let's Get a Wog" chants'.[13] It was a time when, as Pearce argues, 'African American identification, particularly among activists and artists', was a by-product of the exclusion of black Britons from the dominant culture, combined with the 'global dissemination' of US pop culture and the increasing influence of the Black Power movement.[14]

Though male playwrights were to dominate the stage in the 1950s and 1960s, several women played important foundational roles, crucially building the infrastructure of the industry. Pearl Connor ran the Cedric Connor Agency from 1958 until 1974, founding the Negro Theatre Workshop in

[10] Errol John, *Moon on a Rainbow Shawl*, 2nd edn (London: Faber and Faber, [1958] 1963).
[11] Brewster, quoted in King-Dorset, *Black British Theatre Pioneers*, 24.
[12] See Roland Rees, *Fringe First: Pioneers of Fringe Theatre on Record* (London: Oberon, 1992), 96–144, and Malcolm Hay, 'The Black Theatre Co-operative', *Drama*, 149 (Autumn 1983): 11–12.
[13] Helen Thomas, 'The Social and Political Context of Black British Theatre: 1950s–80s' in Brewer et al. (eds.), *Modern and Contemporary*, 22–9; 18–19, 22.
[14] Michael Pearce, 'Kwame Kwei-Armah's African American Inspired Triptych' in Brewer et al. (eds.), *Modern and Contemporary*, 128–47; 130.

1963; Carmen Munroe worked with the West Indian Students' Drama Group in the 1950s and later became a co-founder of Talawa. Path-breaking African American women playwrights such as Adrienne Kennedy and Alice Childress do not appear to have made an impact, though Lorraine Hansberry's *A Raisin in the Sun* was performed in 1959, and, more than thirty years later, in 1992, Talawa's first production of a woman-authored play was American Ntozake Shange's *The Love Space Demands*.

In the 1970s, black British theatres blossomed as the works of Matura, Edgar Nkosi White, and Michael Abbensetts established a growing black repertoire through their 'plays of exodus and exile'.[15] A Trinidadian of Indian origin, Matura (1939–) first brought the black experience in Britain to the stage; his *Black Pieces* shorts, staged as part of Inter-Action's Ambiance Lunch Hour theatre, were heralded as a new voice, written in the vernacular and seen as authentically representing black Caribbean working-class immigrants. Matura's 1971 play *As Time Goes By*, depicting the conflict between a Caribbean immigrant and his British-born son 'Skinheads', was directed by Roland Rees and played at the Edinburgh Festival before transferring to the Royal Court and winning the John Whiting and George Devine awards. This was the first of a string of successes for Matura: he won the *Evening Standard*'s Most Promising Playwright Award in 1974, *Play Mas* was performed at the Royal Court, and in 1978 he co-founded the Black Theatre Co-operative (BTC), whose first production was his celebrated 1979 play about the disaffection of four black teenagers in London, *Welcome Home Jacko*.

Another important writer to emerge in the 1970s was Tunde Ikoli (1955–), whose *Short Sleeves in the Summer* was staged at the Royal Court in 1974 and *On the Out* at the Bush Theatre in 1978. His work highlighted youth culture, but unlike other black dramatists of the 1970s Ikoli was a second-generation British citizen of mixed Cornish and Nigerian ethnicity. Anticipating the concerns of a later generation of British-born playwrights who came to prominence in the 1990s, Ikoli's 1980 play *Scrape Off the Black* (about an interracial family in the East End) explores themes such as conflicts over race, family loyalty, and identity.

Despite the successes of Matura and Ikoli, black practitioners still found few opportunities in mainstream theatre. The touring Temba Theatre Company was founded by actors Alton Kumalo and Oscar James in 1972, specifically to create better roles for black actors. Under Kumalo's artistic direction, the company produced new plays including Barrie Keefe's *Black*

---

[15] Chambers, *Black and Asian Theatre*, 147.

Lear (1980) and White's *The Boot Dance* (1984), as well as revivals of work by Matura, LeRoi Jones, Athol Fugard, and others. Known for its anti-racism and robust political commitment, Temba was the first black British theatre company to secure an annual Arts Council subsidy, which began in 1974–1975.[16] Its fortunes turned in the mid-1980s, following the Arts Council's decentralisation programme, and it lost its core funding in 1990, folding two years later.

Black British theatres flourished during the heady cultural and political milieu of the 1970s, spurred on by the racism on the streets and the influence of liberation movements in Africa, the Caribbean, and the United States. Theatre practitioners worked energetically during these years to improve the cultural and material circumstances of their communities, establishing arts centres that were also safe havens. As Chambers observes: 'At a time when black youngsters could not walk the streets without fear of police harassment, places such as Keskidee offered a vital refuge and place to meet, learn, develop skills, and express oneself.'[17] Dark and Light, which Frank Cousins founded in 1969, became the Black Theatre of Brixton by 1975, reflecting a political outlook better aligned with the working-class audiences it sought to attract. Oscar Abrams founded the Keskidee Center in 1970, with the motto 'a community discovering itself creates its own future'. Keskidee attracted prominent visitors such as Nina Simone and Bob Marley, but its Theatre Workshop addressed grassroots audiences with plays like White's *Lament for Rastafari* (1977) and Walcott's *Remembrance* (1980).

Debates also persisted over approaches that stressed integration with the power-centres of mainstream theatre, and more separatist approaches that saw the theatre as a community-oriented space from which to explore issues of difference, authenticity, and self-validation. These initiatives were also affected by patterns of migration and different community needs. This was particularly evident in the contrast between the needs of post-Partition labour migrants, many of whom arrived from Pakistan and Bangladesh (then East Pakistan) in the early 1960s, and those of the Kenyan and Ugandan Asians expelled by Idi Amin in the late 1960s. Comprising a higher proportion of middle-class professionals and artists, this later group were often English-speakers and conversant with European forms of theatre. It is no accident that the first British Asian theatre company, Tara Arts, was established in 1977 by Jatinder Verma, who was born in Tanzania and raised in Kenya.

[16] Ibid., 148. [17] Ibid., 146.

Yet, as Graham Ley and Sarah Dadswell note, 'a thriving and diverse South Asian arts scene' existed during the 1960s and 1970s even before the founding of Tara. Although these community-based 'language theatres' received no state funding and remained culturally isolated, they served an important strategic function, providing cohesion and identity: 'Own-language theatre, in Urdu, Bengali, Gujarati, Hindi, and Marathi [. . .] tended to validate values and traditions of the home culture and [was] aimed at distinct home language groups, not at other Asian-language communities, let alone non-Asian audiences.'[18] Language remained a critical issue for producers of South Asian theatre well into the 1980s, when Verma conceptualised 'Binglish': new forms of culturally and linguistically hybrid theatre that represented a distinctly British Asian performance aesthetic and ideology.

Tara Arts was formed in direct response to the racist killing of a young Sikh boy, Gurdip Singh Chaggar, and more generally as a reaction to National Front violence.[19] It was not only the first British Asian theatre company to be publicly funded, in 1982, but has remained the one with the longest history in Britain and the organisation that has made the most significant interventions into postcolonial debates around diaspora, difference, and inclusion. Tara's earliest, community-oriented work eschewed mainstream venues, remaining on the 'margins' in relation to both critical recognition and public funding. Key aims of its first productions were to retell histories of the subcontinent; to perform the hidden histories of Asians in Britain long before the period of postwar immigration; and, like the parallel work of black British theatres, to bring second-generation experiences and perspectives to the foreground. Tara's inaugural production *Sacrifice* (1977), adapted from Rabindranath Tagore's play *Balidaan*, sought somewhat unsuccessfully to draw parallels between Tagore's story about 'ideological extremism' and contemporary Thatcherism.[20] Later productions made connections more explicit, such as *Inkalaab, 1919* (1980), depicting the 1919 Jallianwala Bagh massacre and highlighting the similarity between repressive colonial practices and contemporary 'sus laws' (discussed below).

Committed to building a community of British Asian practitioners and theatre-goers, Tara followed a policy of Asian-only casting.[21] Its original

---

[18] Ibid., 109.
[19] See the company's website: 'Tara History', *Tara Arts* (n.d.). Available at www.tara-arts.com/about-us/history.
[20] Hingorani, *British Asian Theatre*, 19–22.
[21] See Chambers's discussion of Equity debates concerning 'integrated' and 'colour-blind' casting; *Black and Asian Theatre*, 154–6.

meetings functioned, like Keskidee's, as a community space, a place where 'you could actually go and have a laugh and talk about your parents and people would understand what you mean', as Verma put it.[22] Despite its insistence on Asian actors, Tara rejected the narrow communal foci of Asian-language theatres, seeking a pan-South Asian audience that was multilingual and multicultural, as well as a British-born generation that spoke English. As Verma explained in 1978, the company '[chose] to do their work in English' because no organisations addressed 'all Asians' regardless of creed and language: 'We feel that for us all, in Britain, it is vital to begin to think of ourselves as Asians.'[23] Verma's 1998 essay on 'Binglishing' highlights Tara's pioneering role and the 'particular negotiation between English and Indian languages and sensibilities' that Tara Arts initiated and continues to practise, an approach that came to characterise much Asian theatre in Britain.

Hanif Kureishi (1954–) was perhaps the only British Asian playwright in the 1970s and early 1980s to achieve mainstream success. His work focused from the outset on the lives of characters whose often failed dreams were set against a fractured social world and decaying urban landscape.[24] Remarkably, his early plays *Borderline* and *Outskirts*, both staged in 1981 at the Royal Court, did not overtly speak for Asian communities in their exploration of contemporary racism: *Outskirts* depicted no Asian characters and *Borderlines* no Asian languages or accents. Kureishi shifted his perspective in his screenplays, *My Beautiful Laundrette* (1984) and *My Son the Fanatic* (1997; first published as a short story in 1994), whose characters, whether immigrant or British-born, are complexly transnational and irreducible to type.

The Thatcher Years: 1979–1990

The publication of Naseem Khan's 1976 report *The Arts Britain Ignores* was an important turning point for arts practitioners in both the black and Asian communities (see Chapter 25). Khan's intervention is widely credited with igniting public interest in and funding for ethnic and minority arts, especially theatre; in fact, by the early 1980s, black theatre was acknowledged as distinctive. Calling the 1980s a 'transformatory decade', Kwesi Owusu describes a radical and expansive movement of cultural practitioners,

---

[22] Quoted in Hingorani, *British Asian Theatre*, 19. Originally published in Naushaba Khan's interview with Jatinder Verma, 30 March 2001 (*Summary of History into Tara's History, 1997–2001*, Tara Arts Archive, 2001).

[23] Quoted in Ley and Dadswell (eds.), *British South Asian Theatres*, 16.

[24] Hingorani, *British Asian Theatre*, 167.

intellectuals, communicators, and politicians, which began to emerge 'as the new intellectual voice of Black Britain', responding to the racism of the Thatcher era.[25] By then, although nearly half the UK's black population was British-born – many had never been to their ancestral homes – they encountered racist street violence and aggressive policing, governed by the notorious 'sus' law, on a daily basis.[26] This law permitted arrests of those who were suspected of intending to offend and it was used disproportionately against black and Asian Britons. The law was not abolished until 1981, the year of the Brixton riots and the Scarman Report on them (see Chapter 25). However, more than a decade later, the racist murder of Stephen Lawrence in 1993 as well as the crucial 1999 Macpherson Report on the failures of the murder investigation highlighted that institutional racism was still evident in the Metropolitan Police (see: Chapters 12 and 25). The continuing injustices of racism fuelled the emergence of new forms of black and Asian political activism, which are prominent in the theatre of the period.[27]

The new arts funding created as a result of the 1981 Scarman Report and the groundbreaking Greater London Council (GLC; 1981–1986) policies under Ken Livingstone provided significant opportunities for a variety of black and Asian artists in the first half of the 1980s, until the GLC was abolished by Margaret Thatcher. An extraordinary range of companies were founded: the Black Theatre Forum, Black Arts Alliance, Carib Theatre, Imani-Faith, Umoja, Tamasha, Theatre of Black Women, the Black Mime Theatre Company and Black Mime Women's Troupe, Munirah, Siren, the Double Edge Theatre Company, and others. BTC produced Matura's *One Rule* (1981), Jacqueline Rudet's *Money to Live* (1984), and several plays by Edgar White and the Asian playwright Farrukh Dhondy. Writers like Caryl Phillips and Michael McMillan produced major plays, including Phillips's *Strange Fruit* (1980), *Where There Is Darkness* (1982), *The Shelter* (1983), and *All Or Nothing at All* (1988), and McMillan's *Carve Your Name* and *Day of Action* (both 1981) and *On Duty* (1983).

Phillips has commented that this 'unbridled enthusiasm for the theatre' first drew him to writing plays but that – like Kureishi, Fred D'Aguiar, and Jackie Kay – he soon found more satisfying creative outlets and larger

---

[25] Kwesi Owusu, 'Introduction' in Kwesi Owusu (ed.), *Black British Culture and Society: A Text Reader* (London: Routledge, 2000), 1–18; 6.

[26] Thomas, 'Social and Political Context', 27.

[27] See Meenakshi Ponnuswami, 'The Social and Political Context of Black British Theatre: 1980–90s' in Brewer et al. (eds.), *Modern and Contemporary*, 79–94.

audiences with fiction and poetry; he notes that 'the theatre never came into its own' in the 1980s for second-generation practitioners.[28] But the record suggests otherwise; many black writers did find a home in playwriting. Productions from this time include Ikoli's *Sink or Swim* (1982) and *Please and Thank-You* (1987); Winsome Pinnock's *Leave Taking* (1987), *A Rock in Water* and *A Hero's Welcome* (both 1989), and *Talking in Tongues* (1991); Bernardine Evaristo's *Silhouette* (1983) and *Pyeyucca* (1984); Jackie Kay's *Chiaroscuro* (1985); Jacqueline Rudet's *Basin* (1985); and Maria Oshodi's *The 'S' Bend* (1985) and *Blood, Sweat and Fears* (1988). Many of these playwrights were female and as, Gabriele Griffin notes, the majority were not only highly educated but '[worked] across a range of media'; few black and Asian women could afford to work exclusively in theatre.[29] Nevertheless, the 1980s were a fruitful decade for female practitioners. In 1982, the year that Brewster became the first black woman drama officer at the Arts Council, Patricia Hilarie, Paulette Randall, and Bernardine Evaristo co-founded Theatre of Black Women, the UK's first black women's theatre company, which focused on experimental works around female experience and identity. At the same time, black women playwrights were frequently drawn to naturalism as they tackled topical concerns including violence directed at women, the vulnerability of the poor, and generational conflict, as well as social and political issues including the 'sus' law and aggressive policing, the history of migration, sickle-cell anaemia, and the effects of Thatcherism. Kay's *Chiaroscuro*, produced by the Theatre of Black Women in 1986, adapts the choreopoem form of Ntozake Shange's *for colored girls* (1975) and is one of relatively few plays at this time to experiment with form. Like *Chiaroscuro*, Rudet's *Basin* (1985) and Kay's *Twice Over* (1988) centre on the black lesbian experience and homophobia.[30] These feminist works were important challenges to both white feminist claims of 'global sisterhood' as well as 'complacent notions of a homogeneous [. . .] Black community'.[31]

Thatcher-era funding cuts had a strong impact on new talent in the mid-1980s, prompting serious debates about strategy, purpose, and direction. Temba's experience offers a useful case-study. In 1986, Alby James became its artistic director and steered it in new directions, focusing on untested authors like Trish Cooke, Felix Cross, and Benjamin Zephaniah, all of whom

[28] Caryl Phillips, 'I Could Have Been a Playwright' in Davis and Fuchs (eds.), *Staging New Britain*, 37–47; 43.
[29] Griffin, *Contemporary Black and Asian Women*, 1.
[30] For a discussion of black lesbian theatre, see Goddard, *Staging Black Feminisms*.
[31] McMillan and SuAndi, 'Rebaptizing the World', 52.

became successful. Whereas Temba was founded by immigrant practitioners, James was British-born and middle class, and Temba's new direction reflected a cultural shift from immigrant perspectives towards second-generation black British experiences. As Chambers argues, James's effort was to 'reposition the company within the theatrical mainstream by looking beyond (without ignoring) what he saw as the limiting focus of much black theatre on racism and a uniquely black experience'. Thus, when Temba lost funding in 1990, James resigned, feeling that the Arts Council 'preferred Temba to focus [narrowly] on black communities and black audiences' and not to 'trespass on the classics'.[32]

Similar questions vexed other practitioners. In 1983, Anton Phillips and Parminder Vir of the GLC Ethnic Arts sub-committee spearheaded the important Black Theatre Season at the Arts Theatre in the West End. The Season lasted for six years; its many productions included Trevor Rhone's *Two Can Play* and Abbensetts's *Outlaw* (both 1983); Earl Lovelace's *The Hardware Store* (1985); Barbara Gloudon's *The Pirate Princess* (1986); and Walcott's *Beef, No Chicken* (1989). A consequence of the season was the assembly of several key groups into the Black Theatre Forum (initially the Black Theatre Alliance). Formed in 1985 at the beginning of the second season, it included representatives from seventeen theatre companies; this key coalition gave weight and credibility to minority theatre at a crucial moment and contributed to the increasing visibility of plays by black British writers in the West End.[33]

The Black Theatre Season survived the abolition of the GLC by the Thatcher government in 1986, but the GLC's successor, the Greater London Authority, withheld funding and blocked venues, bringing the burgeoning of black theatre to an end by the close of the decade. The issues confronting the Black Theatre Forum concerned other minority theatres more widely. All were concerned with finding a means of bringing new audiences to mainstream theatres and deciding whether to abandon the difficult goal of taking theatre to the communities whose lives were depicted on stage. Whilst funding offered a 'lifeline' to many, the agenda of funding bodies meant risking autonomy as creative practitioners and succumbing to the essentialist categorisation that underpinned the minimal support that was offered. They wanted to be seen as artists first and foremost; their diverse cultural heritages were an important but not necessarily determining

---

[32] Chambers, *Black and Asian Theatre*, 149, 150.
[33] Alda Terracciano, 'Mainstreaming African, Asian and Caribbean Theatre: The Experiments of the Black Theatre Forum' in Godiwala, *Alternatives*, 22–50; 49.

element of their artistic vision. Despite these caveats, state funding played an important role in fostering the growth of organisations dedicated to promoting black and Asian voices.

One of the last GLC projects to be supported before its demise was the funding of Talawa, a company that had been a vital force since its founding in 1985 by Brewster, Mona Hammond, Carmen Monroe, and Inigo Espejel. Starting with a revival of C. L. R. James's *The Black Jacobins* in 1986, the company staged a series of path-breaking productions, including Dennis Scott's *An Echo in the Bone* (1986), Derek Walcott's *O Babylon* (1988), and an all-black version of Oscar Wilde's *The Importance of Being Earnest* (1988). As Victor Ukaegbu notes, Talawa focused from the outset on 'establishing black performance traditions in mainstream theatre', as well as on 'multicultural productions and the development of black theatre audiences'.[34] Its productions in the 1980s and 1990s by now major writers such as Walcott, Soyinka, and Earl Lovelace highlighted black identities and histories. At the same time, Talawa's mainly black productions of works by Shakespeare, John Ford, and Wilde sought to affirm the Britishness of black British heritage. Ukaegbu also notes the company's significant role in the training and education of new talents.[35] Although it has not been able to secure a permanent venue, Talawa continues to serve as Britain's premier black theatre company, organising script development programmes for new writers, running a summer school for emerging practitioners, and hosting Talawa Firsts, an annual festival of new plays.[36]

A Theatre of 'New Ethnicities': The 1990s

The late 1980s and early 1990s was an energetic period for British Asian theatre.[37] Tara Arts was flourishing, producing *Chilli in Your Eyes* (1984), for which the company interviewed young South Asians, the police, social services, and others in the London Borough of Newham, as a way of exploring recent attacks on South Asians by National Front supporters. The play was aimed at critiquing both racist bigots and the conservative voices of immigrant culture, which was equally reprimanded for an array of vices

---

[34] Victor Ukaegbu, '*Talawa* Theatre Company: The "Likkle" Matter of Black Creativity and Representation on the British Stage' in Godiwala (ed.), *Alternatives*, 123–51; 123.

[35] Ukaegbu, '*Talawa* Theatre', 127.

[36] 'Talawa's Mission', *Talawa*. Available at http://www.talawa.com/about/talawas-mission/.

[37] See Ponnuswami, 'Social and Political Context', 86 ff.

including casteism, sexism, rape, and male violence. As noted above, several Asian theatre companies were established in the wake of Tara's success including Sahar (1978); the Hounslow Arts Cooperative and the British Asian Theatre Company in 1982; and the Asian Theatre Co-operative (modelled on the Black Theatre Cooperative) and Actors Unlimited in 1983. By the end of the decade, two companies emerged that would, like Tara, become pillars of British Asian theatre: Tamasha (1989) and Kali Theatre Company (1991). All three are still in operation today.

Tamasha was founded in 1989 by Sudha Bhuchar and Kristine Landon-Smith. Though not designed solely as a women's theatre, it made it clear from the outset that 'the lives and experiences of women were dramatically prominent in [its] productions'.[38] Landon-Smith's experience of directing a Delhi adaptation of Mulk Raj Anand's 1935 novel *Untouchable* became the touchstone for Tamasha's artistic philosophy: 'to bring contemporary work of Asian influence to the British stage'.[39] Tamasha's first productions sought to recreate an authentically Asian experience, focusing on social problems in India: an adaptation of Meira Chand's novel *House of the Sun* (1991), examining the lives of Sindhi families in Bombay; Ruth Carter's *Women of the Dust* (1992), which drew attention to the plight of exploited migrant construction workers in Delhi; and Abhijat Joshi's *A Shaft of Sunlight* (1994), which explored communal pressures confronting a Hindu–Muslim couple in India.

Unlike Tara Arts, which translated western classics from an Asian perspective and developed a hybridised 'Binglished' aesthetic, Tamasha embraced naturalism as a means to bring Asian difference to the stage. For Tamasha's production of *Women of the Dust*, for example, Bhuchar, Landon-Smith, and Ruth Carter visited India to interview 'real' women workers, whose language and style of speaking they translated and sought to render realistically. The result was a performance style that was credible to British audiences but seemed parodic to immigrant South Asians. This kind of difficulty with representation continued to stalk British Asian theatre and film well into the twenty-first century, impacting the reception of important productions like Ayub Khan-Din's *East Is East* (1996), Gurpreet Kaur Bhatti's *Behzti* (2004), and BBC comedy shows *Goodness Gracious Me* (1999) and *Citizen Khan* (2012), which featured caricatures of immigrant Asians created by second-generation South Asians (see Chapter 32). Many saw these images as self-directed

---

[38] Graham Ley, 'Women in British Asian Theatre' in Arya Madhavan (ed.), *Women in Asian Performance: Aesthetics and Politics* (Abingdon; New York: Routledge, 2017), 187–99; 191.

[39] http://www.tamasha.org.uk/.

mockery by a new generation confident enough in its Britishness to satirise 'itself' whilst others viewed the performances as self-alienation by second-generation Asians desperate to dissociate themselves from the particular social and sartorial practices of their immigrant parents.[40]

The emergence of Tamasha and Kali is tied to the proliferation of British Asian artists in the 1980s and the activist feminism of the period. Established by Rukhsana Ahmad and Rita Wolf in 1991, Kali had the particular aim of nurturing British Asian women's talents. Like Tara Arts, Kali was born in the wake of violence, specifically the murder of an Indian woman, Balwant Kaur, by her husband at a London women's shelter in 1985. Shocked by this event, Ahmad was to join a protest march for the first time and this moment 'played a big role in politicising' her writing.[41] Kali's first production, directed by Wolf, was Ahmad's dramatisation of the Balwant Kaur murder in her well-received 1990 play *Song for a Sanctuary*, which in effect silences the abusive husband by declining to explore the psychology of male violence, focusing instead on cultural and class differences amongst women at the shelter. The play juxtaposes the conservatism of the Punjabi Sikh victim Rajinder, represented as being too deeply concerned about her family's community status to be able to rebuff the value-system that victimised her, against the leftist feminism of Kamla, a younger mixed-race British Asian woman who has rejected the community's values and who is consequently hostile and impatient towards Rajinder. Ahmad's nuanced portrayal of these differences suggests that women's inability or unwillingness to support each other can perpetuate patriarchal violence, a theme explored in several later works by British Asian feminists, including Meera Syal and Gurinder Chadha's film *Bhaji on the Beach* (1993) and, more recently, Gurpreet Kaur Bhatti's *Behzti* (2004), Yasmin Whittaker-Khan's *Bells* (2005), and Emteaz Hussain's *Sweet Cider* (2008). Whereas many of the later works are premised on a gendered dichotomy in which immigrant conservatism is pitted against British modernity in ways that preclude solidarity between mothers and daughters, Ahmad's subtler appraisal explores the potential for feminist collaboration and resistance across generations.

---

[40] See for example Godiwala's criticism of Tamasha's slice-of-life plays in 'Genealogies, Archaeologies, Histories: The Revolutionary "Interculturalism" of Asian Theatre in Britain' in Godiwala (ed.), *Alternatives*, 101–19; 112.

[41] Quoted in Hingorani, *British Asian Theatre*, 120–1.

Kali's political emphasis is apparent in its radical feminist choice of name. Taken from the Hindu goddess venerated for what Ahmad has described as 'female power, regeneration, fertility and strength',[42] 'Kali' also means 'black' in several South Asian languages. As Ley and Dadswell note, Ahmad's early association with the influential Asian Women Writers' Collective, founded in 1984, paved the way for Kali's emphasis on writer development, as well as its multilingualism, political priorities, and attention to cultural complexities. By 1994, Kali had initiated an influential programme of 'open theatre workshops' dedicated to script development.[43] These and other strategies such as drama- turgical workshops have positioned Kali as the company that has had the greatest impact upon the development of new British Asian playwriting since the 1990s.

While Tara, Tamasha, and Kali grew in strength and influence during the 1990s, many new black and Asian companies were formed, including the Posse, Bibi Crew, Aarawak Moon Productions, Moti Roti, Chandika Arts, Mehtab, Tiata Fahodzi, Man Mela, Half Moon Young People's Theatre, Push, and more. British-born writers also brought several productions to stage: Trish Cooke, Benjamin Zephaniah, Valerie Mason-John, Paul Boakye, Kwame Kwei-Armah, Roy Williams, Jenny McLeod, Femi Elufowoju, Dona Daley, Zindika, Sol B. River, Parv Bancil, Ayub Khan-Din, Tanika Gupta, Harwant Bains, and others. Their work tackles head-on the second- generation struggle for the 'platform' that Caryl Phillips felt had been absent from the culture of the stage in the 1980s.[44]

Identity and authenticity are prominent concerns in both black and Asian playwriting of the period, as are interrelated issues of language and style – specifically the search for idioms and rhythms capturing the living language and vernacular of the first British-born generation. As many critics have noted, this emphasis on black expressive culture is particularly notable in works by Parv Bancil (*Ungrateful Dead*, 1993; *Made in England*, 1998), Ayub Khan-Din (*East Is East*, 1996), Roy Williams (*Lift Off*, 1999; *Clubland*, 2001), and Kwame Kwei-Armah (*Elmina's Kitchen*, 2003), which capture street vernacular while touching on contemporary issues of identity and belonging, signalling the arrival of a distinctly post-immigrant voice. Chambers argues that nat- uralism maintained its 'historic function of being a remedial and provocative

---

[42] Ahmad, 2004 correspondence with Godiwala, quoted in Godiwala, 'Kali: Providing a Forum for Asian Women Writers', in Godiwala (ed.), *Alternatives*, 328–46; 329.

[43] Ley and Dadswell (eds.), *British South Asian Theatres*, 139. For a full description of this process, see also 139–44.

[44] Phillips, 'I Could Have Been', 43.

force, offering counter images to those that confirmed marginalization and discrimination'.[45] However, the 1990s also saw creative experimentation with form, especially in performance art and poetry, by adventurous black poets interested in stretching genre boundaries, such as Patience Agbabi, SuAndi, McMillan, Dorothea Smartt, and Zephaniah.[46]

The integrity of the black family and its ability to withstand the cultural shock of exile and reinvention continued to be predominant themes in the 1990s. Black and Asian plays approached this dynamic from somewhat different perspectives. Whereas black theatres were critical of the compromises made by the immigrant generation (see Roy Williams's 2003 *Fallout* and Kwei-Armah's 2004 *Fix Up*), their plays frequently evoked the memory of a shared legacy of slavery and racism linking members of different generations. This is not the case in Khan-Din's *East Is East*, Bhatti's *Behzti*, and other similar plays about conflicts between immigrant and British-born Asians, which position the second generation alongside white British culture and in opposition to an unassimilable immigrant generation. A notable exception is Bancil's *Made in England*, which as Hingorani observes '[takes] a sceptical position on the appropriation of Asian culture by the mainstream', exploring the pressure on British Asians to conform to stereotypes of 'Asian cool' in order to succeed in the entertainment industry.[47] Here issues of loyalty and 'selling out' are situated within a critique of the systemic degradation and colonisation of Asianness by consumer culture, which serves as a reminder of the oppressions that unite Asians.

Somewhat fewer plays connect black British concerns to contemporary international, diasporic ones. British Asian theatre has focused more explicitly on these cultural interconnections, perhaps because, as Verma claimed earlier, those who launched it were often British Kenyans who arrived in the heated moment of 1968, for whom the process of self-reinvention in England was a more critical issue than for immigrants who had arrived earlier from the subcontinent.[48] Nevertheless some black British plays such as Pinnock's *Talking in Tongues* (1991) and Trish Cooke's *Running Dream* (1993) did engage

---

[45] Chambers, *Black and Asian Theatre*, 196.

[46] See McMillan and SuAndi, 'Rebaptizing the World', 57–61; Goddard, *Staging Black Feminisms*, 133–78; and Catherine Ugwu (ed.), *Let's Get It On: The Politics of Black Performance* (London: Institute for Contemporary Arts, 1996).

[47] Hingorani, *British Asian Theatre*, 174–5.

[48] Jatinder Verma, '"Binglishing" the English Stage' in Richard Boon and Jane Plastow (eds.), *Theatre Matters: Performance and Culture on the World Stage* (Cambridge: Cambridge University Press, 1998), 125–32; 127.

directly with global diasporic pasts, including histories of slavery, imperialism, and independence movements.

A different type of stage, sometimes described as 'commercial black theatre', such as Oliver Samuels's 'bawdy Jamaican comedy' and performances by the Blue Mountain Theatre, is almost entirely bypassed by scholarship. These popular performances attract large audiences, drawn in by the lively humour and the promise of a 'good night out'. As a result, audience engagement at such shows is 'the envy of the theatre world'.[49] Drawing attention to the vital community element of these shows, McMillan comments that the audiences of Caribbean popular theatre inhabit a special position: they are not 'alienated by the form or condescended to by didactic messages, but are allowed to comment, cuss, participate, own, belong, reclaim'.[50]

Conclusion

The turning point in black and Asian theatres was the identification of institutionalised racism across all levels of British society in the 1999 Macpherson Report (see Chapter 25) and the subsequent 2001 Eclipse Theatre Conference focusing on diversity and black arts. Designed explicitly to tackle racism in the theatre industry, the Eclipse report cited Macpherson's definition of institutional racism as its epigraph.[51] Each theatre organisation was required to design a precise diversity plan, to be implemented two years later, which would outline clearly how to 'foster greater inclusion of black practitioners in mainstream theatre' and a commitment to the recognition of black and Asian cultural production.[52] In 2009, counting twenty-eight 'writers of colour' whose work had been produced in 'theatres over the last two years', playwright Roy Williams enthused that 'black British theatre is in quite a healthy state. In fact, it's bloody exciting.'[53]

Whilst such comments were uplifting, many were acutely aware that integration inevitably meant the end of a discrete sector of black British

---

[49] Chambers, *Black and Asian Theatre*, 194–5.

[50] McMillan and SuAndi, 'Rebaptizing the World', 56.

[51] www.artscouncil.org.uk/sites/default/files/download-file/Eclipse_report_2011.pdf.

[52] Lynette Goddard, 'Cultural Diversity and Black British Playwriting on the Mainstream, 2000–2012' (n.d.), National Theatre Black Plays Archive. Available at www.blackplaysarchive.org.uk/featured-content/essays/lynette-goddard-rennaisance-black-british-drama-1990s.

[53] Roy Williams, 'Black Theatre's Big Breakout', *The Guardian*, 27 September 2009. Available at www.theguardian.com/stage/2009/sep/27/black-theatre-roy-williams.

theatre, and with it the funded networks of support and mentoring essential to supporting new talent. As Rukhsana Ahmad was to put it: in the 1980s, 'multiculturalism was a very popular thing, it was the buzzword [. . .] But there has been a lot of regression [. . .] there is a lot of anti-immigration feeling now.'[54] In this 2014 interview, Ahmad calls to mind the crisis of Muslim identity that unfolded following the *Satanic Verses* controversy of the late 1980s. Evoking the 11 September 2001 World Trade Center attacks in New York and the 7 July 2005 bombings in London, she references the escalating animosity towards a cultural diversity that was seen as potentially divisive and had grown out of the multiculturalism of the 1980s. Resistance, as she put it, would soon devolve into neo-isolationist political standpoints and increasing public disavowals of Britain's imperial past (see Chapter 38).

Despite these complexities, there is no doubt that twenty-first-century black and Asian British theatres are ready to confront such challenges as they continue to occupy a bold, radical, countercultural position as a 'theatre of trespass'. Recent work by young playwrights from a wide range of ethnicities – Bola Agbaje, debbie tucker green, Emteaz Hussain, Alia Bano, Yasmin Whittaker-Khan – offers a new generation of narratives: youthful rejections of conventional pieties, quests for new languages and modes of expression, and defiant affirmations of a Britishness that no state has the power to withdraw.

---

[54] 'Rukhsana Ahmad (British South Asian Theatre Memories)', interview by Foundation for Indian Performing Arts, FIPA British South Asian Theatre Memories Oral History project, 25 March 2014, video, 15:53. Available at www.youtube.com/watch?v= RO31Phmm2eY&t=1038s&index=20&list=PL9FnDIEX2woU50vB1VbvYeVDa8SenM PiN.

23

The Writer and the Critic
Conversations between Literature and Theory

VIJAY MISHRA

I have before me a copy of a photograph taken in November 1942, at the request of George Orwell.[1] It remains the only visual record of the poetry programme *Voice*, which Orwell curated for the BBC's Eastern Service. The central figure in the photograph is Una Marson (1905–1965), also presenter of *Calling the West Indies*, a programme run by the BBC's Empire Service from 1939. Renamed *Caribbean Voices* in 1944, this programme featured a number of soon-to-become great writers like George Lamming, V. S. Naipaul, Samuel Selvon, Edward Kamau Brathwaite, Edgar Mittelholzer, Andrew Salkey, and Derek Walcott. Marson, playwright, poet, and author of the seminal poem 'Nigger' (1940), was also one of the great figures of Jamaican feminism (see Chapter 7). A number of key writers and critics are gathered around her. On her right is seated T. S. Eliot who is looking, not a little bemusedly it seems, at a number of sheets in Marson's hand and three or four volumes of works beside them. Behind her stand Orwell, peering into those very sheets and the books, and Nancy Barratt, secretary to Orwell. Standing to her left is the eminent literary critic William Empson, here clean-shaven and without his trademark moustache and Confucian whiskers. Seated around the table (from left to right facing the camera) are four Indians, Venu Chitale (assistant producer), M. J. Tambimuttu (poet and editor of *Poetry London*), Mulk Raj Anand (novelist and co-curator of the *Voice* programme), and Narayana Menon (writer and broadcaster). C. Pemberton, a member of BBC staff, is seated next to Anand.[2]

---

[1] Susheila Nasta, 'Between Bloomsbury and Gandhi? The Background to the Publication and Reception of Mulk Raj Anand's *Untouchable*' in Robert Fraser and Mary Hammond (eds.), *Books Without Borders*, vol. 2: *Perspectives from South Asia* (Basingstoke: Palgrave Macmillan, 2008), 151–69; 154.

[2] For a reprint of the photograph, see James Procter, 'Una Marson at the BBC', *Small Axe* 19:3 (2015): 1–28; 3 Available at https://muse.jhu.edu/article/602408.

During the war years, the BBC directed energies to the war effort and addressed the armed forces, but programmes such as *Caribbean Voices* and its Eastern counterpart engaged with new waves in literature, too. In the words of Lyn Innes, this photograph points to a 'fascinating history' – as yet unwritten – 'of the involvement of writers from the Indian subcontinent, Sri Lanka, Africa and the Caribbean in the formulation of an international British-based culture which was then disseminated overseas to various countries by the BBC'.[3] The image of the writers gathered together in the photograph and the exchanges intimated in its capture of the *Voice* programme point to the main concern of this chapter, which is to highlight how such cross-cultural conversations and alliances between a wide range of writers, critics, and texts offer productive insights in terms of how black and Asian British writing should be read as part of a wide reading commons. The image also anticipates the translocal and transnational quality of much of today's writing, its production, and its reception – now almost taken for granted.

As previous chapters on the history of *Caribbean Voices* and the Eastern Service broadcasts intimate, the figures in the photograph function as a timely reminder about origins, influence, and intertexts (see Chapter 9). Orwell, Eliot, and Empson figured prominently in the early postcolonial imaginary and the poets discussed in the six-part *Voice* series (Dylan Thomas for one) likewise were important touchstones. Often, though, metropolitan writers from the periphery of the 'Empire' needed a literary patron of sorts. Thus, W. B. Yeats was instrumental in persuading Macmillan & Co. to publish Rabindranath Tagore's translation of *Gitanjali* (1912), a manuscript which Yeats kept on him for days, 'reading it in railway trains, or on the top of omnibuses and in restaurants'.[4] The introduction, which denied Tagore's Indianness in favour of a universal humanism, seems to have played a large part in Tagore winning the Nobel Prize for Literature that year. E. M. Forster likewise wrote a preface to Mulk Raj Anand's *Untouchable* (1935), which he praised for its thoroughly modernist aesthetic frame of reference and its 'refreshingly frank' engagement with caste in the treatment of the character Bakha.[5] To the novel, added Forster, Anand brought just the right 'mixture of insight and detachment'[6] because he eschewed the generalising tendencies of philosophical abstraction in favour of concrete reality, itself

[3] C. L. Innes, *A History of Black and Asian Writing in Britain, 1700–2000* (Cambridge: Cambridge University Press, 2002), 217.

[4] Rabindranath Tagore, *Gitanjali* (New York: St Martin's Press, [1912] 1965), xiii.

[5] Mulk Raj Anand, *Untouchable* (London: Bodley Head, [1935] 1970), 10–11.   [6] Ibid., 11.

a very modernist characteristic. When Marson, who had joined the BBC full-time in 1941 as a programme assistant in the 'Empire Programmes', fell seriously ill and had to stop working in 1945, with her went the concept of critical endorsement by established English authors as a prelude to publication.[7] In many ways it was after 1948, post-*Empire Windrush* (see Chapter 12), that postcolonial works, initially by West Indians, began to reshape English modernism's monocultural environment. Their presence can be distinguished from that of Tagore and Anand, and although essays continued to appear on 'new' writing, often writers themselves wrote about their processes of composition. Regarding commentary by writers on their own practice, on which this chapter focuses, we enter into the realm of critical discourses of a different order. A seminal starting point is George Lamming (1927–) who had come to England on the same ship as Trinidadian Sam Selvon (1923–1994) in 1950. Soon after, Lamming published his remarkable novel *In the Castle of my Skin* (1953), revisiting it through the composition of an extended theoretical preface almost forty years later for the Ann Arbor edition. What we get from the content of Lamming's preface is evidence of the emergence of new critical frameworks and a dramatic shift away from readings of texts as relatively autonomous works with a 'central individual consciousness'.[8] This shift is also indicative of the important move away from text to textual production and context, indeed to the sociology of literature and cultural studies, anticipating what Avtar Brah would later theorise as the diasporic location of the cultural Other in England.[9] Lamming's commentary on his seminal novel is now shaped by his experience as a diasporic West Indian who also became part of the 'African' British diaspora. And it is from 'the frozen heart of London' that he reconstructs the world of his childhood captured so vividly in his novel. It is worth recalling a pivotal passage here because of its importance:

> I was among those writers who took flight [in 1950] from that failure [to create a collective West Indian consciousness]. [. . .] We simply thought that we were going to an England which had been planted in our childhood consciousness as a heritage and place of welcome. It is the measure of our innocence that neither the claim of heritage nor the expectation of welcome

---

[7] As Nasta observes in 'Between Bloomsbury and Gandhi?' (164), prefaces by major writers can also suggest the proximity of these different writers' voices, especially when the preface and text have continued to appear together for several decades, as in the case of Anand.

[8] George Lamming, *In the Castle of my Skin* (Ann Arbor, MI: University of Michigan Press, [1953] 1991), xxxvi.

[9] Avtar Brah, *Cartographies of Diaspora* (London: Routledge, 1996).

would have been seriously doubted. England was [...] the name of a responsibility whose origin may have coincided with the beginning of time.

T oday I shudder to think how a country, so foreign to our own instincts, could have achieved the miracle of being called Mother [...]. The English themselves were not aware of the role they had played in the formation of these black strangers. The ruling class were serenely confident that any role of theirs must have been an act of supreme generosity. Like Prospero, they had given us language and a way of naming our own reality.[10]

The passage is revealing on a number of counts. First, it strengthens the case that Lamming's point of view has become one of diaspora, and a diaspora that not only looks back nostalgically but discovers that in England there is need for a greater political solidarity between West Indians and Africans. Second, it spells out a consciousness about writing in English in the shadow of the metropolitan centre even as black West Indians felt that they were children of the English motherland. Third, there is the question of representation of identities: who or what is the West Indian or the African in England? These theoretical concepts were first explored in Lamming's 1960 collection of essays, *The Pleasures of Exile*, a work that signalled the entry of the postcolonial writer into the hitherto exclusive discourse of English literary criticism, the exemplars of which, so far, had been the modernist writers in the 1942 *Voice* programme image. The essays collected in Lamming's early book were prescient and remain crucial for the genesis of theorisations on postcolonial black and Asian British writing. They also reflect an anxiety about the place of a target text (here, the postcolonial text) in the source text (the text of the metropolitan canon).

Critical Self-Reflection and Wilson Harris's Proto-Poststructuralism

Writers like Lamming and Selvon were key intellectuals with a commitment both to opening up the canon of Euro-American modernism and the position of the exile and their revolutionary self-affirmation. In the 1960s the Empire was being gradually dismantled or, in British terms, a decolonisation process was underway. Black and Asian writers were 'a new breed' and the great challenge was how to write in the language of the metropole and yet express both in language and thought something distinctive. Here the works of C. L. R. James (1901–1989) were decisive. James's two key works – *The Black*

---

[10] Lamming, 'Preface' (1991) in *In the Castle of my Skin*, xxxvii.

Jacobins (1938) and *Beyond a Boundary* (1963) – as well as his only novel, *Minty Alley* (1936), shadow Lamming's essays; notably, the introduction to Lamming's collection effectively begins with James's idea of black consciousness as the product of Toussaint L'Ouverture's Haitian revolution which began in 1791, merely two years after the French Revolution itself. What is striking is the turn to suppressed religious rituals, primarily African in origin, as a corrective to the idea of European law. James, whom Lamming called 'one of the most energetic minds of our time [. . .] a spirit that came to life in the rich and humble soil of a British colony of the Caribbean',[11] had also rephrased Rudyard Kipling's line 'And what should they know of England who only England know?' to read '*What do they know of cricket who only cricket know?*' in his own preface to *Beyond a Boundary*.[12] For Lamming a similar, cryptic reformulation is the subtext: *What do they know of the black who only the West Indian know?* In order to understand Lamming's formulation of black consciousness, one has to turn to Shakespeare's Caliban. In *The Pleasures of Exile*, Lamming laid the groundwork for this postcolonial reading of Shakespeare's *The Tempest*, speaking of 'a certain state of feeling which is the heritage of the exiled and colonial writer from the British Caribbean'.[13] The migration of the native from the kingdom of Caliban to the 'tempestuous island of Prospero's and his language' is both confronting and a challenge.[14] For the black writer, Caliban must be 'accorded the power *to see*' and Prospero's ownership of language can be dismantled only when the descendants of 'languageless and deformed slaves' can 'christen language afresh'.[15] And here again it is C. L. R. James's Toussaint who functions as the exemplary figure, 'a slave who was a great soldier, a Caliban as Prospero had never known him',[16] and a figure who touched the imagination of the great poet Wordsworth who, in a sonnet addressed to the revolutionary, had written, 'Thou hast left behind / Powers that will work for thee' ('To Toussaint L'Ouverture').

It is fitting to begin by highlighting the dialogue between Lamming and C. L. R. James because his thoughts capture the black British writer as a colonial with a certain relation to colonisation, a relation best captured in the idea of exile and in a growing identification of black

---

[11] George Lamming, *The Pleasures of Exile* (Ann Arbor, MI: University of Michigan Press, [1960] 1992), 150.
[12] Rudyard Kipling, 'The English Flag' in *The Complete Verse* (London: Kyle Cathie, [1891] 1996), 181; C. L. R. James, *Beyond a Boundary* (Durham, NC: Duke University Press, [1963] 2013), xxvii.
[13] Lamming, *The Pleasures of Exile*, 9.   [14] Ibid., 13.   [15] Ibid., 107, 118.   [16] Ibid., 150.

Britons with their African and Caribbean heritages; a point also made in C. L. R. James's foreword to the 1980 revised edition of *The Black Jacobins*. As James puts it: 'the book was written not with the Caribbean but with Africa in mind'.[17] James's intellectual affiliations are more directly evident in relation to Wilson Harris (1921–2018), also from the Caribbean, with whom he shared a philosophical commitment to Heidegger and a poetic passion for Hölderlin. Harris arrived in London some nine years after Lamming, in 1959, having acquired an unusual grasp of Amerindian cultures during his tenure as a land surveyor in Guyana's hinterland. From his first novel, *Palace of the Peacock* (1960), Harris informed his writing with elements drawn from aboriginal Guyanese cosmologies as well as classical western archetypes (see Chapter 14). Importantly too, he sensed that the European realist novel for the West Indian and for the non-English writer generally lacked, to use a phrase popularised by T. S. Eliot, an 'objective correlative' because it failed to capture non-European lived experiences. His understanding of ethnographic difference was important; and further, the landscape of the mind required an intuitive grasp of being and time, a consciousness of form and of the musicality of language, its abstractions and poetic ambivalences. Andrew Bundy, editor of Harris's essays, writes that 'Harris's exceptional command of the questions underlying the culture and circumstance of the English language makes him one of the most gifted writers of the era.'[18] Harris had a uniquely global outlook and an interest in abstract thinking that anticipated a kind of proto-poststructuralist discourse rather than the language of orthodox postcolonialism, that is, what might be called the postcolonialism of resistance, of anti-imperial, oppositional struggle, and identity politics. In his illuminating essay 'Tradition and the West Indian Novel', Harris avoided taking the more obvious path of a political reading of the West Indian novel.[19] Instead he spoke about native traditions, about broken histories, about the absence of an individual self in slave (and later indentured) lives where bodies were inarticulate. To capture such alternative, vernacular histories one needed not the verbal sophistication of a Lamming

---

[17] C. L. R. James, *The Black Jacobins: Toussaint L'Ouverture and the San Diego Revolution* (London: Allison & Busby, [1938] 1980), vi.

[18] A. J. M. Bundy (ed.), *Selected Essays of Wilson Harris: The Unfinished Genesis of the Imagination* (London: Routledge, 1999), 7.

[19] The lecture was delivered to the London West Indian Students' Union on Friday 15 May 1964, an event attended by C. L. R. James, who wrote a critical reply.

but the intense meditation on a 'common picture of humanity',[20] the kind found in Naipaul's classic *A House for Mr Biswas* (1961).

There are two flight paths, after Harris, that might be usefully noted here. The first is the unacknowledged or even silent homage to Harris evident in Zadie Smith's *White Teeth* (2000), a work that has been described as an instance of 'hysterical realism' (James Wood) and even the 'maximalist novel' (Stefano Ercolino).[21] These are critical reflections that Harris would have recognised as repudiating the conventions of the classical European novel. The second appears in Homi K. Bhabha's much cited essay 'The Commitment to Theory'. Here, cultural theorist Bhabha aligns the historical dimension of the enunciation of what he has famously termed the 'Third Space' with Harris's observations in his other notable essay, 'The Writer and Society' (1967).[22] The important theoretical point is that Bhabha's argument, after Harris, is that even when a presumed assimilation of contraries has taken place, a certain 'void' remains and it is through an entry into this 'void' (which Bhabha calls the 'Third Space') that participation in an alien territory begins to take shape. Bhabha has in mind minorities leading a 'double life' as they translate 'between cultures, renegotiating traditions'.[23] Yet the spectres of Harris remain in Bhabha's thinking when he later, in 2000, returns to invoke the concept of 'vernacular cosmopolitans' who move 'in-between cultural traditions' to reveal 'hybrid forms of life and art that do not have a prior existence within the discrete world of any single culture or language'.[24] It is his focus on hybrid forms without a single precedent that marks Bhabha's work

---

[20] Wilson Harris, 'Tradition and the West Indian Novel' in *Tradition, the Writer and Society* (London: New Beacon Books, [1967] 1973), 28–47; 40.

[21] James Wood, 'Human, All Too Human', *The New Republic Online*, 24 July 2001; Stefano Ercolino, *The Maximalist Novel: From Thomas Pynchon's 'Gravity's Rainbow' to Roberto Bolaño's '2666'* (New York: Bloomsbury, 2014). I owe both these references to my PhD student David Wright. For Zadie Smith's reply to Wood see Zadie Smith, 'This is How it Feels to Me', *The Guardian*, 14 October 2001. Available at www.theguardian.com/books/2001/oct/13/fiction.afghanistan.

[22] Wilson Harris, 'The Writer and Society' in *Tradition, the Writer and Society* (London: New Beacon Books, [1967] 1973), 48–64. Bhabha's quote from Harris, given in the notes to *The Location of Culture* as from pages 60–3, is in fact from page 62 (to the ellipsis in the quotation), followed by pages 60–1. Homi K. Bhabha, *The Location of Culture* (London: Routledge, 1994), 38. Apart from inverting the order of the sentences, Bhabha misquotes 'mythical' (he writes 'mythological') and does not place two of the three instances of the word 'void' in quotation marks.

[23] Homi Bhabha, 'The Vernacular Cosmopolitanism' in Ferdinand Dennis and Naseem Khan (eds.), *Voices of the Crossing* (London: Serpent's Tail, 2000), 133–42; 141.

[24] Ibid., 141.

from *The Location of Culture* (1994) onwards, a theme that emerges in dialogue with Harris's creative fiction and his critical writings.

The Writer-as-Critic: Enunciation and Postcolonial Selfhood

Lamming and Harris were fine writers and astute cultural critics in the tradition of C. L. R. James who worked as individual critics without formal institutional attachments. Both self-taught men, they wrote without formal scholarly training and remained outside academia. However, even as Harris, for instance, wrote his novels and essays, critical cultural and literary studies were taking a new turn with the establishment of the Birmingham Centre for Contemporary Cultural Studies by Richard Hoggart in 1964. It quickly established itself as a powerful voice in post-Gramscian cultural studies. The figure who stood out in that group was not British-born but another post-*Windrush* émigré Stuart Hall (1932–2014), who became the Centre's director (1969–1979). In *Figures of Dissent* (2003), Terry Eagleton calls Hall 'one of the most significant voices in the discourses of Britishness, ethnicity and multiculturalism of our post-imperial twilight'.[25] He had arrived in England from Jamaica in 1951 but, unlike Lamming and Selvon, was a Rhodes Scholar reading English at Merton College, Oxford, coincidentally T. S. Eliot's old college. Hall was to embark on a doctoral thesis on Henry James, a project he never completed. As with many others of his generation, Hall had received a traditional English education in Jamaica, which included studying Euro-American modernists like T. S. Eliot and James Joyce. Unlike other literary members of the post-*Windrush* generation, Hall gravitated towards cultural politics. Influenced by the already well-known publications on race and identity by Frantz Fanon and W. E. B. Du Bois, he soon made the compelling case that in creating counter-discourses many black Britons had in fact arrived at their own subject status – largely forging a new critical language on their own terms.

In an illuminating interview with Julie Drew, Hall expressed his thoughts on the grammar of ethnicity and the discursive turn.[26] As is now well known, a key term for Hall was 'identity' – the word with which he began his deliberations in the interview. Hall began to argue here against the static

---

[25] Terry Eagleton, *Figures of Dissent* (London: Verso, 2003), 215.

[26] Stuart Hall, 'Cultural Composition: Stuart Hall on Ethnicity and the Discursive Turn' in Gary A. Olson and Lynn Worsham (eds.), *Race, Rhetoric, and the Postcolonial* (Albany, NY: State University of New York Press, 1999), 205–39.

notion of identity being 'fixed', stressing that it is always fluid, always in process. This did not imply, he qualified, that identity is completely relative or that identity works within an 'open-ended horizon' that we choose 'intentionally'.[27] Rather, it is a studied and self-conscious process that 'becomes', so to speak, through writing. For the purposes of this discussion of the writer-as-critic, Hall's reference to the ways in which identity grows out of our investments in language is especially important.

Definitions and meanings of ethnicity and class come to us already sedimented in language. Foundational black thinkers and writers, whether Du Bois, C. L. R. James, Lamming, or Harris, have therefore already entered into the sedimented order of language. The writer's role is to reactivate earlier meanings, deprive them of their historical fixity, and reproduce them at any given time. We do not insert a prior, given identity into language but reproduce it through language and, in this act of reproduction, reiteration, and recirculation, 'discover what we are'.[28] From this perspective, literature becomes a place of enunciation, a recovery and rediscovery of selves which can then be subjected to further critique. In this constellation of writings about selves, in the gradual morphing of identities, something else emerges and this something else is never fixed. Writing the self is a process and each enunciation of identity draws on what has gone before. For Hall, careful archival retrospection and analysis, the uncovering of meaning, within a Gramscian materialist understanding of history, were important and avoided 'misrecognizing' how 'class intersects with race'.[29] This important point has since gained much prominence under the sign of Kimberlé Crenshaw's term 'intersectionality' and has become highly relevant in contemporary critical practice.

The Pluralisation of Cultural Forms

The dialectics between the pluralisation and innovation of literary form and emerging theoretical paradigms have allowed writers like Salman Rushdie to influence cultural theorists who in turn have left traces in literary texts. In the 1970s and 1980s, 'Multiculturalism emerged as a result of the realization [. . .] that the melting pot does not melt', as Floya Anthias and Nira Yuval-Davis have suggested, observing that 'ethnic and racial divisions get reproduced from generation to generation'.[30] What remained unresolved or unaddressed

[27] Ibid., 207. [28] Ibid., 208. [29] Ibid., 218.
[30] Floya Anthias and Nira Yuval-Davis, *Racialized Boundaries* (London: Routledge, 1992), 158.

was the impact of black and Asian migration on 'the racially exclusive narcissism of the nation'.[31] The literature of the new migrants filled that void by addressing the nation's discrepant, indeed contradictory, forms of social representations and national identity. The British multiethnic and multicultural nation state has grown out of 'prior conditions of existence under colonialism',[32] but given the nation's belief in its own unified culture, a culture into which admission for the colonised outsider was a non-issue, the UK simply worked on the presumption of final assimilation of the racial Other. What happened, however, was that black and Asian diasporic communities offered a 'novel cultural configuration' (as 'cosmopolitan communities') contrary to the logic of full assimilation.[33] They were also seen both as a relic of the communal sense that 'liberal society is supposed to have lost'[34] and as exemplifying the 'borderline time' of minorities who reproduced not only 'residues' of the past (such as a return to earlier realist and retrospective writing) but a 'localism' that offered itself as 'something new'.[35] This argument received its theoretically astute formulation in Avtar Brah's classic work, *Cartographies of Diaspora: Contesting Identities* (1996), in which she rethought ethnic difference through the category of 'diasporic space', a concept which, she forcefully argued, decentred 'the subject position of "native", "immigrant", "migrant", the in/outsider, in such a way that the diasporian is as much a native' because 'the native now becomes a diasporian through this mutual entanglement'.[36] The case of mutual entanglement found its most succinct articulation in Caryl Phillips (1958–), whose key novels *The Final Passage* (1985) and *Crossing the River* (1993) move the black British diaspora towards a larger black transatlantic concept, one that C. L. R. James was aware of and which Paul Gilroy (1956–) used as the central metaphor of the diaspora interchange in his later works.

The idea of the 'increasing pluralization of cultural forms' and the decoupling of ethnicity from '*essentialist* discourses of "race", "nation" or "culture"'[37] had already taken a slightly different articulation in Paul Gilroy's earlier book *There Ain't No Black in the Union Jack* (1987). Its first substantive chapter begins with a quotation from C. L. R. James's *Black Jacobins*, a quotation that establishes the broad outlines of the debates on

---

[31] Barnor Hesse, 'Introduction' in Barnor Hesse (ed.), *Un/settled Multiculturalisms* (London: Zed Books, 2000), 1–30.

[32] Stuart Hall, 'Conclusion: The Multi-Cultural Question' in Hesse (ed.), *Un/settled Multiculturalisms*, 209–41; 212.

[33] Ibid., 221. [34] Ibid. [35] Ibid., 230. [36] Brah, *Cartographies of Diaspora*, 242.

[37] Ibid., 240.

race and class while it at the same time also signals a longer tradition of black thinking in Britain: 'The race question is subsidiary to the class question in politics, and to think of imperialism in terms of race is disastrous. But to neglect the racial factor as merely incidental is an error only less grave than to make it fundamental.'[38] In classic Marxist theory, the working class's mode of production produces surplus capital from which the agents of labour, that is the working class, are systematically excluded. The presumption here is that labour has no colour and therefore the ways in which racial groups partici-pate in labour differently have little or no bearing on the larger struggle to be participants in the history of the movement of capital. Gilroy reads the social movement of race somewhat differently but without denying completely the value of class analysis. Gilroy's archive is the black British population; by this he means the African British (and not the Asian British, although British racism has affected both, albeit not uniformly), who grew into a separate 'underprivileged class' and have been victims of the historical 'character of racism'.[39] Race for Gilroy, who unlike James, Lamming, Harris, and Hall is British-born, is therefore a 'distinct order of social phenomena *sui generis*'.[40] This is especially so for West Indian migrants for whom, given their status in the history of plantation slavery, race was always linked to economic coer-cion and to the rise of capital.[41] Because diaspora space is occupied differently by black and Asian Britons, respectively, it requires a more subtle theorisation than that provided by Brah; likewise, black British writing and Asian British writing engage with British racism in slightly different ways.

Cockney Translation

Paul Gilroy's close readings, through the lens of a wide range of cultural theory, valorise popular cultural forms, including music and youth culture. His contribution to debates about ethnic absolutism, racial exclusivism, and the general compartmentalisation of cultures (your body designates your standing in a nation) frequently takes the form of the everyday, 'organic' relationship between black and white Britons. Through black music, dance, and variations on the use of English, he argues, black residents have been 'structured into the mechanisms of British society'.[42] This structuration, in the area of music, is noted in the role played by soul, disco, reggae, hip-hop, bebop, and swing in British working-class subcultures, both white and black.

---

[38] C. L. R. James, quoted in Paul Gilroy, *There Ain't No Black in the Union Jack* (Chicago, IL: University of Chicago Press, [1987] 1991), 15.
[39] Ibid., 21.   [40] Ibid., 27.   [41] Ibid., 38.   [42] Ibid., 155.

There were individual black artists too, such as Bob Marley, who popularised 'Rastafari ideology in Britain and throughout the world'.[43] It is productive to explore these interconnections between black and white, ambiguous and contradictory as they are, as Gilroy posits through the singular example of Smiley Culture's 1984 hit 'Cockney Translation'. Black music has always held some sense of difference and an understanding of its own special roots (which were primarily in West Indian culture) – notwithstanding white youths being significant consumers. What Gilroy finds in the case of 'Cockney Translation' is a wider legitimation of the vernacular, that is black people's own idioms, which had hitherto been used as a way of marking out racial difference and grounding them in an exclusive collective identity. Gilroy offers a remarkable commentary on the redefinition of 'black and white urban sub-cultures' with reference to Smiley Culture's song: '"Cockney Translation" conveys a view of these languages as genuinely interchangeable alternatives disrupting the [familiar] racial hierarchy [. . .] It presents them as equivalent "nation languages" facing each other across the desperate terrain of the inner city.'[44] This reading suggests equivalence where difference is often seen to prevail; Gilroy goes on to stress this correspondence between blackness and Cockney when insisting that to 'be black and to express that political identification in the use of black language is, it says, nothing more nor less than what it means to be a Cockney in the city'.[45] A look at the final verse of the song bears out this analysis:

> But sometimes me shake out and leave me home town
> And that's when me travel a East London
> Where I have to speak as a different man
> So that the cockney can understand
> [. . .]
> Cockney say scarper, We say scatter
> Cockney say rabbit, We chatter
> [. . .]
> Cockney say Alright? We say Ites!
> We say pants, Cockney say strides
> Sweet as a nut, just level vibes. 'Sayin?

Race and class, says Gilroy, have different uses, different values, and indeed different functions even if on questions of labour and its abuse there is considerable overlap in meaning. But race, as it enters into cultural formations, ceases to be fixed, its walls crumble, it borrows and then transforms its

---

[43] Ibid., 169.   [44] Ibid., 195.   [45] Ibid.

borrowings. In creating new forms, it often displaces the old ones for both black and white speakers. The new forms that arise affect other diasporas too – in Britain notably the two dominant Asian diasporas, Indian and Pakistani, are both subject in equal measure to the semantics of the 'Paki'. In addressing modernity or even critiquing it, black and Asian British cultural productions have been faced with the task of both recovery of one's past and validation of one's present. Sadly, as Gilroy notes in his later critical study *Postcolonial Melancholia* (2005), the routes taken in expressive culture towards modernity and vibrant pleasures, interconnectedness, and hybridity have 'not been brought into politics or government'.[46] Conviviality (Gilroy's term) abounds, while the more formalised areas of culture, policymaking, govern-ance, and the law lag behind lived experience.

Whereas soul, disco, reggae, hip-hop, bebop, and swing, all primarily black forms, have entered British working-class subcultures, black British grime music has followed a more radically exclusive path (see Chapter 36). Grime is a twenty-first-century British music genre that draws on ragga, hip-hop, and rap but is musically more aggressive, its rapid breakbeats of 140 per minute complementing its more defiant and often racially charged rhetoric. The music of Dizzee Rascal [Dylan Kwabena Mills] (1984–) is exemplary of a different kind of engagement with Brah's diaspora space and a different imagining of Smiley Culture's cross-cultural Rastafarian optimism. A quick look at Dizzee Rascal's June 2017 livestreamed teaser trailer of his single 'Space' (by February 2018 already viewed by over two million on YouTube) shows how grime challenges Brah's benign diasporic space by changing the space's exclusivity and primacy as a privileged white domain.

> Ain't no point in playin' it safe
> Gotta know your role, better state your case
> When it all falls down better know your place
> Just give me three feet and an ounce of
> Space, space, space ...

Grime lyrics work on internal rhymes (ravage, damage, baggage, package; established, saddest; malice, fallacies, chalice, Alice; and many more) bor-rowed from the language of popular rap and urban subculture. Dizzee Rascal extends the rhymes to make the political point about racial exclusion from space, a point made all the more dramatic through space (and here one uses space in its extra-terrestrial sense) as the domain of imperialist strength. The

---

[46] Paul Gilroy, *Postcolonial Melancholia* (New York: Columbia University Press, 2005), 151.

latter is clearly designated by the voice of actual rocket lift off ("'Three, two, one, zero, and lift off' [. . .] "The first flight of the Orbiter Discovery"') and of John F. Kennedy ("'We choose to go to the moon [. . . and do the other things,] not because they are easy, but because they are hard'").

Grime's radical agenda finds echoes in black British LGBTQ writing, of which *Come Let Us Sing Anyway* (2017) by Leone Ross (1969–) may be read as an example (see Chapter 34). From this collection, three short stories can be isolated – 'Love Silk Food', 'Drag', and 'Minty Minty' – to show black British lives as lived British experience, lives both defiant and lost, lives that push beyond the boundaries of Lamming as well as Phillips. In 'Drag' Josephine reverizes 'trusting me in my own space',[47] a phrase that implies accommodation and ease with one's own body. Josephine will make her black body transsexual which, although black, will function within a charged sexual language, graphic in details, but defiantly human. The 'Other' as black body no longer sees itself in political, postcolonial terms (from Lamming to Gilroy this has been the case) but as the signifier of the new multicultural Britain. If 'Drag' signifies that new spirit, in 'Love Silk Food' Neecy Brown's Jamaican British body can find momentary solace from a loveless marriage in the cramped space of the London underground train where another passenger, travelling from Jamaica to visit his daughter and grandchild, gives her attention. 'Well, them tell me England people shy', he says. The triumphalism expressed in 'Drag' (this is my body, I can do what I want with it) is muted in these other stories. The chief character in 'Minty Minty', Jeannie, is remarkably like the author; she is a 'toubab', that is of white and black ancestry, who finds that her turn to Africa in search of her cultural roots leads to disappointment as she feels doubly cheated. Not fully accepted by Africans as black (although the fact that she has a black mother is a plus), she is accused of stealing a baby which she thought she had bought legitimately 'from the smiling woman for everything in her purse'.[48]

Writing within Diasporic Space

A distinction can be drawn between UK-born black and Asian British writers, who worked almost exclusively from within the diasporic space of Britain, and migrant writers, for example Lamming, Harris, and C. L. R. James, who (even in Britain) wrote with a greater sense of distance, as their starting point had always been some idea of a lost West Indian homeland. This is borne out

---

[47] Leone Ross, *Come Let Us Sing Anyway* (Leeds: Peepal Tree Press, 2017), 32.   [48] Ibid., 61.

by a telling passage in Hanif Kureishi's 1992 essay 'The Rainbow Sign', which captures the ambiguous nature of any narrative of 'belonging', the diasporic narrative that looks back and seeks a better place where the 'belonging' might be 'total': 'It is not difficult to see how much illusion and falsity there is in this view. How much disappointment and unhappiness might be involved in going "home" only to see the extent to which you have been formed by England and the depth of attachment you feel to the place, despite everything.[49] Kureishi (1954–) had to make a journey to his ancestral 'home-land', Pakistan, to discover on returning to England that he had come 'home [...] to my country'.[50] That said, the ever-recurring question 'Where do you come from?' remains annoyingly persistent in England (see Chapter 28).[51]

Kureishi echoes Salman Rushdie's 1982 essay 'The Empire Writes Back with a Vengeance', which requires a closer look.[52] Not born in Britain, Rushdie (1947–) could never claim England as his own in the same way as Kureishi could. Nevertheless, he too wished to embrace and claim it. Arriving in England barely aged fourteen, he made it his home, living there until he moved to New York in 1999. Rushdie begins with the metaphor of the *chamcha* (literally 'spoon' in Hindi and Urdu), the term used to describe those who sucked up to the Empire rulers and who were used by the British for effective indirect rule in many parts of the Empire. These *cham-chas*, however, were also the first Indian masters of English, a language they imitated rather well. But in doing so they could only mimic and imitate; at best they could parody; at worst they were appallingly derivative. Now there is a new breed, an assertive breed who, like the great masters before them

---

[49] Hanif Kureishi, 'The Rainbow Sign' in *London Kills Me: Three Screenplays and Four Essays* (London: Penguin Books, 1992), 35.

[50] Ibid., 32.

[51] Ibid., 33–4. A personal note is in order here. In 2016 I was invited by Murdoch University's Vice Chancellor for pre-Christmas drinks. Two other academics had entered the house before me and both spoke with Irish or Scottish accents. Upon my entry, however, even before I could introduce myself, the Vice Chancellor's husband (or partner) asked, 'Where do you come from?' I froze and replied 'Why do you ask? Wouldn't you rather like to know what I do?' Taken aback (I suspect the Vice Chancellor and her spouse were not prepared for such a retort from a 'wog') the Vice Chancellor, Finnish in origin, said 'I'm asked that question all the time', forgetting so easily that she could enter the grand white narrative of assimilation in ways in which I never could. Australian universities declare their multicultural ethos, their sense of inclusion, but in practice, if this example is in any way typical, one senses that even there the 'wog' remains a 'wog' and should be put in his place (especially if he sounds too 'white') and what better way of doing it than with the leading question 'Where do you come from?'

[52] Salman Rushdie, 'The Empire Writes Back with a Vengeance', *The Times* [London], 3 July 1982: 8.

who also came from 'elsewhere' – Melville and Joyce, for instance – are refashioning the English language by infusing it with new idioms and rhythms. Rushdie concludes: 'In the work of Mustapha Matura, Hanif Kureishi and the reggae poet Linton Kwesi Johnson, the new voice is beginning to emerge; but there's still a lot of work to be done, and with other implements than spoons.'[53] 'And V. S. Naipaul,' writes Rushdie elsewhere, 'by now, is something else entirely'.[54] As noted in my introductory remarks, Naipaul (1932–2018) was an early presence on *Caribbean Voices*. Rushdie's aside penetratingly suggests that Naipaul himself stands apart in the context of black and Asian British writing. Especially inasmuch as his writing separated the East Indian experience from that of the black West Indian, as his father Seepersad Naipaul had done before him in his Indo-Trinidadian tales, often read on the BBC Caribbean Service by his son. This is a pity as the shadow of Naipaul, even in its inadmissible form, fell on both black British and Asian British writing. His corpus has been generically diffuse, his observations on writing and cultural norms often unacceptable to many, but his is a towering presence in any discussion of alliances between writer and critic. In his short monograph on writing (*Reading and Writing*, 2000) he notes that he turned to fiction to transform his material (often painful, often based on memory) to make it accessible to an alien British sensibility, an act not uncommon among other West Indian writers. In the end, though, the novel form itself was no longer capable of representing his own experience as a displaced writer, Naipaul comments, echoing Wilson Harris. 'It is the vanity of the age (and of commercial promotion)', he observes, 'that the novel continues to be literature's final and highest expression'.[55]

Conclusion

Necessarily selective, this chapter on dialogues between literature, cultural theory, and criticism has developed a productive explanatory model of current black and Asian British writing which eschews the familiar binary of particularism versus universalism. Instead it proposes to read culture against the grain, that is to read culture and people's investment in it as the condition of what has been called the mutually entangled space of diaspora, the space of the cultural logic of translation, the mark of the place of the incommensurable. It follows, then – to rephrase Stuart Hall – that the terms

[53] Ibid.   [54] Salman Rushdie, *Imaginary Homelands* (London: Granta, 1991), 17.
[55] V. S. Naipaul, *Reading and Writing* (New York: New York Review of Books, 2000), 63.

'black' and 'Asian' have to be disarticulated from their 'older discursive configuration' and placed in 'the deconstructive moment'.[56] This deconstructive moment has been the subtext of the 'writer-as-critic' discussed in this chapter. It is the moment when one subverts 'positive concepts [. . .] in order to think with' them, 'rather than waiting for some new dispensation' such as another language.[57] The writer as critic bends language beyond recognition so that what might be silenced by the English language becomes sayable. In his influential work *Beyond a Boundary*, C. L. R. James said that race, caste, and class have stimulated West Indian cricket. As one 'entered the sporting arena' one left behind the 'sordid compromises of everyday existence'. It was on the field that 'selected individuals played representative roles [. . .] charged with social significance'.[58] Years before, in 1942, Marson possibly felt the same even if, in that panopticon space then occupied by the great modernists, she may have had to work from a prepared script because the gaze of the pre-eminent modernists was so strong. And yet, from Marson through Lamming, Harris, Walcott, and more recently Leone Ross and the grime lyricists, a clear pattern begins to emerge, as all these writers negotiate what Hall called (invoking the French theorist Derrida) the 'spectrum of *différance*, in which disjunctures of time, generation, spatialization and dissemination refuse to be neatly aligned'.[59] Visible minorities will carry the mark of diaspora, their 'vernacular cosmopolitanism' (after Bhabha), which imposes another burden on them in that their relationship to the past will always have to be a critical one. In contemporary black and Asian British writing, modernity continues to create a dynamic space for cultural diversity, a rejection of exclusionary closure in all cultural representations rather than a turn to regressive absolutisms.

---

[56] Stuart Hall, 'Cultural Composition', 229. [57] Ibid., 230.
[58] James, *Beyond a Boundary*, 66.
[59] Stuart Hall, 'Conclusion: The Multi-Cultural Question', 227.

24

Forging Connections
Anthologies, Collectives, and the Politics of Inclusion

NICOLA L. ABRAM

The late twentieth century saw a remarkable phase of collaborative activity by writers of black and Asian heritage in Britain. Individuals worked together to share resources and secure audiences, in groups configured by location or common identity. This was also a period of concentrated anthologising; such publications were often a direct output of specific collectives. This chapter reflects on the politics of inclusion – the complex questions of definition, naming, and participation – that inform these rich histories. Inevitably, such a task involves its own acts of exclusion and omission; this chapter cannot pretend to offer an exhaustive account. Not only are the following pages necessarily finite in scope, but some source material is simply unavailable: various texts are out of print, and some of the information in circulation is contradictory. Instead, this chapter seeks to signal the range and diversity of the field it surveys – echoing a sentiment expressed in many of the anthologies discussed.

Developing and Defining the Field

The habitual celebration of particular literary figures (such as Salman Rushdie and Zadie Smith) obscures the broader picture of black and Asian arts activity in Britain. As James Procter laments, such 'solitary writers [. . .] have almost been canonised out of, or at least seem peculiarly resistant to, incorporation within a communal black British framework'.[1] To correct the over-representation of such individuals, this chapter remembers some of the many relevant writers' groups, theatre companies, and other arts co-operatives, informed by and examining some of their collective publications.

---

[1] James Procter (ed.), *Writing Black Britain 1948–1998: An Interdisciplinary Anthology* (Manchester: Manchester University Press, 2000), 6.

Perhaps the earliest of these groups was the All-India Progressive Writers' Association, formed in London in 1935.[2] Although many members were resident in England the association focused on Indian literature and politics, looking to India as home: founding member Sajjad Zaheer returned there in 1936, taking the organisation with him. As earlier chapters in this volume demonstrate, there followed a dramatic increase in migration from both South Asia and the Caribbean in the years after World War II, as Commonwealth citizens encouraged by the 1948 Nationality Act 'voyaged in'. It took some time before these new Britons began to organise politically, and required a shift in self-perception: from migrant workers in a temporary home to permanent citizens planning a future. Specific – and, sadly, tragic – events were eventually to catalyse action: the vicious attacks by so-called 'Teddy Boys' against members of the Caribbean population in Notting Hill in 1958, to which Trinidad-born activist Claudia Jones responded by organising the first Carnival; the racist murder of Gurdip Singh Chaggar in Southall in 1976, after which Jatinder Verma founded British Asian theatre company Tara Arts. Most of the early organisations focused directly on addressing community issues rather than developing creative practices – though the Organisation of Women of Asian and African Descent (founded in 1978) did incorporate poetry readings as part of their conferences.[3] The cultural historian Kwesi Owusu records the growth of a 'rich infrastructure of community self-help projects, supplementary schools, advice centres, study groups and campaigns [. . .] newspapers or news sheets [. . .] workshops and stalls in the community'.[4] Such groups gathered by necessity, working towards a common goal; their shared experiences of racism preceded and produced their (racialised) collectives.

The 1960s saw the formation of the Caribbean Artists Movement in 1966 (see Chapter 15) along with the earliest anthologies of writings by black and Asian Britons. Many of these first publications prioritised poetry: examples include P. L. Brent's *Young Commonwealth Poets '65* (1965) and John Figueroa's *Caribbean Voices: An Anthology of West Indian Poetry* (1966). The titles of these texts not only describe the content but name the contributors' relation to Britain, using identities particular to the emigrant such as 'Caribbean',

---

[2] Ruvani Ranasinha, *South Asian Writers in Twentieth-Century Britain: Culture in Translation* (Oxford: Clarendon Press, 2007), 19, 39; see also Chapter 6 of this volume.

[3] Beverley Bryan, Stella Dadzie, and Suzanne Scafe, *The Heart of the Race* (London: Virago, 1985), 208–9.

[4] Kwesi Owusu, *The Struggle for Black Arts in Britain: What Can We Consider Better than Freedom* (London: Comedia, 1986), 58.

'Commonwealth', 'Africa', and 'Asia'. Such terms subsume allegiance to a singular nation, mobilising instead a political solidarity with which to speak back to post-imperial Britain. Brent's anthology, for example, gathered works by writers from the diverse locations of Australia, India, New Zealand, Northern Ireland, Pakistan, Sri Lanka, and Zambia, among others. Demonstrating the struggle for appropriate terminology, a phase of some awkward collocations ensued: examples include the idiosyncratic 'Westindian-British' adopted by James Berry for his 1984 poetry anthology *News for Babylon*.

Perhaps inevitably, London was a centre for this collaborative activity. Its migrant populations enjoyed a liberal political climate shaped by the Greater London Council (led by Labour from 1973 to 1977 and from 1981 to 1986) and relatively ready funding from the Greater London Arts Association (1966–1996).[5] But beyond the capital other artists were also forging connections. To promote black writers in the north-west Lemn Sissay formed Cultureword – a sub-group of the writing development association Commonword – in Manchester in 1986. Out of Cultureword came Identity writers' group and the women's collective BlackScribe. Manchester was also home to Black Arts Alliance (BAA), formed in 1985, which curated mixed-media shows and ran training events and conferences; BAA's legacy continues today in the form of National Black Arts Alliance, which maintains a library and resource centre in Manchester dedicated to documenting black arts in the region. In Liverpool the black women's theatre company Assati was formed, whose productions included *Soul Sisters Melody* (1993, Everyman Theatre, directed by Deborah Yhip). Birmingham enjoyed ten years of Brumhalata Intercultural Storytelling Theatre (1996–2006), founded by Vayu Naidu. One of the longest-running South Asian arts organisations is Kala Sangam in Leeds, which maintains a successful arts centre today. Recognising the importance of regional outreach, the Asian Women Writers' Collective (1984–1997) pioneered a postal membership service so that writers outside London could receive feedback on their work; as a result, their 1994 anthology *Flaming Spirit* features stories authored in Sheffield, Birmingham, Manchester, and Cardiff.[6]

The 1980s witnessed a significant shift in self-identification, as both arts collectives and anthologies adopted the (often capitalised) term 'black'.

---

[5] See Chapter 17 where Gail Low details the appeal of postwar London for writers and artists seeking metropolitan as well as local audiences.

[6] Rukhsana Ahmad and Rahila Gupta (eds.), *Flaming Spirit: Stories from the Asian Women Writers' Collective* (London: Virago, 1994), xiii.

This functioned as a strategically inclusive description of all who shared experiences of racism in Britain – rather than a common origin, and regardless of wide-ranging histories and heritages. As one interviewee asserts in *The Heart of the Race: Black Women's Lives in Britain* (1985), the term 'doesn't describe skin colour, it defines our situation here in Britain. We're here as a result of British imperialism, and our continued oppression in Britain is the result of British racism.'[7] In this understanding, 'black' was an identity to be consciously claimed rather than a biogenetic fact. It was a contextualised response to a prior problem, rather than an articulation of an ahistorical essence. Although the term remained subject to continuous critique, it functioned as a necessary fiction – an example of what Gayatri Chakravorty Spivak has memorably termed 'strategic essentialism' – serving to effect unity and solidarity.[8] As Rhonda Cobham observes of the Indian, African, and Caribbean-heritage contributors to her co-edited collection *Watchers and Seekers: Creative Writing by Black Women in Britain* (1987), 'the further the writers got from "Home" the more responsive they seemed to become to the possibilities of interconnection between a range of Black voices that extended far beyond their immediate cultural experience'.[9] The concept of a diasporic 'black' community indexed a further shift in status for Britain's migrant populations and their descendants, towards a self-consciously oppositional stance. As Fred D'Aguiar explains of his 'black British' section in *The New British Poetry* (1988), the term articulates 'a strong sense of being "other" than what is lauded as indigenous and capitally British'.[10]

This inclusive use of the term 'black' worked not only to promote horizontal allegiances among peer populations in Britain, but also to compress history and geography. In Paul Anthony's poem 'The History Maker' – collected in the anthology *Times Like These* (1988), produced by the Obatala publishing collective, of which Sandra Agard was a member[11] – the shared designation 'black' enables the speaker to identify across centuries and

---

[7] Bryan et al., *The Heart of the Race*, 170.

[8] Gayatri Chakravorty Spivak, 'Subaltern Studies: Deconstructing Historiography' in *In Other Worlds: Essays in Cultural Politics* (New York; London: Routledge, 1988), 197–221; 205.

[9] Rhonda Cobham, 'Introduction' in Rhonda Cobham and Merle Collins (eds.), *Watchers and Seekers: Creative Writing by Black Women in Britain* (London: Women's Press, 1987), 3–11; 9.

[10] Fred D'Aguiar, 'Black British Poetry' in Gillian Allnutt (ed.), *The New British Poetry 1968–1988* (London: Paladin, 1988), 3–4; 3.

[11] Cobham and Collins (eds.), *Watchers and Seekers*, 154.

continents with the citizens of ancient Egypt, Greece, and Israel.[12] This practice was not reserved only for the poetic imagination; the editors of the sociological study *The Heart of the Race* adopt the first person plural 'we' in their historical introduction, collating the experiences of centuries of black people across Africa and the Caribbean. This collective identity inscribes an enduring connection between the people of the diaspora, and asserts continuing resistance to the spectrum of white supremacist violence, from historical European colonialism and practices of enslavement to the related hostility of postwar Britain.

But the experiential usefulness of the term 'black' proved limited; while it powerfully aligns those who share the experience of racism, lived experience also demands recognition of the specificity of nation, language, culture, and religion. Resistance to the subsuming effects of the term 'black' gradually grew, among British Asians in particular. The Asian Women Writers' Collective chose not to include 'black' as part of its designation when it formed in 1987,[13] and in 1988 the Commission for Racial Equality advised that the term should no longer be used to describe people of South Asian origin. No term is totally stable, however, and 'South Asian' has also been interpreted variously; in *The Redbeck Anthology of British South Asian Poetry* (2000) its usage refers not only to poets from India, Pakistan, Bangladesh, and Sri Lanka but also to those from Caribbean and African countries with a significant Indian population, justifying the inclusion of the Guyanese writers David Dabydeen and Zorina Ishmail-Bibby.

Despite such usages passionately dividing opinion, some post-millennial anthologies continue to invest in a political definition of 'black'. Most recently, the term features in the titles of Peepal Tree's *Filigree: Contemporary Black British Poetry* (2018) and its earlier partner anthology *Closure: Contemporary Black British Short Stories* (2015). Contributors to the latter include Monica Ali, born in Bangladesh, and Lynne E. Blackwood, who self-describes as Anglo-Indian. Editor Jacob Ross does not discuss his operative definition of the titular term, commenting instead that anxiety over identity has faded.[14] Such attempts to refocus public debate may be motivated to make new conversations possible, and heterogeneous solidarity certainly remains vital. However, given the racialised fissures widening in the

---

[12] Paul Anthony, 'The History Maker' in Obatala Press (ed.), *Times Like These* (London: Black Rose, 1988), 40.

[13] Ranasinha, *South Asian Writers*, 60.

[14] Jacob Ross (ed.), *Closure: Contemporary Black British Short Stories* (Leeds: Inscribe, 2015), 11.

contemporary world – the inhumane treatment of people fleeing conflict zones in the Middle East to seek refuge elsewhere; the impenitent displays of Islamophobia by the 45th President of the United States of America – nuanced discussions of 'race' and racism seem more necessary than ever.

Anthologising as Activism

With a shared identity established – however provisional – arts collectives sought to cultivate appropriate audiences. Anthologies proved a particularly popular medium, demanding little prior knowledge and introducing readers to a body of work at relatively low cost. Anthologies establish both presence and credence; as Barbara Korte has observed, they 'shape readers' conceptions of what [literature] is (or is not)'.[15] Some black and Asian writers were included in mainstream anthologies, giving guaranteed access to a white audience; Korte comments of *The New British Poetry* (1988), for example, that it 'helped to establish "Black" poets as a voice in British poetry'.[16] But between 1970 and 2000 more than sixty anthologies of black British and Asian British writing were published, making this visible as a substantial, cohesive, and independent literary field. The urgency was palpable. Such publications were understood as a political intervention, a necessary response to the under-representation and misrepresentation of Britain's black and Asian populations. As the publishing collective Black Womantalk (established in 1983) expressly stated, its mission was to 'creat[e] the space and the means for our voice to be heard'.[17] An anthology can be understood as a form of public protest; its chorus of voices is the literary equivalent of a mass of people demonstrating in the street.

Anthologies promote writings that may otherwise go unpublished, and preserve those which may otherwise become ephemeral. T. S. Eliot recognised the format to be important for those he called the 'minor poets', though we might also understand *minority* writers as particularly at risk of being forgotten – especially those published by specialist presses, with a small circulation, in texts unlikely to be reprinted.[18] Anthologies thus fulfil the

---

[15] Barbara Korte, 'Flowers for the Picking: Anthologies of Poetry in (British) Literary and Cultural Studies' in Barbara Korte, Ralf Schneider, and Stefanie Lethbridge (eds.), *Anthologies of British Poetry: Critical Perspectives from Literary and Cultural Studies* (Amsterdam: Rodopi, 2000), 1–32; 7.

[16] Korte, 'Flowers', 11.

[17] Da Choong, Olivette Cole Wilson, Bernardine Evaristo, and Gabriela Pearse (eds.), *Black Women Talk Poetry* (London: Black Womantalk, 1987), 7.

[18] T. S. Eliot, 'What is Minor Poetry?', *Sewanee Review*, 54:1 (1946): 1–18; 2.

first objective of cultural production, as identified in Stuart Hall's famous essay 'New Ethnicities': 'the question of *access* to the rights to representation'.[19] The emphasised term also appears in Zhana's introduction to *Sojourn* (1988), an anthology motivated 'to provide access to publishing for women who might not otherwise have it'.[20] Unfortunately the publishing industry has not changed substantively in the decades since these statements; in her introduction to *Ten: New Poets* (2010) Bernardine Evaristo identifies continuing barriers, including the enduring expectation that a writer will represent 'The Black Voice'.[21] Refusing this and other burdens, anthologies return control directly to black and Asian writers and their advocates. Along with independent presses and publishing networks (see Chapter 17), anthologies provide visibility and vital means of self-representation.

What anthologies achieved through publication and print circulation, performance poetry accomplished with a live audience. This immediate and relatively inexpensive platform offered poets the opportunity to connect directly with their publics. The Radical Alliance of Poets and Players (RAPP) was founded in 1972 by Jamal Ali, to produce group-devised poetry, drama, and music rooted in the Brixton environment. Importantly, its work had an audience of both fellow Caribbean migrants and the white British population.[22] Another collective, African Dawn, was formed in the 1980s to recover the pan-African principles of orature in reaction to the western privileging of the written word. As the Wazalendo Players it mounted several productions including Ngũgĩ wa Thiong'o and Micere Githae Mugo's *The Trial of Dedan Kimathi*, performed at London's Africa Centre in 1984. African Dawn also issued cassette recordings of poetry recitals with musical accompaniment.[23] Co-founder Kwesi Owusu recalls that audience interaction was vital to the collective's work, as part of the process of developing a piece and in the form of spontaneous commentary and invited call-and-response during the resulting production.[24] Engaging directly with audiences politicised the community and began a dialogue that could be continued in

---

[19] Stuart Hall, 'New Ethnicities' in David Morley and Kuan-Hsing Chen (eds.), *Stuart Hall: Critical Dialogues in Cultural Studies* (New York: Routledge, 1996), 441–9; 442. Emphasis original.

[20] Zhana, 'Introduction' in Zhana (ed.), *Sojourn* (London: Methuen, 1988), 11–33; 19.

[21] Bernardine Evaristo, 'Introduction' in Bernardine Evaristo and Daljit Nagra (eds.), *Ten: New Poets* (Tarset: Bloodaxe Books, 2010), 11–16; 13.

[22] James Berry (ed.), *News for Babylon: The Chatto Book of Westindian-British Poetry* (London: Chatto & Windus, 1984), 211.

[23] Owusu, *Struggle for Black Arts*, n.p.; Kwesi Owusu (ed.), *Storms of the Heart: An Anthology of Black Arts and Culture* (London: Camden Press, 1988), 303.

[24] Owusu (ed.), *Storms of the Heart*, 303.

print. In some cases live poetry events were a necessary precursor to publication: as the editors of *Black Women Talk Poetry* (1987) recall, 'We held several open readings for Black women and slowly they were persuaded to part with their writings.'[25] The same editors ran a more formal programme of short-story writing courses, funded by Greater London Arts, to develop material for their next collection.[26]

Grouping contributors by their shared experience of racism in Britain gave anthologies a didactic purpose: to educate a naive audience. As Earl Lovelace wrote in his cover note for *Burning Words, Flaming Images: Poems and Short Stories by Writers of African Descent* (1996), the poems sought to ignite 'an aesthetic fire that will announce their presence certainly to Britain'.[27] Similarly, one of the few commonalities Fred D'Aguiar admits of his eclectic selection of black British poetry is that 'All these poets have a sense of public address.'[28] The lesson of some texts was self-conscious and clearly stated. For example, *Merely a Matter of Colour* (1973) – an anthology of Ugandan Asian prose and poetry – responded directly to the 1968 Immigration Act, which prohibited Asians expelled from East Africa from entering Britain. The collection was explicit in its efforts to 'contest media stereotyping',[29] defuse popular misconceptions, and disprove unfavourable and exaggerated reports.[30] The unnamed author of the introduction to *Black and Priceless: The Power of Black Ink* (1988) also demanded a particular perspective of its readers: to '"read" the thoughts between the lines and see the ways in which racism affects our lives'.[31] Other anthologies educated indirectly, inducting readers into unfamiliar worlds by glossing non-English terms and non-canonical cultural references.

The audience imagined by anthologists was not always antagonistic: some editors address their collections to ancestors or global contemporaries. In the foreword to *Times Like These* (1988) Edward Kamau Brathwaite positions the contributors as writing back to peers still resident in the Caribbean,

---

[25] Da Choong et al. (eds.), *Black Women Talk*, 8.
[26] Black Womantalk Collective, 'Introduction' in Da Choong, Olivette Cole Wilson, Sylvia Parker, and Gabriela Pearse (eds.), *Don't Ask Me Why: An Anthology of Short Stories by Black Women* (London: Black Womantalk, 1991), v–vi; v.
[27] Earl Lovelace in Kadija Sesay (ed.), *Burning Words, Flaming Images: Poems and Short Stories by Writers of African Descent* (London: SAKS, 1996), n.p.
[28] D'Aguiar, 'Black British Poetry', 4.
[29] Deirdre Osborne (ed.), *The Cambridge Companion to British Black and Asian Literature (1945–2010)* (Cambridge: Cambridge University Press, 2016), xv.
[30] Ranasinha, *South Asian Writers*, 52.
[31] Anonymous, 'Introduction' in Rushiraj Munshi, Valerie Bloom, Fiona Walker, and Fitz Lewis (eds.), *Black and Priceless: The Power of Black Ink* (Manchester: Crocus, 1988), xii–xiii; xii.

attempting to maintain an aesthetic connection across the diaspora.[32] Anthologies mediate between cultures, symbolically compressing the distance travelled by migrants themselves.

Other anthologies address peers closer to home. Editor Zhana presents *Sojourn* (1988) as a tool to educate fellow black women, cautioning that 'she who does not learn from others' experience will be condemned to repeat it'.[33] One contributor to *Black and Priceless*, Nayaba Aghebo, similarly sought 'to strike a chord of unity with the [. . .] Black readers of this book'.[34] Introducing *Motherlands: Black Women's Writing from Africa, the Caribbean and South Asia* (1991), Susheila Nasta advises that 'women writers living in Britain need to mother each other into a solid literary community'.[35] Some such texts supply their readers with specific tools to facilitate this work: *Sojourn* ends with a list of community groups, while *Motherlands* points towards other published sources of comfort and insight, listing recent anthologies that 'focus on the collective elements of women's experience'.[36] Other texts hoped their readers would go on to participate in the act of writing. The introduction to *Flaming Spirit* (1994) celebrates the growth and diversification of membership precipitated by the previous publication of the Asian Women Writers' Collective.[37] Editor Kadija George presents the contributors to *Six Plays by Black and Asian Women Writers* (1993) as 'models' for 'Young Black women [. . .] to look towards', considering the book part of a wider outreach effort to schools by writers and performers.[38] Some writings by children and young adults were incorporated into other anthologies: *Black and Priceless* included four young writers aged from fourteen.[39]

Many anthologies inscribe educating the next generation as an explicit motivation. Representatives from Centerprise – a publisher, community centre, and specialist bookshop in Hackney – commend *Breaking the Silence* (1984) for its potential use in schools to prompt dialogue between pupils of Asian and non-Asian backgrounds, as well as in Asian families to facilitate understanding between the generations.[40] A few collections were compiled specifically for young people; editor Grace Nichols describes *Black Poetry*

---

[32] Edward Kamau Brathwaite, 'Foreword' in Obatala Press (ed.), *Times Like These*, 7.

[33] Zhana (ed.), *Sojourn*, 32.

[34] Nayaba Aghebo, 'Biography' in Munshi et al. (ed.), *Black and Priceless*, 91.

[35] Susheila Nasta (ed.), *Motherlands* (London: Women's Press, 1991), xxviii.

[36] Nasta (ed.), *Motherlands*, xxviii–xxix.   [37] Ahmad and Gupta (eds.), *Flaming Spirit*, xi.

[38] Kadija George, 'Introduction' in Kadija George (ed.), *Six Plays by Black and Asian Women Writers* (London: Aurora Metro, 1993), 5–7; 5.

[39] See Chapter 33.

[40] Centerprise Trust, 'Preface' in *Breaking the Silence: Writing by Asian Women* (London: Centerprise, 1984), n.p.

(1988) as an effort to correct the 'omission and neglect [of black writers] by the literary establishment'.[41] Such activity follows in the tradition of Kenneth Ramchand and Cecil Gray's *West Indian Poetry: An Anthology for Schools* (1971, 1989), which not only brings the selected poems to the attention of teachers and their pupils but also attempts to educate that audience in how to read: the editors offer commentary and questions for each set of poems, and advise 'repeated oral readings' in the classroom.[42]

By the 1980s, cognisance of gender politics had fractured the provisional unity of the umbrella term 'Black' and subject matter was increasing in specificity. Several anthologies and periodicals dedicated to women emerged, often associated with particular organisations: Brixton Black Women's Group (1973–1985) produced the newsletter *Speak Out*; OWAAD produced *FOWAAD!*; Black Womantalk (1983–1991) published *Black Women Talk Poetry* (1987) and *Don't Ask Me Why: An Anthology of Short Stories by Black Women* (1991). Female writers and editors rapidly became a numeric majority. It is clear that women performed much of the work to establish a black British identity that is now readily recognised in the official language of censuses, even if not yet reflected in equal access to the privileges of citizenship.

The differentiation of gay and lesbian voices brought further diversification. These increasingly specific political agendas not only exposed the fragility of an inclusive 'black' identity but also motivated acts of solidarity with other intersecting groups from beyond the black and Asian communities. For example, Jackie Kay's writing found a comfortable home in anthologies like *Stepping Out: Short Stories on Friendships Between Women* (1986) and *Beautiful Barbarians: Lesbian Feminist Poetry* (1987), and her play *Chiaroscuro* was given a rehearsed reading by Gay Sweatshop in 1985 before being produced by Theatre of Black Women in 1986.

Post-millennial anthologies demonstrate a definite – perhaps even defiant – distance from the earlier motivation of explicit anti-racist education. Kwame Dawes's *Red* (2010) playfully announces itself as 'a different kind of anthology'.[43] Its constitutive poems are united not by the self-reflexive subject of blackness in Britain but instead variously interpret the title colour: as symbolic of passion, anger, blood, and violence; as a prompt for particular images; and as an allusion to a Caribbean term for a particular shade of skin

---

[41] Grace Nichols (ed.), *Black Poetry* (London: Blackie, 1988), 7.

[42] Kenneth Ramchand and Cecil Gray, 'Foreword' in Kenneth Ramchand and Cecil Gray (eds.), *West Indian Poetry: An Anthology for Schools* (Harlow: Longman, 1971), n.p.

[43] Kwame Dawes, *Red: Contemporary Black British Poetry* (Leeds: Peepal Tree Press, 2010).

and presumed lineage.[44] Similarly, submissions to *Closure* responded to the title of the proposed anthology rather than centring on their authors' identities.[45]

Writing as Warfare

For many members of collectives and contributors to anthologies, writing was an act of social survival: it enabled their experiences to be heard. Zhana explicitly invited biographical readings of her 1988 edited collection: '*Sojourn* is a record of some of the many-sided experiences of some Black women in Britain.'[46] As Kobena Mercer recognised, it was important that many such stories were collated: 'Collaborative writing was a strategic means of interruption, or *breaking the silence* as we used to say, in which the act of publication makes public experiences that have been lived as privatised, individualised and pathologised *problems*.'[47] The phrase 'breaking the silence' circulated repeatedly, becoming a call to arms – or to anthologise: it named a book published by Centerprise in 1984, collecting anonymised writings detailing the personal experiences of Asian women living in Britain, and also titled a section in Susheila Nasta's edited collection of critical essays, *Motherlands*.[48]

Editors also broke the formal convention of 'criticizing in silence' advocated of anthologies by Arthur Quiller-Couch.[49] The objective presentation of uncontextualised texts is arguably appropriate only for writers whose status *as* writers is uncontested. In the 1980s, with black and Asian people still battling in many ways simply to be recognised as British, many editors took the opportunity to assert their contributors' authorial status explicitly. Rukhsana Ahmad and Rahila Gupta describe *Flaming Spirit* as part of 'an ongoing process of recognition of Asian women writers'.[50] Pratibha Parmar and Sona Osman commend the four contributors to *A Dangerous Knowing: Four Black Women Poets* (1984) for their 'courage' in identifying themselves as poets.[51] The collective Black Womantalk similarly acknowledge the

---

[44] For a discussion of this anthology see Chapter 31.   [45] Ross (ed.), *Closure*, 12.

[46] Zhana (ed.), *Sojourn*, 33.

[47] Kobena Mercer, 'Back to My Routes: A Postscript to the 1980s' in Procter (ed.), *Writing Black Britain*, 285–93; 288. Emphasis original.

[48] Nasta (ed.), *Motherlands*, 1.

[49] Arthur Quiller-Couch, 'Preface' in Arthur Quiller-Couch (ed.), *The Oxford Book of English Verse* (Oxford: Oxford University Press, 1953), vii–xi; viii.

[50] Ahmad and Gupta (eds.), *Flaming Spirit*, vii.

[51] Pratibha Parmar and Sona Osman, 'Introduction' in Barbara Burford, Gabriela Pearse, Grace Nichols, and Jackie Kay, *A Dangerous Knowing: Four Black Women Poets* (London: Sheba, 1984), vii–ix; vii.

'courageous act' of black women submitting their writing to a publisher,[52] while the editors of *Breaking the Silence* thank contributors for their 'bravery'.[53] Framing commentaries by established authors further validate the contributors as part of a literary coterie. *Black and Priceless* begins with a preface by Benjamin Zephaniah, who had by then published two poetry collections and was celebrated on the performance circuit. Audre Lorde endorsed *A Dangerous Knowing*, writing that the poems 'give me something I need, an affirmation of myself as a black woman, feminist, poet'.[54] In Deirdre Osborne's collections of plays *Hidden Gems* (2008; 2012), each playtext is preceded by a critical essay or interview, establishing the writers as part of a scholarly community.[55] Just as arts collectives and anthologies participated in the naming and evolution of shared identities, the act of publication ascribed to the contributors the status of 'author'.

The anthology form usefully provides 'a window for new writers' – to borrow a phrase from Kadija Sesay's introduction to *Burning Words, Flaming Images*.[56] Note, though, that the meaning of the term 'new' has been curiously fluid; Evaristo frames *Ten* as a collection that 'showcases [the writers'] promise and talent', despite the fact that these eponymous 'new poets' had all been published previously in magazines or pamphlets.[57] Anthologies published in the 1980s frequently included work by people who had no previous publishing record. They often included personal biographies (remarking on place of birth, education, and family life) and were sometimes illustrated with portrait photographs. This paratextual material gave a vivid snapshot of contemporary cultural activism but it also acted as a chronological freeze-frame, producing a rather unfortunate sense of black British and Asian British writing as belonging to a perpetual present – as if it is *always* 'new'. As James Procter notes, there has been 'a pervasive "forgetfulness" within the field'.[58] Few of those anthologised writers went on to publish individually, leaving the impression of a mass of authors suddenly disappearing. It should be noted, though, that many had been included as a result of special circumstances – such as participation in short courses or competitions – rather than out of a sustained commitment to professional writing. For

---

[52] Da Choong et al. (eds.), *Don't Ask Me Why*, v.

[53] Centerprise Trust, *Breaking the Silence*, n.p.

[54] Audre Lorde in Burford et al., *A Dangerous Knowing*, outside rear cover.

[55] Deirdre Osborne, 'Introduction' in Deirdre Osborne (ed.), *Hidden Gems: Contemporary Black British Plays* (London: Oberon, 2008), 7–16; 12.

[56] Kadija Sesay, 'Introduction' in Sesay (ed.), *Burning Words*, n.p.

[57] Evaristo (ed.), *Ten*, 15.

[58] James Procter, 'General Introduction' in Procter (ed.), *Writing Black Britain*, 1–12; 8–9.

example, a number of the contributions to *Black and Priceless* originated as entries to a creative writing competition organised by Cultureword in 1986. Historians of black and Asian writing would therefore do well to recall that the process of enabling people to publicly come to voice was as significant as the resulting publications.

Rather than publishing work by new writers, some anthologies sought to inscribe a historical tradition. Of those collecting previously published pieces, Lynette Goddard's *The Methuen Drama Book of Plays by Black British Writers* (2011) is exemplary; it brings together six plays first produced between 1979 and 2007, selected from the several generations of black British playwrights.[59] In other cases editors articulated a literary lineage in their introductions. Yvonne Brewster's first (1987) collection of black British plays catalogues recent performances by black actors and productions of works by black playwrights while her second (1989) collection constructs a record dating back to 1907, listing a series of touchstones with the urgency of establishing a new canon.[60] Debjani Chatterjee's introduction to *The Redbeck Anthology of British South Asian Poetry* looks further back,[61] offering 1794 as the primary moment for British South Asian literature with reference to Sake Dean Mahomed.[62] James Berry's *News for Babylon* provides a brief history of plantation culture to explain the contemporary use of creole, before tracing some key literary figures and forms from the eighteenth-century Jamaican Francis Williams to the dialect verse of Louise Bennett. Editors recognised their anthologies as constituting literary history, too; Berry's *Bluefoot Traveller* (1976) was revised and reissued in 1981 'to rectify previous omissions', correcting the lack of female contributors and writers born in Britain.[63]

What unites anthologies across the decades is the editors' insistence on the diversity of the contributors and their texts. Bhikhu Parekh affirms that his 1974 study 'show[s] that immigrants do not constitute a solid and cohesive group thinking and feeling alike on the issues affecting their life'.[64] Zephaniah celebrates the works collected in *Black and Priceless* as representing the 'many

---

[59] Lynette Goddard, 'Introduction' in Lynette Goddard (ed.), *The Methuen Drama Book of Plays by Black British Writers* (London: Methuen, 2011), vii–xxvi; xxv.

[60] Yvonne Brewster, 'Introduction' in Yvonne Brewster (ed.), *Black Plays: Two* (London: Methuen, 1989), vii–xiv.

[61] Debjani Chatterjee, 'Foreword' in Debjani Chatterjee (ed.), *The Redbeck Anthology of British South Asian Poetry* (Bradford: Redbeck, 2000), 11–12; 11. See also Chapter 31.

[62] There are different spellings of his name, ranging from Mahomed to Mahomet. Preferred usage here is Sake Dean Mahomed.

[63] James Berry (ed.), *Bluefoot Traveller* (London: Harrap, [1976] 1981), 6.

[64] Bhikhu Parekh, 'Introduction' in Bhikhu Parekh (ed.), *Colour, Culture and Consciousness: Immigrant Intellectuals in Britain* (London: George Allen & Unwin, 1974), 11–12; 11.

shades of Black'.[65] Evaristo writes that the poems selected for *Ten* 'cannot be reduced to [...] a homogeneous "black voice" or "Asian voice"'.[66] And Ross characterises *Closure* by its 'diversity of subject matter, and the varying stances of the writers'.[67] Grace Nichols expresses this sentiment with poetic vision:

> I can write
> no poem big enough
> to hold the essence
> of a black woman
> [...]
> and there are black women
> and black women
> like a contrasting sky
> of rainbow spectrum.[68]

Nichols's frequent repetition of 'black women' demonstrates that, despite a superficial sameness, meaning is dependent on context and is never identical from one line – or one person – to the next. This is analogous to the work of the anthology, and its associated collective: though gathered under one title, naming the contributors and members with an ostensibly fixed identity, what is contained within is multitudes.

Black British and Asian British anthologies have resisted the 'burden of representation', to use Kobena Mercer's term: the expectation that a single work by a minority figure can be read as representative of a whole community.[69] The anthology format is by definition 'a *mixtum composition*' – as Korte writes – 'whose assembled parts [...] have been woven together to form a new textual whole'.[70] Capable of containing diverse works, it gathers together that which is ostensibly alike precisely in order to reveal the 'profane differences' within.[71] The heterogeneity of the materials in any one anthology insists on the provisionality of the terms that title it, refusing any essentialist explanation. These fascinating texts can therefore be understood as actively articulating a Britain that is richer for its diversity and wiser for its complexity.

---

[65] Zephaniah, 'Preface' in Munshi et al. (eds.), *Black and Priceless*, ix.

[66] Evaristo (ed.), *Ten*, 15.   [67] Ross (ed.), *Closure*, 10.

[68] Grace Nichols, 'Of Course When They Ask for Poems about the "Realities" of Black Women' in Burford et al., *A Dangerous Knowing*, 48–50; 48.

[69] Kobena Mercer, 'Black Art and the Burden of Representation', *Third Text*, 4:10 (1990): 61–78.

[70] Korte, 'Flowers', 18.

[71] Paul Gilroy, *Small Acts: Thoughts on the Politics of Black Cultures* (London: Serpent's Tail, 1993), 1.

25

Reading the 'Black' in the 'Union Jack'

Institutionalising Black and Asian British Writing

ROGER BROMLEY

In February 2017, Reni Eddo-Lodge wrote that she was no longer going to engage with white people about race, adding that this did not refer to *all* white people but 'just the vast majority who refuse to accept the legitimacy of structural racism and its symptoms'.[1] Knowingly or not, her use of the term 'structural racism' evokes strong echoes of controversies around terminologies such as 'multiculturalism' and 'anti-racism' which had sparked debate in the 1970s and 1980s. Some, like the Institute for Race Relations (IRR), had made the case that multiculturalism with its emphasis on ethnic cultural forms did little to address the fundamental roots of systemic racism in British society. Three publications by the IRR in the 1980s – *Roots of Racism* (1982), *Patterns of Racism* (1982), and *How Racism Came to Britain* (1985) – attempted to teach about racism in accessible illustrated booklets. Popular with local education authorities, these provoked a predictable backlash from the New Right and Margaret Thatcher's government. Persistent attempts to undermine what was then dubbed 'the Anti-Racist Tendency' followed, loudly orchestrated by the media.

Anti-racism was seen at the time as a struggle at grassroots level by black and Asian working-class activists as part of a wider political engagement, not just of a change in attitudes. 'Structural racism' was never fully acknowledged, until, with the killing of Stephen Lawrence in 1993, a belated public inquiry conducted by Sir William Macpherson finally gave credibility to the concept of 'institutional racism', vindicating the long struggles of the anti-racist movement.[2] Not published until 1999, the turn of the century, Macpherson's important report declared that 'institutional racism had played

---

[1] Reni Eddo-Lodge, *i* [newspaper], 5 July 2017, n.p.

[2] Stephen Lawrence was an 18-year-old black British student killed by five young white men at a bus stop in Eltham on 22 April 1993. It took four years before the re-opened inquest on his death returned a verdict of unlawful killing. A public inquiry, headed by Sir William Macpherson, was ordered and the subsequent Macpherson Report was

a part in the flawed investigation by the police' and that 'there must be [. . .] unequivocal acceptance of institutional racism [. . .] before it can be addressed'.[3]

Regarded as a milestone in race relations in Britain, the Macpherson Report helped to change the environment in which black British and Asian British writing was produced.[4] There is obviously no direct correlation between this report and the persistent lack of recognition of black and Asian British writing across the twentieth century. But it could certainly be argued that the murder of Stephen Lawrence and the profile of the subsequent government enquiry provided the catalyst that gave rise to a public more receptive to recognising the structural inequalities across all industries and to issues of diversity, including across the publishing industry, arts, and culture.

The Macpherson Report touched the edge of a much bigger story. The 1970s and 1980s had witnessed the proliferation of a range of initiatives that sought to address manifest racialised inequalities in education, employment, and housing.[5] Some were specifically cultural, and originated in actions led by the Arts Council, the Inner London Education Authority (ILEA), and the Greater London Council (GLC), though the latter was suspended by the Conservative government in 1986. Alongside these more formal initiatives, evident in influential publications such as *The Arts Britain Ignores* (Naseem Khan, 1976), as well as the substantial Swann Report (1985), there was a gradual growth of publishing companies, journals, conferences, lobbying groups, and curriculum developments that attempted to give space and prominence to black and Asian British writers as part of the broader cultural landscape. For example, the GLC was the main funder for the first four issues of *Wasafiri*, now the 'magazine of international contemporary writing' but known then as the 'magazine of African, Caribbean, Asian and associated literatures'. London and other urban centres, such as Birmingham and Leeds, were also focal points for a range of dynamic community arts movements.[6] To varying degrees, all of these were committed to promoting multiculturalism and the arts. Interestingly, many of these

---

published in February 1999. It was not until 2012 that two of the original suspects were found guilty and sentenced to the equivalent of a life sentence.

[3] Jenny Bourne, 'The Life and Times of Institutional Racism', *Race & Class*, 43:2 (2001): 7–22; 7.

[4] Ibid., 13.

[5] *The Brixton Disorders, 10–12 April 1981: Report of an Inquiry by [. . .] Lord Scarman*, Cmnd.8427 (London: HMSO, 1981).

[6] *Wasafiri* is a quarterly literary magazine originally founded in 1984 as the ATCAL journal and published in the UK. It covers international contemporary writing and is now housed at Queen Mary University of London and co-published by Taylor & Francis.

developments evolved from the activities of particular groups or individuals in key educational institutions, or cultural centres, such as the British Council, the Africa Centre, the Minority Arts Advisory Service (MAAS), and other collectives detailed in previous chapters (see Chapters 17 and 24).[7]

Political protests against endemic racism and police harassment in the 1970s and 1980s were frequently focused in the first instance around the concerns of Britain's African and Caribbean communities. Most often provoked by the violence of far right racist gangs, discriminatory policing, and widespread inequalities, further uprisings and disturbances emerged from urban South Asian and Muslim areas in the late 1990s and new millennium. The 2001 Ouseley and Cantle Reports were attempts to investigate the causes of these uprisings. Both introduced the idea that white and Asian communities living in northern British towns – the main focus of both reports – were leading 'parallel lives'. Importantly, it was not a case of either community growing or moving away from the other, but that the two groups had developed separately in their own spheres. The findings of these reports saw the gradual replacement of the notion of 'multiculturalism' by 'cultural diversity' as official government policy.[8] The media and political debates around these fraught issues were accompanied by less direct literary responses, as Rehana Ahmed demonstrates in *Writing British Muslims: Religion, Class and Multiculturalism*.[9] The cultural and literary responses to the earlier 'disturbances' of the 1980s had largely placed emphasis on black British (of African heritage) experience, with far less attention paid in the first instance to British Asians. For example, the name of the charitable educational organisation ATCAL (discussed below) was an acronym originally referring primarily to Caribbean and African literature, with Asian and Associated Literatures only added in 1983.

As earlier chapters in this volume detail, a number of writers and intellectuals migrated to Britain from Africa, the Caribbean, and South Asia in the 1950s and 1960s. Many stayed on and became residents, publishing, as noted

[7] Naseem Khan, *The Arts Britain Ignores: The Arts of Ethnic Minorities in Britain* (London: Community Relations Commission, 1976); The Swann Report, Education for All – Report of the Committee of Inquiry into the Education of Children from Ethnic Minority Groups (London: HMSO, 1985).

[8] Ted Cantle, *Community Cohesion: A Report of the Independent Review Team* (London: Home Office, 2001). The Ouseley Report: Sir Herman Ouseley, 'Community Pride not Prejudice' (2001). Report commissioned by Bradford Vision, 2001.

[9] Rehana Ahmed, *Writing British Muslims: Religion, Class and Multiculturalism* (Manchester: Manchester University Press, 2015).

by Gail Low, in Britain (see Chapter 17). The volume of published work is apparent in the lists of established presses such as Heinemann, Longman, André Deutsch, and Faber, but also lesser-known independent publishers such as Allison & Busby (1967), New Beacon (1966), and Bogle-L'Ouverture (1968), who emerged partly to facilitate the creative works of these cultural communities and with a remit to publish Caribbean and, later, black British writers. John La Rose founded New Beacon Books and the George Padmore Institute, whose valuable archive now covers the black British experience from the 1960s to the 1990s.[10] The Institute of Race Relations launched the influential black political periodical *Race Today* (1969), published from 1973 by the Race Today Collective made up of a grouping influenced by C. L. R. James and George Padmore, who, like their predecessors, become major activists. Darcus Howe was *Race Today*'s first editor but the grouping included Farrukh Dhondy, who began his writing career there in 1970, later becoming a commissioning editor at Channel 4, and the poet Linton Kwesi Johnson, who joined in 1974. These activities were followed by several other initiatives, such as the launch of feminist houses, influenced by the growth of African American writing in the United States, the Women's Press (1978) and Sheba (1980).[11]

This chapter explores the emergence of black and Asian British writing as it began to become institutionalised: taught in UK schools, established in higher education, and made more readily available on the lists of educational publishing houses. Focusing on the second half of the twentieth century, especially the turbulent political period from the late 1970s onwards, it will lead up to the present day. Given the uneven nature of this history, any imposed chronology or periodisation is fairly arbitrary, though it is important to view the emergence of this writing alongside specific political and cultural contexts, in particular, anti-racism, multiculturalism, and cultural diversity.

The Beginnings

As the scholar and poet Kwame Dawes once observed, reflecting from the United States on the reception of black writing in Britain: 'Nobody talked

[10] For further information on the George Padmore Institute and archive visit www.georgepadmoreinstitute.org/.
[11] Many of these organisations joined together to participate in the International Book Fair of Radical Black and Third World Books (1982–1995); see Sarah White, Roxy Harris, and Sharmilla Beezmohun (eds.), *A Meeting of the Continents: The International Book Fair of Radical Black and Third World Books – Revisited* (London: New Beacon Books/George Padmore Institute, 2005).

much about Black British writing until the early nineteen seventies.'[12] Moreover, the context for its evolution was not an easy one. Although Dawes was writing in 1999, his words were borne out in Naseem Khan's 1976 survey, entitled *The Arts Britain Ignores*. Commissioned by Arts Council England, it concluded that Britain's 'immigrant' communities largely existed in 'ghettoes' and that the diverse range of their arts remained 'invisible to the mainstream'.[13] Although the Caribbean Artists Movement (CAM), which ran from 1966 to 1972, had been made up of several Caribbean writers long resident in Britain, it was not in any sense constituted as a forum for black British artists. Nevertheless, as one commentator noted: 'the movement [was to have] an enormous impact on Caribbean arts in Britain [. . .] [I]t set the dominant artistic trend, at the same time forging a bridge between West Indian writings and those who later came to be known as Black Britons.'[14] No other formal groupings existed at the time – though Tara Arts, an Asian British theatre company, was set up by Jatinder Verma in 1977, prompted by an increasing number of racially motivated attacks and the tragic murder of the 18-year-old student Gurdip Singh Chaggar in Southall in 1976. It was also during this period that crucial artistic collaborations such as the Minority Arts Association (1976–1988), which produced *Artrage*, an arts journal, the Asian Women Writer's Collective (1984–1999), Southall Black Sisters (1979–present), and *Wasafiri* (1984–present), initially founded as a literary and artistic forum for the Association of the Teaching of African and Caribbean Literatures (ATCAL), began to flourish.[15]

As detailed by Chris Campbell, CAM held its early conferences at the University of Kent, until some members objected to the link with the 'white establishment' (see Chapter 15). It would be premature to speak of an established field of black and Asian British writing in universities at this time, though undergraduate courses at Leeds, Kent, Sussex, and Edinburgh all included books by African, Caribbean, Asian, and Commonwealth writers, however marginal they may have then appeared to be to the established curriculum. The first conference in Britain dedicated to what was still termed

---

[12] Kwame Dawes, 'Negotiating the Ship on the Head: Black British Fiction', *Wasafiri*, 29 (1999): 18–24; 18.

[13] Khan, *The Arts Britain Ignores*.

[14] Angela Cobbinah, 'A Caribbean Hothouse for the Arts in a Cold Climate', *Camden New Journal Review* (25 October 2007), n.p.

[15] For more information on some of these associations please follow the web links: Asian Women Writers' Collective (AWWC): http://sadaa.co.uk/archive/literature/asian-women-writers-collective; Southall Black Sisters: www.bl.uk/learning/histcitizen/sisterhood/clips/race-place-and-nation/civil-rights/143172.html; *Wasafiri*: www.wasafiri.org/about/background/.

Commonwealth Literature, at which the Nigerian Nobel Laureate Chinua Achebe spoke, was held in 1964 at the University of Leeds. The Association for Commonwealth Literature and Language Studies (ACLALS), a precursor and sister of the later UK-based Association for the Teaching of Caribbean, African, Asian and Associated Literatures (ATCAL, 1978) with a wider international remit, was founded at this time. ACLALS still holds successful triennial conferences today, as do the many regional affiliates that were subsequently founded. Many founding members of CAM were already established writers and artists; however one of CAM's key functions in the context here was to begin to make space for and connect with the next generation. Race Today and Bogle-L'Ouverture publishers – both with CAM affiliations – were among the first outlets for the now distinguished poet Linton Kwesi Johnson. Born in Jamaica but resident in London from age eleven, Johnson was one of the first writers to be thought of as 'black British'.

A specifically British organisation, the Association for the Teaching of Caribbean, African, Asian and Associated Literatures, emerged out of this context. Though the idea was launched at a 1978 University of Kent conference, entitled 'The Uses of African Literature', the main drivers for the inauguration of a formal association came from schoolteachers, librarians, and students.[16] Whilst key figures like Denis Brutus, the South African poet, and Louis James and Lyn Innes (both University of Kent academics who had links to CAM) were passionately committed, the aims of the organisation were pedagogic: to make British teachers and librarians aware of the range of writing available in order to introduce now world-famous writers such as Derek Walcott, Sam Selvon, Chinua Achebe, and Anita Desai onto British school and university curricula. ATCAL's inaugural conference was held in 1979 at the Africa Centre in London. Its title, 'How to Teach Caribbean and African Literature in Schools', was consonant with its aim to influence Ordinary-level (now GCSE) and Advanced-level examination boards by producing reading guides and newsletters, foregrounding new and 'non-canonical' writing. The organisation went on to hold seven annual conferences, producing a series of annotated reading lists of African, Caribbean, and South Asian literatures and resources for teachers. Conferences also provided

---

[16] Elsewhere in Europe, initiatives pursuing similar aims and strategies unfolded during the same period; in Germany, Austria, and Switzerland, for example, annual conferences engaging with 'new' anglophone literatures and cultures were held from 1978 onwards, with the Association for the Study of the New Literatures in English (ASNEL) being founded in 1989. The organisation, renamed GAPS (Association for Anglophone Postcolonial Studies) in 2012, continues to promote research and teaching through conferences and publications; see www.g-a-p-s.de.

a platform for African, Caribbean, Asian, and black British writers based in the UK and overseas. ATCAL was a powerful pressure group and many of its founding members remained engaged until it ceased activity in 1985.[17]

ATCAL initially campaigned to change the content of GCE O-level and A-level syllabuses to reflect a more diverse society. Although some of the writers who spoke at conferences were black or Asian British, black British writing was not an explicit theme until the final conference in Aston in 1985. By chance, the Greater London Literature Competition (LLC) launched the same year was the first of its kind to focus on black writing in Britain. With six categories of prizes, all named after major figures and awarded by James Baldwin, the LLC was a landmark event, even though the term 'black British' was still not actively used.[18] The last ATCAL conference in Aston also marked a turning point. Not only was the keynote address given by Wilson Harris, a Guyanese migrant and British resident since 1959, but the British-born black poet Benjamin Zephaniah gave an impassioned reading. Though ATCAL ceased to function in its original capacity as an educational charity after this, a literary magazine, *Wasafiri*, had been launched by Susheila Nasta the previous year with the aim of continuing the work of the organisation by enabling a forum for the discussion of African, Caribbean, South Asian, black British, and diasporic migrant writing in Britain, offering its writers networks to reach a wider readership and critical audience.[19] As Nasta says in 'Looking Back to Look Forward', ATCAL was situated at a particular conjuncture in the 1970s and early 1980s; this period saw the proliferation of small presses and collectives (such as Dangaroo, Akira, Karia, Peepal Tree, and Karnak House), the publication of James Berry's pioneering black British poetry anthology *News for Babylon* (1984), and Hanif Kureishi's groundbreaking film *My Beautiful Laundrette* (1985).[20] The moment saw convergence across a number of 'minority' arts activities, including music, film, literature, and dance, which contributed to

[17] Early members were predominantly schoolteachers (Christine Archer, Robert Bush, Joan Goody, Jenny Scott, Liz Gerschel, Susheila Nasta) as well as arts administrators (Maggie Williams, Commonwealth Institute), librarians, and publishers (James Currey and Vicky Unwin from Heinemann, Anne Walmsley and Gill Stacey from Longman); writers such as David Dabydeen, Abdulrazak Gurnah, Lauretta Ngcobo, and Prabhu Guptara were also key (Susheila Nasta, personal communication).

[18] Prabhu Guptara, 'Editorial: "Happening At All Was a Triumph" – The London Literature Competition', *Wasafiri*, 3 (Autumn 1985): 4.

[19] Susheila Nasta, Robert Fraser, and Christine Archer (eds.), *Wasafiri*, 1:1 (1984).

[20] Susheila Nasta, 'Looking Back to Look Forward: Celebrating Thirty Years of *Wasafiri*', *Wasafiri*, 29:3 (2014): 1–3.

a growing sense of Britain as a multicultural society, and the confidence that this might start to be taken for granted.[21]

The 1980s was an important crucible, then, from which present-day policies and practices in anti-racist and multicultural education emerged. And as has been intimated, these policies emerged alongside the increasingly fraught and exclusionary political climate of Margaret Thatcher's Conservative government. The first multicultural policies, stemming out of the race relations 'industry' of the 1960s, had developed from a series of government reports and commissions, responding to what were seen to be social problems with 'second-generation' Britons and the perceived educational deficit amongst these groups. At an official level, multiculturalism was at its best an attempt to recognise difference and diversity rather than continuing to push the already unsuccessful postwar attempts at assimilation and integration. Yet some of the guidelines for educational institutions – often too hastily formulated – glossed over quite sharp differences in respect to gender, class, culture, generation, and sexuality. The Inner London Education Authority (ILEA), catering then to half of all Britain's black school students, was a leader in introducing multiculturalism in schools, but its 1977 Multi-Ethnic Education Report was just one example of the naive culturalism which came to be criticised by anti-racist activists who wanted more attention drawn to disadvantage across all levels of society and to embedded and pernicious structural racisms.[22] ILEA's 1982 carefully named 'Anti-Racist School Policy' was partly produced in response to these criticisms, implicitly drawing attention to the pitfalls and the patronising effects of 'saris, samosas and steel band' approaches.

Reports by other charitable bodies such as the Runnymede Trust, still active today, addressed both education and unemployment in black communities. And in the Scarman Report (1981), commissioned following the so-called 'riots' in Brixton that year, education was cited once again as a major factor. However the report failed to address the wider factors of disadvantage and discrimination that had provoked the 'uprisings' amongst black communities in London, Birmingham, and Bristol, uprisings which in fact echoed earlier revolts by disgruntled black and Asian minorities as early as 1919.[23] In

---

[21] Naseem Khan, 'The Arts of Ethnic Minorities in Britain', *Journal of the Royal Society of Arts*, 128:5290 (September 1980): 676–88.
[22] The Stephen Lawrence Inquiry: Report of an Inquiry by Sir William Macpherson of Cluny, Cm 4262–I (London: HMSO, 1999).
[23] The 1919 Aliens Restriction Act extended the powers of the wartime Act of 1914 which obliged foreign nationals to register with the police, enabled their deportation, and

1985, Lord Swann, who had been appointed Chair of a specialist committee accounting for disadvantage in ethnic minority children, published the 851-page *Education for All* document (known as the Swann Report), which 'became the official incarnation of multicultural education policy'.[24] The report offered seventy-five recommendations which made it adamantly clear that not only was the UK a multiracial and multicultural society but that education must be the force for change and the means to 'combat racism and attack inherited myths and stereotypes'. Swann expressed significant concern at the under-representation of ethnic minorities across the teaching profession, stressing that the implementation of a multicultural curriculum would enable 'all ethnic groups, both minority and majority, to participate fully in shaping society [. . .] whilst [. . .] assisting [. . .] ethnic minority communities in maintaining their distinct ethnic identities within a framework of commonly accepted values'.[25] Thirty or more years later, the question of 'commonly accepted values' still remains contested in Britain, perhaps even more so since the results of the Conservative government's EU membership referendum ('Brexit') in 2016 to exit the European Union have sadly resulted in an upsurge in the articulation of a narrow nationalist (and often racist) discourse.

Inevitably, the Swann Report attracted criticism from many sides but, as well as the fact that it gave official recognition to the existence of racism in schools and at all levels of society, it provided a useful context for those lobbying for the inclusion of African, Caribbean, and Asian literature as an integral part of the school curriculum. It thus marked a significant step on the road to 'institutionalisation'.

It is difficult to establish precise causal links between events which take place in society and their cultural impacts. Context and history are always crucial. However, as the cultural historian David Olusoga recently reflected in *Black and British: A Forgotten History* (2016), the 1980s 'uprisings' created 'a strong sense' amongst black people of 'being under siege [. . .] of the need to fight for a place and a future in the country'.[26] One possible response was for Britain's black and Asian communities to reclaim their pasts and affirm their own histories by inventing new cultural and artistic conduits in

restricted where they could live. The 1919 Act continued these restrictions in peacetime and continued till the 1970s.

[24] Paul Warmington, *Black British Intellectuals and Education: Multiculturalism's Hidden History* (London: Routledge, 2014), 79.

[25] The Swann Report, *Education for All*, 5.

[26] David Olusoga, *Black and British: A Forgotten History* (London: Macmillan, 2016), 518.

a contested present. Though Olusoga's history is one of several new books by black British scholars intervening in the present-day narration of the nation's history to present a more inclusive perspective, it is worth remembering that many of the debates raised by Olusoga, Afua Hirsch, and others, are regrettably still having to engage with some very familiar issues around race, citizenship, identity, and belonging already rehearsed in the 1970s and 1980s.[27] It is here that the work of the sociologist and cultural theorist Stuart Hall is important, as he and a younger generation of scholars, including now distinguished figures such as Paul Gilroy, Hazel Carby, and Errol Lawrence, and linked with the Centre for Contemporary Cultural Studies in Birmingham, began to articulate a new wave of thinking in black British cultural studies.

By the 1980s, cultural studies permeated a range of academic disciplines and it 'helped shift the gaze of black British writing because [it] understood Britain not in terms of exile and migration, but from the standpoint of a permanent black presence'.[28] Controversies over multiculturalism and anti-racist education, the presence of black music, art, and cinema, and the publication of pioneering critical interventions, such as Hall's co-written Birmingham Centre's *Policing the Crisis* (1978), *The Empire Strikes Back* (1982), and Paul Gilroy's *There Ain't No Black in the Union Jack* (1987), were critical, if controversial, contributions to the exploration of anti-black racism in Britain. Similarly, highlighting the long history of black Britain, Peter Fryer's *Staying Power* (1984) provided an extensive account of the depth and range of black and Asian settlement, demonstrating that racist struggles stretched back over centuries. These studies were not explicitly literary but, together with Stuart Hall's vision of a fluid diasporic identity in his 1988 'New Ethnicities' essay and the advent of postcolonial studies in universities, they combined to transform the landscape in which black and Asian British writing was debated.[29] As Kobena Mercer put it in *Welcome to the Jungle* (1994), speaking powerfully about 'black' as a specifically new signifier and emphasising that identity was not something exclusively individual but something born out of common experience and political struggle, 'When various peoples – of Asian, African, Caribbean descent – interpellated themselves

---

[27] Afua Hirsch, *Brit(ish): On Race, Identity and Belonging* (London: Penguin, 2018).
[28] Paul Warmington, 'Critical Outlooks' in Deirdre Osborne (ed.), *The Cambridge Companion to British Black and Asian Literature (1945–2010)* (Cambridge: Cambridge University Press, 2016), 256–69; 256.
[29] Stuart Hall, 'New Ethnicities' in Kobena Mercer (ed.), *Black Film/British Cinema: ICA Document 7* (London: Institute of Contemporary Arts, 1988), 27–30.

and each other as /black/ they invoked a collective identity predicated on political and not biological similarities [. . .] alliance and solidarity among dispersed groups of people sharing common historical experiences of British racism'.[30]

Institutional Responses

A panel discussion, held at University College London on 10 March 2014, and provocatively titled 'Why Isn't My Professor Black?', interestingly returned to many of the issues which had been of key concern in the 1980s and 1990s.[31] Focusing on race and gender inequalities within the academy, it was initially set up to debate issues of inclusivity and diversity, examining the institutional racism which militated against this.[32] Generating considerable national interest, the topic was extended by the NUS (National Union of Students) campaign 'Why Is My Curriculum White?'. The issues circulated across UK campuses, drawing attention not only to questions of why black and Asian British writing was not always readily visible on courses but also to black and Asian history. Results were tangible, with Oxford University soon making available (May 2017) a paper on black and/or Asian histories for its history students.[33] Adding papers to examinations or simply introducing more black and Asian literary texts is a fairly superficial response, but it did, at least, indicate the growing awareness at the centre of the British establishment of the need to reflect the diversity of British society and provide a more representative curriculum. And, as anyone engaged in the implementation of postcolonial studies in university departments will know, a more systematic analysis of the 'white curriculum' would need to deploy the arguments of 'decolonial' thinking.[34] Only six months after the decision at Oxford

---

[30] Kobena Mercer, *Welcome to the Jungle: New Positions in Black Cultural Studies* (London: Routledge, 1994), 291.

[31] The Re-Inventing Britain Conference in 1998 was led by a British Council initiative and a manifesto by Homi Bhabha. See Nick Wadham Smith, 'Re-Inventing Britain', *British Studies Now*, 9 (1998): 107–9.

[32] 'Why Isn't My Professor Black?', live panel discussion, University College London, March 2014. For more details, see Shanell Johnson, 'Structures of Dis/Empowerment: My Year as the UK's First Black and Ethnic Minorities Student Office' in Felipe Garrido Espinoza, Caroline Koegler, Deborah Nyangulu, and Mark U. Stein (eds.), *Locating African European Studies: Interventions – Intersections – Conversations* (London: Routledge, forthcoming).

[33] Mariya Hussain, 'Why Is My Curriculum White?', 11 March, 2015. Available at www.nus.org.uk/news/why-is-my-curriculum-white/.

[34] A representative selection of essays on decolonialism can be found in Walter D. Mignolo and Arturo Escobar (eds.), *Globalization and the Decolonial Option* (London: Routledge, 2010).

University, a fake news story in the popular press claimed that all white male authors were to be dropped from the Cambridge University English literature syllabus. Whilst the university issued a clear refutation of this claim, it had to respond to an open letter, signed by one hundred students, calling for 'non-white authors and "postcolonial thought" to be incorporated'. Significantly, the students were not asking for the exclusion of white males from reading lists but for the inclusion of a less Eurocentric and more diverse global range of texts and authors.[35]

A handful of UK universities and polytechnics had certainly begun to teach courses in African, Asian, and Caribbean literature by the 1980s, with a few black British writers included. With the growth of the 'modern' universities after 1992, literature departments further expanded and began to employ a new generation of staff with expertise in 'Commonwealth', postcolonial, and area studies. As the field gained in profile both in Britain and internationally, syllabuses were extended to include black and Asian British texts, now more readily available due to the work of independent presses as well as the mainstream publishers Heinemann, Longman, and Nelson. A number of author studies (some initially sponsored by the British Council in their 'Writers and their Works' series), monographs, and anthologies began to further build the field. This marked a substantive shift from the period when Prabhu Guptara's first annotated bibliography of *Black British Literature* (1986) and David Dabydeen and Nana Wilson-Tagoe's *A Reader's Guide to West Indian and Black British Literature* (1987) were isolated but key resources.[36]

If, as claimed, the 2015 launch of an MA in Black British Writing at Goldsmiths, University of London was the first postgraduate programme of its kind in the UK, the inevitable question as to whether it is possible to speak of the 'institutionalisation' of black and Asian British writing even today must necessarily follow.[37] Another 'first' was claimed for an undergraduate degree set up in Black Studies at Birmingham City University and launched in September 2017. Moreover, with the exponential growth of postcolonial studies in universities since the 1990s, many texts by black and Asian British

[35] Jasmin Gray, 'Cambridge University Professors will not be "Forced" to Drop White Authors from the Curriculum', *Huffington Post*, 25 October 2017. Available at www.huffing tonpost.co.uk/entry/cambridge-university-white-authors_uk_59f05b7be4b0bf1f8836eb09.

[36] Prabhu S. Guptara, *Black British Literature: An Annotated Bibliography* (Sydney: Dangaroo, 1986); David Dabydeen and Nana Wilson-Tagoe, *A Reader's Guide to West Indian and Black British Literature* (London: Hansib, 1987).

[37] Sarah Cox, 'Introducing the MA Black British Writing – "It's a Story that Hasn't Really Been Told"', *Goldsmiths University of London*, 26 October 2015. Available at www.gold.ac.uk /news/introducing-the-ma-black-british-writing/.

writers are also included in syllabuses with specific regional emphases. Importantly, therefore, it has proved extremely difficult to quantify just how much teaching of black and Asian British writing actually takes place.

The universities most associated with the pioneering of courses in African and Caribbean literatures – Kent, Sussex, Leeds, Birmingham, the Open University, the School of Oriental and African Studies, Warwick, Edinburgh, Queen Mary University of London – continue to offer modules in these areas, together with black and Asian British texts. The University of Kent was one of the first to launch the teaching of black British writers, mainly in special topic options (such as 'The Black Experience' and 'The Migrant Experience') in the late 1970s and early 1980s. *News for Babylon*, James Berry's landmark 1984 anthology, which was one of the earliest to use the term 'Black British', was on the syllabus at Kent.[38] It also included poetry by then up-and-coming writer Fred D'Aguiar and, like him, the writers Valerie Bloom, Sandra Agard, and Amryl Johnson were coincidentally students in African and Caribbean Studies at Kent.

Of the seventy-eight English departments in the UK today, a large number do offer modules including black and Asian British texts, though few actually name courses in this way. In part, this is a question of categorisation. For example, work by D'Aguiar (a poet and novelist, born in Guyana, resident in London from 1972 but based now in the USA) can be taught in classes focused on black British, Caribbean, migrant, diasporic, and postcolonial writing, as well as several other areas. Similarly, work by notable South Asian writers such as Salman Rushdie, Romesh Gunesekera, or Kamila Shamsie might feature differently in, for example, a course on the South Asian diaspora (such as the one launched and run at Queen Mary University of London in the 1990s) than a course on contemporary global or world writing (such as the MA in National and International Literatures which ran at the London Institute of English Studies from the late 1990s). It would be problematic to claim that black and Asian British texts should primarily be taught under that label, as opposed to the many alternatives. In fact, if black and Asian British writing has now finally become established, it is arguably more positive to see it permeated across classes on contemporary drama, diaspora novels, queer writing, British poetry, British contemporary writing, and so on. There is a similar situation in some GCE A-level syllabuses for schools where, along with African American, Caribbean, and African texts, now well-known black and Asian British writers such as Monica Ali, Zadie Smith, Andrea Levy, and

[38] Lyn Innes, personal communication, February 2017.

Jackie Kay are sometimes taught. Even if these are only prize-winning authors who have already achieved a measure of celebrity, their inclusion in mainstream syllabuses is positive.

Notably, the new Goldsmiths' and Birmingham City University's programmes focus primarily on writers of African heritage, not as yet including British Asian writing. At a Goldsmiths' conference in 2009, the writer and professor Joan Anim-Addo and the sociologist Les Back were both to argue that the continuing absence of black British literature as a field in the curricula of British educational institutions remains 'a result of a genteel racism' that continues to sway 'intellectual judgements'. It is because of this continuing climate that black authors, already little-known and undervalued by colleagues, are not widely taught.[39]

Publicity material for the Goldsmiths MA emphasises that it is telling 'a story that hasn't been told', claiming that, whilst modules incorporating black British writing may be taught at UK universities, works by black British writers have ironically gained far more attention overseas than in the UK.[40] In the absence of any existing systematic evidence quantifying the range of black British writing taught in UK higher education institutions today, this can as yet only be speculation.

At least a dozen British universities now have dedicated units, or modules, in black or Asian British writing, while a number of others include these texts on a wide range of other period or genre courses. At the level below the university, a radical initiative has been developed in respect to GCE syllabuses. EdExcel-Pearson, the UK's largest qualifications awarding organisation, commissioned a University of London academic, Dr Deirdre Osborne, to rewrite the A-level Literature syllabus to include a black British list (published June 2017) followed by an Asian British list. This initiative, which in fact echoes work done by ATCAL and other educational bodies such as the Inner London Educational Authority in the 1970s and 1980s, promises to transform once again the teaching of literature at secondary level.[41] Whilst it is sometimes argued that it was not possible to include such texts on the curriculum until a significant mass of critical material became available, this absence is certainly no longer due to a scarcity of available

---

[39] Joan Anim-Addo and Les Back, 'On Whose Terms? Critical Negotiations in Black British Literature and the Arts', conference panel, Goldsmiths, University of London, March 2008.

[40] Cox, 'Introducing the MA Black British Writing'.

[41] This list was sent to me in a personal communication from Dr Deirdre Osborne, Goldsmiths, University of London, June 2017.

sources but rather to a continuing failure to perceive the works of these writers as integral to the diverse canon of British writing.

Despite its continuing struggle to win adequate representation, there is one major area where black and Asian writing does show signs of significant progress and that is in the realm of literary festivals, literary prizes, and overseas writers' tours. While only 4 per cent of the 2,000 writers' names listed at mainstream festivals such as Hay, Cheltenham, or Edinburgh (2014 study) were classifiable as black Caribbean, black African, or South Asian,[42] on British Council overseas tours or live events held at the Southbank Centre, London, the British Library, or smaller arts venues or festivals, the black and Asian presence is much more marked, with some writers making a number of return visits. Bernardine Evaristo, for instance, has participated in over 50 tours in the past 20 years and has received more than 150 invitations. The black poets Malika Booker, Kadija George, and Patience Agbabi as well as the South Asian writers Kamila Shamsie, Nadeem Aslam, and Romesh Gunesekera have also been frequent tour participants. A specifically black British writers' tour was organised to the USA in 2015, funded by the Arts Council, which showcased ten established and up-and-coming female and male writers, whose work is now beginning to appear on the curriculum in universities and schools.[43] The Arts Council and British Council also offer funds to promote black British writers internationally. To end on an optimistic note, there is evidence from wider arts programming, and not just at metropolitan venues, that increasing space is being made for the platforming of writers from black British and Asian backgrounds.[44] It is hoped that such ongoing initiatives to publicly fund and promote diversity will continue to flourish; and, that they will continue the work of all the pioneering publishers and activists, who have found it necessary for several decades to continue to raise the visibility and profile of black and Asian British writers whose voices have not always been recognised as an integral part of Britain's dynamic and diverse literary culture.

---

[42] Mel Larsen, 'Side Show or No Show' in Danuta Kean with Mel Larsen (eds.), *Writing the Future: Black and Asian Writers and Publishers in the UK Market Place* (London: Spread the Word, 2015), 34–5.

[43] Spread the Word, the London Writers Network: An Arts Council England National Portfolio Organisation.

[44] Speaking Volumes: Live Literature Productions was set up in 2010 by Sharmilla Beezmohun and Sarah Sanders. Their Arts Council England-funded 'Breaking Ground' project showcases British diversity in literature as shown in the publication *Breaking Ground: Celebrating Writers of Colour* (March 2017).

PART III

★

WRITING THE CONTEMPORARY

Preface

Black and Asian British writing has continued to shape our perception of the past as much as it fashions the future. New idioms, new cultural forms, new questions, and complex affiliations characterise the contemporary post-millennial era. Although the 1990s witnessed a scramble for the black and Asian British novel in particular, many then prominent writers and texts had disappeared by the noughties. And whilst black theatre is continuing to grow, a 2004 report on publishing opportunities for black and Asian poets found this group to be under-represented, both in the publishing industry and on the printed page. Black and Asian writers regularly win literature prizes but this does not change the fact that success in the creative industries requires very substantial social, cultural, and economic capital, more unevenly distributed now than ever before. While texts are increasingly marketed to a wide range of audiences, 'prizing Otherness' and the consumption of writing associated with minoritised communities continues in the twenty-first century, almost obscuring how white the publishing industry has remained. Paradoxically, perhaps, South Asian Muslim writers have felt the need to strategically complicate their wide-ranging affinities and affiliations, responding to the rather insistent demand for coherent and unambiguous knowledge about the Islamic world. Nevertheless, writers are wearing their 'burden of representation' more lightly, which has entailed new forms of life-writing and poetry as well as an increase in 'post-ethnic' texts that explore and display the workings of positionality. An increasingly diverse body of writing now shows the ways in which queerness disturbs categories of race, class, gender, and nation, defying not only the 'straightening effects' of the mainstream but concomitantly the marginalisation of racialised communities. In dialogue with urban youth culture and still transcending the confines of social realism, popular genres like estate fiction respond to architectural forms and pulsating rhythms, creating multimedial texts. Fields such as children's literature are reworked by black and Asian writing, presenting a multicultural Britain both in speculative as well as in realist modes. Stage, TV, and film are powerfully affected by the challenge posed by new types of media with which they partially intersect. Providing space for challenging Britishness and engaging the fallout from colonialism, these institutions and their productions have retained if not enhanced their cultural and political significance today. That the contemporary moment has been marked, in part, by the UK's 2016 decision to exit the European Union and to exert greater control over its cultural composition, does not bode well for this field. At the same time, such moves have been accompanied by the articulation of popular demands to decolonise the academic syllabus and for the restitution of cultural artefacts misappropriated during colonialism, held in major British museums. It is in this context that Black and Asian British writing provides a forum for reinventing the nation and charting multidirectional genealogies for the twenty-first century, inhabiting with confidence a central and formative position in British cultural production.

(I)

★

LOOKING BACK, LOOKING FORWARD

26

Diasporic Translocations
Many Homes, Multiple Forms

PETER MOREY

In her first speech to the Conservative party conference as Prime Minister, Theresa May verbalised the renewed spirit of nationalism that had swept across the west in the tumultuous year of 2016.[1] Decrying an internationalism that, she suggested, weakened bonds of citizenship and shared responsibility, she asserted: 'if you believe you're a citizen of the world, you're a citizen of nowhere. You don't understand what the very word "citizenship" means.'[2] May's words were a further repudiation of the pluralist discourse of multiculturalism – seen in the political representation of minorities and the valorisation of cultural difference – which had been a feature of the British political landscape from the 1980s to the early years of the twenty-first century. In the new nationalist vision, nebulously defined 'British values' were now to be asserted against the weakening effects of values and traditions born in other cultures.

May's intervention can be viewed as articulating the latest twist in a much longer story of migration and diaspora in Britain: one that reveals shifting attitudes and positions. The literature produced by black and Asian diasporic writers over that same period grapples with a double-faced approach towards newcomers – at once officially welcoming but, in practice, marked by prejudice and discrimination – while articulating a growing political confidence and literary sophistication. In this chapter, I will explore how the resulting plural literary forms collectively demand that Britain be recognised once and for all as a racially mixed, postcolonial nation. They do so in part by inscribing the challenges to a sense of identity and home posed by the diasporic condition and translocation processes. We can see a spectrum of writings

---

[1] 2016 saw the so-called 'Brexit' vote for the UK to leave the European Union, and the election in the United States of President Donald Trump on an explicitly anti-migrant, anti-multiculturalism platform.

[2] 'Theresa May's Conference Speech in Full', *Daily Telegraph*, 5 October 2016.

over the period, from those positing the traveller and the migrant as a representative Everyman figure for the late twentieth century, to others emphasising the marginality and mental and material vulnerability attendant on shifting locations and a decentred sense of self. Such work is always attentive to the deeply felt legacy of colonialism (especially racism); the sense of home and belonging as split, and its implications for identity; and the compulsion to tell (and retell) stories as a way of making sense of the past and its shaping impact on the present. Such themes offer challenges to form and writers grapple with these to produce distinctive and often innovative styles and registers. I will consider these features as they appear in the works of Caryl Phillips (1958–), Salman Rushdie (1947–), Hanif Kureishi (1954–), Hari Kunzru (1969–), V. S. Naipaul (1932–2018), Sunetra Gupta (1965–), Monica Ali (1967–), Abdulrazak Gurnah (1948–), and Romesh Gunesekera (1954–).

Theorising and Writing Diaspora

As the 1980s gave way to the 1990s there was an increasing realisation in critical circles that diasporic groups formed a distinct set of communities across the countries of the west. Emmanuel S. Nelson noted how the concept of diaspora offered a new way of thinking, beyond the usual categories of the nation. Instead, 'the diasporic paradigm enables a global approach and initiates a new perspective'.[3] Theoretical definitions of diaspora were advanced, most notably by William Safran and James Clifford. Safran's model and Clifford's modification of it offer us a good starting point. Safran remarks on the breadth of contemporary uses of the term, and gives some defining features, including: the experience of dispersal from an original 'center' to two or more 'peripheral' regions; shared collective memories and myths of home; a continued commitment to the homeland and fantasies of return; and a sense of marginality in the new host society.[4] Safran's ideal type is the Jewish diaspora and, in his intervention, Clifford points out that not all aspects of this model apply to other diasporas. In particular, the fantasy of a return cannot really be applied to, for instance, the South Asian diaspora in the west, which has operated on the ability to recreate

---

[3] 'Introduction' in Emmanuel S. Nelson (ed.), *Reworlding: The Literature of the Indian Diaspora* (Westport, CT: Greenwood Press, 1992), ix–xiv; xi.

[4] William Safran, 'Diasporas in Modern Societies: Myths of Homeland and Return', *Diaspora*, 1:1 (1991): 83–99; 83–4.

aspects of South Asian cultures in diverse locations rather than seeking a return.[5]

Both Safran and Clifford likewise recognise that an important distinction must be made between the black African diaspora – particularly in the circumstances of its forced migration to the Americas in slavery – and the subsequent results of indentured labour schemes or economic migration. Safran concedes that the African homeland myth can no longer be precisely focused in geographical terms and that what he calls African 'Zionist' efforts, such as the establishment of Sierra Leone and Liberia, do not resonate across the whole diaspora.[6] Clifford, in turn, draws on the work of Paul Gilroy in *The Black Atlantic*, with its emphasis on crossings and migrations, to describe how '[e]xperiences of unsettlement, loss and recurring terror produce discrepant temporalities – broken histories that trouble the linear, progressivist narratives of nation-states and global modernization'.[7]

Clifford might almost be describing here the interests and techniques of Caryl Phillips. Along with Salman Rushdie and Hanif Kureishi, Phillips emerged in the 1980s as one of the most articulate voices narrating the experience of diaspora subjects in the face of a renewed white nationalist patriotism evoked by Thatcherism. Born in St Kitts, educated in Britain, and now resident in the United States, Phillips explores exile, alienation, and identity with an emphasis on the importance of a thorough historical understanding of contemporary injustices. The focus of much of his early work is on the Caribbean diaspora, since its story begins in translocation – the movements of the Ciboney, Arawak, and Carib peoples subsequently decimated by the Spanish invaders – and the forced migrations brought about by colonialism through slavery and indentured labour. Phillips's novels chart the movements of black subjects caught up in historical powerplays such as colonialism and war, understanding, in the words of Stuart Hall, that '[i]dentity is formed at the unstable point where the "unspeakable" stories of subjectivity meet the narratives of history, of a culture'.[8]

Phillips is a master of voices and differing perspectives. In novels that are often segmented by discrete but interlocking stories, we hear from figures as diverse as an educated slave on the Caribbean plantations in the eighteenth century (in *Cambridge*, 1991); an incarcerated young civil rights firebrand in

---

[5] James Clifford, 'Diasporas', *Cultural Anthropology*, 9:3 (1994): 302–38; 306. See also Amitav Ghosh, 'The Diaspora in Indian Culture', *Public Culture*, 2:1 (1989): 73–8; 76–7.
[6] Safran, 'Diasporas', 89–90.   [7] Clifford, 'Diasporas', 317.
[8] Stuart Hall, 'Minimal Selves' in *Identity: The Real Me*, ICA Documents 6 (London: Institute of Contemporary Arts, 1987), 44–6; 44.

1960s America (in the second story of *Higher Ground*, 1989); and a nineteenth-century slave-owner and the black missionary he has sent to West Africa (in the first section of *Crossing the River*, 1993). Phillips's debut novel, *The Final Passage* (1985), tells the story of Leila, a young woman from an unnamed Caribbean island, and her migration to 1950s England with her philandering husband, Michael, and their baby son. In England, Leila is abandoned by Michael, and her strained relationship with her sickly mother is a factor in her inability to respond to the few gestures of kindness she receives in this cold, grey country.

The polyphonic structures Phillips favours ensure that the victims of established injustices get to tell their story. This technique is perhaps most effective in *Crossing the River*, a novelistic tetralogy rendering different aspects of black experience from the eighteenth to the twentieth century, such as the middle passage, West African resettlement by freed slaves, and the neglected black presence in the expansion of the American West. These narratives are bookended by a transhistorical choric presence – what Phillips calls 'the many-voiced chorus of the common memory'[9] – reflecting on the panorama of experience we have seen: '[t]here are no paths in water. No signposts. There is no return.'[10] Here, diaspora and translocation are seen as producing an endless, if painful, dissemination of black culture and experience: a kind of necessary sharing.

Phillips's highly innovative technique reflects the need to shape form to the requirements of unprecedented experiences. Susheila Nasta notes the same urge reflected in the variety of literary strategies employed by South Asian writers of the period: from picaresque *Bildungsromane*, to intimate autobiographies, to postmodern fables.[11] Salman Rushdie is probably the best-known South Asian writer of this era and his early works especially have been taken to epitomise the exuberant, magical realist style – 'full of the disrespectful energies of exaggeration, travesty and masquerade'.[12] They offer what Bryan Cheyette, in another context, calls the 'creatively disruptive impurity' characteristic of diasporic life.[13] In novels and essays Rushdie has also been keen to reflect on the perspectival shifts that occur in writing about a lost imaginary homeland from outside; the writer is necessarily dealing in

[9] Caryl Phillips, *Crossing the River* (London: Picador, [1993] 1994), 235.   [10] Ibid., 237.

[11] Susheila Nasta, 'Homes Without Walls: New Voices in South Asian Writing in Britain' in Ralph J. Crane and Radhika Mohanram (eds.), *Shifting Continents / Colliding Cultures: Diaspora Writing of the Indian Subcontinent* (Amsterdam: Rodopi, 2000), 83–101; 97.

[12] Steven Connor, *The English Novel in History* (London; New York: Routledge, 1996), 34.

[13] Bryan Cheyette, *Diasporas of the Mind: Jewish and Postcolonial Writing and the Nightmare of History* (New Haven, CT; London: Yale University Press, 2013), xiii.

'broken mirrors, some of whose fragments have been irretrievably lost'.[14] For him, there is a certain freedom that comes with this uprooting, allowing the migrant author to float 'upwards from history, from memory, from Time'.[15] However, there is arguably a degree of complacency in this view, over-looking the privileges of Rushdie's class background.[16] It also tends to elide the crucial differences between voluntary and forced movements. Especially in *Shame* (1984) and *The Satanic Verses* (1988) characters are faced with the effects of migration – whether they are ripped from their homes by Partition or undergo bestial metamorphoses in the racist gaze of the English.

Performing Translocation

Indeed, one of the distinctive qualities of Rushdie's writing is its effort to challenge the (self-) deceiving narratives peddled by cultural and national purists. Against their disabling solipsism stand those who articulate the realities and challenges of a multicultural nation: teenagers like the Sufyan sisters, fully anglicised daughters of an immigrant café owner, who proble-matise monocultural allegiance: 'What do you think we are [. . .] Bangladesh in't nothing to me. Just some place Dad and Mum keep banging on about';[17] or the black activist Dr Uhuru Simba who comments of the migrant experi-ence: 'We have been made again: but I say that we shall also be the ones to remake this society, to shape it from the bottom to the top.'[18]

Another writer and film-maker who emerged in the eighties and took this notion of chronicling and thereby remaking contemporary Britain even further was Hanif Kureishi. In his essay 'The Rainbow Sign', published in 1986, Kureishi insists, 'It is the British, the white British, who have to learn that being British isn't what it was. Now it is a more complex thing, involving new elements.'[19] After starting out as a playwright and with two highly successful state-of-the-nation films, *My Beautiful Laundrette* (1985) and *Sammy and Rosie Get Laid* (1987) – which also feature the politically and sexually transgressive energies of youth and popular culture to present an

[14] Salman Rushdie, *Imaginary Homelands: Essays and Criticism 1981–1991* (London: Granta, 1991), 11.

[15] Salman Rushdie, *Shame* (London: Picador, 1984), 86.

[16] Aijaz Ahmad dissects the class dimensions of these claims in his book *In Theory: Classes Nations Literatures* (London; New York: Verso, 1994), 135–7.

[17] Salman Rushdie, *The Satanic Verses* (Dover, DE: The Consortium Inc., [1988] 1992), 259.

[18] Ibid., 414.

[19] Hanif Kureishi, *'My Beautiful Laundrette' and 'The Rainbow Sign'* (London: Faber and Faber, 1986), 101–2.

alternative view of modern Britain to that simultaneously being promulgated by Thatcherism – Kureishi turned his hand to novels. Karim Amir, protagonist of *The Buddha of Suburbia* (1990), famously uttered the rallying cry of the second generation of British-born authors, whose diasporic family backgrounds remain formative if sometimes superseded by other concerns: 'I am an Englishman born and bred, almost.'[20] In the novel the mixed-parentage Karim, much like his creator, has to contend with the hostility of 1970s Britain, experienced in its harshest form in direct racist abuse and violence, but also in the patronising guise of liberal exoticism, when he is treated as a pet by his father's new girlfriend Eva, and patronised by a liberal theatre director who casts him for 'authenticity' as Mowgli in a production of *The Jungle Book*.

At the same time, this theme of performance – and particularly performing ethnicity in the white racist gaze – is central to the book, not least in Karim Amir's father, the eponymous Buddha, who exploits white Britons' inability to tell the difference between a Buddhist and a Muslim to perform the role of suburban guru.[21] There is a sense in which the father's excessive performance of a type of expected 'Asian-ness', together with his son's strategic exaggerations and hamming when playing Mowgli, are politically subversive gestures, suggesting the possibility of using textually apprehended stereotypes against the colonial master. Kureishi thus stands opposed to the more essentialist articulations of black political identity being promoted at the time.[22] This is of a piece with the rejection of Islamic purism we see in his next novel, *The Black Album* (1995), and in the related short story and screenplay *My Son the Fanatic* (1997), which is foreshadowed in *Buddha* by Karim's own sense of being alienated from his 'Indian side'. Instead, Kureishi stands for hybridity and mixing, suggesting that identity itself is subject to ceaseless translocations of one kind or another and that the individual voice and vision must take precedence over the demands to stand as a representative of black or Asian diaspora experience.

[20] Hanif Kureishi, *The Buddha of Suburbia* (London: Faber and Faber, [1990] 1991), 3.

[21] Mark U. Stein explores the strategic uses of performance and 'posed ethnicity' of Karim and his father Haroon Amir in *Black British Literature: Novels of Transformation* (Columbus, OH: Ohio State University Press, 2004), 114–22.

[22] As James Procter says, 'As a label of racial pride, "black" did not emerge as a category internal to the British nation, but was imported from America during the new social movements of the 1960s and 1970s. However, if "black" is increasingly recognised as a dispersed, diasporic signifier, then it does also have a locally, accented history, peculiar to Britain'; *Dwelling Places: Postwar Black British Writing* (Manchester; New York: Manchester University Press, 2003), 5.

The importance of the look and the notion that diasporic identity is, at least in part, attained through the gaze of an Other is also central to Hari Kunzru's novel *The Impressionist* (2002). On one level, the book launches a characteristic postcolonial attack on Manichean identity structures and the desire for purity and a sealed-off sense of self, in the translocations of the central character Pran – offspring of an English colonial forester and a Hindu moneylender's daughter – at the turn of the nineteenth and twentieth centuries. Pran's journeys take in Agra, Lahore, Bombay, Oxford, the capitals of Europe, and 'darkest Africa'. Yet there are also journeys into different selves as this versatile shape-shifter constructs and inhabits a series of identities in the interests of self-preservation and advancement: as 'Rukhsana', a transvestite courtesan to the ruler of a princely state; 'Bobby', an orphan raised by Christian missionaries; and finally – when he steals the identity of an Englishman killed during riots in Bombay – as 'Jonathan Bridgeman', in which guise he sails off to start a new life in the England he has long idealised from afar.

The Impressionist is in some ways a postcolonial version of *Tom Jones*; an illegitimate child is thrown out of his protector's house and engages in a series of bawdy adventures as part of an unfolding journey of discovery as to identity. However, unlike Fielding's hero, Pran does not return as a rightful heir, nor does he settle fully or comfortably in any of the identities he has 'parsed'. Each section of the novel ends in a conflagration of sorts, from which Pran emerges in a new guise, ready for the next instalment in his peripatetic life. Although this most theoretically aware of novels rehearses some familiar ideas about the destabilising effects of colonial mimicry and recognises mutability as key to diasporic identity, it nonetheless probes the unease of in-between identities, rather than celebrating them. Late in the novel, Pran reflects on the emptiness that may lurk beneath his various performances: '[T]hen becoming is flight, running knowing that stopping will be worse because the suspicion will surface again that there is *no one running*. No one running. No one stopping. No one there at all.'[23] In the final scene, with his various veneers of identity stripped away, we witness Pran as a nomad, walking out into the desert to start the next leg of his adventures: 'For now the journey is everything. He has no thoughts of arriving anywhere. Tonight he will sleep under the enormous bowl of the sky. Tomorrow he will travel on.'[24]

---

[23] Hari Kunzru, *The Impressionist* (London: Penguin, [2002] 2003), 463. [24] Ibid., 481.

Textual Returns

A self that is created through the legacy of colonial education and value systems, enshrined in textually derived notions of England and Englishness yet irrevocably altered through translocation, is something *The Impressionist* shares with the stylistically very different work of V. S. Naipaul. To some younger writers, Naipaul – with his often caustic diagnoses of the ills of postcolonial societies – has come to seem a kind of edifice to be overcome in the search for a voice with which to write about diaspora. Kunzru's Pran is, as we have seen, something of a mimic man, and on his arrival in London he at first rents a room in Bayswater, recalling Ralph Singh in Naipaul's *The Mimic Men* (1967), whose talents as a natural impersonator also come in useful in forging a character for himself later in life.[25] Naipaul's terrain is the uncertainty of postcolonial identity and the quest for a literary style in a world of decline, his subject-matter the frustrated efforts of decolonised peoples to forge an authentic space in it.

Naipaul draws on his background as a Trinidadian Hindu who won a scholarship to Oxford at the age of eighteen, and his work reflects the pull of at least three worlds: India, the Caribbean, and Europe. This also forms the subject-matter of many of Naipaul's books. For Vijay Mishra, his writing is fed by the longer history of the end of Caribbean slavery and its replacement by indentured labour from South Asia. It is representative of what Mishra calls 'the old diasporas of classic capitalism', where the old world was imaginatively reclaimed, whereas the late twentieth-century diasporas of advanced capitalism retain family networks and produce those 'hyphenated subjects' celebrated in the work of Rushdie and Kureishi.[26] Naipaul's early fiction often rehearses imaginative returns to origins. Places – islands, streets, and houses – become important as real and symbolic locations, but they and their inhabitants are always acted upon by their colonial heritage. Indeed, one recurring theme is the evolution of the writer himself and the attempt to forge a style that is no longer derivative or second-hand. Nowhere is this theme mined more thoroughly than in *The Enigma of Arrival* (1987), which tells of Naipaul's sojourn in a rural part of Wiltshire, a stay marked by the cycle of the seasons, agricultural patterns, and a gradual lifting of the veil of nostalgic, textually apprehended understandings of the people and places he encounters.

[25] V. S. Naipaul, *The Mimic Men* (London: Penguin, [1967] 1969), 20, 134.
[26] Vijay Mishra, 'The Diasporic Imaginary: Theorizing the Indian Diaspora', *Textual Practice*, 10:3 (1996): 421–47; 421–2.

The Enigma of Arrival is in part a fictionalised autobiography. Its slow, elegiac, pastoral qualities allow the author to weave in reflections on change and loss, and also the journey that has brought him to this point. Gentle echoes and prefigurings crisscross the five sections of a text whose middle part describes the arrival in England of the young writer and his search for appropriate subjects for fiction. The book offers an aesthetic of space characteristic of diasporic writing: an attempt to come to terms with loss and change while making a new home in the world. The particular problem for the Naipaul persona in such an ancient landscape is, as Susan Spearey points out, that 'he cannot take credit for its inauguration into history, nor can he perceive it as a world awaiting his gesture of naming'.[27] For Naipaul, the word 'estate' – used about the manorial lands on which his cottage stands – is more familiarly applied to the plantations of his native Trinidad; 'a sugar estate didn't hold any idea of grandeur or style, carrying connotations instead only of size and sameness, and many small lives and small houses at the edges'.[28] However, he recognises that both kinds of estate are products of empire and reflects on his current location:

> Fifty years ago there would have been no room for me on the estate; even
> now my presence was a little unlikely. But more than accident had brought
> me here [. . .] there was a clear historical line. The migration, within the
> British Empire from India to Trinidad had given me the English language as
> my own, and a particular kind of education. [. . .] The history I carried with
> me, together with the self-awareness that had come with my education and
> ambition, had sent me to England with a sense of glory dead: and in England
> had given me the rawest of raw nerves.[29]

Andrzej Gasiorek has commented that the novel 'marks something of a departure for Naipaul because it problematises the role of perception'.[30] Certainly, Naipaul has to learn how to invest what he sees with appropriate meaning, rather than relying on those canonical country texts of English Literature – by Wordsworth and Gray, Hardy and Cobbett, Shakespeare and Malory – that lull him into reading his environment as timeless, instead of subject to mutability. Such well-worn paradigms come to be rejected by the more practised eye as time and reflection bring things into the field of vision

---

[27] Susan Spearey, 'Shifting Continents/Colliding Cultures: Spatial Odysseys in Diaspora Writing' in Crane and Mohanram (eds.), *Shifting Continents*, 151–68; 158.
[28] V. S. Naipaul, *The Enigma of Arrival: A Novel in Five Sections* (London: Penguin, 1987), 177.
[29] Ibid., 51–2.
[30] Andrzej Gasiorek, *Post-War British Fiction: Realism and After* (London: Edward Arnold, 1995), 57.

to be re-read more accurately. The book is as much about understanding one's context for looking as about what one sees. The writer must create the landscape, invest it with significance, piece it together, and call it into being through meticulous observation. What Michael Gorra calls an 'understanding of the constancy of change allows Naipaul to place himself within a history that had once seemed to have no place for him'.[31] Thus, what we witness is a process of maturing in both the man and the writer: 'the writer defined by his discoveries, his ways of seeing, rather than by his personal adventures, writer and man separating at the beginning of the journey and coming together again in a second life just before the end'.[32]

The book's strongest image, from which it derives its title, is one that sums up the idea of translocation. It comes from Giorgio De Chirico's 1912 painting 'The Enigma of Arrival and the Afternoon'. The two shrouded figures passing one another obliviously and the wall at the end of the piazza, behind which the sails of a ship are visible but forever out of reach, resonate with Naipaul's predicament. The picture starkly renders the impossibility of return and Naipaul reflects: 'we had made ourselves anew [. . .] we couldn't go back. There was no ship of antique shape now to take us back. We had come out of the nightmare; and there was nowhere else to go.'[33]

If, as Bakhtin informs us, appropriation is a feature of all language, then it is especially important for the postcolonial diasporic writer, struggling to come to terms with the histories of colonialism in the very language through which it was rationalised.[34] For the Indian diasporic author Sunetra Gupta, the strongest inheritance is that of European modernism, in particular its sophisticated experiments with formal unities, psychological emphasis, and the random intrusion of memory. Lyrical and dreamlike, Gupta's first novel *Memories of Rain* (1992) tells the story of a middle-class Indian woman, Moni, as she prepares to leave her English husband, Anthony, and their life together in London to return to her family in Calcutta. The narrative flows between past and present: the couple's first meeting and blossoming romance, their marriage and move to England, his small infidelities and the beginning of a more serious affair with an artist. Gupta's stream-of-consciousness style creates a rich, impressionistic tapestry of sensation that shifts between characters' thoughts with an almost Woolfian rhythm. Images of water and immersion abound, from the description of the couple's early

[31] Michael Gorra, *After Empire: Scott, Naipaul, Rushdie* (Chicago, IL: University of Chicago Press, 1997), 164.

[32] Naipaul, *Enigma*, 309.   [33] Ibid., 317.

[34] See Graham Allen, *Intertextuality* (London; New York: Routledge, 2000), 28.

courtship during Calcutta's monsoon season, through the flow and ebb of their feelings for each other, to the suffocating sensation of drowning as the marriage falters and escape becomes imperative. In a dense web of poetic allusion, drawing on both Bengali and English Romantic traditions, the novel reveals how lives and stories are woven fast in the fabric of shared experience and memory, as if to show that our sense of self is created from the cumulative weight of past experiences lodged in the mind's recesses and constantly retold, wherever in the world we may move.

Moni's story is one of failure: a failed relationship and failed acclimatisa-tion, redeemed by decisive action as she gathers her child and a few belong-ings and makes her escape. Somewhat unusually for a contemporary diasporic writer, there is no doubt about 'home' here: for Moni it means Calcutta, and the heaviness she feels as she boards the plane at Heathrow – 'as if the tendrils of this land were pulling at her feet, finally pleading with her not to leave, an indifferent parent entreating a prodigal child'[35] – seems related to the weight of disappointed expectations. As befits its style, the intensely personal experiences shown in *Memories of Rain* are rendered unique by characters' consciousness. Other types of experience appear only sporadi-cally, seen from the outside, as when Moni recalls a visit to another family in Bristol whose story reflects that of countless other first-generation migrants:

> how they had landed upon English soil with a mere five pounds to their name, the first difficult years, on weekends they had shared curried shad with other couples and reminisced of hilsa fish, cradling their children, they had rubbed their eyes in the damp heat of the coin-operated gas fires, and absorbed heavy texts, and now they basked in their hard-earned success, in detached suburban homes, their children amassing A-levels.[36]

Gupta's novel conveys the risk and the price of following a love that will lead one away from home and into diaspora. It is particularly attentive to the minute shifts of feeling by which love may grow but also be lost. Yet, for all their hyperconsciousness, her characters always have the means to uproot themselves and undertake international journeys as mood and opportunity take them, and our focus is on the effect of dislocation on their finely tuned sensibilities. As such they carry an air of privileged malaise about them. Gupta's protagonists are never pressed hard by material needs, as are char-acters in Monica Ali's tale of love and autonomy, *Brick Lane* (2003). In the rundown, claustrophobic streets of Ali's novel we find ourselves a world

---

[35] Sunetra Gupta, *Memories of Rain* (London: Phoenix, [1992] 1993), 174.   [36] Ibid., 186.

away from the ebullience of Rushdie's migrants, the detached yet observant self-awareness of Naipaul's fledgling writers, or the erudite ennui of Gupta's heroines. Here, the marginalisation of the diasporic Bangladeshi community in east London is experienced first-hand by the protagonist, Nazneen, when she is brought to England as a young bride in the mid-eighties. The word 'estate', and the place it describes, here implies something very different from the faded manorial splendour of Naipaul's Wiltshire retreat or its shadow in the plantations of Trinidad. Living a financially constrained existence with her increasingly embittered husband Chanu, Nazneen finds herself cooped up on a derelict council estate, where the paper-thin walls of the flats reinforce the feeling of exposure to the censure of a defensive diasporic group already under threat. She experiences tragedy when her baby son dies, and dreams of escape and romance, fortified by the giddy allure of the professional ice-skaters she watches twirling away on television and by occasional letters from her sister back in Bangladesh whose admirable spirit and impulsiveness nonetheless leads her into a series of disastrous relationships in that vigorously patriarchal society. In the second half of the book Nazneen acts on her desires, beginning a passionate but ultimately unfulfilling relationship with a local firebrand who leads an Islamic revivalist group in verbal skirmishes with local fascists.

The real story in *Brick Lane*, however, comes to be about Nazneen's rejection of romantic love and diasporic community solidarity in favour of self-realisation through economic empowerment and sisterhood when, at the end, she forms a clothing collective with female friends. As Rehana Ahmed comments, the book stages a battle between cultural repression and individual freedom: 'a submission to patriarchal culture on the part of the Muslim woman is counterposed to an individual dissent and withdrawal from culture and community'.[37] Ali's somewhat utopian resolution has baffled some critics, but is a good indicator of the ways in which, after 9/11 and the beginnings of a backlash against multiculturalism, perceived community conservatism and segregation became matters of concern.[38] Indeed, *Brick Lane* is one of the key documents outlining this shift.

---

[37] Rehana Ahmed, *Writing British Muslims: Religion, Class and Multiculturalism* (Manchester: Manchester University Press, 2015), 134.

[38] See Dave Gunning, *Race and Antiracism in Black British and British Asian Literature* (Liverpool: Liverpool University Press, 2012), 16. See also Sara Upstone, 'Representation and Realism: Monica Ali's *Brick Lane*' in Rehana Ahmed, Peter Morey, and Amina Yaqin (eds.), *Culture, Diaspora, and Modernity in Muslim Writing* (New York; London: Routledge, 2012), 164–79; 165.

Stories and Memory

The various concerns and features we have seen – questions of belonging, home, and identity; the urge to weave stories; and an understanding that diaspora experience presents certain challenges to form – are memorably brought together in the work of Abdulrazak Gurnah. His novels compulsively revisit his native Zanzibar in the era of his childhood, tracing the legacies of colonialism, independence, and migration. Themes of translocation and abandonment loom large, from his debut, *Memory of Departure* (1987), through to *Gravel Heart* (2017). Gurnah's narrators often tell their tales with hindsight, from exilic positions where they gain perspective on their previous experiences. For instance, in *Desertion* (2005) the protagonist Rashid reflects on the discrepancy between the romanticised notions of England inculcated by the colonial schoolmasters of East Africa and the cold, hostile, and lonely reality he encounters, while the unnamed narrator of *Admiring Silence* (1996) undergoes a full-scale existential crisis caused by his inability to explain the two very different worlds he inhabits to those nearest to him in each. This sardonic text is about the difficulties of narrating diaspora experience. Mimicking this uncertainty, the text shuttles back and forth between the narrator's youth and upbringing in Zanzibar, and life with his partner, Emma, and daughter in England. In tailoring stories of these lives for different audiences – including Emma's latently racist parents – he experiences the lure of editing, embellishment, and outright fabrication: fantasising about a loving family upbringing when, in fact, his father had abandoned them and taken off on a trading ship bound for England.

Indeed, the legacies of trade and the old pre-colonial trade routes loom large in Gurnah's stories, underlining the multiple forms of translocation in his work. From the young boy ransomed to a rich merchant and taken on a trading expedition into the interior during colonial times in *Paradise* (1994), to the devious trader who persuades a character to put up his house as security against a new business venture with disastrous results in *By the Sea* (2001), East African and Indian Ocean trade routes determine patterns of movement. *By the Sea* is in some ways the most sophisticated of Gurnah's novels, employing a shuttling temporality between 'present day' England and 1960s Zanzibar, which gives a fluidity to events and draws our attention once more to the partial and self-serving nature of memory. Houses and their ownership, as well as kinds of door- or gate-keeping, symbolise those imaginary homelands from which people are forcibly evicted and between which they move. Exile shapes the narrative and is repeated in the lives of various minor characters: a European woman whose life has been marked by the forced migrations of World War II; a Jewish refugee worker whose own family history is filled with expulsions.

At one point in *By the Sea* the principal narrator reflects: 'It's a dour place, the land of memory, a dim gutted warehouse with rotting planks and rusted ladders where you sometimes spend time rifling through abandoned goods.'[39] Stories are a bridge across time, from the present to the past, and also across space. They may not always be consoling but they are a way of making sense of life and loss. In a situation where 'home is a wilful fiction' for the migrant,[40] and where journeys never really end, the power of telling one's story often involves struggle and trauma, but it can in the end be redemptive.

The recuperative power of storytelling also permeates the fiction of Romesh Gunesekera, a writer whose first book, *Reef*, was shortlisted, along with Gurnah's *Paradise*, for the Booker Prize in 1994. Deriving from a very different history and Sri Lankan diasporic context, Gunesekera's fictions similarly address questions of loss, memory, reclamation, attempting to create homes in fiction even though, as he once put it, the 'real world is constantly invading'.[41] In *Reef* we are warned early on of the vulnerability of the coral encircling the island, a metaphor pointing to both the broad theme of human frailty and the fratricide likely to break out within the newly independent island nation. As Mister Salgado tellingly warns Triton, the cook narrator, after their move to London: 'we are only what we remember, nothing more ... all we have is the memory of what we have done or not done'.[42] Whilst Gunesekera's subsequent fictions reflect a continuing desire to discover a poetics of reclamation, whether in their depiction of despoiled paradises or the migrant's disappointed love, they remain committed to the vital role of the imagination in transforming the politics of the present. The relation of the artist to the past, as the carrier of memory – like Chip, who holds other people's stories in

[39] Abdulrazak Gurnah, *By the Sea* (London: Bloomsbury, [2001] 2002), 86.

[40] Abdulrazak Gurnah, *Admiring Silence* (London: Penguin, [1996] 1997), 89.

[41] Maya Jaggi, 'Lost Horizons' [interview with Romesh Gunesekera], *The Guardian*, 5 May 2007.

[42] Romesh Gunesekera, *Reef* (London: Granta, 1994), 190.

The Sandglass (1998) – is a recurrent concern. Gunesekera is acutely aware of the problematics in writing such histories and frequently addresses the question directly through his characters. As Prins puts it, in *The Sandglass*: 'Trouble is when I look back I see [. . .] everything [. . .] through so many filters. Nothing you can be sure of.'[43] Similarly, Gunesekera's epigraph to *The Match* (2006), drawn from Henri Cartier-Bresson, points directly to the camera's ability to freeze a moment, frame a memory, a passion that drives his cricket-obsessed protagonist Sonny Fernando to Lord's cricket ground to capture the Sri Lankan game.[44] In *Noontide Toll* (2014), set soon after the end of Sri Lanka's 28-year civil war, Gunesekera was to face head-on the complex ethics of writing the stories of a traumatised nation.[45] Through the viewpoint of his van man narrator, the reader is offered a multiple range of perspectives, ranging from voyeuristic war tourists, soldiers, and aid workers to acquisitive businessmen, all transported in the van from the ravaged north to the renewed south. Though ostensibly a simple man, Vasantha is a wry pragmatist and his words point ironically to the challenges facing the writer who seeks to engage with the silences of a nation once destroyed by civil war and devastated by the natural disaster of the 2004 tsunami: 'What they saw, what they thought, what they remembered was their problem, not mine. A driver's job is to stay in control behind the wheel [. . .] The past is what you leave as you go. There is nothing more to it.'[46]

The vitality of diasporic fiction in English inheres in the diverse stories and experiences it captures, and in the varieties of narrative strategy employed to render them. Taken together they illustrate a much greater degree of complexity in ways of being British – and thinking about national and transnational identities – than are to be found in the rhetoric of most of today's politicians. Diasporic subjects have spent too long in establishing a place in Britain to have it taken away by political whim or fiat. Avtar Brah makes the point that the 'question of home [. . .] is intrinsically linked with the way in which processes of inclusion and exclusion operate [. . .]. It is centrally about our political and personal struggles over the social regulation of

---

[43] Romesh Gunesekera, *The Sandglass* (London: Granta, 1998), 239.

[44] Romesh Gunesekera, *The Match* (London: Bloomsbury, 2006).

[45] I am grateful to Susheila Nasta for her observations here.

[46] Romesh Gunesekera, *Noontide Toll* (London: Granta, 2014), 25.

"belonging".[47] In telling alternative stories of departure and arrival, location and translocation, settling but also feeling unsettled, diasporic writers contest officially sanctioned notions of belonging that demand a kind of uniformity, at the same time revealing something central about the modern experience of living in a globalised world.

[47] Avtar Brah, *Cartographies of Diaspora: Contesting Identities* (London; New York: Routledge, 1996), 192.

27

Reinventing the Nation
Black and Asian British Representations

JOHN McLEOD

On 27 July 2012, during the opening ceremony of the London Olympic Games, a large model of the *SS Empire Windrush* was carried around the perimeter of the Olympic stadium as part of the carnival celebrating the history of the British Isles. Speaking of the ceremony four years later during a BBC documentary, its director, the distinguished film-maker Danny Boyle, spoke passionately about the *Windrush* as marking 'one of the great transformational moments – of music, culture, of our history – [that] arrives when our past joins us; y'know, when what we've built our Empire on turns up. [...] So we built the *Windrush*.'[1] Along with the Grimethorpe Colliery Band, a phalanx of Pearly Kings and Queens, a model of The Beatles' yellow submarine, and a throng of Pankhurst's suffragettes, Boyle's surreal visual tableau proposed an inclusive populist rendition of the British nation, boastful of the social and cultural range of its people, grateful for its long and energising history of immigration and the diverse society it has forged, and proud of its progressive political vision (from women's rights to the National Health Service). Although some have warned against a too-celebratory reading of the ceremony – Steven Blevins viewed it, perhaps rather harshly, as 'overflowing with the comforting signs of an inflated national history utterly emptied of historical consciousness'[2] – the positioning of the *Windrush* not primarily as an icon of a discrete 'black British past' but as a talismanic moment in a collective multiracial *national* history was of particular significance and value.[3]

---

[1] Boyle's comments appear in Angie Mason (dir.), *One Night in 2012 – An Imagine Special* (BBC, 2016).

[2] Steven Blevins, *Living Cargo: How Black Britain Performs its Past* (Minneapolis, MN; London: University of Minnesota Press, 2016), 32.

[3] Eva Ulrike Pirker, *Narrative Projections of a Black British History* (New York; London: Routledge, 2011), 50. Pirker offers a useful account of the emergence of the iconicity of the *Windrush* from the mid-1990s (see 47–52).

At the same time as Boyle and his team were being interviewed for the documentary, the British Government was about to hold a referendum regarding the nation's membership of the European Union (EU), the result of which, as became clear in the early hours of 24 June 2016, was won by those pushing for a British exit (or 'Brexit') who were keen to recover a perceived loss of control to the European Parliament and curtail immigration. One of the key images from this Brexit campaign, a poster of a queue of immigrants under the headline 'Breaking Point', underlined the extent to which it stimulated and preyed upon misconceptions about race and immigration.[4] In the light of the successful Brexit vote and the vision of Britain it endorsed, sourced in a nostalgia for imperial greatness profoundly at odds with the facts of history, Boyle's Olympic egalitarian rendition of the nation retrospectively appeared depressingly out of sync, either as marking a democratising vision of the nation fast losing its influence in an increasingly intolerant present or as projecting a wished-for equality and diversity still yet to be realised and never more urgently needed in prejudicial times.

Few readers and writers of black and Asian writing, I suspect, would have been surprised by the piously prejudicial character of the Britain that Brexit projected. As this literature has persistently portrayed over several recent decades, Britain has made little room for its black and Asian citizens to participate in the daily business of the nation (beyond the familiar contexts of entertainment and sport), and gains in social, cultural, and political life have been hard won. Black and Asian British literature has contributed a significant critical consciousness of the efforts of such Britons and their supporters to establish life in the British Isles on an equal footing for all and to challenge the minoritisation visited upon those considered as within but not *of* the national community. These attempts at recasting and reinventing the nation in recent years have taken place amidst the cross-currents symbolised by the London Olympics ceremony and the Brexit vote. On the one hand, we find a determined attempt to uncover, portray, and explore the seminal contribution made by black and Asian peoples to the fortunes of Britain over several centuries (not only since the arrival of the *Windrush* in 1948). On the other hand, writers have remained cautious of and vigilant towards any progressive or festive narrative of the nation as having shifted from imperial metropole to postcolonial democracy, and have spotlighted the ongoing refurbishment of prejudice that constitutes, in Tabish Khair's sobering

---

[4] See Heather Stewart and Rowena Mason, 'Nigel Farage's Anti-Migrant Poster Reported to Police', *The Guardian*, 16 June 2016.

term, the 'new xenophobia' of our constrained neoliberal contemporaneity, as well as the difficulties encountered when seeking to marshal opposition to it.[5]

The nation is, famously, an 'imagined community', in Benedict Anderson's well-worn phrase: 'imagined as both inherently limited and sovereign' and 'conceived as a deep, horizontal comradeship'.[6] Literary production is a key component of such imaginings, part of the wider cultural negotiation and declaration of the nation's identity, paraphernalia, and insignia that collectively contribute to the perpetual formation of the nation as a political, concrete entity. But as Anderson's phrases also betray, the nation is always something of a precarious notion, caught unsteadily between competing or contrary ambitions – delimitation *and* empowerment, exclusivity *and* inclusivity – which Anderson anxiously seeks to stabilise in yoking together the usually antithetical ideas of the 'deep' and the 'horizontal' in his championing of national comradeship. Representations of the nation, then, are forever fated to be pulled between demotic and illiberal tendencies, shaping comradely modes of inclusion but always complicit in the rendering of borders and perimeters between national peoples. While black and Asian British writing of the nation can never entirely free itself from complicity in setting such limits, its democratising commitment to extending sovereignty and membership to all, regardless of race and ancestry, has crucially kept buoyant the liberal, demotic imagining of the nation in terms of political equality and full participation. For many such authors, this commitment to writing the nation has also propelled the critical presentation of the fortunes of their ancestral homes (particularly in the Caribbean, Africa, and South Asia), and led to the insistence that Britain's history, fortunes, and future cannot be fully faced, as we shall see, without reference to the colonised locales of the British Empire and the wider world beyond.

Slaving Nation

Blevins has argued that black British writing from the late 1980s and early 1990s was often characterised by a particular kind of historical turn, as a new generation of writers looked back into the archive of British history in order to create 'works that instead place these narratives of [postwar] migration within a long historical context, that *historicize* postcolonial migrations within

---

[5] See Tabish Khair, *The New Xenophobia* (New Delhi: Oxford University Press, 2016).
[6] Benedict Anderson, *Imagined Communities: Reflections on the Origin and Spread of Nationalism*, rev. edn (London; New York: Verso, 1991), 6, 7.

the long colonial past'.[7] We can understand this turn as an important moment when writers sought to open an interface between the seemingly distinctive and discrete preoccupations of minoritised black and Asian Britons – migration, prejudice, race, violence, disenfranchisement, resistance – and the wider creation and conduct of the British nation as indebted to the central, not marginal, significance of Empire. As Caryl Phillips (1958–) remarked in an interview, reflecting on his early years in Leeds in the 1960s,

> [o]ne of the problems that one had growing up in Britain [. . .] is a real lack of understanding of one's own history because so much of British history took place in the colonies. One was encouraged to see Britain through a rather narrow lens, not understanding that British history had to be seen in the context of Africa, had to be seen in the context of Asia, had to be seen in the context of the Caribbean, because that's what's fed British history.[8]

Phillips was one of several writers, which also included David Dabydeen (1955–) and Fred D'Aguiar (1960–), whose early work helped open a wide-angled encounter with Britain by focalising its colonial and especially slave-trading contexts. In Abigail Ward's view, these writers' 'return to this past [arose] from an urgent need to understand the racial anxieties of twentieth- and twenty-first-century Britain'.[9] In his novel *Cambridge* (1991), Phillips interlaces the narrative of Emily, daughter of an absentee plantation landlord who travels from England to her father's West Indian estate, with that of an African-born slave who assumes a range of names (Olumide, Thomas, David Henderson, and eventually Cambridge) during a life that takes him from Africa to Georgian England, and on to the Caribbean, where he works on Emily's father's estate. The paralleling of Emily's and Cambridge's experiences – each has travelled abroad, both are under the authority of powerful white men – is part of the novel's poetics of proximity, which deliberately draws together seemingly remote figures so that readers think about the contiguity rather than the detachment of Britain and its colonies. The novel's entanglement of Emily's and Cambridge's grim fortunes on the plantation indexes the wider historical enmeshing of colonising and colonised subjects, while at the same time calling into question the tidiness and simplification of viewing colonial history always through the bifocal lenses of master and

---

[7] Blevins, *Living Cargo*, 12.

[8] Caryl Phillips and John McLeod, 'The City by the Water: Caryl Phillips in Conversation with John McLeod', *Interventions: International Journal of Postcolonial Studies*, 17:6 (2015): 879–92; 887.

[9] Abigail Ward, *Caryl Phillips, David Dabydeen and Fred D'Aguiar: Representations of Slavery* (Manchester: Manchester University Press, 2011), 1.

slave, native and foreigner, centre and margin. As Phillips shows, Britain and the colonies are closely bound as part of a knotted, webbed, and matted historical weave which cannot be neatly disentangled. This point is further emphasised in his next novel, *Crossing the River* (1993), where lines of connection rooted in the African slave trade are, amongst others, traced to the supposed humanitarianism of the nineteenth-century American Colonization Society's resettlement schemes and a love-affair between an African American GI, Travis, and an Englishwoman, Joyce, during World War II. Phillips exposes a cat's-cradle of connections that bind the fortunes of Britain with Africa and the Americas, born from colonial 'discovery', settlement, and slavery, and reminds us that the emotional life of a white Yorkshirewoman in 1940s England has something to do with the legacies of dispossession overseas. Britain's identity does not stand on a distant shore from the fortunes of Empire: indeed, it cannot be properly understood without its remediation in terms of colonialism and its consequences, just as the phenomenon of postwar migration from once-colonised locations can only be fully understood in terms of the *longue durée* of contact between those racialised as white and black.

Phillips's writing exposes two missing histories of the nation: a consciousness of Britain as fundamentally founded in relation to imperial exploits, and a recognition that Britain had long been host, if not readily home, to black peoples. Significantly, his choice of an early 1940s example of a multiracial British encounter in *Crossing the River* deliberately predates the talismanic docking of the *Windrush* in 1948 – an advent which, as James Procter has noted, risks concealing the much longer 'prewar black presence in Britain'[10] – while his characterisation of Cambridge draws substantially and quite deliberately upon the life-writing of Olaudah Equiano, whose bestselling *The Interesting Narrative of the Life of Olaudah Equiano, or Gustavus Vassa, the African* (1789) made an influential contribution to the cause of abolitionism in the late eighteenth century. Indeed, the pastiche of Equiano is significant not least in reminding readers that a consciousness of Britain's entangled black presence is as much cultural as it is historical, and evidence of it can be found across the full spectrum of British literary and creative works, if one cares to look.

In a similar vein, David Dabydeen's long poem 'Turner' (1994) contends with J. M. W. Turner's famous painting *Slavers Throwing Overboard the Dead*

---

[10] James Procter, 'General Introduction' in James Procter (ed.), *Writing Black Britain 1948–1998: An Interdisciplinary Anthology* (Manchester: Manchester University Press, 2000), 1–16; 3.

and *Dying, Typhoon Coming On* (1840), specifically the sidelining of its primary context – the traffic and murder of the enslaved aboard the *Zong* in 1781 who were thrown alive into the sea when their water supplies declined – in its celebration as a work of artistic genius by esteemed British figures such as John Ruskin. In giving the captain of the slave ship the same name as the artist, 'Turner', Dabydeen challenges readers to think about the complicity between culture and imperialism, the extent to which the nation's most prestigious creative artists constrained and silenced the colonised through their very representation, and perhaps even offered a sadistic spectatorship of black suffering. At one level, Dabydeen's poem foregrounds the unspeakable conditions of colonisation and enslavement, not least in imagining the fictional Turner's sexual exploitation of the slaves aboard ship, so that the painting is returned to us as framing a scene of inhumane violence rather than the sublime power of nature (the oncoming typhoon) or the artist's exceptional talents with oil and canvas. At another level, and crucially, Dabydeen confronts (as does Phillips) the difficult writerly and ethical task of seeking to represent those lost to history who have left little, if any, trace of their own. Ostensibly narrated by the drowning slave whose head is glimpsed in the painting, the poem brings to the surface something of the cultural domains from which such figures were seized and underlines the obscenity of their enslavement, while at the same time recognising the dangerous business of requisitioning the dead for the present purposes of revision, critique, and accusation. The poem's narrator is in search of a 'redemptive song', a new future conceived in an amniotic imagination that throws history overboard, but struggles to escape the concrete legacies of race that render such hopes stillborn: 'my face was rooted / In the ground of memory, a ground stampeded / By herds of foreign men who swallow all its fruit / And leave a trail of dung for flies / To colonise'.[11] In remembering such historical grounds today, even for the urgent purpose of reinventing the nation, to what extent do we risk our own complicity in the sadism of the past, or constrain the dead once again within visions not of their own making? And how do we begin to mourn those who went before us, forgotten or misrepresented, destroyed by the nation we seek to claim as our own?

Like others from this moment, Dabydeen was suspicious '[n]ow that peasantry is in vogue', as he put it in his poem 'Coolie Odyssey' (1988), of how tales of colonial horrors entertained 'congregations of the

---

[11] David Dabydeen, 'Turner' in *Turner: New and Selected Poems* (London: Cape Poetry, 1994), 1–40; 39.

educated / Sipping wine, attentive between courses'.[12] For black and Asian British writers, the establishment of a consciousness of black suffering as central to the story of the nation was no straightforward task, but opened up a range of vitally important artistic, philosophical, and ethical challenges. No wonder, then, that Dabydeen's important novel of black Britons in eighteenth-century England, *A Harlot's Progress* (1999), focuses upon the tensions between its central character Mungo, London's oldest black inhabitant, and those abolitionists who wish to appropriate his story for their own designs. Similar issues also preoccupy Fred D'Aguiar's 1990s writing, as in his novel *Feeding the Ghosts* (1997), which also exposes Britain's dark colonial history while at the same time wondering how it can ever be laid to rest in the interests of a postcolonial, post-racist futurity. Also based on the *Zong* incident of 1781 and the subsequent legal wranglings – the insurers refused to pay out in lieu of the human cargo thrown murderously into the sea – D'Aguiar's novel fictionalises the life of a female slave, Mintah, who survives being tossed overboard and produces a written account of the voyage, only for it to be dismissed in the court case as 'a fabrication by the insurers'.[13] She ends the novel living in Jamaica in 1833, now an old woman, having produced a series of carvings which memorialise the slaves thrown overboard and written about her experiences, aware of the grip that such violent pasts can hold in the present. As Stef Craps has argued, the novel explores how '[t]he present can will the past away but cannot actually rid itself of its haunting power' and, as in Dabydeen's writing, it mobilises the *Zong* massacre to expose the continuities between Britain's colonial past and its allegedly postcolonial present: such works 'demonstrate how [past and present] are imbricated in one another, as the past continues to structure the present. Thus, they unsettle triumphalist accounts of the postcolonial that deny the continuing effects of racial and colonial trauma.'[14] In seeking to re-present the nation, then, these writers urgently demand a recognition of how black lives have mattered in the past, but also insist upon something more complex and challenging than simply slotting forgotten figures and incidents into the grand narrative of the Great British nation (where

---

[12] David Dabydeen, 'Coolie Odyssey' in *Coolie Odyssey* (London: Hansib/Dangaroo, 1988), 9–13; 9, 13.

[13] Fred D'Aguiar, *Feeding the Ghosts* (London: Chatto & Windus, 1997), 168.

[14] Stef Craps, *Postcolonial Witnessing: Trauma Out of Bounds* (Basingstoke: Palgrave Macmillan, 2013), 68, 71.

Equiano would join Wordsworth and Defoe on the same canonical plinth). Rather, they demand that *all* take 'ethico-political responsibility'[15] for the barbarities of the British past which continue to traumatise and structure the racist present, call into question the prevailing narratives of British nationhood in which such incidents have been conveniently screened off, and begin with caution the hard task of remembering the lives of those lost to history without glibly envisaging their unimaginable experiences or instrumentalising them yet again.

Continental Nation

Much late twentieth-century writing focused exclusively on past British colonial happenings as a way of reinventing the nation for the future, although in novels such as *Higher Ground* (1989) and *The Nature of Blood* (1997) Caryl Phillips intercalated these histories with Jewish and African American contexts. In a related vein, Salman Rushdie linked his account of South Asian migration to Britain in *The Satanic Verses* (1988) to the British presence in South America and, indeed, to the Norman Conquest of 1066. This way of situating British history within a wider, cross-hatched complex of culturally diverse pasts can be understood in terms of Michael Rothberg's notion of multidirectional memory.[16] The reinvention of the nation in twenty-first-century black British writing has often advanced in a deliberately multidirectional frame, for two particular purposes: to challenge the counterpointing or separation of the two key twentieth-century British contexts of World War II and the decolonisation of Empire, and to situate a refreshed rendition of the nation within a specifically *European* frame as part of a pan-continental rather than narrowly nationalist agenda. As regards the former, Bill Schwarz has asked if popular memories of British wartime 'greatness' and victory 'worked to screen other historical realities, not least the end of empire',[17] while Paul Gilroy has discussed the neurotic return to the 'anti-Nazi War' as a 'privileged point of entry into national identity and self-understanding [. . .]. It explains not only how the nation remade itself through war and victory but can also be understood as a rejection or deferral

---

[15] Ibid.
[16] See Michael Rothberg, *Multidirectional Memory: Remembering the Holocaust in the Age of Decolonization* (Stanford, CA: Stanford University Press, 2009).
[17] Bill Schwarz, 'End of Empire and the English Novel' in Rachael Gilmour and Bill Schwarz (eds.), *End of Empire and the English Novel since 1945* (Manchester: Manchester University Press, 2011), 1–37; 7.

of its present problems.'[18] To refuse the splitting of the 1939–1945 conflict from the consequences of decolonisation – of war from *Windrush*, if you will – is to challenge one of the key manoeuvres of postwar British national imagining.

A key novel that does exactly this is *Small Island* (2004) by Andrea Levy (1956–2019), which uses the iconic occasion of the docking of the *Windrush* in Tilbury in 1948 to entangle a multidirectional tale of wartime service, *Windrush* and migration, the beginning of Empire's end, and the first steps of Britain's multiracial futurity. The suitability of the *Windrush* for this literary task of national reimagining is historically apposite of course (even if the novel does not make it explicit): the celebrated ship that carried migrants from the Caribbean to the UK was originally a German-built cruise ship named the *Monte Rosa*, which had been requisitioned during the war to carry German troops, was subsequently captured by British forces in 1945, and renamed with its imperial title. In the novel, Levy intertwines the tale of two couples, Queenie and Bernard Bligh and Gilbert and Hortense Joseph, whose entangled fortunes figure the multidirectional travails of the nation at large. The 'small island' is both the Jamaica of the Josephs' birth and the Britain of the Blighs, with whom the Josephs come to lodge in 1948. Gilbert Joseph has served in the Royal Air Force as part of the war effort and has returned to the UK on the *Windrush*; his narrative touches upon the often unacknowledged contribution made by colonial servicemen to the nation's 'finest hour' and invites us to recognise the proximity of war, decolonisation, and migration which cannot be readily disentangled. In a similar vein, Bernard Bligh has seen service in the Far East and witnessed the last days of British India on his way back home, a set of circumstances which further bind tightly the novel's multidirectional tapestry. Hortense's story helps to expose the fortunes of migrant women in Britain, experiences often left out of the predominantly male-oriented narratives of arrival and settlement in the 1950s and 1960s. Queenie's tale reveals the racism that characterises Britain in the war and its aftermath, as well as uncovers the many contacts, connections, and intimacies that traversed racial divides during the time. Indeed, her conceiving of a child with another RAF serviceman, Michael Roberts (who is a distant cousin of Hortense, although this is not revealed to the characters), highlights the fertile possibilities of Britain as a small island of multiracial intimacies; yet her unhappy decision to surrender the child to the Blighs for

---

[18] Paul Gilroy, *After Empire: Melancholia or Convivial Culture?* (Abingdon: Routledge, 2004), 97.

adoption also marks the seemingly insoluble parameters of race that will come to structure the fate of postwar Britain.[19] Through this multidirectional tale of war and *Windrush*, Levy offers a significant rewriting of Britain's national past, one which recognises the long-standing intimacies and relations of Britain and the colonies as well as the central contribution which black and Asian people made to the war effort, but also grimly reminds us of the missed opportunities and failures (both personal and political) that have arrested the birth of a genuinely multiracial and postcolonial nation. That kind of 'small island' remains both a missed opportunity in times past and suspended from the future, despite the multiracial realities which were definitive of, not detrimental to, the nation's survival.

The global reach of Levy's re-presentation of British history is given a distinctly European and transcontinental turn in the work of Bernardine Evaristo (1959–), who also seeks to rewrite Britain as a nodal point on a wider multidirectional network of crossing, passages, arrivals, and transformations – a reimagined island, as the eponymous narrator of her novel-in-verse *Lara* (1997, rev. 2009) puts it, with 'the "Great" Tippexed out of it, / tiny amid massive floating continents'.[20] Much of Evaristo's work offers a strategically witty, inventive, and playful representation of Britain in both trans- and pan-continental terms, emphasising its European connectedness as much as its colonial foundations in a series of novels which fuse poetry and prose as part of a literary aesthetic as diverse and multifaceted as the nation itself. A novel of family discovery, *Lara* traces filial connections through the narrator's father's ancestry to Nigeria and the plantations of Brazil, while her mother's family tree beckons stories of German and Irish migration to Britain as part of the nation's singularly plural fortunes. These tales are embedded in a semi-autobiographical tale of identity crises, prejudice, and fortitude, especially for Lara, a girl of mixed parentage. Indeed, Lara's struggles to understand the historical legacies that shaped her birth and structured her experience of growing up as a black Briton in late-twentieth-century London are offered as indexing the enduring problems of the nation but also the possibilities for reinventing it; as with other writers, the clues to a genuinely democratised national futurity may reside in a reconceived relationship, political and ethical, to its suppressed pasts.

---

[19] I have explored elsewhere the possibilities and problems of Levy's imagining of transcultural adoption in *Small Island*. See John McLeod, *Life Lines: Writing Transcultural Adoption* (London: Bloomsbury Academic, 2015), 57–66.

[20] Bernardine Evaristo, *Lara* (Tarset: Bloodaxe Books, 2009), 188. This edition is a revised version of the original 1997 publication.

These matters are pursued with playful if serious-minded irreverence in Evaristo's novel-in-verse *The Emperor's Babe* (2001), inspired in part by her tenure in 1999 as Poet in Residence at the Museum of London, which depicts the life of feisty Zuleika in third-century Roman 'Londinium'. Here the country is presented as an outpost of another European empire, one which hosts arrivals from the Middle East and Africa as a key node of transport for the classical world's circulation of peoples and cultures. Given such historical antecedents, however mischievously portrayed as in this novel, it becomes increasingly difficult to imagine Britain's origins in terms of national or racial purity or to think of migration to the country as a modern phenomenon. The European positioning of Britain is also emphasised in Evaristo's *Soul Tourists* (2005), which uses a road journey of two black Britons across late 1980s Europe to locate the work of retrieving forgotten black Britons from history within a wider pan-continental frame. Hence, during his travels one of the central characters, Stanley Williams, is visited by ghostly visions not only of Lucy Negro from Elizabethan England but also of Louise Marie-Thérèse (the mixed-race daughter of the Queen of France) and the Russian writer Alexander Pushkin who had African ancestry, amongst others. Evaristo thereby emphasises the particularity but not exclusivity of Britain as a European country that boasts a history of black presence, and crucially challenges the rendition of the nation in crudely national*ist* terms of splendid isolation or as remote from its continental partners. Given the increasing demonisation of Europe in twenty-first century Britain, climaxing in the EU referendum, Evaristo's attention to the UK as a part of a common multi-cultural *continental* domain continues to retain important political and critical traction in its insistence that we recognise the shared international histories that traverse and conjoin European space.

Corporate Nation

A cognisance of Britain as a site of international and intercultural contact has been no guarantee of the emergence of a racially inclusive sense of the nation. As Hanif Kureishi (1954–) memorably and importantly depicted in his novel *The Buddha of Suburbia* (1990), an acknowledgement of Britain as an inter-nationalised site of multicultural creativity does not necessarily dislodge the political establishment. Indeed, as is evidenced by the narrator Karim Amir's experiences as an aspiring actor of mixed parentage forging a career amidst London's middle-class white intelligentsia in the 1970s, such radical endeavour could quickly be co-opted as part of a facile depiction of a diverse 'cool

Britannia' which left very little unchanged. Several recent black and Asian British writers have explored the contradictions between the corporate depiction of a Britain of tolerance and prosperity open for business and welcoming to all and the austere and precarious lives of many minoritised or migrant figures – especially in the context of the 2008 global financial crisis, which impacted inordinately upon minoritised Britons and recent migrants who had fled for their lives from unimaginable circumstances.

For example, *In the Kitchen* (2009) by Monica Ali (1967–) unearths a range of tensions and fractures within Britain in its story of Gabriel Lightfoot, executive chef at London's Imperial Hotel, whose multiracial staff also includes trafficked workers from Eastern Europe, one of whom is found dead in the kitchen's basement. Gabriel's enquiry into the death leads him ultimately to discover and experience the precarious lives of migrant workers living hand-to-mouth, pursuing some of the worst and most poorly paid jobs available. At the same time, he travels frequently back to his home town of Blantwistle in Lancashire to see his ailing father, and is reminded of a very different version of the nation 'up north': working-class, often racist, disdainful of metropolitan mores. The deeply fractured, unequal, and profoundly divided nation that the novel depicts is epitomised by the oleaginous and media-friendly New Labour politician Fairweather, one of the backers of a new restaurant which Gabriel is keen to open, whose love of a business opportunity and penchant for Savile Row suits is in keeping with a corporate entrepreneurialism that cares more about securing profits than supporting people. Ali undercuts the glitzy spectacle of millennial multicultural British chic by exposing its dependency on cheap migrant labour trafficked from mainland Europe, its familiar racial hierarchies, and its depiction of the widening gap between the working poor, so often immigrants, and a new class of slick politician-entrepreneurs. *In the Kitchen* reinvents the nation from the standpoint of those on the receiving end of postcolonial prejudice and neoliberal capitalism, while taking the temperature of a confused and separated nation blundering towards the very discord and disunity that would be exploited by those calling for 'Brexit'.

Soberingly, a Danny Boyle-like rendering of a proudly multicultural nation seems remote in the Britains we encounter across several recent works. Caryl Phillips's *In the Falling Snow* (2009) depicts a nation deeply fractured by conflicts between racisms, generations, genders, and migrants old and new. The bleak view of austerity Britain presented by Zadie Smith (1975–) in *NW* (2012) exposes the frustrations of upward mobility for black Britons seeking to make their way on an equal footing in the 'world city' of contemporary

London, as well as the deprivations and fatality created when one is forced to dwell cheek by jowl with signs of the very affluence and opportunity that have passed one by. The impact of the toxic admixture of neoliberal economics, austerity, race, and migration on Britain has been powerfully measured in representations of precarious and so-called illegal immigration, such as *The Year of the Runaways* (2015) by Sunjeev Sahota (1981–). This novel follows the fortunes of three Indian male migrants as well as a British Sikh woman who live a tense and shadowy existence in Sheffield, and dwells upon the various sobering and often painful reasons why each has ended up in South Yorkshire, scraping together a meagre living while dogged by prejudice, the suspicious eyes of officialdom, and those on all sides willing to exploit the vulnerable. The novel powerfully confronts the media's demonising and two-dimensional clichés of 'illegal' immigrants as exploiting the bureaucratic structures of student and marriage visas, and presents a vision of Britain as deeply inhospitable and happily exploitative of vulnerable people who are as complex as they are injured. As such, the novel joins other representations of those seeking refuge in Britain by reflecting, to borrow Agnes Woolley's words, 'a disavowal of British hospitality to immigration in a post-millennial context'.[21] Black and Asian Britons are also complicit in these unequal relations between host and newcomer. Zadie Smith's short but powerful narrative *The Embassy of Cambodia* (2013) depicts the travails of Fatou, a West African immigrant in London whose job as a domestic servant for the affluent Derawal family is presented as a mode of modern-day slavery, while Leila Aboulela's *Minaret* (2005) tells the story of Najwa, daughter of a Sudanese politician, who is forced to flee after a coup and becomes a cleaner in London for a cosmopolitan Muslim family. Taken together, these literary works sustain the long-standing attention to ethico-political responsibility in black and Asian British writing by focusing on the precarious lives of the present as well as the past, and offer an often grim rendering of the enduring impact of capital, wealth, and impoverishment as inhibiting the emergence of a properly equal, inclusive nation where all might find recognition and security.

It might seem, then, that twenty-first-century writing offers a distinctly muted enthusiasm for the likelihood of reinventing the nation progressively for the future – something borne out, perhaps, by the 'Brexit' vote and its dismal anti-immigration platform. But this would be to miscalculate the

---

[21] Agnes Woolley, *Contemporary Asylum Narratives: Representing Refugees in the Twenty-First Century* (Basingstoke: Palgrave Macmillan, 2014), 30.

ongoing stubborn commitment to ensuring that Britain acknowledges its colonial history and realises the possibilities that might still emerge from the legacies of a dark past. Daljit Nagra (1966–) offers a fascinating and profound example of this sensibility in his depiction of one of the most popular sites of British national public culture in the poem 'Meditations on the British Museum' (2017). The speaker regards the British Museum as a storehouse of treasures that have arrived, migrant-like, from and through conflicts waged overseas: 'a back street open-ended Bloomsbury bazaar / where every marvel / migrant, in the four-wing three-floor stone, is guarded quaint'.[22] In pursuing the conceit of 'museum as nation, // as a fragment of varnished Britannica', he unflinchingly acknowledges the wretched colonial contexts of many of the artefacts, which may be suppressed in their display as objects of aesthetic beauty, an 'exotic sublime'.[23] But he strives, too, to find another way of valuing the amassed collections, strategically future-facing, not simply as Benjaminian documents of barbarism that call civilisation into question.[24] At the poem's climax the British Museum is mooted as a progressively migratory space, a cultural hub which guards the insurgent potential of the imagination and creativity across cultures, symbolised by its diverse artefacts, from being thoroughly demolished by 'the art of rubble': war, conflict, faction, and feud. In this museum-as-nation all of Britain's diverse peoples, long-standing or recently arrived, may find evidence of 'the unconquerable climate of our cultures [. . .] safe in this fortress' that is both welcoming and unhomely all at once: 'We're at home, albeit lost, while roaming among our kind / in Cuerdale, Yarlung, Shang, Ashanti, Aulong, Kush, Thule, Ur.'[25]

Nagra's poem offers a clear-eyed vision of a potentially reinvented Britain: aware of its worldly past, acknowledging the global cultural variety housed at its centre, committed to bringing people together through a shared contemplation of both the worst and best activities of 'our kind'. It engages a number of the issues that have preoccupied a wealth of black and Asian writers of Britain for decades, as we have seen, in its consciousness of the *longue durée* of Empire and its centrality to the construction of Britain's image, in its curation of the intertwined and overlapping histories in which the nation has been

---

[22] Daljit Nagra, 'Meditations on the British Museum' in *British Museum* (London: Faber and Faber, 2017), 49–53; 49.

[23] Ibid., 50, 51.

[24] See Walter Benjamin, 'Theses on the Philosophy of History' in *Illuminations*, trans. Harry Zohn, ed. Hannah Arendt (New York: Shocken Books, 1968), 253–64.

[25] Nagra, 'Meditations on the British Museum', 53.

always enmeshed, and in its cognisance of the fugitive lives and ongoing inequalities that continue to prohibit a truly demotic and inclusive vision of imagined comradeship from being fully realised at large. Nagra's vision, as we have seen, is only the latest cautious but determined attempt to reimagine the nation anew in black and Asian British writing. He joins the ranks of many others who remain aware of the enormity of this task and of the political and ethical challenges it brings, but are fully committed to inaugurating a pluralised and democratised Britain that refuses the narrow, nostalgic, imperious ignorance of race, class, or cultural privilege. Like those who hoisted the model of the *Windrush* at Danny Boyle's Olympic ceremony, black and Asian British writers continue to hold forth a vital, valuable consciousness of Britain's past failures and future possibilities in the face of those who, when confronted with images of the nation properly alert to its compound racial and cultural composition, would rather run hastily for the exit.

28

Reclaiming the Past
Black and Asian British Genealogies

TOBIAS DÖRING

In *Brit(ish): On Race, Identity and Belonging* (2018), Afua Hirsch describes experiences of unbelonging – and what consistently triggers her sense of exclusion: 'If I were to single out the most persistent reminder of that sense of not belonging, it would be The Question. The Question is: where are you from?' Hirsch has been confronted in this way since growing up as a child of mixed parentage during the 1980s and 1990s in the UK: 'Although I have lived in five different countries as an adult, nowhere have I been asked The Question more than right here where I started, where I *am* from, in Britain.'[1] Importantly, this is a personal as well as a collective experience; it unsettles the right to belong and directs attention to the past, an experience that has been written about by many. Seven decades earlier, George Lamming was greeted with the same question by the young son of an English family he was visiting. Lamming relates the anecdote in his essay 'In the Beginning', which opens the seminal *The Pleasures of Exile* (1960). His short answer – 'The Caribbean' – prompts the boy to locate the islands on his map while the visitor launches into a lengthy narrative of their eventful history, the 'sad and hopeful epic of discovery and migration', only to spur the child to the next, inevitable question: 'But what happened before?'[2]

Published ten years after his arrival in England, Lamming's book about New World modernities can be read as an attempt to address 'what happened before' – and how this generates new ways of seeing. Who I am, where I am positioned, can only ever be made out by establishing a clear sense of the past – who I was, who my parents and in turn their parents were, and where they have come from. Belonging, then, concerns not just the individual; personal belonging intersects with processes of cultural and political identification. This imperative has long been a major driving force in postcolonial,

---

[1] Afua Hirsch, *Brit(ish): On Race, Identity and Belonging* (London: Jonathan Cape, 2018), 32.
[2] George Lamming, *The Pleasures of Exile* (London: Allison & Busby, [1960] 1984), 16–18.

diasporic, and transcultural writing. Lamming's anecdote thus stands for the larger, complex, and often contradictory acts of self-questioning and self-locating through which black and Asian British genealogies have taken shape until today.

This chapter traces such processes, working with five distinct perspectives from which writers have responded to this challenge: People with History, The Other Story, Family Matters, Echo Chambers, and Historiographic Metafiction. These five categories are all porous but they indicate shared tendencies. A key concern of black and Asian British writing, the exploration of the past by tentative probing or active reclamation and the construction of individual or communal histories has taken many forms, across all media and genres. But for reasons explored more fully below, the dominant form is the novel. This comprises adoptions and adaptions of American slave narratives, for instance in the works of Caryl Phillips, Fred D'Aguiar, Andrea Levy, and David Dabydeen. It also includes sophisticated historiographic allegories for intertwining the personal with the national, as in Salman Rushdie's *Midnight's Children* (1981), a novel which turns the difficulties of ever narrating, let alone containing, history into its central trope: its errant narrator Saleem Sinai attempts to seal India's history into pickle jars that leak because they can never be tight enough for their fermenting contents.

Midnight's Children remains a landmark both in postcolonial Indian and in Asian British writing, just as other works and writers in this chapter are part of more than one tradition, given their multiple heritage and often plural sense of cultural belonging, unsuited to exclusive claims of nationalism. Therefore they in some way exemplify what Paul Gilroy has termed 'double consciousness',[3] and what the narrator of Hanif Kureishi's *The Buddha of Suburbia* (1990), with refreshing confidence, introduces as 'a new breed' that has 'emerged from two old histories [. . .], [an] odd mixture of continents and blood, of here and there, of belonging and not'.[4] History, then, rarely figures in the singular and its pursuit takes many shapes. However, what all these works have in common is their shared commitment to an imaginative impulse Rushdie has described as crucial to the composition of *Midnight's Children*. The book 'was really born when I realized how much I wanted to restore the past to myself' in an act of personal restoration with strong

[3] In the title of his study *The Black Atlantic: Modernity and Double Consciousness* (Cambridge, MA: Harvard University Press, 1993).
[4] Hanif Kureishi, *The Buddha of Suburbia* (London: Faber and Faber, 1990), 3.

political implications: 'description is itself a political act. [. . .] So it is clear that redescribing a world is the necessary first step toward changing it.'[5] For Rushdie, in 1981, reclaiming the past was the necessary first step towards claiming, and changing, the present, a goal that all writers mentioned in this chapter share.

How are such claims made, remade, or questioned? What rhetorical strategies are employed, what narratives developed to establish what happened before? How does the past impact the present? And how can we really make out, in Lamming's words, what happened 'in the beginning'?

Answers to these questions are as compelling as they are elusive. Any attempt to identify beginnings immediately provokes the question posed to Lamming by the English boy. Outside myths of genesis, therefore, beginnings are better suspended in favour of the complementary question of 'what happened next' – a conventional narrative ploy that Saleem Sinai, with reference to the female interlocutor who keeps interfering in his tale, calls 'bowing to the ineluctable Padma-pressures of what-happened-nextism'.[6] In this way, narratives can stitch together what would otherwise remain an incoherent mess of isolated incidents into a clear chronology and pattern, constructing the kind of meaningful unity with suggestive cause–effect relations that we associate with history.

However, this also introduces some anxiety. History is always difficult to come to terms with. Not only is the term ambiguous, denoting both actual occurrences and the cultural record that is supposed to take account of them, it also has an unmistakable affinity with *story*, as though historical events were somehow the product of storytelling acts that relate them, blurring any distinction between representation and what is being represented. This may be a reason why the constructed order of historical narration can also be constricting, even oppressive, as indicated in the epigraph to Lamming's book: 'History is a nightmare from which I am trying to awaken [sic].'[7] At the start of an exile's reflections whose project is to recover historical consciousness, this declaration comes as a surprise. Quoted from Stephen Dedalus, James Joyce's alter ego in *Ulysses*, the aphorism reminds us that history may be a promise as much as a problem.[8] The problem lies in burdening the present with a legacy, especially one of violence and suffering, that weighs on all contemporary predicaments and future ventures, possibly

---

[5] Salman Rushdie, 'Imaginary Homelands' in *Imaginary Homelands: Essays and Criticism 1981–1991* (London: Granta, 1991), 9–21; 13–14.
[6] Salman Rushdie, *Midnight's Children* (London: Picador, [1981] 1982), 39.
[7] Lamming, *Pleasures*, 9. [8] James Joyce, *Ulysses* (New York: Vintage, [1922] 1986), 23.

diminishing any creative space of self-invention. This is why some writers, especially from the Caribbean, have been wary of reclaiming the past – Derek Walcott's essay 'The Muse of History' (1974) is the best-known case in point – and remain sceptical as to the benefits of memory and historical recovery. Therefore, in making black and Asian British genealogies, and in making them matter, the task is to balance dreams of an *em*powering past with nightmares of an *over*powering past.

Lamming's reference to a modernist classic may be paradigmatic of such a double strategy: he acknowledges a given legacy without submitting to its pressure. In just this way, throughout *The Pleasures of Exile*, he draws on another classic text as a paradigm for Caribbean–English entanglements: Shakespeare's *The Tempest* (c. 1611) provides him with a repertoire of figures to consider present-day concerns both in relation, and in resistance, to the early modern play. When Lamming discusses *Black Jacobins* (1938), C. L. R. James's pioneering study of the Haitian revolution, he calls this chapter 'Caliban Orders History'. In Shakespeare's play, Caliban embodies rather the antithesis of order, a 'savage and deformed slave', who foments rebellion and defies authority.[9] And yet he is made to acknowledge in a famous speech that he must rely on this very authority for his own powers of articulation: 'You taught me language, and my profit on't / Is I know how to curse.'[10] A model for postcolonial intellectuals to negotiate their stance towards English and colonial authority, Caliban thus provides an ambiguous precedent, and *The Tempest* is both a constricting legacy – in defining canonical roles of black–white relations – and potentially a liberating text, opening such roles to critical rewriting. History, then, is never simply given, but subject to changing views, reviews, and revisions. As much as the present is made by the past, we should never forget that the past is, in turn, constantly made through present acts of reinterpretation.

This insight is captured by the key concept *genealogy*. Michel Foucault's term signifies the critical practice of tracing the history of concepts commonly believed to have no history, such as sexuality. As Foucault argues, genealogy 'must record the singularity of events outside of any monotonous finality; it must seek them in the most unpromising places, in what we tend to feel is without history – in sentiments, love, conscience, instincts'.[11] That is to

---

[9] William Shakespeare, *The Tempest*, ed. Virginia Mason Vaughan and Alden T. Vaughan (London: Bloomsbury, [1999] 2011), 162.

[10] Ibid., 1.2.364–5.

[11] Michel Foucault, 'Nietzsche, Genealogy, History' in *Language, Counter-Memory, Practice: Selected Essays and Interviews*, ed. D. F. Bouchard (Ithaca, NY: Cornell University Press, 1977), 139–63; 139–40.

say, genealogy insists that these notions are not timeless entities, but social constructs changing over space and time, determined by concrete practices and contingent upon specific social conditions. At the same time, Foucault draws on Friedrich Nietzsche to argue that the term genealogy 'opposes itself to the search for "origins"',[12] that is, the longing for a singular authentication in the past from which all present signification derives: 'Why does Nietzsche challenge the pursuit of the origin [. . .]? First, because it is an attempt to capture the exact essence of things, their purest possibilities, and their carefully protected identities, because this search assumes the existence of immobile forms that precede the external world of accident and succession.'[13] Genealogy, then, resists the ideology of pure and single origins, just as it rejects the longing for essentialised identities and unbroken continuities. Instead, it emphasises accident, contingency, discontinuity, and rupture. It recognises that everything may well be different and change quite unpredictably. How, then, can literature engage with it?

People with History

The title of Eric Wolf's 1982 study of pre-colonial African societies, *Europe and the People without History*, draws on a cliché of colonial discourse, the prejudice that historical agency, and therefore cultural status, is a prerogative of Europeans and their settler descendants. This notion was directed against Africans, who were seen as beasts or, at best, children of nature, without civilisation, cultural achievement, or historical consciousness. For centuries, the imperial powers justified their slave trade with this convenient view. Without history, Africans did not attain full humanity and so simply did not count. As Chinua Achebe put it in 1965, 'I would be quite satisfied if my novels (especially the ones set in the past) did no more than teach my readers that their past – with all the imperfections – was not one long night of savagery from which the first European acting on God's behalf delivered them.'[14] As is well known, literature, storytelling, and especially the historical novel thus confront and confound this central topos of European colonial discourse.

This point has a bearing on black British culture, too. Many novels, poems, films, performances, and artworks aim to establish the reality of an age-old black presence in British society. In this way they counteract what Stuart Hall has called the 'profound historical forgetfulness' of racism and prove wrong

[12] Ibid., 140.   [13] Ibid., 142.
[14] Chinua Achebe, 'The Novelist as Teacher' in *Morning Yet on Creation Day* (London: Heinemann, 1975), 42–5; 45.

the populist slogan 'there ain't no black in the Union Jack'.[15] Historical novels like S. I. Martin's *Incomparable World* (1996) or David Dabydeen's *A Harlot's Progress* (1999) are complex imaginative ventures, steeped in scholarship and intertextual networks, and full of self-reflexive acts of literary invention. Yet a fundamental point they make concerns the programmatic claim that black people have a history, that this is an inalienable part of British history, and that it predates twentieth-century events like the Windrush arrival in 1948 (see Chapter 12). Important as such dates in recent times certainly are, black presences reach back much further.

Both Dabydeen and Martin focus on the later eighteenth century, the subject of important scholarly work by both authors as well. Dabydeen seeks to trace the human presence behind the stereotypical and strictly marginal depictions of black figures in eighteenth-century English art, like the celebrated Hogarth engravings of London life that lend the novel its title. Martin follows the fortunes of two protagonists in the 1780s, former slaves on American plantations and Black Loyalists fighting on the side of the British in the American War of Independence; now trying their fortunes in the imperial metropolis, they become part of a struggle to reimagine British culture as inclusive, 'constructing their identities in direct response to their material world'.[16] This choice of historical period is highly pertinent: the time when the black population in England was at a pre-Windrush peak, it was also the point at which black authorship emerged in print.[17] Eighteenth-century writers like Olaudah Equiano, Ottobah Cugoano, and Ignatius Sancho, who make cameo appearances in Martin's narrative, were pioneers in setting down their lives and views in writing and getting published, with considerable sales (see Chapters 1 and 4). Historical fiction that returns contemporary readers to this period, then, establishes that black British history is not a vision but a given.

In fact, the eighteenth century was far from the beginning of this history. Black British presence dates back a long way, via the Tudor era,[18] to the first to the fifth century AD, when the island was a far-off province of the Roman Empire, and Londinium was a military stronghold with an army that

---

[15] Stuart Hall, 'Racism and Reaction' in *Five Views of Multi-Racial Britain* (London: Commission of Racial Equality, 1978), 23–35; 25.

[16] Dave Gunning, 'S. I. Martin's *Incomparable World* and the Possibilities for Black Historical Fiction', *Journal of Postcolonial Writing*, 43:2 (2007): 203–15; 205.

[17] See C. L. Innes, *A History of Black and Asian Writing in Britain, 1700–2000* (Cambridge: Cambridge University Press, 2002), ch. 2.

[18] See the recent study by Miranda Kaufmann, *Black Tudors: The Untold Story* (London: Oneworld, 2017).

included African soldiers. In an exuberant, moving, and very funny novel-in-verse, *The Emperor's Babe* (2001), Bernardine Evaristo has reimagined this cultural mix through the voice of a young daughter of Sudanese immigrants, bored in her arranged marriage to a rich old Roman and discovering the thrills of a vibrant multicultural city. She is also bored by the canonical literature she is taught (Homer, Virgil) and so decides to tell her own story by writing poetry: 'you see Dad, what I really want to read / and hear is stuff about us, about now, // about Nubians in Londinium'.[19] Delighting in anachronism to highlight the constructedness of history, this meta-poetical comment provides a rationale for contemporary black writing. Indeed Evaristo's literary project takes inspiration from a seminal history, Peter Fryer's *Staying Power: The History of Black People in Britain* (1984), whose famous opening reads: 'There were Africans in Britain before the English came there.'[20] It is historical truths like this, simple but widely forgotten, in which present-day claims of belonging can ground themselves. As Evaristo's narrator reflects: 'my father spoke pidgin-Latin, / we ate off our laps in the doorway, // splattered with mud. Yet I was Roman too. / Civis Romana sum. It was all I had.'[21]

The Other Story

The history of the Roman Empire long served as a useful, if ambiguous, model for imagining English imperial destiny, too. The ambiguity lies in anxieties about the decline following imperial glory, as articulated in Joseph Conrad's *Heart of Darkness* (1899), with its persisting analogies between the Romans in Britain and the British in Africa. They were reactivated in 1968 in a speech by Tory MP Enoch Powell conjuring a dire vision of Britain's future torn apart by racial rioting. Quoting a prophecy from Virgil's *Aeneid*, Powell provided a memorable phrase, 'rivers of blood', that has since become a byword for racist rhetoric. It has also become a challenge taken up by black and Asian British writers: rejecting its message by reversing its premise. In Rushdie's *The Satanic Verses* (1988), for instance, we find a London writer called 'Hanif Johnson' appreciatively mocking fellow writer Joshi and his poem 'Rivers of Blood':

---

[19] Bernardine Evaristo, *The Emperor's Babe* (London: Hamish Hamilton, 2001), 85.
[20] Peter Fryer, *Staying Power: The History of Black People in Britain* (London: Pluto, 1984), 1.
[21] Evaristo, *Emperor's*, 54.

'He says a street is a river and we are the flow; humanity is a river of blood, that's the poet's point. [. . .] In our very bodies, does the river of blood not flow?' *Like the Roman*, the ferrety Enoch Powell had said, *I seem to see the river Tiber foaming with much blood*. Reclaim the metaphor [. . .] Turn it; make it a thing we can use.[22]

This reclaiming and transcoding of offensive terms so they become less harmful and even positive expressions remains one of the most potent strategies of black and Asian British writing.

'The Other Story' was the title of the first art show to present Asian, African, and Caribbean artists based in the UK, curated by Rasheed Araeen in 1989 at the Hayward Gallery in London. Its aim was to make visible an important strand of postwar British creativity that had not received any attention. As indicated by the title, its strategy was primarily an act of narrative: telling 'the other' story means retelling a familiar story from a different point of view to demonstrate dimensions or uncover aspects of the seemingly familiar version that have so far remained hidden or repressed. Therefore, such a retelling involves rereading existing records, searching for their silences and trying to complement, as well as to contest, the one-sided account. The reclamation of black and Asian British presences by way of such revisions and rewritings is a major literary project. It proceeds on the recognition that these histories are already being told – but from a skewed angle, with a biased eye, from a dominant perspective that shows only marginal and/or distorted views, and therefore must be turned around. In the words of Rushdie's poet figure, perpetuated and exclusivist or downright racist stories must be made 'a thing' to 'use'.

The strategy is widespread in postcolonial writing and is just as central for black and Asian British literature. David Dabydeen, Abdulrazak Gurnah, Kazuo Ishiguro, Hari Kunzru, Caryl Phillips, and others have all responded to well-known texts (or, especially in Dabydeen's case, images) so as to explore what other stories are implied in them and need to be teased out. Two of the most powerful examples, however, are by women writers with Caribbean connections: *Wide Sargasso Sea* by Jean Rhys, published in 1966, and *Indigo, or, Mapping the Waters* by Marina Warner, published in 1992, the year of the Columbian quincentenary. They both take specific works from the English canon and re-examine the acts of exclusion on which their symbolic structures rest.

[22] Salman Rushdie, *The Satanic Verses* (Dover, DE: The Consortium, [1988] 1992), 186.

Wide Sargasso Sea presents itself as prequel to Charlotte Brontë's *Jane Eyre* (1847), a tale of female emancipation in which the titular figure's social progress is predicated on the suppression of a Caribbean character, Mr Rochester's first wife. Bertha Mason is a creole woman from the Jamaican planter class, married off to a hapless English gentleman and transferred to his country house, where she is imprisoned in the attic like a beast, disavowed by her husband, henceforth haunting his life and wrecking his planned second marriage before finally killing herself when setting the house on fire. It is this so-called 'madwoman in the attic', a crucial but marginal figure in Brontë's symbolic economy, whose story Rhys reinvents through a dialogue of voices and a subtle interweaving of her own text with the one she has inherited. The textile metaphor is apt, indeed highlighted in an early scene where the heroine is shown engaged in needlework, 'cross-stitching silk roses on a pale background',[23] as if to comment on the way in which Rhys's text crosses a given pattern, while retracing creole history as a thread in larger textures.

The prefix *re-* in *rewriting* signals repetition at the same time as resistance. In just this way, *Indigo* revisits Shakespeare's *The Tempest* and its career through postcolonial rewritings, especially by Caribbean authors like Lamming, Aimé Césaire, or Dabydeen, who use the figure of Caliban as a means of self-positioning. What Warner adds to this tradition is her focus on a figure not previously considered: Sycorax, Caliban's enigmatic mother. In Shakespeare, she is significantly absent, only talked about, appealed to, cursed, or slandered. And yet what we can glean about her backstory – a so-called witch, banished from her home and sent to live on a solitary island where she raised her child – suggests intriguing parallels to what we learn of Prospero. On this basis, Warner reimagines the history of New World conquest from a Caribbean perspective, drawing further parallels with female figures between colonial frontlines, such as Pocahontas, while exploring the use of storytelling in colonial contact zones. She also complements her early modern storyline with a narrative of post-imperial Britain where the trauma of the past must finally come to rest. As the black British present-day embodiment of Caliban says to his white English girlfriend, a present-day Miranda: 'I'm so tired, as the poet [Walcott] said, of our fucking envy and your fucking guilt'[24] – thus trying to put history to rest.

---

[23] Jean Rhys, *Wide Sargasso Sea* (Harmondsworth: Penguin, [1966] 1968), 44.
[24] Marina Warner, *Indigo, or, Mapping the Waters* (London: Vintage, 1992), 394.

Significantly, for a history of black and Asian British writing, Rhys and Warner offer borderline and test cases. Neither 'black' nor 'Asian' themselves, both writers nevertheless have a place in this history because of their creative work as much as their personal connectedness. The place of Rhys in Caribbean literature was the subject of a fierce debate between Kamau Brathwaite and Peter Hulme, whereas Warner commented on her unacknowledged creole family connections, which she addressed through the novel, 'interloping on territory from which accidents of history had morally barred' her.[25] However, history can be a bar as much as it can be a bridge – such category problems are characteristic of a field in which dichotomies are often questioned and distinctions blurred in favour of acknowledging porosity and ongoing entanglements.

Family Matters

Coming to terms with traumatic family histories is a challenge not exclusively for black and Asian British writing. Other diasporic literatures, above all Jewish writing, also address a history of pain and plight, and they frequently seek to focus on the author's family. Such cultural work of memory – and, for subsequent generations, post-memory – fuses autobiographical with historiographical impulses, often aided by specific media such as images or photographs. Marianne Hirsch, the daughter of holocaust survivors, has described this process as the construction of a 'familial gaze' that 'situates human subjects in the ideology, the mythology, of the family as institution', with this institution itself occupying a precarious place: 'structurally a last vestige of protection against war, racism, exile, and cultural displacement, [the family] becomes particularly vulnerable to these violent ruptures, and so a measure of their devastation'.[26] In this way, family matters combine personal with public history and new modes of autobiographical writing can 'open up the symbolic borders of new or previously contested national histories'.[27]

---

[25] See Denise deCaires Narain, 'Caribbean Creole: The Real Thing? Writing and Reading Creole in a Selection of Caribbean Women's Texts' in Susheila Nasta (ed.), *Reading the 'New' Literatures in a Postcolonial Era* (Cambridge: D. S. Brewer, 2000), 105–27. Marina Warner, 'Between the Colonist and the Creole: Family Bonds, Family Boundaries' in Anna Rutherford and Shirley Chew (eds.), *Unbecoming Daughters of the Empire* (Mundelstrup: Dangaroo, 1993), 197–203; 199.

[26] Marianne Hirsch, *Family Frames: Photography, Narrative, and Postmemory* (Cambridge, MA: Harvard University Press, 1997), 11, 13.

[27] Susheila Nasta, 'Editorial', *Wasafiri*, 21:2 (2006): 1–2; 1.

Examples abound. Family photographs are an acknowledged inspiration for Rushdie's *Midnight's Children*, as for Edward Said's memoir *Out of Place* (1999), Kureishi's *My Ear at his Heart* (2004), and Vikram Seth's *Two Lives* (2005); the last is a monumental tribute to his great-uncle, Indian in origin, and his great-aunt, German in origin, with whom he lived in England in the early 1970s, after their turbulent lives across three continents and several decades of the twentieth century. Family matters also give substance to many black and Asian British novels – often debut novels – that use such relationships as a narrative structure in which, and against which, an emerging sense of self must be defined. Zadie Smith's *White Teeth* (2000), Evaristo's *Lara* (1997), and Andrea Levy's *Fruit of the Lemon* (1999) all present quests for self-knowledge, between England and various other places, through journeys exploring family histories and dislocation.[28] As Levy's narrator explains: 'The country where I live, among people so unaware of our shared past that all they would see if they were staring at my aunt would be a black woman acting silly'.[29] It is such ignorance and a glaring lack of historical consciousness that such black and Asian British literary genealogies attempt to remedy.

As part of this broader trend, there are cases when the self is barred from knowledge of its own past, as for instance in *The Adoption Papers* (1991), the debut poetry sequence by black Scottish poet Jackie Kay (see Chapter 20). Here, a constellation of three poetic voices – a daughter, a birth mother, and an adoptive mother – stages a search for connections beyond accidents of birth and across lines of belonging. At the same time, families made by cultural affiliation rather than biological parentage (like Sycorax's family in Warner's *Indigo*) counter heteronormative conceptions of the family as a form of natural order, as in English tales of orphans like *Jane Eyre*. These are even more powerfully challenged, however, in narratives of queer family life, like Kay's *Trumpet* (1998) or Evaristo's *Mr Loverman* (2013).

Literary bonds also produce genealogies, as in Kureishi's *My Ear at his Heart: Reading my Father* (2004) and V. S. Naipaul's *Letters Between a Father and a Son* (1999), his actual family correspondence from the 1950s. In both cases, the writers stage a process of initiation and emancipation, by which they triumph precisely where their fathers failed: in successful authorship. Both fathers entertained literary ambitions that never found fulfilment, except in legacies left to their sons. In Kureishi's book, this is an actual novel in

---

[28] For this reason, Mark U. Stein reads these and other novels as *Bildungsromane* in *Black British Literature: Novels of Transformation* (Columbus, OH: Ohio State University Press, 2004).

[29] Andrea Levy, *Fruit of the Lemon* (London: Review, 1999), 326.

manuscript; in Naipaul's book, it is the father's advice collected in letters to his son in England, who now brings him posthumous publication. Both fathers, who also figure prominently in the novels by which the sons first made their names, *The Buddha of Suburbia* (1990) and *A House for Mr Biswas* (1961), represent a personal history that must be at once reclaimed and rejected, as a family inheritance that is both enabling and restricting. 'Writing this book I wonder what my self consists of', Kureishi declares. 'I feel inhabited by others, composed of them. Writers, parents, older men, friends, girlfriends, speak inside me.'[30] For all the urge, then, to recover the past in writing, the act of writing may itself demand that the inhabitants of this past be exorcised or silenced.

Echo Chambers

The feeling described by Kureishi turns out to be a fundamental and familiar predicament, theorised by poststructuralist philosophers. Just as history is neither uniform nor unambiguous, so the self is never singular nor independent from the cultural and verbal repertoires that inform its formation. Thus, individuality may simply be the fetish of uncertain cultures in need of self-assurance. And literary projects like the exercises in autobiographical writing just considered may be significant not because they provide a given self the chance to speak, but because they actually produce this sense of self by means of such generic speech acts as the right to say 'I'. From this perspective, autobiographies are primarily performative texts, not so much descriptive as productive: they do things with words. What they are doing can be characterised as self-formation by self-formulation.[31] Through writing his or her own life, the autobiographer turns into the author of his or her own self (see Chapter 30).

This issue has particular relevance for slave narratives and their afterlives in contemporary literature. The character of Thomas Pringle in Dabydeen's *A Harlot's Progress* recalls the editor of the first slave narrative published by a woman, *The History of Mary Prince* (1831), provoking debates on what profits, moral and financial, such a publication project may yield. Fred D'Aguiar's

---

[30] Hanif Kureishi, *My Ear at his Heart: Reading my Father* (London: Faber and Faber, 2004), 55.

[31] Ulla Haselstein, *Die Gabe der Zivilisation: kultureller Austausch und literarische Textpraxis in Amerika, 1682–1861* (Munich: Fink, 2000), ch. 4. See also Anthony Carrigan, 'Negotiating Personal and Cultural Memory in Olaudah Equiano's *Interesting Narrative*', *Wasafiri*, 21 (2006): 42–7.

Feeding the Ghosts (1997) is an engagement with the 1781 case of the slave ship *Zong* where Africans were thrown overboard so as to claim insurance for them as 'goods lost at sea', while his *The Longest Memory* (1994) is a polyphonic exploration of Virginian plantation life around 1800; Andrea Levy's *The Long Song* (2010) is set on a Jamaican sugar plantation and uses the form of a slave memoir. All these examples do not simply retrace historical narratives of suffering but also interrogate the ways in which such narratives were constructed and are perpetuated.

The same holds, with particular force, for Caryl Phillips's interest in historical fiction as a vehicle to revision the past. Novels such as *Higher Ground* (1989), *Crossing the River* (1993), and *The Nature of Blood* (1997) are part of this project, as is *Cambridge* (1991), perhaps the strongest example of his tendency to abandon the notion of a controlling narrative authority for a kaleidoscope of different views, sometimes converging but often conflicting. *Cambridge* tells the story of Emily Cartwright, a young Englishwoman, and her encounter with West Indian plantation life, full of brutality and sexual undercurrents, specifically her fascination with the estate overseer Mr Brown and a devoutly Christian slave, the eponymous Cambridge – a story that ends with an illicit pregnancy, a violent death, a murder charge, and an execution. As readers we are never given a full account of what has actually happened and may only seek for answers in the two journals, Emily's and Cambridge's, that constitute most of the novel's text, like fragmentary documentary evidence from which no comprehensive history can be reconstructed. The task of reclamation ultimately remains with each reader.

Framed by a prologue and epilogue in present-day language, the two divergent accounts are marked as historical by their language, redolent of traditional journal writing. Indeed, they are largely composed of actual citations from such literature – such as Janet Schaw's *Journal of a Lady of Quality* (1770s), Mrs Carmichael's *Domestic Manners and Social Conditions of the White, Coloured, and Negro Population of the West Indies* (1833), and 'Monk' Lewis's *Journal of a West Indian Proprietor* (1834) – a 'palimpsest which assembles specific passages from older texts in an artistic montage' to form an intertextual patchwork of historical plantation accounts.[32] Cambridge's journal, in turn, draws on slave narratives and related sources, for instance Equiano's *Interesting Narrative* (1789) and Ignatius Sancho's *Letters* (1782). When writing the book, Phillips in fact corresponded with Paul Edwards,

---

[32] Lars Eckstein, *Re-Membering the Black Atlantic: On the Poetics and Politics of Literary Memory* (Amsterdam; New York: Rodopi, 2006), 69.

modern editor of Equiano's and Sancho's texts and eminent historian of eighteenth-century black British life, who took an active interest in the question of how to shape literary characters from such material from the colonial archive. *Cambridge* can therefore be read as an experiment in making historical texts matter again by transforming them into present-day fiction.

According to Lars Eckstein, 'the specific mnemonic design of *Cambridge* thus encourages, or even demands, the incorporation of its source-texts into a negotiation of contemporary values'.[33] This novel makes us realise that reclaiming the past is necessarily an act of the present. Through its intertextual composition and the integration of diverse and distinct voices, historical fiction like Phillips's forms an echo chamber in which no single note can sound unbroken.

Historiographic Metafiction

In the different ways outlined above, black and Asian British writing has engaged with history and historical memory, inviting readers to consider their own relations to the past and their efforts in remembering or forgetting and denying 'what happened before'. The politics of memory are crucial here, typically shifting with the changing circumstances to which they respond. In immigrant communities, especially, a characteristic pattern of remembrance often emerges over different generations, with first-generation immigrants actively keeping memories of their homeland alive, while the second generation growing up in the host country may just as actively try to forget them, whereas the third generation may in turn consciously try to revive connections to the place their grandparents once left behind. Such differences are, for instance, featured in Timothy Mo's novel *Sour Sweet* (1982) about a Hong Kong family settling in 1960s London. They are also crucial, in different and perhaps more complex ways, for a recent travelogue like *Looking for Transwonderland: Travels in Nigeria* (2012), in which Noo Saro-Wiwa goes in search of everyday realities in the country that formed, and eventually killed, her father. This has painful relevance for diasporic subjects, whose search for their own past literally takes them into countries that are thought to be familiar but often turn out to be utterly foreign.

---

[33] Ibid., 106.

Memory, this goes to show, may be less a personal capacity than a cultural function, in the sense established by Maurice Halbwachs:[34] collective memory results from social acts; it is less inherited from the past than inhabited by the present, actively constructed, communicated, and circulated in the daily cultural practices of a particular community. For this reason, novels are crucial here: they contribute to the shaping and reshaping of what a particular community chooses to remember and what it chooses to forget. Notions of nationhood, it has been argued, ground themselves in such collective acts, especially the stories people tell themselves of a shared past.[35] Therefore, memory and history are political categories, bound up in those power struggles that determine which version – or rather, *whose* version – of the past is passed on.

In the seventh of his 'Theses on the Philosophy of History' (1940), Walter Benjamin formulated this connection between the partiality of memory and history as a consequence of power:

> Whoever has emerged victorious participates to this day in the triumphal procession in which the present rulers step over those who are lying prostrate. [. . .] There is no document of civilization which is not at the same time a document of barbarism. And just as such a document is not free of barbarism, barbarism taints also the manner in which it was transmitted from one owner to another.[36]

It is this manner of transmission, formative of cultural tradition, that is often foregrounded, explored, and questioned through black and Asian British genealogies. To reclaim the past means, above all, to claim a different kind of past and a historiography that allows contrapuntal views and versions. In Benjamin's phrase, they mean 'to brush history against the grain'.[37]

Many of the novels discussed here counter conventional historiographies. But perhaps the most enduring example of a narrative that dramatises the wayward workings of memory and the forward makings of history is Rushdie's *Midnight's Children*. With its unreliable narrator Saleem, who commences 'the business of remaking my life from the point at which it really began', only to discover that his whole existence is 'mysteriously

---

[34] See Jan Assmann, 'Communicative and Cultural Memory' in Astrid Erll and Ansgar Nünning (eds.), *A Companion to Cultural Memory Studies* (Berlin; New York: de Gruyter, 2008), 109–18.

[35] See Homi K. Bhabha, 'Introduction: Narrating the Nation' in Homi K. Bhabha (ed.), *Nation and Narration* (London; New York: Routledge, 1990), 1–7.

[36] Walter Benjamin, *Illuminations*, trans. Harry Zohn, ed. Hannah Arendt (New York: Schocken Books, 1968), 256.

[37] Ibid., 257.

handcuffed to history', the book combines a search for the personal past, as found through family histories, with an interrogation of the public past, as presented in nationalist rhetoric.[38] Its most powerful metaphor, however, derives from the kitchen: what the novel calls 'the chutnification of history'.[39] Saleem produces pickle jars, corresponding to the chapters of his narrative, as containers and sustainers of a past which may thus be putatively preserved, but only at the cost of continuous change: 'I reconcile myself to the inevitable distortions of the pickling process. To pickle is to give immortality, after all [. . .]. The art is to change the flavour in degree, but not in kind.'[40] From this vantage point, pickling and writing go together: both provide ways of making things last, contributing to cultural memory. But the result is never pure, preservation necessitates transformation; in order to keep anything it must be changed in a 'constant and endless' process of revision.[41] Precisely *as* history, then, the past is necessarily transformed and creatively corrupted. Rushdie uses chutney as a trope for this revised understanding of history, a critical tool to highlight ongoing and indeed *meaningful* corruptions, against the ideology of purity that riddles nationalist discourses.

This makes the project to reclaim the past even more complex. Whenever literature manages to address, explore, and reflect such complexities, its strategies are best described by Linda Hutcheon's term 'historiographic metafiction'. *Historiographic* novels do not present definite histories, but engage with the ways in which history is written; and they are *metafictional* when they reflect on their own strategies of constructing a world. Historiography and fiction come together in that they both '*constitute* their objects of attention', according to Hutcheon, deciding 'which events will become facts'.[42] In this sense they constitute narratives that matter.

These affinities between postmodern and postcolonial strategies are sufficient grounds for rethinking postmodern philosophies in postcolonial terms, shaped as they are by diasporic authors like Jacques Derrida. At the very least they prompt us to place black and Asian British literary engagements with history into a larger framework. As genealogy in the Foucauldian sense, metahistorical writing does not provide seamless, unbroken, and continuous tales of cause–effect relations within a broad framework. Instead it questions the desire for such tales by exposing the costs and consequences incurred by their production. An example of this broader trend is Julian Barnes's novel *A History of the World in 10½ Chapters* (1989), which offers a series of apparently

---

[38] Rushdie, *Midnight's*, 9, 10.   [39] Ibid., 459.   [40] Ibid., 461.   [41] Ibid., 460.
[42] Linda Hutcheon, *A Poetics of Postmodernism: History, Theory, Fiction* (London; New York: Routledge, 1988), 122.

unconnected anecdotal chapters whose supposed significance we must gauge ourselves. The only clue that the authorial voice offers lies in a critique of history given in the half-chapter – the incomplete chapter, the chapter full of spill-overs – included there, like Saleem Sinai's extra pickle jar, to suggest that no schema can accommodate everything: 'The history of the world? Just voices echoing in the dark; images that burn for a few centuries and then fade; stories, old stories that sometimes seem to overlap; strange links, impertinent connections.'[43]

The issue, therefore, is pervasive and also concerns this *History*: can our book provide a sense of order and, if so, how? Furthermore, Barnes's 'impertinent connections' have special relevance for representations of mainstream British history because of the impertinence by which so much that should be of key importance, such as *colonial* histories, traditionally eludes the local eye and grasp. In the words of Mr Sisodia, the stuttering film producer in *The Satanic Verses*, 'the trouble with the Engenglish is that their hiss hiss history happened overseas, so they dodo don't know what it means'.[44] To broaden the horizon, to restore a sense of worldly interconnectedness and ongoing cultural entanglement to our understanding of history, by making readers see what strange links and impertinent connections colonialism has bequeathed us: *this* is what black and Asian British writers, each in their own different way, achieve with their creative takes on genealogy.

[43] Julian Barnes, *A History of the World in 10½ Chapters* (London: Vintage, 1989), 242.
[44] Rushdie, *Satanic*, 343.

29

Expanding Realism, Thinking New Worlds

TABISH KHAIR

The world of Salman Rushdie's 1981 novel *Midnight's Children* is often cited as exemplary of a new wave of experimentation in British writing, a tradition drawing (as some have argued) on world-famous figures like Gabriel García Márquez, or earlier mentors from the 1930s such as G. V. Desani. Rushdie's so-called reinvention of 'magical realism' is sometimes said to have sparked the publication of a series of similarly hyper-realist, 'maximalist', or 'big' novels by other subcontinental and British Asian writers. However, Rushdie has himself claimed in various interviews that *Midnight's Children* was not surrealistic but 'realist' and drew on the jangling contradictions of the India of his childhood. Similarly other writers covered here, such as Helen Oyeyemi, have on several occasions refused to be categorised as magical realist.

Despite disclaimers by Rushdie, Oyeyemi, and others, it is important to engage with the notion of 'magical realism' because, even before Rushdie, magical realism had a strangely colonial *and* postcolonial lineage, so that its 'surrealism' was often rooted in the *jangling contradictions* of a particular, and particularly non-European, reality. If Alejo Carpentier's 'lo real maravilloso Americano' is accepted, as often acknowledged, as the progenitor of literary magical realism, then it is not incidental that Carpentier not only located the elements of magical realism in the colonies but was himself returning after an extended sojourn in Europe.[1] Latin America was seen by Carpentier as essentially a mix of the marvellous and the real, which, by obvious implication, Europe was not.

One can argue that this way of seeing non-Europe was *not* a twentieth-century development. Historically, European writers (all the way back to Herodotus, and beyond) have tended to read non-European spaces in terms

---

[1] Lois Parkinson Zamora and Wendy B. Faris (eds.), *Magical Realism: Theory, History, Community* (Durham, NC; London: Duke University Press, 1995), 87.

of a mixture of the real and the magical: hence, for instance, reports and 'histories' of the hybrid beasts of not just Latin America in the recent past (as in the voyages of Columbus), but also of Asia and Africa all the way back to the Greek and Roman empires. But there *is* a difference. Earlier European writers, from the classical period to the late medieval and early Enlightenment periods, found a similar admixture *in Europe* too: witches, vampires, unicorns. It is only with the establishment of Enlightenment perspectives that such hybrid beings started to disappear from European spaces – to be found largely in non-European ones. (Though here too, the matter remains far more complex in literature, as I intend to indicate at the end with just one example: Laurie Lee's twentieth-century 'realist' memoir *Cider with Rosie*.) One can argue, with reference to texts by Salman Rushdie (1947–), Ben Okri (1959–), Pauline Melville (1948–), and Helen Oyeyemi (1984–), that this tendency distinguishes and frames what is called 'magical realism'. This marks a fraught but necessary attempt to write about non-European experiences and spaces in their difference, which was seen as an otherness not reduced to negativity, and outside the dominant paradigms of European literary speech, commonly identified with realism.

Contending the Real

Magical realism is a literary version of a larger twentieth-century challenge to the 'reality' of an assumed universal rationality, which was often revealed to be particularly European. As Sandra Harding puts it in a restrained critique of the assumption of a universal, single, coherent reality, 'social reality depends in part on us, is open, structured, possesses emergent powers, and is intrinsically dynamic and processual'.[2] Apart from the fact that 'reality' can be seen as (partly) a construct or, at the very least, not singular and unchanging, magical realism is also a reaction to the literary narrative mode of realism, as it developed in the eighteenth, nineteenth, and twentieth centuries.

Realism was often identified by European, particularly anglophone, critics as a defining aspect of the modern novel. Perhaps its most influential and advanced exposition is by Ian Watt in *The Rise of the Novel*. Watt argues that before the rise of the novel in the eighteenth century, literature was conditioned by an 'Aristotelian' conception of 'reality', which dealt with universals and abstractions. These, not the concrete objects of sense perception, were

---

[2] Sandra Harding, 'Representing Reality: The Critical Realism Project', *Feminist Economics*, 9:1 (2003): 151–9; 152.

considered true realities. Watt states that modern realism, building on the philosophical traditions arising from Descartes, began in the late eighteenth century with 'the proposition that the truth can be discovered by the individual through the senses'.[3] Connected to this and growing out of it is the notion of 'realism' as a general philosophical doctrine that considers reality as quite distinct from (various) representations (of reality), and only to be determined on the basis of objective, repeatable, and verifiable parameters.

In itself the 'realist' tradition in literature could be considered narrower than the reality of the European novel – leaving out, for instance, Franz Kafka – but it was experienced as particularly restrictive in post/colonial non-European spaces. This was partly because, as noted earlier, non-Europe was seen as exceeding or escaping the European 'real'. The matter of creolisation obviously played a part, and impelled even largely realist writers, like Raja Rao in *Kanthapura* (1938), as the foreword, language, and structure of that seminal Indian English novel indicate. The need to disrupt ontological certainties – European particulars passed for universals – was always part of the anti-colonial endeavour, and it was brought home to the 'centre' when writers like Rushdie started consciously writing back to the empire *from* the west. Strangely, however, this bid to describe new realities was also for some writers, especially those coming from or relating to significantly oral cultures, such as Ben Okri, rooted in older non-European realities. The Pacific writer and critic, Albert Wendt, notes, 'So now we have a complex and expansive blend of realism and magical realism in our writing. But at the heart of all this are the indigenous ingredients: the techniques of oral storytelling and other oral traditions; art, dance and music; and indigenous philosophies and visions'.[4]

In black and Asian British fiction, when these supposedly non-European elements – 'indigenous ingredients' in Wendt's words – are used by diasporic writers, there is an immediate effect of Otherness. As this engagement with Otherness runs through most of postcolonial literature – which, at its best, has to contend against the negativised 'Othering' of post/colonial realities in colonial literature while allowing space for their essential Otherness at the same time – one finds magical realist texts merging with other kinds of texts too. For instance, Hanif Kureishi (1954–), essentially a realist novelist, combines traces of magical realism with traces of science fiction in the title story

---

[3] Ian Watt, *The Rise of the Novel* (London: Hogarth Press, 1993), 12.
[4] Albert Wendt, 'Introduction' in Albert Wendt (ed.), *Nuanua: Pacific Writing in English Since 1980* (Auckland: Auckland University Press, 1995), 1–8; 4.

of *The Body* (2002), built on the central conceit of an ageing man stumbling across a kind of surgery that enables his brain to be transplanted into the body of a young man. The fact that Kureishi avoids dwelling on the technology of the surgery, as science fiction would, in order to concentrate on his meditative exploration of the issues, is enabled by a readership used to magical realism. Recently, Hari Kunzru (1969–) and, to an extent, Mohsin Hamid (1971–) in *Exit West* (2017), discussed later, have also toyed with speculative fiction in tandem with magical realism, while Romesh Gunesekera's (1954–) engagement with exile, dreams, and nightmares in *Heaven's Edge* (2002) is consciously poised between a fragile mythic/magical realm and violent reality.

In any of these cases, whatever the specific rubric employed by critics, the attempt by the author is to engage with some version of non-Eurocentric Otherness. Oyeyemi has addressed this directly in some interviews, noting that she wants her reader to experience the Other. Rushdie's *Midnight's Children*, for instance, uses the trick to narrate an entire nation's birth (and partition): magical realism allows space for the narrative to encapsulate all loose ends and contradictions, including those of the narrator, of a nation that escapes 'reasoned' (Cartesian?) reality. Interestingly, though, this endeavour contests one of the tenets of magical realism as a genre proposed by some theorists. In order to make any sense of magical realism – and segregate it from surrealism, fairy tales, and so on – critics have propounded that the magical elements should be rooted in reality and irreducible.[5]

From the necessary if narrow perspective of critical nit-picking, it should not be possible to reduce the magic to reality, for instance as psychological aberration or parable. From that angle, a magical realist novel should not be an allegory – but *Midnight's Children*, while being undoubtedly magical realist, is nevertheless widely read (with good cause) as a 'national allegory'. In this sense, much of black and Asian British magical realism contests not just realism but also escapes definitions of magical realism, suggesting modes of reading that draw upon both these generic trends. It is this innovative element that, as I shall argue later in this chapter, gives postcolonial magical realist fiction much of its impetus and impact.

Returning to Rushdie, it can be argued that in generic terms *The Satanic Verses* (1988) is more of a magical realist novel than *Midnight's Children*.

---

[5] Lois Parkinson Zamora and Wendy B. Faris, 'Introduction: Daiquiri Birds and Flaubertian Parrot(ie)s' and Wendy B. Faris's 'Scheherazade's Children: Magical Realism and Postmodern Fiction' in Zamora and Faris (eds.), *Magical Realism*, 1–14, 163–90.

Though *The Satanic Verses* was read as partly a novelisation of the birth of Islam, among other things, it is a novel that resists allegorical readings. The 'magical' elements in *The Satanic Verses* do not just controvert the reality of 'faith' (including certain Islamic interpretations) but also the realities of the ex-colonial centre: it is fruitful to read the novel as a 'multicultural London novel' following along a path initially cut by Sam Selvon's *The Lonely Londoners* (1956). Selvon's novel is not magical realist in a specifically generic sense, but it shares with *The Satanic Verses* a similar contention of both London's inherited space (reality) and the form in which it can be narrated. While noting the class and generational differences between Rushdie and Caribbean writers like Sam Selvon (1923–1994), Susheila Nasta also states that 'Rushdie's description [. . .] of England as the dubious fulfilment of an illusory "colonial" dream is not markedly dissimilar from Caribbean writers who migrated to London in the 1950s.'[6]

That *The Satanic Verses* led to the biggest controversy over a book in recent decades, with the author being threatened with death by Islamists and the Islamist regime of Iran, highlights the effectiveness of magical realism as a contention of reality, and also shows that such contention can be absorbed for very different political ends. For instance, in retrospect, the controversy (including attacks, threats, and book burnings) over *The Satanic Verses* in the UK led to the consolidation of reactionary positions among sections of the Muslim diaspora in Britain as well as of racist positions among sections of white Britons. In the process, it is questionable whether the novel widened the space for thinking about faith, culture, and nationality that it obviously intended to open up. The fact that this collision occurred due to an admixture of religious belief on the one side and magical realism as a narrative mode on the other is significant: religions have traditionally depended on the magical (miracles, for instance) as a confirmation of their higher and final 'reality' – quite often opposed to Cartesian reality – and religious establishments have drawn power from their ability to impose authoritative interpretations on stories. *The Satanic Verses* employed a similar strategy for the counter-purpose of opening up reality and interpretation – turning them plural and provisional.

However, part of the Islamic indignation over *The Satanic Verses* also related to a matter highlighted earlier. The novel was condemned as primarily an attack on a faith seen as non-European, and sometimes abused – using

---

[6] Susheila Nasta, *Home Truths: Fictions of the South Asian Diaspora in Britain* (Basingstoke; New York: Palgrave, 2002), 147–8.

similar interpretations of its sacred stories – in and by Europe. This was by no means a full summary of the novel, and yet the narrative mode of magical realism – because it so often sees non-European experiences as magical realist, posed unconsciously against the Cartesian reality of Europe – made such a reading also partly viable. In *Midnight's Children*, Rushdie had powerfully used the mode to narrate a teeming subcontinent outside Europe. In *The Satanic Verses*, he used the mode to engage with a certain religious history from outside Europe, in the past and in a Pakistani present – and even when the novel moved to London, the 'magical' elements adhered to characters from outside Europe, in particular Gibreel Farishta and Saladin Chamcha. This tendency is not restricted to Rushdie. Okri's *The Famished Road* (1991), for instance, is difficult to imagine as set in Europe, as are a number of other stories and novels, such as the narratives of Amos Tutuola, if defined as 'magical realist'. At its best, though, this way of narrating the Otherness of non-Europe can have a powerful impact, as it does in *The Famished Road*. Okri's novel is a first-person narrative by and of Azaro, an *ábíkú* or spirit-child, in an unnamed ghetto of Africa: it enables the author not just to cover large swathes of sociopolitical 'reality' but also to introduce other ways of understanding and seeing the world – ways that critics continue to dispute as best contained in the labels 'magical realist' or 'traditional African religious' perspectives. Once again, though, despite the fact that Okri's *The Famished Road* resists, as we have seen above, an allegorical reading far more than Rushdie's *Midnight's Children*, it too has been read as an allegory – in that sense, escaping the magical realist commandment of irreducibility.

In Pauline Melville's collection *The Migration of Ghosts* (1998) too, the magical realist stories have to do with the non-west, or with someone from the non-west, most brilliantly in 'The President's Exile'. This is a story that seems to begin with an exiled dictator-president from a developing country reliving the site of his education in London, but it gets murkier as the president returns home and is revealed to be a kind of ghost-zombie. He has died – been murdered? – during a foreign visit, and at the end of the novel he is a bleeding dead body on a horse in a forest outside his capital: 'There, beneath the trees, the horse continued to graze patiently, until such time as his sleeping burden should wake again.'[7] The ability of such a story to reflect obliquely and shockingly on the repetitive brutalities of power in many developing countries and their obscure links to the 'west' has a lot to do with its narrative mode; a realist narrative would have failed to evoke that

[7] Pauline Melville, *The Migration of Ghosts* (London: Bloomsbury, 1998), 24.

exact effect. It also, at the same time, turns such magical realist texts into allegories.

Thinking in Stories

However, it is misleading to read black or Asian British magical realism only in contrast to realism, if realism is seen as having a largely European provenance, just as it is misleading to associate reason only or largely with Europe. As was evident in the reception of *The Satanic Verses*, an attempt to insist on a particular reality as definitive is by no means only a European prerogative. And the combination of 'magic' with 'reality' need not be either enabling or corrosive of power. After all, religious fundamentalists often dismiss 'science' in words that are not too different from those employed by poststructuralists or postmodernists who question 'reality'. Creationists claim that evolution is just a story, and that their own stories are at least as good and as real as that of Darwinian evolution. The reality of human rights can be opposed in the name of the 'greater' reality of some god or holy book. This list is long: a simple championing of magical realism against realism, or of 'realities' against 'reality', or of stories against history, or magic against reason, does not achieve much.

I would argue that it also reduces magical realism – and literature as a whole. Either we are left with stories that have nothing to do with 'reality' unless the storyteller so wishes, or we are left with a Plato-like, mimicry-based understanding of art and literature. Both are reductive. Magical realism and literature in general are served better if one stops to look at the way in which human beings have used stories to think. It is this attempt that makes black and Asian magical realist texts significant: they open up new ways to think about ourselves and society.

As suggested, this is not a matter confined to magical realist texts but extends to all of literature. For instance, a fundamentalist reading of the Book of Job stresses Job's 'true' faith. But to leave the Book of Job there is to stop thinking about it. Because the narrative of Job is secondary to its problematic. One can even argue that the narrative is misleading: in the restoration of Job's children, health, and wealth we have a resolution that fails in our terms. We do not expect such magic / miracles in real life. Hence, it is not the narrative of Job that is significant. What is significant and useful are the problems of the story.

Religions (theology, as against fundamentalism) have always known that human beings think in stories. That is why religions consciously think through stories: the 'facts' and 'details' of these stories change with changing human circumstances, but what does not change is the bid and ability to make us contemplate, imagine, reason, induce, examine – in other words, think. Returning to *The Satanic Verses*, it can be argued that, despite what they said, Islamic fundamentalists were angry at Rushdie more for his bid to think differently about the 'magic' of their faith, than the liberties that they claimed he took with their 'realities'. In this context, the strange similarity between religious texts and magical realism is not just an accident.

Magical realist texts are not simply a contention with Cartesian reality or with literary realism; they are primarily an attempt to make the reader think anew or differently. If to read the Book of Job as about faith is to reduce it to fundamentalist singularity, to read the alternation of magic/fantasy and reality in black or Asian magical realism as primarily a gripping or different narrative is to do something similar. It is also reductive to celebrate the magical against the real, perhaps as the overturning of a purportedly colonial binarism, in such fiction. Something much more complex happens in the best magical realist texts. Both reality and magic, as well as their specific admixture, are necessary for this in such cases. What these texts do is make it possible to think about what is unthinkable, or think anew about what has been thought in fixed ways.

That might be the reason why, increasingly, magical realism either combines with other subgeneric trends in black and Asian British fiction, or exists as a strong trace rather than a full subgenre. Such novels can be difficult to label and slot – unless one remembers that easy labels are not conducive to new thinking. Such a trend could be discerned in earlier postcolonial novels too, for instance, in Jean Rhys's brilliant use of the gothic to reveal the hidden colonial secrets of race and identity in *Wide Sargasso Sea* (1966), a novel published when much of the Caribbean was still colonised.

Magical Realism as Storied Thought

Among recent novels, Brian Chikwava's *Harare North* (2009) does something similar to Rhys's *Wide Sargasso Sea*: it skirts the edges of the magical and reality, though with a more clearly psychological resolution. Chikwava (1972–) clearly toys with the reader's expectations from the subgenre of magical realism. The unnamed hero of his novel lands in London, carrying a cardboard suitcase and a longing to be reunited with his childhood friend Shingi. As one reads on, various discrepancies attract the reader's attention, so that the reality of either the hero or Shingi or both starts looking doubtful.

Various options cross the reader's mind, mostly associated with magical realist premises, such as the existence of spirits, before, right at the end, the novel is given a powerful, credible, and overwhelmingly rational resolution as well. Chikwava's narrative seems to be magical realist until his protagonist is revealed as having a kind of split personality, though even this is difficult to pin down to a neat psychological paradigm. The unresolved element in this brilliant novel makes it rise above other 'multicultural London' novels of its generation by unsettling convictions about not just London but also Zimbabwe, not just 'mixed immigrant' identities but also human identity. Just as Chikwava plays with magical realist elements in the novel, he also presents a contemporary version of London: his novel is a darker, more violent, highly twisted successor to Sam Selvon's *The Lonely Londoners*.

One can also place *A Wicked Old Woman* (1987) by Ravinder Randhawa (1952–), a pioneering but sadly overlooked novel, in this category: this contains no magical element at all, but it plays on the magic of appearance and reality. The wicked old woman of the title is an Asian immigrant in England who pretends to be much older than she is, as that enables her to escape the conscription of niceness imposed on her both as an immigrant and as a young woman. A number of other novels, such as Hari Kunzru's *Gods Without Men* (2011), while not being clearly magical realist, nevertheless follow in the wake of magical realism by flouting expectations of a straight reality and of a holistic narrative unity. In fact, authors like Kunzru and Zadie Smith (1975–), at least in *White Teeth* (2000), often display magical realist traces – paradoxes, contradictions, a joyous sort of multiculturality, verbal play, narrative expanse or narrative disjunction, a questioning of given European realities – in their novels. Smith's *White Teeth*, of course, was famously described as an example of hysterical realism rather than magical realism by James Wood, but it is a distinction better left out of the purview of this chapter. Other novels, by authors not known as magical realist, also sometimes employ magical realism: *Paradise* (1994) by Abdulrazak Gurnah (1948–) and *Salt and Saffron* (2000) by Kamila Shamsie (1973–) come to mind. While probably an engagement with Joseph Conrad's *Heart of Darkness* and distinguished by the predominant register of a kind of historical realism, Gurnah's *Paradise*, shortlisted for the Booker Prize, nevertheless contains elements reminiscent of magical realism: a boy who has strange dreams, tales of wonder, an earthly paradise. Such novels might not be generically magical realist, but they are definitely permeated by its spirit. Evidently, magical realism can as often be discerned as an influence rather than pinpointed as a definitive subgenre in recent black and Asian British fiction.

The insertion of magical realist elements in such novels seems to be aimed at opening up new areas of thought. A good example of this is Mohsin Hamid's *Exit West*. Hamid had not employed a clearly magical realist device in his earlier novels, though he had skirted around the subgenre in at least two of them. *Exit West*, too, seems to open along those lines, presenting a pithy but basically realistic account of a man and a woman falling in love in an unnamed 'city swollen by refugees but mostly at peace, or at least not yet openly at war'.[8] The man, Saeed, is the son of a professor and a teacher, and brought up to be open, accepting, somewhat religious: he *sometimes* says his evening prayers. The woman, Nadia, is fully veiled, but turns out to ride a motorcycle, live on her own, and not to believe in religion: veiling, for her, is a personal choice for entirely pragmatic reasons.

There is very little of magical realism until a bit later in the novel, though there are occasional 'episodes' – in other, richer countries – of people emerging from 'black' doorways and disappearing into the light. These are not explained until later in the main narrative – that of Saeed and Nadia – when war and violence take over the unnamed city, and Saeed's mother is killed by a stray bullet. Then rumours began 'to circulate of doors that could take you elsewhere, often to places far away, well removed from this death trap of a country'.[9] At first dismissed as 'superstitions of the feeble-minded',[10] it turns out that such doors do exist – and Saeed and Nadia pay their way to escape through one to Greece, and from there, after a while, they are helped to escape through another door to London. Much of the rest of the novel realistically describes the experiences and deprivations of seeking refuge in our world, but the doors remain as undoubtedly magical devices.

As is the case with magical realism at its best, these black doors of escape – which also lead back into the 'global South', though fewer people travel that way in the novel – serve various purposes. For instance, they enable Hamid to avoid the nitty-gritty of trafficking in refuge – the crammed containers of people, the leaking rafts in the Mediterranean, the icy routes across Eastern Europe – and focus on his main concerns, which have to do with human beings who cannot live at 'home' and what happens to them when they arrive 'elsewhere', not with how they get there. This can be criticised by some, but it enables focus and concentration. The magic doors are not inert and the people who pass through them are not left unchanged: 'It was said in those days that the passage was both like dying and like being reborn.'[11] What

[8] Mohsin Hamid, *Exit West* (London: Hamish Hamilton, 2017), 1.   [9] Ibid., 69.
[10] Ibid., 70.   [11] Ibid., 98.

happens on the other side – both good and bad (such as attacks by national-ists, policemen, and others) – is also Hamid's concern. Moreover, the magic doors enable Hamid to jack up the matter of refuge and immigration to a kind of futuristic scenario – millions start pouring out of these doors – where it cannot be tinkered with or swept under political carpets; it has to be faced up to and lived with, unless of course one chooses genocide. Hence, the magical realist element in *Exit West* enables Hamid to think about identity, refuge, and violence, to analyse the state of the world today – all of it pushed to levels that make the extremes and options starker, and hence turn the novel into an excellent example of speculative fiction. Here speculative fiction has to be understood not just as fiction whose setting is not in the 'real world' but also, significantly, fiction that comments on and speculates about the real world from this other- or non-worldly setting.

Another clearly magical realist novel that does something similar to such novels is Helen Oyeyemi's *The Icarus Girl* (2005). Jess is the 8-year-old daughter of an English father and a Nigerian mother, brought up in England, sensitive, stubborn, and whimsical. During a visit to her mother's family in Nigeria, she meets a mysterious and ragged girl of her own age, Titiola, who reveals to Jess things unknown to her, as well as the ease with which others can be hurt. When TillyTilly, as Jess calls her, unexpectedly (magically) crops up in Jess's English neighbourhood as well, the two girls compulsively unpeel the 'reality' of their life: a novel that seems to be about mixed identities develops into a personal quest for lost halves and meaning, thus (like *Harare North*) partly escaping the straitjacket of just another 'multicultural London' novel.

Oyeyemi makes a particularly acute use of the insertion of fantasy into reality, because she ensures that the fantasy is not given an allegorical interpretation. This is sustained throughout her novel, as in the scene where TillyTilly and Jess fall through the staircase of Jess's house, to the amazement of two onlookers (Lidia and Dulcie):

> Jess saw Lidia's mouth open to address her, then both Lidia's and Dulcie's mouths stretched wider in amazement and shock as TillyTilly's arms enfolded her [Jess] from behind and pulled her
>
> d
> o
> w
> n

and *through* the staircase, the carpet and the actual stair falling away beneath her feet.[12]

When Jess resurfaces again, and everything is intact, Dulcie connects the magical dis/appearance to Africa ('You weren't like this before you went abroad!') while Lidia tries to explain it in a rational way ('You just ... ran away and hid, didn't you?').

Another significant novel in this regard is Nadeem Aslam's *Maps for Lost Lovers* (2004), which is consciously generic in its magical realism, though not as obviously so as some of the fictions of Rushdie, Okri, and Oyeyemi. The setting of Aslam's novel is a British town known only by the name given it by its Asian-born residents (Dasht-e-Tanhaii, or Desert of Loneliness). Its narrative revolves around the disappearance of Jugnu, a naturalist specialising in rare butterflies (who has phosphorescent hands), and Chanda, his younger lover. Along with the rich metaphorical language used, which is itself in excess to reality, as well as other unlikely events (such as Jugnu's phosphorescent hands and a human heart found in town), *Maps for Lost Lovers* consciously employs magical realist elements. Again, the attempt is to open up spaces between mainstream narratives, either British or non-British, either secular or religious, of what is 'normal' and, by that token, 'real'.

In all these texts, the magical elements – whether they remain irreducible or are partly explained by reality – are not used simply to oppose the Cartesian realities of Europe but to make us think again about given notions: such as the nature of power, identity, culture, violence, refuge, love, and narration. I argue that this is what makes black and Asian British magical realism significant: in general, at least the best of postcolonial magical realism is not, as some critical readings imply, about contesting Cartesian reality/realism; it is about expanding reality. To realise this is to see the complexity of not just magical realism as a literary genre, but also of realism, which, at its best, has never been simply about 'universal rational European thinking', whatever that might be, a fact that should be adduced from the point that any successful realist fiction, by its very nature, is also imaginative and hence at least residually magical.

---

[12] Helen Oyeyemi, *The Icarus Girl* (London: Bloomsbury, [2005] 2006), 146. Emphasis original.

Conclusion

Published in 1959, Laurie Lee's *Cider With Rosie* predates the 'official' rise of magical realism and has been considered a 'vivid memoir of childhood in a remote Cotswold village, a village before electricity and cars', as the blurb of the 2014 edition puts it. Neither fiction nor magical realism, this very European and very English memoir nevertheless contains lines like these:

> Jones's terrorist goat [a mythical creature just seen by the narrator and his friends] seemed to me a natural phenomenon of that time, part of a village which cast up beasts and spirits as casually as human beings. All seemed part of the same community, though their properties varied widely – some were benevolent, some strictly to be avoided; there were those that appeared at different shapes of the moon, or at daylight or midnight hours, that could warn or bless or drive one mad according to their different natures.[13]

This is a 'white' British text; it is a memoir, and hence generically a realist account. And yet it contains passages that merge the magical with the real in magical realist ways – the magic is irreducible, rooted in and growing from the reality described. One needs to take into account texts like these before celebrating magical realism in reductive ways, either as being automatically 'non-European' or being essentially opposed to realist writing. What happens seems to happen, as my above discussion highlights, between these various spaces and across them.

But what does not happen, might also not happen across these different spaces. Magical realism might not automatically provide answers that realism cannot. Here, it is useful to take a detour through Amitav Ghosh's contention in his 2017 non-fictional collection *The Great Derangement* that realist fiction has failed to address the (almost gothic) uncanniness of climate change, and magical realism has not fared any better. Ghosh argues that one of the reasons why realism failed is the fact that climate change escapes rational imagination, and also carries echoes of repressed guilt, as a gothic secret does too. If that is so, one would expect magical realism to cope better, but Ghosh notes that it has failed just as much – unless, of course, one expands the rubric to sci-fi and fantasy fiction (though even here, it can be argued, climate change is used for effect or to further the narrative tension, and not really grappled with as a subject on its own).

If Ghosh's thesis is substantiated, then, evidently both realism and magical realism have failed to address fully the threat of climate change. A simple

[13] Laurie Lee, *Cider with Rosie* (London: Vintage Books, [1959] 2014), 24.

celebration of the one against the other does not suffice. It can be argued that colonial gothic fiction allowed the Otherness of the colonised to be high-lighted, at the risk of giving it a negative colouring, while many postcolonial identity novels end up explaining away this Otherness, in their laudable bid to narrate it. Similarly, black and Asian British magical realist fiction does not simply go beyond the Cartesian limitation of realism; it can also encumber itself with given assumptions about the domain of the magical, its (unproble-matic) relationship to reality, and so on, some of which might have a colonial provenance or be identical to various kinds of non-European discursive hegemonies (such as religious fundamentalism's dismissal of scientific ration-ality), as argued at the start of this chapter. The creation of new worlds seems to demand an ironic engagement with and/or an ironic rejection of certain-ties of 'magic' *and* 'reality' rooted in old worlds, thus achieving the aimed-at ontological and social or political disruptions. Evidently, this can be done from a critical realist position or, as the best magical realist texts discussed above demonstrate, from a critically fantastic/magical one. Finally, at its best, we are not talking of a binarism, overturned or not, but a productive inter-section that cuts across both terms and enables us to think anew.

30

Writing Lives, Inventing Selves
Black and Asian Women's Life-Writing

OLE BIRK LAURSEN

This chapter examines the ways in which black and Asian women writers have invented themselves through autobiographies, autobiographical novels, and memoirs, focusing primarily on the decades of the late twentieth and early twenty-first centuries. The rather capacious term of 'life-writing' is used here to signal the diversity of the forms of autobiography employed, which will be distinguished in the textual analysis to follow. As readers of this history will know (see Chapters 1–4), life-writing was already popular with eighteenth-century black and Asian writers, who turned to the genre (whether through autobiographies, letters, or memoirs) partly as a strategy to challenge dominant discourses of race, slavery, and empire. Ignatius Sancho's *Letters of the Late Ignatius Sancho, an African* (1782), Olaudah Equiano's *The Interesting Narrative of the Life of Olaudah Equiano* (1789), and Sake Dean Mahomet's *The Travels of Dean Mahomet* (1794) are all concerned with inventions and reinventions of self, making plain the early impulse to inscribe black and Asian histories into British life. These early works appeared in the same era as Jean-Jacques Rousseau's landmark text *Confessions* (1782–1789), often heralded as the first modern autobiography. Offering evidence of early correctives to Rousseau's Orientalist narrative of the self, these pioneering black and Asian works challenged orthodox views of autobiographical subjectivities.[1] A few decades later, Prince's *The History of Mary Prince: A West Indian Slave* (1831) and Seacole's *Wonderful Adventures of Mrs Seacole in Many Lands* (1857) expanded this early historiography of black British writing, as texts once again demonstrating explorations of subjectivity and selfhood.[2] Such works derived, however, from a significantly different historical context

---

[1] Bart Moore-Gilbert, 'Western Autobiography and Colonial Discourse: An Overview', *Wasafiri*, 21:2 (2006): 9–16.
[2] Mary Prince, *The History of Mary Prince, a West Indian Slave, related by Herself* (London: F. Westley and A. H. Davis, 1831); Mary Seacole, *Wonderful Adventures of Mrs Seacole in Many Lands*, ed. Sara Salih (London: Penguin Classics, [1857] 2005).

from the largely contemporary texts under scrutiny in this chapter. Given the early period of their composition, it is perhaps not surprising that autobiographical fictional narratives were not commonly used to challenge ideologies of race or gender, though challenges there certainly were.

Autobiographical works by black and Asian writers have long reconstructed specific subjectivities whether in personal, public, or historical contexts. Notably, many of them engage with themes of self-discovery alongside spatial politics, frequently exploring broken geographies as well as the traumatic legacies of colonial amnesia common in postcolonial histories. At times, questions of genealogy, biogenetic heritage, and broken family histories surface directly through the recounting of personal memories. However, they are also represented metaphorically and evoked through the writing process itself, signalling the challenges of representing a larger transnational condition of displacement and opening up questions of widespread inequalities and uneven global relations.

Over the past four decades, black and Asian women writers, such as Beryl Gilroy (1924–2001), Andrea Levy (1956–2019), Jackie Kay (1961–), Shyama Perera (1976–), and Diana Evans (1971–), have turned to this broad genre – whether through memoir, verse, testimony, or autobiographical fiction – to express individual subjectivities and establish communal identities with great force and urgency. In fact, given that the postwar migratory narrative of Britain has predominantly been articulated by men, it is not surprising that black and Asian British women have turned to these forms of literary expression to not only *author* themselves but also *authorise* their own voices and subjectivities.[3] Established male figures, such as Caryl Phillips, Hanif Kureishi, and Vikram Seth, have also of course employed a range of autobiographical forms to explore and narrate issues of selfhood in Britain and beyond. Written over a period of twenty years, Phillips's collection of non-fictional autobiographical essays *Colour Me English* (2011) starts from his experience of growing up in Leeds, but mixes in travelogue and reflects on his later development as a writer. Kureishi's memoir of his father, *My Ear At his Heart* (2004), is also a device to reflect on the author's own artistic development, though the archives he discovers from his father's secret writing life open up a different perspective on the diasporic geographies of his South Asian British history. In similar ways, Seth

---

[3] Pallavi Rastogi, 'Women's Fiction and Literary (Self-) Determination' in Deirdre Osborne (ed.), *The Cambridge Companion to British Black and Asian Literature (1945–2010)* (Cambridge: Cambridge University Press, 2016), 77–94; 79.

uses family papers, photographs, and interviews in his book *Two Lives* (2005) to trace the eponymous two lives of his great-uncle and great-aunt, with whom he came to live in Tonbridge at the age of seventeen. Interweaving his own story with theirs, Seth uncovers a larger and previously hidden family history that enmeshes disparate narratives of displacement and migration to Britain. Phillips, Kureishi, and Seth all investigate issues of migration, belonging, subjectivity, Britishness, and cultural identity. What is important, however, is that these authors were already well established, commercially successful, and publishing in a range of other genres before turning to non-fictional autobiography and memoir. And though Kureishi's well-known *Bildungsroman*, *The Buddha of Suburbia* (1990), and Phillips's early novel, *The Final Passage* (1985), certainly address issues of growing up black or brown in Britain, these partly autobiographical fictions were not necessary vehicles to authorise their own legitimacy. For black and Asian women writers on the other hand, especially in the 1980s and 1990s, the genre provided an accessible frame to counter erasure, represent their lives, and articulate the complexity of their multiple subject positions. Bearing these elements in mind, this chapter's primary focus is on the role life-writing has played in the emergence and consolidation of what is now a significant field of contemporary black and Asian women's life-writing. As will become evident, there continues to be an ongoing need to challenge the still sometimes impermeable boundaries of race, gender, and class and embed the stories of black and Asian women's histories into British life.

Writing Selves: Autobiography, Autobiographical Fiction, and Memoir

Many of these writers experiment with diverse means of expression to narrate their collective and individual experiences in modes which are distinct from more mainstream white texts. Writing by black and Asian women has frequently been marginalised by dominant Anglo-American readings; however, this critical context has also been invigorating, offering opportunities not only to experiment but also to extend the conventional boundaries of the genre. The complex issue of unpacking such autobiographical texts, and distinguishing their political and aesthetical visions, is by now well rehearsed in the field of feminist autobiography studies. For example, scholars such as Liz Stanley and Sidonie Smith have persuasively claimed that, as women's stories have often been silenced in patriarchal culture, women have necessarily turned to fiction to produce accounts of the self.[4] As is now well known, such feminist interventions have opened up the field of autobiography studies through offering interpretations that challenge orthodox, masculine definitions of autobiography and male subjectivities. In the context of black and Asian women's writing, such definitions, despite their value, are also potentially problematic because they tend to privilege the essential category 'woman' without adequately considering the multiple ways in which such identities are also shaped by issues of race, ethnicity, and culture.

Linda Hutcheon, for example, warns us of the limitations of a feminist critique that does not combine a challenge to the legacies of colonialism:

> The current post-structuralist/postmodern challenges to the coherent, autonomous subject have to be put on hold in feminist and post-colonial discourses, for both must work first to assert and affirm a denied and alienated subjectivity: those radical postmodern challenges are in many ways the luxury of the dominant order which can afford to challenge that which it securely possesses.[5]

Indeed, at the very same time that white feminist critics were wresting the male autonomous self away from orthodox notions of subjectivity, there was a further risk of masking other racialised forms of subjectivity. As Sara Ahmed explains: 'autobiography as individuation never quite takes place. It is precisely those marginalized and abject figures, which return to haunt the authorial self [reminding] her of her immersion in a violent sociality [. . .]. Black women are present as a trace of the impossibility of female signature, or of any *ontologically secured* category of "women's writing"'.[6] What Ahmed importantly notes is that black and Asian British women's autobiographical texts emerge in exactly those gaps and silences created by the dominant structures of power that surround them. These did not only interrogate questions of race and gender but were to open up wider issues of national

---

[4] Liz Stanley, *The Auto/Biographical I: The Theory and Practice of Feminist Auto/Biography* (Manchester: Manchester University Press, 1992), 59–62; Sidonie Smith, *A Poetics of Women's Autobiography: Marginality and the Fictions of Self-Representation* (Bloomington, IN: Indiana University Press), 50.

[5] Linda Hutcheon, '"Circling the Downspout of Empire": Post-Colonialism and Postmodernism', *ARIEL: A Review of International English Literature*, 20:4 (1989): 149–175; 151.

[6] Sara Ahmed, '"It's a Sun-Tan, Isn't It?": Auto-biography as an Identificatory Practice' in Heidi Safia Mirza (ed.), *Black British Feminism: A Reader* (London: Routledge, 1997), 153–67; 154.

and transnational identification, combined with an urgent need to give voice to stories previously silenced or erased by traumatic histories. Life-writing, as Ahmed continues, may be of 'interest to black feminism precisely because it renders explicit the subject's immersion within the social and political. It is a critical reflection on the self – and its history or becoming – that may dramatize the unstable but determinate relation between the subject and its others.'[7] Interventions by theorists such as Ahmed, who represented a new 1990s generation of black and Asian feminist critics, have been important. Not only did such scholars offer a younger generation of women writers alternative frames through which to view their lives but they actively encouraged and legitimised often painful personal engagements with the trauma of racial violence and erasure bred by a colonial past. Discovering appropriate frameworks in which to express such experiences was not an unproblematic process. As Suzanne Scafe reminds us: the 'instability of [. . .] selves that black British women's autobiography constructs' should act 'as a caution against [any] insistence on marginalised voices'. In other words: 'safeguards need to be erected' in our critical thinking 'against [. . .] the articulation of either an exceptional exemplar or an overdetermining "we"'.[8]

Whilst there is no doubt that life-writing by women in the diaspora responds in part to wider pressures of migration, racism, and sexism, to black and Asian women it offers a potent means of challenging the dominant discourses of race that continue to construct them as 'Others' within Britain today.[9] The very diversity of the genre, which offers opportunities for the writing of personal histories, travelogues, family quests, fiction, and the possibility through testimony of opening up the gaps and silences of trauma, allows each author to negotiate her individual subjectivity in the face of an institutionalised racism often predicated on prejudice. This, in turn, enables the authors to define their own specific lives against the restrictive frame of a sometimes self-imposed cultural identity from within 'black' collective representations, allowing the construction of alternative versions of subjectivity and fragmented identities. That is, if the political category 'black' was once positively invoked to challenge racist power structures, it also tended as an overarching concept to elide individual expressions of blackness in Britain.

---

[7] Ibid.

[8] Suzanne Scafe, 'Black Women's Subjects in Auto/biographical Discourse' in Osborne (ed.), *Cambridge Companion to British Black and Asian Literature*, 144–58; 144–5.

[9] Jenni Ramone and Suzanne Scafe, 'Editorial: Women's Life Writing and Diaspora', *Life Writing*, 10:2 (2013): 125–8.

This situation was particularly apparent during the heated debates to differentiate and distinguish black and Asian identities in the 1980s.

Becoming Black and Asian British, 1970s–1980s

Despite the many examples of life-writing across the long history of black and Asian writing in Britain, it would be simplistic to imply a neat linear progression or tradition. Significantly, as other chapters in this history demonstrate, it was primarily in the decades after World War II that black and Asian British writing began to gain any significant critical and commercial attention (see Chapters 25 and 34). And in fact it has been only since the beginning of the twenty-first century that black, Asian, or mixed heritage British women writers, such as Zadie Smith and Monica Ali, have begun to be recognised in the mainstream, selling in excess of one million copies of their debut novels, *White Teeth* (2000) and *Brick Lane* (2003). This spurt of attention was repeated when Andrea Levy published her highly praised autobiographical fiction, *Small Island*, in 2004. Presenting the Windrush histories of Levy's parents, the novel, which was a WH Smith bestseller, attracted attention for embedding their story and that of a later UK-born generation into the fabric of postwar Britain. The book won numerous awards, including the Orange Prize for women's fiction, and was swiftly turned into a primetime TV series (see Chapters 27 and 32). Whilst interest was partially prompted by a fast-growing literary prize culture and the belated recognition of Britain's rich migrant history, the telling of the Windrush story through the voice of a woman was significant, placing 'herstory' centre stage in the memory of the nation. Such novels did not emerge out of a vacuum but grew out of an earlier generation which had already laid the ground for things to come. Whilst some books by black and Asian women, such as Joyce Gladwell's *Brown Face, Big Master* (1969), Louise Shore's *Pure Running* (1982), and Sharan-Jeet Shan's *In My Own Name* (1985), had begun to be published, there were a few voices that broke through in the 1970s and 1980s that warrant specific mention here.

As direct predecessors to writers who are now read widely like Zadie Smith or Monica Ali, Bernardine Evaristo or Jackie Kay, early figures such as Beryl Gilroy, Buchi Emecheta (1944–2017), and Joan Riley (1958–) all explored a variety of autobiographical forms to depict the harsh realities of their early experiences in Britain. These narratives provided a counter to the gender inequalities and racism these writers encountered on a daily basis, challenging orthodox conventions and offering readers a fresh and little-known perspective on the difficulties of being black, female, and British in the 1970s and 1980s. Gilroy's memoir *Black Teacher* (1976), which experiments with several voices and forms, offers the reader a vivid (and often humorously sardonic) portrait of her early experiences as a 1950s student at London University, her encounters with the 'colour bar', her fierce resilience as she continued to confront issues of gender, especially on becoming the first black head teacher of a London school. Born in British Guiana (now Guyana) in 1924, Gilroy is seldom featured as one of the well-known and predominantly male group of Windrush writers, as discussed by other contributors. Arriving in 1951 and studying for a Diploma in Child Development at the University of London, she qualified as a teacher in 1968. Her memoir, which shifts from historical account to educational philosophy, anecdote, and personal history, speaks directly to E. R. Braithwaite's earlier *To Sir, With Love* (1959), an autobiographical novel that painfully evokes Braithwaite's life as a young teacher in a tough east London school. Like Braithwaite – a black fellow countryman who served in the RAF in World War II – Gilroy writes with some disdain about the strategies she adopted to survive: whether navigating the city, asserting her identity, or confronting the daily barrage of discrimination she faced. Gilroy's experiences are located firmly *outside* what John McLeod has described as the 'imagined community' of 1950s Britain, and such challenges are further accentuated when she becomes London's first black head teacher. Forced to operate within a predominantly white, male environment, Gilroy recounts how she devises a range of educational strategies, including writing and publishing children's stories (her Nippers series) to deconstruct reductive racial and class stereotypes in mixed multicultural classrooms.[10] While male contemporaries from the Caribbean, such as V. S. Naipaul, Andrew Salkey, Sam Selvon, and George Lamming, had achieved significant literary recognition by the 1960s, Gilroy's memoir was initially praised for its sociological and educational insights rather than any literary value. As a result, Gilroy continued to struggle for a recognition that came late in life. Her debut novel, *In Praise of Love and Children*, written in the 1960s, first appeared in 1996 and was followed by several others.[11]

[10] Beryl Gilroy, *Black Teacher* (London: Cassell, 1976); E. R. Braithwaite, *To Sir, With Love* (London: Bodley Head, 1959).
[11] Sandra Courtman, 'Not Good Enough or Not Man Enough? Beryl Gilroy as the Anomaly in the Evolving "Black British Canon"' in Gail Low and Marion Wynne-Davies (eds.), *A Black British Canon?* (Basingstoke: Palgrave Macmillan, 2006), 50–73; Sandra Courtman, 'A Black British Canon?: The Uses of Beryl Gilroy's *Black Teacher* and Its Recovery as Literature', *Wasafiri*, 17:36 (2002): 51–5.

Nigerian-born Buchi Emecheta similarly recounted her early experiences of being a black Nigerian woman living in Britain in her early fictions. A new arrival in 1960s London, her first two novels, *In the Ditch* (1972) and *Second Class-Citizen* (1974), were semi-autobiographical and based on the trials of her life before she turned to more conventional autobiography in *Head Above Water* (1986). Written in the third-person voice of Adah, her first novels paint the tawdry and claustrophobic pressures of her life as a black woman, her entrapment both as immigrant woman and amidst the rigid patriarchal codes she was to confront within her own Nigerian community. These novels demonstrate, as Chris Weedon explains, 'how the internalised class and gender identities [. . .] shaped by customs and practices in Nigeria, and that make up one woman's sense of self and her aspirations for equality, are challenged, transformed, and realised by experience acquired in London'.[12] Rather than offering a unified subjectivity common in more orthodox auto-biographies, her 1970s novels create identities that can straddle multiple histories and are able to navigate the newly found challenges of class, sexism, and racism she was forced to confront.[13] Emecheta's urban landscape is relentlessly one of immiseration in these early books; yet her future invest-ment, as with Gilroy, is with the next generation. As Adah emphatically tells us in *Second Class Citizen*: 'Her children were going to be different. They were going to enjoy being black, be proud of being black, a black of a different breed.'[14]

Publishing almost a decade later, British Jamaican Joan Riley's debut, *The Unbelonging* (1985), depicts the consequences of a history of childhood trauma on the psyche of a young Jamaican girl recently arrived in Britain. Set partly in a children's home and written in the first person, the narrative relentlessly describes the girl's bodily reactions to a growing sense of disempowerment and dislocation. An important precursor to a body of 1990s novels that followed, Riley was one of the first black women to engage directly with abuse, foster care, adoption, and orphanhood, conditions which afflicted many women in the black community. As with Emecheta, Riley's subsequent books, *Waiting in the Twilight* (1987), *Romance* (1988), and *A Kindness to Children* (1992), also have a strong autobiographical component, mapping Riley's life and providing uncomfortable insights into the violent legacies of

[12] Chris Weedon, 'Migration, Identity, and Belonging in Black British and South Asian Women's Writing', *Contemporary Women's Writing*, 2:1 (2008): 17–35; 22.
[13] Stuart Hall, 'Cultural Identity and Diaspora' in Jonathan Rutherford (ed.), *Identity, Community, Culture, Difference* (London: Lawrence & Wishart, 1990), 222–237; 222.
[14] Buchi Emecheta, *Second Class Citizen* (London: Heinemann, [1974] 1994), 148.

colonial politics in 1970s and 1980s Britain.[15] As James Procter sees it, pioneering writers like Riley, Gilroy, and Emecheta exploited 'the authority and transparency of autobiographical discourse' in order to document and authorise their own stories and their own (dis)locations within Britain through memoir and narrative non-fiction.[16] Forced, often in unforgiving conditions, to negotiate an 'insider–outsider' status, such writings were significant in opening up a legitimate space for testimony and an ethics which allowed the exposure, acceptance, and reconfiguration of stories by black and Asian women that had previously been unheard.[17]

In retrospect, these publications not only complemented but also contributed to what was fast becoming a growing body of work, helping to create a market for writing by black and Asian British women at the time. Publishers such as the Women's Press, Virago, and Sheba Feminist Publishers established new lists, focusing on Britain and diversifying from the existing and stable African American market, a movement supported by the politics of organisations such as the Brixton Black Women's Group, Southall Black Sisters, Asian Women Writers' Collective, Camden Black Sisters, and the Organisation of Women of Asian and African Descent (OWAAD). As Aamer Hussein notes: 'the [women] writers that emerged during this period were to establish their individual "credentials" over the second half of the eighties'.[18] Often crossing boundaries between autobiography, fiction, poetry, sociology, and anthropology, and including non-fictional essays and short stories, pioneering collaborations such as *The Heart of the Race* (Beverley Bryan, Stella Dadzie, and Suzanne Scafe; 1985), *A Dangerous Knowing* (Barbara Burford, Gabriela Pearse, Grace Nichols, and Jackie Kay; 1984), *Watchers and Seekers* (edited by Rhonda Cobham and Merle Collins; 1987), *Let it be Told* (edited by Lauretta Ngcobo; 1987), *Right of Way* (the Asian Women Writers' Workshop; 1988), and *Charting the Journey* (edited by Shabnam Grewal, Jackie Kay, Liliane Landor, Gail Lewis, and Pratibha Parmar; 1988) were to further diversify and open up black and Asian women's histories. Often deriving from black or

[15] Sandra Courtman, 'From Mary Prince to Joan Riley: Women Writers and the "Casual Cruelty" of a West Indian Childhood' in Abigail Ward (ed.), *Postcolonial Traumas: Memory, Narrative, Resistance* (London: Palgrave Macmillan, 2015), 30–47.

[16] James Procter, *Dwelling Places: Postwar Black British Writing* (Manchester: Manchester University Press, 2003), 94.

[17] John McLeod, 'Postcolonial Writing in Britain' in Ato Quayson (ed.), *The Cambridge History of Postcolonial Literature* (Cambridge: Cambridge University Press, 2015), 571–603.

[18] Aamer Hussein, 'Changing Seasons: Post-Colonial or "Other" Writing in Britain Today', *Wasafiri*, 10:20 (1994): 16–18; 16; Valerie Amos, Gail Lewis, Amina Mama, and Pratibha Parmar, 'Many Voices, One Chant: Black Feminist Perspectives', *Feminist Review*, 17 (Autumn 1984): 1–2.

Asian feminist collectives and workshops, the multi-vocal nature of these anthologies offered readers a new form of truth-telling, designed to complicate unitary perspectives and establish alliances across difficult racial and ethnic divides.[19] Influenced by the popularity of African American writers such as Alice Walker, Toni Morrison, and Maya Angelou, the experimental subject-matter of these anthologies began to map out a path for a home-grown tradition of black and Asian British writing in the 1990s.

New Ethnicities and New Voices, 1990s–2000s

With notable exceptions, the task of representing and reimagining black and Asian women's lives in 1980s Britain was largely delivered through collective efforts and anthologies. Yet, as was signalled by the 1982 split within OWAAD, the necessary activism of these collectives sometimes masked significant cultural differences between individual writers and their histories, thus inadvertently falling into the trap of perpetuating dominant discourses around race, gender, and ethnicity. As Kobena Mercer was to famously argue in his 1994 essay, 'Black Art and the Burden of Representation': 'when artists are positioned on the margins of the institutional spaces of cultural production, they are burdened with the impossible task of speaking as "representatives", in that they are widely expected to "speak for" the marginalised communities from which they came'.[20] In other words, black and Asian writers were often tasked with the imperative to speak for everyone simultaneously, to carve out public spaces through writing and art, and to remain inclusive across ethnic, class, religious, and sexuality differences. Moving on from identity politics and calls for collective activism, Stuart Hall had begun to suggest a need, by the early 1990s, for a shift in vision and urgently emphasised a move forward from the 'struggle' over 'relations of representation' to 'a politics of representation itself'. This was not to replace earlier activism but to '*displace*, reorganise, and reposition the different cultural strategies in relation to one another'.[21] If black and Asian British writers had been part of the struggle to be heard collectively in the 1970s and 1980s, the 1990s was the moment to inscribe new British stories, present the

---

[19] Pratibha Parmar, 'Other Kinds of Dreams', *Feminist Review*, 31 (1989): 55–65.

[20] Kobena Mercer, 'Black Art and the Burden of Representation' in *Welcome to the Jungle: New Positions in Black Cultural Studies* (London: Routledge, 1994), 233–58; 235.

[21] Stuart Hall, 'New Ethnicities' in Houston A. Baker, Jr., Manthia Diawara, and Ruth H. Lindeborg (eds.), *Black British Cultural Studies: A Reader* (London; Chicago, IL: University of Chicago Press, 1996), 163–72; 165.

complexity of diasporic life-histories, and subvert stereotypical portraits that reduced the diversity of the black experience in Britain. Narrating this turn, life-writing, autobiography, and memoir were not only flexible enough to write difference but also offered a potentially subversive model by which to revision and reframe the cultural landscape of black and Asian Britain.

Growing up Black and Asian British: The Bildungsroman

Those who began publishing in the context of post-Thatcherism and New Labour multiculturalism frequently focused on the challenges of growing up in the diaspora and coming to terms with an extended but often broken or disjointed family history. Perhaps not surprisingly, as is evident from Hanif Kureishi's landmark 1990s novel *The Buddha of Suburbia*, which confidently heralded the hybridity of its mixed heritage British Asian narrator, Karim – 'I'm an Englishman born and bred, almost' – the *Bildungsroman* was a readily accessible frame to extend and challenge the dominant narrative of black, Asian, and mixed-race lives. As Mark U. Stein notes in his 2004 monograph, *Black British Literature: Novels of Transformation*: 'while many novels of formation – black British or otherwise – are autobiographical, autobiographies cannot be considered novels of formation by the same token'.[22] And while the universal motif of generational conflict was also key in black and Asian British autobiographical fictions, a younger generation of writers was beginning to paint different portraits of their lives. Though works by this new generation covered a wide range of different content and contexts, it will be useful here to focus our attention on three recurrent preoccupations: home and return; orphanhood, adoption, and foster care; and the often transatlantic and diasporic search for lost family histories.

Drawing primarily on the form of the *Bildungsroman*, a series of novels were to appear in the 1990s which portrayed young black and Asian women growing up in Britain. These include: Atima Srivastava's *Transmission* (1992) and *Looking for Maya* (1999), Meera Syal's *Anita and Me* (1996) and *Life Isn't All Ha Ha Hee Hee* (1999), Andrea Levy's *Fruit of the Lemon* (1999), and Shyama Perera's *Haven't Stopped Dancing Yet* (1999). Many of these novels chart a move away from home, the beginnings of a career, and the process of discovering a new sense of self and place. Able to interrogate the past and invent new British selves, the protagonists in these works often resist the cultural pressure of traditional family expectations and challenge the

---

[22] Mark U. Stein, *Black British Literature: Novels of Transformation* (Columbus, OH: Ohio State University Press, 2004), 26.

hegemony of the racist power structures that have restricted them during their formative years. In Syal's *Anita and Me* (1996), for example, Meena wants in part to be like an English girl, eat fish and chips, and enjoy a white Christmas. Constantly having to shift between the cultural festivities of her parents' Punjabi household, the white working-class culture at school, and the racist attitudes of her white schoolfriend Anita, Meena begins to claim and assert a liberated sense of an undivided self which is fully accepting of her mixed heritage and location in Tollington, a fictional Midlands town: 'The place in which I belonged was wherever I stood and there was nothing stopping me simply moving forward and claiming each resting place as home.'[23]

Apart from issues of growth, belonging, and self-development, the mapping and naming of new spaces are central to such stories. Accounts by the 1950s Windrush writers, as well as later renditions by Emecheta and Riley, often dwell primarily on the difficulties of voyaging in to the 'Mother Country' and being reluctantly accommodated on arrival in dilapidated houses, flats, and rooms. On the edge of the nation's threshold, many of these migrant narratives portray their protagonists as disappointed guests, unable to find the Britain dreamt up by the false expectations of their colonial education. Instead, as Dillon Brown and others show us earlier in this volume, they are confronted by the realities of a pernicious racism (see Chapters 13 and 17).[24] By contrast, the next generation, including figures like Levy, Syal, Perera, and Srivastava as well as more recently Zadie Smith and Monica Ali, have marked out regional affiliations within specific areas, creating a sense of local connection with the histories and communities of a particular location and place, whether in north London as with Srivastava and Zadie Smith, west London (Perera), the East End (Monica Ali), or the Midlands (Syal).[25] As Bart Moore-Gilbert argues in his study of postcolonial life-writing, the 'relation between writers with diasporic histories and their location is often fraught and contested, varying between a desire to establish a stable socio-spatial identity (roots) and a liberating migrant identity (routes)'.[26]

---

[23] Meera Syal, *Anita and Me* (London: Flamingo, 1996), 303.

[24] For more on 'dwelling places', see Procter, *Dwelling Places*, 21–68.

[25] Andy Wood, '"New Forms": Towards a Critical Dialogue with Black British "Popular" Fictions' in Low and Wynne-Davies (eds.), *A Black British Canon?*, 105–25; 113.

[26] Bart Moore-Gilbert, *Postcolonial Life-Writing: Culture, Politics and Self-Representation* (London: Routledge, 2009), 66.

The full acknowledgement of a non-hyphenated black and Asian citizenship remains a contentious issue. In *Brit(ish)* (2018), a meditation on and analysis of race, identity, and belonging in twenty-first-century Britain, Afua Hirsch, an author and a Ghanaian Irish British woman, reflects on the conflicts she faced coming of age in 1980s Britain and their recurrence in the present. She reminds us of the seemingly inevitable question posed to British citizens of black or Asian backgrounds, even today: 'Where are you from? Where are you from really?'[27] Even more apparent in the conflict-ridden atmosphere of the 1970s, such questions have not only been unashamedly connected to race but linked to hotly contested legal enforcements, manifested by the so-called 'sus' laws that disproportionally targeted young black and Asian men on British streets. Building on Stuart Hall's warnings in *Policing the Crisis* (1978), the cultural theorist Paul Gilroy was to argue over two decades later that we must 'confront the extent to which the cultural politics of "race" reveals conflict over the production of urban meaning and situate [those] meanings which have already been identified as constitutive of "race" in their proper place, as contending definitions of what city life is about'.[28] In other words, if dominant British society continued to pigeonhole black and Asian stories in relation to crime within London's inner city areas such as Brixton or Tower Hamlets in east London, the question of 'race', as Gilroy notes, would inevitably become a marker of urban social movements in conflict with British political systems and state institutions.

Set on north London's council estates, Levy's first three novels, *Every Light in the House Burnin'* (1994), *Never Far from Nowhere* (1996), and *Fruit of the Lemon* (1999), do address racial and class inequalities. However, they are significantly more invested in enabling Levy to explore the generational conflicts of her parents' generation and to make her own story as a black British woman key to Britain's cultural landscape. In contrast to the insular and often narrow immigrant world of Emecheta, Levy creates the sense of an open urban landscape, depicting the texture of London's streets as well as its outside spaces and laying claim to her place in the city. When Faith, in *Fruit of the Lemon*, is challenged by a colleague to explain the complex nature of her diasporic sense of belonging, her response is indicative: 'As I was born a bred in Haringey I could only suppose that I had some sort of collective unconscious that was coming through from my slave ancestry.'[29]

[27] Afua Hirsch, *Brit(ish): On Race, Identity and Belonging* (London: Jonathan Cape, 2018), 8.
[28] Paul Gilroy, *There Ain't No Black in the Union Jack: The Cultural Politics of Race and Nation* (London: Routledge, [1987] 2002), 311.
[29] Andrea Levy, *Fruit of the Lemon* (London: Review, 1999), 31.

In comparable ways, Perera's *Haven't Stopped Dancing Yet*, set in late 1960s and 1970s Bayswater, west London, employs a linear chronology to create a sense of London as 'home'. Interspersed with 1960s pop references, like Kureishi's *The Buddha of Suburbia*, *Haven't Stopped Dancing Yet* defies conventional expectations of black and Asian writers by eschewing the essentialism of certain renditions of 'black' politics at the time and writing Perera's 'self' into mainstream British social space. As is apparent from the outset, Perera establishes the subjectivity of the main character, Mala Fonseka, in relation to friends and class politics: 'Four little girls in a Paddington playground. Four rounds of free dinners, four different social workers, four strains of family problems. It is 1966 and only one has a bag of sweets – and I wasn't going to be her friend unless she gave me one.'[30] In that sense, as Perera's novel reinscribes London's spaces with new meaning, the genre of the black and Asian British *Bildungsroman* is as much about the transformation of British society as the transformation of the self.[31]

Srivastava's novels, *Transmission* and *Looking for Maya*, set in 1980s and 1990s London, both engage with the historical rift of diaspora from the perspective of young adults struggling to set themselves apart from an earlier, more traditional generation. Mirroring Srivastava's own professional career in film, her protagonists, young film-makers, navigate London's savvy media world and in the process reinvent themselves. Abandoning any overt need to engage with a politics of representation, these novels, rather, write Srivastava's individual Asian diasporic perspective and vision into Britain's urban spaces. The fictional format allows Srivastava the opportunity to explore all the dimensions of her modern female Asian British identity; not as a fragmented or divided British Asian child, torn between her parents' colonial memories and their experiences of migration but rather as a part of London's furniture and its mixed multicultural spaces.

Fictions of Orphanhood, Adoption, and Foster Care

Adoption, it has been noted, is a particular kind of 'social practice' and plays 'a central, if under-acknowledged, role in the social negotiation of discourses of national, cultural and racial affiliation'.[32] Further developing this idea and the notion that texts of 'transcultural adoption [...] bravely chart new bearings of personhood', it is not surprising that such explorations

---

[30] Shyama Perera, *Haven't Stopped Dancing Yet* (London: Sceptre, 1999), 1.

[31] Stein, *Black British Literature*, xiii.

[32] John McLeod, 'Postcolonial Fictions of Adoption', *Critical Survey*, 18:2 (2006): 45–55; 45–6.

experiment with and extend the potentiality of life-writing as a genre.[33] In their own ways, Isha McKenzie-Mavinga and Thelma Perkins's *In Search of Mr McKenzie* (1991) and Jackie Kay's *The Adoption Papers* (1991) were seen to break new ground for black and Asian British writers by openly addressing this subject. Almost written as a biography of their father – like Kureishi's *My Ear at his Heart* – McKenzie-Mavinga and Perkins's book is ostensibly more autobiographical, establishing 'a discursive framework within which their excluded blackness can be reclaimed and reinscribed'.[34] The text opens with a letter from their father and such documents sit alongside the fictional narrative, merging objectivity and subjectivity into multifaceted selfhoods and allowing their own story to emerge from the story of their father.

Told from three perspectives – the birth mother, adoptive mother, and adopted daughter – *The Adoption Papers* experiments with life-writing in verse and invents the self through a polyphony of voices, emphasising the multi-faceted subjectivity of the author. At the time of writing her long verse poem Kay had not yet traced her biological parents, and the text speaks to the process for Kay of creatively filling in gaps and imagining origins; it thus narrates the invention of a lost self, embedding it within the wider discourses of national, cultural, and racial belonging in Britain. Reading *The Adoption Papers* alongside Kay's later memoir, *Red Dust Road* (2010), written in prose and completed almost a decade after Kay had journeyed to Nigeria in search of her lost biological father, we are given a broader insight into the enmeshed histories of Britain and its former colonies across Africa and the Caribbean. *Red Dust Road* opens with the statement: 'I had been told they met in 1961 in the dance hall in Aberdeen', emphasising the partiality of narratives that are passed on. The memoir-cum-travelogue that Kay is subsequently able to construct places herself centre stage in the story. When she is 'about to have a conversation with [her] birth father for the first time', the metaphor of the absent father, also key in other black and Asian autobiographical texts such as Charlotte Williams's travelogue *Sugar and Slate* (2002), points to lost coun-tries and foreclosed cultural origins.[35] Her connection to Nigeria, to Africa, which she herself sought and which interlocutors, triggered by her skin tone, projected on to her, becomes a viable bond once she meets her father and

---

[33] John McLeod, *Life Lines: Writing Transcultural Adoption* (London: Bloomsbury Academic, 2015), 181.

[34] Suzanne Scafe, '"Let Me Tell You How It Really Was": Authority, Legitimacy and Fictive Structures of Reality in Contemporary Black Women's Autobiography', *Changing English*, 17:2 (2009): 129–40; 134.

[35] Jackie Kay, *Red Dust Road* (London: Picador, 2010), 3.

extended family. While the eponymous Red Dust Road does not take Kay back to putative beginnings, the construction of the narrative helps to merge fantasy with concrete reality.

Fictions of transcultural adoption are frequent, their subjects often determining the character, form, and shape of the narratives.[36] Different challenges come to mind, however, when we examine constructions of the family around notions of race. As Suki Ali observes: 'transcultural adoption is often bound up with concerns about "national" and "ethnic" identifications as it implies that black people (for example) must automatically have a different and bonded culture that came from different "roots" than those of white Britons, and that this cultural knowledge is passed on through "the family"'.[37] Given the realities of the absence of family connections and 'roots', such fictions importantly seek to invent alternative family models, which both challenge and open up narrowly defined notions of Britishness, belonging, and race.

Similar in theme to Alex Wheatle's The Seven Sisters (2002), but often overlooked in studies of black and Asian writing, Joanna Traynor's Saga Prize-winning Sister Josephine (1997) explicitly exposes the brutality of foster care as it documents its subject's entrapment in a particular manifestation of the latent racist violence in postcolonial Britain. As sociological research has shown, the generation of mixed-race children who grew up in the 1960s often 'lived socially isolated and at times extremely emotionally abusive childhoods' in foster homes.[38] Whereas fictions of adoption often centre, sometimes metaphorically, on lost family ties, black and Asian novels about foster care tend to focus explicitly on the traumatic experiences of growing up within the social care system in Britain. Traynor's Josephine knows little about her origins, except the ever-present reminder of her appearance through systematic racism and sexism. The novel overtly challenges orthodox ideas of family patterns, offering alternative models. The complex relationship between adoption and traditional family structure is abandoned in Traynor's novel, creating instead a self-constructed world in relation to friends, colleagues, and lovers after leaving the foster home: 'After the door on my history closed leaving me rattling around in my future', the narrator says, 'I paused for a breath.'[39] Unapologetic and almost confessional, the act

---

[36] See McLeod, Life Lines.

[37] Suki Ali, Mixed-Race, Post-Race: Gender, New Ethnicities and Cultural Practices (Oxford: Berg, 2003), 8.

[38] Jayne O. Ifekwunigwe, Scattered Belongings: Cultural Paradoxes of 'Race', Nation and Gender (London: Routledge, 1999), 68.

[39] Joanna Traynor, Sister Josephine (London: Bloomsbury, 1997), 97.

of writing allows Traynor to work through the experience of growing up in various foster homes, subject to racism and sexual abuse, and to forge alternative forms of familial relations.

Lucinda Roy's 1998 novel *Lady Moses* illustrates a similar pattern. Yet, whilst Traynor rejects both foster parents and her biological parents, Roy begins a passionate search for the threads of family histories, particularly her father's, the late Maroon author Namba Roy, to narrate her own story as part of a longer history of slavery, colonialism, migration, and diaspora. A victim of racist abuse in 1960s and 1970s Britain, Roy's mixed-race protagonist struggles to establish her identity through family histories that have been buried with her father's death. Crossing genres and mixing diary entries, *testimonio*, and fiction to try to invent different versions of the self, Roy's novel breaks through the conventions of standard autobiography not only to point to its limitations but to show how the author has been constructed, contained, and represented by dominant discourses in Britain. As we are told:

> The African Americans in [the United States] fascinated me because they took this land as their own. Black Briton's didn't do that in the same way. We were always aliens [. . .] in the corner of our eyes was the fear of repatriation. I wanted to find a home like the Africa of [my father's] stories – a place where no one would question my right to put down roots.[40]

The breaks and fissures in Roy's life necessitate other ways of representing and inventing the self and this fragmentation is encapsulated in the novel's non-linear structure. Whilst the novel adheres in part to the conventions of the *Bildung*, like many other texts already discussed, its focus is more significantly on foster care and the protagonist's quest for a larger family history across Britain, America, Africa, and the Caribbean. Roy's attempts to connect with a wider transatlantic history of diaspora and geography is a familiar trait in contemporary black and Asian life-writing.

Life-Writing, Trauma, and the Politics of Remembering Across the Diaspora

Rifts caused by broken histories of diaspora, the search for lost family memories, and the discovery and establishment of multiple identities remain key preoccupations in many black and Asian British autobiographical texts. If, as Marianne Hirsch suggests, memories are always passed down from one generation to the next, this path of connection becomes less than

---

[40] Lucinda Roy, *Lady Moses* (London: Virago, 1998), 216.

straightforward in the context of a recurrent amnesia combined with the geographical fractures of colonialism.[41] As Leela Gandhi argues, 'the emergence of anti-colonial and "independent" nation-States after colonialism is frequently accompanied by a desire to forget the colonial past'. This desire is impelled by various cultural and political motivations, but this form of amnesia 'is symptomatic of the urge for historical self-invention or the need to make a new start'.[42] Given this context, it is not surprising that family memories of colonial hardship or the subordination of slavery are always uneven and full of gaps and silences. Casting the net more widely, Paul Gilroy challenges the idea that traumatic memories bear only on their immediate family victims, and proposes that the effects not only reverberate but involve perpetrator and victim, coloniser and colonised, whites and blacks. He concludes that all such histories remain a ghostly, transgenerational part of the broader history of Britain.[43]

Much like Roy's *Lady Moses*, Andrea Levy's *Fruit of the Lemon*, Jenny McLeod's *Stuck up a Tree* (1998), and Bernardine Evaristo's *Lara* (1997) are impelled in different ways by similar urges for self-invention. Cut off from a colonial past and surrounded by a nationwide culture of amnesia, these authors single-mindedly pursue individual family histories to clear new spaces and inscribe their diasporic stories into British history. This process of giving voice to collective lost histories was also evident of course in other 1990s texts, such as Caryl Phillips's *Cambridge* (1991) and Fred D'Aguiar's *Feeding the Ghosts* (1997), where the retrieval of the past becomes an act of 'postmemory', bringing to light the forgotten realities of a history of slavery, colonialism, and migration.[44]

Levy's *Fruit of the Lemon* traces Faith's journey from Britain to Jamaica and back to London in search of her family history. Comprising three parts, and using diary entries, the novel's non-linear and non-chronological narrative encapsulates Faith's fragmented sense of her past. Despite using the conventional 'I' often found in autobiography, Levy's novel creates a hybrid sense of self that can simultaneously straddle various historical narratives, as Faith recovers from her parent's understated traumas and the consequent silences

---

[41] Marianne Hirsch, *Family Frames: Photography, Narrative, and Postmemory* (Cambridge, MA: Harvard University Press, 1997), 22.

[42] Leela Gandhi, *Postcolonial Theory: A Critical Introduction* (St Leonard, NSW: Allen & Unwin, 1998), 4.

[43] Paul Gilroy, *Between Camps: Race, Identity and Nationalism at the End of the Colour Line* (London: Allen Lane, 2000), 114.

[44] Ole Birk Laursen, '"Telling Her a Story": Remembering Trauma in Andrea Levy's Writing', *EnterText*, 9 (2012): 53–68; 54.

of expression. After Faith returns from Jamaica, where she traces family members across Africa, America, and the Caribbean, the narrator proclaims: 'I am the bastard child of Empire and I will have my day.'[45] This meshing of histories is also apparent in *Small Island*, almost a form of biography, written from the daughter's perspective, of her parents' migration during the Windrush era and how they are almost entirely stultified by white postwar British culture.

McLeod's novel interestingly highlights ways in which a cultural and historical amnesia can inadvertently continue to sustain racist colonial legacies in Britain today. Using a third-person narrative, McLeod is able to distance herself from a younger self, who is unaware of the traumatic history of colonialism, and a present autobiographical self, where author, protagonist, and narrator merge. Upon her mother's death, the main character, Ella, breaks down and is faced with secrets from the past. Ella's later return to her childhood home also represents a return to repressed memories, forcing her to create a new sense of identity. Much like *Small Island*, the ambition of *Stuck up a Tree* is to re-inscribe black subjectivities into Britain, making them part and parcel of the nation today.

Evaristo struggled for several years to find an appropriate form for her family memoir, *Lara*, which traverses three continents as its British Nigerian protagonist escapes from a restricted childhood in London into a conflicted young adulthood. Comparable to *Lady Moses* and Williams's *Sugar and Slate*, *Lara* provides a wide-angled portrait of the intertwined relationship between histories of slavery, colonialism, and migration, a transatlantic legacy which helps to define the complexity of being black in Britain today. As Pilar Cuder-Dominguez suggests, the ongoing search in Evaristo for 'clues' to individual pasts is also, 'metaphorically, a *re*-turn, since the characters' physical and psychological journey of self-discovery traverses Africa as the location where they must piece together their paternal heritage'.[46] Lara not only profits from travelling to places previously inhabited by her ancestors; more significantly she becomes more assertive and resourceful, resolving to author and authorise her own history. By researching and collecting together these wider transatlantic family stories and creatively inserting her own subjectivity into them, Evaristo challenges dominant narratives of Britishness. By the end of her narrative, Lara has grown in stature and decides to return to

---

[45] Levy, *Fruit of the Lemon*, 327.
[46] Pilar Cuder-Dominguez, '(Re)Turning to Africa: Bernardine Evaristo's *Lara* and Lucinda Roy's *Lady Moses*' in Kadija Sesay (ed.), *Write Black, Write British: From Post Colonial to Black British Literature* (London: Hansib, 2005), 300–13; 300.

a telescoped Britain, 'my island – the "Great" Tippexed out of it', ready to claim the land of her birth and to step 'into my future'.[47] Much like Kay, who revisits her verse poem *The Adoption Papers* several years later to write *Red Dust Road*, Evaristo continues to dig further for her history, a pursuit which resulted in the publication of an expanded version of *Lara* in 2009, adding to the British, Brazilian, and Nigerian side of her story its Irish Catholic and German components.

Inscribing and Inventing Selves: The Twenty-First Century

Tapping into New Labour's politics of multiculturalism, writers such as Levy, Srivastava, Perera, and Traynor were to partly establish the context for the commercial breakthroughs of Zadie Smith's *White Teeth* (2000) and Monica Ali's *Brick Lane* (2003). Although not overtly autobiographical, these books were signed up as part of an impulse to create new spaces for women's writing, though the more fundamental challenge of exploring new genres of life-writing for black and Asian women's writing did not recede.

For Diana Evans (1971–), for instance, the tragic death of her twin sister was key to the writing of *26a* (2005), her first novel. Drawing attention to the forgotten bonds between sisters, family, and continents, the book follows sisters Georgia and Bessi to Neasden in north London as well as to Nigeria. Attuned to the challenges of racism against those of mixed heritage, the novel expertly conjoins the broken histories of the twin sisters, exploring at the same time issues of mental health and loss (as is also the case in Levy, McLeod, Roy, and Evaristo). Twins, as Pallavi Rastogi notes in relation to Smith's *White Teeth*, also act as a symbolic trope that does not necessarily just signify twin kinship but can also suggest a well-known 'reformulation', as in Homi Bhabha's 'Janus-faced discourse of the nation'.[48] Twins feature centrally again in Helen Oyeyemi's early novel *The Icarus Girl* (2005), a book which garnered considerable public attention and pointed to the difficulties of being doubly affiliated to both Nigeria and Britain and being both outside and of the nation. Notably Smith, like Oyeyemi, has extended the landscape of her fiction from the black and Asian communities in *White Teeth* to Jewish Chinese characters in *The Autograph Man* (2002) and African Americans in *On Beauty* (2005). Whilst this was in part due to Smith's move away from Britain

---

[47] Bernardine Evaristo, *Lara* (Tunbridge Wells: Angela Royal, 1997), 140.
[48] Rastogi, 'Women's Fiction', 86.

to the USA, the shift in perspective to wider global issues and subjects was also significant.

More recently, a growing generation of Asian British writers such as Nikita Lalwani (1973–) and Roopa Farooki (1974–) have picked up where predecessors such as Perera, Srivastava, and Syal left off. Born in India and raised in Cardiff, Lalwani unearths the generational conflict between parents and their children in her debut novel, *Gifted* (2007). Set in Cardiff and Oxford, where the 'gifted' young protagonist is sent to study by her ambitious Asian parents, the novel maps new territories for black and Asian fictions, as it locates the self in overlooked diasporic urban spaces beyond London. Farooki's *Bitter Sweets* (2007) also paints a widely angled picture of three generations of entangled family history linking Britain with its long South Asian past. Written in a comic vein, it brings in elements from Farooki's own life. Like Kureishi's *My Ear at his Heart* and Levy's *Small Island*, Farooki's *The Flying Man* (2012) was inspired by her father, the author Nasir Farooki (1929–2002), and portrays the wayward life of an unsympathetic anti-hero. Initially intended as a father's memoir which never materialised, Farooki uses the form of fictional biography to bring her father to life. Now author of five successful books, Farooki remains outspoken about the need to address the difficulties still facing black and Asian women writers even in the twenty-first-century literary marketplace:

> All artists fight for the right to practice their craft, and we, as Asian writers, fight more than most. We fight for our places on publisher's lists, for our places on the prize lists, for our places in the promotions. We writers, both men and women, may be dismissed because of our appearance, because of the boxes we have been put in, the brands that publishers have built. Accused of being too political, or not political enough. Too Asian, or not enough.[49]

Conclusion

Continuing to respond to pressures of racism, sexism, and historic erasure, black and Asian British women's writing is frequently self-determinedly autobiographical, allowing for the recording of traumatic histories. Enabling the reinvention of black and Asian female subjectivities and

---

[49] Roopa Farooki, 'Keynote: The Asian Writer Festival', 24 October 2017. Available at https:// theasianwriter.co.uk/2017/10/24/roopa-farooki-keynote-the-asian-writer-festival/.

a range of perspectives from which to confront the silences of history, the diverse possibilities of the autobiographical form have enabled a number of writers over the past four decades to engage with, transcend, and counter such pressures, not only writing themselves into the narrative of British history but continuing to create new voices and contexts from which to reconfigure their lives.

31

Black and Asian British Women's Poetry
Writing Across Generations

DENISE DECAIRES NARAIN

'Why is it Still Rare to See a Black British Woman with Literary Influence?'

In her introduction to *Ten: New Poets*, Bernardine Evaristo (1959–) explains the publication's origins: concerned by the lack of submissions by black British poets for the Poetry Book Society Prize in 2004, Evaristo prompted the Arts Council of England to commission a report which, when published in 2005, concluded that only 1 per cent of all poetry books published in Britain were by black and Asian poets. That statistic galvanised the launch of 'The Complete Works', a two-year national mentoring project for poets which resulted in *Ten: New Poets* (2010), edited by Evaristo and Daljit Nagra, and *Ten: The New Wave* (2014), edited by Karen McCarthy Woolf. In her preface to the second collection, the project's manager, Nathalie Teitler, reports an upward trend (by 10 per cent in 2016) in publications by black British poets; this trend is visible in a spate of recent successes: the Forward Poetry Prize was won by Kei Miller in 2014, Claudia Rankine in 2015, and Vahni Capildeo in 2016; in 2016 Tiphanie Yanique won the Felix Dennis prize for best first collection, while in 2017 Malika Booker was shortlisted for the best single poem category and Richard Georges for the best first collection category. Although these successes have raised the profile of black British poets (male and female) considerably, they are still statistically under-represented.

In a piece in *The Guardian* in 2013, whose title I borrow above, Evaristo comments ruefully on the continuing dearth of influential black women in British literary culture and expresses nostalgia for the fiery radicalism of the 1980s, rather than the 'polite acceptance'[1] of the status quo that, in her view,

---

[1] Bernardine Evaristo, 'Why is it Still Rare to See a Black British woman with Literary Influence?', *The Guardian* (13 December 2013), n.p.

characterises the contemporary poetry scene. Evaristo invokes some of the key anthologies that black women published in response to publishers' claims that there was no market for their work: *Watchers and Seekers* (1987), *Black Women Talk Poetry* (1987), and *Charting the Journey* (1988). One of the four editors of *Black Women Talk Poetry*, Evaristo quotes a key assertion from their joint introduction, 'As black women we experience oppression due to our race, sex, class and sexuality on a daily basis and this is reflected in every area of our lives.'[2] This sentiment resonates strongly with the manifesto-like declarations of several other texts published in the 1980s, which articulated a strong collective identity in the face of black and Asian women's under-representation in mainstream publishing. As dub poetry rose in prominence in the 1980s, women poets also found themselves increasingly marginalised from a male black British poetry scene that assumed hard-hitting, political poetry and robust performers as the norm. But where curating a collective sense of black and Asian women's identity in response to these challenges was largely viewed as a necessary and productive strategy in the 1980s, the shared purpose that mobilised solidarity then is much more elusive now. As Evaristo puts it, 'If it all seems a bit over the top today, this early outrage was the engine that powered us.'[3]

Nostalgia for an idealised black revolutionary moment resonates strongly with feminist nostalgia for the 1970s as a time of (presumed) universal, global sisterhood. But, rather than succumb to such nostalgia, we might recall the risks of invoking 'difference' as the foundation of *any* identity, the common-alities too readily and definitively asserted, and the exclusions on which that hinges. Perhaps, indeed, we should be suspicious of all genealogies of poetry, recognising that they tend to be driven by critical and categorising agendas that poetry and poets may well resist. In writing this piece, for example, it is tempting to make quick generalisations about the contemporary generation of women poets: more irreverent and experimental, with a preference for fragmented rather than narrative forms; with less emphasis on 'identity' and 'voice' in favour of pluralising or, indeed, unravelling those concepts; more ecologically attuned and global in reach, and so on. While poetry by black and Asian women produced in the last two decades aligns *somewhat* with these arcs, there is a degree of overlap with the 'previous generation' that results in a messier genealogy; a 'mashed-up genealogy', if you will, that is not without its attractions. Black and Asian women's poetry as it is written *across the generations* indicates a criss-crossing traffic in ideas and forms at the

[2] Ibid.   [3] Ibid.

detailed granular level, which belies the magisterial overview that critical summary demands.

The Anthology as Poetic Platform

One obvious continuity across generations is the prominence of the anthology as a platform for increasing visibility. Several publications in the last decade recognise the ongoing need for such platforms for black and Asian poets, while also indicating a more modulated and less strategically confrontational rationale than, say, the iconic *News for Babylon* edited by James Berry in 1984. These newer anthologies are less invested in finding *a* voice than in accommodating all kinds and registers of voices and diversifying the very category, 'black and Asian British poetry'. In his introduction to *Red: Contemporary Black British Poetry* (2010), Kwame Dawes argues that 'The term Black British is an evolving one' and one that veers between 'a fairly broad definition, predicated on the idea of minority status, with some relationship to the term "people of colour" and a more exclusive one where "Black British" often refers to British people of African descent'.[4] To manage this spectrum of positions, Dawes invited poets who self-identified as black British to contribute on the theme of 'red'. The ironies of seeking to evade the limiting identity politics associated with 'black' by using a 'colour' – red – are obvious; while 'red' is aligned with rage and passion, it is also the colour of blood with the added significance in Caribbean contexts that 'red' is used to describe those who are 'light-skinned' or 'brown'. *Out of Bounds: British Black and Asian Poets* (2012), edited by Jackie Kay, James Procter, and Gemma Robinson, takes a different tack, extending and complicating the category by organising the contributions by region within the United Kingdom, rather than assuming a concentration in London. This manoeuvre aims to reorient questions of belonging, marginality, and home to acknowledge that many poets are second or third generation, that they are, indeed, as the title of the anthology indicates, *British* black and Asian (rather than black and Asian British), and that Britain, in all its regional diversity, is *their* place. Here, 'geography' eclipses 'biology' as the main anthologising principle. In providing 'an alternative A–Z of poetic Britain',[5] the anthology engages both

---

[4] Kwame Dawes, 'Preface' in Kwame Dawes (ed.), *Red: Contemporary Black British Poetry* (Leeds: Peepal Tree Press, 2010), 17–21; 19.

[5] Jackie Kay, James Procter, and Gemma Robinson, 'Introduction' in Jackie Kay, James Procter, and Gemma Robinson (eds.), *Out of Bounds: British Black and Asian Poets* (Newcastle upon Tyne: Bloodaxe Books, 2012), 13–26; 26.

with the geographic regions of the UK and with an increasing environmental awareness among black and Asian poets. In both *Red* and *Out of Bounds*, women poets are well represented and without fanfare, arguably suggesting that the 'outrage' of the 1980s is no longer required to ensure parity.

Women poets are also very well represented in the two *Ten* collections. What distinguishes these two anthologies from both *Red* and *Out of Bounds* is their strong mentoring function, with each poet's contribution prefaced by a short commentary from their designated mentor. In the second volume, former mentees are now themselves mentors, indicating a poetic legacy established through practical passing on of knowledge and craft, alongside whatever else might be assumed to hold the poets together. The mentors are not exclusively black and Asian and their pairing with poets appears to be driven by affinities in relation to poetic *form*, rather than to a shared cultural or political agenda. Karen McCarthy Woolf, editor of *Ten: The New Wave*, and herself one of the poets mentored in the first, neatly embodies the anthologies' success. Her introduction is tellingly equivocal about pinning down just what 'binds these multicultural poets together': 'If anything, I might suggest a certain confidence: a confidence to pursue idiosyncratic avenues; to embrace, ignore or transcend the political; to write from or for a community if they so choose; to cast the net of cultural and literary influence wide.'[6]

This generously accommodating spirit conveys an apt approach to gathering together 'black and Asian women poets' across the generations. The category remains strategically useful in foregrounding a gendered perspective on key concerns (migration, ethnicity, gender, belonging, language, ecological devastation), but the attitudes to these concerns and the range of forms and styles in which they are explored have proliferated in increasingly idiosyncratic and quirky ways.

Migration Blues

As many pieces in this history suggest, the exclusive focus on the arrival of the *Windrush* in black British migration history does not include Asian or other less well-documented arrivants; neither does it resonate with the precarity and chaos of recent migrations to Europe, which, in complicated ways, have amplified the diverse colonial 'push factors' that propel people away from

---

[6] Karen McCarthy Woolf, 'A True Fellowship' in Karen McCarthy Woolf (ed.), *Ten: The New Wave* (Newcastle upon Tyne: Bloodaxe Books, 2014), n.p.

home. Jay Bernard (1988–), a poet of Caribbean ancestry (featured in *Ten: The New Wave*), speaks to a long history of ocean crossings that includes both the middle passage and the arrival of the *Windrush*. In 'Cadence' the speaker troubles ideas of continuity and lineage:

> I should consider this cold British soil
> an island for a funeral like you do.
> But in the cusp between the middle passage
> and the Windrush something changed
> in the chronology of things.

The speaker briefly considers the possibility of thinking back to a time before nations 'when people saw what made them different / and fell in love with it', before concluding:

> Being young is an oxymoron -
> our genes are old and gnarled as the moon.
> They are genes only: we're columns of blood
>   biding time,
> caught by the delicate cadence that binds us, yes,
> but that doesn't mean I owe a thing to you.[7]

Here, blood ties *don't* bind and the histories they trail can be *refused*; it is the more subtle ways in which they inflect the rhythm and cadence of the poet's voice that Bernard highlights. In 'Migration', Bernard returns to this theme to provide an equally melancholic account of how layers of generational journeying leave an affective residue that haunts the speaker's bus-journey through London:

> . . . and it is that blue
> of stagnant blood beneath the skin,
> that blue of clouded eyes and dried tongues,
> that blue of migration that I recognised
> in the wastes of this evening.[8]

Historical periods are palpably porous, 'the translucent sheet / that hangs between eras', suggesting that what is passed, backwards and forwards, across generations is the melancholic ambience of longing and unbelonging, a shared emotional legacy of migration.[9] The 'stagnant blood' indicates stasis, rather than the movement and vitality often associated with migration, or with cross-generational 'passing on' narratives.

[7] Jay Bernard, *Your Sign is Cuckoo, Girl* (London: Tall-Lighthouse Publications, 2008), 10.
[8] Ibid., 8.   [9] Ibid., 9.

Bernard's interest in embodiment is equally nuanced when the focus is directly on sexuality, as it is in 'One Night', describing the afterglow of a sexual encounter, when a woman has tenderly entered their (female) lover with their fist:

> I turned to lie beside you.
> I watched the morning swell
> With quiet gold, held my
> Hand up to the light.[10]

Shifting from the palpably intimate present of this poem, we might turn to Bernard's queer engagement with a more distant past in their narrative poem, *The Red and Yellow Nothing* (2016), a prequel to the thirteenth-century middle-Dutch story 'Morien'. In their boldly playful handling, the story of the black knight becomes one that transgresses genre, gender, and sexualities. The postmodern panache with which Bernard juggles identities, including their own as a gay, black British woman poet, gives them a confidence to rifle though the archive freely and fearlessly; migration appears to authorise an eclectic 'right to roam' and in their poetry, queer is less an identity than a queering *process*.

Warsan Shire (1988–), another *Ten* poet, brings a similarly confident and varied, nomadic range to 'migration'. Born in Kenya to Somali parents, Shire was appointed as the first Young Poet Laureate of London in 2013. Her poetry addresses more recent and desperate arrivals than those associated with Windrush, documenting the dangerous crossings in precarious boats, trains, and trucks that have characterised recent migrations from across Africa to Europe. 'Conversations About Home', opens, 'Well, I think home spat me out, the blackouts and curfews like tongue / against loose tooth' and goes on to offer an intensely embodied image of what losing a homeland and language might entail:

No one leaves home unless home is the mouth of
a shark. I've been carrying the old anthem in my mouth for so long that
there's no space for another song, another tongue or another language.
I know a shame that shrouds, totally engulfs. I tore up and ate my own
Passport in an airport hotel. I'm bloated with language I can't afford to
Forget.[11]

---

[10] Ibid., 13.
[11] Warsan Shire, *Teaching My Mother How to Give Birth* (London: Mouthmark, 2011), 24.

Shire's poetry conveys the violent circumstances that propel so many to leave home on hazardous quests for better lives. Her work is punctuated by startling metaphors and unexpected juxtapositions that convey the 'extra-ordinary ordinariness' of violence for some of the world's citizens. Caught between European hosts who bark their greetings, *'fucking immigrants, fuck-ing refugees',*[12] and the dangers of 'back home', Shire's arrivants appear suspended in a protracted and perilous liminality.

Vahni Capildeo's reflections on migration in *Measures of Expatriation* (2016), which won the Forward Poetry Prize, resonate with the dislocated disembo-diment noted in Bernard and Shire. Capildeo (1973–), an Indo-Trinidadian, now lives in the UK and *Measures of Expatriation*, her seventh collection, displays her characteristic formal and thematic eclecticism and hybridity: it ranges widely across both expected and unexpected poetic terrain, deploys fragmented and aphoristic forms as well as longer narrative and free verse structures, and is often driven by whimsical associations. Rather than the precision implied in 'Measures of Expatriation', the collection revolves around the diffuse emotions of diverse experiences of being away from, or between, homes.

So, for example, the familiar question, 'where are you from?', posed between strangers on a train to Lancaster in 'Slaughterer', generates an exchange that juxtaposes the mechanical, large-scale killing of cattle in the north of England with the warmth and familiarity of somewhere green and warm in the southern hemisphere. 'Fire & Darkness: And Also / No Join / Like' (Capildeo's titles are often oblique 'clues' to the poem's meaning), offers meditations on disparate experiences that veer vertiginously from Guy Fawkes bonfires and effigies in 'this country' to a 'street in Trinidad', to a two-generational Hindu family watching the news of the liberation of Kuwait on television. The family are joined by a visiting Muslim friend, whose outsider status, the narrator notes, derives from 'a lunatic reverbera-tion' triggered by Partition in 1947. Capildeo, with typically laconic wit, describes the uneasy grouping as they watch Kuwait's 'liberation' unfold, 'We sat on our nice imported sofa with the delicate novel unicorn visitant who looked just like us.'[13] As the visitor's anguished response to the news becomes evident, the speaker reflects:

> I tried to see with his eyes. Brownskinned people with strong features and children of adorable gravity were being killed from the air; and en masse they

[12] Ibid., 27.
[13] Vahni Capildeo, *Measures of Expatriation* (Manchester: Carcanet Press, 2016), 14.

looked more like us than anyone else on television, local or international in those days. My insides flipped. People who looked like they could be family were being killed from the air.[14]

The poem concludes with a repetitive counterpoint of phrases that performs the equivocation about identifying *with* – or *as* – 'brownskinned people', a category the poem identifies as a 'lunatic reverberation' spawned by the geopolitical fallout of colonialism:

Our soft brown young man sat, and sat, until he could get himself home.

> no join
> no join
> no join
> and also
>   like
>   like
>   like[15]

The uncertainty signalled here invites an equally tentative reading: are we being admonished *not* to join or is the speaker insisting that there *is* no join? The 'And also' could be read as 'and another thing' or, more emphatically, 'and don't forget' while the repetition of 'like' might be read as an imperative *to* like. It also acts as a reminder that the poem's subject – the likeness 'brownskinned people' supposedly share – is as erratic as the use of simile throughout the poem itself. The poem both recognises and refuses the identity-category around which it turns. The preference for a scattering of the particulars and particles that may momentarily comprise identity is a fascinating characteristic of Capildeo's work; 'no join' might also be read as an enjoinder *not* to join the dots, to be open to assembling rather than fixing identity.

In 'Too Solid Flesh', the speaker, *'four-thousand-miles-away-across-the-ocean'*[16] – the approximate distance between Trinidad and England – invites the reader to imagine her as:

a pointillist vision given an order of dismissal: the dots of colour that vibrate until the eye interlinks them and learns the trick of making sense of the person or the landscape depicted, these dots would obediently dance apart, disperse, making image into worse than nonsense, hurting the eye that tries to focus into questing after a scattering in which each particle is adamantine, uncollectable.[17]

---

[14] Ibid., 15.   [15] Ibid.   [16] Ibid., 20.   [17] Ibid., 13.

Here, Capildeo mines the ontological implications of a pointillist point of view that, in turn, invites the reader to read and *assemble*, rather than *identify*.

'Language Is My Home, I Say; Not One Particular Language'

Like Bernard and Shire, Capildeo explores the complex and diverse meanings that accrue to but cannot be contained by the currency of words such as, migrant, refugee, expatriate, and exile and, like them, she also turns these words around to push at new horizons of meaning. In 'Word by Word', the speaker mocks her inability to play the word-association party game before word-associating 'refugee' with Bach's fugues, 'migrant' with geese and other birds, 'exile' with various expulsions, and 'expatriate' with *'unhousèd free condition'*.[18] The collection is punctuated throughout with word-play of various kinds, so that the reader is well prepared for the manifesto that appears in the penultimate section:

> Language is my home. It is alive other than in speech. It is beyond a thing to be carried with me. It is ineluctable, variegated and muscular. [. . .]

> Language is my home, I say; not one particular language.[19]

Where Capildeo's poems reference Trinidadian demotic, European, Shakespearean, and Norse words and culture, Shire's poems are frequently punctuated by Somali and Arabic words and proverbs, London slang, and references to popular culture. Language has never been a taken-for-granted medium for black and Asian women poets, but a vigorously contested one. In *News for Babylon*, James Berry (1924–2017) claimed that Louise Bennett's pioneering use of Jamaican creole 'launched a people's voice'.[20] And *i is a long memoried woman* (1983) by Grace Nichols (1950–) is widely read as endorsing the empowerment and vocal agency of black women: the treacherously smiling silent woman of her epigraph gives way to the 'new tongue' signalled in the epilogue:

> I have crossed an ocean
> I have lost my tongue
> from the root of the old one
> a new one has sprung[21]

---

[18] Ibid., 103. [19] Ibid., 100–1.
[20] James Berry, 'Introduction', in Berry (ed.), *News for Babylon: The Chatto Book of Westindian–British Poetry* (London: Chatto & Windus, 1984), xvi.
[21] Grace Nichols, *i is a long memoried woman* (London: Karnak, 1983), 87.

While, as Evaristo suggests, black and Asian women poets continue to struggle for a platform from which to be heard, their poetry now seems less exclusively invested in finding *a* voice than in experimenting with *voices*. Returning to the pointillist metaphor, we might say that they appear less insistent on 'joining the dots' or in tracing lines of genealogy across generations, and more interested in experimenting with forms and voices across diverse migratory and cultural routes. The confident linguistic promiscuity that distinguishes this poetry demands readings that refuse the old binary of *either* standard English *or* creole. It also prompts us to question the presumed opposition between experimental and expressive poetic forms.

The Expressive and the Experimental

In thinking about how we might most productively read women's poetry across the generations to arrive at the provisional or 'mashed-up' genealogy I referred to earlier, we need to avoid an account in which poets are seen as 'progressing' from the expressive to the experimental, or, to put it another way, from finding a voice to playing with voices. If we align Bennett and Nichols exclusively with an expressive vocality and, by contrast, Capildeo and Shire with an experimental, aestheticised poetics, we write out the messy intersections across their work. R. Victoria Arana argues that anthologies of new black British writing invariably focused on 'the socio-political emergence of the voices, but drew little or no attention to what the voices were saying and no attention whatsoever to *how* they were crafting their messages'.[22] Anthony Reed also warns against reading black poetry exclusively as an *expressive* mode in which the realities of black experience (presumed as an identifiably shared one) must (and *can*) be simply relayed on the 'presumption that black writers' condition of intelligibility is addressing a narrowly conceived social problem'.[23] I share Reed's sense that these 'genealogies rely either on the idea of "finding a voice" or participating in a transhistorical project' and agree that the focus on resistance often occludes attention to aesthetics and is insufficiently receptive to 'the radical implications of formal innovation as a mode of social engagement'.[24] But where Reed favours poetry that is strikingly and obviously 'experimental' over poetry that is

---

[22] R. Victoria Arana (ed.), *'Black' British Aesthetics Today* (Newcastle upon Tyne: Cambridge Scholars, 2009), i.

[23] Anthony Reed, *Freedom Time: The Poetics and Politics of Black Experimental Writing* (Baltimore, MD: Johns Hopkins University Press, 2014), 3.

[24] Ibid., 8.

'expressive', I would argue for a messier, intersectional approach and argue that 'horizons of intelligibility'[25] can be challenged by poetry that criss-crosses expressive/experimental modes. A brief discussion of *Zong!* by Marlene NourbeSe Philip (1947–) suggests ways in which this might be effected.

Zong! (2008) offers an intimate engagement with the transcript of the legal record pertaining to the claim for insurance by the ship's owner, following the killing of 130 (or possibly as many as 150) enslaved Africans, thrown overboard mid-Atlantic at the command of Captain Collingwood in 1781. In 'Notanda', Philip includes a facsimile of the legal document and a detailed account of the sources, processes, and difficulties involved in writing the book; 'Notanda' opens, 'There is no telling this story: it must be told.'[26] The collection unfolds through six sections in which the reader is immersed in a sea of text, sometimes comprised of syllables (as in the example below), recognisable words and occasionally sentences, all drawn from the 1783 legal documents that Philip 'cut ... into pieces', 'mutilates', and reassembles.[27] Some pages conjure a palimpsest effect with traces of words scrolling faintly across the page while on others the imagined names of the drowned Africans scroll across the bottom.

Zong! #1
```
    w  w  w        w              a    wa
       w      a              w a        t
    er             wa                   s
        our                        wa
    te r  gg                  g        g   go[28]
```

Philip works over the legal document, picking it apart, dismantling it, and reassembling fragments of it, in an attempt to convey *something* of the drowned African souls. Rather than attempting to fill the silence and make the drowned Africans *speak*, Philip exposes the violent history that pre-empted speech then – *and* now. In doing so the poem, to use Reed's evocative phrase, provides a 'broken witness'[29] to the event.

Returning to the expressive and experimental, it seems to me that *Zong!* navigates across both poetic modes. The process of *writing* the text, at least as Philip outlines it in 'Notanda', involves an immersive, patient *reading* and *sounding* of the legal source documents which the reader is then invited to

---

[25] Ibid.
[26] Marlene NourbeSe Philip, *Zong! As Told to the Author by Setay Adamu Boateng* (Middletown, CT: Wesleyan University Press, 2008), 187.
[27] Ibid., 193–5. [28] Ibid., 3. [29] Ibid., 23.

empathetically mimic in her reading of *Zong!* itself. Reading *Zong!* becomes an ethical and performative event that is corporeally engaging and expressive, requiring the reader to inhabit syllable, sentence, and sound in an affectively, aesthetically immersive reading. In recorded performances easily available online and at several live events I have attended, Philip's presentation of sections of the poem makes the intersection of expressive and experimental more readily visible and audible. Often dressed in white and with minimal stage props, her appearance on stage resonates with that of the traditional Griot, the community historian, poet, and storyteller of West African cultures. The radical experimentation with words, sounds and meanings that is (perhaps intimidatingly) visible in the written text is immediately audible in performance, even if the appearance of the poet might suggest a more 'traditional' poetic role.

This hybrid intersection of experimental and expressive poetic practices is evident, in different registers, in the work of several other contemporary women poets who mine archives of various kinds. In *The Fifth Fugue* (2006), Jean 'Binta' Breeze (1957–) uses the European quadrille dance form to structure her reflections on five generations of Jamaican women. Grace Nichols writes back to, and through, several of Picasso's paintings in *Picasso, I Want My Face Back* (2009) and *Telling Tales* (2014) by Patience Agbabi (1965–) loosely frames its account of twenty-first-century south-east England on Chaucer's *Canterbury Tales*. As well as their foray into medieval culture (see above), Jay Bernard's *Beacon of Hope: New Beacon in Poetry and Prose* (2016) is the generically hybrid result of their engagement with the New Beacon archives of the New Cross Massacre (the firebombing in 1981 that killed thirteen young West Indians at a party in New Cross Road, for which no one has ever been charged). What is striking about Bernard's response is the intimacy, humility, and hesitancy with which they engage with their sources. In the preface they write:

> I wanted to explore the aftermath of the fire – the silence, the separation, the charred remains, the loss and the mystery of what happened in those early hours on January 18th 1981. I also wanted to create something protean, mutable, never-ending – a kind of conversation I could keep having with myself about who I am and who I speak to.[30]

[30] Ruth Bush and Jay Bernard, *Beacon of Hope: New Beacon in Poetry and Prose* (London: New Beacon Books, 2016), 55–6. Bernard was awarded the Ted Hughes Award for new poetry for 2017 for their multimedia sequence, *Surge: Side A*, which focuses on the New Cross Fire.

It is this nuanced and careful engagement with the past as it is felt in the present that continues to distinguish contemporary black and Asian women poets, informing their poetics so that the expressive and experimental invariably intersect. The particular contours of these intersections may vary, but the commitment to protean poetic forms is shared as is a willingness to both construct and deconstruct identities and narratives. Vahni Capildeo provides a powerful image of this poetic élan and flair; her poem 'Sycorax ~~Whoops~~' concludes:

> Mother! plunge your tongue where ever with brokenness we're ~~deaf~~
> ~~en'd defend~~ fed. Take ~~apart~~ our part. Launch in sighted
> darkness our pack of languages, fluid as hounds,
> all ready: bathed: riteful: already intending chase:[31]

The brilliance of this metaphor – it, like the hounds, is straining at the leash for what lies beyond its immediate horizon of intelligibility – is its unexpectedness. It yokes power with unknown poetic possibilities while the colon with which the poem ends signals a futurity that might be read, 'watch this space'. This compelling image of a bold openness to *whatever* poetic possibilities may emerge resonates strongly with the tenor and tone of black and Asian women's poetry.

---

[31] Capildeo, *Measures of Expatriation*, 121.

(11)

★

FRAMING NEW VISIONS

32

Through a Different Lens
Drama, Film, New Media, and Television

FLORIAN STADTLER

Drama, film, new media, and television play key roles in the representation of black and Asian British experiences. This has raised a series of questions about how these narratives have been offered up for consumption to the wider public. As D. Keith Peacock observes in relation to drama, 'when social diversity does not translate into socially proportionate theatre-going demographics, this reveals much about the theatre complex itself.'[1] Peacock gestures towards wider issues around aesthetics, the availability and politics of funding, as well as distribution and access, which are also relevant to film, new media, and television. These elements, then, have shaped debates around the creation and reception of these cultural productions and highlight the difficult path to wider mainstream representation of Britain's cultural diversity.

Linking back to a history of performance earlier in the century, this chapter looks at how leading writers and their productions – by actor, playwright, and artistic director Kwame Kwei-Armah (1967–), actress and writer Meera Syal (1961–), and playwrights like Roy Williams (1968–), Tanika Gupta (1963–), Hanif Kureishi (1954–), and Ayub Khan-Din (1961–) – have taken Britain's multiculture centre stage. The first decade of the twenty-first century saw an upsurge in black and Asian British writing for stage, radio, film, and television, with productions receiving increased attention and recognition. Among the biggest successes were the production of a triptych of plays (2003–2007) by Kwei-Armah at the National Theatre (NT) and Gurinder Chadha's film *Bend It Like Beckham* (2002). The widespread success of these works led some commentators to conclude that the way Britain conceived of itself as a nation had effectively been transformed, while others saw this

---

[1] D. Keith Peacock, 'Stages of Representation' in Deirdre Osborne (ed.), *The Cambridge Companion to British Black and Asian Literature (1945–2010)* (Cambridge: Cambridge University Press, 2016), 110–26; 110.

breakthrough as marking a moment of arrival for black and Asian British productions in the cultural mainstream.

Circumstances are far more complex than this would suggest and these assertions are increasingly challenged, especially by directors and actors from black, Asian, and minority ethnic (BAME) backgrounds; actor Lenny Henry's campaign on diversity in the media, which aims to increase the number of roles for BAME acting talent on British screens, exemplifies this. Writers, too, have joined this heated debate linking to earlier discussions of citizenship and cultural investment in the artistic life of the UK. These concerns have received new urgency in the wake of the 2018 Windrush scandal. Members of the Windrush generation, long resident in Britain, were stripped of citizens' rights due to a lack of documentation, which led to the withholding of jobs, housing, and medical treatment and, in some instances, to deportation. This was compounded by the government's failure to preserve ship landing cards.

Long-standing barriers to processes of representation dating back to the 1970s and 1980s still resonate today. There is much evidence to suggest that narratives of black and Asian British lives are not yet equitably represented in the mainstream. The focus in this chapter on a wide range of artistic expression including television, which Stuart Hall describes as 'the mass medium of social interpretation', offers a useful way of tracing the sense of arrival as well as alienation for these cultural productions.[2] For example, while popular serial dramas, such as *EastEnders, Emmerdale, Casualty,* and *Coronation Street,* feature black and Asian British characters, the number of writers from these backgrounds commissioned to work on them is low.

Drama, film, radio, and television are all *collaborative* endeavours and this raises important questions of classification. Is a film like *My Beautiful Laundrette* (1985), written by Kureishi and directed by Stephen Frears, a British Asian film? Similarly, is the Windrush musical *The Big Life* (2004), written by English dramatist Paul Sirett and directed by British Caribbean director Clint Dyer (1968–) at Theatre Royal Stratford East, with a West End transfer, to be seen as a black British production? And does the make-up of the audience play a role in categorising a cultural product, too? In other words, are story and subject matter more important than the writer, director, or producer in making such distinctions? Such collaborative productions, then, challenge the primacy of the position of the writer and further complicate the

[2] Sarita Malik, *Representing Black Britain: A History of Black and Asian Images on Television* (London: Sage, 2002), vii.

categories black British and British Asian. As the push for access to and recognition in the wider cultural landscape is premised on the very cross-pollination that disrupts binary distinctions, these works must be considered through a wider prism and focus on the collaborative creative processes by which black and Asian British stories are presented to multiple audiences through a range of media. By taking account of networks between cultural practitioners and organisations, a more nuanced picture can be drawn of the successes and failures of these endeavours to question notions of British national identity. In the post-millennial moment, then, it is important to account for what Jen Harvie terms 'the UK's multiple identities and practices', from which emerge a series of 'power dynamics', which revolve around an axis of 'identities, practices and power'.[3]

The first decade of the twenty-first century witnessed an increased visibility of these productions, following an agenda to widen audiences. The second decade offers perhaps a more sobering picture with its distinct reduction in the number of plays by black and Asian British playwrights on the major national stages and on UK broadcasting channels. In the aftermath of racial tensions and erupting violence in northern towns such as Bradford, Burnley, and Oldham in 2001 and the London terrorist attacks on 7 July 2005, there has also been a representational shift in depictions of black and Asian British life that often panders to stereotypes. Audiences, practitioners, and funding bodies are here confronted with complex questions of which stories to focus on and how to present them. Indeed, when revisiting these debates in the contemporary context, it becomes clear that the questions around representation and, more specifically, the 'burden of representation' that Kobena Mercer (1960–) asked in relation to black art still ring true:

> If, after many years of struggle, you arrive at the threshold of enunciation and are 'given' the right-to-speak and a limited space in which to tell your story, is it not the case that there will be an overwhelming pressure to try and tell the whole story all at once? If there is only one opportunity to make your voice heard, is it not the case that there will be an intolerable imperative to try and say everything there is to be said, all in one mouthful?[4]

This is most certainly relevant to the films that emerge in the 1980s and 1990s, such as *My Beautiful Laundrette* or Chadha and Syal's *Bhaji on the Beach* (1993). Throughout the 1990s, the representation of diasporic identities on screen

[3] Jen Harvie, *Staging the UK* (Manchester: Manchester University Press, 2005), 13.
[4] Kobena Mercer, 'Black Art and the Burden of Representation', *Third Text*, 4:10 (1990): 61–78; 62.

shifted from an arthouse cinematic aesthetic to commercial film-making, exemplified by the film adaptation of Khan-Din's play *East is East* (1999), *Bend It Like Beckham*, and *Bride and Prejudice* (Chadha, 2004). These recalibrated the stories through commercially successful formats, such as comedy dramas and romantic comedies. Although writers and directors from black and Asian British backgrounds work across different media, there remains a distinct lack of opportunity for their work to be heard and seen. The experience of actors is similar. This raises key questions about the remit of Arts Council-funded organisations like the Royal Shakespeare Company (RSC) and the NT to represent Britain in all its diversity. Such considerations are also contingent on funding and the process of building an audience for theatrical productions, which is true for television as well.

In the 1990s, the powerful satirical sketches written by Anil Gupta (1974–), Syal, Sanjeev Bhaskar (1963–), Sharat Sardana (1968–2009), Sanjeev Kholi (1971–), Richard Pinto, Nina Wadia (1969–), and Kulvinder Ghir (1965–) in the radio and television show *Goodness Gracious Me* became an important vehicle to challenge stereotypes through their subversive humour. This is encapsulated by the sketch 'Going for an English', in which a group of young Mumbaikars decide to end their night out in an establishment serving English food, mirroring the visit to curry-houses by groups of youths in the UK after a drunken night out. Other television programmes, like the situation comedy *Desmond's* (1989–1994), the drama series *Babyfather* (2001–2002), and the crime drama *Luther* (2010–present) starring Idris Elba (1972–), attracted equally large audiences. More recently, adaptations of black and Asian British novels, like *Life Isn't All Ha Ha Hee Hee* (2005), *Small Island* (2009), and *NW* (2016), have brought these narratives to wider audiences. This is not without controversy, as demonstrated by the sitcom *Citizen Khan* (2012–2016), created by Adil Ray (1974–), and the chat show *The Kumars at No 42* (2001–2006), both of which had mixed receptions and faced accusations of offensiveness or 'Uncle Tom-ism'.

As Isaac Julien (1960–) and Mercer point out in 'Introduction: De Margin, De Centre':

> the point of contestation is no longer between multiculturalism and anti-racism, but inside the concept of ethnicity itself. Within dominant discourses, 'ethnicity' is structured into a negative equivalence with essentialist

versions of 'race' and 'nation' which particularizes its referent, as the pejorative connotation of 'ethnic minority' implies (who after all constitutes the 'ethnic majority'?).[5]

Indeed, the crucial debates around marginalisation and representation signalled here have been usefully extended by Harvie in her 2005 study, *Staging the UK*, where she explores how 'performance has produced national and related identities in the United Kingdom'.[6] The move into accelerated visibility on mainstream stages has coincided with a deeper debate about notions of national identity in Britain. A discussion of the major impact these writers have had in a variety of media as well as their successful creative collaborations across the industry reveals the complex conditions and means by which challenging new works began to capture the imagination and empathy of a more diversely conceived British audience.

During the 1990s and 2000s, black and Asian British film, television, and theatre productions started to gain increasing traction in the cultural mainstream. This includes many popular cultural modes, whether commercial theatrical productions, soap operas, television miniseries, or, increasingly, new digital online provisions. Very evident here is how institutions like the NT and the RSC have sought to restage the UK. Such an impetus is to some extent state-led, in so far as eligibility for state funding comes with the requirement to represent inclusively the national life of the United Kingdom. While this has led to a diversification of audiences in these houses and to a more representative screen presence of a wide range of communities on television and in new media, many of the productions place identity politics at their centre.

A larger question emanating from such increased visibility is whether this push for recognition at the centre has in fact enabled more nuanced representations and pulled the writer in from the margins. Indeed, it is here where perhaps a murkier underside can be detected. If black writers are only asked to write on black subjectivity, can we really consider this sense of arrival a success? Avril Russell, one of the co-writers of the popular miniseries *Babyfather*, notes in a 2014 interview that the programme made her fall 'into a deep, dark pigeonhole' and that, whereas before she had written on long-running continuing dramas like the police series *The Bill*, she now found

---

[5] Isaac Julien and Kobena Mercer, 'Introduction: De Margin and De Centre', *Screen*, 29:4 (1988): 2–11; 6.
[6] Harvie, *Staging the UK*, 1.

herself losing out on commissions.[7] How then does contemporary Britain engage with the African and African Caribbean community living in Britain and vice versa? In what ways do these productions articulate black and Asian British experiences and in the process challenge questions of a monolithic British identity and an idea of multicultural Britain? These issues need to be addressed in order to investigate how a greater awareness of Britain's multi-cultural, multiethnic self has allowed these cultural productions to reach broader audiences, while binary distinctions that undercut their full accep-tance as 'British' cultural productions still remain.

Drama

Black and Asian British drama's push onto mainstream stages accelerated from the mid-1990s onwards (see Chapter 22). The late 1990s and first two decades of the twenty-first century have seen a string of successful theatre productions presented nationally by large repertory companies and in the West End. Khan-Din's *East is East* started out as a theatre play before being adapted into a successful Brit comedy film released in 1999. First produced by the theatre company Tamasha in collaboration with the Royal Court and Birmingham Repertory Theatre, the play premiered in 1996 and then transferred to London's Ambassadors Theatre for three sell-out runs. Set in Salford, the play centres around the Khans, a family of mixed heritage who run a fish and chip shop. It is as much about community and class as it is about generational conflict. Firmly rooted in the milieu of the early 1970s in the wake of Enoch Powell's 'Rivers of Blood' speech, it confronts questions of national identity, citizenship, and belonging. In 2015, the play was revived at Trafalgar Studios in London's West End before embarking on a UK tour.

Kwei-Armah's foray into playwriting came on the heels of starring roles in continuing BBC medical dramas *Holby City* and *Casualty*. His triptych of plays *Elmina's Kitchen*, *Fix Up*, and *Statement of Regret* shaped much black drama representation at the NT in the early part of the century by considering multiple aspects of the black British experience for the first time on one of Britain's major stages. *Elmina's Kitchen* transferred to the West End's Garrick Theatre in 2005, a first for a black Briton. As Aleks Sierz writes, 'it became clear that much of the energy in British new writing was now coming from

---

[7] Ian Burrell, '"Babyfather" Stereotyping by the BBC Cost Me Career, Says Writer Avril Russell', *The Independent*, 9 June 2014. Available at www.independent.co.uk/arts-entertainment/tv/news/babyfather-stereotyping-by-the-bbc-cost-me-career-says-writer-avril-russell-9517841.html.

black writers whose point of view was critical of both established society and the black subcultures within it'.[8] Artistic directors of major playhouses picked up on this dynamism and the late 1990s and early 2000s saw a number of black and Asian British playwrights receive major commissions, including Kwei-Armah, debbie tucker green, and Roy Williams, who, as Lynette Goddard remarks, 'are widely acknowledged as the most significant black British playwrights of the early 2000s'.[9] Their work was showcased at theatres such as the Royal Court, NT, Hampstead Theatre, Soho Theatre, and Young Vic, and in 2017 it was announced that Kwei-Armah would take over as the Young Vic's new artistic director. Some works were also adapted for radio and television, including tucker green's *random* for BBC Radio 3 (2010) and Channel 4 (2011).

Kwei-Armah's triptych was written for the NT and produced between 2003 and 2007. Commissioned by artistic director Nicholas Hytner, the staging of these plays offered new insights into the role of black British theatre in the context of the NT, which aspires to reflect the diversity of national culture. The critical acclaim and box office success of these plays in subsidised houses as well as commercial theatres point to a shift in perspective that allows the narration of black British stories on their own terms. In this respect, Kwei-Armah's plays serve as a useful case study of how theatre as a medium can articulate hybrid and minority identities for a wider audience. NT reports suggest that these plays have brought in a younger and more diverse demographic that is more representative of the UK population and, more specifically, London. They are an example of how the NT is working towards a more diverse programme that reflects the reality of contemporary British life. Rufus Norris, who replaced Hytner in 2015, continues pushing this agenda. This is most pressing in relation to black and Asian British theatre but also indicative elsewhere. For instance, until February 2016, when the NT staged *The Solid Life of Sugar Water* (directed by Amit Sharma; co-produced with Graeae theatre company), the theatre had never programmed a play with a cast entirely led by disabled actors.

In 2001, Hytner argued that 'any consensus of what our national identity is has evaporated in recent years, and it is with that that the National Theatre

---

[8] Aleks Sierz (ed.), *The Methuen Drama Book of Twenty-First Century British Playwrights* (London: Bloomsbury, 2010), xi.

[9] Lynette Goddard, *Contemporary Black British Playwrights: Margins to Mainstream* (Basingstoke: Palgrave Macmillan, 2015), 5.

should start'.[10] He set out to change the perception of the NT by broadening access, moving boldly away from the concerns of a white, middle-aged, middle-class audience by programming plays that signalled a new openness and also by working with a larger group of writers, actors, directors, and other theatre companies. The new regime required an interrogation of the NT's role, re-evaluating the functions of a *national* theatre in an evolving multireligious, multiethnic, and multicultural Britain, and in the context of emergent organisations that help this process of reformulation. As Hytner states in a *Guardian* interview in September 2003:

> High standards have always been the cornerstone of the National's identity, but that doesn't wash any more. [...] We can't claim a monopoly of high standards. Very often small itinerant nibble organisations achieve amazing things. The National should also be about vitality that reflects the vitality of the nation and the diversity and energy of its interlocking communities.[11]

The strategies Hytner put in place – such as initiating the Travelex season in which two-thirds of tickets in the Olivier theatre are sold at a reduced price; collaborations with other theatres and arts organisations including Birmingham Rep, Tamasha, Tara Arts, Talawa, and Battersea Arts Centre; a focus on new writing and revivals relevant to the state of the nation – have successfully attracted a younger and more diverse audience, allowing the NT to question and explore the idea of nation. This has been further complicated in recent years with the inauguration of a National Theatre for Scotland and the creation of an English-speaking National Theatre for Wales.

Over the past few years, new communities and younger audiences have found a platform from which their voices demand to be heard, not only on the theatrical and societal fringe but within the mainstream too. For the NT to inhabit the heart of the nation's theatre life, it needs to engage this broad spectrum of voices – and make them heard by the widest possible audience. These developments have led to several co-productions, such as a stage version of Kureishi's novel *The Black Album* (2009), directed by Jatinder Verma (1954–) and co-produced with Tara Arts; Khan-Din's *Rafta, Rafta ...* (2007) based on Bill Naughton's *All in Good Time*, which embarked on a national tour in collaboration with Birmingham Repertory Theatre and The Lowry in Salford and was also turned into a film which used the title of

---

[10] Fiachra Gibbons, 'Hytner Looks to New Identities for National', *The Guardian*, 26 September 2001. Available at www.guardian.co.uk/uk/2001/sep/26/arts.highereducation.

[11] Fiachra Gibbons, 'The Guardian Profile: Nicholas Hytner', *The Guardian*, 26 September 2003. Available at www.theguardian.com/stage/2003/sep/26/theatre.

Naughton's play; and Inua Ellams's *Barber Shop Chronicles* (2017), co-produced with Fuel and the West Yorkshire Playhouse.

As Goddard notes, 'Mainstream representations of black experience are shaped to address dual audiences, the typical, predominantly white, middle-class theatre-going audience and the new, young, black and working-class audiences that are targeted to attend these productions.'[12] Perhaps addressing multiple audiences entails a differently articulated understanding of how minority-ethnic concerns can be represented on stage and to what extent these plays do not just raise questions about minority experiences but more broadly address key issues of the contemporary moment. Indeed, this cen-tring of the margins is crucial for the different media that this chapter addresses, as are the intense debates around increasing the visibility of and enabling broader access to cultural production for those who often remain marginalised. Such concerns have been most hotly contested by visual artists and film-makers.

Film

The emergence of black and Asian British cinema dates back to the 1970s. Horace Ové's *Pressure* (1975) is a landmark and has been the trail-blazer for the cinema that followed. The 1970s, 1980s, and early 1990s saw an increase in black and Asian British independent film-making, with several films, such as the collaborations between Kureishi and Frears (1941–) or Julien and John Akomfrah (1957–), characterised by an arthouse aesthetic. This allowed for a recalibrated view of black and Asian life in Britain that lay outside of social realism and shifted towards a different representative vocabulary. *My Beautiful Laundrette* was a break-out hit and in many ways paved the way for films that followed in the early 2000s using more popular modes of storytelling, such as *Bend It Like Beckham*, a coming-of-age comedy set in Southall centring on Jess and Jules who dream of playing women's football professionally. In the wake of the 1980s riots across the UK, including Brixton, Handsworth, and Toxteth, a more favourable funding climate evolved for film-makers of minority ethnic backgrounds. The wider state-led push cre-ated funding opportunities for black and Asian British cultural producers through, for example, Channel 4 Films, BBC Films, the British Film Institute, and the UK Film Council (set up in 2000). The unexpectedly wide success of *My Beautiful Laundrette*, then, helped to open doors in unforeseen ways.

[12] Goddard, *Contemporary Black British Playwrights*, 11.

Cultural commentators such as Hall and Mercer were quick to consider these forms of cultural expression in relation to representations of black and Asian subjectivities on screen and how they related to the wider body politic of Britain as it moved into the 1990s. A further shift can however be identified as Britain changed government in the mid-1990s, with the ascent of 'New Labour' and its new form of state-led multiculturalism focusing on celebrating diversity and inclusivity. These ideological shifts were to be severely tested in the decades that followed.

While black and Asian film-making came to wider prominence in the 1980s and the 1990s, trail-blazing works were already evident in the 1970s, most notably the first black and Asian British full-length feature films: *A Private Enterprise* (1974), directed by Peter Scott and written by Dilip Hiro, and *Pressure*, directed by Ové, who developed the screenplay with the novelist Sam Selvon. These feature films followed on from short films of the 1960s. Directors, screenwriters, and actors particularly addressed the tensions of making a home in Britain and highlighted policies of exclusion, which led to a radical form of film-making beyond established conventions. In that sense, this formed part of an evolutionary process responding to the politics of the decades. Many discussions centred around the wider questions of identity as they relate to the complexities of the diasporic experience and the process of establishing a home in Britain. This is especially reflected in the diversity of genres and film forms. As Sarita Malik has noted, 'Films as diverse as *Handsworth Songs* (John Akomfrah, Black Audio Film Collective, 1986), *Bhaji on the Beach* (Gurinder Chadha, 1993) and *Young Soul Rebels* (Isaac Julien, 1991) have raised vital questions about ethnicity, identity and the cultural politics of difference, while also re-examining notions of "Britishness" and national cinema.'[13]

These considerations have influenced not only the contents of film production but also its forms, which are intimately bound up with the sociopolitical context in which these films were first released. Here, a tension between the aesthetically provocative and challenging works of collectives and workshops like Sankofa, the Black Audio Film Collective, and Ceddo can be discerned alongside more popular modes of film-making. Black and Asian British film is characterised by a wide range of genres and styles – be they the social realist dramas of the mid-1970s and 1980s or experimental short films. Especially notable in this context is Ové's *Pressure*, which dramatised

[13] Sarita Malik, 'Beyond "The Cinema of Duty"? The Pleasure of Hybridity: Black British Film of the 1980s and 1990s' in Andrew Higson (ed.), *Dissolving Views: Key Writings on British Cinema* (London: Cassel, 1996), 202–16; 202.

complexities around race and racism, cross-generational conflict, and belonging. The film centres on Tony and his family in Notting Hill; born in England to parents of the Windrush generation, he struggles to find employment despite his good educational achievements. Despondent at the prejudice he experiences, he and his brother become involved in the Black Power movement. The film raises pertinent questions about political commitment and activism in the face of hostile state structures, constant police suspicion, and discrimination. Although a moderate success at the box office, the film was difficult to finance with limited funding made available through the British Film Institute as well as private funders.

A game changer for film production was the 1976 report *The Arts Britain Ignores* by Naseem Khan. It led to the establishment of the Minority Arts Advisory Service to assist with the redistribution of resources to foster better representation in the media.[14] Funding was increased in the 1980s as a result, facilitated through the Arts Council, the British Film Institute, or local government institutions, such as the Greater London Council. The expensive nature of film-making hampered many, which explains the scarcity of productions in the preceding decades. Nevertheless, notable early films include Lionel Ngakane's *Jemima and Johnny* (1963) and Ové's *Baldwin's Nigger* (1969) and *Reggae* (1970). Mostly filmed in a social-realist style, they focused on the social issues faced by black and Asian communities. Documenting lived experience despite being fictional, they challenged received perceptions of the diaspora experience.

The early 1980s, when 'Raj nostalgia', the longing for Britain's lost imperial past in India, first peaked, marked the moment when, as Julien notes, 'black British cinema became the cutting edge of independent British film culture because [. . .] some of the black people working in film, wanted to make oppositional work'.[15] Yet he is sceptical of whether this momentum will be maintained in the 1990s. What characterised the film-making of the 1970s and 1980s were the deep-seated political interests of the artists. This is especially important in relation to black independent film-making in the UK and the production of black films of fiction and drama. One of the hallmarks of 1980s scriptwriting was the foregrounding of stories that were otherwise ignored and instead generating, as Malik states, 'new ways of seeing Black people in the context of wider society and the newly developing cultural politics'.[16]

---

[14] Ibid., 203.
[15] Isaac Julien, 'Burning Rubber's Perfume' in June Givanni (ed.), *Remote Control: Dilemmas of Black Intervention in British Film and TV* (London: British Film Institute, 1995), 55–62; 55.
[16] Malik, 'Beyond "The Cinema of Duty"?', 206.

The mid-1980s was an important moment, then, for black British film production. The founding of several independent production companies and a range of collectives together with increasing financial support from funders such as the British Film Institute and the newly founded Channel 4, which regularly commissioned production companies such as Kuumba, Anancy Films, Penumbra, and Social Film and Video, enabled debates around film form and aesthetics, between experimentation and popular narrative. The politics of representation remained high on the agenda and was important to collectives such as Sankofa, Retake, Ceddo, and the Black Audio Film Collective. Perhaps this is best exemplified by the debates following the release of *Handsworth Songs*. This landmark documentary, created by the Black Audio Film Collective for Channel 4 as part of their 'Britain: The Lie of the Land' series, is structured as a film essay and directly engages with the complexities of representation by refusing a linear narrative. Instead, it presents distinct viewpoints on the 1985 riots in the Handsworth area of Birmingham to generate a much more nuanced vision of social exclusion and what it means to be black and British.

In autumn 1994, the *Black Film Bulletin* produced an issue that further extended their ongoing engagement with what June Givanni terms the 'diaspora experience'.[17] What is encapsulated by notions such as 'Asian British film' or 'Asian Diaspora film' and how such terminology relates to identity constructions and increasingly location were vital questions that emerged. Co-editor Atif Ghani argues that:

> the diaspora functions as a space where the negotiation of meaning, the exchange of experiences and strategies of representation takes place between cultural practitioners located in the west. It is not a literal 'piece' of space, but a figurative 'piece' of mind where one can attempt understanding of our contemporary moment and project a politics into the future.[18]

In the wake of the surprise success of *My Beautiful Laundrette*, the 1990s saw an upsurge in the production of films – David Atwood's *Wild West* (1992), Chadha's *Bhaji on the Beach*, and Ruhul Amin's *Rhythms* (1994) are notable examples. Uniquely, *My Beautiful Laundrette* complicated the way in which the South Asian community was represented on screen, highlighting the complexities of distinct minority identities in Britain, be they related to race, class, gender, or sexual orientation, and how their negotiations impact generations differently in Thatcherite Britain's new 'enterprise culture'.

[17] June Givanni, 'Editorial', *Black Film Bulletin*, 2:3 (1994): 2.
[18] Atif Ghani, 'Projecting the Diaspora', *Black Film Bulletin*, 2:3 (1994): 3–4; 3.

Indeed, short films such as Yugesh Walia's *Mirror, Mirror* (1980) had already repositioned some of these issues. The film focuses on Jo, a young woman of Punjabi heritage who, while house-sitting for a friend, considers moving out of her parents' home to live with her English boyfriend. She has to navigate the pressures put on her by the expectations of her traditional family and by her secret boyfriend, Mike. These pressures to conform to familial and societal norms are contrasted with the greater freedoms her brother enjoys.

Ahmed Jamal's *Majdhar* (1984) also engages with gendered explorations of cultural identity, very much focusing on women's experiences. Marking Syal's film debut, the film revolves around Feroza, played by Rita Wolf (1960–), a young Pakistani woman who arrives in Britain for an arranged marriage. When her husband leaves her for a relationship with a white woman, she renegotiates her life, leaving behind cultural, religious, and social constraints. After her marriage breaks down, she refuses to return to Pakistan, has an abortion, finds a part-time job, and gets an English boyfriend. The charting of her journey to independence is contrasted with that of her husband who struggles to become fully accepted in English society and to meet the demands placed on him by traditional expectations. Funded by Channel 4, the Greater London Council, Camden Council, and Greater London Arts Association, the film was produced by the Retake Film and Video Collective. Set up in the 1980s, it was the first all-Asian film workshop and told stories about the British Asian experience for film and television audiences at a time when these were absent from popular culture. The Collective also made a series of documentaries for Channel 4, including *Living in Danger* (1984), *Hotel London* (1987), and *An Environment of Dignity* (1987). The Collective did not focus on experimental works, but its collaborative working practice and the creation of culturally and politically aware films made their work stand out as attempts by British Asian film-makers to complicate and explode some of the myths around race and integration and Britain's emergent multiculture by combining dramatic and documentary styles. Both *Majdhar* and *Mirror, Mirror* are, however, limited and have been criticised for the centrality of their conflicted protagonist. As a consequence, as Sarita Malik argues, they 'reduc[e] the diasporic experience to a confused "in-betweenness"'.[19]

In the wake of more populist films such as Ové's *Playing Away* (1986), scripted by the writer Caryl Phillips (1958–), the 1990s saw more films reach mainstream audiences. *Playing Away* centres on a black cricket team from

---

[19] Malik, 'Beyond "The Cinema of Duty"?', 208.

south London, invited to play a match in a picturesque fictional village in Suffolk. While the film focuses on the cultural clashes between the teams, and works hard to eschew stereotypes of both black and white Britons, the more light-hearted content moves away from the deeper social commentary of *Pressure*. Films like *Young Soul Rebels*, *Wild West*, *Bhaji on the Beach*, and *East is East* are also examples of films that use popular modes of storytelling. They deploy a more multidimensional form of storytelling on the one hand, but also a differently modulated use of genre and style. For example, *Bhaji on the Beach* uses elements of family drama, comedy, road movie, romantic comedy, and Hindi cinema and yet also bears hallmarks of realist traditions of British film-making. This more hybrid cinematic form, then, as well as the quintessential setting of the film in the seaside town of Blackpool, enabled a questioning of ideas of Englishness in the context of complexly articulated, irreducible notions of identity, race, and class.

This trend continued throughout the 1990s, for example with Ngozi Onwurah's *Welcome II the Terrordome* (1995), the first feature film by a female black British director to receive a wide cinema release. Taking its title from the 1990s track by US rap artists Public Enemy, it opens with a sequence based on a historical incident of 1652 in North Carolina, when a shackled Igbo family, rather than being enslaved, walks into the sea to drown. In its title card, this is conflated with the 1803 Legend of Igbo Landing, the location of another mass suicide. Importantly both incidents are read as an act of resistance and defiance that has transcended into myth. The film then flashes forward to a dystopian landscape in the future, an inner-city slum, the Terrordome, blighted by police brutality, crime, drugs, racism, and gang violence. While the film received many negative reviews on release, it is a striking, visually imaginative piece of film-making.

By contrast, *Babymother* (1998) adopted a different mode and style. Produced by Parminder Vir (1955–) and written and directed by Julian Henriques (1955–), it portrays how singer Anita frees herself from Byron, the father of her two children. When he steals some of her lyrics, she decides to compete against him to become queen of the dancehall and displace him. Shot as a musical, rather than as a film with music, the film is part of the revival of the 1990s film musical genre. Henriques set it entirely in Harlesden's black British environment, a decision that some critics identified as a weakness and that led advertisers and promoters to the assumption that the film 'would never have cross-over potential'.[20] Yet by 2002, when *Bend It*

---

[20] 'Parminder Vir in Interview' in Barbara Korte and Claudia Sternberg, *Bidding for the Mainstream? Black and Asian British Film since the 1990s* (Amsterdam: Rodopi, 2004), 233.

Like Beckham was released, such cross-over potential was recognised and *Babymother* began to be re-evaluated in the context of British cinema. According to Vir, it only achieved this status after it had been screened abroad. *Babymother* is an instructive example of the complex journey of black and Asian British film-making in order to gain recognition as an important component of the British film industry. This has led to further reformulations of genre and style – for example, Noel Clarke's trilogy *Kidulthood* (2006), *Adulthood* (2013), and *Brotherhood* (2016) – that evaluate the question of being black and British through complex narratives of city life and the urban environment (see Chapter 36).

The production of black and Asian British films in the UK is intimately intertwined with the financing and support of organisations such as Channel 4 Films (now Film4 Productions) and BBC Films, both linked to major television channels. In many ways, television and its funding have been a major driver for black and Asian British film and the way in which it has managed to achieve wider recognition.

Television

Television became more and more popular between the 1950s and 1970s, a development that coincided with large-scale migration from Britain's former colonies. The ensuing relationship between film and television and multicultural identity remains complex. While there has been positive change in the 1980s and 1990s, especially through the influence of Channel 4 and its 'minority broadcasting' remit, stereotypes persist. As Mercer points out, 'it is this process of simplification and reduction, whereby television depicts only a fixed and narrow view of black experiences, that is at issue, not only because it denies the rich diversity and differences among black people, but also because it burdens each image with the role of being "representative".'[21]

Television executives seeking to reflect the diversifying comedy scene in Britain became more creative in their commissioning. For example, the first black sketch series on BBC television, *The Real McCoy*, ran on the BBC from 1991 to 1996 for five series. The show featured a series of comedy skits, including BBC programmes like *Dr Who* and *The Generation Game* dubbed for Jamaican audiences, or Hortense Pretentious who, blue-costumed,

---

[21] Kobena Mercer, 'General Introduction' in Therese Daniels and Jane Gerson (eds.), *The Colour Black: Black Images in British Television* (London: BFI Publishing, 1989), 1–11; 3–4.

handbagged, and with full Thatcher bouffant hair, addresses the Conservative party conference. Along with *Desmond's*, a situation comedy set in a barbershop in Peckham, these shows looked towards challenging the stereotypical representations of the 1970s and 1980s. As *Real McCoy* cast member Llewella Gideon highlights: 'It was successful in [...] that black audiences had never seen themselves portrayed in a way that wasn't patronising.'[22]

When *Goodness Gracious Me* first aired on radio in 1996, there was no real precedent for the comedy this show pioneered. Syal had also penned and starred in the radio drama *Masala FM*, first broadcast in the same year. Set in an Asian radio station, this show was a radio first, being performed by an all-Asian cast, and featured many of the creative team who would go on to work on *Goodness Gracious Me*. *Goodness Gracious Me* gave the writers and actors creative control, but the support of producer Jon Plowman was critical to champion the show at the BBC. The show managed to come clearly and distinctly from the perspective of Britain's Asian community, but significantly presented characters that resonated across communities. For example, Dinesh and Shashi Kapoor, who adopt the alias Dennis and Charlotte Cooper, and Surjit and Veena Rabindranath, who present themselves as St John and Vanessa Robinson, engage in a game of one-upmanship exposing their ambitions of social climbing. They are recognisable types reflective of class and snobbery, but added to this is a rivalry to be more English than the English. The show also confronts issues of representation head-on – a sketch, for example, set in the commissioning room of the Indian Broadcasting Corporation, features a pitching session for a new series on England and calls out in reverse the exoticising travelogue programme on India; another sketch features a white ethnic minority representative to highlight the station's lack of 'white' representation. *Goodness Gracious Me*'s characters have endured, from the Bhangra muffins, to Mr 'Everything Comes From India' or Smeeta Smitten Showbiz Kitten, and, while highlighting stereotypes, the show was remarkable for its subtle subversion of them. In fact, the series' success rested on a strategic subversion of British Asian stereotypes, turned inside out by puns, visual gags, and parody. What made *Goodness Gracious Me* unique was also, as Malik highlights, its

[22] 'What is the Legacy of the Real McCoy?', *Ariel: Online News for All BBC Staff*, 1 May 2012. Available at www.bbc.co.uk/ariel/17898802.

'omniscient cultural politics', centred on 'an implicit self-awareness of popular perceptions of British Asians and an acknowledgment that British racism and, for that matter, liberal political correctness exists'.[23]

These TV shows were milestones; however, at a cast reunion of *The Real McCoy* in 2012 for the BBC Black and Asian Forum, Syal pertinently stated: 'I think we've gone backwards from the 1990s. I know so many black and Asian actors who have gone to the States because they can't get acting jobs here. If we wanted to play terrorists we would be busy all the time.'[24] The actor Riz Ahmed echoes Syal's sentiments. In his essay 'Airports and Auditions' he argues that the depictions of ethnic minorities in the aftermath of the 9/11 terrorist attacks were stratified into three categories, which Ahmed likens to a necklace of constricting and decorative labels neither chosen nor created by the actor:

> Stage One is the two-dimensional stereotype – the minicab driver/terrorist/cornershop owner. It tightens the Necklace.
> Stage Two is the subversive portrayal, taking place on 'ethnic' terrain but aiming to challenge stereotypes. It loosens the Necklace.
> And Stage Three is the Promised Land, where you play a character whose story is not intrinsically linked to his race. In the Promised Land, I'm not a terror suspect, nor a victim of forced marriage. In the Promised Land, my name might even be Dave. In the Promised Land there is no Necklace.[25]

It would seem clear from these interventions that there is a persistence in the industry of these stereotypical, constraining, and ultimately damaging forms of representation. And they were a major driver for the campaigns of 2016 and 2017 for greater and more subtle representations of black and Asian voices in television. In this respect, as Sarita Malik has pointed out, television has not overcome what Stuart Hall describes as a 'racialized regime of representation'.[26] The process of reformulation is ongoing, however, and changing funding remits have led to a reconfigured representation of Britain on television in the second decade of the twenty-first century. Here, television has importantly helped to open up and disseminate debates around British

---

[23] Malik, *Representing Black Britain*, 103.   [24] 'What is the Legacy of the Real McCoy?'.
[25] Riz Ahmed, 'Airports and Auditions' in Nikesh Shukla (ed.), *The Good Immigrant* (London: Unbound, 2016), 159–68; 160.
[26] Stuart Hall (ed.), *Representation: Cultural Representations and Signifying Practices* (London; Thousand Oaks, CA; New Delhi: Sage Publications in association with The Open University, 1997), 245.

history, most recently through the BBC's 2016 Black and British and 2018 Great Big Asian Summer seasons of programmes.

New Media

The persistence of stereotypes and clichéd representations has led to scant and narrow roles for black and Asian British actors, an exodus of many stars to the USA, and several campaigns that challenge commissioning processes. The rise of new media platforms offers a unique response to these issues. Although these new spaces are a symptom of the fragmentation of broadcasting, making a push for the centre much harder to ascertain, they also open up new opportunities for differently engaged forms of storytelling, which may help to create an alternative mainstream by circumventing the commissioning constrictions of established broadcasters.

The advent of fast mobile internet connections has significantly changed the ways in which media products are disseminated, accessed, and consumed. As Seth Giddings and Martin Lister point out, 'new media are the product of the digital transformation of communication, information, entertainment media, including television, the press, cinema, telephones, photography and so on'.[27] It is also worth noting that these different types of media production have their separate histories of development, calling into question the homogenising adjective 'new' in relation to media. In addition, it is clear that these technologies continue to innovate, rapidly influencing both processes of representation and the way in which audiences interact with them in their everyday lives.

New media offers a variety of platforms that can circumnavigate the stringent commissioning process of organisations like the BBC. Platform viewing through Netflix, YouTube channels, the BBC's iPlayer, and the move of the television channel BBC Three to an online-only platform has helped further diversify the media landscape. An example of this diversification is the artist and film-maker Cecile Emeke and her numerous web series, from the sitcom *Akee and Saltfish* (2014), later broadcast on BBC Three, to the video poem *Fake Deep* (2014) and the series of documentary shorts *Strolling*. With a particular focus on the lives of young black women, *Fake Deep* harnesses a video platform that situates itself outside the mainstream to present black lives beyond the restrictive objectives of the commissioning

---

[27] Seth Giddings with Martin Lister (eds.), *The New Media and Technocultures Reader* (Abingdon: Routledge, 2011), 2.

room. However, it also highlights the potential of online platforms to make innovative work more widely accessible.

Starting off in the UK (2014–2015), *Strolling* highlights the connections across black diasporas and documents the realities of black British lives. Emeke also filmed shorts on a similar theme in France, the Netherlands, Italy, Jamaica, and the USA. Each episode focuses on one individual and recounts their thoughts and reflection as they stroll through their neighbourhoods. They confront wide-ranging topics, from philosophy to art, capitalism to civil rights, and feminism to the politics of race. But they also offer an important snapshot of what it means to be black at a certain temporal, social, and cultural moment and capture this lived experience. These shorts distinguish themselves through their clear focus on their subject, but they are slickly edited with intricately interwoven sound cues and music. In an interview with the online magazine *Vice*, Emeke expands on the uses of online platforms:

> I think, to some people in film circles, the online space devalues the work. But that comes from an ahistorical understanding of film in a wider context. What does it mean when we devalue film in the online space, when the industry of film is largely set up to only support, distribute, and serve whiteness? [...] I know not all black filmmakers will operate with these things in mind. But thinking of the online space as a format is important for someone like myself – a black woman.[28]

The stand-up comedian Guz Khan (1986–) similarly takes up the issue of access and alternatives to the mainstream. Khan came to prominence on the stand-up circuit and through his YouTube channel where he developed his comedy alter ego, Mobeen. On the back of the success of these routines, Steve Coogan's production company Baby Cow commissioned Khan to make a BBC comedy short. He has subsequently hosted radio shows for the BBC Asian Network and been commissioned by online channel BBC Three to co-write and star in *Man Like Mobeen*. This character comedy is set in the Small Heath area of Birmingham, focusing on a 28-year-old Asian Muslim, Mobeen, and his two friends, Nate and Eight. The show's wry humour addresses larger questions about being a British Muslim. Confronted with police suspicion and racial profiling, Mobeen's actions and reactions, as well as the dialogue, display

---

[28] Ashley Clarke, '"Strolling" is a Thoughtful Walk through the Joys and Struggles of Black People across the World', *Vice*, 26 November 2015. Available at www.vice.com/en_uk/article/9bgvg7/strolling-is-a-thoughtful-walk-through-the-joys-and-struggles-of-black-people-across-the-world-555.

a subtlety that explodes stereotypes still common on the small screen. Yet *Man Like Mobeen* also highlights the difficulties of nuanced representations of black and Asian British lives at the centre, being one in a series of black and Asian British-led series on BBC Three in 2017, alongside *Enterprice, five by five*, and *Coconut*. It appears that here, in these alternative, off-centre, online broadcasting spaces, differently articulated representations of black and Asian British subjectivities are becoming possible.

Conclusion

Black and Asian British film, television, and drama production have become central to contemporary debates around Britishness and the ongoing process of decolonisation. These productions constitute important cultural markers that investigate further what Paul Gilroy terms a continuing 'post-imperial melancholia' – in other words Britain's inability to confront honestly its colonial heritage and conceive of itself as a networked and transnationally connected diverse nation.[29] In this context, narratives of the black and Asian British experience are fundamental to these debates. That said, it requires the continued commitment of artistic directors, funding bodies like Arts Council England, Film 4, BBC Films, and the British Film Institute, and commissioning institutions such as BBC television and radio or Channel 4, to facilitate their ongoing representation in Britain's multiplexes, television screens, online platforms, radio, and subsidised and commercial theatres. While we may consider black and Asian British stories as major contributors to Britain's cultural and creative industries, their position within the mainstream still cannot be taken for granted and remains less secure than one would hope.

---

[29] Paul Gilroy, *After Empire: Melancholia or Convivial Culture?* (London: Routledge, 2004), 98.

33

Children's Literature and the Construction of Contemporary Multicultures

SUSANNE REICHL

Introduction

All children, irrespective of their cultural backgrounds, can benefit from engaging with a range of different literary worlds. These may share demographic structures and other correspondences with their own lives whilst also providing a range of alternative positions to empathise with or emulate. Finding themselves reflected in the literary worlds with which they engage is vital for children's sense of self and their literacy education.[1] This chapter, then, focuses on questions of representation and the construction of multicultures in black and Asian British literature for children and young adults. Labelling a text as black or Asian British is problematic, as is frequently pointed out in this volume, because such labels are suspected of homogenising an array of diverse histories, backgrounds, as well as social realities and perpetuating privileged norms. This chapter suggests that, despite the apparent limitations of the category, there is great diversity and heterogeneity within black and Asian British literature for young readers. Like the category of children's and young adult literature, black and Asian British writing constitutes a broad, strategic label that enables a discussion of a diverse body of writing which remains underexplored: literature for a young British readership, written predominantly, but not exclusively, by black or

---

[1] See Emily Drabble, 'Why We're Holding a Diversity in Children's Books Week', *The Guardian*, 13 October 2014. Available at www.theguardian.com/childrens-books-site/2014/oct/13/diversity-in-childrens-books-week; Catherine Johnson, 'The Books World is a Massive Diversity Fail – Here's How we Change it', *The Guardian*, 17 June 2016. Available at www.theguardian.com/childrens-books-site/2016/jun/17/childrens-books-diversity-change-inclusive-minds; Rosemary Stones, 'Multicultural Publishing in Britain: How Did it Happen?', *Wasafiri*, 24:4 (2009): 60–3.

Asian British authors and concerned with at least one protagonist of black or Asian British origin.[2]

While I would not construct a neat genealogy of thematic or stylistic clusters, several trends can be observed over recent decades, the most obvious being genre diversification. A glance at the literature bears out its thematic variety and its strategic and ideological attachments to both black and Asian British writing and British children's and young adult literature. Black and Asian British writing has often been caught up within the familiar and reductive discourse of centre and margin, and the struggle of writers to position themselves within the mainstream. Children's and young adult literature has been confronted with similar questions: its position vis-à-vis literature for adult readers, the question of its literary merit as opposed to its social and educational value, and its relation to the canon. It is usually the adult who selects, buys, or borrows for and often reads the book to the child:[3] this power imbalance in children's literary production, dissemination, and reception has led some specialists to consider children as the 'most colonised persons on the globe'.[4] This argument is highly problematic, since it conflates various discourses of power and powerlessness that are different from one another and also because it is reminiscent of historical analogies between children and colonial subjects.

Black and Asian British writing for children and young adults is under-represented in critical discourse: *Wasafiri: The Magazine for International Writing* tried to redress the balance by dedicating a special issue to 'New Generations: Writing for Children and Young Adults' in 2009. The *Dictionary of Literary Biography* volume on *Twenty-First-Century 'Black' British Writers* includes a section on Malorie Blackman, the only children's writer selected, and mentions the work for children by writers such as Jackie Kay, Ravinder Randhawa, and Benjamin Zephaniah.[5] While Beverley Naidoo, Malorie Blackman, and Grace Nichols have received some critical attention in the

---

[2] This careful definition allows for cases of white British writers and illustrators producing representations of black and Asian children and teenagers. Examples include Jan Needle's *My Mate Shofiq* (1979) and picturebooks by Helen Oxenbury such as *Tickle, Tickle* (1995) and *Clap Hands* (1995). See also Karen Sands-O'Connor, *Children's Publishing and Black Britain, 1965–2015* (New York: Palgrave Macmillan, 2017), 19–21, which references early young adult literature that includes black teenagers by white writers such as Josephine Kamm's *Out of Step* (1962) and Eric Allen's *The Latchkey Children* (1963).

[3] See, for instance, Jacqueline Rose, *The Case of Peter Pan or The Impossibility of Children's Fiction* (London: Macmillan, 1984), 1–2.

[4] Roderick McGillis, 'Postcolonialism, Children, and their Literature', *ARIEL*, 28:1 (1997): 7–15; 7.

[5] R. Victoria Arana (ed.), *Twenty-First-Century 'Black' British Writers* (Dictionary of Literary Biography, vol. 347) (Detroit, MI: Gale Cengage Learning, 2009).

field of children's literature,[6] there has been limited interest from within postcolonial or children's literature studies, considering the sheer volume of books published for children by black and Asian British writers.[7]

Towards a Tentative History of Black and Asian British Writing for Young Readers

Tracing a history of writing for children and young adults multiplies the difficulties that a genealogy of black and Asian British writing itself implies: the debates around the signifiers 'black' and 'Asian' are repeated in attempts at defining children's literature; the question of whether young adults are implied in the category 'children' is reminiscent of similar debates about the inclusiveness of the term 'black'. Deciding whom to include in the corpus investigated is not made any easier by the permeable borders between writing for adults and writing for younger readers. In most cases the publishing house or imprint is a pragmatic and relatively reliable indicator of children's literature, even if the categorisation of the texts themselves is not always clear-cut.

In many respects, then, constructing a provisional history of such a diverse body of texts is a problematic endeavour: while it is possible to write with relative certainty about the beginnings – Karen Sands-O'Connor identifies 1965 as a starting point for her investigation of black British publishing for children – the field has not only become extremely diversified thematically and generically, but also with respect to its visibility and availability.[8] While some texts are easily available in the mainstream book market (examples include top-sellers such as former Children's Laureate Malorie Blackman (1962–) and the equally active and popular Bali Rai), others, especially those published before 2000, are out of print, such as the picturebooks of Beverley

---

[6] See, for instance, Pat Pinsent, 'Language, Genres and Issues: The Socially Committed Novel' in Kimberley Reynolds (ed.), *Modern Children's Literature: An Introduction* (London: Palgrave Macmillan, 2005), 191–208, and Lissa Paul, 'Multicultural Agendas' in J. Maybin and N. J. Watson (eds.), *Children's Literature: Approaches and Territories* (Basingstoke: Palgrave Macmillan in association with The Open University, 2009), 84–99.

[7] See the work of Karen Sands-O'Connor, Pat Pinsent, and Blanka Grzegorczyk. Sands-O'Connor's recent *Children's Publishing and Black Britain* is the only substantial book-length study to date and a fascinating account of publishing for black children in Britain after 1965. Note that Sands-O'Connor focuses on black British rather than black and Asian British writing.

[8] See Sands-O'Connor, *Children's Publishing*, 2–4.

Naidoo (1943–), Jackie Kay's *Strawgirl* (2002), and early work by Jacqueline Roy (*Fat Chance*, 1994; *Playing it Cool*, 1997).

Thematic clusters cannot be easily identified for certain historical periods without doing injustice to the variety on offer and to the diversity of the target group, whether toddlers or teens. Generally, though, picturebooks for the very young, such as Trish Cooke's *So Much!* (1994) and *Full, Full, Full of Love* (2003) or Errol Lloyd's *Nini at Carnival* (1978) and *Nandi's Bedtime* (1982), tend to centre on the warmth and support of a loving family and community. In young adult novels, the power struggle between adults and minors at the centre of any teenage narrative extends to conflicts of racism, or to inter-generational negotiations about cultural belonging. The child or teenager's identity is often not only constructed in relation to the adults' hegemony but also in relation to the majority of the protagonists' white and middle-class peers as well as a global culture that clearly privileges these subjectivities. This works as a structural, rather than a thematic, parallel and can even be found in non-realistic stories, such as Blackman's fantasy and science fiction (*Trust Me*, 1993, or *Robot Girl*, 2015, discussed below).

In terms of writing and publishing strategies, I would identify three aims that writers, illustrators, and publishers have pursued. The first is to make visible children and teenagers of black, Asian, and mixed heritage; the second is to thematise racism and engage in anti-racist education; and the third is to extend the subject positions available to them. I do not link these strategies to specific historical moments but instead trace these patterns from the 1960s to the 2010s.

Black and Asian British Children and the Issue of (In-)Visibility

Much black and Asian British writing for children has emerged as a result of a strong dissatisfaction with the reading material available. As Sands-O'Connor points out, educational reports and reforms from the 1940s onwards had an impact on the education of black and Asian British children, most notably the Plowden Report of 1967 and the Swann Report of 1985, both of which identified a gaping lack of suitable reading material for young children at school.[9] In 1967, Leila Berg founded the *Nippers* and *Little Nippers* series with Macmillan to provide a more inclusive reading scheme for working-class and migrant children. Contrary to earlier literacy schemes,

---

[9] Ibid., 27–32.

the *Nippers* had storylines focusing on diverse rather than white middle-class family and school settings.[10] Beryl Gilroy (1924–2001), a schoolteacher and London's first black head teacher in the 1970s, contributed a number of short books for both series. Sands-O'Connor criticises how, in this and other series, the focus was on 'a multi-ethnic society whose children, though they looked different, all spoke exactly the same'.[11] Despite the problematic levelling of language diversity and a willingness to leave the prevailing social hierarchies unquestioned, the publications were a major achievement in the early 1970s, presenting classrooms with black, Asian, and white teachers and pupils in word and image, thus normalising a culturally diverse society for young readers. The stories touch rather forgivingly on the widespread racism of the 1970s, and any fears of discrimination are easily dispelled for the sake of harmony. In *A Visitor from Home* (1973), Roy throws a tantrum at school, complaining to his white teacher that the other children are laughing at him because he is black, to which she replies: 'Nobody is picking on you. Nobody cares if you are bright yellow, bright green or covered with polka dots. [. . .] You're picking on me because I'm pink.'[12] Even for the 1970s, this is a surprisingly insensitive and disparaging response. Roy's outburst is explained by his being overtired, and the story brushes conflict aside rather than insisting on strengthening the child's identity and acknowledging racism.[13]

In the 1960s and 1970s, some Caribbean writers addressed their adventure stories to a British audience: C. Everard Palmer, who lived in the West Indies, and James Berry and Andrew Salkey, who both lived in the UK when their stories for children were published, construct implied readers who are largely ignorant of life in the West Indies. Salkey (1928–1995) even added glossaries to some books, explaining terms such as 'ackee' and 'The Daily Gleaner'.[14] During the 1960s and 1970s, private publishing houses such as the newly founded New Beacon Books (1966) and Bogle-L'Ouverture (1968) published a range of children's books on black history, Caribbean folk tales, and black biographies, aimed at a specific market for children with a West Indian

[10] For a detailed history of the *Nippers* series, see ibid., 37–49.

[11] Karen Sands-O'Connor, *Soon Come Home to this Island: West Indians in British Children's Literature* (New York: Routledge, 2008), 118.

[12] Beryl Gilroy, *A Visitor from Home* (Basingstoke; London: Macmillan Education, 1973), 14.

[13] See Sands-O'Connor's detailed analysis of *A Visitor from Home* in *Children's Publishing*, 45–6.

[14] Andrew Salkey, *Earthquake* (Harmondsworth: Puffin, 1965), 125. See Sands-O'Connor, *Soon Come Home*, 144–9, for a detailed discussion of the question of Palmer's and Salkey's implied readership.

background. Writers such as Andrew Salkey and Valerie Bloom were responsible for a number of publications from the 1970s to the 1990s. Tamarind Press was founded by the author Verna Wilkins in 1987; it aimed at representing black characters for a British readership, producing books for young readers into the 2000s, when Tamarind was bought by Random House and Wilkins withdrew from publishing.

Over the past four decades, British writers and illustrators of all backgrounds have contributed greatly to the representation of very young children from visible minorities, simply by putting them at the centre of their illustrated work: Jamila Gavin's *Kamla and Kate* (1983; illustrated by Thelma Lambert), Allan Ahlberg's *Happy Families* series of the 1980s (for example, *Mr Biff the Boxer*, 1980; illustrated by Janet Ahlberg), Beverley Naidoo's 1994 picturebook series (illustrated by Petra Röhr-Rouendaal), Trish Cooke and Helen Oxenbury's *So Much!* (1994), and Floella Benjamin and Margaret Chamberlain's *My Two Grannies* (2007) and *My Two Grandads* (2011). Significantly, none of these focuses in any way on racism or anti-racist strategies but on a peaceful coexistence of diverse communities.

It is not only visual representation that creates literary presence, though. Grace Nichols (1950–) has written children's poetry (*The Poet Cat*, 2000; *Everybody Got a Gift*, 2006) and edited a number of anthologies of poems and nursery rhymes for children (*Can I Buy a Slice of Sky?*, 1991; with John Agard, *No Hickory, No Dickory, No Dock*, 1991); these employ Caribbean Englishes, either validating or opening up new linguistic experiences to children. Conversely, the poetry of Benjamin Zephaniah (1958–) does not reference a Caribbean setting when he uses oral non-standard forms: his 'Talking Turkeys' ends on these lines: 'Be nice to yu turkey dis christmas / An spare dem de cut of de knife, / Join Turkeys United and dey'll be delighted / An yu will mek new friends "FOR LIFE".'[15]

Same and Other: Racism, Conflict, and Dialogue

While books for very young readers highlight the positive aspects of diversity and often focus on uncontroversial culinary or sartorial differences, in many teenage novels dialogue is preceded or prevented by conflict. *Strawgirl* by Jackie Kay (1961–), her only novel for young readers to date, follows an 11-year-old girl of mixed parentage, Maybe (so called because she

[15] Benjamin Zephaniah, *Talking Turkeys* (London: Viking, 1994), 89. See Sands-O'Connor's analysis of the poetry of John Agard and others, and the way they deal with language varieties (*Soon Come Home*, 160–3).

cannot ever decide to say yes or no), struggling with being bullied in a Scottish farming community. A magical corn doll come to life helps her cope with the bullying and save the farm she lives on from being sold to a supermarket chain. Her intervention brings the local community closer together, dialogue suddenly becomes possible, and Maybe finally learns how to say yes.

In a number of novels, the social barriers that children and teenagers experience seem insurmountable. The institutional racism of the 1970s and 1980s sparked a number of publications, such as Farrukh Dhondy's realist stories in *East End at Your Feet* (1976). Mary Hoffman's popular *Amazing Grace* (1991) is a picturebook in which a resourceful girl works extra hard so that she can reach her goals, as if she has to compensate for being black. The oppositional sides of a segregated society are often conveyed through dialogic narrative voices: in Malorie Blackman's celebrated *Noughts & Crosses* (2001), Sephy and Callum are two star-crossed lovers whose alternating narratives construct an image of a divided society (a reversal of the established black and white social stratification) and enable readers to see two sides of the conflict. *You're Not Proper* (2015) by Tariq Mehmood (1956–) shows the dividing lines in a northern English army town made insecure and anxious by terrorism, right-wing politics, and the British army presence in Iraq and Afghanistan. Two 14-year-old girls, who attend the same school and develop an intense dislike of one another, tell their stories in alternating chapters. As the demands of the young adult genre stipulate, these novels usually end on a conciliatory note, demonstrating that understanding and dialogue are possible even in the most dire situations, or that love surpasses racial segregation: in spite of the fact that Sephy has to watch Callum being hanged at the end of *Noughts & Crosses*, there is hope in the shape of their daughter; the two warring girls in Mehmood's novel find out that they are sisters and reconcile. Mehmood draws attention to the diversity of female teenage Muslim characters who try to make sense of the place that religion has in their lives. This is similar to the novels by Na'ima B. Robert (1977–), *Boy vs. Girl* (2010) and *She Wore Red Trainers* (2014), in which young male and female Muslim characters reflect on the version of Islam they want to live by. While *Boy vs. Girl* is concerned with the development of twins, who both see themselves on different trajectories in life, *She Wore Red Trainers* is a Muslim teenage love story that celebrates Muslim traditions, among others the wearing of the hijab and niqab. All three books extend the repertoire of teenage Muslim characters and emphasise the diversity of their lives and the complexity of their choices and allegiances.

Just as interethnic conflict and dialogue are a constant presence in black and Asian British novels for young readers, so too is intergenerational conflict. Often, the conflict centres on the degree to which teenagers adapt to their peer groups, while their parents feel they should abide by the rules of their religious or ethnic communities. Frequently, another relative re-establishes harmony within the family. In *Artichoke Hearts* (2011) by Sita Brahmachari (1966–), it is Mira's grandmother who helps her find a sense of belonging. In the sequel, *Jasmine Skies* (2014), a stay with her grandfather's family in Kolkata makes her discover family secrets at the same time as she gains important insights into herself and her ambitions. In the *Bindi Babes* quartet (2003–2008) by Narinder Dhami (1958–), intergenerational dialogue is enabled through the arrival of the aunt of the three sassy protagonists, who are more adapted to life in a neoliberal capitalist Britain than their father would like to see.

Family life is an endless source of conflict and resolution. The less teen-age protagonists are supported by loving families, the grittier the social realism becomes. Examples range from bleak urban tales of gang warfare, such as Bali Rai's *The Crew* (2003) and *The Whisper* (2005), to stories of individuals struggling against a hostile environment, such as Beverley Naidoo's *The Other Side of Truth* (2000) and *Web of Lies* (2004), Farrukh Dhondy's *Run* (2002), and Benjamin Zephaniah's *Refugee Boy* (2001). Most of these novels end on a hopeful note, promising their protagonists a better future. An exception is *Hello Mum* (2010) by Bernardine Evaristo (1959–), which is a moving farewell letter ending on the death of a teenager killed in gang warfare. Even here, there is a moment of reconciliation when he explains posthumously that he 'hadn't been mixed up in badness for a long time – just for twenty-five minutes of my fourteen years of life'.[16] *Liccle Bit* (2015) and its sequel, *Crongton Knights*, Alex Wheatle's (1963–) Guardian Children's Fiction Prize winner of 2016, combine the very real dangers of gang warfare on the fictional estate of Crongton with light-hearted and comic teenage banter. Wheatle creates what has been called an 'invented, acrobatic dialect' for his south London novels, which might not be the most authentic, up-to-date black youth language, but contributes much to the humour.[17]

---

[16] Bernardine Evaristo, *Hello Mum* (London: Penguin, 2010), 81.

[17] See Homa Khaleeli, 'Alex Wheatle: "I Felt Like the Token Black Writer who Talks about Ghetto Stuff"', *The Guardian*, 18 November 2016. Available at www.theguardian.com/books/2016/nov/18/alex-wheatle-interview-guardian-childrens-fiction-prize-crongton-knights.

Zephaniah's *Refugee Boy* is an example of a bleaker social realism entirely devoid of humour: 10-year-old Alem and his father flee to London from the war in the Horn of Africa. On appealing for asylum in the UK they have to experience the harsh realities of British bureaucracy: their appeal is rejected on the grounds that millions of other Eritreans and Ethiopians are unaffected by the war. Alem loses both his parents in the course of the novel but experiences generous help from people at school, the Refugee Council, and a foster family. Beverley Naidoo's *The Other Side of Truth* (2000) narrates a similar story of Nigerian children becoming refugees in London and its sequel, *Web of Lies* (2004), continues their story, showing that the teenagers' development is far from an easy ride, despite all the support they receive. Urban crime and gang violence are recurring motifs in novels by Victor Headley, Courttia Newland, and the early works of Alex Wheatle, which were not published as books for children and teenagers (see Chapter 36). Bali Rai (1971–) picks up this topic, too: *The Crew* and its sequel, *The Whisper*, are about a gang of underprivileged teenagers who run into problems with the inner-city authorities over guns and drugs. London is constructed as a nightmarish jungle in which the boys need to survive against all odds, but even in this bleak setting the focus is on friendship and solidarity. Rai demonstrates how conflict is based on the intersection of race and class, and by stressing the teenagers' humanity and individuality, he gives fictional access to a social group that is usually either ignored or censured in mainstream British media.

Imaginary and Magical Homelands: Histories and Mythologies

While realistic contemporary settings clearly dominate a great deal of children's and young adult literature, history and mythology play an important role, too. Young protagonists often draw strength from their parents' or grandparents' histories and stories as they discover or reconstruct them, in turn promoting intergenerational dialogue and understanding.

As is true of recent Asian British writing for adults, the chapter in Indian history that most frequently figures is Partition: in Brahmachari's *Jasmine Skies*, Mira's desire to know about Partition comes with a metafictional criticism of British education: 'it's not like they teach about it in school'.[18] Partition features more prominently in the *Surya* trilogy (1992–1997) by Jamila

---

[18] Sita Brahmachari, *Jasmine Skies* (Chicago, IL: Albert Whitman, 2014), 627.

Gavin (1941–), a historical saga in which a Sikh family is shown suffering from and living with the impact of Indian Partition over two generations. Gavin's greatest commercial and critical success, *Coram Boy* (2000), winner of the Whitbread Children's Book Award and adapted very successfully for the National Theatre, reconstructs eighteenth-century London, complete with references to slavery and a focus on the social conditions that surrounded illegitimacy.

Slavery is frequently addressed in historical novels: for instance, *A Breath of Fresh Air* (1987) by Geraldine Kaye (1925–2010) features a time-travelling character who becomes an eyewitness to slavery, and Malorie Blackman's collection *Unheard Voices* (2007) brings together stories by writers including James Berry, John Agard, Grace Nichols, and Benjamin Zephaniah for the bicentenary of the abolition of the slave trade in the British Empire. Catherine Johnson (1962–) writes historical novels that place their black or mixed-parentage characters in eighteenth- and nineteenth-century settings and follow their struggles to survive and develop a voice (*Stella*, 2001; *A Nest of Vipers*, 2008; *Sawbones*, 2013). While Johnson's and especially Gavin's historical fiction has a complexity that would be too demanding for pre-schoolers, Trish Cooke and Anni Axworthy package history appropriately and unproblematically for a young audience with *Hooray for Mary Seacole!* (2007).[19] All these inscribe the child, teenager, or adult of black, Asian, or mixed parentage firmly into British history, setting the record straight and drawing attention to the fact that people of colour have long been present in Britain.

Some writing for children and adults focuses on the mythological powers of storytelling: for the very young, Trish Cooke and Anna Violet have produced a picturebook entitled *How Anansi Got His Stories* (2011), in which the notorious African trickster figure features prominently. Beverley Naidoo and Piet Grobler's *Who is King? Ten Magical Stories from Africa* (2015) contains illustrated stories for young readers from a variety of African countries. Further up the age spectrum, in *Haroun and the Sea of Stories* (1990) and *Luka and the Fire of Life* (2010) Salman Rushdie (1947–) sets his tales of magic realism in fictional versions of India, interweaving a variety of stories, including Indian legends, the Arabian Nights, Greek mythology, native American characters, and elements from Anglo-American literature and popular culture. *Aditi and the One-Eyed Monkey* (1986) by Suniti Namjoshi (1941–) tells a magical adventure tale about a strong girl character with a great sense of very contemporary streetwise humour. Questions of children and

---

[19] See Sands-O'Connor's criticism of this publication (*Children's Publishing*, 147–8).

teenagers constructing their precarious identities are as dominant in these novels as in the more contemporary and realistic ones.

Conclusion: Post-Ethnic Perspectives on and Metaphors for a Racist Society

In which ways does writing for children and young adults reflect a post-ethnic stance? Around the same time that Hanif Kureishi was writing *Intimacy* (1998), a novella referred to as 'post-ethnic' for its pronounced refusal to engage with questions of ethnic identity, Malorie Blackman and Verna Wilkins were pursuing similar strategies in their publications for children and young adults.[20] While we can infer from paratexts, illustrations, or passing comments that all their protagonists are black or Asian, ethnic identity and racism are not an issue here. Their characters are black in the same way that characters in novels by white authors tend to be white. Black children and teenagers go on adventures, are visited by the tooth fairy, learn how to spell, become vampires, crack computers, undergo heart transplants, and experience all the agency and the limitations that white characters usually do, rather than being victims to racism and discrimination.[21] This can be seen as a strategy to normalise the presence of black and Asian British children and teenagers, but it can also be seen as ignoring institutional and individual racism, which for the past decades has been a reality for young people of black, Asian, or mixed parentage living in the UK.

A new strategy can be observed in more recent black and Asian British writing: racist environments are defamiliarised by abstract or metaphorical rather than realist representation. In *Face* (1999), Zephaniah tells the story of a white boy who, after a car crash that burns his face, suffers from what he himself calls 'facial discrimination'.[22] Blackman chooses a variety of speculative settings to defamiliarise our social contexts: in her *Noughts & Crosses* series, she turns our notions of black and white, of dominated and dominant, completely on their heads. The result is a dystopia closely resembling the world we know and yet unrecognisable in how its denizens are arranged on

[20] See Mark U. Stein, 'Posed Ethnicity and the Postethnic: Hanif Kureishi's Novels' in H. Antor and K. Stierstorfer (eds.), *English Literatures in International Contexts* (Heidelberg: Winter, 2000), 119–39; 139.

[21] For more detail see Sands-O'Connor, *Soon Come Home*, 117–18 and Susanne Reichl, 'Reading Race in British Young Adult Fiction: Malorie Blackman and Benjamin Zephaniah' in W. Kriegleder et al. (eds.), *Jugendliteratur im Kontext von Jugendkultur. Wiener Vorlesungen zur Kinder- und Jugendliteratur 1* (Wien: Praesens, 2016), 201–24.

[22] Benjamin Zephaniah, *Face* (London: Bloomsbury, 1999), 135.

the social scale. Readers cannot easily identify with one particular social group, nor is one side privileged as a narrative voice. The distance that this creates between readers and characters allows for a better understanding of the structures of this society and its history, and for seeing parallels with a variety of historical and geopolitical settings across the globe.[23] Her *Chasing the Stars* (2016) is an adventure-packed science fiction story set in outer space. In a futuristic society divided by social norms, a love story develops between the female commander of a spaceship and a male subaltern refugee, whom she has saved from certain death. The negative responses by their social environment destroy the relationship, inviting readers to draw possible parallels to the intertext, *Othello*, and their own lifeworlds. Similarly, characters forced to live at the fringes of society feature in Blackman's vampire story *Trust Me* and in the science fiction *Robot Girl*, which slowly reveals the first-person narrator to be an android who is confronted with a reconstructed humanoid, thousands of years after humans were destroyed by a virus that left only androids on planet earth. These stories do not enforce, but clearly invite, parallels with our lifeworlds. Blackman and Zephaniah abstract race and racism from the contexts we know, providing an analytical, almost universal, view of Othering processes and structures. This representational strategy allows for mechanisms of segregation, intersectionality, and racism to surface from the speculative settings.

Like literature addressing adults, black and Asian British texts for children and young adults refuse to follow a predefined, narrow path. These works continue to surprise with their range, diversity, and powers of innovation. Whether through realistic or speculative settings, young readers are offered a range of subject positions and experiences. Writers no longer restrict themselves to reconstructing realistic multicultures but instead engage all kinds of genres, from fantasy via historical novel to thriller and gritty urban realism, employing a variety of modes, from speculative to realistic, from 'chick-lit' to hard-boiled (see Chapter 36). Frequently they steer a careful path between an anti-racist agenda and an entertaining mode. They put black and Asian British characters firmly on the map, which is indeed important to *any* young person growing up in the UK, because they need to see themselves and the multicultural society in which they live represented in literature.

---

[23] See Christine Wilkie-Stibbs, *The Outside Child In and Out of the Book* (London: Routledge, 2008), 128; Alison Flood, 'Malorie Blackman: Developing Negatives', *The Guardian*, 10 November 2008. Available at www.theguardian.com/books/2008/nov/10/malorie-blackman-double-cross-noughts-crosses; Reichl, 'Reading Race'.

34

Redefining the Boundaries
Black and Asian Queer Desire

KATE HOULDEN

Any reference to black and Asian queer desire immediately necessitates certain caveats and qualifications, not least because many black and Asian individuals historically have found themselves torn between racial and sexual identifications potentially at odds with one another. Kobena Mercer and Isaac Julien, for example, write movingly of finding no voice for their sexuality in contexts of racial solidarity, and no acknowledgement of their race within the gay community, while similarly Ashley Tellis claims that to 'be a British South Asian queer subject [. . .] is to face a repressive family within and a hostile society outside'.[1] Nevertheless, as this chapter goes on to attest, the twenty-first century has seen more black and Asian writers than ever exploring same-sex desire in their fiction, leading to a vibrant body of work that demonstrates the ways in which queerness unsettles racial, national, class, and gendered categories. In fact, queer writing might even be said to have obvious resonance with black and Asian British writers, and more generally, writers of colour, who often themselves transgress the imposition of narrow, racially determined physical and discursive boundaries in forms akin to the 'slanting' or 'oblique' positionalities discussed by Sara Ahmed.[2] Ranging across diverse literary forms to look at authors including Bernardine Evaristo, Kei Miller, Neel Mukherjee, Diriye Osman, Jay Bernard, and Saradha Soobrayen, this chapter raises questions about the interrogation, blurring, and translation of racial and sexual identities across a range of orientations. In so doing, it charts the uneven evolution and heterogeneous

---

[1] Kobena Mercer and Isaac Julien, 'Race, Sexual Politics and Black Masculinity: A Dossier' in Jonathan Rutherford and Rowena Chapman (eds.), *Male Order: Unwrapping Masculinity* (London: Lawrence & Wishart, 1988), 97–164; Ashley Tellis, 'The Well of Homeliness: South Asian Queers in Britain' in Kate Chedgzoy, Emma Francis, and Murray Pratt (eds.), *In a Queer Place: Sexuality and Belonging in British and European Contexts* (Aldershot: Ashgate, 2002), 40–9; 41.

[2] Sara Ahmed, *Queer Phenomenology: Orientations, Objects, Others* (Durham, NC; London: Duke University Press, 2006).

quality of queer black British and Asian writing, framing it against Stuart Hall's 'refusal to represent the black experience in Britain as monolithic, self-contained, sexually stabilised and always "right on"'.[3]

As the introduction to this collection has already made clear, the labels 'black' and 'Asian' are not without both their limitations and their detractors. For the purposes of this chapter, the terminology is used tenuously, critically, and with the recognition that: 'different heritages can be juggled within the same neighborhood, within the same household, and within the same person'.[4] In practical terms, some of my chosen authors use these labels and some do not; some have spent extended periods in the UK, whereas others have lived there since birth; while the fictional settings of my selected texts range across Britain and abroad. In similar fashion, 'queer' also stands as a conflictual or problematic term, with there being some concern that it has little valence for raced invocations of same-sex loving. As Emily Taylor rightly cautions, we must be wary of 'the potential imperialism' of analytical modes that 'might assume Eurocentric notions of the subject and categories of gender and sexuality that have their basis in Western epistemologies'.[5] More specifically, Jin Haritaworn, Tamsila Tauqir, and Esra Erderm outline how 'queer' frequently signifies white, gay male, with the visibility of controversial figures such as Peter Tatchell – criticised for the troubling racial tenor of his queer activism – signalling less, progress on gendered and sexual concerns and more, racial and national conservatism.[6] I therefore use 'queer' with some wariness, and only in the absence of preferred nomenclature by any particular author. Yet some writers do claim the term. Valerie Mason-John, for example, explains:

> '[Q]ueer' doesn't just mean 'homosexual', it encompasses a range of identities, gay and straight. It includes bisexual and transgender people. 'Queer' covers a whole range of sexualities and genders. It means 'other' or 'different'. It's a political term that permits greater freedom around gender and

---

[3] Stuart Hall, 'New Ethnicities' in David Morley and Kuan-Hsing Chen (eds.), *Stuart Hall: Critical Dialogues in Cultural Studies* (Abingdon: Routledge, 1996), 441–9; 449.

[4] Mark U. Stein, *Black British Literature: Novels of Transformation* (Columbus, OH: Ohio State University Press, 2004), xii.

[5] Emily Taylor, 'Introduction: Reading Desire Between Women in Caribbean Literature', *Contemporary Women's Writing*, 6:3 Special Issue: Caribbean Queer (November 2012): 191–3; 191.

[6] Jin Haritaworn, Tamsila Tauqir, and Esra Erdem, 'Gay Imperialism: Gender and Sexuality Discourse in the "War on Terror"' in Adi Kuntsman and Esperanza Miyake (eds.), *Out of Place: Interrogating Silence in Queerness/Raciality* (York: Raw Nerve Books, 2008), 71–95.

sexuality. 'Queer' indicates identities that are fluid. It loosens the attachment to binaries.[7]

Of course, as Thomas Glave warns, this 'linguistic and intellectual fluidity and expansiveness' means 'almost anything can be "queer"-ed or "queery"-ed';[8] words that alert us to the hazards of poststructuralist wordplay watering down the political or material realities at stake. Nevertheless, this chapter remains committed to the idea that racial and sexual questioning can, and do, happen in tandem, in keeping with Hall's assertion that 'the new politics of representation' crosses 'the questions of racism irrevocably with questions of sexuality'.[9] Over the pages to follow, I therefore emphasise the undeniable presence of what might tenuously be called black and Asian queer British lives.

Although increasing scholarly attention has been paid to black and Asian cultural production over the last fifteen years, sexuality has not featured prominently in many studies. In fact, amidst the raft of monographs encompassing Asian and/or black fiction that have appeared since the new millennium, few devote substantive attention to questions of sexual desire.[10] Gabriele Griffin is careful to probe the racialised sexualities depicted by her subjects in *Contemporary Black and Asian Women Playwrights in Britain* (2003) and, interestingly, both Dimple Godiwala's *Alternatives within the Mainstream: Black British Black and Asian Theatres* (2006) and Geoffrey V. Davis and Anne Fuchs's *Staging New Britain* (2006) include coverage of the topic, suggesting that discussion of sexuality is perhaps more prevalent within theatre scholarship. R. Victoria Arana oversees some acknowledgement of same-sex loving

[7] Emma Parker, '"Odd Girl Out": An Interview with Valerie Mason-John, aka Queenie', *Textual Practice*, 25:4 (2011): 799–822; 811.

[8] Thomas Glave (ed.), *Our Caribbean: A Gathering of Lesbian and Gay Writing from the Antilles* (Durham, NC: Duke University Press, 2008), 189 n. 4.

[9] Hall, 'New Ethnicities', 445.

[10] The following texts include little to no mention of sexuality: C. L. Innes, *A History of Black and Asian Writing in Britain, 1700–2000* (Cambridge: Cambridge University Press, 2002); Susheila Nasta, *Home Truths: Fictions of the South Asian Diaspora in Britain* (Basingstoke: Palgrave, 2002); Sukhdev Sandhu, *London Calling: How Black and Asian Writers Imagined a City* (London: HarperCollins, 2003); James Procter, *Dwelling Places: Postwar Black British Writing* (Manchester: Manchester University Press, 2003); John McLeod, *Postcolonial London: Rewriting the Metropolis* (London; New York: Routledge, 2004); Stein, *Black British Literature*; John Clement Ball, *Imagining London: Postcolonial Fiction and the Transnational Metropolis* (Toronto: University of Toronto Press, 2004); Gail Low and Marion Wynne-Davies (eds.), *A Black British Canon?* (Basingstoke: Palgrave Macmillan, 2006); Lars Eckstein, Barbara Korte, Eva Ulrike Pirker, and Christoph Reinfandt (eds.), *Multi-Ethnic Britain 2000+: New Perspectives in Literature, Film and the Arts* (Amsterdam; New York: Rodopi, 2008); Claire Chambers, *British Muslim Fictions: Interviews with Contemporary Writers* (Basingstoke: Palgrave Macmillan, 2011).

in *'Black' British Aesthetics Today* (2007, 2009), while John R. Gordon and Rikki Beadle-Blair's anthology *Black and Gay in the UK* (2014) is the first UK-focused collection to address the experiences of gay black men. Finally, Kanika Batra offers a timely chapter on 'British Black and Asian LGBTQ Writing' in Deirdre Osborne's 2016 *The Cambridge Companion to British Black and Asian Literature (1945–2010)*. Aside from these works, stand-alone essays and author-specific collections are the only source of academic insight into queer Asian and black British fictional lives.

Early Examples

Yet this scarcity is not because such desires are absent from black and Asian British writing. Osborne, for example, rightly notes the 'rarely acknowledged Black and Asian LGBTQ literary continuities to be found in a broad spectrum of poetry, drama and fiction'.[11] The nomenclature and cultural understandings of sexuality might have changed, but queer sexual readings can be applied to texts from as early as the eighteenth and nineteenth centuries, by those who journeyed to, and found fame in, Britain. In line with Daniel O'Quinn we might, for example, consider the male libidinal impulses and bodily masochism of Olaudah Equiano's *The Interesting Narrative and Other Writings* (1789).[12] The sadism, sexual silences, and narrative strictures of *The History of Mary Prince* (1831) can, likewise, be both queried and queered, not least in their undermining of normative, white, domestic heterosexuality. Despite the fact that Mary Seacole's memoir (1857) asserts her personal adherence to the norms of English femininity, these are revealed to be premised on the rejection of gendered nonconformity espoused by 'those French lady writers', in a veiled reference to the kinds of female sexual transgression demonstrated by George Sand amongst others.[13] These works might reflect period trends in the creation and formalisation of autobiography as a genre, as well as the instantiation of the slave narrative as a recognised form, but they also speak to a twenty-first-century interest in

---

[11] Deirdre Osborne 'Introduction' in Osborne (ed.), *The Cambridge Companion to British Black and Asian Literature (1945–2010)* (Cambridge: Cambridge University Press, 2016), 1–21; 13.

[12] Daniel O'Quinn, 'The State of Things: Olaudah Equiano and the Volatile Politics of Heterocosmic Desire', *Praxis: Historicizing Romantic Sexuality* (2006): n.p. Available at www.rc.umd.edu/praxis/sexuality/oquinn/oquinn.html.

[13] Mary Seacole, *Wonderful Adventures of Mrs Seacole in Many Lands*, ed. Sara Salih (London: Penguin, [1857] 2005), 26.

queer life-writing and the significance of the personal in political self-fashioning. Furthermore, whether it be O'Quinn's emphasis on Protestant myth-making and the sexual habits of shipboard culture in Equiano's case, or Sara Salih's argument as to how the abolitionist cause tried to present Mary Prince as sexually pure and sufficiently Christian, what these early examples also have in common is their linkage of sexual propriety, racialised colonial violence, and religion.[14]

In the twentieth century, queer readings can be coaxed from a number of unexpected texts by authors who moved between the UK and abroad. Rahul Rao discusses Rabindranath Tagore's 1915 work *Ghare Baire* in terms of the politics of the *zenana* (women's space) and notions of 'coming out', highlighting how the 'Woman Question' is 'always already queer'.[15] In a similar vein, Cornelia Sorabji's engagement with the zenana in *India Calling* (1934) can be read for its 'depiction of the easy intimacy between women, the rituals of touch, grooming, affection, and pleasure', despite what Gayatri Gopinath describes as the author's determination to 'position herself as a cosmopolitan, modern nationalist subject' in opposition to the women on whom she gazed.[16] Claude McKay's novels *Home to Harlem* (1928) and *Banjo* (1929) can also be read in overtly queer terms. Michelle Ann Stephens discusses the former through 'a queer reading that explores how constructions and discourses of sexuality shape McKay's ultimate turn away from stories of home' and the latter as 'a gendered story of the formation of alternative male desires'.[17] Furthermore, Josh Gosciak points to McKay's reliance on radical Victorian intellectual traditions such as Fabian socialism and the Arts and Crafts movement, which reflected a blurring of queer, political, and patronage relations.[18] These writers' complex renderings of gendered and sexual lives attest to both their own internationalism and the difficulties of navigating the sexual proscriptions of British rule in an era of increasing anti-colonial sentiment. As Stephens makes clear, figures such as McKay struggled 'to

---

[14] O'Quinn, 'The State of Things'; Sara Salih, 'Introduction' in *The History of Mary Prince* (London: Penguin Books, [1831] 2004), vii–xxxiv.

[15] Rahul Rao, 'Queer Questions', *International Feminist Journal of Politics*, 16:2 (2014): 199–217; 204. DOI: 10.1080/14616742.2014.901817.

[16] Gayatri Gopinath, *Impossible Desires: Queer Diasporas and South Asian Public Cultures* (Durham, NC: Duke University Press, 2005), 121.

[17] Michelle Ann Stephens, *Black Empire: The Masculine Global Imaginary of Caribbean Intellectuals in the United States, 1914–62* (Durham, NC: Duke University Press, 2005), 131, 169.

[18] Josh Gosciak, *The Shadowed Country: Claude McKay and the Romance of the Victorians* (New Brunswick, NJ: Rutgers University Press, 2006).

chart a course' for the rendering of sexual desire 'somewhere in the interstices between empire, nation, and state'.[19]

Postwar Shifts

Although black and Asian individuals have asserted their influence over
British life and culture for centuries, postwar migration to the UK served,
as Osborne puts it, to alter the country's 'demographic composition more
markedly than in any other period in its history'.[20] This led inevitably to
a greater number of texts being set (at least in part) within the shores of
England, as authors began to lay claim to what Mark U. Stein calls 'British
cultures *in Britain*'.[21] Within this body of work, references to black and Asian
queer characters can be discerned with some frequency, albeit that a certain
veiled allusiveness still pertains; unsurprising given the moral panic and
aggressive policing typical of the period before legalisation in 1967. Even so,
V. S. Naipaul's *In A Free State* (1971) and *Guerrillas* (1975), along with Neville
Dawes's *The Last Enchantment* (1960) can be read for their conflictual, and
occasionally hostile, treatment of male same-sex desire. Unusually, George
Lamming devotes persistent attention to female homosexuality across
a number of his novels, demonstrating the intense heteronormative pressure
faced by women at the time.[22] Andrew Salkey and Oscar Dathorne, meanwhile, place men desiring other men at the heart of their narrative concerns.
Salkey's *Escape to an Autumn Pavement* (1960), in particular, constitutes an
important early intervention in the formation of a black British queer canon
through its framing of protagonist Johnnie as '*both* sexual and racial
outsider'.[23] Many of these texts demonstrate considerable difficulties with
the stereotyping of black male sexuality, skewering the racialised sexual
fantasies of white British society at the same time as they share parallels
with Kobena Mercer's discussion of 'ambivalent' structures of feeling.[24]
Despite their tentative portrayal of a range of peripheral lives, these works
more commonly reveal the negative emotions of 'nostalgia, regret, shame,
despair, *ressentiment*, passivity, escapism, self-hatred, withdrawal, bitterness,
defeatism, and loneliness' identified by Heather Love as characterising the

[19] Stephens, *Black Empire*, 2.   [20] Osborne, 'Introduction', 1.
[21] Stein, *Black British Literature*, xv.
[22] See *The Emigrants* (1954) and *Of Age and Innocence* (1958).
[23] Kate Houlden, *Sexuality, Gender and Nationalism in Caribbean Literature* (Abingdon:
Routledge, 2016), 154. See also O. R. Dathorne's *The Scholar-Man* (1964).
[24] Kobena Mercer, *Welcome to the Jungle: New Positions in Black Cultural Studies* (London;
New York: Routledge, 1994).

queer canon – in contradiction to the more celebratory and assertive render-ings of same-sex loving visible in twenty-first-century writing.[25] The chief exception to this is Aubrey Menen, whose satirical novels not only provide consistent critique of heteronormativity but, as Leela Gandhi puts it, also imagine: 'a dissident alternative world populated by irreverent Wildean figures who find themselves in sympathetic counterallegiance with, among others, trees, "orientals," children, criminals, and "primitives"'.[26]

The latter part of the twentieth century saw diverse expressions of same-sex desire become far more prevalent, Kanika Batra going as far as to describe the 1980s as a 'threshold generation' for whom the 'social and cultural visibility of sexual subjectivity and diversity in Britain increased'.[27] From Hanif Kureishi, Rikki Beadle-Blair, Caryl Phillips, and DeObia Oparei through to Suniti Namjoshi, Barbara Burford, Jacqueline Rudet, Jackie Kay, Dorothea Smartt, Patience Agbabi, Valerie Mason-John, Bidisha, and Meera Syal, expressions of queer desire are more easily traced in these concluding decades. In the world of film, Stephen Frears and Hanif Kureishi's seminal work, My Beautiful Laundrette (1985), along with Isaac Julien's Looking for Langston (1989) and Young Soul Rebels (1991), seemed to usher in a new era of queer black and Asian loving on the big screen, which continued through to the 2002 film of Syal's Anita and Me (1996). The trajectory between these movies gestures towards two key fictional trends of the period: first, greater numbers of black and Asian women gaining access to the cultural domain; and second, an accompanying increase in emphasis on lesbian lives. Accordingly, much of this work chimes with Audre Lorde's argument as to the generative possibilities of eroticism between women of colour and the radical potentiality of shared connection with another.[28] Jackie Kay's 1986 drama Chiaroscuro is emblematic of both these tendencies. Detailing the friendship between four friends of diverse racial and familial back-grounds, this 'political play centres on issues of naming, belonging and self-definition, particularly in relation to the labels "black" and

---

[25] Heather Love, Feeling Backward: Loss and the Politics of Queer History (Cambridge, MA; London: Harvard University Press, 2007), 4.

[26] Leela Gandhi, 'Loving Well: Homosexuality and Utopian Thought in Post/Colonial India', in Ruth Vanita (ed.), Queering India: Same-Sex Love and Eroticism in Indian Culture and Society (New York: Routledge, 2002), 87–99; 94.

[27] Kanika Batra, 'British Black and Asian LGBTQ Writing' in Deirdre Osborne (ed.), The Cambridge Companion to British Black and Asian Literature (1945–2010) (Cambridge: Cambridge University Press, 2016) 159–76; 164.

[28] Audre Lorde, Sister Outsider: Essays and Speeches by Audre Lorde, ed. Audre Lorde and Cheryl Clarke (Berkeley, CA: Crossing Press, 2007).

"lesbian"'.[29] In similar fashion, the lesbian-feminist poet, myth-maker, and fabulist Suniti Namjoshi's work explores the consequences of being both lesbian and Indian, detailing the 'problems of self-conception that arise when a decision to adopt a particular identity has to be carefully negotiated with a resistant and unwieldy universe'.[30] Towards the close of the 1990s, Valerie Mason-John's provocative play *Sin Dykes* (1998) claims black lesbian identity in out and proud fashion, invoking S&M sexual dynamics between women in a repudiation of sexual shame that 'seeks to overcome the booby traps of a simplistic racial or sexual politics through the corporeality of sexual desire'.[31] Finally, on the cusp of the millennium, the poet and activist Patience Agbabi's lyrical collection *Transformatrix* (2000) plays wittily with gendered and sexual expectations, signalling a more confident fluidity as she moves between masculine and feminine gendered subjects. Her work reflects an outward and globalised experience of queerness, where 'the queer diasporic subject troubles issues of both gender normativity and of national and geographical stability'.[32]

In the present moment, more black and Asian writers than ever are exploring queer desire in their fiction. Authors of note whom I have not been able to discuss due to space constraints include: Dean Atta, Malorie Blackman, Maya Chowdhry, Yrsa Daley-Ward, Thomas Glave, Marlon James, NSR Khan, Ash Kotak, Adam Lowe, Seni Seneviratne, Andra Simon, and Luke Sutherland, as well as there being a number of black and Asian queer writers in Adam Lowe's *SPOKE: New Queer Voices* (2015) – all of whom reveal in playful ways how 'the question of the black subject cannot be represented without reference to the dimensions of class, gender, sexuality and ethnicity'.[33] In particular, the twenty-first century sees greater questioning of toxic black and Asian masculinities, along with intensified recognition of sexual and familial silences. Gendered constructions are increasingly

---

[29] Lynette Goddard, 'Introduction' in Lynette Goddard (ed.), *The Methuen Drama Book of Plays by Black British Writers* (London: Methuen Drama, 2011), vii–xxvi; x. *Chiaroscuro* (1986) is available in Goddard's *Methuen Drama Book*.

[30] Anannya Dasgupta, 'Interrogating Identity in Suniti Namjoshi's Fables' in Vanita (ed.), *Queering India*, 100–10; 100.

[31] Ashley Tellis, 'We Sinful Dykes: Lesbian Sexuality in Valerie Mason-John's *Sin Dykes*' in Dimple Godiwala (ed.), *Alternatives within the Mainstream: British Black and Asian Theatres* (Newcastle upon Tyne: Cambridge Scholars, 2006), 239–47; 241. *Sin Dykes* (1998) appears in Mason-John's *Brown Girl in the Ring* (London: Get a Grip Publishers, 1999).

[32] Manuela Coppola, 'Queering Sonnets: Sexuality and Transnational Identity in the Poetry of Patience Agbabi', *Women: A Cultural Review*, 26:4 (2015): 369–83; 370.

[33] Hall, 'New Ethnicities', 444.

destabilised, as are the boundaries between text and image. In addition, the groundwork laid by Dorothea Smartt, Malika Booker, Patience Agbabi, and others has led to an exciting new generation of poets who traverse written, musical, and performative modes as much as gendered and sexual barriers.

The Twenty-First Century: Caribbean Losses

Known for her engagement with histories of the African diaspora and her light-footed experimentation with genre, in 2013 Bernardine Evaristo (1959–) brought out the wryly comic, London-based novel *Mr Loverman*. In keeping with well-known texts like *White Teeth* (2000) by Zadie Smith and *Small Island* (2004) by Andrea Levy, this work returns to previous generations, providing a new inflection on foundational narratives of black Britain. In Evaristo's case, she looks to the Windrush era, excavating the queer voices obscured at the time, in line with J. Dillon Brown and Leah Reade Rosenberg's interest in 'unsettling and overturning the potent originary myths' of the period.[34] *Mr Loverman* tells the story of two closeted gay men in their seventies from Antigua: dandyish Barrington and his gentle-natured lover Morris. A wise-cracking and somewhat affected autodidact, Barry has the self-educated man's joy with words and much of the novel's pleasure comes from his verbal showmanship (his character has echoes of Sam Selvon's Moses in his London trilogy).[35] Told through the alternating viewpoints of Barry and his long-suffering wife, Carmel, *Mr Loverman* brings movingly to life the shared damage of a lifetime clouded by fear and shame. At the same time, it does not shy away from Barry's masculine failings, illustrating the cost borne by the women closest to him of his deceit. Like many queer novels before, it reflects back on the innocence of the boyhood fumblings between the two men. Caught in a compromising position by Barry's brother, Larry, the elder boy keeps their secret, simply warning the pair to take better heed – in what is perhaps a gentle nod to a similarly understanding character named Larry in Salkey's *Escape*.[36] The novel is also at pains to show Barry as a man who cares for children (both his own and those of others), countering what Cecil Gutzmore

---

[34] J. Dillon Brown and Leah Reade Rosenberg (eds.), *Beyond Windrush: Rethinking Postwar Anglophone Caribbean Literature* (Jackson, MS: University Press of Mississippi, 2015), 5.

[35] These include *The Lonely Londoners* (1956), *Moses Ascending* (1975), and *Moses Migrating* (1983). For a more detailed analysis of Selvon's works, see Chapter 13.

[36] Bernardine Evaristo, *Mr Loverman* (London: Penguin, 2013), 162.

describes as the tendency within certain Caribbean communities to associate homosexuality with paedophilia.[37] In fact, in some ways, it is the unexceptionality of Barry and Morris's relationship that stands out, making this a novel for the generation of LGBTQ marriage and what has been termed 'homonormativity'.[38] Yet, despite their celebration by a younger generation of gay men as '*living* history', there is some poignancy to the men's belated sexual freedom, Barry himself recognising that '75 percent' of his life has passed and that 'this is the story of we lives. Hellos and goodbyes'.[39] While not depicting quite the suffering of Heather Love's queer canon, Evaristo's novel does, nevertheless, remind her readers that there have been costs to attaining the sexual freedoms many now take for granted. As a London-born woman of Nigerian background, in *Mr Loverman* Evaristo demonstrates similar linguistic dexterity and confident multiculturality to Zadie Smith, supporting her critical lauding as an author who says 'things about modern Britain that no one else does'.[40] Given this prescient eye, one can only wonder at the noticeable paucity of scholarly writing on *Mr Loverman*, despite its positive reception from reviewers.[41]

The novelist, poet, and short-story writer Kei Miller (1978–) has come to greater public prominence in recent years as a result of his Forward Prize-winning collection, *The Cartographer Tries to Map a Way to Zion* (2014). In tandem with figures such as Marlon James and Thomas Glave, his writing heralds a new generation of black, gay, male Caribbean literary talent, whose work builds on precursors such as H. Nigel Thomas, as well as Caribbean women authors of the late twentieth century who challenged gendered and sexual norms. The fiction of these men works to contest stereotypes of Caribbean homophobia, Miller, for example, proving alert to the hazards of 'queer imperialism' as he points out: 'It is very obvious that several well-meaning white North Americans would like (ever so earnestly) to bear witness to the suffering that LGBT people experience in the Caribbean [. . .] And this

---

[37] Cecil Gutzmore, 'Casting the First Stone! Policing of Homo/Sexuality in Jamaican Popular Culture', *Interventions*, 6:1 (2004): 118–34.

[38] See Jasbir K. Puar, *Terrorist Assemblages: Homonationalism in Queer Times* (Durham, NC: Duke University Press, 2007).

[39] Evaristo, *Mr Loverman*, 259, 134, 5.

[40] Maggie Gee, '*Mr Loverman* by Bernardine Evaristo – Review', *The Guardian*, 31 August 2013. Available at www.theguardian.com/books/2013/aug/31/mr-loverman-bernardine-evaristo-review.

[41] As of December 2017, I could find no published journal articles or essays addressing *Mr Loverman*.

kind of advocacy is deeply problematic.'[42] Yet, at the same time, James, Glave, and Miller alike have all left the region themselves, highlighting the continued difficulties of queer Caribbean experience and echoing previous, exilic male traditions. Two earlier works by Miller deal overtly with same-sex desire: the 2006 short story collection *Fear of Stones and Other Stories* and the novel *The Same Earth* (2008). Both employ a folk vernacular interspersed with warm humour to bring to life small-town Jamaica and its attendant religious-sexual proscription. *Fear of Stones* contains two striking tales about the challenges facing queer Caribbean men. 'This Dance' reveals how social pressure and restrictive masculine codes combined mean that 'some men in this island will never dance the way they want to dance', while the titular story's dextrous narrator teases out the 'something else would have happened' that never actually does, both sentiments reflecting Glave's description of 'that erotic-emotional desire for people of our own gender that it seemed no one – not anyone at all – ever spoke about'.[43] In *The Same Earth*, meanwhile, Miller's 'matter-of-fact narration of the sex-life of Eulan Solomon, a man-loving actuary [...]' marks an important expansion of the Caribbean novel's sexual world', this despite the fact that all three stories are haunted by the erotic possibilities left unfulfilled.[44]

The Twenty-First Century: Queer Escape

The novelist Neel Mukherjee (1970–) published *Past Continuous* – known as *A Life Apart* in the UK – in 2008. It focuses on the life of a young gay man, Ritwik Ghosh, who flees Kolkata for England, heading first for Oxford University before experiencing a life of precarity amidst London's undocumented workforce. Mukherjee claims that he 'consciously wanted to have a gay protagonist in my novel', believing the topic to be 'a trend in India'.[45]

---

[42] Cited in Annie Paul, 'If a Gay Man Screams in the Caribbean and a White Man Isn't There to Hear Him, Has He Still Made a Sound?', *Active Voice* [website], 13 July 2015. Available at https://anniepaul.net/2015/07/13/if-a-gay-man-screams-in-the-caribbean-and-a-white-man-isnt-there-to-hear-him-has-he-still-made-a-sound/.

[43] Kei Miller, *Fear of Stones and Other Stories* (Oxford: Macmillan Education, 2006), 158, 137; Glave, *Our Caribbean*, 3.

[44] Alison Donnell, 'Sexuality and Gender in the Anglophone Caribbean Novel' in Simon Gikandi (ed.), *The Oxford History of the Novel in English*, vol. 11: *The Novel in Africa and the Caribbean since 1950* (Oxford: Oxford University Press, 2016), 152–66; 163.

[45] Anon, 'I Wanted a Gay Protagonist in my Novel: Neel Mukherjee', *News18* [website], 27 July 2009. Available at www.news18.com/news/books/i-wanted-a-gay-protagonist-in-my-novel-neel-mukherjee-321410.html.

Accordingly, Ritwik's sexual experiences are rendered in matter-of-fact, explicit, and detailed fashion, this despite the author's further description of his character's homosexuality as 'a sideshow. The novel is not a "gay novel" [. . .] His sexuality is what it is, a given.'[46] The book concentrates on the protagonist's isolation in pitiless fashion, emphasising Ritwik's outsider status both at home and abroad. In so doing, Mukherjee rejects 'both a nostalgic vision of the nation and an understanding of freedom as Westernization-at-home or emigration-to-West'.[47] In contrast to Evaristo's and Miller's more private and domestic portrayals, Ritwik's primary sexual experiences come through the public realm of cottaging and gay cruising culture. His first forays into this world are portrayed as a dance or game, before gradually we are told that his activities have become: 'a habit, an addiction, and he is powerless to break out of its grip [. . .] he has the clinical gambler's dopamine-addicted brain, hooked to the tyranny of uncertain and random rewards'.[48] Mukherjee is careful to reflect the exoticism of which Ritwik is victim, echoing trends within postwar fiction, as his protagonist recognises: 'his is a type of minority appeal, catering to the "special interest" group rather than the mainstream'.[49] As the book's original title suggests, this is also a text fixated on questions of time. Ritwik takes the view that cottaging 'is to experience time in its purest form; he understands how viscous, like treacle, it is in its unadulterated state' – words with echoes of Jack Halberstam's discussions of queer temporality.[50]

The work of short-story writer and visual artist Diriye Osman (1983–) deals with themes of sexuality and mental health. His debut collection, *Fairytales for Lost Children* (2013), is a striking mixture of text and Osman's own illustrations (which weave in Arabic calligraphy). It concentrates on the voices of displaced young gay and lesbian Somalis attempting to make their way both in the world and in love, in keeping with Brenna Munro's claim that: 'A new figure has begun to appear in the anglophone African novel: the gay African is being written into literary existence, and more often than not, is being represented

---

[46] Aditya Sudarshan, 'An Interview with Neel Mukherjee', *Aditya Sudarshan* [website], 30 September 2009. Available at http://adityasudarshan.blogspot.co.uk/2009/09/interview-with-neel-mukherjee-author-of.html.

[47] Rao, 'Queer Questions', 206.

[48] Neel Mukherjee, *A Life Apart [Past Continuous]* (London: Constable and Robinson, [2008] 2010), 182.

[49] Ibid., 127.

[50] Ibid., 128; Jack Halberstam, *In a Queer Time and Place: Transgender Bodies, Subcultural Lives* (New York: New York University Press, 2005).

sympathetically.'[51] Osman's rendering of diverse African sexualities works to challenge one-note depictions of the continent as sexually regressive, while also showing the very real familial tensions generated by coming out. His stories range across ages, backgrounds, and orientations, from queer-curious children to sexually adventurous adults, judgemental grandparents, and understanding mothers who recognise the sexual tolerance that 'my generation was not capable of'.[52] As was the case with Miller's work, Osman acknowledges that: 'In Somali culture many things go unsaid: how we love, who we love and why we love that way.'[53] Countering this, his stories are 'sensual, erotic, explicit', as Evaristo recognises.[54] One character, for example, states unequivocally that 'I've always loved being gay. Sure, Kenya was not exactly Queer Nation but my sexuality gave me joy', words instantiating Audre Lorde's assertion of the erotic potential of desire (as further signalled by Osman's choice of a Lorde quotation for his epigraph).[55] Finally, *Fairytales* ranges across both male and female same-sex desire – a surprisingly unusual tendency across this body of work.[56]

The Twenty-First Century: Poetic Forms

The twenty-first century has also seen an efflorescence of exciting black and Asian poets addressing same-sex desire in both written and performative fashion, including figures such as Dean Atta, Maya Chowdhry, Adam Lowe, Seni Seneviratne, Andra Simon, and Yrsa Daley-Ward. In closing, I reference two: Jay Bernard (1988–) and Saradha Soobrayen (1974–). Bernard is a self-described 'writer, film-programmer and inter-disciplinary artist' who explores themes of the body, the archive, technology, and history.[57] Their 2016 pamphlet *The Red and Yellow Nothing* combines poetry with Bernard's own images to reimagine the tale of Morien, a Moorish knight of Camelot, 'skeletal and genderqueer'.[58] This gendered nonconformity is representative

---

[51] Brenna Munro, 'Sexuality and Gender in the African Novel' in Gikandi (ed.), *The Novel in Africa and the Caribbean Since 1950*, 176–80; 167.

[52] Diriye Osman, *Fairytales for Lost Children* (London: Team Angelica, 2013), 3–4.

[53] Osman, *Fairytales for Lost Children*, 3.

[54] Bernardine Evaristo in Osman, *Fairytales for Lost Children*, frontmatter.

[55] Osman, *Fairytales for Lost Children*, 33–4; Audre Lorde, *Sister Outsider*.

[56] Evaristo includes a minor plot strand about a lesbian couple in *Mr Loverman* and queer undertones can be read into Mukherjee's secondary story that reimagines a female character from a Tagore text.

[57] See www.jaybernard.co.uk.

[58] Jay Bernard, *The Red and Yellow Nothing* (London: Ink, Sweat and Tears, 2016), 29.

of Bernard's œuvre as a whole, which, as Kei Miller recognises, is also grounded in the world of 'London in all of its messy multi-lingual, multi-dialectal, multi-racial, multi-sexual and relentlessly modern complexity'.[59] Like Miller's, Bernard's work considers the violent legacies troubling Caribbean culture. In the poem 'Fake Beach', for example, they ponder on the crossover between 'fucking / discipline' and parenthood, suggesting that 'Your dad's stance   thigh muscles tight   as he lowers / himself' onto your mother 'is the same   as when he draws back his arm' to beat you.[60] As the spacing here suggests, Bernard's complex wordsmithery offers a challenging reading experience, one rendered incantatory in their compelling live readings. Finally, Saradha Soobrayen's lyrical poems explore questions of desire, the body, silence, and historical injustice. Her much-anthologised poem 'My Conqueror' reimagines the colonisation of Mauritius – Soobrayen later redrafts it to include reference to the Chagos Islanders[61] – and genders conquest as female, albeit with no lesser a 'lust for breasts and thighs'.[62] This imagined world is populated with 'cross-dressing captains and girls in white breeches. Boys who like boys who like collars and chains', its insistent references to 'tongues' and 'sucking' in keeping with the poet's ongoing exploration of language and desire. Her conqueror's claim to be 'no one and everyone', meanwhile, reflects Soobrayen's assertion that 'I like to remain in the unknowingness. I aim to stay for as long as possible with what is not being understood or expressed' – words appropriate to the questioning and restless nature of both her and Bernard's work.[63]

In *Queer Phenomenology* (2006), Sara Ahmed discusses the 'straightening' effect of the orientations provided by the heteronormative world, whereby 'we not only have to turn towards the objects that are given to us by heterosexual culture' but 'we must "turn away" from objects that take us off this line'.[64] Those inhabiting a queer orientation are framed as existing in 'slanting' or 'oblique' ways to the norm, facing pressure to fall 'in line'. In a similar fashion to the ways in which black and Asian writers come into conflict with the narrow physical and discursive boundaries of nationhood

[59] Kei Miller, 'Comment' in Karen McCarthy Woolf (ed.), *Ten: The New Wave* (Tarset: Bloodaxe Books, 2014), 127–8; 127.

[60] Bernard, 'Fake Beach' in McCarthy Woolf (ed.), *Ten*, 129.

[61] Nicole Fordham Hodges, 'Interview: Saradha Soobrayen', *Disability Arts Online* [website], 28 June 2012. Available at www.disabilityartsonline.org.uk/Festival-of-the-world-southbank-Saradha-Soobrayen.

[62] Saradha Soobrayen, 'My Conqueror', *Disability Arts Online* [website], 29 June 2012. Available at http://www.disabilityartsonline.org.uk/Saradha-Soobrayen.

[63] Soobrayen, 'My Conqueror', n.p.; Fordham Hodges, 'Interview', n.p.

[64] Ahmed, *Queer Phenomenology*, 21.

and race in Britain, Ahmed shows in *The Cultural Politics of Emotion* (2004) how ideas of national belonging work 'to transform whiteness into a familial tie, into a form of racial kindred, that recognizes all non-white others as strangers'.[65] Countering both the straightening effects of mainstream culture, and the construction of persons of colour as 'strangers' to Britain, the texts discussed in this chapter illustrate the heterogeneous quality of Asian and black British queer lives, embodying Hall's still salient point as to such communities' refusal to perform 'respectable' sexuality.[66]

[65] Sara Ahmed, *The Cultural Politics of Emotion* (Edinburgh: Edinburgh University Press, 2004), 2.
[66] Stuart Hall, 'New Ethnicities'.

35

Prizing Otherness
Black and Asian British Writing in the Global Marketplace

SARAH BROUILLETTE AND JOHN R. COLEMAN

In Graham Huggan's foundational work on the prizing of Otherness in the British literary field, he highlights the irony in the Booker company using its wealth, which originated in Guyanese sugar plantations, to back a prize that has so often been awarded to writers born in former colonies or born to parents who were.[1] In his account this irony is a species of an ambivalence general to postcolonial literature: authors who set out to resist standard narratives about colonial history and identity write books that become commodities sold to predominantly white readers looking to access apparently 'exotic' locations and experiences. For Huggan, white readers' exoticised consumption of Otherness is a driving force within the field. Their tastes shape what kind of work publishing houses will take on as well as what is defined as worthy of reward.

In this chapter we develop this line of analysis in some perhaps unfamiliar directions. Considering that prizing Otherness is an activity characteristic of the literary field more than the mass market, we suggest this is because it is within the literary field that there is a marketing emphasis on writers' individual biographies and unique expressive lives. The distinction of association with a minoritised community, and attendant controversies around representation and authenticity, have proven important sources of language that is useful in promotional materials, including journalistic commentary. It is also within the mainstream literary field where one finds a creative elite eager to adhere to a liberal ideal of multicultural diversity and attentiveness to global issues. We argue in addition that, especially in more recent years, prizing Otherness has involved an attempt on the part of UK governments and media corporations to channel people into certain kinds of consumer activity and certain kinds of work. Put briefly: the literary prize is supposed to

[1] Graham Huggan, *The Postcolonial Exotic: Marketing the Margins* (New York: Routledge, 2001), 105–23.

sell books and make work in the literary industries seem glamorously appealing. As it arises from these various forces – the importance of writers' identities to the marketing of their work, the activity of liberal self-fashioning, and industry development – a major implication of the highlighting of minoritised writers is its tendency to obscure the extraordinary whiteness of the book industries overall. In fact, prizing Otherness has served as a kind of cover, hiding the fundamental social barriers that delimit who can pursue remunerative creative work in the UK.

The Reality of Publishing Industry Homogeneity

Elsewhere we have considered the example of the *decibel* programme, which started as a 2003–2004 Arts Council England initiative designed to address under-representation of non-white people in the British arts scene.[2] Five million pounds were allocated to support African, Asian, and Caribbean artists and arts managers, as well as arts programmes involving people of African, Asian, or Caribbean origin now living in Britain. Initiatives developed during 2003–2004 included a high-profile performing arts showcase, a fellowship programme for promising cura-tors, and the annual *decibel*-Penguin prize, which was co-sponsored by the British Book Awards and Penguin Books. The prizing of literary Otherness by the *decibel* programme was a means of encouraging those who are sometimes called 'BAME' people (Black, Asian, and Minority Ethnic) to buy literary books, and to look at the publishing industry as relevant to their interests and available to them as potential employment.

Nevertheless, a follow-up report published in 2015, *Writing the Future*, reveals that the *decibel* programme and related initiatives basically had no effect. In fact, the UK book industries are in a period of decline, with diversity negatively affected. In light of the economic downturn, publishers have in the report's words 'retrenched and become more conservative in their editorial and employment choices'.[3] They have resorted to 'a risk-averse culture' due to declining sales, in which 'the demands of major retailers [. . .] pressure [publishers] to focus on obvious markets rather than anything more

---

[2] Sarah Brouillette, *Literature and the Creative Economy* (Stanford, CA: Stanford University Press, 2014), 117–19.

[3] Danuta Kean with Mel Larsen (eds.), *Writing the Future: Black and Asian Writers and Publishers in the UK Market Place* (London: Spread the Word, 2015), 2. Available at http://spreadtheword.org.uk/resources/view/writing-the-future.

nuanced'.[4] The supported pathways into the field that *decibel* resulted in were entry level. People from BAME backgrounds working in publishing remain in junior positions and tend not to be involved in decision-making around manuscripts and overall lists. The report features a survey of 203 UK-based published novelists; 30 per cent of these put themselves in the BAME category. It reveals that BAME writers are less likely to have agents for their first or subsequent novels, and that they are more likely to feel as though their work is not commercially viable. There is a 'BAME angle' that surveyed novelists often understand as an imposed focus on ethnicity that betrays the 'more universal' aspects of their work.[5]

Literary publishers have not traditionally been interested in large profits. They were forced to reorient, however – albeit with the backing of increased marketing budgets – when they were subsumed by media corporations and conglomerates beginning in the 1960s. These were global trends, though with implications particular to each local literary milieu. Across the board, mainstream literary publishing is now clearly dependent on corporate advertising, at the heart of which is a boisterous desire for brand recognition. In the 1980s and 1990s, bookstore chains decorated their salesroom floors and walls with large quantities of bestselling paperbacks written by famous authors and packaged with attractive covers. Functioning like warehouses, they could commit to providing the capital necessary for massive print runs, functioning as corporate publishers' main customers.[6] In the UK in 1993 these companies together sold about 40 per cent of adult trade books,[7] and this only escalated after the dissolution of the Net Book Agreement in 1995, which abolished price maintenance and ushered in the 'freedom to discount' for these stores and, increasingly, online retail sites.[8]

A creative elite specialising in the production and management of literary curation and promotion oversaw this expansive moment. These were boom years for the B-format literary paperback, which is slightly larger than a mass-market book. It was during this time that literary prizes proliferated and became major means of product circulation; the Booker Prize became an annual televised spectacle watched by millions of people; other sorts of list-making and prize-giving came to prominence (selection for inclusion in the Richard and Judy Book Club for instance); and nothing guaranteed sales like winning a literary prize.

---

[4] Ibid., 14.   [5] Ibid., 8.
[6] Eric de Bellaigue, *British Book Publishing as a Business since the 1960s: Selected Essays* (London: The British Library, 2004), 188–9.
[7] Ibid., 24.   [8] Ibid., 189.

The risk associated with a product that is definitively 'creative' – not produced by a machine but rather by an individual with a unique and unpredictable expressive life – requires management. A key technique has been intensive marketing of writers' most apparent biographies. This fact is not itself explanatory, since a given strategy is only workable because of, and in tandem with, what audiences perceive literature to be: that is, the expression and manifestation of the individual psychic life, the product of genius, and the close articulation of an individual experience. BAME writers are drawn into this marketing in an extraordinary way. In their own perception, they are unfairly burdened with 'voicing the voiceless', with representing their communities, and so on. This focus indicates that publishers are assuming an otherwise monocultural white mainstream – for whom is the given work an articulation of what was heretofore unknown? – constantly in need of sources of newness. It also indicates that marketing departments are compelled to devise what Claire Squires has called 'marketing stories' to circulate with the work, accumulate journalistic capital, and become subject to debate.[9] In the case of BAME writers, questions of authenticity and representation – 'speaking for the community' (whether sanctioned to or not) and 'telling untold stories' – have proven especially appealing, and portable catchphrases have occasioned publicity-generating controversies.

Another finding of the 2015 *Writing the Future* survey was that '42 per cent of respondents from a BAME background wrote literary fiction'.[10] The next biggest genre was young adult fiction, at 26 per cent, with women's commercial fiction (including romance) at 8 per cent of respondents.[11] Of the biggest selling genres, crime accounted for only 4 per cent of BAME novelists' output.[12] 'Science fiction and fantasy was written by eight per cent of respondents and horror by 10 per cent.'[13] So there seems to be a marked 'propensity of the industry to publish writers of colour under the "literary" banner'.[14] It is of course possible that people who are not white are not writing as many manuscripts in other genres; these statistics are not available. What the report claims is that BAME writers are effectively confined within the literary niche, and that the possibility of making a decent living as writers is stymied because they cannot get at the mass-market book sales. A BAME writer setting out to make a decent living as a full-time novelist is at a disadvantage, then. According to Nielsen BookScan, 'Crime, romance and YA books make up almost half of the adult fiction market in the UK'; while as

[9] Claire Squires, *Marketing Literature: The Making of Contemporary Writing in Britain* (New York: Palgrave Macmillan, 2007), 119–46.
[10] Kean and Larsen (eds.), *Writing the Future*, 9.   [11] Ibid.   [12] Ibid.   [13] Ibid.   [14] Ibid.

we know books that are more deliberately literary are 'witnessing a decline in market share'.[15]

In light of these findings, we suggest that the relative success of BAME figures within the literary niche, and their prizing within that niche – that is, relative to other niches, not to the literary field as a whole – is evidence that within the industry there has been a certain liberal cosmopolitan self-fashioning at work in the devising of specifically *literary* lists. Richard Todd's *Consuming Fictions*, the first full-length academic study of the rise of the Booker and related escalated marketing efforts, is a telling instance of what we mean. Todd presents a thriving literary culture energised by its new entrants. Citing Rushdie's 1981 Booker win for *Midnight's Children*, Todd argues that the Booker effect in this case ultimately 'created a precedent [. . .] offering English-speaking readers a panoramic, international and intensely *current* view of "fiction in Britain"'.[16] This in turn 'led to an increasingly global picture of fiction in Britain during the course of the 1980s. It is now the case that the line-up of half or more of a typical late 1980s or 1990s Booker shortlist is not centred on Britain. This reflects a new public awareness of Britain as a pluralist society.'[17] This flattering image of the industry presents as non-problematic the ongoing dominance of the London-based Anglo-British literary market-place. For Todd, it is not the acquisitive adjudicating centre of literary value, and the market to which postcolonial writers from disparate locales must appeal if they hope to earn a substantial living, but rather a welcoming, pluralising, panoramic embrace. He depicts the highly competitive world of literary authorship, epitomised by prize culture, as a microcosm of an inclusive multicultural society. He ignores the fact that BAME writers have so often felt pressured to parrot stereotypes of their cultures to gain publication and consecration in this field, and that they are also vastly under-represented in non-authorial roles in publishing, especially in the upper tiers of management.

In more recent years, scholars have deviated from Todd's take, instead following Huggan's lead in attending to imbalances in the literary industries in terms of the flow of literary talent from the peripheries to the core. Dobrota Pucherová's excellent work on the Britishness of the Caine Prize for African writing is a notable example.[18] She points out how the prize

---

[15] Ibid.

[16] Richard Todd, *Consuming Fictions: The Booker Prize and Fiction in Britain Today* (London: Bloomsbury, 1996), 82; Todd's emphasis.

[17] Ibid., 83.

[18] Dobrota Pucherová, '"A Continent Learns to Tell its Story at Last": Notes on the Caine Prize', *Journal of Postcolonial Writing*, 48:1 (2012): 13–25. DOI http://dx.doi.org/10.1080/17449855.2011.595157.

consolidates the power of the London literary establishment to determine how writing in English from Britain's former colonies is valued. The Man Booker International Prize could be read in similar terms, of course. What deserves more attention, in particular, is precisely the startling number of publishing industry professionals – those charged with administering and adjudicating prizes – who are white and 'drawn from the English upper middle classes'.[19]

There remains a remarkable level of independent wealth behind the publishing industry. Eighty-nine per cent of the 2015 survey respondents agreed that personal contacts and recommendations were a 'significant source of new clients'; and 80 per cent of industry staff 'hold a post-graduate diploma, higher degree or industry-specific accredited qualification'.[20] The *Writing the Future* report suggests that 'novelists able to finance a creative writing degree, will be better placed to meet literary agents whom they may approach at a later date with a finished manuscript'.[21] Of course, given 'post-graduate university fees at £9,000 a year and entry-level salaries in publishing very low', accumulated debt may discourage those from less elite backgrounds from considering publishing as a viable career.[22]

A survey of the Society of Young Publishers further revealed that '19 per cent of respondents achieved their first job in publishing through an unpaid internship'; another 19 per cent through paid internships, and a 'further 13 per cent achieved their first job through a personal contact, such as a family member or friend'.[23] So some of the primary routes into the publishing business are barriers 'to those outside the affluent professional classes and [this] explains why the industry remains dominated by White, public school educated, "Oxbridge" graduates, even though [members of] this group represent a tiny fragment of the overall UK population'.[24] Only 11 per cent of the survey respondents had ties with non-Oxbridge universities or more market-facing colleges. In terms of employees in non-authorial roles in publishing houses and literary agencies, 80 per cent have a 'post-graduate diploma, higher degree or industry-specific accredited qualification'.[25] According to the Social Mobility and Child Poverty Commission for 2014, 7 per cent of the UK population attended public schools; less than 1 per cent went on to Oxbridge.[26] A 2010 Race for Opportunity Campaign 'found that only 11.1 per cent of Oxford students and 10.5 per cent of Cambridge students have a BAME background'.[27]

---

[19] Kean and Larsen (eds.), *Writing the Future*, 14. [20] Ibid., 22. [21] Ibid. [22] Ibid.
[23] Ibid. [24] Ibid. [25] Ibid. [26] Ibid., 23. [27] Ibid.

The Role of Universities as Gateways to the Industry

What we see here is a picture of the UK literary industry in which the advantages of gaining an education in the UK's most elite universities are available only to some. These people come to hold high-salaried positions of decision-making power in publishing firms with the most significant market share, and in turn influence the content that circulates in the form of mainstream literary works, and infect the way works and their authors are represented in high-profile marketing stories. This relatively homogeneous creative class is made up of university-educated people trained to define and broker marketable taste, and assigned powerful roles in a situation of general industry contraction, which entails the whittling down of publishers' lists and the intensive marketing focus on particular titles. The reproduction of this creative elite is deeply rooted in a matrix of social, economic, and cultural forces that link mainstream British literary publishing both to a history of whiteness and to the neoliberal educational establishment in Britain. This establishment is now characterised by the dramatic split between its lofty heights, where exposure to liberal-humanistic educational ideals is still available to the most elite students, and an ever-growing market-facing training rung where creative-economy workplace skills are the priority. People from minoritised communities are at a disadvantage at either end of the spectrum.

The Department for Culture, Media and Sport (DCMS) reported that in 2013, 69.1 per cent of UK publishing workers had some higher education, with 62 per cent having university-degree or equivalent qualifications.[28] The percentage of BAME people employed in the entire creative economy was only 10.2 per cent; this means that of the 2,616,000 employees, 2,348,000 identified as white.[29] *Writing the Future* suggests BAME representation in publishing is similar to that reported by a recent survey of over 1,000 UK publishing workers, which found that over 90 per cent of these workers identified as 'white British'.[30]

This data reveals the dramatic failure of recent educational policy, which has since the early 2000s not opened up access but rather constructed a 'more

---

[28] Department for Culture, Media and Sport (DCMS), *Creative Industries: Focus on Employment* (London: DCMS, 2014), 57. Available at https://assets.publishing.service .gov.uk/government/uploads/system/uploads/attachment_data/file/324530/Creat ive_Industries_-_Focus_on_Employment.pdf.

[29] Ibid., 35.

[30] Alison Flood, 'UK Publishing Industry Remains 90% White, Survey Finds', *The Guardian*, 6 September 2017. Available at www.theguardian.com/books/2017/sep/06/ uk-publishing-industry-remanins-90-white-survey-finds.

formal, more directed, and more calculating relationship' between higher education and the creative industries than ever before.[31] In another study, while only 22.13 per cent of people with so-called 'Bohemian credentials'– training in arts and culture disciplines – graduated from schools in the Greater London area, 34.21 per cent of people with creative occupations were working there.[32] The proportion of creative graduates working in creative fields in regions across the UK varied depending on the specific industry; many were highly concentrated in London, like publishing, and others, like craft production, were concentrated in South East and West Midlands creative clusters.[33] But overall, the trend is that creative labour conducted by graduates of arts and design fields mostly occurs in and around London, whether or not they earned their degrees there. Moreover, there is a London-centric anchoring of creative-economy employees overall – 28.1 per cent of all creative economy jobs.[34] So in addition to having the right credentials, being keyed into London's network of creative professionals is clearly crucial to success in the industry. A person who has not attained the right media industry credentials and does not live in London experiences cascading disadvantages.

The importance of internships is perhaps the clearest instance of the combined force of education, location, and social connections within the field. By some measures unpaid internships are *the* primary route into creative work, and they have permeated British higher education in the form of work placements in exchange for course credit. Standard in nearly all programmes, the lucrative experience, relationships, and development of 'soft skills' that internships offer attract students to arts and design courses branded as avenues into jobs. However, based on empirical research into the experiences of ITPS television industry employees, David Lee argues that networks 'actually act as mechanisms of exclusion, favouring individuals with high levels of cultural and social capital', resulting in 'a structural class-based inequity in our labour market'.[35] Kate Oakley argues that, despite attempts to promote diversity in work placement schemes, they often do not teach

---

[31] Kate Oakley, '"Making Workers": Higher Education and the Cultural Industries Workplace' in Daniel Ashton and Caitriona Noonan (eds.), *Cultural Work and Higher Education* (New York: Palgrave Macmillan, 2013), 25–44; 26.

[32] Roberta Comunian et al., 'Winning and Losing in the Creative Industries: An Analysis of Creative Graduates' Career Opportunities Across Creative Disciplines', *Cultural Trends*, 20:3–4 (2011), 291–308; 300. DOI http://dx.doi.org/10.1080/09548963.2011.589710.

[33] Ibid., 302.   [34] DCMS, *Creative Industries*, 18.

[35] David Lee, 'Creative Networks and Social Capital' in Ashton and Noonan (eds.), *Cultural Work and Higher Education*, 195–213; 195–6.

students how to discuss or deal with inequality when experienced or witnessed; instead, they are encouraged to fit in.[36] And the gender inequality of creative production that some scholars have pointed out seems realistic in light of the fact that 5,000 women, compared with 750 men, left the creative industries between 2006 and 2009.[37] Essentially: '[T]he discursive construction of the ideal work placement student and potential creative worker – with a currency on flexibility, enterprise and self-sufficiency – privileges whiteness, middle classness, masculinity and able-bodiedness.'[38]

Still, these programmes were sold across the UK as opportunities for students whose parents did not attend university, as local creative 'clusters' and higher education were co-opted into regeneration initiatives.[39] New Labour financed a 'geographical spread of HEIs [higher education institutions] providing creative courses' across the UK,[40] and many staff and researchers were hired to promote equal opportunity on the ground and in policy. The presence of university students has been used to attract the creative elite and entrepreneurs to productive clusters 'by giving them somewhere to tune into industry "noise"'.[41] Britain's higher education institutions continue to play a large role in maintaining and solidifying these hipster scenes, which increase downtown property values and attract jet-setting impresarios from around the world. While youth culture has always been a part of the university experience, it used to be a by-product or spin-off effect; now it is something universities are directly engaged in making and selling.[42] What started with Tony Blair's 'Third Way' New Labour government has only intensified under Conservative leadership. In Stefan Collini's words, the 2010 Browne Report on higher education intimates that universities are now best viewed as 'engines of economic prosperity and as agencies for equipping future employees to earn higher salaries'.[43] Many of the Browne Report's recommendations affirm those of the DCMS-funded *Looking Out*, completed by the Art Design Media Subject Centre within the Higher Education Academy. Eighty-five per cent of art and design departments were said to employ teacher-practitioners who develop and oversee

---

[36] Oakley, 'Making Workers', 32.   [37] Ibid., 38.

[38] Kimberly Allen et al., 'Doing Diversity and Evading Equality: The Case of Student Work Placements in the Creative Sector' in Yvette Taylor (ed.), *Educational Diversity: The Subject of Difference and Different Subjects* (Basingstoke: Palgrave Macmillan, 2012), 180–200; 185.

[39] Oakley, 'Making Workers', 27.

[40] Comunian et al., 'Winning and Losing in the Creative Industries', 305.

[41] Oakley, 'Making Workers', 30.   [42] Ibid., 26.

[43] Stefan Collini, 'Browne's Gamble', *London Review of Books*, 31:21 (2010), 23–5; 25. Available at www.lrb.co.uk/v32/n21/stefan-collini/brownes-gamble.

the knowledge-transfer projects that serve as university's 'selling point', and 81 per cent of English universities were said to have identified the creative industries 'as a target sector for outward activities' including, for instance, increased intellectual property commercialisation.[44]

But access was never as diversified as the dreamy language of inclusion might lead one to believe, and for many students – especially those without prior connections to the creative elite – the credentials they acquired at great cost defaulted in oversaturated labour markets. A capacity for mobility and comfort with impermanence are crucial here. Needless to say, this culture has a tendency to exclude people who do not have supports to fall back on between jobs or if they are not successful over the longer term; this includes minoritised populations first and foremost, if they even manage to gain admittance to the programmes offering the prized credentials. Penny Jane Burke and Jackie McManus reveal that people from less affluent socioeconomic backgrounds, enticed enough to apply for school, may never have a chance to begin with. They analysed processes of subjective misrecognition that are discursively produced in the admissions procedures of five UK arts and design higher education institutions. They found that applying 'requires the individual applicant to subject herself to a range of institutional technologies of assessment'; application forms, presenting work portfolios, and stringent interview processes 'are entangled in complex relations of power' through which 'the subject is individualized, categorized, classified and provoked to disciplinary practices of self-surveillance'.[45] In one admissions interview they observed, which is representative of their entire data set, Nina, 'a Black working class young woman from a poor inner-city area' applying to a Fashion Design BA, stated her influences were hip-hop and that she would like to design sports tops; as such, she 'was not recognized as a legitimate subject of art and design studies because she cited a form of fashion seen as invalid in the HE context'.[46] In contrast, they observed an interview of a male candidate, who was admitted, who 'knew how to cite the

---

[44] Caitriona Noonan, 'Constructing Creativities: Higher Education and the Cultural Industries Workforce' in Kate Oakley and Justin O'Connor (eds.), *The Routledge Companion to the Cultural Industries* (New York: Routledge, 2015), 442–51; 443.

[45] Penny Jane Burke and Jackie McManus, 'Art for a Few: Exclusions and Misrecognitions in Higher Education Admissions Practices', *Discourse: Studies in the Cultural Politics of Education*, 32:5 (2011): 699–712; 705.

[46] Ibid., 707.

discourses that would enable him to be recognized as a legitimate student subject'.[47]

The Commercial Case for Staging Diversity

Recall now that the motivation of the collection of publishing industry diversity statistics is the effort to keep the industry economically viable. The *Writing the Future* report's opening states that 'in an industry that operates increasingly on a global level, the absence in most publishing houses of staff at a senior level with Indian or Chinese heritage – especially in international sales – risks putting the UK trade at a disadvantage for working in these significant and growing markets'.[48] More importantly, it states that by 2051:

> one in five people in the UK is predicted to be from an ethnic minority; a rise from 14 per cent in 2011 to at least 30 per cent. In London, the proportion of BAME people is already 40 per cent. Those with a mixed heritage are in the fastest growing ethnic group in the UK: over one million (two per cent) of the population are of mixed race and this is expected to more than double over the next 30 years.[49]

In this light, the book industry 'risks becoming a 20th century throwback increasingly out of touch with a 21st century world'.[50] It is thus no wilful reading on our part to understand these reports, and the collection of diversity statistics on which they are based, as efforts to respond to industry contraction. It is their directly stated purpose.

Since the galvanising release of *Writing the Future*, several new prizes and initiatives have arisen in response to the overwhelming whiteness of publishing's executive ranks.[51] These include the #diversedecember Twitter campaign, which the writer Nikesh Shukla spearheaded in response to the anger that emerged when the list of titles for 2016 World Book Night did not include a single BAME writer.[52] Shukla also co-founded, with Sunny Singh, the Jhalak

[47] Ibid., 708. [48] Kean and Larsen (eds.), *Writing the Future*, 3. [49] Ibid. [50] Ibid.
[51] See, for example: Arifa Akbar, 'Could There Really Be Only One New Black Male Novelist in Britain?', *The Guardian*, 17 November 2016; Bobby Nayyar, 'The Beauty of Belonging? Diversity in UK Publishing', *Publishing Perspectives*, 14 January 2016, available at http://publishingperspectives.com/2016/01/the-beauty-of-belonging-diversity-in-publishing-in-2016/#.WGvkY4WcGYN; and Shaffi's 'Seeing in Colour', a collection of essays commissioned for *The Bookseller* by HarperCollins' Natalie Jerome, available at www.thebookseller.com/insight/seeing-colour-426046.
[52] See Nikesh Shukla, 'Where Are World Book Night 2016's BAME Writers?' *The Bookseller*, 24 November 2015. Available at www.thebookseller.com/blogs/where-are-world-book-night-2016s-bame-writers-317041.

prize in February 2015 to recognise BAME writers.[53] The SI Leeds prize is another instance. It partners with the Ilkley Literature Festival and Peepal Tree Press, and is designed as a 'loudspeaker for Black and Asian women's voices' in particular.[54]

Nor have the major houses been inactive. In partnership with three of Arts Council England's 'National Portfolio Organisations' – Spread the Word (based in London), Commonword (based in Manchester), and Writing West Midlands – Penguin Random House launched a writing workshops programme called Write Now, designed to scout out, mentor, and publish new authors from under-represented communities; it also formally removed the requirement that job applicants hold university degrees. Hachette announced that it would henceforth pay its interns, and offered internships targeting BAME applicants. *The Guardian* paired with 4th Estate, a HarperCollins imprint, to introduce a short story prize for BAME writers; *The Guardian* has also secured its dominance among a liberal readership by publishing many of the most 'liked' and 'shared' and page-viewed polemics on the whiteness of the industry.[55]

What becomes apparent in this context is that, though their limitations are widely recognised – they are not a direct enough means of fostering 'boardroom diversity' and they cannot delink the reading and writing of literature from socioeconomic privilege – the creation of new ways of prizing 'Otherness' is one way people in the literary industries are attempting to address a stark whiteness. We have been suggesting in addition that it is a generalised panic in the face of the various threats to the health of the literary field that has induced new attention to the industry's demographics. We can expect the current trends to continue, as the industry continues to be pinched by the economic stagnation and climate of austerity that have affected everything from the size of the advances that writers can expect to receive to the amount that potential readers are willing to spend on books. If the literary field continues to be largely made up of a creative elite eager to adhere to a liberal ideal of multicultural diversity, we can also expect a continued focus on overcoming the industry's whiteness in response to

[53] Sian Cain, 'Chair of BAME Prize Slams British Publishers After Lack of Submissions', *The Guardian*, 19 November 2016. Available at www.theguardian.com/books/2016/nov/19/bame-prize-slams-uk-publishers-sunny-singh-jhalak-diversity-britain.

[54] SI Leeds Literary Prize, 'Welcome', *SI Leeds Literary Prize*, 2017. Available at www.sileedsliteraryprize.com/.

[55] See most recently Hanif Kureishi, 'Diversity in Publishing is Under Attack', *The Guardian*, 15 June 2018. Available at www.theguardian.com/commentisfree/2018/jun/15/diversity-publishing-culture-minority-writers-penguin.

the rightist emphases in Brexit-era politics. The opening up of the Man Booker Prize in 2014 to American writers – it was previously restricted to British, Irish, Commonwealth, and Zimbabwean writers – can be read in these terms. While it may have been a ploy to renew interest in the prize by generating a scandal, it also indicates the British literary field's surface reaction against a certain kind of parochial Britishness: not the limitation of a largely white elite workforce, in this case, but that of being too parsimonious with its largesse and restricting what it will consider identifying as praiseworthy.

We should note in conclusion that the reality of the British literary field's contraction sheds new light on James English's important work on literary prize culture. He argues that after the marked proliferation and growing importance of literary prizes in the 1960s and 1970s it became less possible to take on the position of the 'incorruptible refusenik' positioning oneself against prize culture. Instead every moment of refusal started to become just another scandal contributing to the prize's value, and everyone began to see this and reflect on it.[56] What is clear now is the way in which English's analysis is a symptom of wealth, or of a moment of relative expansion within the cultural fields. Now that conditions have changed we can see the literary prize in a different light. For contemporary British literary culture, 'diversity' has become a code word for what is potentially newly commercially viable, and the prizing of Otherness is one of several ways of attempting to stimulate a diverse population's incorporation into a kind of consumption that is simply outmoded. Whiteness can no longer be depended upon as a basis for expansion of the literary industries. The literary prizing of Otherness has been one way of trying to turn the reality of a less white and less wealthy British population overall into new sources of revenue within a struggling and risk-prone industry which has been at the same time increasingly pressured to increase profit margins. The highlighting of prized 'creatives' disguises the fundamental truth: those lacking the right entrée into the field – a social network already connected to the industry, and sufficient resources to be able to weather unemployment or work without pay for a while – find only precarious footing; and those who are disadvantaged in these various respects are predominantly non-white.

It is clear that there is a crucially determining relationship between the existence of literary prizes and the literary marketplace as a whole: prizes are

---

[56] James English, *The Economy of Prestige: Prizes, Awards, and the Circulation of Cultural Value* (Cambridge, MA: Harvard University Press, 2005), 221.

an effort to increase the circulation of literary commodities by drawing attention to particular writers and particular works. What is not often acknowledged, and what we have sought to highlight, is the further connection between the literary marketplace and the economy writ large: prizes are in part efforts to encourage people to work in certain sectors and to consume culture that many people want to believe can be a source of ongoing – because 'immaterial' – economic dynamism. These functions of prizes and other drivers of circulation within the literary industries have become clear only as, in light of the global economic crisis and attendant regimes of stagnation, austerity, and precarity, the conditions of possibility for thinking the cultural economy have radically changed.

36

Frontline Fictions
Popular Forms from Crime to Grime

FELIPE ESPINOZA GARRIDO AND JULIAN WACKER

This chapter charts the turbulent history of black and Asian British popular forms since the 1980s. As other contributors to this history have noted, there was a noticeable increase in opportunities for black publishing in the postwar period. Such platforms, however, were predominantly for writers whose work spoke to easily identifiable 'literary' sentiments. It was only in the decades following the 1980s that the vast field of what is now known as black and Asian British popular or genre fiction began to generate traction.[1] When the establishment of specialist presses provided increased visibility for these works in the late 1980s and 1990s, such genre fictions encountered a pernicious, racialised resistance for their portrayal of multiethnic, working-class experience. Not only did the texts meet general prejudices for their representations of diasporic cultures but they also had to face long-standing biases against popular, allegedly lowbrow fiction. As this chapter focuses its attention on popular texts that are often condensed, homogenised, and racialised under the umbrella terms 'street' or 'urban' fiction, it simultaneously explores the problematic relationship between the diverse genre of inner-city fiction and dominant readings of these as mimetic, realist texts. Moving from the late 1980s to the 1990s, the first section revisits texts by, among others, Mike Phillips (1941–), Victor Headley (1959–), Sheri Campbell (1977–), and Courttia Newland (1973–), whose work in part surfaced as a counter-movement to highbrow literary texts that increasingly portrayed the migrant as a stylised representative of late twentieth-century modernity. Reaching into the twenty-first century, the second part of this chapter will address more recent black and Asian British popular textualities, like grime

---

[1] A notable exception is the first novel published by a black writer born in Britain, Norman Samuda Smith's *Bad Friday* (1982), whose protagonist is constantly torn between his aspirations for a professional basketball career and the easy money life of petty crime; Norman Smith, *Bad Friday* (Birmingham: Trinity Arts, 1982). A revised version was published in 1985 by New Beacon Books.

music and contemporary estate novels, as well as the films of Noel Clarke (1975–) and Menhaj Huda (1967–). All of these undoubtedly owe a great deal to popular inner-city novels but also define their own distinct artistic trajectories. While the emphasis here is on inner-city fictions, there are, of course, several other versions of the popular which warrant attention: such as afro- and retrofuturisms, neo-Victorian imaginaries, and romantic formats such as 'chick lit'. The same holds true for other literary forms whether popular theatre or performance poetry. When writing about black *and* Asian British popular forms, it is necessary to treat each area as a separate and unique strand. Both draw upon a multitude of experiences and heritages and each comprises a heterogeneous field of written and audiovisual material. Despite this they can be read comparatively through the concept of the frontline. In considering how these distinct textualities contest dominant representations of marginalised inner-city communities, this focus will enable a productive analysis across a variety of genres.

Popular Nobrow and the Frontline: Spaces of Contestation

The texts discussed here have most often been located in a tradition of writing that is considered as 'committed to realist representations, drawing on genres developed by the classical realist tradition and adhering to a mimetic ontological agenda'.[2] The emphasis on these presumably 'authentic' representations of inner-city, multiethnic, working-class experience usually comes with a strong focus on content, neglecting the texts' investment in narrative form. In contrast, white nineteenth-century realist novels are commonly interpreted as artful literary constructions, and critics repeatedly praise contemporary white social realist films for their arthouse qualities. The difference regarding these black realist texts, according to Victor Headley, is the degree of artistry and abstraction granted the authors in their craft: 'The assumption is that black authors writing about gangsters have lived the life, while white writers have done some research.'[3] In limiting black and Asian popular texts to their realist dimension, scholarship has thus racialised pre-existing hierarchies between 'the literary' and 'the popular'.

---

[2] Magdalena Maczyńska, 'The Aesthetics of Realism in Contemporary Black London Fiction' in R. Victoria Arana (ed.), *'Black' British Aesthetics Today* (Newcastle upon Tyne: Cambridge Scholars, 2007), 135–49; 135.

[3] Quoted in Andy Wood, 'Contemporary Black British Urban Fiction: A "Ghetto" Perspective?', *Wasafiri*, 17:36 (2006): 18–22; 22.

Heavily influenced by the Birmingham Centre for Contemporary Cultural Studies, British cultural studies have long re-evaluated popular forms as art forms unto themselves. This tradition also continues to provide a frame of reference for reading contemporary black and Asian popular fiction. It will be useful here to consider Peter Swirski and Tero Eljas Vanhanen's concept of 'nobrow culture' which

> situates itself outside the high-, middle-, and lowbrow divisions, even as it crisscrosses them all. As an aesthetic and creative strategy, it borrows freely from on high and from down below and shamelessly combines them into a seamless whole. This is to say that [. . .] nobrow embraces both the artistic strategies of high culture and the genre aesthetics of popular art.[4]

Describing how black and Asian popular forms plunder, manipulate, and bend cultural forms as well as literary conventions, this chapter acknowledges that these texts 'must be seen to represent a diverse and distinctive strand in contemporary Asian and black British expressive cultures' and that they must be read against 'hegemonic and reductive' interpretations.[5] In other words, such genre fiction is often driven by an emancipatory thrust, writing back against portrayals of a white hegemonic Britain. Acknowledging the complexities of black and Asian British experiences, these texts continually seek out new modes that challenge well-established literary norms, navigating their unique positionalities on the margins of Britain's various textual canons.

Such 'nobrow' sensibilities that are visible across a range of different media and genres are complemented by the frontline as a theoretical vantage point. Originally a military term, it was adopted in police jargon to designate urban 'no-go areas' where 'illegal' activities flourish. Since the 1980s, it has been transcoded by London's multiethnic communities and, most importantly here, by black British writers. Perceived as a hostile, racialising ascription to black and Asian communities as a whole, the (literary) frontline is most prominently exemplified by Railton Road in south London, which was the site of violent clashes between protesters and police during the 1981 Brixton Riots. It features heavily in David Simon's *Railton Blues* (1983), a partly disillusioned, partly defiant story of the racism that Caribbean migrants and

---

[4] Peter Swirski and Tero Eljas Vanhanen, 'Introduction: Browbeaten into Pulp' in Peter Swirski and Tero Eljas Vanhanen (eds.), *When High Brow Meets Low Brow: Popular Culture and the Rise of Nobrow* (New York: Palgrave Macmillan, 2017), 1–9; 8.

[5] Andy Wood, '"New Forms": Towards a Critical Dialogue with Black British "Popular" Fictions' in Gail Low and Marion Wynne-Davies (eds.), *A Black British Canon?* (Basingstoke: Palgrave Macmillan, 2006), 105–25; 123.

their British-born children encounter in Thatcher's Britain. Railton Road is also a key setting in the novels *Brixton Rock* (1999) and *East of Acre Lane* (2001) by Alex Wheatle (1963–). While the former retrospectively captures the lurking tensions before the riots, the events in *East of Acre Lane* unfold around the actual escalation along the frontline. Despite obvious political implications, the novel portrays the frontline as a dwelling place of black communal life threatened by the encroaching, racist police forces. The frontline is not simply a space that divides; it is a space where alternative lives can thrive beyond official, discriminatory confinements. This is uniquely expressed in David Miller's upbeat Brixtonian reggae anthem 'Swing & Dine': its chorus line, 'Swing an' dine, dance all the time / That's how we do it 'pon de Front Line', which also finds its way into *East of Acre Lane*, writes back to the police's official, punitive interpretation of the term.[6]

While the literary idea of the frontline originates in black British fiction, its conceptual relevance clearly extends to, and makes for productive readings of, Asian British literature as well. Many texts covered in this chapter are concerned with imaginaries of marginalised inner-city spaces. Given that several writers we discuss here come from Britain's traditionally multiethnic social housing communities and some, like Wheatle, even grew up around the frontline, there are multiple biographic, thematic, and aesthetic overlaps between these two strands. This is particularly true in the case of crime and inner-city novels and contemporary film-making. The frontline grasps how these texts have continuously pushed the boundaries of popular forms, of literary, cinematic, and musical aesthetics, publishing standards, and ultimately the politics of representing black and Asian British communities. In both its political and literary dimensions, the frontline, we suggest, is first and foremost a liminal zone where black and Asian Britons are able to generate novel imaginaries and claim their ground.

Black and Asian British Crime Fiction

The gradual influx of Black and Asian British popular fiction into the book market is often traced to *Blood Rights* (1989), the debut novel from black Britain's most influential crime fiction writer, Mike Phillips. With protagonist Samson 'Sam' Dean, Phillips inscribes a counter-figure into the hegemonically white canon of British detectives, and also adds to the existing palette of

---

[6] David Miller, 'Swing & Dine Dance All the Time'; cited in Alex Wheatle, *East of Acre Lane* (London: HarperPerennial, [2001] 2006), 279–80.

black private eyes in American crime fiction. Sam Dean is far from the archetypal all-knowing, imperial detective: like Phillips himself, Dean is of Guyanese descent, a black British journalist who operates outside official investigative structures. It is his liminal position as an educated black man of the press that enables him to move between Britain's diasporic communities and its white upper-class circles. His unique location allows the text to comment on the systemic injustices of the novel's 1980s frontline setting.

In *Blood Rights* and *The Late Candidate* (1990), Dean roams between a variety of settings, ranging from culturally diverse underground spaces to exclusively white upper-class neighbourhoods. Despite Dean's ability to cross rigid thresholds, he still faces some of the novel's larger sociopolitical issues: institutional racism, unwarranted police violence based on racial profiling, and the disproportionate incarceration of black people. The novels' political dimension is also evident in their subversion of the classic detective format. The fact that Phillips's protagonist is an expert on Victorian art can be read as a commentary on how the text borrows from the conventions of Victorian detective fiction.[7] Moreover, *Blood Rights* explores black British fatherhood through the complex metaphorical structure of the double: Roy Akimbola, the suspect Dean searches for, comes to resemble the detective's own son, and ultimately himself. Reminiscent of the classic Victorian addict-detective, dreamlike episodes, which take him to childhood memories or see him contemplate his own aspirations, interlace Dean's trips through black and Asian British milieus and his encounters with characters from various cultural backgrounds. The search for clues and truths in what is an intricate subversion of genre traditions becomes an interrogation, at times unpleasant, of the complexities of black British selfhood.

Among authors who have followed in Phillips's footsteps to produce innovative black British crime fiction is Zimbabwean-born writer Tendai Huchu (1982–). He extends the genre in his 2014 novel *The Maestro, The Magistrate & The Mathematician*, a murder mystery that eschews a classic detective figure and manipulates the rules of the genre. A story about the diasporic experiences of three expatriate Zimbabweans in Edinburgh, the novel's central crime, the murder of the mathematician Farai, only occurs towards the end of the text. In contrast to standard detective fiction, the reader is tasked not with solving but with anticipating it. Throughout,

---

7 Patricia Plummer, 'Transcultural British Crime Fiction: Mike Phillips's Sam Dean Novels' in Christine Matzke and Susanne Mühleisen (eds.), *Postcolonial Postmortems: Crime Fiction from a Transcultural Perspective* (Amsterdam; New York: Rodopi, 2006), 255–70; 262.

untranslated passages written in Shona offer critical clues about the murderer's secret identity, creating a second, closed-off narrative that escapes the Eurocentric frames of reference which so often prevail in canonical British detective fiction. The novel thus rewards readers with knowledge of Shona language and culture – and signals the inadequacy of reading *The Maestro* solely from a white, anglophone perspective. Other clues are only detectable with a precise knowledge of popular culture. The text uses the antagonists of the Pac-Man videogame series, a number of murderous ghosts, to foreshadow Farai's murder. These ghosts are not described, but printed as icons within the text. Introduced early on as symbols for Farai's many virtual deaths in an arcade he would visit in his youth in Harare, the reappearance of the ghosts in increasingly close intervals during his death-scene equates Farai's life with that of the player who is caught by the monsters.[8] The earlier the reader understands these clues, the earlier they solve the novel's central riddle. Huchu's radical blend of diasporic struggles and the detective genre, his mixture of Zimbabwean oppositional literature and black Scottish murder mystery relies heavily on this multimodal nobrow pastiche. *The Maestro* thus not only pushes the boundaries of the detective genre, but in so doing seeks out new literary forms of representing black diasporic experience in Britain.

In the less well-known field of Asian British crime fiction, several authors have brought forth a range of novels and series. Amer Anwar's thriller *Brothers in Blood* (2018) leads accidental detective Zaq Khan through Southall's multiethnic and multireligious neighbourhoods in search of a missing girl.[9] Kia Abdullah's *Child's Play* (2009) is equally gritty, despite its staggering density of light-hearted pop-cultural references. Her crime thriller about trapping paedophile sex offenders is provocative, often erotic, and at times grotesque, hyperbolically addressing uncomfortable questions about the infantilisation of Asian British women in contemporary culture. Abir Mukherjee's historical Sam Wyndham series about a traumatised World War I veteran plays out in 1919 Calcutta against the background of the British Raj.[10] Similarly, Vaseem Khan (1973–) draws on his British Indian upbringing in his storytelling. *The Unexpected Inheritance of Inspector Chopra* (2015), as well as subsequent novels, playfully explores more fantastic modes of crime fiction through the eyes of an Indian investigator and his companion

---

[8] Tendai Huchu, *The Maestro, The Magistrate & The Mathematician* (Cardigan: Parthian, [2014] 2015), 68, 278–9.

[9] The novel was previously published as *Western Fringes* in 2017.

[10] Abir Mukherjee, *A Rising Man* (London: Harvill Secker, 2016) and *A Necessary Evil* (London: Harvill Secker, 2017).

Ganesh, a small elephant. Khan's novels can be read as metaphysical detective stories that interrogate their own position as an Indian British variety of the genre. Retired inspector and self-proclaimed anglophile Ashwin Chopra receives the elephant as a gift from his uncle. In an accompanying letter, the elephant takes on a playful allegorical function, commenting on the text itself: 'elephants, like humans, are self-aware. They understand that they exist, and that they are individuals. An elephant can be taught to recognize itself in a mirror, just as a human child comes to this awareness.'[11] The elephant, like the text, understands that its own condition depends on its cultural location. When a veterinarian tells Chopra that perhaps 'this new environment has upset him' and that Ganesh 'may begin to settle', the text brings to the fore its own status as a metaphysical detective story transplanted into a new frame.[12] In knitting together crime plots with such self-reflexive episodes, Khan's Asian British crime fiction draws on and subverts the orthodoxies of mainstream detective fiction.

The X Press: Publishing Black British Pulp

The fact that we are even able to sketch the history of popular black and Asian British texts owes much to the independent publisher The X Press. The increasing presence of black British popular literature throughout the 1990s is inextricably tied to this press, founded in 1992 by journalists Oludotun 'Dotun' Adebayo and Steve Pope. In the pre-Zadie Smith era, the visibility of black and Asian British authors either depended on large mainstream publishers – who shied away from what were considered lowbrow manuscripts – or a small number of independent presses. Among these were New Beacon Books, Bogle-L'Ouverture, and Allison and Busby, which had all been set up during the 1960s with a commitment to publishing black and Asian writers.[13] Their demands for more traditional, or highbrow, literary merit, however, meant that overall they, too, excluded genre fiction for decades. The emergence of The X Press changed these modes of publication radically, churning out pop-fiction across a variety of genres such as romance, melodrama, and crime. Its output was immense and it quickly became a key platform for young, aspiring black British writers. In 2007, Adebayo estimated that The X Press had published more than 200 books by first-time authors,

[11] Vassem Khan, *The Unexpected Inheritance of Inspector Chopra* (London: Mulholland Books, 2015), 61–2.
[12] Ibid., 117.   [13] See Chapters 8 and 17.

many of whom had seen their manuscripts rejected by major publishers.[14] One such formerly rejected novel, Victor Headley's *Yardie* (1992), brought instant success to both press and author. Now described as heralding 'a new wave of black British pulp fiction',[15] *Yardie* – as well as its sequels *Excess* (1993) and *Yush!* (1994) – not only secured the budding X Press's survival but spawned what has arguably become the most recognisable black British popular genre, the inner-city novel. Within a few years, stories of second- or third-generation youths longing for better economic opportunities while tempted by the ambiguous structures of organised crime became increasingly popular: among others, Courttia Newland's and Alex Wheatle's fiction, *Rude Girls* (1996) by Vanessa Walters (1978–), and Stephen Thompson's *Toy Soldiers* (2000) would later help fashion the inner-city novel into a distinct genre. Although London stories made up the bulk of publications, some, like Karline Smith's Manchester-set *Moss Side Massive* (1994) and *Full Crew* (2002), decentred the genre's focus on the capital. With the arrival on the scene of BlackAmber (the publisher of Wheatle's *Brixton Rock*) in 1998 and Brown Skin Books in 2003, such popular presses 'carved out a niche for themselves on the fringes of the British publishing industry as specialist publishers of a wide range of black interest books', fundamentally transforming the publication of black and Asian British popular fiction.[16]

Fostering a transnational community in both author- and readership, The X Press signed up writers from various geographical backgrounds and, although they were overwhelmingly black, their fictional milieus were decidedly multiethnic, often including Asian British characters as well. Nevertheless, they predominantly link up the black diaspora across the UK, the Caribbean, and North America.[17] Its publications draw upon 'lived experience in Britain, avid reading in anticolonial and Black Power literature,

---

[14] James Silver, '"We Don't See Ourselves Represented on Screen at All" – Britain's First General Interest Black Internet TV Station Launches Later This Month. Founder Dotun Adebayo Talks to James Silver', *The Guardian*, 2 July 2007. Available at www.theguardian.com/media/2007/jul/02/mondaymediasection8.

[15] James Procter, 'Headley, Victor' in Alison Donnell (ed.), *Companion to Contemporary Black British Culture* (London; New York: Routledge, 2002), 139.

[16] Philippa Ireland, 'Laying The Foundations: New Beacon Books, Bogle L'Ouverture Press and the Politics of Black British Publishing', *E-rea* [En ligne], 11:1 (2013), n.p. Available at http://journals.openedition.org/erea/3524; DOI: 10.4000/erea.3524.

[17] Curdella Forbes, 'X Press Publications: Pop Culture, "Pop Lit" and Caribbean Literary Criticism: An Essay of Provocation', *Anthurium: A Caribbean Studies Journal*, 4:1 (2006): article 2; 5.

and immersion in Jamaican popular music, from roots reggae to ragga or jungle', allowing for critical analyses of the entwined histories of Caribbean and African immigration to Britain's cities.[18] The X Press published texts that often fuse popular forms such as crime fiction, 'street literature', romance, and erotica. These 'crossovers' playfully challenge borderlines in a literal, but also a figurative sense.[19] In this vein, Michael Maynard's *Games Men Play* (1996) and Patrick Augustus's *Baby Father* (1994)[20] use strategies common in Caribbean writing, such as 'multiple narrators, first person vernacular voices, musical rhythms and tropes, parody, rewriting and carnival laughter' to consciously 'modify the traditional pop approach to literature, in which the direction of the text is towards the story telling/exciting event rather than outwards "artistic" manipulations of form as aesthetic'.[21] The texts' capacity to manipulate and exploit literary conventions and popular forms creates its very own nobrow aesthetics. The X Press's investment in pushing boundaries manifested itself in selection, production, and circulation processes that ultimately upended distribution standards and advertising strategies. Whereas contemporary artists turn to YouTube channels and social media platforms to promote and circulate their work, it took more inventive ideas to advertise popular fiction before 2000. An infamous example is the press's advertising of Donald Gorgon's revenge fantasy *Cop Killer* (1994), which gained particular notoriety because it was sent out to buyers alongside empty bullet shells. Furthermore, individual X Press publications regularly announced events – such as Adebayo's own radio show – in the back of the books.

Despite these challenges to orthodox modes of production and advertising, the reception of Headley's *Yardie* trilogy epitomised the problematic assumption that black British popular fiction was only defined by mimesis and was thus distinct from 'highbrow' narrative fiction and its heightened emphasis on form. Andy Wood points to common misreadings of the trilogy, which mark it as either 'an "authentic" gangsta narrative or a morally damning indictment of black life'.[22] Contrary to these reductive, binary engagements, the novels' portrayal of communal life and black musical cultures, in particular, allows for more optimistic readings. Music assumes an almost tactile quality in *Yardie*: 'A heavy bass was thumping its way right through the walls,

---

[18] Loretta Collins, 'Raggamuffin Cultural Studies: X-Press Novels' Yardies and Cop Killers Put Britain on Trial', *Small Axe*, 5:1 (2001): 70–96; 72.

[19] Forbes, 'X Press Publications', 5.

[20] For a discussion of the TV series *Babyfather* based on Augustus's novel, see: Chapter 32.

[21] Forbes, 'X Press Publications', 12.   [22] Wood, 'Contemporary Black', 20.

spreading into the cold night air and guiding the late arrivals to the venue like a musical lighthouse.'[23] Much like Wheatle's work a few years later, Headley's novels use reggae tunes and dancehall raves as links across the trilogy that create dwelling places for Britain's black inner-city population to celebrate, interact, and bond. Rather than perpetuating stereotypes of black life in the metropolis, Headley's *Yardie* trilogy interrogates the multifarious problems that newly arrived black working-class migrants from the Caribbean had to face. While employing music as 'both a soundtrack and harbinger of metropolitan meltdown',[24] the novels' communal spaces and contoured, sympathetic characters, on the one hand, and their environment of crime and struggle, on the other, destabilise the early 1990s perception of inner cities as inherently violent and ruthless.

Although The X Press publications were accused of glamorising clichéd, toxic masculinities, reinforcing negative stereotypes, Sheri Campbell's often neglected erotica challenged the publisher's reputation as a purely male platform.[25] As Forbes writes, 'her books are at once a feminist manifesto (assertion of women's right to sexual enjoyment and expression) and an exploitation of male attitudes to women and sex'.[26] Her novels, such as *Rude Gal* (1997) and *Wicked in Bed* (1994), relish the exploration of multifaceted sexual fantasies in which black female desire can be played out uncondition-ally. Campbell's texts, however, are also acutely aware of their representa-tional dynamics as they address and distance themselves from fetishisations of the black body, both female and male. For instance, *Wicked in Bed* allows its hunky protagonist, Michael, to slip in and out of the role of a 'black stud fantasy', while it constantly expands and undermines what the text labels an incomplete, distinctly white, middle-class view of black masculinity.[27] As such, the book undercuts the power of the white gaze while imagining, for some at least, an ideal lover for a distinctly black female audience. Campbell's work paved the way for black female erotica mostly published and distrib-uted by small publishing houses like Vastiana Belfon's London-based Brown Skin Books. Never shy of deviant kink, graphic sex, *and* self-reflexivity, black female erotica complements the often complex narratives of insecure black male sexuality in the 1990s inner-city novels. This subgenre has, however, fallen short – with a few exceptions such as Saran Thornton's dream-like

[23] Victor Headley, *Yardie* (London: Pan Books, [1992] 2017), 87.
[24] Sukhdev Sandhu, *London Calling: How Black and Asian Writers Imagined a City* (London: HarperCollins, 2003), 342.
[25] Procter, 'Headley', 193.   [26] Forbes, 'X Press Publications', 10.
[27] Sheri Campbell, *Wicked in Bed* (London: The X Press, [1994] 1995), 5.

story 'Hotel Room' – of representing non-heteronormative relations and non-binary sexualities.[28]

While texts like Headley's exploit Caribbean, hypermasculine rudeboy culture as a significant storytelling device and female erotica mostly avoids the ganglands altogether, Vanessa Walters's *Rude Girls* is a confident roar against the otherwise male-dominated estate fiction of the 1990s. As their lives are slowly invaded by gang violence, the cocky female protagonists Shree, Paula, and Janice lend the novel an upbeat feminist touch that resonates with the girl power movement of the 1990s. It can be understood, in Paula's thoroughly self-conscious reflection, as 'a lecture about friendship being bigger than boyfriends'.[29] After Shree loses her unborn child when she gets caught up in a fight during the novel's gruesome climax, it is her friends that help alleviate her grief and tentatively begin to restore her good spirits, as is evident in the novel's final paragraph. In their company Shree manages to laugh again and, despite her trauma, the sunlit scene promises a glimmer of hope for their futures.[30] In contrast to most male-centred fiction – and notwithstanding the personal costs for each protagonist – the novel keenly stresses the redemptive capacity of adolescent female solidarity.

Courttia Newland and Alex Wheatle: Estate Fiction

The second half of the 1990s witnessed a steady increase in inner-city genre fiction. Authors like Alex Wheatle and Courttia Newland began to express their frustrations with how narrowly political think-tanks, the press, and even other literary texts had represented black working-class experience in London. In response, these writers began to forge their own fictions of the frontline. While Wheatle revisited Brixton's Railton Road and negotiated persistent issues of institutional racism at the turn of the century, Newland's novels established the estate as a key setting in popular black and Asian British fiction. While it is true, as Wood suggests in relation to Newland, that the 'characters and the voices [. . .] clearly reflect the ethnic make-up of the West London he was born and brought up in', these frontline fictions also explore the complex and often contradictory dynamics between the social realities of multiethnic Britain and the literary fiction they inspire.[31]

Newland's *The Scholar: A West Side Story* (1997) and its sequel, *Society Within* (1999), are not only foundational texts of the estate genre, but also

---

[28] These, as Kate Houlden shows in Chapter 34, are increasingly represented elsewhere.
[29] Jennifer Walters, *Rude Girls* (London: Pan Books, 1996), 321.   [30] Ibid., 322.
[31] Wood, 'Contemporary Black', 21.

highly self-referential novels that play with and deconstruct the cliché of the estate as a lawless space of rampant criminality and the breeding ground for generations of black delinquent teenagers. Central to such an understanding is these novels' sustained deliberation about their own status as works of art that undercut and contextualise their focus on the crime-related downward spiral that most of their protagonists inhabit. On a basic level, *The Scholar's* steady evocation of other texts, even in its subtitle, stresses an awareness of its literary and cinematic sources. We find the same self-awareness in its connection of space and multiperspectivity: *The Scholar* and, even more so, *Society Within*, build their narrative forms around the estate, mirroring the council housing's dense architecture, with each multi-unit block comprising numerous flats. Similarly, storylines are focalised through different characters and blend into each other, creating a patchwork of enclosed yet interlocked segments. Set in different flats and a range of other spaces in and around the fictional Greenside Estate, Newland's novels embrace a kaleidoscopic multi-perspectivity that mirrors the estate's physical appearance yet resists simplistic perceptions of estate life. Even though such novels have often been defined by their 'brutalist' and less than optimistic realism,[32] Fatima Kelleher reminds us that, 'within each shadowy, brick-laden tale of grim reality, is the vestige of hope'.[33] Newland provides rich insights into the multicultural estate community and engages with the estate as a vital space within the city, successfully creating its own microcosm. In opening up this vision, Newland's work connects with larger political issues such as police misconduct and local crime networks that flourish in the face of governmental neglect.

Newland's visceral and at times almost unbearably gory realism has overshadowed other features of his work, such as frequent text-within-a-text structures. A key sequence in *The Scholar*, for example, sees the protagonist Sean relate the events of the novel to a friend. He reflects on the very possibility of narrating estate life, which invariably becomes an abstraction, a 'tale' that is 'divorced from reality'.[34] Here, *The Scholar* clearly acknowledges the distinction between the reality of growing up around the estate's criminal structures – as Newland did – and the novel's artistic reimagination

---

[32] Modhumita Roy, 'Brutalised Lives and Brutalist Realism: Black British Urban Fictions (1990s–2000s)' in Deirdre Osborne (ed.), *The Cambridge Companion to British Black and Asian Literature (1945–2010)* (Cambridge: Cambridge University Press, 2016), 95–109; 96.

[33] Fatimah Kelleher, 'Concrete Vistas and Dreamtime Peoplescapes: The Rise of the Black Urban Novel in 1990s Britain' in Kadija Sesay (ed.), *Write Black, Write British: From Post Colonial to Black British Literature* (London: Hansib, 2005), 241–54; 246.

[34] Courttia Newland, *The Scholar* (London: Abacus, [1997] 2009), 136.

of this experience. Sean's hesitation thus anticipates and criticises readings of his story – and, by extension, the novel itself – as a direct, realist representation of his as well as Newland's life. Concluding, however, that '[u]nless you're *in* [the estate], you can't feel anything *about* it', the text addresses its own realist double bind, caught between abstraction and re-presentation: even though it is fiction, it is a fiction whose authorship is intimately reliant upon estate experience.[35] *The Scholar* emphasises that the margins of society, exemplified by estate communities, must write themselves to avoid being silenced, for which the novel chooses a distinctly popular form. The novel's constant explication of its protagonists' inner workings – their unspoken fears and motivations – consequently approximates being *of* their world. Similarly, and possibly evoking the author's own dilemmas, the fictional black writer Michael Weathers debates internally his rejected book proposals in *Society Within*. The novel interrogates the situation in which many writers of black popular fiction have found themselves, while the novel's very existence attests to the changes in the publishing industry. As both texts muse on the conditions of their own existence, they produce self-conscious estate narratives whose gritty realist descriptions are constantly punctured by reflections on the nature of their own genre allegiance to popular fiction.

As a counterpoint to its own, often clichéd representation of black working-class existence, *The Scholar* also draws on Victorian culture. Relying on the nineteenth-century literary figure of the double, the text deftly inverts the roles of the 'scholar' Sean and the 'criminal' Cory, signalling its intertextuality and structural indebtedness to canonical pre-texts such as Robert Louis Stevenson's *The Strange Case of Dr Jekyll and Mr Hyde* (1886) and Charlotte Brontë's *Jane Eyre* (1847). The conflict in Brontë's novel between Jane and her racialised Other, Bertha Mason, is referenced when Cory is torn between the sensible, pious, and supportive Rosie and the 'mad woman', his girlfriend and partner in crime, Tanya.[36] However, *The Scholar* places this romantic conflict out in the open and, unlike Bertha, we get to know and like Tanya. Such references are framed and interrogated by the text's frequent juxtaposition of London's surviving Victorian spaces and the contemporary housing estate. By using such strategies, the novel positions itself as a deliberately anti-canonical revision of English literary history while at the same time emphasising its own literariness and fictionality. *The Scholar*'s central Manichean binaries such as 'Jane' vs 'Bertha', Victorian London vs the

---

[35] Ibid.   [36] Ibid., 66.

estate, school vs crime warn the reader away from taking the story for a direct reflection of estate life.

Newland's investment in the genre of the black British popular ventures beyond the containment of the novel form. Some editions of *Society Within* came with a CD, capturing a broadcasting session of the novel's pirate radio station Midnight FM.[37] As with *Yardie*, *Brixton Rock*, and *East of Acre Lane*, Newland's novels pulsate with black British musical sounds. *The Scholar's* textual soundscape is laced with jungle rhythms that fuse ragga, rave, and pop, whereas the timbre of its sequel, *Society Within*, is set to British garage. This shift from dub and reggae to those black British musical forms emergent in the 1990s symbolised an important 'coming of age', as Kelleher puts it, 'for a generation of Black descendants born and bred within the British urban landscape'.[38] Similarly, *Junglist* (1995), by Two Fingers (Andrew Green) and James T. Kirk (Eddie Otchere), first published in Boxtree's 'Backstreets' series, is an experimental, almost Joycean trip through London's underground.[39] The novel employs jungle as a literary soundscape to create an alternative form of black subjectivity for its characters. While listening to jungle, the protagonists are transported into an alternative, imaginary environment and find themselves in a state free from social norms and oppressions. Like *Yardie*, these texts point to the sonic experience of the estate but in ways that transcend music, particularly in their attention to spoken language.[40] They capture the vernacular of 1990s black youth culture on the page, along with a range of other Caribbean and Asian British versions of street language. It is especially in its attentiveness to musical forms and spoken languages that estate fiction grasps the complexities of multiethnic working-class experience beyond reductive interpretations as criminal 'urban' or 'street' culture.

While Newland sets his fiction in the 1990s, Alex Wheatle's *Brixton Rock* and *East of Acre Lane* look back to the repression of the early Thatcher years and the growing tensions that eventually erupted during the so-called Brixton Riots in April 1981.[41] *East of Acre Lane* nods to Wheatle's personal experience of the disturbances by including the semi-autobiographical DJ Yardman Irie (Wheatle's real stagename at the time) in its ensemble cast. The novel's realist

---

[37] Wood, 'Contemporary Black', 21.   [38] Kelleher, 'Concrete Vistas', 250.

[39] Sukhdev Sandhu, 'The Strange Case of Rave-Culture Pulp-Fiction', *Frieze*, 20 June 2013. Available at https://frieze.com/article/music-26.

[40] See Chapter 19 on sonic solidarities and dub.

[41] See Chapter 33 for more information on Wheatle's later novels *Liccle Bit* and *Crongton Knights*.

settings and style, however, owe as much to historical documentation as they do to deliberate, transparent fictionalisations.[42] Jah Nelson, a Caribbean Rastafari first introduced in *Brixton Rock*, reappears in *East of Acre Lane* to comment on the novel's fragile balance between history and fiction. Speaking to the protagonist Biscuit about the philosophical question of historical truths, Nelson counsels that he 'affe unlearn wha' you 'ave learned'[43] and instead he devises a collage-like account of a global black history that ranges from precolonial African civilisations to the fictional origins of the sphinx, and from the mythical Nubian king Memnon's involvement in the siege of Troy to contemporary identifications of black British youths as African. Nelson's tour de force exposes the trappings of linear, allegedly rational, and objective histories written about, not by, black people and that have continually marginalised their existence. Through Nelson, *East of Acre Lane* argues for the value of speculative, sometimes even counterfactual, black narrations that challenge, counterbalance, and rewrite white hegemonic historiographies. In devising such a semi-fictional, empowering history of black experience, *East of Acre Lane* makes transparent its own approach: like Nelson, the novel, too, reclaims contested histories because it reimagines the early Thatcher years, and particularly the so-called Brixton Riots, from the marginalised perspective of the local black community. Apart from the realism of Wheatle's historical settings and the range of black vernaculars in his texts, his early novels provide potent, self-reflexive, historical black British counter-narratives that testify to estate fiction's ability to reclaim the prerogative of interpretation over marginalised inner-city spaces and their communities.

Estate of the Art: Grime and Contemporary Inner-City Fictions

By the early twenty-first century, grime music and video culture had become one of the most productive art forms negotiating black experience within inner-city estate communities, inspiring both literature and film. Originating from the Crossways 'Three Flats' council estate in east London, grime emerged as a counterpoint in the early noughties to UK garage's increasingly shiny and commodified rave culture, which by the late 1990s had lost much of

---

[42] Wheatle acknowledges not only his own lived experience of the Brixton Riots, but in particular the Government's Scarman Report into the Brixton Riots, which served as an inspiration for the novel; Wheatle, *East of Acre Lane*, 308.

[43] Wheatle, *East of Acre Lane*, 161.

its edge. With its experimental fusion of self-made electronic beats and rap techniques, grime provided a fruitful ground for young, aspiring black musicians to explore new ways of expression. Its fast-paced breakbeats that are influenced by garage, jungle, and dubstep as well as its sharp, angry, and defiant audiovisual characteristics speak out against the disenfranchisement of the estate's working class. Since then, grime has increasingly started to reclaim the estate as both a spatial entity and a signifier in public discourse. Already, in its initial stages, grime achieved a heightened self-awareness as a subversive, popular black British art form. On his 2004 track 'Wot Do U Call It?', Wiley (Richard Kylea Cowie; 1979–) pokes fun at attempts to label his music, implying that preconceived categories such as 'garage' or 'two-step' deny his prototypical grime tracks their novelty value. Playing on classic call-and-response structures, the song's hook 'What do you call it, "urban"?' disarms this term as a racialised signifier that homogenises and devalues black cultural production.[44] In so doing, the lyrics bring out Wiley's awareness of the loaded relationship between popular black British musical forms and the mainstream public. Through its confidence, estate aesthetics, and verbal mocking of critics and authorities, grime has amplified the affirmative narratives of black inner-city life and more optimistic moments which already permeated 1990s frontline fictions. Although many tracks tackle issues specific to the realities of black communities in post-recession Britain, the grime scene has produced an inclusive sound that bridges differences among disenfranchised, multiethnic, working-class youths. More recently, grime, as a popular form, has not only been torn between commodification and the struggle to represent estate life but has followed in dub's footsteps and gained political weight as a voice for marginalised inner-city communities.[45] In particular, grime artists' reactions to the fire at Grenfell Tower reinforced this perception among the public. On 14 June 2017, a fire broke out at Grenfell Tower in North Kensington, west London, turning the multiethnic social housing block into a death trap. Dozens of people were injured and killed during the incident. Prior to the fire, the government had long ignored residents' demands for refurbishment and safety measures. The incident bears parallels to the 1981 New Cross fire in south-east London, during which thirty-one people were killed without anyone being charged. Like the resulting Black People's Day of Action after the New Cross fire, the incident at Grenfell Tower has mobilised community residents and activists

[44] Wiley, 'Wot Do U Call It?', *Treddin' on Thin Ice* (XL Recording, 2004).
[45] See Chapter 19 for dub poetry's political impact and the distinct sound of resistance.

alike. In an act of solidarity, Stormzy (Michael Omari; 1993–) performed a medley at the 2018 BRIT Awards in which the vocal supporter of Labour leader Jeremy Corbyn fired lyrical shots at Prime Minister Theresa May, asking her directly about the government's lack of financial aid for the victims: 'Where's the money for Grenfell?'[46] Stormzy and other fellow grime artists have since actively contributed to keeping alive the discussion around the tragedy at Grenfell Tower, repeatedly accusing political representatives of neglecting the affected estate community and their demands.

Grime's political impact is intimately linked to the ways it foregrounds questions of race and, if often more subtly, gender. Following suit with earlier forms of rudeboy culture, grime often provides yet another 'pugilistic context for the theatrics of masculinity to be played out', encouraging 'young black men to assert themselves using the most valuable currency available: masculinity'.[47] At the same time, a number of grime tracks and videos explicitly subvert the stereotype of the aggressive male black body and critique its public perception, among them 'Shutdown' (2016) by Skepta (Joseph Junior Adenuga; 1982–).[48] The track is interrupted by sonic and thematic breaks, sampling a complaint call that ITV received after a performance by Kanye West and a large number of grime MCs at the 2015 BRIT awards: 'A bunch of young men all dressed in black dancing extremely aggressively on stage, it made me feel so intimidated and it's just not what I expect to see on prime time TV.'[49] Through their sheer numbers, and two flamethrowers intersecting with the bleak grey background imagery, West's performance not only made a massive black presence visible at such a popular event but provocatively overemphasised the supposed dangers of a large, predominantly black and male crowd. With many prominent grime artists including Skepta, Stormzy, and Krept & Konan present, and given the regulated setting of a major awards show, the performance subverted the racialisation of the male black body as dangerous and 'always already

---

[46] Stormzy, 'Blinded by Your Grace Pt. 2 & Big for your Boots [Live at the BRITs 18]', *YouTube*, 22 February 2018. Available at https://www.youtube.com/watch?v=ReY4yVkoDc4, 02:29–02:31.

[47] Jeffrey Boakye, *Hold Tight: Black Masculinity, Millennials and the Meaning of Grime* (London: Influx, 2017), 359.

[48] Skepta appropriates 'shutting down' (read: selling out) as a direct reference to the infamous Form 696, which made it legal for authorities such as the Metropolitan Police to cancel concerts on suspicion of a heightened crime risk. This legislation affected grime artists and other black British musicians in significantly higher proportions than white artists.

[49] Skepta, 'Shutdown', *Konnichiwa* (Boy Better Know, 2016).

weaponized'.[50] Performed to be televised, it made visible the constant surveillance, profiling, and racialisation of the male black body when the group on stage eventually dropped down, almost crouching to West's lyrics 'Get low, alright / [. . .] / Stay low, alright'. Looking left and right, and reaching out and holding on to one another as if to protect themselves, the overtly masculine, faux-aggressive spectacle of the show shifted in tone to expose the misconception and generalisation of black men as threatening. The music video to Skepta's track, which refers to the show directly through the aforementioned sample, further undercuts the fear of what is constructed as a hooded black 'mob'. After opening with a diverse, cheerful crowd, the sampled call visually homogenises and racialises the group as an indistinguishable, dangerous Other, reflected in their all-black attire. While some male artists challenge the toxic masculinities that haunt grime, female MCs are gradually rising through the ranks with feminist acts of subversion. Femcee Lady Leshurr (Melesha O'Garro) plunders meme culture and exploits Queen Elizabeth II for her own character Queen L, while Nadia Rose in her eponymous track reclaims the street from the largely male groups featured in most grime videos with her female 'Skwod'.

Just as reggae, dub, and jungle were central to inner-city fiction in the 1990s, recent novels have started to incorporate grime and contemporary British rap. In Alex Wheatle's *Liccle Bit* (2015), the youths now chill and listen to 'rap, grime, and R&B',[51] and for young Ardan, one of the protagonists in Guy Gunaratne's estate novel *In Our Mad and Furious City* (2018), grime changes the way he perceives his surroundings, as the estate setting transforms into a 'place of ill-purpose, full of sketchy humour and distinction' while he listens to Skepta's tracks.[52] Complementing these literary contacts with grime, Nigerian German London-based author Olumide Popoola (1975–) tells a long overdue story in *When We Speak of Nothing* (2017): set against the 2011 London 'riots', the novel centres on Karl, its black transgender protagonist, and his best friend Abu. Traversing this new frontline, the text queers the estate and responds to its typical portrayals as a hypermasculine space with Karl slowly embracing his transgender identity. Read against grime culture's literally loud proclamation of masculinity, Popoola's use of silence as a motif stresses the importance of

---

[50] Christina Sharpe, *In the Wake: On Blackness and Being* (Durham, NC; London: Duke University Press, 2016), 16.
[51] Alex Wheatle, *Liccle Bit* (London: Atom, 2015), 23.
[52] Guy Gunaratne, *In Our Mad and Furious City* (London: Tinder Press, 2018), 59.

voices like Karl's that are often drowned out in discussions of estate experience as well as grime culture as a whole.

This revisiting of the estate novel genre perhaps also occurs in response to the significant inner-city relocation that Britain's cities have undergone since New Labour's increasing privatisation of social housing and the resulting gentrification that the country continues to witness today. Nikesh Shukla (1980–) tackles this issue in *Run, Riot* (2018), in which a group of teenage friends expose a high-level con-spiracy between a property development company, corrupt policemen, and the local government to relocate estate residents. Rapping prota-gonist Taran's lyric 'However it starts, it has to be loud' sparks the residents' protest against their forced relocation and functions as a metaphor for music to ignite grassroots movements and give a voice to estate residents.[53] Shukla's earlier young adult novel *Coconut Unlimited* (2010) uses music to explore the identity formation of its three protagonists through their shared desire for a rap career. Moving back and forth between a predominantly white private school and multiethnic backstreets, its Asian British characters defy the strictly racialised oppositions of insider and outsider, tradition and progression. Balancing bhangra tunes and US hip-hop, the novel acknowledges cultural heritages that inform British Asian musical styles, amalgamating these in its literary songscape. Whilst grime as we have seen has started to seep into literary texts, black and Asian British popular film also displays a strong preoccupation with its music video culture.

Popular Black and Asian British Film

Courttia Newland's multi-unit forms have been neatly translated into the music-video aesthetics of the film *Kidulthood* (2006) along with its sequels, *Adulthood* (2008) and *Brotherhood* (2016). *Kidulthood*, a black and Asian British co-production, written by Noel Clarke and directed by Bangladeshi-born director Menhaj Huda, is a distraught collage of entangled teenage lives in central London. Told from various perspectives, like Newland's novels, *Kidulthood* negotiates estate life between expressions of community, escap-ism, and catastrophe. In remediating music video's fast-paced edits, the film interweaves black popular culture to establish its own distinct aesthetics,

---

[53] Nikesh Shukla, *Run, Riot* (London: Hodder Children's Books, 2018), 7.

creatively undermining the orthodoxies of a predominantly white British social realism. Britain's early 2000s rap artists, such as Shystie (Chanelle Scott Calica) and Akala (Kingslee James Daley), provide the beats for this film's racy storyline. For example, Dizzee Rascal's (Dylan Mills) grime music is present both sonically and in its visual 'boy in the corner' aesthetics.[54] As a device, it creates a cheeky and upbeat mood that contributes to the film's subversive, distinctly black and Asian British realist mode. When Trevor, the main protagonist, dies after being attacked by his rival Sam, we are provided with a powerful commentary on the persistent issue of violence in intra- and inter-estate community clashes.

Several other films have been influenced by *Kidulthood*, including Somali British director Mo Ali's *Shank* (2010). The film is set on estates in the wastelands of a post-apocalyptic London, a scenery reminiscent of Ngozi Onwurah's *Welcome II the Terrordome* (1995).[55] The decaying metropolis now houses ravaging street gangs that compete, knife, and kill over the most valuable good, 'munchies' (food). Pop-cultural references to music videos and video games are as much part of the film as its allusions to *Kidulthood*, with which it shares a production company. Borrowing heavily from the aesthetics of the zombie film genre, *Shank* is reminiscent of other now-canonical London horror films (such as *28 Days Later*) in its critique of neoliberal capitalism's corrosion of British society. However, *Shank*'s mixture of estate drama and horror movie projects the common misrepresentation of council estates as violent, morally decaying spaces into an immediate dystopian future; this ultimately unmasks political neglect and socioeconomic inequality as the actual horrors that result in, among others, violence between marginalised, multiethnic communities.

While Clarke wrote, directed, and starred in the subsequent films of the *Kidulthood* trilogy, Huda went on to direct *Everywhere + Nowhere* (2011). Diving into the world of DJ-ing and staying true to Huda's emphasis on musical styles, the film uses its underground setting to

---

[54] See Chapter 23 for more information on the use of diasporic space in Dizzee Rascal's lyrics. Dizzee Rascal's debut album, *Boy in Da Corner*, has today assumed cult status as *the* grime classic; it has influenced the scene and other engagements with grime significantly through its experimental, quirky aesthetics. In particular, its black and yellow colour scheme has found its way onto the covers of primary and secondary texts, among them Wheatle's *Liccle Bit*, Boakye's *Hold Tight*, and Dan Hancox's *Inner City Pressure: The Story of Grime* (London: WilliamCollins, 2018), which even copies the font used on *Boy in Da Corner*.

[55] For more information on *Welcome II the Terrordome*, see Chapter 32.

negotiate Asian British subjectivities through its protagonist, Ash. His development, from wandering through raving crowds to performing centre stage, mirrors Asian British film's current, steadily growing attraction to popular musical forms. Ash's DJ-ing suggests agency in a multiethnic setting and the film also features an Asian British actor, James Floyd. The fusion of Indian sounds and popular breakbeats connects Asian British youths to one another; but Ash also reaches out to other communities, establishing new alliances as well as creating a confident, empowering, and original soundtrack for a generation of young Asian Britons, which has become a vital part of the UK's inner-city soundscapes. In its intermedial aesthetics, *Everywhere + Nowhere* is paradigmatic for both black and Asian British popular film, whose meaning-making processes increasingly depend on their capacity to remediate and seamlessly venture between film, music, and literary fiction.

Conclusion

Black and Asian British popular forms deserve readings that go beyond the established critical focus on realism. As we have seen, such texts are weaving (however unevenly) their own cultural and literary genealogies by way of intertextual and intermedial connections, by echoes and citations, by endorsement and repudiation. Inescapably subject to narrowly racialised readings, these frontline fictions are in dialogue with their corresponding real-life settings, developing self-reflexive narratives that engage with and subvert discourses of the 'street' or the 'urban'. While Phillips's protagonist Sam Dean undercuts the white hegemonic canon of British detectives, Headley's deliberate exploration of rudeboy and sound cultures is complemented by Campbell's erotica and Walters's focus on women's unity. By way of contrast, the form of Newland's estate fiction draws heavily on multi-unit estate architecture and explores inner-city life as much as it debates the divide between low- and highbrow culture and its own 'popular' position. Recent literary and cinematic texts such as Huda's films or Gunaratne's and Popoola's novels are heavily indebted to these aesthetics and have themselves drawn attention to the porosity of such distinctions. Cross-pollination between different media is a key feature of these popular texts, which often draw on current musical trends and constantly test the boundaries of their representational forms. Just as dub and reggae were key influences for earlier estate fiction, today grime has started to open conversations about the state of post-recession Britain, a theme that contemporary directors, writers, and poets have incorporated. Acknowledging such developments, it will be productive for future scholarship to draw on the manifold creative – and often highly sub-versive and self-reflexive – strategies of black and Asian British popular textualities.

37

Reimagining Africa
Contemporary Figurations by African Britons

MADHU KRISHNAN

Early in the pages of *Trumpet* (1998) by Jackie Kay (1961–), narrator and grieving widow Millie Moody finds herself musing over the strange fact that, despite its central presence in her late husband's work and their lifetime of world travels, neither she nor he had ever seen the African continent:

> We never actually got to go to Africa. Joss had built up such a strong imaginary landscape within himself that he said it would affect his music to go to the real Africa. Every black person has a fantasy Africa, he'd say. Black British people, Black Americans, Black Caribbeans, they all have a fantasy Africa. It is all in the head.[1]

Here, this notion of a 'fantasy Africa' renders itself as something of a site of longing, an aspiration whose realisation would be its undoing. Yet, at the same time, there is another side to this fantastical, imagined place, one echoed in the sardonic observations of the unnamed narrator at the centre of *Harare North* (2009) by Brian Chikwava (1972–). Observing the audience at a London concert, he notes how:

> Southbank is crawling with them Africans in they colourful ethnic clothes it make you feel like you is not African enough. Many of them is also them lapsed Africans because they have live in London from the time when it was OK to kill kings, queens and pigs. You can tell because they carry smiles like they have take over the palaces at last. We is only one wearing jeans.[2]

These two quotations come from two very different novels written by authors who may be thought of as African Britons; each text, in its own way, contends with the lived presence of characters from African backgrounds within the United Kingdom and the spectre of the continent in daily life. Despite this broadly defined shared heritage and preoccupation, however,

---

[1] Jackie Kay, *Trumpet* (London: Picador, [1998] 2011), 34.
[2] Brian Chikwava, *Harare North* (London: Vintage, [2009] 2010), 137.

the significant differences between *Trumpet* and *Harare North* attest to the inherently problematic nature of any attempt to define or delineate the parameters of 'African' experience, writ large, in Britain. The one, a story of love and mourning set largely in Scotland and told through a multiracial panoply of narrative voices which together invoke a kind of jazz, and the other a tale of dissociation and paranoia voiced by the spectral consciousness of an unrepentantly malicious narrator in a hybridised form of English, Shona, Ndebele, Caribbean patois, and slang, these two texts invoke the polarities that seem to define the presence of 'Africa' as a symbolic and material entity in black British writing, simultaneously reifying and deconstructing the myths of homogeneity and immutability which apparently accompany its emergence. At the same time, these texts, when read together, attest to the wide range of strategies, purviews, and conceptual frameworks which translate the lived experience of Britons of African heritage in the twentieth and twenty-first centuries, gesturing towards the dynamic complex through which 'Africa' is both felt and realised in this larger body of work.

In *The Africa That Never Was: Four Centuries of British Writing about Africa*, Dorothy Hammond and Alta Jablow highlight 'the existence of a governing literary tradition in European and American popular writing on Africa'.[3] Based on an analysis of over 500 works of fiction and non-fiction, the authors stress the extent to which the 'Africa that emerges from the British tradition is a myth', used more often to 'support cultural values and mediate points of stress' in Britain itself than to reflect meaningfully on Africa.[4] Noting the ways in which 'Africa [has] remained a free field for the play of European fantasy' since the classical times,[5] the study identifies two sets of projections through which Africa has been represented in British writing: on the one hand, Africa is 'the pejorative negation of all the good traits of the British. [. . .] lewd, savage, instinctual, thoughtless', while, on the other, Africa 'represent[s] the former, now lost, values of the British' through the concept of the 'noble savage'.[6] In both cases, the onus of representation remains on the British subject, for whom Africa serves as little more than what Nigerian writer Chinua Achebe once termed 'a foil [. . .] a place of negations at once remote and vaguely familiar, in comparison with which Europe's own state of spiritual grace will be manifest'.[7] Hammond and Jablow are by no means alone in their observations. More recently, Achille Mbembe characterises the

---

[3] Dorothy Hammond and Alta Jablow, *The Africa That Never Was: Four Centuries of British Writing about Africa*, reprint edn (Long Grove, IL: Waveland Press, 1992), 8.
[4] Ibid.   [5] Ibid., 12.   [6] Ibid., 11.
[7] Chinua Achebe, *Hopes and Impediments* (New York: Anchor Books, 1998), 3.

representation of the African continent in Euro-American discourse through the two interlocking signs of 'the strange and the monstrous' and the intimately known, of whom we can 'give an account [. . .] in the same way we can understand the psychic life of the *beast*', so pervasive in their repeated emergence as to create a discursive field almost impossible to escape.[8] Implicitly tied to the realm of the material through the ways in which 'meaning emerges from and accrues to the discursive object, "Africa"' such that it 'becomes located and defined as an object of knowledge', the 'tradition' of writing Africa in Britain emerges as a field of contradictions and fissures.[9]

While the pernicious tensions which accompany the act of writing – or writing about – Africa in the British context have been discussed primarily through the lens of race and racism, foregrounding the persistent patterns and often-arbitrary rhetorical categorisation of the so-called 'dark' continent by white authors, they simultaneously may be read as the backdrop against which black and Asian British writers engage with the continent in all of its diversity. Africa's literary genealogies – both as token and signifier but also as a real, material geography that has entered the literary imagination – remain closely intertwined; this is irrespective of whether they are viewed through the 'writing back' paradigm or through a more complex aesthetic engagement with the a priori image of Africa and its attendant representations. Indeed, even the delineations of what constitutes an 'African Briton' in this context attest to the complexity of its genealogical and rhetorical history, with a significant risk of reifying the homogenising impulse which undergirds exoticist objectifications in ostensibly postcolonial contexts.[10] What, that is to say, are the stakes at play and risks associated with proposing a subjective category in which figures as diverse as Nigerian émigré Ben Okri (1959–) and half-Scottish, half-Sierra Leonean Aminatta Forna (1964–) stand as equivalents? Or second-generation British writers such as Helen Oyeyemi (1984–) and Britons of African heritage such as Abdulrazak Gurnah (1948–)? These are questions which remain both present and unresolvable, reflecting the futility which accompanies any effort to create straightforwardly unproblematic

---

[8] Achille Mbembe, *On the Postcolony* (Berkeley, CA: University of California Press, 2001), 1–2.

[9] Kadiatu Kanneh, *African Identities: Pan-Africanisms and Black Identities* (London: Routledge, 1998), 1; see also James Ferguson, *The Anti-Politics Machine: 'Development', Depoliticization, and Bureaucratic Power in Lesotho* (Cambridge: Cambridge University Press, 1990), 18.

[10] Graham Huggan, *The Postcolonial Exotic: Marketing the Margins* (London: Routledge, 2001), 18–19.

declarations about a landmass larger than Europe and North America, containing vastly different cultural traditions, historical genealogies, and ecosystems.[11] Equally, it is vital not to erase the longer history and tradition of Africans and peoples of African heritage writing in and from Britain, with a view to exposing their reality as individuals attaching simultaneously and variously to both places.[12] From Olaudah Equiano's *The Interesting Narrative*, published in 1789, to Ernest Marke's *Old Man Trouble* (1975), these early writings, memoirs, and reflections demonstrate the *longue durée* of entanglement that has defined Britain's relationship with the African continent, and vice versa. Noting the importance of these foretexts, in what remains of this chapter my focus will turn to twentieth- and twenty-first-century texts that foreground the tensions, dynamics, and multiplicities which have come to define what it is to write Africa as a Briton, tracing the ways in which contemporary writers build upon the legacies and genealogies of writing, aesthetic production, and rhetoric from which their work springs, sometimes enabling and sometimes subverting the 'image of Africa' in Britain with its elision of the discursive and the material, the incommensurable and the already-known, the strange and the familiar.

De-Territorialising and Re-Territorialising 'Fantasy Africa'

In his 1925 poem 'Heritage', Harlem Renaissance poet Countee Cullen asks the question, 'What is Africa to me?', a query that captures the spectral presence of the continent in the imaginative landscapes of the Black Atlantic, and emphasises the particularities of displacement which resonate in the African American context within which he works. In the context of black Britain, it is perhaps more apt to consider the notion that, in the words of Jackie Kay's novel *Trumpet* quoted earlier, 'every black person has a fantasy

---

[11] The difficulty of periodising writing and writers in this manner is explored in Mark U. Stein, *Black British Literature: Novels of Transformation* (Columbus, OH: Ohio State University Press, 2004), 5–6; the geographical problems which arise in attempts to delineate 'Africa' as a bounded space are discussed in Ziad Bentahar, '"Continental Drift": The Disjunction of North and Sub-Saharan Africa', *Research in African Literatures*, 42:1 (2011): 1–13.

[12] Excellent and comprehensive histories of early writing by African Britons can be found in C. L. Innes, *A History of Black and Asian Writing in Britain*, 2nd edn (Cambridge: Cambridge University Press, 2008); David Dabydeen (ed.), *The Black Presence in English Literature* (Manchester: Manchester University Press, 1985); Paul Edwards and David Dabydeen (eds.), *Black Writers in Britain, 1760–1890* (Edinburgh: Edinburgh University Press, 1991).

Africa', a refrain which has resounded across the landscape of African British writing from its earliest incarnations to the present day. Though largely focused on the interlinked notions of grief, love, and loss, *Trumpet*, which explores the aftermath of the death of Joss Moody, a mixed-parentage jazz trumpeter exposed on his death as a transgender man, is haunted by the shadow of this fantasy of the continent, metonymically connected to its larger exploration of the dialectics of loss and belonging. Africa the continent, as ancestral home to black diasporas the world over, comes to function as a signifier of unfulfilled desire, articulated at one point in the novel by Colman, Joss's adopted son, whose own search for acceptance functions as a counterpoint throughout the novel:

> If I'd got the chance, I'd have probably liked to see a photograph of my mother and one of my father. I don't even know which one was black or where the black one came from. Haven't got a clue. People are always coming up to me and asking if I'm from Morocco, Trinidad, Tobago, Ghana, Nigeria, Sierra Leone, Jamaica.[13]

In *The Postcolonial Exotic*, Graham Huggan argues that there exists a tendency, when approaching the global South, to conflate geographies in a manner which 'creates an impression of *interchangeability* of highly discrepant cultural/historical experiences'.[14] Marking a failure of nuance and a bland homogenisation of 'the Other' in which the exigencies of experience are placed under erasure, this is a tendency that has been repeatedly cited by critics as emblematic of the British approach to the African continent. On first appearance, then, Coleman's expression of a desire for origins, articulated through the metonymic slippage between the absent space of the biological parent and the litany of places potentially read as home, might be read under this same system of meanings, reduced to an externalisation of the internalised 'oppression of the image'.[15] Yet, it is equally possible to perceive another interpretation, one in which the simultaneous yearning for a place and denial of its possibility transforms into a call for trans-Atlantic black solidarity which foregrounds the 'transcendent cultural commonalities' which cross amongst peoples of African descent.[16] Under this line of reasoning, Colman's bitter ruminations on his lack of origins, the impossibility of materialising and localising 'his' Africa, seem to stand in sharp contrast to Joss's exhortations that he 'make up [his] own bloodline [. . .] Make it up and

[13] Kay, *Trumpet*, 58. [14] Huggan, *Postcolonial Exotic*, 19.
[15] Pius Adesanmi, *You're Not a Country, Africa* (London: Penguin Classics, 2011).
[16] Ibid., 74.

trace it back. Design your own family tree', a move predicated on the performativity of being and the ultimately arbitrary notion of roots.[17] Indeed, when responding to Colman's pleas that he tell him the history of his own father, long dead, Joss only responds:

> I could tell you a story about my father. I could say he came off a boat one day in the nineteen hundreds, say a winter day. All the way from the 'dark continent' on a cold winter day, a boat that stopped at Greenock. Greenock near the port of Glasgow when Glasgow was a place all the ships wanted to go. He came off that ship and although it was cold and grey, he liked it. He liked Greenock so he settled. Or I could say my father was a black American who left America because of segregation [. . .] Or I could say my father was a solider or a sailor who was sent here by his army or his navy. Or I could say my father was from an island in the Caribbean whose name I don't know.[18]

Here, too, is a refusal of the particular, a return to a deterritorialised Africa, a generalised Africa so long thought to be a sign of victimhood and oppression, rewritten through its displacement into a radical site of agency and solidarity. A floating signifier – what Jean-Loup Amselle has referred to as a 'branchement',[19] or deterritorialised entity open to all who connect to it – which simultaneously refuses the fragmentation of postcolonialist visions of materiality, Africa is reframed, reborn, and realigned not as the always-already known space of loss and thwarted fulfilment but as the actualisation of an unspoken future anterior. If, as Kanneh suggests, 'it is vital to resist formations of a holistic African world, culture or worldview which can be discovered, recovered or re-appropriated',[20] then this move gestures towards the alternative potentialities encoded within the writing of black Britons, potentialities in which no such discovery or appropriation is possible because of the very intangibility of subversive and strategic alliance-making amplified by the exigencies of its displacement in British space.

The novel's final pages, titled 'The Last Word', attest to the ambivalent power of this story. Here, through a letter from deceased father to son, Colman is at last told the story of his grandfather, John Moore, a name not his own. Opening with the claim that 'his story could be the story of any black man who came from Africa to Scotland', a story of the diaspora which 'runs into the same river and the same river runs into the sea',[21] Joss's letter

---

[17] Kay, *Trumpet*, 58.   [18] Ibid., 58–9.
[19] Jean-Loup Amselle, *Branchements: Anthropologie de l'universalité des cultures* (Paris: Flammarion, 2001).
[20] Kanneh, *African Identities*, 43.   [21] Kay, *Trumpet*, 271.

outlines his father's journey from Africa – unspecified still – to Britain, given to a Scottish captain at the age of six by his own father to be taken to Scotland for his education. Arriving in a fog that 'the local people called [. . .] a "real pea souper"',[22] John and his journey are described in terms of bewilderment, of confusion. Contrasting the cold, wet greyness of Britain, a land populated with 'shadow people [. . .] insubstantial, no colour', a country described as 'a wet ghost',[23] with his memories of Africa, his own country, 'the hot dust on the red road, the jacaranda tree, his mother's hot breath on his cheek',[24] he tries, and fails, to reach the continent through its hazy image in books and memory. Yet, even in this attempt to materialise Africa, to enliven it through the memory of John Moody, the continent remains oddly diffuse, known only through synechdochal parts which fail to attach to any specific geography: the 'hot dust' and 'red roads' which, in the global imaginary and British tradition outlined at the start of this essay, represent the otherworldly savagery of the continent unsettled through its syntactical contiguity with the universal image of a mother's protective love. Africa, as a totality, resists the urge to be pinned down into a single and fossilised image, while at the same time remaining open and unmoored, signifying only as a form of unfinished play.[25]

The ambivalence captured in the 'fantasy Africa' of Kay's novel is repeated across the larger body of writing by African Britons. Works with settings split between the African continent and Britain, including Helen Oyeyemi's *The Icarus Girl* (2005), Elaine Proctor's (1960–) *Rhumba* (2011), and Aminatta Forna's *The Memory of Love* (2010) and *Ancestor Stones* (2006), emphasise the contradictions at the heart of the imagined vision of the continent, while offering alternative paths towards solidarity both for people of African heritage and their white British compatriots.[26] In *Some Kind of Black* (1996) by Diran Adebayo (1968–), meanwhile, 'Africa' operates as an unwelcome spectre of a cultural nationalism rejected by self-consciously performative protagonist Dele, despite his increasing desire for a space of belonging and refuge.[27] Elsewhere, 'Africa' disappears entirely, replaced by a geographic and temporal specificity which reanimates the continent as a space of diverse – and not always congruent – histories, evidenced in texts such as *Tail of the Blue*

---

[22] Ibid. [23] Ibid. [24] Ibid., 273.

[25] See Henry Louis Gates, Jr., *The Signifying Monkey: A Theory of African-American Literary Criticism* (New York: Oxford University Press, 1988).

[26] Helen Oyeyemi, *The Icarus Girl* (London: Bloomsbury, 2005); Elaine Proctor, *Rhumba* (London: Quercus, 2011); Aminatta Forna, *The Memory of Love* (London: Bloomsbury, 2010); *Ancestor Stones* (London: Bloomsbury, 2006).

[27] Diran Adebayo, *Some Kind of Black* (London: Virago, 1996).

Bird (2009) by Nii Ayikwei Parkes (1974–), Ben Okri's *Famished Road* trilogy (also known as the Azaro trilogy; 1991, 1993, 1998), and *Black Mamba Boy* (2010) by Nadifa Mohamed (1981–).[28] Indeed, the slippages that define the way in which African Briton writers have variously engaged with the continent re-emerge in Kay's 2010 memoir *Red Dust Road*, a chronicle of the author's search to trace her birth parents. In a chapter entitled 'Fantasy Africa', Kay describes the little she knew about her African lineage:

> I was told two things, really. One: [my biological father] studied agriculture at the University of Aberdeen; two: he was from Nigeria. Nigeria was a country in West Africa and West Africa was very far away from Glasgow. Africa itself could only ever be imagined in the way that I imagined my father, with bright picture-book colours and bold outlines. Part of me came from Africa, part of me was foreign to myself, strange to myself since I have never been to the *dark continent* and could only really have it burning away, hot and dusty, in my mind. It is not so much that being black in a white country means that people don't accept you as, say, Scottish; it is that being black in a white country makes you a stranger to yourself.[29]

Where, for Gilroy, the double consciousness that mediates the experience of subjects in and from the Black Atlantic is defined by 'the inescapable hybridity and intermixture of ideas' marked by the forging of 'the stereophonic, bilingual, or bifocal cultural form[s]',[30] this notion of duality appears in Kay's memoir as an uncanny moment of estrangement. Marking the incommensurable simultaneity of two divergent, yet mutually dependent, temporal ecosystems, the African and the Scottish, this strangeness functions on a second level as an interiorisation of displacement.[31] Notable is the speed with which slippages occur in this passage, Nigeria becoming West Africa – measured against Glasgow – which again becomes 'Africa' as a whole. 'Hot and dusty', strange and known, this is an image of Africa in which the horror evoked by Joseph Conrad and the teleological retardation written by Joyce Cary telescope into the very fabric of subjective being, no longer able to act as a passive foil, enlivened in its rescripting of the self. Later in this section, Kay's narratorial voice recalls her discomfort on being taught about Africa – never

---

[28] Nii Ayikwei Parkes, *Tail of the Blue Bird* (London: Vintage, 2010); Ben Okri, *The Famished Road* (London: Jonathan Cape, 1991); Ben Okri, *Songs of Enchantment* (London: Vintage, 1993); Ben Okri, *Infinite Riches* (London: Phoenix House, 1998); Nadifa Mohamed, *Black Mamba Boy* (London: HarperCollins, 2010).

[29] Jackie Kay, *Red Dust Road* (London: Picador, 2010), 38.

[30] Paul Gilroy, *The Black Atlantic: Modernity and Double Consciousness* (Cambridge, MA: Harvard University Press, 1993), xi, 3.

[31] See Mbembe, *On the Postcolony*, 15.

very much – at school, a personal slight taken during lessons on the continent highlighting 'appalling poverty', 'grass skirts and tribal make-up', people with 'strange cuts in their faces to indicate their tribes', 'primitive, unsophisticated', sexualised, and made wild through its association with 'the jungle and bush, lions and elephants' juxtaposed with people no more than 'wild savages', 'bongo drums', 'witch doctors and strange wild dances, lots of chanting and humming and squealing'.[32] Directly addressing the tradition of writing Africa in Britain, that 'familiar colonial rhetoric of the timelessness of Africa, the emptiness of village life, locked in a fixed and lost dimension, the primitive savagery energising the episodic destruction of order',[33] a continent that has remained 'unchanged since the Stone Age, because Africans have neither the creativity nor desire to bring about any change',[34] Kay's recollections of these lessons foregrounds the ways in which the image of Africa betrays a 'generalising tendency to reduce the totality of empire to a type of savagery already known',[35] standing in stark contrast to the tactical, strategic, and solidarity-engendering generalisations articulated by characters like Colman and Joss Moody. Instead, here is a return to the irrationality that lies at the heart of discourse around Africa, the idea that African 'can only be understood through a *negative interpretation*',[36] captured in Conrad's vision of its inhabitants as little more than 'a whirl of black limbs, a mass of hands clapping, of feet stamping, of bodies swaying, of eyes rolling'.[37]

It is in response to this return, however, that 'Africa' eventually disappears in the memoir, replaced instead by Nigeria and, eventually, Igboland and the Igbo ethno-nation, and still more defined, Nzagha, Ukpor, the author's ancestral village and home of her biological father. Telescoping from generality into specificity, a fine texturising of detail emerges which resists the universalising and ahistorical notion of 'Africa' that is tacitly reproduced in its manifestation in Britain under its performative guise, while retaining a trace of its transcendental potentiality. Describing her journey from Lagos to Nzagha as motivated by a desire to 'see how the country changes [...] how one place bleeds into another',[38] Kay's narratorial voice foregrounds the immutable difference of discrete spaces at the same time as it emphasises their interconnectedness in their singularity. Gone is the 'Africa' of schooldays and Conrad, and in its place is a varied, populated, and distinct

---

[32] Kay, *Red Dust Road*, 39.   [33] Kanneh, *African Identities*, 3.
[34] Hammond and Jablow, *The Africa That Never Was*, 15.   [35] Kanneh, *African Identities*, 8.
[36] Mbembe, *On the Postcolony*, 1.
[37] Joseph Conrad, *Heart of Darkness* (Ontario: Broadview Literary Texts, [1899] 1999), 107.
[38] Kay, *Red Dust Road*, 203.

landscape, which operates through its own agency within historical time. If this generalised Africa is a site of discomfort for the young Kay, ashamed at her association, actual Nigeria, for the adult, is a place of protection and comfort, a place where the narrator is able to imagine herself 'walk[ing] through waters'.[39] At the same time, the imagined fantasy of the universal 'Africa' retains its traces in a more situated sense of belonging and desire articulated with greater urgency as the ancestral home nears, embodied in the imagined 'outline of [her] Nigerian grandmother sitting next to [the driver] in the passenger seat', the 'timeless' thrill of the River Niger and the unspoken ease of being in a place where 'the shapes of people's faces change to mirror the shape of [her] own'.[40] Most evocative is a passage which describes her arrival to the village:

> We turn into a road that takes my breath away. The whole time I've been in Nigeria, I've never come across a red-dust road exactly like the one in my imagination until I come to my own village. I ask Pious to stop so that I can get out and walk on it. I take off my shoes so the red earth can touch my bare soles. It's as if my footprints were already on the road before I even got there. I walk into them, my waiting footprints. The earth is so copper warm and beautiful and the green of the long elephant grasses so lushly green they make me want to weep. I feel such a strong sense of affinity with the colours and the landscape, a strong sense of recognition. There's a feeling of libera-tion and exhilaration, that at last, at last, at last I'm here. It feels a million miles away from Glasgow, from my lovely Fintry Hills, but, surprisingly, it also feels like home.[41]

Materialising Africa, localising it so that the continent is no longer that homogeneous void, but now a country, a region, and a village claimed as one's own, this passage crystallises the ways in which *Red Dust Road* inhabits the contradictory discursive tradition around which the continent is written while simultaneously setting it on its head in a manner emblematic of the writing of African Britons more generally. In a landscape in which 'the temptation to continually move from an examination of the particular, the local, to an obsession with the whole, the continent, is prevalent',[42] this act of transformation, a process of home-making in which the red dust roads of Ukpor evoke nothing so much as the affective landscape of Fintry Hills, marks a realignment of the precepts upon which the continent is rendered legible in British discourse, opening space for a form of interdependency in which singular points of reference are unsettled and unmoored. At the same

---

[39] Ibid., 208.   [40] Ibid., 209–10.   [41] Ibid., 213.   [42] Kanneh, *African Identities*, 5.

time, opening itself to a pastoral idiom that foregrounds the natural world and yet remains buttressed by the irreducible singularity of home, whether in Ukpor or Glasgow, this moment of encounter subverts the tradition of writing Africa as a place outside of history, effectively (and affectively) extinguishing its puissance at the source. Though a certain ambiguity remains in which the spectre of that 'other' Africa, the Africa of the tradition, lingers on, its discursive weight is neutralised through an explicit reckoning with the entanglements that define the continent's relationship with the rest of the world and Ukpor's relationship with Glasgow, an 'interlocking of presents, pasts, and futures that retains their depths of other presents, pasts, and futures, each age bearing, altering, and maintaining the previous ones'.[43]

Decentring (Post)colonial Geographies, Remapping Africa and/in the World

If Kay's writing captures many of the tensions and anxieties that accompany the idea of 'Africa' in a global imaginary as resituated in the writing of African Britons, Brian Chikwava's *Harare North* rewrites the very scripts and foundations upon which those tensions are based, gesturing towards the fabrication of radical and experimental traditions in this same field. Born in Zimbabwe and a resident of London since 2004, Chikwava is the winner of the 2004 Caine Prize for African Writing; *Harare North*, his first novel, was published to critical acclaim in 2009. What strikes me as significant about the novel is the extent to which it remains a distinctly London story, inspired, Chikwava has shared, by the underclasses who striate the city with their unseen presence, hidden in plain sight. Yet at the same time, London, transformed into Harare North, is radically decentred, indicating a rewriting of the colonial script, which maintains its presence to the present day, in favour of a vision of the world in which the absolutes of centre and periphery are made mutable and multifocal. Referring to the term actually used by Zimbabweans to describe the British capital, Harare North – and its corollary, Harare South (Johannesburg) – indicates a form of meaning-making in which Zimbabwe remains starkly present, not merely as a trace or vague desire for 'Africa', but materialised in the actual fabric of the former metropole. The novel's very title signals the decentring of the former metropole, marked by the positioning of Harare as the physical and symbolic centre of meaning and valuation. Transforming London to Harare North, that is, the novel does not simply

---

[43] Mbembe, *On the Postcolony*, 16.

conjure up a process of inversion, in which the binary term Africa–Britain is flipped in favour of an Afrocentric world-view, but it also enables an undoing of the very terms of this dichotomy, decentring London – and thus rewriting the binary Africa–Britain that mediates the ways in which geographies and temporalities come to mean. Throughout its course, the novel reinforces the power of language and reference to radically revise existing hierarchies, transforming the BBC from the venerated broadcasting company into 'British Bum Cleaners'; the Red Hot Chili Peppers into the Red Hot Piri Piris; and Britain from the vaunted land of arrival into an unwanted – and ideally temporary – place where 'immigrant people's contribution [. . .] is equal to one Mars bar in every citizen's pocket every year',[44] useful only for finding 'enough pound sterling to equal US$5000',[45] the amount of money the narrator needs to pay off a price on his head back home in Zimbabwe and become 'free man again'.[46]

In a literary and imaginative landscape in which Africa is so often generalised, *Harare North* refuses any such attempt, retaining its contextual specificity. Through the narrator, a former member of the Green Bombers, the youth wing of Mugabe's ZANU-PF, the narrative reorients the normative preconceptions on which images of home and away are predicated, positioning Zimbabwe – and indeed Mugabe – as aspirational sites and turning Britain into a site of bewilderment that comes less from the devastating displacement of the migrant figure in its midst and more from the repulsive strangeness of British life itself. Told through an unstable, malicious, materialistic figure blinded by a patriotism which places him above those 'civilian people' of Harare North, the novel signals a radical departure from the normative world order which underwrites both the tradition of British writing about Africa and its reinscription in the writing of African Britons. Early in the narrative, for instance, the unnamed narrator reports on the strange doings of his cousin, Paul, and wife, Sekai, long-term residents of Harare North fully assimilated into its norms:

> Because Paul and Sekai is doing DIY work on they house when I arrive, they sleep me in spare room that is full of MDF boards, bags of plaster, PVC sheets and all. Everyone on the street is doing DIY to they houses, making noise hammering all weekend and sometimes making small neighbour talk with Paul or Sekai as they unload things from they cars.[47]

---

[44] Chikwava, *Harare North*, 24.   [45] Ibid., 6.   [46] Ibid.   [47] Ibid., 13.

Seen through the narrator's eyes, the norms and points of reference which orient Britain, Africa, and the world are realigned; no longer is the quest for (white) middle-class English decency, parodied in the images of DIY and neighbourly cordiality, upheld as aspiration. Instead, the supposedly aspirational trappings of middle-class (white) British existence become objects of ridicule, bewildering in their primitivity and ritual.

At the heart of *Harare North* is thus a radical performativity that cannot be reduced to any dichotomous form of identitarian thinking and that rescripts the very notion of an African Briton with which this chapter engages. Signalled in the passage quoted near the start of this chapter, this is a performativity which moves beyond the superficial to subvert the hierarchies of geopolitical identity which define 'Africa's' place in the imagined world order. It is no coincidence that this episode is one of the only places in the novel where the narrator makes reference to 'Africans', rather than specific nationalities and ethnic identities. The very idea of 'Africa' – Africa, the continent; Africa, the homogeneous space – the novel seems to suggest, is as hollow as the 'colourful ethnic clothes' of the Southbank crowd, their garish costumes functioning in deep contrast to the enlivened authenticity of 'the Kinshasa boy' on stage, whose guitar playing 'kill all the xenophobia, hippopotomonstrosesquippedaliophobia and yugoslavia that exist in London'.[48] Dressed in a worn out shirt and pair of trousers 'now [...] puckered and getting all out of shape [from over-washing] in that way that make them more African than them thousand cotton garments with blue lizards, green fish and ethnic patterns',[49] the Kinshasa boy stands for a different ordering of things in Harare North, a de-centring of the superficiality of performances in a place where arrivals are compelled to 'flash toothy grin of friendly African native' or risk deportation.[50] Throughout the novel, then, the scripts on which 'Africa' is written in the global imaginary are exposed, alternately inhabited by the narrator in the name of self-interest, and demolished in their parameters and conventions through a refusal to internalise.

It is impossible to generalise the ways in which the cultural histories, genealogies, and entanglements through which Africa emerges in black British writing function. Indeed, as this brief chapter has illustrated, the continent is grappled with in myriad ways which span the imaginative, the material, and the radically transformative across this body of work. If the history of writing Africa in Britain has been marked by contradictions,

[48] Ibid., 138.   [49] Ibid.   [50] Ibid., 4.

then so, too, has the history of writing Africa by African Britons. At the same time, the vision of the continent as both irreducibly diverse, with its sprawling and discrete histories, and simultaneously offering a transcendental site upon which bonds of solidarity and strategic alliance-building may be forged remains significant. Whether a fantasy Africa, a Harare North, or something else entirely, the spatio-temporal entanglements, displacements, and ecologies which mark African diasporic experiences in Britain remain vital and essential battlegrounds upon which the challenge to rewrite the image of Africa is continually being answered.

38

Post-Secular Perspectives
Writing and Fundamentalisms

REHANA AHMED

Introduction

The 2016 election of a Muslim Mayor of London might suggest a shift towards a more inclusive notion of Britishness, one which encompasses religious as well as racial difference, accommodating Islam at its very centre. Yet Sadiq Khan's success in the capital was not prefaced or accompanied by a decrease in Islamophobic hate crimes or diminishing of prejudice against Muslims. On the contrary, Tell MAMA, the organisation that monitors anti-Muslim abuse and attacks in Britain, reported that such incidents rose by 326 per cent in 2015.[1] The 2016 campaign for Britain to leave the European Union, shaped by an anti-immigration discourse, resulted in a notable increase in Islamophobic prejudice, which hardens in the wake of each terror attack perpetrated in Britain or one of its neighbouring European countries.[2] Further, if this Islamophobic racism sits alongside the openness to cultural difference that saw Londoners elect a Muslim mayor, the predominantly secular liberal left continues to valorise certain Muslim identities over others: while private, spiritual approaches to faith are deemed legitimate, visibly and assertively Muslim identities and communities are frequently stigmatised, and a 'post-secular' conception of society remains on the peripheries of political and public discourses about Islam in Britain. Drawing on the work of Jürgen Habermas and Tariq Modood, I understand the term 'post-secular' not simply to indicate a recognition of the relevance, influence, or resurgence of religion in the multicultural societies of contemporary western Europe,

---

[1] Harriet Sherwood, 'Incidents of Anti-Muslim Abuse Up by 326% in 2015, Says Tell MAMA', *The Guardian*, 26 June 2016. Available at www.theguardian.com/society/2016/jun/29/in cidents-of-anti-muslim-abuse-up-by-326-in-2015-says-tell-mama.

[2] 'Race and Religious Hate Crime Rose 41% after EU Vote', *BBC News*, 13 October 2016. Available at www.bbc.co.uk/news/uk-politics-37640982.

but to identify an approach to these societies that recognises the place of religiosity, in particular Islam, within the public sphere, and advocates a mutually respectful dialogue between secularism and faith.[3] This chapter examines a selection of literary texts by black and Asian British writers that explore and interrogate Muslim identities, communities, and cultures in Britain and beyond. In doing so, it asks, centrally, to what extent and in what ways these fictional works offer us a post-secular perspective. Beginning with the 1988 publication of *The Satanic Verses* by Salman Rushdie (1947–) and the protests that it triggered, the chapter works through four themed sections that reflect approximate trends in contemporary 'British Muslim' writing and underline the importance of thinking about religion and race always in combination with gender, class, and place.[4]

The Rushdie Controversy and its Literary Legacy

The controversy triggered by *The Satanic Verses* in 1988 led to the visibilisation of Britain's Muslim minority. As Tariq Modood writes, the stereotype of the 'unassertive, over deferential, and docile' Muslim man shifted to one of inflexibility, aggression, and fanaticism.[5] Further, the dispute exposed the limits of a secular anti-racism which was unable to accommodate grievances rooted in the religiosity of one of Britain's most disadvantaged ethnic minorities.[6] The British Muslims who protested against the novel's representation of Islam and the Prophet Muhammad – the majority of them working class – were largely dismissed or demonised from across the political spectrum. The Rushdie controversy, then, entrenched an absolutist position on freedom of speech, and helped to forge a reductive binary opposition between creative freedom and religious repression which continues to shape

---

[3] Jürgen Habermas, 'Equal Treatment of Cultures and the Limits of Post-modern Liberalism', *Journal of Political Philosophy*, 13:1 (2005): 1–28; 'Religion in the Public Sphere', *European Journal of Philosophy*, 14:1 (2006): 1–25; Tariq Modood, *Multiculturalism: A Civic Idea* (Cambridge: Polity Press, 2007), 78–84.

[4] Inevitably there are writers whose work I have been unable to address in this chapter. These include Aamer Hussein whose beautifully crafted short fiction eschews sensational global events involving Muslims to focus rather on themes such as cosmopolitanism, exile, loss, and love; and Abdulrazak Gurnah whose fictional worlds are subtly infused by Islam which is, however, rarely a key focus or theme. It comes to the surface some more in Gurnah's *Paradise* (1994) and *Desertion* (2005): located in the coastal region of East Africa, their characters' lives are shaped by colonialism, and Islam is portrayed as both sustaining, and – especially in *Desertion* – prohibitive.

[5] Tariq Modood, *Multicultural Politics: Race, Ethnicity and Muslims in Britain* (Edinburgh: Edinburgh University Press, 2005), 14.

[6] Tariq Modood, 'Reflections on the Rushdie Affair: Muslims, Race, and Equality in Britain', in *Multicultural Politics*, 103–12.

constructions of Muslims.[7] The struggle between free speech and religious censure underpins *The Satanic Verses* itself: in the Jahilia sequences of the novel, subversive writerly figures – Baal the poet, Salman the scribe – are pitted against the figure of Mahound; and in the contemporary London sequences, the pious Hind is the oppressive counterpart to her free-thinking, secular husband Sufyan, and the exiled Imam is a Khomeini-like religious dictator. While the complexities of the twinned protagonists open up a range of interpretative possibilities, ultimately it is Saladin Chamcha, characterised by secular doubt, who triumphs over his zealous adversary Gibreel Farishta. The novel's valorisation of a secular individualism against a religious collectivism is, I suggest, in unresolved tension with its commitment to anti-racism, evident in the sections located in late-twentieth-century 'Brickhall' which explore the largely South Asian Muslim community's battle against the racism of Thatcher's Britain. This tension brings us back to the shortcomings of a secular liberal anti-racism unearthed by the Rushdie controversy itself.[8]

The Rushdie controversy cast a shadow not only over perceptions of Muslims in Britain, but also, arguably, over the literary production of British writers of South Asian Muslim heritage. In *The Black Album* (1995), Hanif Kureishi (1954–) makes direct allusion to the controversy. Protagonist Shahid's sexual corruption of prophet-like Riaz's verses is redolent of Salman's corruption of Mahound's in Rushdie's novel, while Riaz and his 'brothers' organise demonstrations, including book-burnings, against an offensive novel.[9] Moreover, Kureishi's representations of British Muslims in both *The Black Album* and the 1997 screenplay *My Son the Fanatic* are shaped by the conceptual framework entrenched by the Rushdie controversy. The theme of censorship and creative freedom threads its way through *The Black Album*: Shahid is pulled between Riaz's zealotry and his lover Deedee's iconoclastic thought and passion for the arts. While Deedee's lifestyle bohemianism does not escape ironisation,[10] and notwithstanding the dialogic, satirical form of the novel which works against a clear interpretation of its politics, Shahid's final tentative choice of 'freedom', combined with an identification of Islam with fundamentalism, prevents it from reaching

---

[7] See Anshuman Mondal's *Islam and Controversy: The Politics of Free Speech after Rushdie* (Basingstoke: Palgrave Macmillan, 2014).

[8] For a detailed reading of the novel and controversy in dialogue with one another, see Rehana Ahmed, *Writing British Muslims: Religion, Class and Multiculturalism* (Manchester: Manchester University Press, 2015), ch. 2.

[9] Hanif Kureishi, *The Black Album* (London: Faber and Faber, 1995), 233–6, 222–6.

[10] Ibid., 44, 57.

beyond the limits of a liberal secularism.[11] Similarly, in *My Son the Fanatic*, individual choice and freedom, aligned with secularism, are pitted against a constraining, communal religiosity. Here, the poverty that afflicts many Muslims in Britain forms a context for the radicalisation of the son Farid.[12] Further, his 'liberal' father Parvez is a flawed character – adulterous, exploitative, and abusive – complicating a clear valorisation of his position against his son's.[13] In spite of this, however, misogynistic and anti-Semitic Farid's two-dimensionality, as opposed to his father's complexity, places him further beyond readerly sympathy.[14]

The dichotomy of free speech versus religious offence was entrenched in the years following the 9/11 terror attacks and the rise of the New Atheist movement which strengthened the construction of Islam as the enemy of art.[15] The 2003 publication of *Brick Lane* by Monica Ali (1967–) and its filming in 2006 offended some Bangladeshi Muslims, triggering a controversy that resonated with the Rushdie controversy; while Sikh protests against Gurpreet Kaur Bhatti's play *Behzti* in 2004 were closely followed by protests against the publication of cartoons depicting the Prophet Muhammad in the Danish newspaper *Jyllands-Posten*. The same year also saw the publication of *Maps for Lost Lovers* by Nadeem Aslam (1966–). Despite its provocative content – including paedophilic sex abuse by an imam and female foeticide[16] – this novel did not precipitate a dispute. Nevertheless, a binary of creative freedom and religious repression can be traced within it, not least in the central couple: non-believer Shamas (enlightened poet and reader of literature) and his pious wife Kaukab (blinkered, literalist reader of the Qur'an). Similarly, in Aslam's subsequent novel, *The Wasted Vigil* (2008), art, literature, and music are counterposed to Islam. Englishman Marcus, in fear of the Taliban, daubs mud over the murals in his house in Afghanistan; while his wife Qatrina has nailed books to the ceiling to protect them from religious zealots.[17] The dichotomy that emerges is partly complicated by the Islamic aesthetic that can be traced in both the

---

[11] See Bart Moore-Gilbert, 'From "the Politics of Recognition" to "the Policing of Recognition"' in Rehana Ahmed, Peter Morey, and Amina Yaqin (eds.), *Culture, Diaspora, and Modernity in Muslim Writing* (Abingdon: Routledge, 2012), 183–99; 189–90.

[12] Hanif Kureishi, *Collected Screenplays 1* (London: Faber and Faber, 2002), 334, 337.

[13] Ibid., 366–9, 297, 351–2, 346–7.   [14] Ibid., 333, 337, 344, 338, 365–6, 378.

[15] Arthur Bradley and Andrew Tate, *The New Atheist Novel: Fiction, Philosophy and Polemic after 9/11* (London: Continuum, 2010).

[16] Nadeem Aslam, *Maps for Lost Lovers* (London: Faber and Faber, 2004), 234, 349.

[17] Nadeem Aslam, *The Wasted Vigil* (London: Faber and Faber, 2008), 12.

content and form of Aslam's work. In *The Blind Man's Garden* (2013), the beauty of the mosque which shelters protagonist Mikal, its walls calligraphed with words from the Qur'an, and that of the angels suspended from the ceiling of the school bombed by terrorists, suggest an aesthetic from *within* Islam.[18] Similarly, in *The Golden Legend* (2017), Islam and creativity are brought together in the mosques designed by architects Massud and Nargis, as well as the presence of models of the Great Mosque of Córdoba and Istanbul's Hagia Sophia in the library in their home in Pakistan; and the destructive 'purity' of extremist brands of Islam is counterposed to a syncretism that comprises faith, including Islam, in the form of Massud's father's precious book.[19] Further, while in *The Wasted Vigil* Qatrina's paintings are firmly antithetical to Islam, 'her comment on the non-existence of God', the rigidity of her non-belief is not valorised;[20] rather, it is Marcus's doubt, which encompasses respect for Islam, that is represented as having the most potential for social justice. It is not insignificant, however, that Marcus is not a believer, despite his respect for belief, while in *The Blind Man's Garden* it is the eponym Rohan's faith that is the source of his most destructive actions. Ultimately, throughout Aslam's work, 'good' Islam is a marginal presence and relegated largely to a private, spiritual sphere.

Evident in Rushdie's 2012 memoir *Joseph Anton* is the hardening of an absolutist valorisation of creative freedom, which mimics and thereby undermines his own blanket equation of faith with absolutist thinking. Literature is repeatedly represented as the antithesis to religion and as a 'counterweight to power'.[21] The equation of Islam and power distorts the offence of disenfranchised working-class British Muslims: their protests are compared to Nazi book-burnings in a reversal of hierarchies that positions the privileged writer as the disempowered victim.[22] Reflections on the Rushdie controversy triggered by the memoir's publication, as well as responses to the terror attacks on the staff of French magazine *Charlie Hebdo* in January 2015, suggest the continuation of a hardline secularist position on free speech and religious offence among media and literary figures.[23] Yet, the objection by six high-

[18] Nadeem Aslam, *The Blind Man's Garden* (London: Faber and Faber, 2013), 151, 267.
[19] Nadeem Aslam, *The Golden Legend* (London: Faber and Faber, 2017), 2, 34–5.
[20] Aslam, *Wasted Vigil*, 201.
[21] Salman Rushdie, *Joseph Anton* (London: Jonathan Cape, 2012), 78.   [22] Ibid., 124.
[23] 'Looking Back at Salman Rushdie's *The Satanic Verses*', *The Guardian*, 14 September 2012. Available at www.theguardian.com/books/2012/sep/14/looking-at-salman-rushdies-satanic-verses.

profile authors to PEN's decision to award *Charlie Hebdo* the PEN/Toni and James C. Goodale Freedom of Expression Courage prize brings hope for a more nuanced understanding of such controversies.[24]

Gender and Islam

Both Ali's *Brick Lane*, focalised through a Bangladeshi woman who settles in London's Tower Hamlets, and Aslam's *Maps for Lost Lovers*, which revolves around an 'honour killing', explore the tensions between women's freedom and an adherence to religious culture. Their publication in the wake of 9/11, when constructions of Muslim women as in need of 'saving' were mobilised as a means of discrediting multiculturalism and even as justifying the invasion of Afghanistan, burdened them with a representative status. *Brick Lane*'s protagonist Nazneen reverses the majoritarian gaze that frequently reduces the Muslim woman to an object of oppression.[25] A similar reversal is effected through the trope of clothing: Nazneen, with her friend Razia, moves beyond her role as exploited labour, sewing clothes for a garment factory, to exploit the exoticisation of South Asian dress by setting up her own clothing business.[26] In this way, Nazneen emerges into subjecthood. Yet her faith is mainly confined to the private sphere, and she dresses in a sari, unlike the two burka-clad women, who remain, significantly, peripheral to the point of anonymity.[27] Further, Nazneen's and Razia's final liberation is attained only once the male Bangladeshi protagonists have departed,[28] and there is little sense of the pressures of class and race acting on the community's men. Hence, the novel's feminist impulse seems constrained by a limited multiculturalist vision – one that neither accommodates a more radical female difference, nor relates gender inequalities within a minority community to inequalities of class, race, and religion more broadly. By contrast, *Maps for Lost Lovers* contextualises its male characters' abusive behaviour in their disenfranchisement. Nevertheless, the saturation of the fictional northern town of Dasht-e-Tanhaii with crimes against women and children committed in the name of Islam reinforces the identification of 'sexual misery' and

---

[24] Alison Flood and Alan Yuhas, 'Salman Rushdie Slams Critics of PEN's Charlie Hebdo Tribute', *The Guardian*, 27 April 2015. Available at www.theguardian.com/books/2015/apr/27/salman-rushdie-pen-charlie-hebdo-peter-carey.

[25] Monica Ali, *Brick Lane* (London: Doubleday, 2003), 210, 326.   [26] Ibid., 328, 402–4.

[27] Ibid., 196–8, 231, 235–7.   [28] Ibid., 294.

'sick' sexualities with British Muslims, characteristic of media coverage of honour-based violence and child sexual abuse.[29] The young women of the community must either succumb to patriarchal abuse, or leave: Chanda, one of the central lovers, is killed by her brothers; Shamas and Kaukab's daughter Mah Jabin escapes; Suraya, exiled in Dasht-e-Tanhaii because of her spirited defence of a woman in Pakistan, becomes a ghostly presence in the town.[30] The characters' entrapment is conveyed formally by the circularity of the novel, which moves through the seasons and begins and ends with a near-identical image.[31] This finds an echo in the novel's entrapment within the blind-alley of a blanket equation of feminism with secularism and patriarchy with Islam, which leaves little space for a post-secular understanding of multiculturalism.

The first two novels by Scottish Sudanese writer Leila Aboulela (1964–), *The Translator* (1999) and *Minaret* (2005), disturb conventional constructions of British Muslim women's subjectivity. Both reverse the trope of a journey from patriarchal religious oppression to secular freedom: in *The Translator*, protagonist Sammar leads the secular Rae towards faith; while in *Minaret* Najwa's journey towards faith is one of liberation and self-realisation. For *The Translator*'s Sammar, prayer and fasting are a form of sustenance.[32] Faith shapes her perspective on life, and any attenuation of this is associated with a 'narrowing' of the world.[33] Far from offering 'freedom' to her, secular British culture is characterised by loneliness, its individualism contrasted negatively with the communal living of Islamic Sudanese culture,[34] while the superior 'objectivity' of her lover Rae's atheism is recast as myopic arrogance.[35] For *Minaret*'s Najwa, the communal nature of a religiously observant life enables a personal development which she could not find within the 'empty space [...] called freedom' that she inhabits before she embraces Islam, while veiling grants her freedom from the sexual objectification that she experiences in everyday London life.[36] The disorientating effect of disaggregating agency from secular individualism reaches its zenith when Najwa renounces her love for the pious Tamer for the sake of his family, and

[29] See Claire Chambers, Richard Phillips, Nafhesa Ali, Peter Hopkins, and Raksha Pande, '"Sexual Misery" or "Happy British Muslims"? Contemporary Depictions of Muslim Sexuality', *Ethnicities* [OnlineFirst] (21 February 2018). DOI https://doi.org/10.1177/1468796818757263.

[30] Aslam, *Maps for Lost Lovers*, 157–60, 365–6. [31] Ibid., 5, 367.

[32] Leila Aboulela, *The Translator* (Edinburgh: Polygon, [1999] 2008), 16, 36, 31, 100, 103.

[33] Ibid., 71. [34] Ibid., 72–3, 155. [35] Ibid., 123.

[36] Leila Aboulela, *Minaret* (London: Bloomsbury 2005), 175, 245–47.

her own education and material independence for hajj. However, the protagonist's fantasy of becoming a concubine for Tamer's family and her submissive attitude more generally are hardly conducive to a secular metropolitan understanding of Najwa as a liberated woman.[37] In *The Translator*, moreover, while Sammar leads Rae to Islam,[38] their relationship remains traditionally gendered, disturbing a reading of the novel as articulating an Islamic feminism.[39] The lack of persuasive alternative voices in both novels means that there is little – if any – sense of a critical disturbance of these gender politics.[40] Hence, while they undermine the identification of female religious observance with patriarchal oppression, thereby reframing thinking about gender and Islam, they struggle to translate an Islamic worldview to the secular metropolitan feminist reader. Aboulela's first novel draws attention to the limits of translation: the untranslatability of certain words, the Qur'an, and faith generally is highlighted.[41] Perhaps, then, there is a self-consciousness on the part of these narratives of their inevitably limited ability to translate across cultures.

In *Love in a Headscarf: Muslim Woman Finds the One* (2009), Shelina Zahra Janmahomed (1974–) self-consciously positions her memoir as a vehicle for cross-cultural translation, articulating its aim to dismantle stereotypes and offering the (implicitly non-Muslim) reader the challenge of friendship with a Muslim woman.[42] Throughout, its emphasis is on the common ground shared by Muslim women and their secular counterparts when it comes to romantic love. One of several British Muslim memoirs published in the first decade of the new millennium, it diverges from its contemporaries by giving voice to a practising Muslim woman who wears the hijab and is guided primarily by her faith. In *We Are A Muslim, Please* (2010) by Zaiba Malik (1969–), the narrator's approach to her inherited faith is primarily private as well as frequently conflictual.[43] And in *The Making of Mr Hai's Daughter* (2008) by Yasmin Hai (1970–), the narrator, while critical of the stereotypes circulating about Muslim women, nevertheless distances herself from and expresses bafflement at her friends' decision to don the hijab.[44] Conversely, faith is an

---

[37] Ibid., 215.   [38] Ibid., 192.   [39] Ibid., 105, 115, 171.

[40] Peter Morey, '"Halal Fiction" and the Limits of Postsecularism: Criticism, Critique, and the Muslim in Leila Aboulela's *Minaret*', *Journal of Commonwealth Literature*, 53:2 (2018): 301–15.

[41] Aboulela, *Translator*, 94, 121, 50.

[42] Shelina Zahra Janmahomed, *Love in a Headscarf: Muslim Woman Finds the One* (London: Aurum, 2009), xiii, 1.

[43] Zaiba Malik, *We Are A Muslim, Please* (London: Windmill, 2010).

[44] Yasmin Hai, *The Making of Mr Hai's Daughter: Becoming British* (London: Virago, 2008), 324, 333.

integral component of Janmahomed's narrator's public identity as a British woman.[45] *Love in a Headscarf* avoids the 'culture clash' clichés into which Hai's and Malik's memoirs occasionally lapse. By bringing together a hijabi and romantic love, it destabilises the binary of individual desire and religious oppression. Further, it emphasises the role of choice in practising Islam, while highlighting the rules that structure any lifestyle,[46] and reframes communal modes of living as enabling. While its post-feminist gender politics are far from radical, it is partly because of their appeal to a chick-lit readership, as well as the affective power of the memoir form, that *Love in a Headscarf* is able to translate religiosity to secular metropolitan culture in an age of Islamophobia.[47]

Transnationalism and Translation after 9/11

While categorising Mohsin Hamid (1971–) as a British Asian writer might be a stretch, it seems important to consider his second novel, *The Reluctant Fundamentalist* (2007), given its high profile in a post-9/11 climate as well as Hamid's role as an 'insider' public intellectual in the British media (he writes regularly for *The Guardian*). Further, the novel's location in North America and Pakistan speaks to the transnational perspective opened out by the 'war on terror' and its fallout. In this period, political and public discourses aligned Britain with North America and its self-proclaimed 'innocence';[48] while Pakistan's role in the 'war' was significant to Britain because of its substantial Pakistani diaspora.

In *The Reluctant Fundamentalist*, Hamid's use of the second person places the reader in uncomfortable alignment with protagonist Changez's anonymous and silent white American interlocutor whose assumptions are interrogated by the powerful but unreliable narrative voice. As well as disturbing the fixity of the term 'fundamentalism' by delinking it from terroristic violence and Islam and aligning it instead with the structural violence

---

[45] Janmahomed, *Love in a Headscarf*, 161.   [46] Ibid., 73–4.

[47] See also Janmahomed's *Generation M: Young Muslims Changing the World* (London: I.B. Tauris, 2016), a creative non-fictional work which breaks down the binary of faith versus modernity, and Sabrina Mahfouz's anthology *The Things I Would Tell You: British Muslim Women Write* (London: Saqi, 2017). For a fuller engagement with these three memoirs, as well as Ed Husain's *The Islamist* (2007), discussed below, see Ahmed, *Writing British Muslims*, ch. 6.

[48] On the rhetoric of American and British innocence in responses to 9/11, see Ana María Sánchez-Arce, 'Performing Innocence: Violence and the Nation in Ian McEwan's *Saturday* and Sunjeev Sahota's *Ours Are the Streets*', *Journal of Commonwealth Literature*, 53:2 (2018): 194–210.

of American capitalist imperialism,[49] the novel undermines the American/ reader's interpretation of Changez himself, of the bearded Pakistani waiter at the café where they meet, and of Pakistan and Pakistanis generally,[50] while at the same time positioning the American/reader as potential aggressor to the narrator's own possible innocence.[51] By making the reader conscious of the assumptions they bring to manifestations of cultural difference, specifically 'Muslimness', the novel dislodges their certainties, and the innocence that derives from these. It thereby opens up the possibility of a translation across difference, of breaking down the boundaries between 'us' and 'them' to acknowledge our 'cross-cultural commonalities' – against the American and British retreat into the 'myths of [. . .] difference' which defined the post-9/11 period,[52] and beyond the 'post-race' exoticisation of privileged brown bodies which characterised metropolitan culture, and which Changez enjoyed, before the terror attacks.[53] As well as blurring the boundary between white secular Anglo-American culture and Muslim culture, the novel destabilises the division between writer and reader. Reading becomes a process of co-creation.[54] As Hamid writes of Antonio Tabucchi's novel *Sostiene Pereira*, an 'interpretative space opens up before us, nags at us, seduces us', and this works against 'absolutist ideologies'.[55] It also works against an 'anthropological' consumption of 'Muslimness', which characterised the reception of Ali's *Brick Lane*, for example, and reifies difference. In *The Reluctant Fundamentalist*, Changez says of his relationship with Erica: 'it is not always possible to restore one's boundaries after they have been blurred and made permeable by a relationship'.[56] The permeability of the boundary between reader and text elicits empathy across difference, disabling the reduction of others 'to simplified (and artificial) mono-identities of religion or nationality or race'.[57]

The hardening of a dichotomised discourse in the wake of 9/11 is captured in the poetry collection by British Pakistani poet Moniza Alvi (1954–), *How the*

[49] Mohsin Hamid, *The Reluctant Fundamentalist* (London: Hamish Hamilton, 2007), 98, 116.
[50] Ibid., 75–6, 6, 108–9, 101, 108.   [51] Ibid., 138.   [52] Ibid., 168.   [53] Ibid., 34, 38, 48.
[54] See Mohsin Hamid, 'Enduring Love of the Second Person' in *Discontent and its Civilizations: Dispatches from Lahore, New York and London* (London: Penguin, [2014] 2015), 77–80.
[55] Hamid, 'Pereira Transforms' in *Discontent and its Civilizations*, 63–6, 66.
[56] Hamid, *Reluctant Fundamentalist*, 173–4.
[57] Hamid, 'A Beginning' in *Discontent and its Civilizations*, 111–13; 111. Hamid's recently published *Exit West* (2017), which explores the condition of refugees, has overlapping concerns. By disturbing readerly expectations (including about Islam), and through its satellite, godlike perspective, which draws connections through time as well as across space, it gestures towards a porosity of borders – between reader and text, as well as between nations, cultures, and religions.

Stone Found Its Voice (2005). In 'How the Words Feared the Mouth', words are configured as vulnerable to the violence of a mouth, which is reduced to a void characterised by aggression and greed: 'that slash in the face, the hole / which could fill with potatoes and beer'.[58] The mouth's subject is anonymous, their identity swallowed by this insatiable 'hole', which spouts monochromatic answers rather than posing questions. If the language of 'them and us' becomes anonymising, reducing individuals to the categories in which they might be placed, so, in 'How a Long Way Off Rolled Itself Up', the anonymity of the enemy enables the reduction of cultural Others to stereotype, the evacuation of their individuality in order to legitimise aggression, even – or especially – when those Others are among us, when their 'otherness' is close enough to 'breathe in'.[59] In the face of this violence, 'half-formed' words, those that refute the certainties of a 'clash of civilizations' discourse, disappear, while others, perhaps those that can be co-opted into such a discourse, are 'cruelly nailed to the air'.[60] But this final, impossible image undercuts itself, suggesting the collapse of a world-view that pits Islam against the 'West', and the potential of the creativity and subtleties of language to contribute to such a collapse. In her novel *Burnt Shadows* (2009), Kamila Shamsie (1973–) also foregrounds language in an exploration of the possibilities and limits of cross-cultural communication. Language lessons are the reason Japanese protagonist Hiroko meets her German fiancé Konrad and later her Pakistani husband Sajjad, while Hiroko and Sajjad's son Raza's linguistic ability grants him the means of speaking across borders of class, ethnicity, and nation. Hiroko is described as 'disrupting hierarchies': not only does she defy categories of belonging, but she challenges power relations by failing to slot into a designated place on the social scale (whether of imperial India, late twentieth-century Pakistan, or contemporary North America).[61] Yet pulling against this possibility is a repeated emphasis on the difficulties of living or speaking across difference. This is highlighted most powerfully in the breakdown in communication that occurs between Anglo-German Elizabeth and Sajjad (which leads to her declaring him a rapist) and, decades later, white American Kim and Afghan refugee Abdullah (which leads to Raza's incarceration in a detention camp at

[58] Moniza Alvi, 'How the Words Feared the Mouth' in *How the Stone Found Its Voice* (Tarset: Bloodaxe Books, 2005), 15, lines 6–7.

[59] Alvi, 'How a Long Way Off Rolled Itself Up' in *How the Stone Found Its Voice*, 16, lines 11–12.

[60] Alvi, 'How the Words Feared the Mouth', 15, lines 8, 11.

[61] Kamila Shamsie, *Burnt Shadows* (London: Picador, 2009), 82.

Guantánamo Bay).[62] Ultimately, *Burnt Shadows* suggests the failure of a cosmopolitan ethics, one that 'begins with the precarious life of the Other'.[63]

By embedding 9/11 in a long global history of colonialism and other forms of subordination – for example, by drawing links between the victims of 9/11 and those of the Atomic bombing of Nagasaki[64] – *Burnt Shadows* refuses the exceptionality claimed for both 9/11 and Islam, locating 'Islamic' terrorism within a complex narrative of oppression and resistance. In this sense, it invokes the necessity of a historicised perspective when considering the responsibilities and rights of Muslims today. Aboulela's 2015 novel *The Kindness of Enemies* also makes connections through historical time (twenty-first-century Scotland and the nineteenth-century Caucasian War) which similarly work to challenge the idea of Islam as inherently and exceptionally repressive and violent. The legendary Chechen Imam Shamil brings together Islam and political resistance, not in the form of the terroristic aggression of twenty-first-century ISIS but as a vehicle for challenging his people's oppression that is shaped by the principles of faith. Islam is not relegated to the private domain, following the prescriptions of secularist thinking; and its presence in the public, political domain is as a legitimate force for justice. The novel's bridging of different historical periods can be understood, then, as an act of translation, in so far as it allows the reader to reinterpret contemporary Islam. At the beginning of the novel, history is, for academic Natasha, a place of refuge from the complexity of the contemporary.[65] Further, 'staunchly secular' historical researchers like herself 'hit against the faith of the characters' they study;[66] for them, religiosity does not fit the narrative they weave out of the archive. Yet, just as her 'communion' with the history of Shamil and her friend Malak's guidance towards the faith of her paternal heritage enable Natasha to weave together the threads of her identity,[67] so the novel offers its reader history as a means of speaking to the contemporary and an understanding of religiosity as legitimately occupying the British public sphere.

---

[62] Ibid., 360–1.
[63] Judith Butler, *Precarious Life: The Powers of Mourning and Violence* (London: Verso, [2004] 2006), xviii.
[64] Shamsie, *Burnt Shadows*, 274.
[65] Leila Aboulela, *The Kindness of Enemies* (London: Weidenfeld & Nicolson, 2015), 41.
[66] Ibid., 216.   [67] Ibid., 311, 175.

Place, Belonging, and Terror after 7/7

Aboulela's novel repeatedly raises questions about belonging. Natasha's journey to Sudan on her father's death is not to claim her inheritance but to assert her belonging there;[68] while student Oz's attraction to radicalism is rooted in an 'ache to belong',[69] as well as the increased hostility towards Muslims following 7/7. Significantly, however, the novel ends by embedding Islam in Britain. Malak completes a sequence of prayers in unlikely spaces across Scotland, including the chapel of Dunnottar Castle, a place that is associated with resistance around faith.[70] Finally, Natasha moves tentatively towards Islam by considering joining Malak in a reading of the Qur'an on an Orkney beach.[71] This resonates with the ending of the novel by Syrian British writer Robin Yassin-Kassab (1969–) *The Road from Damascus* (2008), which also depicts a journey towards faith. Protagonist Sami, like Natasha, is slowly drawn to a 'trembling, contingent' faith, finally joining his observant wife Muntaha at prayer, but in the countryside rather than a mosque.[72] While the location of prayer in external spaces in both novels indicates most obviously their protagonists' hesitant commitment to Islam, it also suggests a *rooting* of Islam in British space, a kind of space-claiming.

A similar concern is at the centre of *Ours Are the Streets* (2011) by Sunjeev Sahota (1981–). Protagonist Imtiaz's alienation is grounded partly in his disenfranchisement in Britain; it is only when he travels to Pakistan and Afghanistan that he feels a sense of rootedness, captured by images of his relationship with the land. At his father's funeral in Pakistan, the communal mourning rituals enable him to feel 'solid, rooted to my earth [. . .] magnificent'; and by placing bricks on the walls of a ruined fort in Afghanistan, he asserts his place in the history of the land and its struggles, gaining a continuity of self that contrasts with the fragmentation of his British identity.[73] On his return to Sheffield, Imtiaz's mental deterioration leads him to seal the windows of his house, thereby cutting himself off from British space. This shrinking of space echoes his father's shrinking form in the Indian restaurant where he is sexually harassed by a drunk woman.[74] Indeed, it is partly his father's failure to become 'part of these streets', to lay claim to Britishness, that drives Imtiaz towards radicalisation.[75] Sahota's novel takes the form of a confessional narrative compared, by the

---

[68] Ibid., 290, 310. [69] Ibid., 208. [70] Ibid., 312. [71] Ibid., 314.
[72] Robin Yassin-Kassab, *The Road from Damascus* (London: Hamish Hamilton, 2008), 347–8.
[73] Sunjeev Sahota, *Ours Are the Streets* (London: Picador, 2011), 94, 162–3, 179.
[74] Ibid., 44. [75] Ibid., 70.

protagonist, to du'a, a 'form of prayer', in so far as it represents a desire 'to be found out', a 'way of wanting to be known'.[76] Throughout, there is a tension between the coherence the narrator wishes to impose on his story and its formal fragmentation,[77] which reflects his attempt not only to order the chaos of his mind but also to move from the margins to the centre of his narrative, to discard his observer status for that of an agent, perhaps to attain a secure place at the centre of a collective that he gets from prayer, and that he believes he can get from an act of terror.[78]

In contrast to Sahota's novel, Ed Husain (1974–) offers the reader a seamless narrative in his memoir *The Islamist* (2007). This, together with the 'insider' perspective of the former Islamist and the split timeframe, which underlines the narrator's acquired knowledge, endows the narrative with authority, leaving little space for interpretative flexibility. As Gillian Whitlock points out, the ability of the autobiographical 'I' to elicit empathy makes memoir especially amenable to deployment as a 'manipulation of opinion and emotion'.[79] Hence, this memoir's self-representation as a 'true' account of radicalisation and salvation has a particular power to shape understanding of Islam in Britain. Just as the young Husain's mind is infiltrated by the ideologies of groups such as Hizb ut-Tahrir, so east London is taken over by Islamism, represented as a dark, ominous force.[80] Further, any public display of Islam is conflated with Islamism and contrasted with a private spirituality that is finally adopted by Husain as the only legitimate form of his faith.[81] This depiction of Islamism as infiltrating British space finds an attenuated echo in Malik's *We Are A Muslim, Please*. Here, the narrator describes Bradford as a place of secrets, where you 'never knew [...] what's happening behind closed doors'.[82] Malik's memoir, punctuated by letters to 7/7 suicide bomber Shehzad Tanweer, offers a vital riposte to the identification of Islam with terror in the wake of the attacks. The narrator emphasises the difference between her Islam and Tanweer's distortion of Islam.[83] She also retreats from the assertiveness of Muslims that emerged during the Rushdie controversy: just as the Muslim community in Bradford 'starts to roar', she falls silent.[84] We might read Malik's loss of voice as representative of the difficulty of articulating a middle-ground between spiritual Islam and politicised

---

[76] Ibid., 17.   [77] Ibid., 151, 170.   [78] Ibid., 182, 212.

[79] Gillian Whitlock, *Soft Weapons: Autobiography in Transit* (Chicago, IL: University of Chicago Press, 2007), 12.

[80] Ed Husain, *The Islamist* (London: Penguin, 2007), 2, 62–3, 112, 114, 265.

[81] Ibid., 67, 265.   [82] Malik, *We Are A Muslim*, 216, 222, 269.   [83] Ibid., 261–3.

[84] Ibid., 148.

Islam – a religiosity that can be practised in the public sphere but is not reducible to extremism. In his memoir *Only Half of Me* (2006), Rageh Omaar (1967–) shows us this middle-ground, thereby troubling secularist orthodoxies. Significantly, the chapter 'Hidden Lives' disturbs the notion of Muslims as a fifth column in Britain that its title might suggest. Instead, Omaar looks beneath the stereotypes to the stories of family members subjected to racial abuse after 7/7 and explores the diversity of London's Somalis. In his narrative, the veil does not signify patriarchal practices in enclaved communities ripe for radicalisation, as in Husain's; rather, the emphasis is on how the media's obsession with it works to veil real issues such as the poverty that blights the lives of many British Muslims, and the integration and success of many women who choose to wear it.[85]

Just Another Jihadi Jane, the 2016 novel by Tabish Khair (1966–), also foregrounds a lack of belonging in its exploration of narrator Jamilla and her friend Ameena's decision to travel to Syria. Jamilla describes the sense of homelessness she experienced as a niqabi woman, following a Wahhabi form of Islam, in her native Leeds.[86] For her, the Islamic State 'seemed to be [...] a country where I thought I could be myself', a sanctuary from the racist abuse she is subjected to at home.[87] While the frame narrative, of Jamilla telling her story to the anonymous writer-interlocutor in Bali, is not as evident as it is in Hamid's *The Reluctant Fundamentalist*, the sporadic use of the second person and allusions to the narrator's own processes of selection and omission when constructing her narrative draw attention to its inevitable partiality, undermining the idea of a 'true' account of radicalisation.[88] The front-cover image of a redacted typescript similarly draws attention to the gaps and silences not just in newspaper headlines and media reports but in any attempt to answer definitively the question of why young British women travel to the Middle East to join terrorist organisations such as Daesh. As Jamilla reminds us, it is certainty, or an ideological purity, that leads to acts of harm; while doubt, or an acknowledgement of the inadequacy of *any* singular narrative, might prevent this.[89] But doubt does not equate to a rejection of faith for Jamilla; rather, it is part of the Islamic self she becomes.[90] This, then, reminds us of the need for a 'moderate secularism', one that has the capacity for self-doubt and can make space for

---

[85] Rageh Omaar, *Only Half of Me: British and Muslim; The Conflict Within* (London: Penguin, [2006] 2007), 225, 231.

[86] Tabish Khair, *Just Another Jihadi Jane* (Reading: Periscope, 2016), 68.   [87] Ibid., 78, 73.

[88] Ibid., 101, 107, 118, 216.   [89] Ibid., 193, 205–6, 217, 219.   [90] Ibid., 140.

religiosity.[91] Like Khair's novel, Kamila Shamsie's recently published *Home Fire* (2017) examines the journey of a young British Muslim towards radicalisation and scrutinises ideas of home.[92] A contemporary reworking of Sophocles' play *Antigone*, it deploys theatricality to explore the roles that Muslims are pressed into performing in a nation that denies this minority their right to be at home within it. Further, the novel's focus on surveillance and ways of seeing more broadly encourages the reader to reflect critically on the ways we see – or read – one another across lines of difference. In this way, *Home Fire* prompts us to think about the possibilities and difficulties of forging productive cross-cultural dialogue and understanding in contemporary Britain. While the stereotyping of Muslims continues, and a secularist position remains dominant within the liberal-left media and publishing spheres, literary fiction by British writers is increasingly pushing beyond prejudice and constraints to offer its readers post-secular perspectives that can help to build a multiculturalism of reciprocity.

[91] Tariq Modood, 'Moderate Secularism, Religion as Identity and Respect for Religion', *Political Quarterly*, 81:1 (March 2010): 4–14.
[92] Kamila Shamsie, *Home Fire* (London: Bloomsbury, 2017).

39

Post-Ethnicity and the Politics
of Positionality

SARA UPSTONE

In 2013, a new wave of black activism swept the United States. Following the death of African American teenager Trayvon Martin and the acquittal of the white police officer implicated in his death, #BlackLivesMatter began trending on Twitter. By 2016, Black Lives Matter had spread from being a slogan to a decentralised, informal movement: an international banner for the demand to recognise the continued presence of racism in twenty-first-century society.

Black Lives Matter seals within its naming an irony. For matter is not an innocent term. It speaks to the materiality of race – the physical reality experienced by black communities persecuted on the basis of their skin tone. It also speaks, conterminously, to the desire to recognise a positive cultural history associated with this materiality – to celebrate and acknowledge black successes, achievements, and cultural expressions. In this latter manifestation, materiality is reclaimed from racist discourse, to signify instead the powerful cultural, creative, economic, and political presence of blackness.

Into the centre of this materiality – both positive and negative – the post-ethnic enters as critique, counter-narrative, and future-possible, suggesting that the materiality of signifiers such as race, religion, and nationality be eschewed for a system of relations beyond such taxonomies. Contemporary black and Asian British authors are at the forefront of imagining the post-ethnic, postulating its existence both as historical and present-day presence, as well as speculative utopian future. These authors also recognise the limitations of the post-ethnic, both as a counter to prejudice and as a means of communal identification. In these terms, post-ethnicity exists not as an uncomplicated or naive assertion, but rather as a highly nuanced engagement with the desire to move beyond notions of ethnic identification, in terms of both the writer's own positioning and wider questions of communal identification and the politics of encounter.

Across the Sea

In speaking of the post-ethnic in the context of British literatures, it is important to recognise both the American origins of the term and the departures from those origins in how the term is employed in relation to conceptions of Britishness. The original American definition as coined by the literary scholar David Hollinger in his work *Postethnic America* (1995) describes not a state beyond the ethnic, but rather one in which ethnicity is but one in a series of identifications, available with a fluid and contingent association implied by the idea of 'affiliation by revocable consent'.[1] Hollinger's notion suggests a move towards a society in which individuals make multiple associations, strongly held and based in fundamental principles but without any sense of inherent belonging. So one can belong to a 'moral community' through either self-identification or communal or familiar socialisation, but this belonging is part of a fluid and transformative cultural matrix in which affiliations inherited through birth or a wider national or racial history are no longer the sole defining features of an individual's identity.[2]

In this respect, the post-ethnic as advanced by Hollinger does not so much erode essentialist identification as acknowledge its contingency. The post-ethnic thus has much in common with Gayatri Spivak's concept of strategic essentialism – the idea that any fundamental identification exists not as genuine subscription to the timeless, but rather as a politically motivated association for a particular moment – what Hollinger refers to as 'strategic enclaving'.[3] This parallel demands a rethinking of what constitutes the 'political' to include activities driven by a desire for social inclusion or individual gain, and where 'motivation' is both conscious and unconscious. While Hollinger is less concerned to emphasise the fluidity within essentialist identities, he nevertheless shares with Spivak the sense of a possible movement between identifications that challenges claims to biological or ancestral ties.

In contrast to Hollinger's idea of the post-ethnic, what emerges as central to British usage is not this definition so much as the work of sociologists such as Suki Ali and Paul Gilroy. British post-ethnicity has less in common with strategic consent to communal identities (including the racial and religious) and is more akin to Gilroy's notion of planetary humanism: Gilroy's term in

[1] David Hollinger, *Postethnic America: Beyond Multiculturalism* (New York: Basic Books, 2005), 188.
[2] Ibid., 113.
[3] See Gayatri Chakravorty Spivak, *In Other Worlds: Essays in Cultural Politics* (New York: Routledge, 1987); David Hollinger, 'The Concept of Post-Racial: How Its Easy Dismissal Obscures Important Questions', *Daedalus*, 140:1 (2011): 174–82; 176.

Between Camps for a way of thinking not only 'beyond race' but also religion, gender, and class, in the service of a universal communality shared across these boundaries.[4] In the US meanwhile, the notion of post-ethnicity has become the subject of extensive critique, entwined with a more specific criticism of ideas of the post-racial and its exploitation by the far right in order to deny continued racism.[5] To some extent these criticisms are based on a misunderstanding of Hollinger's original definition; they suggest that post-ethnicity fails to recognise the value that many communities – particularly those marginalised – continue to place on ethnicity as a source of strategic identification essential to anti-racist and resistance politics, when in fact Hollinger's notion of revocable consent allows precisely this kind of affiliation. These criticisms are, ironically, much more relevant in relation to ideas such as Gilroy's, which are cynical with regard to the positive valence of race. Relevant in both contexts is the criticism of post-ethnicity as a celebratory rhetoric that obscures the continued presence of ethnic prejudice.

Post-Ethnic Aesthetics

It is in this context of post-ethnicity – its competing meanings and controversial reception – that the term has come to be associated with black and Asian British literature, particularly of the past twenty years. It is in Mark U. Stein's landmark publication *Black British Literature: Novels of Transformation* that Hollinger's concept of post-ethnicity is first associated with British writings. For Stein, post-ethnic literature is to be defined not by an eschewal of ethnic themes, but rather by 'an awareness of the expectations that so-called ethnic writing faces [. . .] texts working through these expectations and going beyond them'.[6] Stein's example of this approach is Hanif Kureishi (1954–), whose playful invocation of ethnicity in novels such as *The Buddha of Suburbia* (1990) and *The Black Album* (1995) represents a self-

---

[4] Paul Gilroy, *Between Camps: Nations, Cultures and the Allure of Race*, new edn (London: Routledge, [2000] 2004).

[5] See, for example, Fredrick C. Harris and Robert C. Lieberman, *Beyond Discrimination: Racial Inequality in a Post-Racist Era* (New York: Russell Sage Foundation, 2013); Ta-Nehisi Coates, 'There is no Post-Racial America', *The Atlantic* (July–August 2015). Available at www.theatlantic.com/magazine/archive/2015/07/post-racial-society-distant-dream/395255/; Robert Eddy and Victor Villaneuva, *Language and Power Reader: Representations of Race in a Post-Racist Era* (Salt Lake City, UT: Utah State University Press, 2014).

[6] Mark U. Stein, *Black British Literature: Novels of Transformation* (Columbus, OH: Ohio State University Press, 2004), 112.

conscious awareness of expectations placed on both the black and Asian British author and black and Asian British subjects. Stein sees in these early works by Kureishi a *posed* ethnicity, a recurring engagement with the performative as undermining the idea of stable identities, which gives way in Kureishi's later work, particularly *Intimacy* (1998), to an outright rejection of ethnic affiliation.[7]

Elsewhere, I have offered a less generous counter-reading of Kureishi's work, suggesting that his post-ethnicity is rather a conscious denial of ethnicity in favour of a stridently presented liberal didacticism that goes against the revocable promise of Hollinger's definition.[8] What Stein identifies in Kureishi's fiction is, however, usefully presented in black and Asian British narratives elsewhere: the sense of a post-ethnicity defined not by ironic engagement, but rather by fiction that, in rejecting ethnic themes, is the most noted example of work that 'self-consciously sidesteps and disputes the confines of ethnicity'.[9] For writers such as Mike Gayle (1970–), for example, post-ethnicity is enshrined in a refusal to include ethnic markers that play to the expectations of readers and publishers. Gayle has written nine 'chick-lit' novels with male protagonists, each one eschewing any mention of his central characters' ethnicities. To further this effect, his novels are marketed with covers that frequently feature inanimate household objects such as toasters and armchairs, actively resisting attempts to locate his fiction in ethnic terms. In interview, Gayle has said that he has consciously not written about race because 'It's a burden that's put on every single black novelist that's not put on any white novelist' and that, when an author is black, to be mainstream is 'a political statement'.[10] Unlike Kureishi, Gayle's work comes without an alternative political agenda. As such, it might be seen to be more genuinely post-ethnic in Stein's terms, offering as it does an inclusive multitude of subject positions.

There are limitations to the profitability of contrapuntal readings of absence, such as Kureishi, Gayle, and other writers including Monica Ali (1967–) in *Untold Story* (2011), Bidisha (1978–) in *Seahorses* (1997) and *Too Fast to Live* (2000), Romesh Gunesekera (1954–) in *Heaven's Edge* (2002), and Kazuo Ishiguro (1954–) in *The Buried Giant* (2015) represent. While these

[7] Hanif Kureishi, *Intimacy* (London: Faber and Faber, 1998), 115.
[8] See my discussion of Kureishi in Sara Upstone, *British Asian Fiction: Twenty-First-Century Voices* (Manchester: Manchester University Press, 2010).
[9] Stein, *Black British Literature*, 135.
[10] Suzi Feay, 'Mike Gayle: I'm not the Male Bridget Jones', *The Independent*, 26 July 2000. Available at www.independent.co.uk/news/people/profiles/mike-gayle-im-not-the-male-bridget-jones-709498.html.

interventions are important for pushing against the definition of black and Asian British authors, they offer less subject material when it comes to examining how attitudes to ethnicity have changed in the post-ethnic context. In contrast, works by a new generation of writers such as Diana Evans (1971–) and Helen Oyeyemi (1984–) can be seen as the natural inheritors of Kureishi's earlier perspectives, employing self-referential and ironic mediations on identity which manage to both recognise ethnicity and relativise its significance within the context of multiple cultural affiliations. It is these works, I would argue, that speak more powerfully than Kureishi's later works or Gayle's fictions to the contemporary demands of contexts such as Black Lives Matter, in which there is a need to simultaneously both eschew ethnic absolutism and recognise the continued cultural presence of ethnicity. Each of these works operates post-ethnicity on the level of form as well as theme. Both Evans and Oyeyemi employ magical realist strategies – most notably associated with postcolonial works – with a self-conscious subversion, in order to illustrate its association with a particular ethnic perspective as equally open to post-ethnic questioning.

In both of their debut novels – Oyeyemi's *The Icarus Girl* (2005) and Diana Evans's *26a* (2005) – the authors subtly undercut ideas of ethnic determinism. Examining how they do this is a useful example of the distinctions between post-ethnic and other ethnic fictions, both in thematic and aesthetic terms. Both *26a* and *The Icarus Girl* evoke Nigerian myths around twins and *ábíkú* spirit children – the same myths that play a central role in postcolonial fictions, most notably the *Famished Road* trilogy (1991–1998) by Ben Okri (1959–). In *26a*, the myth is used to account for the powerful psychic connection between Georgia and Bessie, two young girls of mixed parentage growing up in London in the 1980s. In *The Icarus Girl*, likewise, the myth is used to explore the experience of a young girl of mixed parentage called Jess, also in London, whose psychological instability is associated with the presence of a ghost/imaginary friend she names Titiola, a manifestation of her twin who died at birth. In both novels, the acknowledgement of ethnicity that comes through these cultural reference points is combined with a resistance to straightforward associations between those reference points and narrative events. While Georgia and Bessie situate themselves in relation to their Nigerian heritage, when Georgia experiences mental illness this is not as a result of her diasporic positioning, but rather is to be accounted for by her being sexually abused as a young girl while on a visit to Nigeria. Magical realism enters the novel in this Nigerian context, through the ability of Georgia and Bessie's mother to psychically connect with her ancestors. At the end of the novel, however, it is appropriated by Bessie in her connection to Georgia after death, stripping it of these associations. In this transference, the magical is no longer a space of the 'Other', problematising its postcolonial associations. Likewise, *The Icarus Girl* operates in the context of a profound ambivalence in which readers are never certain whether Titiola is a ghost or a manifestation of Jess's imagination. In interview, Oyeyemi has explained her choice of third-person narration for *The Icarus Girl* as an attempt to cement rather than undermine this ambiguity – creating a 'membrane' that prevents unbridled access to the character.[11] While this may seem counter-intuitive, its function illustrates how form works in the service of a strategic post-ethnic intervention. Without access to Jess's consciousness, it is difficult to ascertain her mental health, and this is something the third-person narrative neglects to reveal. Oyeyemi positions readers between the competing simplifications that are western realist rationalism and an African magical realism, thus neither eschewing the ethnic nor adopting it, but working transversally across multiple sites of identification.

Each novel's modification of magical realism is as significant as its presence, for it is the conscious manipulation of the form that announces a creatively ambivalent relationship to the marvellous structures most popularly associated with the postcolonial novel, and with this a similarly problematised relationship to the ethnic inheritance it symbolises. These formal choices mirror each novel's thematic position on identity. When at the end of the novel Jess thinks she may have to choose sides in order to rid herself of Titiola and be mentally healthy, she discovers instead that this choice is not necessary.[12] Likewise, Georgia's and Bessie's lives in London exist in reference to, but not in the service of, ethnic identification. One paradigmatic example of this comes in the girls' development of the 'afro version of the flick': their modification of 1980s hairstyle trends to suit their own hair type. The six-point description of the method of creating the flick denotes a strategic performativity that represents the refusal to shape identification in terms of ethnic binaries.[13] When the girls declare the hairstyle 'saved them from themselves' they mean not from their ethnicity, but rather from their prominent foreheads, which make them subject to 'Spam slaps' in the playground.[14] Evans's ironic pastiche of the language of diasporic identity confusion normalises the girls' identities and enacts a post-ethnic questioning

---

[11] Aminatta Forna, 'New Writing and Nigeria: Chimamanda Ngozi Adichie and Helen Oyeyemi in Conversation', *Wasafiri*, 21:1 (2006): 50–7; 55.
[12] Helen Oyeyemi, *The Icarus Girl* (London: Bloomsbury, 2005), 257.
[13] Diana Evans, *26a* (London: Chatto & Windus, 2005), 79.　[14] Ibid., 80.

of reader assumptions about the association of those ethnic identities with trauma.

Utopian Realisms

While Evans and Oyeyemi recreate postcolonial forms in the service of a post-ethnic playfulness both structural and thematic, elsewhere post-ethnicity is gestured towards by much more subtle shifts in formal emphasis – what I have termed a 'utopian realism' in which the elision of race is paralleled with an elision of the harsh realities of racism in favour of alternative, speculative visions of British society.[15] That these reimaginings come not purely in the form of future-set fictions, but also in those dealing with the present – and perhaps most notably those dealing with the near and distant past – exploits the gap between realism and reality to present a particular social vision. Such awareness counters suggestions that post-ethnic writing is less political than its anti-racist and post-racist counterparts; playing out the post-ethnic within the realm of the identifiable provides a powerful counterpoint through which readers are encouraged to invest in the possibility of post-ethnic futures as achievable social outcomes.

A useful example of this is given by the starkly realist *Some Kind of Black* (1996), the Saga Prize-winning first novel by Diran Adebayo (1968–). The story of Dele, a young black man from London studying at Oxford University, *Some Kind of Black* is firmly rooted in notions of racial identity, yet within this enacts a powerful subversion of notions of racial essentialism. Drawing this into relief, one can compare Adebayo's novel with another landmark black British fiction, *The Scholar* (1997) by Courttia Newland (1973–), which was published just a year later. Both novels are haunted by events in Brixton in December 1995, in which rioting broke out after the death of 26-year-old Wayne Douglas in police custody – in *The Scholar* captured in an opening in which the father of one of the two central male characters is murdered in police custody; in *Some Kind of Black* represented when Dele learns that his sister, Dapo, has been seriously injured in a police incident. Yet while Newland's novel ends 'on the darkest possible note' with the two young boys at the novel's centre lost to crime, Adebayo ends his fiction with Dapo's recovery, and a comic scene of romantic entanglement.[16] In Dele's

---

[15] Sara Upstone, *Rethinking Race and Identity in Contemporary British Fiction* (London: Routledge, 2016).

[16] Susanne Cuevas, *Babylon and the Golden City: Representations of London in Black and Asian British Novels since the 1990s* (Heidelberg: Winter, 2008), 217.

response to his sister's suffering, *Some Kind of Black* contains an announcement of a conscious desire for reimagining: 'Reality mugged Dele', we are told.[17] In his next novel, *My Once Upon a Time* (2000), Adebayo indulges this desire for the speculative in a future-set fiction, infused with Yoruba myth, but setting this influence alongside a world in which it is postcode rather than ethnicity that determines communal belonging.

Not only blackness, but also whiteness is destabilised by these approaches. This is particularly a preoccupation of Bernardine Evaristo (1959–), whose concern for revisionist fictional histories foregrounds the performativity not only of black, but also white ethnicities. Evaristo's focus on the historical blackness of Europe in novels such as *The Emperor's Babe* (2001) and *Soul Tourists* (2005) draws attention to the farcical nature of absolute conceptions of whiteness in contemporary European culture, when its post-ethnic diversity is not new, but rather historically entrenched.

To re-vision histories is an idealistic and speculative strategy, noted by the fact that many authors turn to narratives of childhood experience in the pursuit of post-ethnic imaginaries, filtering the harsh realities of racism through the naive and diffracted viewpoints of child protagonists. In *My Name is Leon* (2016) by Kit de Waal (1960–), for example, a gritty story of child abuse and the foster care system is transformed into post-ethnic political statement by the experience of the novel's central child protagonist. Leon is a boy of mixed parentage, who is placed in foster care alongside his white baby brother, Jake. While his white foster mother, Maureen, explicitly acknowledges that his brother is to be adopted because he is white, Leon's own experience constructs a positive post-ethnic possibility, evident not only in Leon's relationship with Maureen, but also in Leon's interactions with the wider community centred upon his secret visits to a local allotment. The allotment is a model of post-ethnic interaction: West Indian black power followers share the soil with old white men and an Asian couple in traditional dress of sari and turban. The sharing of seeds between the inhabitants is metaphoric of the growth of a shared future, in which ethnicity ceases to define friendship or community. When Leon goes missing, it is the inhabitants of the allotment who, together, combine forces to find him and return him home. As Leon himself says when confronted by a policeman near the novel's conclusion: 'We've been growing things [. . .] that's what we do.'[18]

---

[17] Diran Adebayo, *Some Kind of Black* (London: Abacus, 1996), 71.

[18] Kit De Waal, *My Name is Leon* (London: Viking, 2016), 241.

The Pitfalls of the Post-Ethnic

My Name is Leon in this respect comes in the wake of a number of childhood revisionings, such as *Anita and Me* (1996) by Meera Syal (1961–) and *Vauxhall* (2013) by Gabriel Gbadamosi (1961–). In these narratives, optimism for the future is always tempered: be it by class as in *Some Kind of Black* and *My Name is Leon*, by gender in *26a*, or by educational opportunity in *Anita and Me*. A caveat, therefore, is directed towards an awareness of how embracing the post-ethnic can present an unwelcome complacency towards the continued 'otherness machine' that drives the construction of contemporary identities. In this regard, novelists point not so much to the unreality of the post-ethnic as per American critiques, but rather to the risks in the assumption that ethnicity exists as a static frame of reference, the erosion of which might challenge prejudice.

The author Zadie Smith (1975–) has continually reflected on this problematic in her fiction. Her landmark novel *White Teeth* (2000) is often lauded as a celebratory text of post-ethnicity, but is in fact largely constructed in order to problematise this idea. While readings of *White Teeth* frequently focus on the hybrid fusion of diverse cultural influences reflected in the lives of Millat and Magid, Irie's mixed-race (rather than multicultural) experience is very different – entrapped by her feelings that she must make an absolute identification that she finds impossible because she feels that to be accepted she must be the daughter of Archie *or* the daughter of Clara; that she can be 'Jamaican hourglass' or '*English Rose*', with no other identity possible.[19] This is made concrete by its evolution in Irie's understanding of herself not via the older generation of racist war veterans like Mr Hamilton, or even by her parents' generation, but rather in her relationships with those she feels closest to. Millat runs a hybrid 'crew' of culturally diverse influences; he declares in post-ethnic assertion that he lives 'for the in between'.[20] Yet in terms of racial hybridity his attitude is very different; when considering the results of procreation with Irie he declares the offspring would be 'freaks!'.[21] So Smith points to a Britain in which multicultural identity has become acceptable in the movement between absolute positions, and even in the hybrid fusion of cultural influences, but where the inhabiting of the middle-space in terms of post-racial identification that Irie represents has yet to be fully achieved: possible – yes – but only in the uncertain future of the novel's

---

[19] Zadie Smith, *White Teeth* (London: Hamish Hamilton, 2000), 231.   [20] Ibid., 303.
[21] Ibid., 198.

final pages as represented by a runaway mouse and unborn child with uncertain parentage.

In *NW* (2012), Smith's return to the Willesden of her first novel, readers are ostensibly offered the post-ethnic not as future-possible, as in *White Teeth*, but now twelve years later as having come to pass, embodied in the friendship of Leah (white) and Keisha (black), and their relative fortunes, complicating stereotypes of social mobility by the fact that it is Keisha who has escaped the poverty of their youth, and Leah who has remained on the council estate. Yet other forces continue to create a politics of difference, most notably in terms of gender and class; Leah may be white, but socioeconomic background is the barrier to her professional success as she attempts to compete amongst 'warbling posh boys'.[22] The post-ethnic here is, like the hybrid, revealed as a fetish that fails to account for the complex intersectional politics driving discrimination in Britain today. And Smith is not alone in this regard – we can see similarities in the critique of globalisation offered by Hari Kunzru (1969–) in his novel *Transmission* (2004), which problematises the idea of a post-ethnic, global economy with the stark reminder of economic exploitation on which it rests, or *Londonstani* (2006) by Gautam Malkani (1976–). Malkani's novel is the closest one might get to a vision of a truly post-ethnic reality, with a central character, Jas, who is part of a west London Asian gang, only to be revealed at the end of the novel as white. Yet rather than this signifying the end of ethnic difference, it betrays merely a transference of this difference to new, post-ethnic identities; Asian is no longer birth or skin colour, instead it is a hypermasculine, consumerist culture that leaves those associated with it culturally bereft rather than enriched.

Post-Ethnic Criticism

Novelists who expose the problematic nature of idealised versions of the post-racial are not suggesting that they would rather the post-ethnic did not exist. As warning, however, these novelists do expose its promotion as a panacea for social division as underestimating the multifaceted work into communal relations that must be undertaken. In relation to this exposure, it is important for scholarship to expose its own problematic relation to post-ethnic fictions. Literary critics have become comfortable with Graham

---

[22] Ibid., 27.

Huggan's idea of the postcolonial exotic as the preserve of readerships and publishers.[23] This is an issue that has particular relevance to the post-ethnic where not merely personal identification but also the visual politics of difference is a pertinent factor in how writers are marketed and what burden of representation is placed upon them: the wide thematic range of authors such as Patricia Dunker (1951–) and Helen Walsh (1977–) draws less critical attention because, despite mixed backgrounds, these authors' less obvious linguistic or visual ethnicity suggests their evasion of ethnicity is less politically charged than the similar acts of Kureishi or Gayle. It has been, however, more difficult to recognise the culpability of scholars in the cultivation of particular Othering stereotypes of world literatures. Those writing about such literatures continually confront Spivak's critique of the west's representation of the subaltern and Said's ideas of Orientalising discourse, as they ask to what extent the selection of texts for study and commentary feeds into a particular totalising image of the world outside of the Anglo-American academy. More recently, Chimamanda Ngozi Adichie (1977–) has spoken powerfully about the dangers of a 'single story' of Africa.[24] Adichie's account of her own experience studying in America with a white American roommate who assumed, because of what she had read about Nigeria, that Adichie listened to tribal music and would not be able to speak good English draws attention to the institutional contexts in which such readings take place.

It is in this context that, similarly, it is appropriate to ask questions about whether the choices made by academics foster the post-ethnic. Why is Kureishi's post-ethnicity a matter of comment, and Dunker's or Walsh's is not? How does a complex conjunction of visuality, author-identification, subject matter, and linguistic signifiers such as author name and book title position an author critically as black or Asian British? Are black and Asian British texts reserved in the curriculum and academic discussions for questions of ethnicity or race? Are they present as either token or representative fictions, or are they consigned to themed courses about questions of race, ethnicity, and identity? Such choices are not easily made – the resounding message of Black Lives Matter is that we are not yet at the point to indulge the utopian fantasy that ethnicity is no longer an issue. So it is important that black and Asian British texts are given the space to be received in the context of

---

[23] Graham Huggan, *The Postcolonial Exotic: Marketing the Margins* (London: Routledge, 2001).

[24] Chimamanda Ngozi Adichie, 'The Danger of a Single Story', *TEDGlobal*, July 2009. Available at www.ted.com/talks/chimamanda_adichie_the_danger_of_a_single_story.

ethnic awareness. Without this, they risk contributing to precisely the kind of illusions that critics of the post-ethnic in an American context point towards. There are thus competing needs, complicated by the perspective of particular texts – those that demand the continued presence of race as a positive aspect of cultural identification in post-ethnic terms, versus those that speak for its presence as a marker of continued racism to be questioned and eroded, and of course those that fall between these positions in desiring a positive positioning presented in counterpoint to continued racist violence and prejudice. At the same time, however, it is vital that black and Asian British texts be recognised for their crucial contributions in other respects too, not merely in intersectional terms but also outside of discussions of race, so that there is a critical recognition that these writers are first and foremost authors who, like their white counterparts, might equally be discussed for thematic concerns which fall outside of the narrow borders of racial discourses. For example, where does one find space to discuss the politics of desire or the existential philosophy of *NW*, or the representations of memory and mental illness in *26a*? Until critics can begin to see these texts in planetary terms and mirror their own argument in their practice it seems hard to imagine a wider social world capable of such planetary thinking.

These questions can also be brought to bear on the ways in which race is isolated within mainstream criticism as something identified with particular authors. Again, a problematic terrain must be navigated by the critic in such terms. Suggesting that questions of race are the province of black and Asian British writers is highly problematic. At the same time, however, discussion of these issues in relation to white writers must recognise that allowing the white author a voice on questions of racial prejudice risks again a colonisation of black and Asian British voices by a white authority that will be potentially given greater space than its counterparts. Spivak's questions of representation raise their head again, in the possibility of cultural appropriation. Ultimately, however, it must be seen as a democratising and planetary act to come to the position that voices and themes matter more than the racial identities – often defined by others – of those who create them. For it is only with such acknowledgement that the taxonomies of literary criticism can be eroded so that they might provide in practice a model of the post-ethnic society the literature itself speaks for.

It is at the interstices of these debates that the current volume itself stands – desiring to give voice to black and Asian British writers and recognising the continued need to do so, yet at the same time to suggest that there is a literature of vast theme and interest that in its scope gestures towards a contribution that is post-ethnic in its range of subject matter, aesthetic variety, and formal diversity. As much as one writes for such a volume with enthusiasm, it is therefore also with a hope that such a volume becomes indeed as its name suggests – a 'history'. For the future, it can be hoped, will be in one form or another distinctly more 'post-ethnic'.

Select Bibliography

Primary

Abdullah, Kia. *Child's Play*. Stockport: Revenge Ink, 2009.

Aboulela, Leila. *The Kindness of Enemies*. London: Weidenfeld & Nicolson, 2015.

Lyrics Alley. London: Weidenfeld & Nicolson, 2010.

Minaret. London: Bloomsbury, 2005.

The Translator. Edinburgh: Polygon, 1999.

Adebayo, Diran, *My Once Upon a Time*. London: Abacus, 2000.

Some Kind of Black. London: Virago, 1996.

Agard, John. *Mangoes and Bullets: Selected and New Poems, 1972–84*. London: Pluto, 1985.

Agbabi, Patience. *Telling Tales*. Edinburgh: Canongate, 2014.

Transformatrix. Edinburgh: Payback Press, 2000.

Ahlberg, Allan. *Mr Biff the Boxer*. Illustrations by Janet Ahlberg. Harmondsworth: Kestrel Books, 1980.

Ahmad, Rukhsana. *The Hope Chest*. London: Virago, 1996.

Mistaken: Annie Besant in India. London: Aurora Metro, 2007.

Ahmad, Rukhsana and Gupta, Rahila (eds.). *Flaming Spirit: Stories from the Asian Women Writers' Collective*. London: Virago, 1994.

Ahmed, Rehana (ed.). *Walking a Tightrope: New Writing from Asian Britain*. Basingstoke: Pan Macmillan, 2004.

Ali, Duse Mohamed. *A Cleopatra Night*. Performed at Dundee, 1907.

The Jew's Revenge. Performed at Royal Surrey Theatre, London, 1903.

Lily of Bermuda. Performed at the Theatre Royal, Manchester, 1909.

Ali, Monica. *Brick Lane*. London: Doubleday, 2003.

Untold Story. London: Simon & Schuster, 2011.

Allen, Eric. *The Latchkey Children*. London: Oxford University Press, 1963.

Alvi, Moniza. *At the Moment of Partition*. Newcastle upon Tyne: Bloodaxe Books, 2013.

Blackbird Bye. Newcastle upon Tyne: Bloodaxe Books, 2018.

The Country at my Shoulder. Oxford: Oxford University Press, 1993.

Europa. Newcastle upon Tyne: Bloodaxe Books, 2008.

How the Stone Found its Voice. Tarset: Bloodaxe Books, 2005.

Anam, Tahmima. *A Golden Age*. London: John Murray, 2007.

Anand, Mulk Raj. *Across the Black Waters*. London: Jonathan Cape, 1940.

The Bubble. New Delhi: Arnold-Heinemann, 1984.

Untouchable. London: Wishart, 1935.

Anand, Mulk Raj and Singh, Iqbal (eds.). *Indian Short Stories*. London: New India Publishing Company, 1946.

Anwar, Amer. *Brothers in Blood*. London: Dialogue Books, 2018.

Asian Women Writers' Workshop. *Right of Way*. Ed. Ravinder Randhawa. London: Women's Press, 1988.

Aslam, Nadeem. *The Blind Man's Garden*. London: Faber and Faber, 2013.

The Golden Legend. London: Faber and Faber, 2017.

Maps for Lost Lovers. London: Faber and Faber, 2004.

The Wasted Vigil. London: Faber and Faber, 2008.

Atta, Dean. *I am Nobody's Nigger*. London: Westbourne, 2013.

Augustus, Patrick. *Baby Father*. London: The X Press, 1994.

Bandele, Biyi. *The Street*. London: Picador, 1999.

Bennett, Alvin Gladstone. *Because They Know Not*. London: Phoenix Press, 1959.

Bennett, Louise. *Anancy Stories and Poems in Dialect*. Kingston, Jamaica: Gleaner, 1944.

(Jamaica) Dialect Verses. Kingston, Jamaica: Herald, 1942.

Jamaica Labrish. With notes and introduction by Rex Nettleford. Kingston, Jamaica: Sangster's Bookstores, 1966.

Selected Poems. Ed. Mervyn Morris. Kingston, Jamaica: Sangster's Bookstores, 1982.

Bernard, Jay. *The Red and Yellow Nothing*. London: Ink, Sweat and Tears, 2016.

Your Sign is Cuckoo, Girl. London: Tall-Lighthouse Publications, 2008.

Berry, James. *Hot Earth Cold Earth*. Newcastle upon Tyne: Bloodaxe Books, 1995.

Lucy's Letters and Loving. London: New Beacon Books, 1982.

Windrush Songs. Tarset: Bloodaxe Books, 2007.

(ed.). *Bluefoot Traveller: An Anthology of West Indian Poets in Britain*. London: Limehouse, 1976.

(ed.). *News for Babylon: The Chatto Book of Westindian-British Poetry*. London: Chatto & Windus, 1984.

Bidisha. *Seahorses*. London: Flamingo, 1997.

Too Fast to Live. London: Duck Editions, 2000.

Blackman, Malorie. *Chasing the Stars*. London: Penguin, 2016.

Noble Conflict. London: Doubleday, 2013.

Noughts & Crosses. London: Doubleday, 2001.

Robot Girl. Illustrations by Matthew Griffin. Edinburgh: Barrington Stoke, 2015.

Bloom, Valerie. *Touch Mi! Tell Mi!* London: Bogle-L'Ouverture, 1983.

Booker, Malika. *Absolution*. Performed at the Battersea Arts Centre, London, 1999.

Pepper Seed. Leeds: Peepal Tree Press, 2013.

Bose, Siddharta. *Digital Monsoon*. London: Penned in the Margins, 2013.

No Dogs, No Indians. London: Penned in the Margins, 2017.

Brahmachari, Sita. *Artichoke Hearts*. London: Macmillan, 2011.

Jasmine Skies. Chicago, IL: Albert Whitman, 2014.

Braithwaite, E. R. *Choice of Straws*. London: Bodley Head, 1965.

A Kind of Homecoming. Englewood Cliffs, NJ: Prentice Hall, 1962.

Paid Servant. London: Bodley Head, 1962.

Neighbours. London: Bodley Head, 1972.

To Sir, with Love. London: Bodley Head, 1959.

Brathwaite, Edward [Kamau]. *The Arrivants*. Oxford: Oxford University Press, 1973.

Breeze, Jean Binta. *Riddym Ravings and Other Poems*. London: Race Today Publications, 1988.

Brewster, Yvonne (ed.). *Black Plays*. London: Methuen, 1987.

(ed.). *Black Plays: Two*. London: Methuen, 1989.

Burford, Barbara, Pearse, Gabriela, Nichols, Grace, and Kay, Jackie. *A Dangerous Knowing: Four Black Women Poets*. London: Sheba, 1984.

Bush, Ruth and Bernard, Jay. *Beacon of Hope: New Beacon in Poetry and Prose*. London: New Beacon Books, 2016.

Campbell, Sheri. *Rude Gal*. London: The X Press, 1997.

Wicked in Bed. London: The X Press, 1994.

Capildeo, Vahni. *Measures of Expatriation*. Manchester: Carcanet Press, 2016.

Carew, Jan. *Moscow is not my Mecca*. London: Secker & Warburg, 1964.

Centerprise Trust. *Breaking the Silence: Writing by Asian Women*. London: Centerprise Trust, 1984.

Chatterjee, Debjani (ed.). *The Redbeck Anthology of British South Asian Poetry*. Bradford: Redbeck, 2000.

Chaudhuri, Amit. *Afternoon Raag*. London: Heinemann, 1993.

Chikwava, Brian. *Harare North*. London: Jonathan Cape, 2009.

Chingonyi, Kayo. *Kumukanda*. London: Chatto & Windus, 2017.

Da Choong, Cole Wilson, Olivette, Evaristo, Bernardine, and Pearse, Gabriela (eds.). *Black Women Talk Poetry*. London: Black Womantalk, 1987.

Da Choong, Cole Wilson, Olivette, Parker, Sylvia and Pearse, Gabriela (eds.). *Don't Ask Me Why: An Anthology of Short Stories by Black Women*. London: Black Womantalk, 1991.

Chowdhry, Maya. *Fossil*. Leeds: Peepal Tree Press, 2016.

The Seamstress and the Global Garment. Manchester: Crocus Debuts/Suitcase, 2009.

Cobham, Rhonda and Collins, Merle (eds.). *Watchers and Seekers: Creative Writing by Black Women in Britain*. London: Women's Press, 1987.

Cooke, Trish. *Full, Full, Full of Love*. Illustrations by Paul Howard. London: Walker Books, 2003.

How Anansi Got His Stories. Illustrations by Anna Violet. Oxford: Oxford University Press, 2011.

So Much! Illustrations by Helen Oxenbury. London: Walker Books, 1994.

Craft, William and Ellen. *Running a Thousand Miles for Freedom: Or, the Escape of William and Ellen Craft from Slavery*. Mineola, NY: Dover Publications, [1860] 2014.

Cugoano, Quobna Ottobah [alias John Stuart]. *Thoughts and Sentiments on the Evil and Wicked Traffic of the Slavery and Commerce of the Human Species, Humbly Submitted to the Inhabitants of Great-Britain, by Ottobah Cugoano, a Native of Africa*. Ed. Vincent Carretta. Harmondsworth: Penguin, [1787] 1999.

D'Aguiar, Fred. *Bill of Rights*. London: Chatto & Windus, 1998.

British Subjects. Newcastle upon Tyne: Bloodaxe Books, 1993.

Feeding the Ghosts. London: Chatto & Windus, 1997.

Mama Dot. London: Chatto & Windus; Hogarth Press, 1985.

Dabydeen, David. *Coolie Odyssey*. London: Hansib/Dangaroo, 1988.

Disappearance. London: Secker & Warburg, 1993.

A Harlot's Progress. London: Jonathan Cape, 1999.

The Intended. London: Secker & Warburg, 1991.

Slave Song. Mundelstrup: Dangaroo, 1984.

Turner: New and Selected Poems. London: Cape Poetry, 1994.

Dathorne, O. R. *The Scholar-Man*. London: Cassell, 1964.

Dawes, Kwame. *Red: Contemporary Black British Poetry*. Leeds: Peepal Tree Press, 2010.

Dawes, Neville. *The Last Enchantment*. Leeds: MacGibbon & Kee, 1960.

De Waal, Kit. *My Name is Leon*. London: Viking, 2016.

Dennis, Ferdinand. *Duppy Conqueror*. London: Flamingo, 1998.

Desai, Anita. *Bye-Bye Blackbird*. Delhi: Orient, 1985.

Desani, G. V. *All About H. Hatterr*. London: Aldor Press, 1948.

Dhami, Narinder. *Bhangra Babes*. London: Corgi Yearling, 2005.

    Bindi Babes. London: Corgi Yearling, 2003.

    Bollywood Babes. London: Corgi Yearling, 2004.

    Superstar Babes. London: Corgi Yearling, 2008.

Dharker, Imtiaz. *Over the Moon*. Hexham: Bloodaxe Books, 2014.

Dhingra, Leena. *Amritvela*. London: Women's Press, 1988.

Dhondy, Farrukh. *East End at Your Feet*. Basingstoke: Macmillan, 1976.

    Poona Company. London: Gollancz, 1980.

    Trip Trap. London: Gollancz, 1982.

Donkor, Michael. *Hold*. London: HarperCollins, 2018.

Dover, Cedric. *Half-Caste*. London: Secker & Warburg, 1937.

Edwards, Yvette. *A Cupboard Full of Coats*. Oxford: Oneworld, 2011.

    The Mother. London: Mantle, 2016.

Ellams, Inua. *Barber Shop Chronicles*. London: Oberon, 2017.

Ellams, Inua and Selected Poets. *#Afterhours: Anthology / Diary / Memoir / Poems*. Rugby: Nine Arches Press, 2017.

Emecheta, Buchi. *Head Above Water*. London: Fontana, 1986.

    In the Ditch. London: Barrie & Jenkins, 1972.

    Second Class Citizen. London: Allison & Busby, 1974.

Equiano, Olaudah. *The Interesting Narrative and Other Writings*. Ed. Vincent Carretta. Rev. edn. London: Penguin, [1789] 2003.

Evans, Diana. *26a*. London: Chatto & Windus, 2005.

    Ordinary People. London: Chatto & Windus, 2018.

    The Wonder. London: Chatto & Windus, 2009.

Evaristo, Bernardine. *Lara*. Tunbridge Wells: Angela Royal, 1997. Rev. edn, Tarset: Bloodaxe Books, 2009.

    The Emperor's Babe. London: Hamish Hamilton, 2001.

    Mr Loverman. London: Hamish Hamilton / Penguin, 2013.

    Soul Tourists. London: Hamish Hamilton, 2005.

Evaristo, Bernardine and Nagra, Daljit (eds.). *Ten: New Poets*. Tarset: Bloodaxe Books, 2010.

Farooki, Roopa. *Bitter Sweets*. London: Macmillan, 2007.

    The Flying Man. London: Review, 2012.

    The Way Things Look to Me. London: Pan, 2009.

Figueroa, John. *The Chase: A Collection of Poems 1941–1989*. Leeds: Peepal Tree Press, 1992.

Forna, Aminatta. *Ancestor Stones*. London: Bloomsbury, 2006.

The Memory of Love. London: Bloomsbury, 2010.

Gandhi, M. K. *An Autobiography, or, The Story of My Experiments with Truth*. London: Penguin, [1927–1929] 1982.

Hind Swaraj and Other Writings. Ed. A. J. Parel. Cambridge: Cambridge University Press, [1909] 1997.

Gavin, Jamila. *Kamla and Kate*. Illustrations by Thelma Lambert. London: Magnet, 1983.

Coram Boy. London: Egmont, 2000.

The Eye of the Horse. London: Methuen, 1994.

The Track of the Wind. London: Egmont, 1997.

The Wheel of Surya. London: Mammoth, 1992.

Gbadamosi, Gabriel. *Vauxhall*. London: Telegram, 2013.

George, Kadija (ed.). *Six Plays by Black and Asian Women Writers*. London: Aurora Metro, 1993.

Gibbes, Phoebe. *Hartly House, Calcutta*. Ed. Michael J. Franklin. New Delhi: Oxford University Press, [1789] 2007.

Gilroy, Beryl. *Black Teacher*. London: Cassell, 1976.

In Praise of Love and Children. Leeds: Peepal Tress Press, 1996.

Inkle & Yarico. Leeds: Peepal Tree Press, 1996.

Leaves in the Wind: Collected Writings. Ed. Joan Anim-Addo. London: Mango Publishing, 1998.

Glave, Thomas (ed.). *Our Caribbean: A Gathering of Lesbian and Gay Writing from the Antilles*. Durham, NC: Duke University Press, 2008.

Goddard, Lynette (ed.). *The Methuen Drama Book of Plays by Black British Writers*. London: Methuen, 2011.

Gordon, John R. and Beadle-Blair, Rikki. *Black and Gay in the UK: An Anthology*. London: Team Angelica, 2014.

Gorgon, Donald. *Cop Killer*. London: The X Press, 1994.

Grewal, Shabnam, et al. (eds.). *Charting the Journey: Writings by Black and Third World Women*. London: Sheba, 1988.

Gronniosaw, Ukawsaw. *A Narrative of the Most Remarkable Particulars in the Life of James Albert Ukawsaw Gronniosaw, an African Prince, as Related by Himself*. Bath: Printed by W. Gye in Westgate-Street; and sold by T. Mills, bookseller, in King's-Mead-Square, [1772].

Gunaratne, Guy. *In Our Mad and Furious City*. London: Tinder Press, 2018.

Gunesekera, Romesh. *Heaven's Edge*. London: Bloomsbury, 2002.

The Match. London: Bloomsbury, 2006.

Noontide Toll. London: Granta, 2014.

Reef. London: Granta, 1994.

The Sandglass. London: Granta, 1998.

Gupta, Rahila. *Don't Wake Me: The Ballad of Nihal Armstrong*. Portsmouth: Playdead Press, 2013.

Gupta, Sunetra. *Memories of Rain*. New Delhi: Penguin India, 1992.

Gurnah, Abdulrazak. *Admiring Silence*. London: Hamish Hamilton, 1996.

By the Sea. London: Bloomsbury, 2001.

Desertion. London, Bloomsbury, 2005.

Gravel Heart. London: Bloomsbury, 2017.

Memory of Departure. London: Jonathan Cape, 1987.

Paradise. London, Hamish Hamilton, 1994.

Hai, Yasmin. *The Making of Mr Hai's Daughter: Becoming British*. London: Virago, 2008.

Hall, Stuart with Schwarz, Bill. *Familiar Stranger: A Life Between Two Islands*. London: Allen Lane, 2017.

Hamid, Mohsin. *Exit West*. London: Hamish Hamilton, 2017.

The Reluctant Fundamentalist. London: Hamish Hamilton, 2007.

Hammon, Briton. *A Narrative of the Uncommon Sufferings, and Surprizing Deliverance of Briton Hammon, a Negro Man*. Boston, MA: Printed and sold by Green & Russell, in Queen-Street, 1760.

Harris, Maggie. *In Margate by Lunchtime*. Teynham: Cultured Llama, 2015.

Limbolands. London: Mango Publishing, 1999.

Harris, Maggie. *Sixty Years of Loving*. Royston: Cane Arrow Press, 2014.

Harris, Wilson. *The Angel at the Gate*. London: Faber and Faber, 1982.

Carnival. London: Faber and Faber, 1985.

The Dark Jester. London: Faber and Faber, 2001.

The Far Journey of Oudin. London: Faber and Faber, 1961.

The Ghost of Memory. London: Faber and Faber, 2006.

Heartland. London: Faber and Faber, 1964.

The Infinite Rehearsal. London: Faber and Faber, 1987.

Palace of the Peacock. London: Faber and Faber, 1960.

The Secret Ladder. London: Faber and Faber, 1963.

The Waiting Room. London: Faber and Faber, 1967.

Headley, Victor. *Excess*. London: The X-Press, 1993.

Yardie. London: The X-Press, 1992.

Yush! London: The X-Press, 1994.

Hoffman, Mary. *Amazing Grace*. New York: Dial Books, 1991.

Hosain, Attia. *Phoenix Fled*. London: Chatto & Windus, 1953.

Sunlight on a Broken Column. London: Chatto & Windus, 1961.

Huchu, Tendai. *The Maestro, The Magistrate & The Mathematician*. Bulawayo: amaBooks, 2014.

Husain, Ed. *The Islamist*. London: Penguin, 2007.

Hussein, Aamer. *Another Gulmohar Tree*. London: Telegram, 2009.

Mirror to the Sun. London: Mantra, 1993.

The Swan's Wife. Delhi: Ilqa Publications, 2014.

Ishiguro, Kazuo. *The Buried Giant*. London: Faber and Faber, 2015.

The Remains of the Day. London: Faber and Faber, 1989.

James, C. L. R. *The Black Jacobins: Toussaint L'Ouverture and the San Domingo Revolution*. London: Secker & Warburg, 1938.

Minty Alley. London: Secker & Warburg, 1936.

Toussaint Louverture. Ed. Christian Høgsbjerg. Durham, NC: Duke University Press, 2012.

Janmahomed, Shelina Zahra. *Love in a Headscarf: Muslim Woman Finds the One*. London: Aurum, 2009.

Jekyll, Walter. *Jamaica Song and Story: Anancy Stories, Digging Songs, Ring Tunes and Dancing Tunes*. London: D. Nutt for the Folklore Society, 1907.

John, Errol. *Moon on a Rainbow Shawl*. London: Faber and Faber, 1958.

Johnson, Catherine. *The Curious Tale of the Lady Caraboo*. London: Penguin Random House, 2015.

    A Nest of Vipers. London: Corgi, 2008.

    Sawbones. London: Walker Books, 2013.

    Blade and Bone. London: Walker Books, 2016.

Johnson, Linton Kwesi. *Dread Beat and Blood*. London: Bogle-L'Ouverture, 1975.

    Inglan is a Bitch. London: Race Today, 1980.

Joseph, Anthony. *Desafinado*. London: Poison Engine Press, 1994.

    The African Origins of UFOs. Cambridge: Salt, 2006.

    Kitch. Leeds: Peepal Tree Press, 2018.

    Rubber Orchestras. Cambridge: Salt, 2011.

Kalu, Peter. *Being Me by Adele Vialli*. London: HopeRoad, 2015.

    The Silent Striker. London: HopeRoad, 2015.

Kamm, Josephine. *Out of Step*. London: Hodder & Stoughton, 1962.

Karaka. F. D. *All My Yesterdays*. Bombay: Thacker, 1944.

    Oh! You English. London: Frederick Muller, 1935.

    The Pulse of Oxford. London: J. M. Dent, 1933.

Kay, Jackie. *The Adoption Papers*. Newcastle upon Tyne: Bloodaxe Books, 1991.

    Darling: New and Selected Poems. Newcastle upon Tyne: Bloodaxe Books, 2007.

    Red Dust Road. London: Picador, 2010.

    Strawgirl. London: Macmillan Children's, 2002.

    Trumpet. London: Picador, 1998.

Kay, Jackie, Procter, James, and Robinson, Gemma (eds.). *Out of Bounds: British Black and Asian Poets*. Newcastle upon Tyne: Bloodaxe Books, 2012.

Kaye, Geraldine. *A Breath of Fresh Air*. London: André Deutsch, 1987.

Khair, Tabish. *How to Fight Islamist Terror from the Missionary Position*. London: HarperCollins, 2012.

    Just Another Jihadi Jane. Reading: Periscope, 2016.

    Night of Happiness. New Delhi: Picador India, 2018.

    The Thing about Thugs. New Delhi: Fourth Estate, 2010.

El-Khairy, Omar. *Sour Lips*. London: Oberon, 2013.

El-Khairy, Omar, created with Latif, Nadia. *Homegrown*. London: fly πrates, 2017.

Khalvati, Mimi. *The Meanest Flower*. Manchester: Carcanet, 2007.

Khan, Vaseem. *The Unexpected Inheritance of Inspector Chopra*. London: Mulholland Books, 2015.

Khan-Din, Ayub. *East is East*. Dir. Kristine Landon-Smith. Tamasha Theatre Company / Royal Court, 1996.

Kingsley, Charles. *At Last a Christmas in the West Indies*. London; New York: Macmillan, 1872.

Kunzru, Hari. *Gods Without Men*. New York: Knopf, 2011.

    The Impressionist. London: Hamish Hamilton, 2002.

    Transmission. London: Hamish Hamilton, 2004.

Kureishi, Hanif. *Birds of Passage*. Oxford: Amber Lane, 1983.

    The Black Album. London: Faber and Faber, 1995.

    The Black Album. Dir. Jatinder Verma. Tara Arts / National Theatre, 2009.

Borderline. London: Methuen, 1981.

The Buddha of Suburbia. London: Faber and Faber, 1990.

Collected Screenplays 1. London: Faber and Faber, 2002.

Gabriel's Gift. London: Faber and Faber, 2001.

Love in a Blue Time. London: Faber and Faber, 1997.

'*My Beautiful Laundrette*' *and* '*The Rainbow Sign*'. London: Faber and Faber, 1986.

My Ear at his Heart: Reading my Father. London: Faber and Faber, 2004.

My Son the Fanatic. London: Faber and Faber, 1997.

Sammy and Rosie Get Laid. London: Faber and Faber, 1988.

Kwei-Armah, Kwame. *Elmina's Kitchen*. London: Methuen, 2003.

Fix Up. London: Methuen, 2004.

Statement of Regret. London: Methuen, 2007.

Lalwani, Nikita. *Gifted*. London: Viking, 2007.

Lamming, George. *The Emigrants*. London: Michael Joseph, 1954.

In the Castle of my Skin. London: Michael Joseph, 1953.

The Pleasures of Exile. London: Michael Joseph, 1960.

Water with Berries. London: Longman, 1971.

Levy, Andrea. *Every Light in the House Burnin'*. London: Review, 1994.

Fruit of the Lemon. London: Review, 1999.

Never Far from Nowhere. London: Review, 1996.

Small Island. New York: Picador, 2004.

Lloyd, Errol. *Nandi's Bedtime*. London: Bodley Head, 1982.

Nini at Carnival. London: Bodley Head, 1978.

Lowe, Adam (ed.). *SPOKE: New Queer Voices*. Manchester: Dog Horn Publishing, 2015.

McCarthy Woolf, Karen. *An Aviary of Small Birds*. Manchester: Carcanet, 2014.

MacInnes, Colin. *Absolute Beginners*. London: MacGibbon & Kee, 1959.

City of Spades. London: MacGibbon & Kee, 1957.

McKay, Claude. *Banjo*. New York: Harper & Brothers, 1929.

Constab Ballads. London: Watt & Co., 1912.

Home to Harlem. New York: Harper & Brothers, 1928.

A Long Way from Home. New York: Lee Furman, 1937.

McKenzie-Mavinga, Isha and Perkins, Thelma. *In Search of Mr McKenzie*. London: Women's Press, 1991.

McLeod, Jenny. *Stuck up a Tree*. London: Virago, 1998.

Mahfouz, Sabrina. *Chef*. London. Methuen Bloomsbury, 2016.

How You Might Know Me. London: Out-Spoken Press, 2016.

Mahfouz, Sabrina (ed.). *The Things I Would Tell You: British Muslim Women Write*. London: Saqi, 2017.

Mahomet, Dean. *Shampooing or Benefits Resulting from the Use of Indian Medicated Vapour Bath, as introduced by S. D. Mahomed (A Native of India)*. Brighton: Printed by E. H. Creasy, Gazette-Office, North Street, 1822.

The Travels of Dean Mahomet: An Eighteenth-Century Journey through India. Ed. Michael H. Fisher. Berkeley, CA: University of California Press, [1794] 1997.

Makoha, Nick. *Kingdom of Gravity*. Leeds: Peepal Tree Press, 2017.

The Lost Collection of an Invisible Man. London: Flipped Eye Publishing, 2005.

Resurrection Man. Miami, FL: Jai-Alai Books, 2016.

Malabari, Behramji. *The Indian Eye on English Life; or, Rambles of a Pilgrim Reformer.* London: Constable, 1893.

Malik, Zaiba. *We Are a Muslim, Please.* London: Windmill, 2010.

Malkani, Gautam. *Londonstani.* London: Fourth Estate, 2006.

Malvery, Olive Christian. *Baby Toilers.* London: Hutchinson, 1907.

 The Soul Market, with which is Included 'the Heart of Things'. London: Hutchinson, 1907.

 The White Slave Market. London: Stanley Paul, 1914.

Marath, S. M. *The Wound of Spring.* London: Dobson, 1960.

Markandaya, Kamala. *Nectar in a Sieve.* London: Putnam, 1954.

 The Nowhere Man. New York: John Day, 1972.

 Possession. London: Putnam, 1963.

Marke, Ernest. *Old Man Trouble.* London: Weidenfeld & Nicolson, 1975; republished as *In Troubled Waters: Memoirs of my Seventy Years in England*, London: Karia, 1986.

Markham, E. A. *Human Rites: Selected Poems 1970–1982.* London: Anvil Press, 1984.

 Against the Grain: A 1950s Memoir. Leeds: Peepal Tree Press, 2008.

 'Roots and Roots'. *PN Review*, 29:3 (January–February 2003): 22–8.

 (ed.). *Hinterland: Caribbean Poetry from the West Indies and Britain.* Newcastle upon Tyne: Bloodaxe Books, 1989.

Marson, Una. *The Moth and the Star.* Kingston, Jamaica: the author, 1937; reprinted Kingston: Gleaner, 1937.

 Selected Poems. Ed. Alison Donnell. Leeds: Peepal Tree Press, 2011.

Martin, S. I. *Incomparable World.* London: Quartet, 1996.

Mason-John, Valerie. *Brown Girl in the Ring.* London: Get a Grip Publishers, 1999.

Maynard, Michael. *Games Men Play.* London: The X Press, 1996.

Mehmood, Tariq. *You're Not Proper.* London: HopeRoad, 2015.

Melville, Pauline. *The Migration of Ghosts.* London: Bloomsbury, 1998.

 Shape-Shifter. London: Women's Press, 1990.

Menen, Aubrey. *Dead Man in the Silver Market: An Autobiographical Essay on National Pride.* London: Chatto & Windus, 1954.

 The Prevalence of Witches. London: Chatto & Windus, 1947.

 The Space Within the Heart. London: Hamish Hamilton, 1970.

'Middlesex October Session 1795 'The Examination of Robert Wedderburn a Rogue and Vagabond and the Witnesses against him'. London Metropolitan Archive. MJ/SP/1795/10/034.

Miller, Kei. *Fear of Stones and Other Stories.* Oxford: Macmillan Education, 2006.

 The Same Earth. London: Weidenfeld & Nicolson, 2008.

Mittelholzer, Edgar. *Kaywana Heritage.* London: Corgi, 1976.

 A Morning at the Office. London: Hogarth Press, 1950.

Mohamed, Nadifa. *Black Mamba Boy.* London: HarperCollins, 2010.

Mohanti, P. *Through Brown Eyes.* Oxford: Oxford University Press, 1985.

Moraes, Dom. *Selected Poems.* Ed. Ranjit Hoskote. New Delhi: Penguin Books, 2012.

Mukharji, T. N. *A Visit to Europe.* Calcutta: Newman, 1899.

Mukherjee, Abir. *A Necessary Evil.* London: Harvill Secker, 2017.

 A Rising Man. London: Harvill Secker, 2016.

Mukherjee, Neel. *A Life Apart.* London: Constable and Robinson, 2010 [first published as *Past Continuous*, 2008].

Past Continuous. New Delhi: Picador India, 2008.

Nagra, Daljit. *British Museum*. London: Faber and Faber, 2017.

Look We Have Coming to Dover! London: Faber and Faber, 2007.

Tipoo Sultan's Incredible White-Man Eating Tiger-Toy Machine! London: Faber and Faber, 2011.

Naidoo, Beverley. *The Other Side of Truth*. New York: HarperCollins, 2000.

Web of Lies. London: Puffin, 2004.

Who is King? Ten Magical Stories from Africa. Illustrations by Piet Grobler. London: Frances Lincoln, 2015.

Naidu, Sarojini, *The Bird of Time: Songs of Life, Death & the Spring*. Introduction by Edmund Gosse. London: William Heinemann, 1912.

The Golden Threshold. Hyderabad: Dodo Press, 1905.

Naipaul, Shiva. *North of South: An African Journey*. London: André Deutsch, 1978.

An Unfinished Journey. London: Abacus, 1986.

Naipaul, V. S. *The Enigma of Arrival: A Novel in Five Sections*. London: Penguin, 1987.

Finding the Centre: Two Narratives. London: André Deutsch, 1984.

A House for Mr Biswas. London: André Deutsch, 1961.

Letters Between a Father and Son. Ed. Nicholas Laughlin and Gillon Aitken. London: Little, Brown, 1999.

The Mimic Men. London: André Deutsch, 1967.

Mr Stone and the Knight's Companion. London: André Deutsch, 1963.

The Mystic Masseur. London: André Deutsch, 1957.

A Turn in the South. New York: Vintage, 1989.

Namjoshi, Suniti. *Aditi and the One-Eyed Monkey*. Illustrations by Hanife Hassan.Boston, MA: Beacon, 1986.

Feminist Fables. London: Women's Press, 1983.

Saint Suniti and the Dragon. London: Virago, 1994

Needle, Jan. *My Mate Shofiq*. London: HarperCollins, 1979.

Nehru, Jawaharlal. *An Autobiography*. London: John Lane, 1936.

The Discovery of India. London: Meridian Books, 1946.

Newland, Courttia. *The Scholar: A West Side Story*. London: Abacus, 1997.

Society Within. London: Abacus, 1999.

Ngcobo, Lauretta (ed.). *Let it be Told: Black Women Writers in Britain*. London: Pluto, 1987.

Nichols, Grace. *Everybody Got a Gift: New and Selected Poems*. London: A&C Black, 2006.

The Fat Black Woman's Poems. London: Virago, 1984.

i is a long memoried woman. London: Karnak, 1983.

Startling the Flying Fish. London: Virago, 2005.

Sunris. London: Virago, 1996.

(ed.). *Black Poetry*. London: Blackie, 1988.

Nugent, Maria. *A Journal of a Voyage to, and Residence in, the Island of Jamaica from 1801 to 1805, and of Subsequent Events in England from 1805 to 1811*. 2 vols. London: private circulation, 1839.

Obatala Press (ed.). *Times Like These*. London: Black Rose, 1988.

Okojie, Irenosen. *Butterfly Fish*. London: Jacaranda, 2016.

Speak Gigantular. London: Jacaranda, 2016.

Okri, Ben. *The Famished Road*. London: Jonathan Cape, 1991.

Songs of Enchantment. London: Vintage, 1993.

Omaar, Rageh. *Only Half of Me: Being a Muslim in Britain*. London: Viking, 2006.

Onyeama, Dillibe. *Nigger at Eton*. London: Leslie Frewin, 1972.

Osborne, Deirdre (ed.). *Hidden Gems: Contemporary Black British Plays*. London: Oberon, 2008.

Osman, Diriye. *Fairytales for Lost Children*. London: Team Angelica, 2013.

Owusu, Kwesi (ed.). *Storms of the Heart: An Anthology of Black Arts and Culture*. London: Camden Press, 1988.

Oxenbury, Helen. *Clap Hands*. London: Walker Books, 1995.

Tickle, Tickle. London: Walker Books, 1995.

Oyeyemi, Helen, *The Icarus Girl*. London: Bloomsbury, 2005.

The Opposite House. London: Bloomsbury, 2007.

What Is Not Yours Is Not Yours. London: Picador, 2017.

White is for Witching. London: Picador, 2009.

Parkes, Nii Ayikwei. *The Makings of You*. Leeds: Peepal Tree Press, 2010.

Tail of the Blue Bird. London: Jonathan Cape, 2009.

(ed.). *Filigree: Contemporary Black British Poetry*. Leeds: Peepal Tree Press, 2018.

Pennell, Alice Sorabji. *The Begum's Son*. London: John Murray, 1928.

Children of the Border. London: John Murray, 1926.

Perera, Shyama. *Haven't Stopped Dancing Yet*. London: Sceptre, 1999.

Phillips, Caryl. *Cambridge*. London: Bloomsbury, 1991.

Colour Me English. London: Harvill Secker, 2011.

Crossing the River. London: Bloomsbury, 1993.

The European Tribe. London: Faber and Faber, 1987.

The Final Passage. London: Faber and Faber, 1985.

The Lost Child. London: Oneworld, 2015.

A New World Order. London: Secker & Warburg, 2001.

(ed.). *Extravagant Strangers: A Literature of Belonging*. London: Faber and Faber, 1997.

Phillips, Mike. *Blood Rights*. London: Michael Joseph, 1989.

The Late Candidate. London: Penguin, 1990.

Pitts, Johny. *Afropean: Notes from Black Europe*. London: Allen Lane, 2019.

Popoola, Olumide. *When We Speak of Nothing*. Abuja; London: Cassava Republic, 2017.

Prince, Mary. *The History of Mary Prince: A West Indian Slave*. Ed. Sara Salih. London: Penguin, [1831] 2000.

Procter, James (ed.). *Writing Black Britain 1948–1998: An Interdisciplinary Anthology*. Manchester: Manchester University Press, 2000.

Proctor, Elaine. *Rhumba*. London: Quercus, 2011.

Rai, Bali. *The Crew*. London: Corgi, 2003.

Dream On. Edinburgh: Barrington Stoke, 2002.

Game On. Edinburgh: Barrington Stoke, 2015.

(Un)arranged Marriage. London: Corgi, 2001.

The Whisper. London: Corgi, 2005.

Ramsay, James. *A Letter to James Tobin, Esq. Late Member of His Majesty's Council in the Island of Nevis*. London: printed and sold by James Phillips, George-Yard, Lombard-Street, 1787.

Randhawa, Ravinder. *Hari-Jan*. London: Mantra Lingua, 1992.

A Wicked Old Woman. London: Women's Press, 1987.

Rhys, Jean. *Voyage in the Dark*. London: Constable, 1934.

Wide Sargasso Sea. London: André Deutsch, 1966.

Riley, Joan. *The Unbelonging*. London: Women's Press, 1985.

Waiting in the Twilight. London: Women's Press, 1987.

Riley, Joan and Wood, Briar (eds.). *Leave to Stay: Stories of Exile and Belonging*. London: Virago, 1996.

Robert, Na'ima B. *Boy vs. Girl*. London: Frances Lincoln, 2010.

She Wore Red Trainers. Markfield: Kube Publishing, 2014.

Robinson, Roger. *Adventures in 3D*. London: Lubin & Kleyner, 2001.

Suckle. London: Waterways, 2009.

Suitcase. London: Waterways, 2004.

Ross, Jacob. *The Bone Readers*. Leeds: Peepal Tree Press, 2016.

(ed.). *Closure: Contemporary Black British Short Stories*. Leeds: Peepal Tree Press, 2015.

Ross, Leone. *All the Blood Is Red*. Tunbridge Wells: Angela Royal, 1996.

Come Let Us Sing Anyway. Leeds: Peepal Tree Press, 2017.

Orange Laughter. Tunbridge Wells: Angela Royal, 1996.

Roy, Jacqueline. *Fat Chance*. London: Penguin, 1994.

Playing It Cool. London: Viking, 1997.

Roy, Lucinda. *Lady Moses*. London: Virago, 1998.

Rushdie, Salman. *East, West*. London: Jonathan Cape, 1994.

Grimus. London: Gollancz, 1975.

Haroun and the Sea of Stories. Illustrations by Paul Birkbeck. London: Puffin, 1990.

Joseph Anton. London: Jonathan Cape, 2012.

Midnight's Children. London: Jonathan Cape, 1981.

The Satanic Verses. London: Viking, 1988.

Shame. London: Picador, 1984.

Sahota, Sunjeev. *Ours Are the Streets*. London: Picador, 2011

Salgado, Minoli. *A Little Dust on the Eyes*. Leeds: Peepal Tree Press, 2014.

Salkey, Andrew. *Escape to an Autumn Pavement*. London: Hutchinson, 1960.

Anancy, Traveller. London: Bogle-L'Ouverture, 1992.

Earthquake. London: Oxford University Press, 1965.

Sam-La Rose, Jacob. *Breaking Silence*. Hexham: Bloodaxe Books, 2011.

Sancho, Ignatius. *Letters of the Late Ignatius Sancho, an African*. Ed. Vincent Carretta. Peterborough, Ontario: Broadview Press, [1782] 2015.

Sanghera, Sathnam. *The Boy with the Topknot: A Memoir of Love, Secrets and Lies in Wolverhampton*. London: Penguin, 2008.

Marriage Material. London: Windmill, 2014.

Scott, Lawrence. *Aelred's Sin*. London: Allison & Busby, 1998.

Night Calypso. London: Allison & Busby, 2004.

Witchbroom. London: Allison & Busby, 1992.

Seacole, Mary. *Wonderful Adventures of Mrs Seacole in Many Lands*. Ed. Sara Salih. London: Penguin Classics, [1857] 2005.

Selvon, Samuel. *A Brighter Sun*. London: Allan Wingate, 1952.

Eldorado West One. Leeds: Peepal Tree Press, 1988.

The Housing Lark. London: MacGibbon & Kee, 1965.

The Lonely Londoners. London: Allan Wingate, 1956.

Moses Ascending. London: Davis-Poynter, 1975.

Moses Migrating. Harlow: Longman, 1983.

Ways of Sunlight. London: MacGibbon & Kee, 1957.

Sesay, Kadija (ed.). *Burning Words, Flaming Images: Poems and Short Stories by Writers of African Descent*. London: SAKS, 1996.

Seth, Vikram. *Two Lives*. London: Little, Brown, 2005.

Shahani, Ranjee G. *Indian Pilgrimage*. London: Michael Joseph, 1939.

Shamsie, Kamila. *Burnt Shadows*. London: Picador, 2009.

Home Fire. London: Bloomsbury, 2017.

Salt and Saffron. New York; London: Bloomsbury, 2000.

Shan, Sharan-Jeet. *In My Own Name*. London: Women's Press, 1985.

Sheikh, Farhana. *The Red Box*. London: Women's Press, 1991.

Shire, Warsan. *Teaching My Mother How to Give Birth*. London: Mouthmark, 2011.

Shore, Louise. *Pure Running*. London: Centerprise, 1982.

Shukla, Nikesh. *Coconut Unlimited*. London: Quartet, 2010.

Meatspace. London: The Friday Project, 2014.

Run, Riot. London: Hodder Children's Books, 2018.

Siddique, John. *Poems from a Northern Soul*. Manchester: Crocus, 2007.

The Prize. Norwich: The Rialto, 2005.

Simon, David. *Railton Blues*. London: Bogle-L'Ouverture, 1983.

Sissay, Lemn. *Gold from the Stone*. Edinburgh: Canongate, 2016.

Something Dark. London: Oberon, 2017.

(ed.). *The Fire People*. Edinburgh: Payback Press, 1998.

Smartt, Dorothea. *Connecting Medium*. Leeds: Peepal Tree Press, 2001.

Smith, Karline. *Full Crew*. London: The X Press, 2002.

Moss Side Massive. London: The X-Press, 1994.

Smith, Michael. *It A Come*. London: Race Today, 1986.

Smith, Norman. *Bad Friday*. Birmingham: Trinity Arts, 1982.

Smith, Zadie. *The Autograph Man*. London: Hamish Hamilton, 2002.

NW. London: Hamish Hamilton, 2012.

Swing Time. London: Hamish Hamilton, 2016.

White Teeth. London: Hamish Hamilton, 2000.

Sorabji, Cornelia. *India Calling: The Memories of Cornelia Sorabji*. London: Nisbet, 1934.

Love and Life Behind the Purdah. London: Freemantle, 1901.

Soueif, Ahdaf. *In the Eye of the Sun*. New York: Random House, 1992.

I Think of You. London: Bloomsbury, 2007.

The Map of Love. London: Bloomsbury, 1999.

Soyinka, Wole. *Idanre and Other Poems*. London: Methuen, 1967.

Srivastava, Atima. *Looking for Maya*. London: Quartet, 1999.

Transmission. London: Serpent's Tail, 1992.

Syal, Meera. *Anita and Me*. London: Flamingo, 1996.

Life Isn't All Ha Ha Hee Hee. New York: Doubleday, 1999.

Tagore, Rabindranath. *Gitanjali: Song Offerings*. London: India Society, 1912.

The Home and the World [Ghare Baire, 1915]. Trans. Surendranath Tagore. London: Macmillan, 1919.

Thompson, Stephen. *Toy Soldiers*. London: Hodder & Stoughton, 2000.

Traynor, Joanna. *Divine*. London: Bloomsbury, 1998.

Sister Josephine. London: Bloomsbury, 1997.

Trollope, Anthony. *The West Indies and the Spanish Main*. London: Chapman & Hall, 1859.

Walcott, Derek. *Collected Poems 1948–1984*. New York: Farrar, Straus and Giroux, 1986.

Walters, Vanessa. *Rude Girls*. London: Pan, 1996.

Warner, Marina. *Indigo, or, Mapping the Waters*. London: Vintage, 1992.

Wedderburn, Robert. *The Horrors of Slavery and Other Writings*. Ed. Ian McCalman. Edinburgh: Edinburgh University Press, [1824] 1991.

Wheatle, Alex. *Brixton Rock*. London: BlackAmber, 1999.

Crongton Knights. London: Atom, 2016.

East of Acre Lane. London: Fourth Estate, 2001.

Liccle Bit. London: Atom, 2015.

Wheatley, Phillis. *Complete Writings*. Ed. Vincent Carretta. New York: Penguin, 2001.

Williams, Charlotte. *Sugar and Slate*. Aberystwyth: Planet, 2002.

Yassin-Kassab, Robin. *The Road from Damascus*. London: Hamish Hamilton, 2008.

Young, Kerry. *Gloria*. London: Bloomsbury, 2013.

Pao. London: Bloomsbury, 2011.

Show Me a Mountain. London: Bloomsbury, 2017.

Zephaniah, Benjamin. *Face*. London: Bloomsbury, 1999.

Pen Rhythms. London: Page One, 1980.

Refugee Boy. London: Bloomsbury, 2001.

Talking Turkeys. London: Viking, 1994.

Too Black, Too Strong. Tarset: Bloodaxe Books, 2001.

Zhana (ed.). *Sojourn*. London: Methuen, 1988.

Secondary

Abdelwahid, Mustafa. *Dusé Mohamed Ali (1866–1945): The Autobiography of a Pioneer Pan African and Afro-Asian Activist*. Trenton, NJ: Red Sea Press, 2011.

Adesanmi, Pius. *You're not a Country, Africa*. London: Penguin Classics, 2011.

Adi, Hakim and Sherwood, Marike (eds.). *The 1945 Pan African Congress Revisited*. London: New Beacon Books, 1995.

Adichie, Chimamanda Ngozi. 'The Danger of a Single Story'. *TEDGlobal*, July 2009. Available at www.ted.com/talks/chimamanda_adichie_the_danger_of_a_single_story.

Ahmed, Rehana. *Writing British Muslims: Religion, Class and Multiculturalism*. Manchester: Manchester University Press, 2015.

Ahmed, Rehana, Morey, Peter, and Yaqin, Amina (eds.). *Culture, Diaspora and Modernity in Muslim Writing*. New York; London: Routledge, 2012.

Ahmed, Rehana and Mukherjee, Sumita (eds.). *South Asian Resistances in Britain, 1858–1947*. London: Continuum, 2012.

Ahmed, Sara. *The Cultural Politics of Emotion*. Edinburgh: Edinburgh University Press, 2004.

Queer Phenomenology: Orientations, Objects, Others. Durham, NC; London: Duke University Press, 2006.

Alghamdi, Alaa. *Transformations of the Liminal Self: Configurations of Home and Identity for Muslim Characters in British Postcolonial Fiction*. Bloomington, IN: iUniverse, 2011.

Ali, Ahmed and Singh, Iqbal. 'Editorial'. *Indian Writing*, 1:1 (1940): 3–4.

Ali, Ahmed, Singh, Iqbal, Shelvankar, Krishnao, and Subramaniam, Alagu. 'Commentary'. *Indian Writing*, 1:3 (1941): 125–9.

Ali, Duse Mohamed. Masthead. *African Times and Orient Review*, July 1913.

Ali, Suki. *Mixed-Race, Post-Race: Gender, New Ethnicities and Cultural Practices*. Oxford: Berg, 2003.

Allen, Rick. *The Moving Pageant: A Literary Sourcebook on London Street Life, 1700–1914*. New York; London: Routledge, 1998.

Alleyne, Brian. *Radicals against Race: Black Activism and Cultural Politics*. Oxford; New York: Berg, 2002.

Allnutt, Gillian (ed.). *The New British Poetry 1968–1988*. London: Paladin, 1988.

Anand, Mulk Raj. 'Bombay Mill'. *Left Review*, 2:12 (1935): 374–7.

  Conversations in Bloomsbury. London: Wildwood House, 1981.

  'Manifesto of the Indian Progressive Writers' Association, London'. *Left Review*, 2:5 (1936): 240.

  'On the Progressive Writers Movement' in Pradhan, Sudhi (ed.) *Marxist Cultural Movement in India*, vol. 1. Calcutta: National Book Agency, 1979, 1–22.

  'Review of Ahmed Ali's *Twilight in Delhi*'. *Indian Writing*, 1:3 (1941): 175–7.

  Roots and Flowers. Dharwar: Karnatak University, 1972.

  'Why I Write' in Sharma, K. K. (ed.) *Perspectives on Mulk Raj Anand*. Ghaziabad: Vimal Prakashan, 1978, 1–8.

Anderson, Benedict. *Imagined Communities: Reflections on the Origin and Spread of Nationalism*. Rev. edn. London; New York: Verso, [1983] 1991.

Anim-Addo, Joan (ed.). *Centre of Remembrance*. London: Mango Publishing, 2002.

  (ed.). *Framing the Word: Gender and Genre in Caribbean Women's Writing*. London: Whiting & Birch, 1996.

Ansari, Sarah. 'Subjects or Citizens? India, Pakistan and the 1948 British Nationality Act'. *Journal of Imperial and Commonwealth History*, 41:2 (2013): 285–312.

Anthias, Floya and Yuval-Davis, Nira. *Racialized Boundaries: Race, Nation, Gender, Colour and Class and the Anti-Racist Struggle*. London: Routledge, 1992.

Antor, H. and Stierstorfer, K. (eds.). *English Literatures in International Contexts*. Heidelberg: Winter, 2000.

Appiah, Anthony. *In My Father's House*. London: Methuen, 1992.

  The Lies that Bind: Rethinking Identity. London: Profile Books, 2018.

Araeen, Rasheed. *The Other Story: Afro Asian Artists in Post-War Britain*. London: South Bank Centre, 1989.

  'Preliminary Notes for a Black Manifesto'. *Black Phoenix*, 1 (1978): 3–12.

Arana, R. Victoria (ed.). *'Black' British Aesthetics Today*. Newcastle upon Tyne: Cambridge Scholars, 2007.

Arana, R. Victoria and Ramey, Lauri (eds.). *Black British Writing*. New York: Palgrave Macmillan, 2009.

Austin, Granville. *The Indian Constitution: Cornerstone of a Nation*. New Delhi: Oxford University Press, [1966] 2004.

Back, Les. *New Ethnicities and Urban Culture: Racisms and Multiculture in Young Lives*. London: UCL Press, 1996.

Bailey, B. L. *Jamaican Creole Syntax*. Cambridge: Cambridge University Press, 1966.

Baker, Houston A., Jr., Diawara, Manthia, and Lindeborg, Ruth H. (eds.). *Black British Cultural Studies: A Reader*. London; Chicago, IL: University of Chicago Press, 1996.

Ball, John. *Imagining London: Postcolonial Fiction and the Transnational Metropolis*. Toronto: University of Toronto Press, 2004.

Barlow, Tani (ed.). *Formations of Colonial Modernity in East Asia*. Durham, NC: Duke University Press, 1997.

Beachcroft, T. O. *Calling All Nations*. London: BBC, 1942.

Beckford, Robert. *Jesus Dub: Theology, Music and Social Change*. Abingdon: Routledge, 2006.

Beezmohun, Sharmilla, Sanders, Sarah, and Chapman, Nick (eds.). *Breaking Ground: Celebrating British Writers of Colour*. London: Speaking Volumes, 2017.

Bellaigue, Eric de. *British Book Publishing as a Business since the 1960s: Selected Essays*. London: British Library, 2004.

Benitez-Rojo, Antonio. *The Repeating Island: The Caribbean and the Postmodern Perspective*. Durham, NC: Duke University Press, 1996.

Benjamin, Walter. *Illuminations*. Trans. Harry Zohn, ed. Hannah Arendt. New York: Schocken Books, 1968.

Bennett, Louise. 'Bennett on Bennett – Louise Bennett interviewed by Dennis Scott'. *Caribbean Quarterly*, 14.1–2 (1968): 97–101. Reprinted in Markham, E. A. (ed.) *Hinterland*. Newcastle upon Tyne: Bloodaxe Books, 1989, 45–50.

Benwell, Bethan, Procter, James, and Robinson, Gemma (eds.). *Postcolonial Audiences: Readers, Viewers and Reception*. New York: Routledge, 2012.

Berman, Jessica. *Modernist Commitments: Ethics, Politics, and Transnational Modernism*. New York: Columbia University Press, 2011.

Berman, Marshall. *All that is Solid Melts into Air: The Experience of Modernity*. London: Verso, 2010.

Bery, Ashok. *Cultural Translation and Postcolonial Poetry*. Basingstoke: Palgrave Macmillan, 2007.

Bery, Ashok and Murray, Patricia (eds.). *Comparing Postcolonial Literatures: Dislocations*. Basingstoke: Palgrave Macmillan, 2000.

Bhabha, Homi K. *The Location of Culture*. London: Routledge, 1994.

  (ed.). *Nation and Narration*. London; New York: Routledge, 1990.

Blevins, Steven. *Living Cargo: How Black Britain Performs its Past*. Minneapolis, MN; London: University of Minnesota Press, 2016.

Bluemel, Kristin. *George Orwell and the Radical Eccentrics: Intermodernism in Literary London*. Basingstoke: Palgrave Macmillan, 2004.

Boakye, Jeffrey. *Hold Tight: Black Masculinity, Millennials and the Meaning of Grime*. London: Influx, 2017.

Boehmer, Elleke. *Indian Arrivals, 1870–1915*. Oxford: Oxford University Press, 2015.

Boon, Richard and Plastow, Jane (eds.). *Theatre Matters: Performance and Culture on the World Stage*. Cambridge: Cambridge University Press, 1998.

Booth, Howard J. and Rigby, Nigel. (eds.). *Modernism and Empire*. Manchester: Manchester University Press, 2000.

Bourne, Stephen. *Mother Country: Britain's Black Community on the Home Front 1939–45*. Stroud: History Press, 2010.

Boyce Davies, Carole. *Black Women, Writing and Identity: Migrations of the Subject*. London: Routledge, 1994.

Bradley, Arthur and Tate, Andrew. *The New Atheist Novel: Fiction, Philosophy and Polemic after 9/11*. London: Continuum, 2010.

Brah, Avtar. *Cartographies of Diaspora: Contesting Identities*. London; New York: Routledge, 1996.

Brathwaite, Edward [Kamau]. *The Development of Creole Society in Jamaica 1770–1820*. Oxford: Clarendon Press, 1978.

Brathwaite, Edward Kamau. *History of the Voice: The Development of Nation Language in Anglophone Caribbean Poetry*. London: New Beacon Books, 1984.

Breiner, Laurence. *Black Yeats: Eric Roach and the Politics of Caribbean Poetry*. Leeds: Peepal Tree Press, 2008.

Brennan, Timothy. 'Writing from Black Britain'. *Literary Review*, 34:1 (Fall 1990): 5–11.

Brewer, Mary F., Goddard, Lynette, and Osborne, Deirdre (eds.). *Modern and Contemporary Black British Drama*. London: Palgrave Macmillan, 2015.

Bromley, Roger. *Narratives for a New Belonging: Diasporic Cultural Fictions*. Edinburgh: Edinburgh University Press, 2000.

Brouillette, Sarah. *Literature and the Creative Economy*. Stanford, CA: Stanford University Press, 2014.

    Postcolonial Writers in the Global Literary Market Place. Basingstoke: Palgrave Macmillan, 2007.

Brouillette, Sarah, Nilges, Mathias, and Sauri, Emilio (eds.). *Literature and the Global Contemporary*. Basingstoke: Palgrave Macmillan, 2017.

Brown, Stewart. *Tourist, Traveller, Troublemaker: Essays on Poetry*. Leeds: Peepal Tree Press, 2007.

Bryan, Beverly, Dadzie, Stella, and Scafe, Suzanne (eds.). *The Heart of the Race: Black Women's Lives in Britain*. London: Virago, 1985.

Bucknor, Michael A. and Donnell, Alison (eds.). *The Routledge Companion to Anglophone Caribbean Literature*. London: Routledge, 2011.

Buhle, Paul. *C. L. R. James: The Artist as Revolutionary*. London: Verso, 1988.

Bundy, A. J. M. (ed.). *Selected Essays of Wilson Harris: The Unfinished Genesis of the Imagination*. London: Routledge, 1999.

Burbank, Jane and Cooper, Frederick. *Empires in World History: Power and the Politics of Difference*. Princeton, NJ; Oxford: Princeton University Press, 2010.

Burton, Antoinette. *Burdens of History: British Feminists, Indian Women, and Imperial Culture, 1865–1915*. Chapel Hill, NC: University of North Carolina Press, 1994.

    After the Imperial Turn: Thinking with and through the Nation. London: Duke University Press, 2003.

    Archive Stories: Facts, Fictions, and the Writing of History. London: Duke University Press, 2005.

    At the Heart of the Empire: Indians and the Colonial Encounter in Late-Victorian Britain. Berkeley, CA: University of California Press, 1998.

Butcher, Maggie (ed.). *Tibisiri: Caribbean Writers and Critics*. Sydney: Dangaroo, 1989.

Carretta, Vincent. *Equiano, the African: Biography of a Self-Made Man*. London: University of Georgia Press, 2005.

    Unchained Voices: An Anthology of Black Authors in the English-Speaking World of the Eighteenth Century. Lexington, KY: University Press of Kentucky, 1996; 2004.

Carretta, Vincent and Gould, Phillip (eds.). *Genius in Bondage: Literature of the Early Black Atlantic*. Lexington, KY: The University Press of Kentucky, 2011.

Cassidy, F. G. *Jamaica Talk: Three Hundred Years of the English Language in Jamaica*. London: Macmillan, 1961.

Centre for Contemporary Cultural Studies. *The Empire Strikes Back: Race and Racism in 70s Britain*. London: Hutchinson, 1982.

Chambers, Colin. *Black and Asian Theatre in Britain: A History*. London; New York: Routledge, 2011.

Chambers, Ian. *Migrancy, Culture, Identity*. London: Routledge, 1993.

Chambers, Ross. *Room for Maneuver: Reading (the) Oppositional (in) Narrative*. London; Chicago, IL: University of Chicago Press, 1991.

Chedgzoy, Kate, Francis, Emma, and Pratt, Murray (eds.). *In a Queer Place: Sexuality and Belonging in British and European Contexts*. Aldershot: Ashgate, 2002.

Cheng, Anne Anlin. *The Melancholy of Race*. Oxford: Oxford University Press, 2001.

Cheyette, Bryan. *Diasporas of the Mind: Jewish and Postcolonial Writing and the Nightmare of History*. New Haven, CT; London: Yale University Press, 2013.

Chinweizu, Onwuchekwa Jemie and Madubuike, Ihechukwu. *Toward the Decolonization of African Literature*, vol. 1: *African Fiction and Poetry and their Critics*. London: KPI, 1985.

Clifford, James. *Routes: Travel and Translation in the Late Twentieth Century*. Cambridge, MA: Harvard University Press, 1997.

Cohen, Phil (ed.). *New Ethnicities, Old Racisms*. London: Zed Books, 1999.

Cohen, Robin. *Frontiers of Identity: The British and the Others*. London: Longman, 1994.

Colley, Linda. *Britons: Forging the Nation 1700 1837*. New Haven, CT: Yale University Press, 1992.

Constantine, Learie. *The Colour Bar*. London: Stanley Paul, 1954.

Cooper, Carolyn. *Noises in the Blood: Orality, Gender, and the 'Vulgar' Body of Jamaican Popular Culture*. Durham, NC: Duke University Press, 1995.

Crane, Ralph and Mohanram, Radikha (eds.). *Shifting Continents/Colliding Cultures: Diaspora Writing of the Indian Subcontinent*. Amsterdam: Rodopi, 2000.

Craps, Stef. *Postcolonial Witnessing: Trauma Out of Bounds*. Basingstoke: Palgrave Macmillan, 2013.

Cudjoe, Selwyn R. (ed.). *Caribbean Women Writers: Essays from the First International Conference*. Wellesley, MA: Calaloux Publications, 1990.

Cuevas, Susanne. *Babylon and the Golden City: Representations of London in Black and Asian British Novels since the 1990s*. Heidelberg: Winter, 2008.

Currey, James. *Africa Writes Back: The African Writers Series and the Launch of African Literature*. Oxford: James Currey, 2008.

Dabydeen, David. *Hogarth's Blacks: Images of Blacks in Eighteenth-Century English Art*. Mundelstrup: Dangaroo, 1985.

Dabydeen, David and Wilson-Tagoe, Nana. *A Reader's Guide to West Indian and Black British Literature*. London: Hansib, 1987.

Dabydeen, David (ed.). *The Black Presence in English Literature*. Manchester: Manchester University Press, 1985.

(ed.). *West Indians in Britain: 1948–1998: The Windrush Commemorative Issue of Kunapipi*, 20:1 (1998).

Dabydeen, David and Gilmore, John (eds.). *The Oxford Companion to Black British History*. Oxford: Oxford University Press 2007.

Daniels, Therese and Gerson, Jane (eds.). *The Colour Black: Black Images in British Television*. London: BFI Publishing, 1989.

Davis, David Brion. *The Problem of Slavery in the Age of Revolution, 1770–1823*. Ithaca, NY: Cornell University Press, 1975.

Davis, Geoffrey V. and Fuchs, Anne (eds.), *Black and South Asian British Literatures*. Trier: WVT, 2018.

(eds.). *Staging New Britain: Aspects of Black and South Asian British Theatre Practice*. Oxford: Peter Lang, 2006.

Dawes, Kwame (ed.). *Talk Yuh Talk: Interviews with Anglophone Caribbean Poets*. Charlottesville, VA; London: University of Virginia Press, 2001.

deCaires Narain, Denise, *Contemporary Caribbean Women's Poetry: Making Style*. London: Routledge, 2002.

Dennis, Ferdinand. *Behind the Frontlines: Journey into Afro-Britain*. London: Victor Gollancz, 1988.

Dennis, Ferdinand and Khan, Naseem (eds.). *Voices of the Crossing: The Impact of Britain on Writers from Asia, the Caribbean and Africa*. London: Serpent's Tail, 2000.

Dillon Brown, J. *Migrant Modernism: Postwar London and the West Indian Novel*. Charlottesville, VA: University of Virginia Press, 2013.

Dillon Brown, J. and Rosenberg, Leah Reade (eds.). *Beyond Windrush: Rethinking Postwar Anglophone Caribbean Literature*. Jackson, MS: University Press of Mississippi, 2015.

Donald, James and Rattansi, Ali. (eds.). *'Race', Culture and Difference*. London: Sage, 1992.

Donnell, Alison. *Twentieth Century Caribbean Literature: Critical Moments in Anglophone Literary and Critical History*. London: Routledge, 2006.

(ed.). *Companion to Contemporary Black British Culture*. London; New York: Routledge, 2002.

Donnell, Alison, and Lawson Welsh, Sarah (eds.). *The Routledge Reader in Caribbean Literature*. New York: Routledge, 1996.

Donnell, Alison, McGarrity, Maria, and O'Callaghan, Evelyn (eds.). *Caribbean Irish Connections: Interdisciplinary Perspectives*. Kingston, Jamaica: The University of the West Indies Press, 2015.

Döring, Tobias. *Caribbean–English Passages: Intertexuality in a Postcolonial Tradition*. New York: Routledge, 2002.

Dover, Cedric. *Feathers in the Arrow: An Approach for Coloured Writers and Readers*. Bombay: Padma Publications, 1947.

Doyle, Laura and Winkiel, Laura (eds.). *Geomodernisms: Race, Modernism, Modernity*. Bloomington, IN: Indiana University Press, 2005.

Du Bois, W. E. B. 'The Talented Tenth' in Washington, Booker T. (ed.) *The Negro Problem: A Series of Articles by Representative American Negroes of To-Day*. New York: James Pott & Company, 1903.

Eckstein, Lars. *Re-Membering the Black Atlantic: On the Poetics and Politics of Literary Memory.* Amsterdam; New York: Rodopi, 2006.

Eckstein, Lars, Korte, Barbara, Pirker, Eva Ulrike, and Reinfandt, Christoph (eds.). *Multi-Ethnic Britain 2000+: New Perspectives in Literature, Film and the Arts.* Amsterdam; New York: Rodopi, 2008.

Edwards, Paul and Dabydeen, David (eds.). *Black Writers in Britain, 1760–1890.* Edinburgh: Edinburgh University Press, 1991.

Elias, Mohammed. *Kerala Writers in English: Aubrey Menen.* Madras: Macmillan India, 1985.

Ellis, Markman, Coulton, Richard, and Mauger, Matthew. *Empire of Tea: The Asian Leaf that Conquered the World.* London: Reaktion Books, 2015.

Emery, Mary Lou. *Modernism, the Visual and Caribbean Literature.* Cambridge: Cambridge University Press, 2007.

English, James. *The Economy of Prestige: Prizes, Awards, and the Circulation of Cultural Value.* Cambridge, MA: Harvard University Press, 2005.

Ernest, John. *The Oxford Handbook of the African American Slave Narrative.* Oxford: Oxford University Press, 2014.

Espinoza Garrido, Felipe, Koegler, Caroline, Nyangulu, Deborah and Stein, Mark U. (eds.). *Locating African European Studies: Interventions – Intersections – Conversations.* London: Routledge, forthcoming.

Esty, Joshua. *A Shrinking Island: Modernism and National Culture in England.* Princeton, NJ: Princeton University Press, 2003.

Evans, Lucy, McWatt, Mark, and Smith, Emma (eds.). *The Caribbean Short Story: Critical Perspectives.* Leeds: Peepal Tree Press, 2011.

Finnegan, Ruth. *Oral Poetry.* Cambridge: Cambridge University Press, 1977.

Fisher, Michael H. (ed.). *The First Indian Author in English: Dean Mahomed (1759–1851) in India, Ireland, and England.* New Delhi: Oxford University Press, 1996.

Francis, Vivienne. *With Hope in their Eyes: Compelling Stories of the Windrush Generation.* London: Nia, 1998.

Fraser, Robert. *Lifting the Sentence: The Poetics of Postcolonial Fiction.* Manchester: Manchester University Press, 2000.

Fraser, Robert and Hammond, Mary (eds.). *Books Without Borders, vol. 2: Perspectives from South Asia.* Basingstoke: Palgrave Macmillan, 2008.

Fryer, Peter. *Black People in the British Empire: An Introduction.* London: Pluto, 1988.

The Politics of Windrush. Richmond, Surrey: Index, 1999.

Staying Power: The History of Black People in Britain. London: Pluto, 1984.

Gandhi, Leela. *Affective Communities: Anticolonial Thought, Fin-de-Siècle Radicalism, and the Politics of Friendship.* Durham, NC: Duke University Press, 2006.

Gasiorek, Andrzej. *Post-War British Fiction: Realism and After.* London: Edward Arnold, 1995.

Gates, Henry Louis, Jr. *Figures in Black: Words, Signs, and the 'Racial' Self.* Oxford: Oxford University Press, 1987.

The Signifying Monkey: A Theory of African-American Literary Criticism. New York: Oxford University Press, 1988.

Gerzina, Gretchen. *Black England: Life Before Emancipation.* London: John Murray, 1995.

Black London: Life Before Emancipation. New Brunswick, NJ: Rutgers University Press, 1995.

Black Victorians/Black Victoriana. New Brunswick, NJ: Rutgers University Press, 2003.

Gikandi, Simon. *Maps of Englishness: Writing Identity in the Culture of Colonialism*. New York: Columbia University Press, 1996.

Slavery and the Culture of Taste. Princeton, NJ: Princeton University Press, 2011.

Writing in Limbo: Modernism and Caribbean Literature. Ithaca, NY: Cornell University Press, 1992.

(ed.). *The Oxford History of the Novel in English*, vol. 11: *The Novel in Africa and the Caribbean since 1950*. Oxford: Oxford University Press, 2016.

Gilkes, Michael. *Racial Identity and Individual Consciousness in the Caribbean Novel*. Georgetown, Guyana: National History and Arts Council, 1975.

Gilmour, Rachael and Schwarz, Bill (eds.). *End of Empire and the English Novel since 1945*. Manchester: Manchester University Press, 2011.

Gilroy, Paul. *After Empire: Melancholia or Convivial Culture?* Abingdon: Routledge, 2004.

Between Camps: Nations, Cultures and the Allure of Race. New edn. London: Routledge, [2000] 2004.

The Black Atlantic: Modernity and Double Consciousness. Cambridge, MA: Harvard University Press, 1993.

Black Britain: A Photographic History. London: Saqi, 2007.

Small Acts: Thoughts on the Politics of Black Cultures. London: Serpent's Tail, 1993.

There Ain't No Black in the Union Jack: The Cultural Politics of Race and Nation. London: Unwin Hyman, 1987.

Givanni, June (ed.). *Remote Control: Dilemmas of Black Intervention in British Film and TV*. London: British Film Institute, 1995.

Glissant, Eduard. *Caribbean Discourse: Selected Essays*. Charlottesville, VA: University Press of Virginia, 1989.

Goddard, Lynette. *Contemporary Black British Playwrights: Margins to Mainstream*. Basingstoke: Palgrave Macmillan, 2015.

(ed.). *The Methuen Drama Book of Plays by Black British Writers*. London: Methuen, 2011.

Godiwala, Dimple (ed.). *Alternatives within the Mainstream: British Black and Asian Theatres*. Newcastle upon Tyne: Cambridge Scholars, 2006.

Gopal, Priyamvada. *Literary Radicalism in India: Gender, Nation and the Transition to Independence*. Abingdon: Routledge, 2006.

Indian English Novel: Nation, History, and Narration. Oxford: Oxford University Press, 2009.

Gopinath, Gayatri. *Impossible Desires: Queer Diasporas and South Asian Public Cultures*. Durham, NC: Duke University Press, 2005.

Gorra, Michael. *After Empire: Scott, Naipaul, Rushdie*. Chicago, IL: University of Chicago Press, 1997.

Gosciak, Josh. *The Shadowed Country: Claude McKay and the Romance of the Victorians*. New Brunswick, NJ: Rutgers University Press, 2006.

Goveia, Elsa. 'The Caribbean: Socio-Cultural Framework'. *CAM Newsletter*, 4 (August/September 1967): 2–8.

Grant, Colin. *Bageye at the Wheel: A 1970s Childhood in Suburbia*. London: Jonathan Cape, 2012.

I & I: The Natural Mystics: Marley, Tosh and Wailer. London: Jonathan Cape, 2011.

Negro with a Hat: The Rise and Fall of Marcus Garvey and his Dream of Mother America. London: Jonathan Cape, 2008.

Griffin, Gabriele. *Contemporary Black and Asian Women Playwrights in Britain.* Cambridge: Cambridge University Press, 2003.

Griffith, Glyne A. *The BBC and the Development of Anglophone Caribbean Literature, 1943–1958.* Cham: Palgrave Macmillan, 2016.

Grzegorczyk, Blanka. *Discourses of Postcolonialism in Contemporary British Children's Literature.* New York; London: Routledge, 2015.

Gundara, Jagdish S. and Duffield, Ian (eds.). *Essays on the History of Blacks in Britain.* Aldershot: Avebury, 1992.

Gunning, Dave. *Race and Antiracism in Black British and British Asian Literature.* Liverpool: Liverpool University Press, 2012.

Gupta, Rahila. *Enslaved: The New British Slavery.* London: Portobello Books, 2007.

Guptara, Prahbu S. *Black British Literature: An Annotated Bibliography.* Oxford; Sydney: Dangaroo, 1986.

Gutzke, David (ed.). *Britain and Transnational Progressivism.* New York: Palgrave Macmillan, 2008.

Habekost, Christian. *Verbal Riddim: The Politics and Aesthetics of African-Caribbean Dub Poetry.* Amsterdam: Rodopi, 1993.

Hall, Stuart. 'Minimal Selves' in *Identity: The Real Me.* ICA Documents 6. London: Institute of Contemporary Arts, 1987, 44–6.

Hall, Stuart, Critcher, Chas, Jefferson, Tony, Clarke, John, and Roberts, Brian. *Policing the Crisis: Mugging, the State, and Law and Order.* Basingstoke: Macmillan, 1978.

Hall, Stuart (ed.). *Representation: Cultural Representations and Signifying Practices.* London; Thousand Oaks, CA; New Delhi: Sage Publications in association with The Open University, 1997.

Hall, Stuart, Held, David, and McGrew, Tony (eds.). *Modernity and its Futures.* Cambridge: Polity Press, 1992.

Halloran, Vivian Nun. *Exhibiting Slavery: The Caribbean Postmodern Novel as Museum.* Charlottesville, VA: University of Virginia Press, 2009.

Hamid, Mohsin. *Discontent and its Civilizations: Dispatches from Lahore, New York and London.* London: Hamish Hamilton, 2014.

Hamilton, Elizabeth. *Translation of the Letters of a Hindoo Rajah.* Ed. Pamela Perkins and Shannon Russell. Hamilton, Ontario: Broadview Press, [1796] 1999.

Hansen, Randall. *Citizenship and Immigration in Post-War Britain: The Institutional Origins of a Multicultural Nation.* Oxford; New York: Oxford University Press, 2000.

Harris, Wilson. *Tradition, the Writer and Society.* London: New Beacon Books, 1967.
  The Womb of Space: The Cross-Cultural Imagination. Westport, CT: Greenwood, 1983.

Hena, Omaar. 'Multi-Ethnic British Poetries' in Robinson, Peter (ed.) *The Oxford Handbook of Contemporary British and Irish Poetry.* Oxford: Oxford University Press, 2013, 517–37.

Henriques, Julian. *Sonic Bodies: Reggae Sound Systems, Performance Techniques, and Ways of Knowing.* New York: Continuum, 2011.

Hesse, Barnor (ed.). *Un/settled Multiculturalisms.* London: Zed Books, 2000.

Hinds, Donald. *Journey to an Illusion: The West Indian in Britain.* London: Heinemann, 1966.

Hingorani, Dominic. *British Asian Theatre.* London: Palgrave Macmillan, 2010.

Hiro, Dilip. *Black British, White British*. Harmondsworth: Penguin, 1973. Rev. edn, London: Grafton, 1991.

Hirsch, Afua. *Brit(ish): On Race, Identity and Belonging*. London: Jonathan Cape, 2018.

Hirsch, Marianne. *Family Frames: Photography, Narrative, and Postmemory*. Cambridge, MA: Harvard University Press, 1997.

Houlden, Kate. *Sexuality, Gender and Nationalism in Caribbean Literature*. Abingdon: Routledge, 2016.

Hoyles, Asher and Hoyles, Martin. *Moving Voices: Black Performance Poetry*. London: Hansib, 2002.

Huggan, Graham. *The Postcolonial Exotic: Marketing the Margins*. London; New York: Routledge, 2001.

Ibironke, Olabode. *Between African Writers and Heinemann Education Publishers: The Political Economy of a Culture Industry*. Ann Arbor, MI: UMI Dissertation Publishing, 2009.

Innes, C. L. *A History of Black and Asian Writing in Britain, 1700–2000*. Cambridge: Cambridge University Press, 2002.

Institute of Race Relations. *How Racism Came to Britain*. London: Institute of Race Relations, 1985.

   Patterns of Racism. London: Institute of Race Relations, 1982.

   Roots of Racism. London: Institute of Race Relations, 1982.

James, C. L. R. 'Abyssinia and the Imperialists'. *The Keys*, 3:3 (January–March 1936): 32–40.

   Beyond a Boundary. London: Stanley/Hutchinson, 1963.

   'The Case for West Indian Self-Government' in Grimshaw, Anna (ed.) *The C. L. R. James Reader*. Oxford: Blackwell, 1992, 49–62.

   Letters from London. Ed. Nicholas Laughlin. Oxford: Signal Books, 2003.

Janmahomed, Shelina Zahra. *Generation M: Young Muslims Changing the World*. London: I. B. Tauris, 2016.

Jarrett-Macauley, Delia. *The Life of Una Marson 1905–65*. Manchester: Manchester University Press, 1998.

   (ed.). *Reconstructing Womanhood, Reconstructing Feminism: Writings on Black Women*. London; New York: Routledge, 1996.

Jayakar, M. R. *The Story of my Life*. 2 vols. Bombay: Asia Publishing House, 1958–9.

John La Rose Tribute Committee (ed.). *Foundations of a Movement*. London: John La Rose Tribute Committee, 1991.

Johnson, Linton Kwesi. 'Jamaican Rebel Music'. *Race and Class*, 17:4 (1976): 397–412.

Jordan, Glenn, Weedon, Chris, and Coppock, Christopher. *Clement Cooper: Deep – People of Mixed-Race*. London: Art Data, 1996.

Joshi, Kusum Pant and Joshi, Lalit Mohan (eds.). *A Forgotten Legend & Such is Life: An Autobiography by Niranjan Pal*. Hounslow: South Asian Cinema Foundation, 2011.

Julien, Isaac and Mercer, Kobena. 'Introduction: De Margin and De Centre'. *Screen*, 29:4 (1988): 2–11.

Kalliney, Peter J. *Commonwealth of Letters: British Literary Culture and the Emergence of Postcolonial Aesthetics*. Oxford: Oxford University Press, 2013.

Kamali, Leila. *The Cultural Memory of Africa in African American and Black British Fiction, 1970–2000: Spectres of the Shore*. Basingstoke: Palgrave Macmillan, 2016.

Kanneh, Kadiatu. *African Identities: Pan-Africanisms and Black Identities*. London: Routledge, 1998.

Kaufmann, Miranda. *Black Tudors: The Untold Story*. London: Oneworld, 2017.

Kean, Danuta with Larsen, Mel (eds.). *Writing the Future: Black and Asian Writers and Publishers in the UK Market Place*. London: Spread the Word, 2015. Available at http://spreadtheword.org.uk/writing-the-future.

Keown, Michelle, Murphy, David, and Procter, James (eds.). *Comparing Postcolonial Diasporas*. Basingstoke: Palgrave Macmillan, 2009.

Khair, Tabish. *Babu Fictions: Alienation in Contemporary Indian English Novels*. Oxford: Oxford University Press, 2001.

   The New Xenophobia. New Delhi: Oxford University Press, 2016.

King, Anthony D. (ed.). *Culture, Globalization, and the World-System: Contemporary Conditions for the Representation of Identity*. Rev. edn. Minneapolis, MN: University of Minnesota Press, 1997.

King, Bruce. *The Internationalization of English Literature*. Oxford: Oxford University Press, 2004.

   New National and Post-Colonial Literatures. Oxford: Oxford University Press, 1996.

King-Dorset, Rodreguez. *Black British Theatre Pioneers: Yvonne Brewster and the First Generation of Actors, Playwrights and Other Practitioners*. London: McFarland, 2014.

Korte, Barbara and Pirker, Eva Ulrike. *Black History – White History: Britain's Historical Programme between Windrush and Wilberforce*. Bielefeld: Transcript, 2011.

Korte, Barbara and Sternberg, Claudia. *Bidding for the Mainstream? Black and Asian British Film since the 1990s*. Amsterdam: Rodopi, 2004.

Korte, Barbara and Müller, Klaus Peter (eds.). *Unity in Diversity Revisited? British Literature and Culture in the 1990s*. Tübingen: Narr, 1998.

Kureishi, Hanif. 'Bradford'. *Granta*, 20 (Winter 1986): 149–70.

   Dreaming and Scheming: Reflections on Writing and Politics. London: Faber and Faber, 2002.

Lawson Welsh, Sarah. *Grace Nichols*. Tavistock: Northcote House, 2007.

Ledent, Bénédicte. *Caryl Phillips*. Manchester: Manchester University Press, 2002.

Ledent, Bénédicte and Tunca, Daria (eds.). *Caryl Phillips: Writing in the Key of Life*. Amsterdam: Rodopi, 2012.

Lee, A. R. (ed.). *Other Britain: Other British*. London: Pluto, 1995.

Lee, J. M. 'Commonwealth Students in the United Kingdom, 1940–1960: Student Welfare and World Status'. *Minerva*, 44:1 (March 2006): 1–24.

Ley, Graham and Dadswell, Sarah (eds.). *British South Asian Theatres: A Documented History*. Exeter: University of Exeter Press, 2011.

Lindfors, Bernth. *Ira Aldridge*. 4 vols. Rochester, NY: University of Rochester Press, 2011–2015.

   (ed.). *Africans on Stage: Studies in Ethnological Show Business*. Bloomington, IN: Indiana University Press, 2000.

Low, Gail. *Publishing the Postcolonial: Anglophone West African and Caribbean Writing in the UK, 1948–1968*. London: Routledge, 2011.

   White Skins/Black Masks: Representation and Colonialism. New York: Routledge, 1996.

Low, Gail and Wynne-Davies, Marion (eds.). *A Black British Canon?* Basingstoke: Palgrave Macmillan, 2006.

McLeod, John. *Life Lines: Writing Transcultural Adoption*. London: Bloomsbury Academic, 2015.

Postcolonial London: Rewriting the Metropolis. London; New York: Routledge, 2004.

McMillan, Michael. *The Front Room: Migrant Aesthetics in the Home.* London: Black Dog, 2009.

Maes-Jelinek, Hena and Ledent, Bénédicte (eds.). *Theatre of the Arts: Wilson Harris and the Caribbean.* Amsterdam: Rodopi, 2002.

Majeed, Javed. *Autobiography, Travel and Postnational Identity: Gandhi, Nehru and Iqbal.* Basingstoke: Palgrave Macmillan, 2007.

Making Britain Database [AHRC-funded project led by Susheila Nasta; Open University, 2017]. Available at www.open.ac.uk/researchprojects/makingbritain/content/about-database.

Malik, Sarita. *Representing Black Britain: A History of Black and Asian Images on Television.* London: Sage, 2002.

Marshall, Howard. 'The Voice of Big Ben'. *London Calling,* 10 December 1953: 21.

Matera, Marc. *Black London: The Imperial Metropolis and Decolonization in the Twentieth Century.* Oakland, CA: University of California Press, 2015.

Maxwell, Marina. 'Towards a Revolution in the Arts'. *CAM Newsletter,* 10 (April–June 1969): 1–12.

Mercer, Kobena. *Welcome to the Jungle: New Positions in Black Cultural Studies.* London; New York: Routledge, 1994.

Mercer, Kobena and Julien, Isaac. 'Race, Sexual Politics and Black Masculinity: A Dossier' in Rutherford, Jonathan and Chapman, Rowena (eds.) *Male Order: Unwrapping Masculinity.* London: Lawrence & Wishart, 1988, 97–164.

Miller, Kei. *Writing Down the Vision: Essays and Prophecies.* Leeds: Peepal Tree Press, 2013.

Mirza, Heidi Safia. *Young, Female and Black.* London: Routledge, 1992.

(ed.). *Black British Feminism: A Reader.* London: Routledge, 1997.

Mishra, Vijay. *Annotating Salman Rushdie: Reading the Postcolonial.* New York: Routledge, 2018.

The Literature of the Indian Diaspora: Theorizing the Diasporic Imaginary. New York: Routledge, 2007.

Modood, Tariq. *Multicultural Politics: Race, Ethnicity and Muslims in Britain.* Edinburgh: Edinburgh University Press, 2005.

Mondal, Anshuman. *Islam and Controversy: The Politics of Free Speech after Rushdie.* Basingstoke: Palgrave Macmillan, 2014.

Moore-Gilbert, Bart. *Postcolonial Life-Writing: Culture, Politics and Self-Representation.* London: Routledge, 2009.

Morey, Peter. *Islamophobia and the Novel.* New York; Chichester: Columbia University Press, 2018.

Morey, Peter and Yaqin, Amina. *Framing Muslims: Stereotyping and Representation after 9/11.* Cambridge, MA: Harvard University Press, 2011.

Morley, David and Chen, Kuan-Hsing (eds.). *Stuart Hall: Critical Dialogues in Cultural Studies.* London: Routledge, 1996.

Morris, Mervyn. *'Is English We Speaking' and Other Essays.* Kingston, Jamaica: Ian Randle, 1999.

Making West Indian Literature. Kingston, Jamaica: Ian Randle, 2005.

Msiska, Mpalive-Hangson. *Postcolonial Identity in Wole Soyinka.* Amsterdam: Rodopi, 2007.

Muhlhausler, Peter. *Pidgin and Creole Linguistics.* Oxford: Blackwell, 1986.

Munshi, Rushiraj, Bloom, Valerie, Walker, Fiona, and Lewis, Fitz (eds.). *Black and Priceless: The Power of Black Ink*. Manchester: Crocus, 1988.

Murphy, Neil and Wai-chew, Sim (eds.). *British Asian Fiction: Framing the Contemporary*. Amherst, NY: Cambria Press, 2008.

Myers, Norma. *Reconstructing the Black Past: Blacks in Britain 1780–1830*. London: Cass, 1996.

Naidu, Sarojini. *Selected Letters*. Ed. Makarand Paranjape. New Delhi: Kali for Women, 1996.

Naipaul, V. S. *Reading and Writing*. New York: New York Review of Books, 2000.

Narain, Mona and Gevirtz, Karen (eds.). *Gender and Space in British Literature, 1660–1820*. New York: Routledge, 2016.

Nasta, Susheila. *Home Truths: Fictions of the South Asian Diaspora in Britain*. Basingstoke; New York: Palgrave, 2002.

Writing Across Worlds: Contemporary Writers Talk. New York: Routledge, 2004.

Nasta, Susheila with Stadtler, Florian. *Asian Britain: A Photographic History*. London: Westbourne Press, 2013.

Nasta, Susheila (ed.). *Critical Perspectives on Sam Selvon*. Washington, DC: Three Continents, 1988.

(ed.). *India in Britain: South Asian Networks and Connections, 1858–1950*. Basingstoke: Palgrave Macmillan, 2013.

(ed.). *Motherlands: Black Women's Writing from Africa, the Caribbean and South Asia*. London: Women's Press, 1991.

Nasta, Susheila and Rutherford, Anna (eds.). *Tiger's Triumph: Celebrating Sam Selvon*. Sydney: Dangaroo, 1995.

Nelson, Emmanuel S. (ed.). *Reworlding: The Literature of the Indian Diaspora*. Westport, CT: Greenwood Press, 1992.

Newland, Courttia and Sesay, Kadija (eds.). *IC3: New Black Writing in Britain*. London: Penguin, 2001.

Ngcobo, Lauretta (ed.). *Let it be Told: Black Women Writers in Britain*. London: Pluto, 1987.

Niven, Alastair. 'Black British Writing: The Struggle for Recognition' in Davis, Geoffrey and Maes-Jelinek, Hena (eds.) *Crisis and Creativity in the New Literatures in English*. Amsterdam: Rodopi, 1990, 325–32.

(ed.). *The Commonwealth Writer Overseas: Themes of Exile and Expatriation*. Brussels: Didier, 1976.

Nixon, Rob. *London Calling: V. S. Naipaul, Postcolonial Mandarin*. Oxford: Oxford University Press, 1992.

Okokon, Susan. *Black Londoners, 1880–1990*. Stroud: Sutton Publishing, 1998.

Olusoga, David. *Black and British: A Forgotten History*. London: Macmillan, 2016.

Osborne, Deirdre (ed.). *The Cambridge Companion to British Black and Asian Literature (1945–2010)*. Cambridge: Cambridge University Press, 2016.

Owusu, Kwesi. *The Struggle for Black Arts in Britain: What Can We Consider Better than Freedom*. London: Comedia, 1986.

(ed.). *Black British Culture and Society: A Text Reader*. London: Routledge, 2000.

Paquet, Sandra Pouchet. *The Novels of George Lamming*. London: Heinemann, 1982.

Parekh, Bhikhu (ed.). *Colour, Culture and Consciousness: Immigrant Intellectuals in Britain*. London: George Allen & Unwin, 1974.

Patterson, Sheila. *Dark Strangers: A Study of West Indians in London*. Harmondsworth: Penguin, 1963.

Paul, Kathleen. *Whitewashing Britain: Race and Citizenship in the Postwar Era*. Ithaca, NY: Cornell University Press, 1997.

Pearce, Michael. *Black British Drama: A Transnational Story*. London; New York: Routledge, 2017.

Perry, Kennetta Hammond. *London is the Place for Me: Black Britons, Citizenship, and the Politics of Race*. New York: Oxford University Press, 2015.

Petersen, Kirsten Holst and Rutherford, Anna (eds.) *Displaced Persons*. Mundelstrup: Dangaroo, 1988.

Phillips, Mike and Phillips, Trevor. *Windrush: The Irresistible Rise of Multi-Racial Britain*. London: HarperCollins, 1998.

Pirker, Eva Ulrike. *Narrative Projections of a Black British History*. New York; London: Routledge, 2011.

Platt, Len (ed.). *Modernism and Race*. Cambridge: Cambridge University Press, 2011.

Platt, Len and Upstone, Sara (eds.). *Postmodern Literature and Race*. Cambridge: Cambridge University Press, 2015.

Potter, Simon J. *Broadcasting Empire*. Oxford: Oxford University Press, 2012.

Procter, James. *Dwelling Places: Postwar Black British Writing*. Manchester; New York: Manchester University Press, 2003.

   Stuart Hall. New York: Routledge, 2012.

   (ed.). *Writing Black Britain 1948–1998: An Interdisciplinary Anthology*. Manchester; New York: Manchester University Press, 2000.

Ramazani, Jahan. *A Transnational Poetics*. Chicago, IL: University of Chicago Press, 2009.

Ramchand, Kenneth. *The West Indian Novel and its Background*. London: Faber and Faber, 1970.

Ramdin, Ron. *Reimagining Britain: 500 Years of Black and Asian History*. London: Pluto, 1999.

Ranasinha, Ruvani. *Contemporary Diasporic South Asian Women's Fiction: Gender, Narration and Globalisation*. London: Palgrave Macmillan, 2016.

   South Asian Writers in Twentieth-Century Britain: Culture in Translation. Oxford: Clarendon Press, 2007.

Ranasinha, Ruvani with Ahmed, Rehana, Mukherjee, Sumita, and Stadtler, Florian (eds.). *South Asians and the Shaping of Britain, 1870–1950: A Sourcebook*. Manchester: Manchester University Press, 2012.

Rastogi, Pallavi and Stitt, Jocelyn Fenton (eds.). *Before Windrush: Recovering an Asian and Black Literary Heritage within Britain*. Newcastle upon Tyne: Cambridge Scholars, 2008.

Rees, Roland. *Fringe First: Pioneers of Fringe Theatre on Record*. London: Oberon, 1992.

Reichl, Susanne. *Cultures in the Contact Zone: Ethnic Semiosis in Black British Literature*. Trier: Wissenschaftlicher, 2002.

Rohlehr, Gordon. *Pathfinder: Black Awakening in 'The Arrivants' of Edward Kamau Brathwaite*. Tunapuna: Gordon Rohlehr, 1981.

Romain, Gemma. *Race, Sexuality and Identity in Britain and Jamaica: The Biography of Patrick Nelson, 1916–1963*. London: Bloomsbury Academic, 2017.

Rupp, Jan. *Genre and Cultural Memory in Black British Literature*. Trier: Wissenschaftlicher, 2010.

Rush, Anne Spry. *Bonds of Empire: West Indians and Britishness from Victoria to Decolonization.* Oxford: Oxford University Press, 2011.

Rushdie, Salman. *Imaginary Homelands: Essays and Criticism 1981–1991.* London: Granta, 1991.

Step Across this Line: Collected Non-Fiction 1992–2002. London: Jonathan Cape, 2002.

Rutherford, Anna and Chew, Shirley (eds.). *Unbecoming Daughters of the Empire.* Mundelstrup: Dangaroo, 1993.

Rutherford, Anna, Jensen, Lars, and Chew, Shirley (eds.). *Into the Nineties: Post-Colonial Women's Writing.* Hebden Bridge: Dangaroo, 1994.

Rutherford, Jonathan (ed.). *Identity, Community, Culture, Difference.* London: Lawrence & Wishart, 1990.

Saha, Anamik. *Race and the Cultural Industries.* Cambridge: Polity Press, 2018.

Said, Edward. *Culture and Imperialism.* London: Chatto & Windus, 1993.

Salkey, Andrew. *Havana Journal.* Harmondsworth: Penguin, 1971.

'The Negritude Movement and Black Awareness', 1969. George Padmore Institute GB 2904 CAM/4/3/4.

Samuel, Raphael (ed.). *Patriotism: The Making and Unmaking of British National Identity,* vol. 1: *History and Politics.* London: Routledge, 1989.

Sandhu, Sukhdev. *London Calling: How Black and Asian Writers Imagined a City.* London: HarperCollins, 2003.

Sandiford, Keith Albert. *Measuring the Moment: Strategies of Protest in Eighteenth-Century Afro-English Writing.* Selinsgrove, PA: Susquehanna University Press, 1988.

Sands-O'Connor, Karen. *Children's Publishing and Black Britain, 1965–2015.* New York: Palgrave Macmillan, 2017.

Soon Come Home to this Island: West Indians in British Children's Literature. New York: Routledge, 2008.

Scafe, Suzanne. *Teaching Black Literature.* London: Virago, 1989.

Schwarz, Bill (ed.). *West Indian Intellectuals in Britain.* Manchester: Manchester University Press, 2003.

Segal, Ronald. *The Black Diaspora.* London: Faber and Faber, 1995.

Segalen, Victor. *Essay on Exoticism: An Aesthetics of Diversity.* Trans. and ed. Yaël Rachael Schlick. Durham, NC: Duke University Press, 2002.

Sesay, Kadija (ed.). *Write Black, Write British: From Post Colonial to Black British Literature.* London: Hansib, 2005.

Seshagiri, Urmila. *Race and the Modernist Imagination.* Ithaca, NY: Cornell University Press, 2010.

Sewell, Tony, *Keep on Moving: The Windrush Legacy; The Black Experience in Britain from 1948.* London: Voice Enterprises, 1998.

Sharpe, Christina. *In the Wake: On Blackness and Being.* Durham, NC; London: Duke University Press, 2016.

Shukla, Nikesh (ed.). *The Good Immigrant.* London: Unbound, 2016.

Sivanandan, A. *A Different Hunger: Writings on Black Resistance.* London: Pluto, 1982.

Slate, Nico. *The Prism of Race: W. E. B. Du Bois, Langston Hughes, Paul Robeson and the Coloured World of Cedric Dover.* Basingstoke: Palgrave Macmillan, 2014.

Small, Stephen. *Racialised Barriers: The Black Experience in the United States and England in the 1980s.* London: Routledge, 1994.

Snaith, Anna. *Modernist Voyages: Colonial Women Writers in London, 1890–1945*. Cambridge: Cambridge University Press, 2014.

Sorabji, Richard. *Opening Doors: The Untold Story of Cornelia Sorabji*. London: I.B. Tauris, 2010.

Soyinka, Wole. *Art, Dialogue and Outrage: Essays on Literature and Culture*. Ibadan: New Horn Press, 1988.

Spivak, Gayatri Chakravorty. 'Subaltern Studies: Deconstructing Historiography' in *In Other Worlds: Essays in Cultural Politics*. New York: Methuen, 1987, 197–221.

Squires, Claire. *Marketing Literature: The Making of Contemporary Writing in Britain*. New York: Palgrave Macmillan, 2007.

Stadtler, Florian. *Fiction, Film and Indian Popular Cinema: Salman Rushdie's Novels and the Cinematic Imagination*. New York: Routledge, 2014.

Stein, Mark U. 'Cultures of Hybridity: Reading Black British Literature'. *Kunapipi*, 20:2 (1998): 76–89.

  Black British Literature: Novels of Transformation. Columbus, OH: Ohio State University Press, 2004.

Sutcliffe, David and Wong, Ansel (eds.). *The Language of the Black Experience*. Oxford: Blackwell, 1986.

Swanzy, Henry. Henry Swanzy Diaries (Ichabod), 1 January 1952. Yesu Persaud Centre for Caribbean Studies, University of Warwick.

Tabili, Laura. *Global Migrants, Local Culture: Natives and Newcomers in Provincial England, 1841–1939*. Basingstoke: Palgrave Macmillan, 2011.

Tajfel, Henri and Dawson, John L. (eds.). *Disappointed Guests: Essays by African, Asian, and West Indian Students*. London: Oxford University Press, 1965.

Teverson, Andrew and Upstone, Sara (eds.). *Postcolonial Spaces: The Politics of Place in Contemporary Culture*. Basingstoke; New York: Palgrave Macmillan, 2011.

Thomas, Helen. *Romanticism and Slave Narratives: Transatlantic Testimonies*. Cambridge: Cambridge University Press, 2000.

Todd, Richard. *Consuming Fictions: The Booker Prize and Fiction in Britain Today*. London: Bloomsbury, 1996.

Ugwu, Catherine (ed.). *Let's Get It On: The Politics of Black Performance*. London: Institute for Contemporary Arts, 1996.

Upstone, Sara. *British Asian Fiction: Twenty-First-Century Voices*. Manchester: Manchester University Press, 2010.

  Rethinking Race and Identity in Contemporary British Fiction. London: Routledge, 2016.

Visram, Rozina. *Ayahs, Lascars and Princes: The Story of Indians in Britain, 1700–1947*. London: Pluto, 1986.

  Asians in Britain: 400 Years of History. London: Pluto, 2002.

Viswanathan, Gauri. *Masks of Conquest: Literary Study and British Rule in India*. New Delhi: Oxford University Press, 1989.

Walker, Sam and Elcock, Alvin (eds.). *The Windrush Legacy: Memories of Britain's Post-War Caribbean Migrants*. London: The Black Cultural Archives, 1998.

Walmsley, Anne. *The Caribbean Artists Movement 1966–1972: A Literary and Cultural History*. London; Port of Spain: New Beacon Books, 1992.

Walvin, James. *Passage to Britain*. Harmondsworth: Pelican, 1984.

Wambu, Onyekachi (ed.). *Empire Windrush: Fifty Years of Writing About Black Britain.* London: Gollancz, 1998.

Ward, Abigail. *Caryl Phillips, David Dabydeen and Fred D'Aguiar: Representations of Slavery.* Manchester: Manchester University Press, 2011.

   (ed.). *Postcolonial Traumas: Memory, Narrative, Resistance.* London: Palgrave Macmillan, 2015.

Weedon, Chris. *Identity and Culture: Narratives of Difference and Belonging.* Maidenhead: Open University Press, 2004.

Wheelock, Stefan M. *Barbaric Culture and Black Critique: Black Antislavery Writers, Religion, and the Slaveholding Atlantic.* Charlottesville, VA: University of Virginia Press, 2016.

White, Sarah, Harris, Roxy, and Beezmohun, Sharmilla (eds.). *A Meeting of the Continents: The International Book Fair of Radical Black and Third World Books – Revisited.* London: New Beacon Books, 2005.

Wilkie-Stibbs, Christine. *The Outside Child In and Out of the Book.* London: Routledge, 2008.

Wisker, Gina (ed.). *Black Women's Writing.* Basingstoke: Palgrave Macmillan, 1992.

Woolley, Agnes. *Contemporary Asylum Narratives: Representing Refugees in the Twenty-First Century.* Basingstoke: Palgrave Macmillan, 2014.

Young, Robert J.C. *Colonial Desire: Hybridity in Theory, Culture and Race.* London: Routledge, 1995.

   White Mythologies: Writing History and the West. London: Routledge, 1990.

Zaheer, Sajjad and Afzar, Amina. *The Light: A History of the Movement for Progressive Literature in the Indo-Pakistan Subcontinent.* Oxford: Oxford University Press, 2006.

Zerbanoo, Gifford. *The Golden Thread: Asian Experiences of Post-Raj Britain.* London: Pandora, 1990.

Index

queering (cont.)
  poetic forms, 583
Quiller-Couch, Arthur, 413
Quit India Movement, 112
Qur'an, 174, 638, 641, 646

race, 20, 26, 94, 107, 299, 317, 366, 408, 426, 622,
    635, 652, 656, 660–1
  addressed in autobiography, 502–3
  burden of, 366, 653
  class and, 356, 358–62, 394, 396–8, 402,
    565, 639
  discourses of, 84–5, 363, 395–6, 499, 511
  family constructions and, 514
  Grime's questioning of, 614
  inequalities, 427
  materiality of, 650
  politics of, 555
  represented in film, 547, 548, 549, 550
  study of, 110, 112
  writings on, 568
Race for Opportunity Campaign (2010), 589
race relations, 115, 116, 219, 220, 365, 417–18, 424
Race Today, 318, 420
Race Today Collective, 314, 318, 420, 422
Race Today Publications, 289
racial discrimination, 107, 114, 357, 358, 419
racial violence, 313–14, 354, 358, 371, 376, 404,
    419, 421, 442
  theatre's response to, 374, 379
racialisation, 355, 358, 366, 614
racism, 26, 118, 357, 358–62, 383, 408, 417–18,
    622, 656, 661
  1950s, 17
  engagement with, 132
  Enlightenment philosophy and, 26–8
  in schools, 425
  in universities, 427
  influence on theatre, 373
  institutional, 201, 203, 353, 359, 384, 417, 563
  Islamophobic, 634
  metropolitan, 254
  Mittelholzer's contestation of, 232
  police, 376
  political protests against, 419
  pre- and postwar, shifts in, 362–4
  press criticism of, 136
  represented in film, 547
  social realist writing and, 353, 354–6, 366–7
  structural, 417
  theatre's response to, 375–6, 378, 384
  towards second generation postwar
    settlers, 364–5

writings on, 66, 107, 183, 568, 602, 608
Radhakrishnan, Sarvepalli, 141
Radical Alliance of Poets and Players
    (RAPP), 409
radio, 278–81, *see also* BBC: radio pro-
    grammes: *Caribbean Voices*; *Voice*
Rai, Bali, 559, 564, 565
  Crew, 564, 565
  Whisper, 564, 565
Rai, Himansunath, 185
Railton Road (Brixton), 600, 608
Raine, Kathleen, 109, 141
Raj nostalgia, 547
Rajan, Balachandran, 141
  Modern American Poetry, 141
  Monsoon and Other Poems, 141
  Novelist as Thinker, 141
  *Paradise Lost and the Seventeenth Century
    Reader*, 141
  Sheaf, 141
Ramabai, Pandita, 76–7
  Peoples of the United States, 52
Ramazani, Jahan, 263
Ramchand, Kenneth, 247, 412
  *West Indian Poetry: An Anthology for
    Schools*, 412
Ramsay, James, 72, 73, 74, 76–7, 78
  *Essay on the Treatment and Conversion of
    African Slaves in the British Sugar
    Colonies*, 76
Ranasinha, Ruvani, 130, 149
Randall, Paulette, 377
Randhawa, Ravinder, 493, 558
  Wicked Old Woman, 493
Random House, 562
Rankine, Claudia, 521
Rao, Rahul, 573
Rao, Raja, 141, 201, 487
  Changing India, 141
  Kanthapura, 141, 487
Rao, Santha Rama, 145
Rastafarianism, 254, 316, 319, 397, 398
Rastogi, Pallavi, 12, 198, 518
  *Before Windrush: Recovering an Asian and
    Black Literary Heritage within Britain*,
    12, 198
Ratnavali (Sanskrit drama), 185
Ray, Adil, 540
Read, Herbert, 103, 120, 283
realism, 486–92, 496, *see also* magical realism;
    social realism
  historical, 493
  hysterical, 493